CONTENTS

ABOUT THE AUTHORS

Louise Forsyth has a BA and MA in European history, and has been teaching AP European History at Poly Prep Country Day School in Brooklyn, New York, for the past twenty years. She has been an AP European History examination reader, table leader, and question leader for nearly as long, and served as question leader for the DBQ when core scoring was introduced. She has published several scholarly articles and two other textbook manuals, and made numerous presentations on European and world history. She also teaches AP World History and Psychology.

Lenore Schneider earned her bachelor's and master's degrees at Duke University, and her doctorate in social history at Carnegie-Mellon University. She has taught AP European History for eighteen years at New Canaan High School in New Canaan, Connecticut. She has served as a reader and table leader for the AP European History examination for fourteen years, and also served on the AP European History Test Development Committee for three years. She has taught numerous workshops for teachers, and she mentors AP history teachers in Maine. She also teaches AP World History and AP Art History.

PREFACE

Every history teacher has a favorite quotation about history. Mine was written by Cicero in the second century B.C.E.: "History is the witness of the times, the light of truth, the life of memory, the teacher of life, the messenger of antiquity." You are fortunate to be studying European history, and I have been fortunate to teach it. The AP Exam is the culmination of a year's work, and it should be a positive and intellectually meaningful experience for you. It is my hope that this book will help you have that experience.

Diana Nam, the editorial project manager for O'Donnell Associates, was a pleasure to work with, efficient and thoughtful. I appreciate the valuable comments of the two reviewers, Tom Highton, of Union City Schools in New Jersey, and Jon Bath, of Fresno Unified School District in California. I also want to acknowledge the important support of my colleagues in the History Department of Poly Prep and all my AP European history students, who continue to inspire and challenge me. Lenore Schneider was generous to give her time and expertise to write the multiple choice questions for the three AP model exams; we became friends reading AP exams together, and I have learned a great deal from her and fellow AP readers. Lastly, I dedicate this work to my two wonderful daughters, Leonora and Micaela, who both, like their mother, are entranced by the power of words.

Louise Forsyth
January 2008

Part I

Strategies for the AP Examination

PREPARING FOR THE AP* EXAM

By the time you open this book to help prepare you for the AP Exam, you are fully immersed in the study of European history, most of you in an AP course and a few of you studying independently on your own. AP European history courses are typically deep and rich experiences, demanding a high level of understanding and sophisticated analysis from you not only of textbook material but also of all sorts of primary and secondary sources. Such an experience has great value beyond and above the AP Exam itself. If you have done it right, you will come away with the ability to wrestle with complex ideas, to see connections between the past and the present, and to write cogently and thoughtfully, and you will have the intellectual tools to make meaningful political choices in your adult life. We teachers also hope that you come away with a richer understanding of yourself and of the extraordinary vitality and variety of human beings.

This book is designed to ease your way into a high score on the AP Exam. Many students feel overwhelmed by the amount of material that the exam covers—six centuries of the history of a dozen or so European countries and many, many complex ideas and developments. But do not be daunted; you *can* master it and walk into the exam confident that you have the knowledge and skills to do well and earn a 5.

WHAT IS IN THIS BOOK?

This study guide is designed to go with John P. McKay's *A History of Western Society*, Eighth and Ninth Editions, but it can be used with almost any European history text. The guide follows the organization of the chapters in McKay, with an introduction and list of key concepts, followed by a succinct summary of the text of the chapter. You will see quite a few boxes labeled AP Tips; these are designed to clarify the concepts and terms in the text, make connections forward and backward in time, and illuminate important details. At the end of each chapter are fifteen multiple-choice questions tied to the chapter and two free-response essay questions, followed by answers and explanations. Some of the multiple-choice questions are like AP questions, but others are more specific. If you can do well on these, you will be sure to do well on the multiple-choice part of the AP Exam. The essay questions are typical of AP exams.

In addition, there are three exams modeled on the AP Exam: a diagnostic test and two practice tests, each with answers and

*AP and Advanced Placement Program are registered trademarks of the College Board, which was not involved in the production of and does not endorse this product.

explanations. The best way to use the diagnostic test is to take it, score it yourself, and evaluate your weaknesses and strengths. Do not just get your score and let it go at that. Take the time to look over the exam carefully and read the explanations for the correct answers. Make a list of what you got wrong. Are there subjects where you were particularly weak as indicated by a high proportion of wrong answers? Are there types of questions that you often got wrong, for example, factual recall, interpretation of visual documents like cartoons or art, comparative questions, or all-but-the-following questions? Did you struggle with your essays? You probably already have a sense of your test-taking skills from your assessments in your class; are those confirmed or challenged by your score on the diagnostic test? Once you have a better sense of what you need to work on, you will organize your exam preparation better. Do not be shy about asking your teacher, too; he or she is likely to be able to recommend what you should focus your energies on.

REGISTRATION FOR THE EXAM

Most likely the school will be taking care of this for you, but if not, make sure that you register in time, sometime during the month of February. If you are home schooled, you need to contact the College Board by March 1 to find out the name of an AP coordinator near you; you will have two weeks to make contact. If you qualify for extra time, make sure that all your paperwork is in order and that the AP coordinator at your school is aware of your special needs. He or she will have to submit a SSD form by February 22 if documentation is needed or March 7 if it is not. If your family is struggling to pay the examination fee of $84, it can be reduced by $22 by the College Board through your school, so check up on this early on. In addition, many states subsidize the cost of the exams; this information is available on the College Board website in February. You want to make sure all your ducks are in order way before the exam. For all these issues, go to www.collegeboard.com and navigate until you get to the European history site. There is also a useful *Bulletin for AP Students and Parents* at the site, which you can easily download. If you have questions, go to apexams@info.collegeboard or call AP Services at 609-771-7300 or 888-225-5427.

FAMILIARIZE YOURSELF WITH THE EXAM

If your teacher has not given you AP Exam questions or old AP Exams as practice, then you need to go to the AP website provided by the College Board and examine the exams they have posted there. There are some sample multiple-choice questions and essay questions from 2001 to 2007. In a nutshell, the exam is three hours and five minutes long; it consists of eighty multiple-choice questions, varying in their degree of difficulty, to be done in 55 minutes and three essays for which you will have 15 minutes of mandatory reading time and 125 minutes of writing time. The Document-Based Question (DBQ) is a specific question to be answered only on the basis of the documents—somewhere between eleven and fourteen documents total—and a brief paragraph of historical background, which is included with the documents. You are expected to write the DBQ essay in 45 minutes. You will also write answers to two free-response questions (FRQs), choosing one from each of two groups with three questions in each. The two groups of FRQs are sometimes organized chronologically, and sometimes thematically. You are expected to write each FRQ essay in 35 minutes.

SETTING UP A REVIEW SCHEDULE

Your teacher will almost certainly organize review sessions or review in class, but often that is insufficient for a student to feel really ready. Some students like to reread the textbook to prepare, but for most students, that's impossible because of time constraints. A study guide like this one is an excellent way to prepare, as it crystallizes the information in a textbook and allows you to hear a fresh voice.

The ideal time to allot for review would probably be three weeks or so, but in most cases, your teacher will still be trying to complete the curriculum—which goes through 1990—in April. Therefore, you have to begin review while you are still learning new material. How to do this?

Ideally, take the three weeks and do one chapter of the study guide a night, which, if you focus your attention, should be about an hour's work or less. As there are twenty-one chapters, that is three weeks of review. If that is impossible, try to set up a schedule before the end of April to do two or three chapters a night.

The time before the AP Exams is often very hectic for students. If you are on an athletic team, you may have play-offs or championship games, and the workload in all your classes may be getting intense as the year is coming to its conclusion, with major assignments like research papers or big labs. So an absolute key to success is *time management*. While this is always useful, it is *crucial* in the period before AP Exams. Otherwise, you will not prepare much and have to rely on your innate abilities and your memory, and in the vast majority of cases, these will not bring you to more than a 3. If you want the 5, you need to pay your dues and spend the time preparing. That means the week or two before the AP Exams are going to be ones in which you will give up some of your activities and socializing. Is it worth it? Absolutely!

In almost every college, a score of 5, and in some places a 4 too, will bring you three or four credits, and if not credit, then placement in an advanced-level history course which can be a phenomenally exciting experience for a first-year student. It was for me!

For some students, particularly seniors, the spring brings other interests to prominence at the expense of schoolwork. While this is understandable, you do not want to let this get in the way of earning a 5 on the exam. You want to do honor to the hard work you have done all year and, I hope, to your teacher, by giving the exam your best effort. It is not a good feeling to sit for three hours taking an exam for which you are not prepared, and at the very least, feeling good about the AP Exam in May will help you end your school year on a very positive note.

The AP Exam is also physically grueling: an hour's worth of multiple choice and two of writing. If you are not used to writing by hand, be sure to practice some in the weeks before the exam; otherwise your hand might cramp up or get tired. Be sure to eat well, stay away from sweets and junk food, and get enough sleep the night before, so that your body will be an ally and not a detriment. And be sure to have a good and healthy lunch before the exam, so your energies will not flag in the last hour or so. Do not drink too many liquids; you don't want to lose valuable exam time by the need for bathroom visits. Take a snack in with you to the exam for the break if that's allowed, wear comfortable clothes and shoes, and bring a sweater or jacket in case the room is too cold. You do not want *anything* to interfere with your ability to concentrate on the exam.

Lastly, make a couple of mantras to help you remember what to do on the exam. My students chant *T, 3P, 3G* (see below) as they walk in; that's for the DBQ. SPRITE (social, political, religious, intellectual, technological, economic) is a commonly used acronym to help you remember how to write a comprehensive FRQ essay.

How the Exams Are Scored

It helps to know how the exams are scored, so that you can understand how to earn the highest score. The multiple-choice question answers are scored electronically, but the essays are read by humans. Your score on the multiple-choice section counts for half of your exam score. In June, some 400 readers, university professors and high school teachers of AP European history, meet for a week in a central location to read and score the three essays. Readers are organized into groups of six or seven at a table, chaired by a table leader who is responsible for quality control. For each question, the DBQ and the six FRQs, a question leader (QL) meets with a small group before the reading begins to create a specific scoring rubric for each essay question. The QL trains the table leaders, who then train the readers; the table leaders check that scores given by readers are accurate and that the rubric is being applied competently and fairly. Everything possible is done to ensure that the scoring rubrics and their application by readers are fair and consistent. To see the scoring guidelines for AP Exams from 2004 to 2007, go to www.collegeboard.com/student/testing. After the reading, the raw scores are evaluated by statisticians at Educational Testing Services (ETS) in Princeton, and with the chief faculty consultant, always a university professor, the cutoffs for the 5, 4, 3, 2, and 1 final scores are created.

The exams are scored in June and the scores are sent out in July. You can call for your score after July 1 if you cannot wait to get it in the mail.

You should not need this but just in case: If the exam proves to be a disaster—which it certainly should not—you can legally cancel the score. You will need to do this in writing to AP Services by June 15—before you get your score.

WHO AM I?

The AP European history exam's DBQ (see below) stresses point-of-view analysis, commonly called POV analysis, to train you to ask every time you face a document or a text if the author is a reliable witness and what the author's biases might be. So here is a very brief autobiography, so you can do a POV analysis about this text, too. I was born and raised in Brooklyn, New York, and live there now. I took AP European history in the 1960s, and it was the single most important course I ever took, even considering college and graduate school. I earned a B.A. in history at the University of Rochester, an M.A. in European history from City College, CUNY, and completed most of the course work for the Ph.D. but did not finish the dissertation. I worked on several historical research projects and then began to teach, first in college for seven years and now at Poly Prep Country Day School, an independent school in Brooklyn. I have been teaching AP European history, and now AP world history as well, for some twenty years. I also have been an AP reader for more than a dozen years and have been question leader for the DBQ and for the FRQs as well, so I know the exams and how they are scored very well. I have published several scholarly articles, frequently make presentations on historical and contemporary issues, and have participated in numerous teacher programs, such as NEH Summer Institutes and Seminars, and teacher trips organized by the American Forum for Global Education and the Goethe Institute. I am politically progressive and of middle-class origin—these are important for POV analysis!—although I have done my very best to be balanced and nuanced in this book as I do in my classes.

The multiple-choice questions for the three AP Exams, diagnostic and practice, were written by Lenore Schneider who teaches AP European and AP world history in New Canaan, Connecticut, and is an expert on the AP Exam, having served for three years on the AP European Test Development Committee.

Taking the AP European History Exam

If you are well prepared, you will do well on the AP Exam; this is a simple but accurate statement. However, there are key test-taking skills that will guarantee that you get the score that your level of mastery should bring you.

The single most common problem is not reading the question carefully or ignoring parts of a question. Read the question carefully and answer it in all its parts. Students sometimes answer the question they know or the one they wished had been asked, rather than the one that has been asked; this is particularly true on the essays but can be true on multiple-choice questions too. Do not rush and assume you understand the question before you read it carefully.

Strategies for the Multiple-Choice Section

1. *Pace yourself.* You are expected to answer the questions in an average of three-quarters of a minute per question. So do not spend a long time on any one question; if you are struggling to select the correct answer, leave it and return to it at the end of the allotted time.
2. Make sure that you *key in your answers accurately*. If you skip a question to come back to it later, be sure that you skip an answer on the answer sheet. Periodically, check that you are filling in the circles on the correct line. You do not want to find that at the end of the exam you have miskeyed your answers, as you may not have time to correct that. And if you do it in haste, you could be compounding your error.
3. About guessing: If you can eliminate one of the five options for sure, then it is worth your while to guess. You earn a point for each correct answer, but there is a guessing penalty—one-quarter of a point off for each wrong answer. In other words, you lose one whole point for every four incorrect answers. If you eliminate one option, then you have a 25 percent chance of getting it right and earning a point. But *do not make wild guesses*; the odds are against you.
4. Some questions will be quite straightforward and easy for you; *do not assume that there is a trick* in such questions to make them difficult. The eighty questions offer an array of difficulty, and a number of them in each exam are answered correctly by the vast majority of students. Similarly, there will be a few multiple-choice (MC) questions that are really tough, with only a small percentage of students getting them right.
5. Remember that to earn a 3 or higher, you generally need to answer about half the MC questions correctly. The higher your score on

the MC section, the greater the likelihood of a high score on the exam. The MC section counts for half of your final score.

6. *Read the questions and the answer choices carefully* and be sure to notice if the question is an *except* question. Use the *process of elimination* method; as you read the choices—you can write on the exam booklet—cross out ones you know for sure are wrong. General rules of thumb: Absolute answers, all or none, are usually wrong. Remember that a multiple-choice question is designed to elicit the best answer from you of the five options. Typically of the five options, one will be clearly and definitively wrong, three might be correct or partially true, but one is the most accurate or complete answer to the question.

TYPES OF MULTIPLE-CHOICE QUESTIONS

1. *Factual recall:* There are relatively few of these on the exam, but here it is a matter of knowing the answer or not, as it is not open to interpretation. *Example:*

   The king of England replaced by the Glorious Revolution of 1688 was
   (A) James I.
   (B) Charles I.
   (C) James II.
   (D) Charles II.
   (E) William III.

ANSWER: (C) James II. William, husband of Mary, the Protestant daughter of James II, became king of England in 1688.

2. *Best answer:* Here you are to select the best option of five. As noted above, one or two of the choices will be nearly right. *Example:*

   The Thirty Years' War began when
   (A) a Holy Roman Emperor began persecuting Protestants for the first time.
   (B) the nobles of Bohemia rejected the Holy Roman Emperor as their new king.
   (C) the Protestants of Bohemia, mostly of bourgeois origin, attacked the nobility of Bohemia, who were mostly Catholic.
   (D) Cardinal Richelieu of France sent troops against the Habsburgs.
   (E) the nobles of Bohemia tried to appoint one of their own to be their king.

ANSWER: (B) Option D is clearly wrong, as Richelieu sent troops against the Habsburg only in the third stage of the war. It is also the only answer that refers to something outside the Holy Roman Empire. Option A is also out of the question if you remember that Charles V, the Holy Roman Emperor, fought against Protestants during his entire reign, so the beginning of persecution of Protestants by the Holy Roman Emperor was much earlier than 1618. Assuming you remember that the war began with the defenestration of Prague in 1618, you will know that it cannot be C. Who threw whom out of the window? It was the nobles of Bohemia, largely Calvinists, who rejected the Holy Roman Emperor Ferdinand and asked the Protestant king of the Palatinate, Frederick IV, to be their king, not one from their own group. The middle classes of Bohemia were hardly involved in starting the war. If you read the answers too quickly, you might have selected C or E.

3. Except *questions:* In these questions, all options but one are correct. Often, if you detect a consistent element among four options but not the fifth, you should choose the distinct one—even if you do not know the answer—as it is likely the correct answer. Careful reading here can usually bring good results. Remember that in these questions, four choices are right and only one is wrong; that is the one you need to find. *Example:*

   The results of the Thirty Years' War included all of the following *except*
   (A) economic dislocation in the Germanic states.
   (B) weakening of the Holy Roman Empire.
   (C) loss of population within the Holy Roman Empire.
   (D) enhancement of the personal prestige of the Holy Roman Emperor.
   (E) France and Denmark acquiring territories formerly within the Holy Roman Empire.

ANSWER: (D) It is the only one that shows the Holy Roman Empire to have had a gain. Even if you do not know the answer, you can guess this one by seeing the inherent connections between the four other answers.

4. *Graphs and charts:* Sometimes, these questions ask you to interpret the results of information, rather than calling on what you know. Other times, they will ask you to use your knowledge to interpret the results of a graph or chart. *Example* of the first type:

Figure 19.3 Exports of English Manufactured Goods 1700–1774

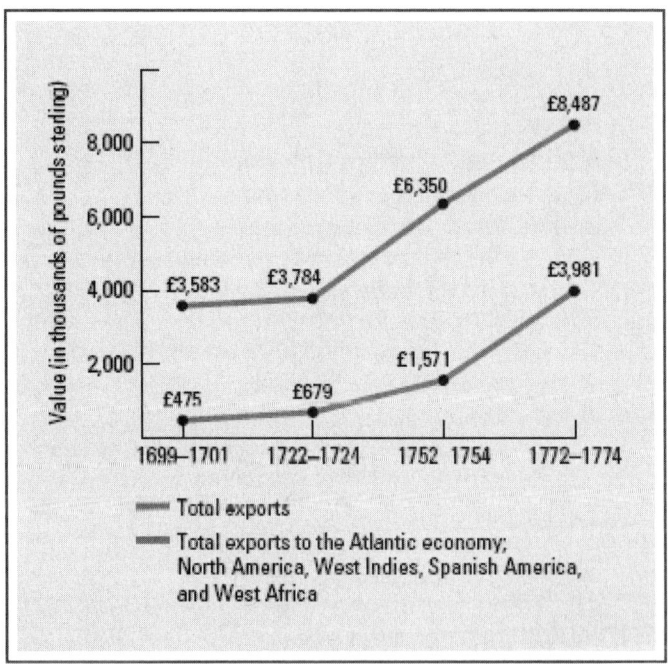

The best interpretation of the data on the chart above is
(A) English exports to the Atlantic economy declined as a percentage of its total trade from 1699 to 1752 but increased after that.
(B) English exports to the Atlantic economy and its total exports both grew at their highest rate between 1724 and 1754.
(C) after the 1750s, English total exports grew less rapidly than did their exports to the Atlantic economy.
(D) English exports to Europe remained constant as a percentage of their total exports.
(E) the main reason for the growth of English exports in the eighteenth century was the dramatic increase in their exports to the Atlantic economy.

ANSWER: (C) From 1754 to 1774, English exports to the Atlantic economy more than doubled while its total exports increased by only a quarter.

5. *Cartoons:* Similar to graphs and charts. These are frequently from the eighteenth through the twentieth centuries.

Turkey's Struggle for EU Membership
Source: Cartoon Stock Limited

The cartoon above refers to the
(A) threat of extremism.
(B) struggles Turkey faces in joining the European Union.
(C) problems within Turkey's government.
(D) struggles between the Turkish government and Turkish Kurds.
(E) strength of the Turkish people.

ANSWER: **(B)** The general population of Turkey wants to "join Europe," but the road to membership in the European Union (EU) is proving difficult. The EU has requested many changes of Turkey's government. Some Turks now believe that the real roadblock is anti-Muslim sentiments in Europe.

6. *Map questions:* Usually these are designed to test your knowledge of the changing borders of European states. Make sure you look carefully at either the borders or the date(s) on the map. *Example:*

This map describes the Balkans in
(A) 1673 after the Turkish siege of Vienna.
(B) 1815 after the Congress of Vienna.
(C) 1853 after the Crimean War.
(D) 1878 after the Congress of Berlin.
(E) 1919 after the Paris Peace Conference.

ANSWER: (D) How can you tell? The Ottoman Empire still has part of the Balkans but Romania, Bulgaria, and Serbia are independent and Austria has occupied Bosnia-Herzegovina; this happened in 1878. By the 1919 treaty, the Ottoman Empire had lost all its European territories except the part of the city of Istanbul on the European side of the Bosporus.

7. *Reproductions of art:* Usually these questions ask you to identify either the school of art that they represent or the time period in which they were likely to have been made. To prepare for these questions, make sure you have looked at the artworks in your textbook and know the major schools of art: Renaissance (fifteenth and sixteenth centuries); mannerism (sixteenth century); Baroque (sixteenth and seventeenth centuries); classicism (eighteenth century); realism, romanticism, and impressionism (nineteenth century); and expressionism, surrealism, and abstractionism (twentieth century). *Example:*

Gentile and Giovanni Bellini: Saint Mark Preaching in Alexandria (1504–1507)
Source: Scala/Art Resource, NY

This painting by the Italian Bellini, "Saint Mark Preaching in Alexandria" 1504–1507, most likely reflects
(A) Renaissance fascination with Greek culture.
(B) European support for Greek independence.
(C) fears of Muslim conquests in Europe.
(D) respect and fascination with the Ottoman Empire.
(E) European glee over their naval victory over the Ottomans at Lepanto.

ANSWER (D) Europeans grew increasing impressed by the city of Constantinople and with the Ottoman Empire as a whole. Contacts, both political and economic, grew in the sixteenth century. Alexandria is in Egypt, not Greece, and was part of the Ottoman Empire. The Greek war of independence took place in the nineteenth century. The battle of Lepanto in 1571 was more than sixty years later than the painting.

THE ESSAYS

As noted above, you will write three essays in about two hours. You will have an additional 15 minutes of reading and preparation time, which generally students use for the DBQ. It is a good idea to pick out the two FRQs you will answer in these 15 minutes as well.

The scoring scale for each essay is 0 to 9, with 0 being a real score, for those essays that make some sort of effort to answer the question, perhaps just restating it, but do almost nothing right in doing so. If a student fails to answer a question or writes something completely irrelevant, then it does not even get a zero. If you want a score of 5 on the exam, you want to make sure that you get a 7, 8, or 9 on the DBQ and at least a 5 or 6 on each of the two FRQs. This means that you have to stay focused, concentrate well, and work assiduously for the two hours.

The AP European history (APEH) exam essays are scored according to two different methods, at least as of this writing. The DBQ is scored according to core scoring (see below) while the FRQs are scored in a more holistic way in order to accommodate the great variety of student responses. There are key elements for a competent FRQ essay even if they are not as specifically identified as they are in the core (see below).

However, both types of essays require a thesis statement. It is this that seems so problematical to some students, so be sure you understand what it is and what it is not. Too often an essay which reveals substantial knowledge on the part of the student fails to get a high score because it lacks a clear thesis. Without one, an essay reads more like a report. A thesis statement is a short, one- or two-sentence, articulation of what the essay will argue, the points you will try to prove in the essay. It is not a description or a rewording of the question. A good thesis statement is often strengthened by a thesis paragraph in which the student lays out some of the key points of the arguments to be made in the essay. While it is acceptable for a thesis statement to be found in the conclusion, you do not want the essay readers to have to search for it, so start out the essay with a strong thesis statement.

EXAMPLES:

Question: Analyze the political, economic, and religious factors that stimulated European exploration and conquest in the fifteenth and sixteenth centuries.

Answer A: There were many political, economic, and religious factors that stimulated Spain and Portugal to explore and conquer in the New World and Asia in the fifteenth and sixteenth centuries.

Is this a thesis statement? No! Mostly, it is a rewording of the question, with the addition of naming the European countries mostly involved in the exploration and conquest in the time period.

Answer B: Although there were many factors that stimulated exploration and conquest, it was economic motives which were more important in leading Spain and Portugal in that direction in the fifteenth and sixteenth centuries.

Is this a thesis statement? Yes! The student tells the reader what she or he will try to prove in the course of the essay. The essay can be evaluated on the degree to which it proves the thesis. This is a basic thesis statement but perfectly acceptable.

Answer C: Although the drive to spread Christianity was highly important to the kings of Spain and Portugal who began the period of European exploration and conquest in the fifteenth century, and certainly it was relevant to the desire to outmaneuver the Muslims who controlled the spice trade in Asia, ultimately it was economic issues which led Spain and Portugal to seek new routes to Asia. The need to find new sources for gold and cheaper access to spices and other valuable goods from Asia spurred Henry the Navigator's push down the coast of Africa and Ferdinand and Isabella's sponsorship of the voyages of Columbus.

Is this a thesis statement? Yes. It has the same thesis as Answer B above, but is more detailed, more fleshed out, and more nuanced. This is a strong thesis statement.

THE DOCUMENT-BASED QUESTION

The DBQ in each of the three AP history examinations is different, so if you have already taken AP world or AP U.S. history, you have to retrain for the AP European history DBQ. The AP U.S. history DBQ expects you to answer the question with the documents and bringing in outside knowledge, but *no* outside knowledge is required or expected in your answer on the European history DBQ. The AP world history DBQ asks you to come up with one additional document that would help answer the question; this is neither expected nor required in APEH.

Sometimes the European history DBQ is on a topic about which you may have substantial knowledge, but quite often it deals with relatively obscure issues, such as nineteenth-century Pan-Slavism or the treatment of juvenile delinquents in England in the seventeenth and eighteenth centuries. So *don't worry at all* if you know nothing at all about the subject; you need not bring in one iota of outside knowledge. Everything you need to write an excellent DBQ essay can be found in the documents themselves.

Another way the AP European history exam is different from the AP world history exam is that in the AP world history exam, all essays are scored according to core scoring. In the AP European history case, only the DBQ essay is scored according to the core—as of this writing. What is core scoring?

CORE SCORING

The basic premise of core scoring is that there are specific and identifiable skills that can be articulated as demonstrations of competence in DBQ essay writing. There are six core points, listed individually, with one point earned for meeting each one. If you earn *all* six points, then and only then can you earn additional points, a score of 7, 8, or 9, for going beyond the minimum. But if you miss a core point, it does not matter how good your essay is; the maximum score you can get on the DBQ is 5. So *learn the core, internalize each point, and be sure to do each one.*

The six core points, as they stand for the May 2008 and May 2009 exams, are

1. **The thesis statement is explicit and addresses all parts of the question**. A thesis statement that is general does *not* earn a point for thesis statement. *Do not simply repeat the question.* It is best to derive your thesis statement in some manner or other from the documents themselves.

2. **The answer uses a majority of the documents, individually and specifically.** This is an easy point to get. Divide the number of documents in half and add one; that's the minimum number to use. What does it mean to use a document? It means referring to the document by name or by reference to its content. It will *not* count if you make a list of documents that support a point, for example, documents 3, 5, and 7. You must made individual use of each of the majority of documents to earn this point.

3. **The answer demonstrates understanding of the basic meaning of the documents.** You are allowed one and only one major error in your analysis of the documents to earn this point. What is a major error? It is an error that leads you to group a document inappropriately or to draw an erroneous conclusion. Minor errors are tolerated, such as misstating the name of the author of a document or writing a date incorrectly.

4. **The answer supports the thesis using a majority of the documents with appropriate interpretations.** If you do not get point one, you cannot get this point.

5. The answer analyzes the documents by using **point-of-view analysis for at least three documents** (see below).

6. **The answer analyzes the documents by explicitly organizing them into three or more appropriate groups.** A group is a minimum of two documents. How to group them? By identity of author (e.g., Germans, socialists, peasants, aristocrats, Protestants, or government officials), by type of document (e.g., letters, diary entries, government reports, cartoons, or speeches), by views expressed or similarity of positions taken, by time period, or by issue addressed.

POINT-OF-VIEW (POV) ANALYSIS

Not doing this well is the single most common reason why students do not earn more than a 5, and therefore this is the most important skill you should work on to prepare for writing the DBQ essay.

Point-of-view analysis is different from point of view. The point of view of a document is the opinion expressed by the author, in other words, his or her viewpoint. Point-of-view *analysis* either questions the reliability of the document or evaluates the degree to which the views expressed in the document reflect or contradict the likely views of similar authors. It is not expected that you can come up with the type of sophisticated POV analysis as might be made by a professional historian but that you make the attempt to show that you have learned to think historically. Every document in the DBQ will be identified by author, name, type of document, date, and something about the author. The task is to connect something within the document with something in the identification. The information given about the author and about the document will offer many opportunities for POV analysis.

Reliability refers to how accurate is the description or how valid is the opinion expressed in the document in view of either the type of document it is or who the author is. For example, if an aristocrat or merchant is describing the life of peasants, one can query whether the views are accurate because it is likely that she or he had little direct experience of peasant life. Similarly, if a tract written during a peasants' revolt vilified aristocrats as greedy, you can query if the depiction of aristocrats is biased because of strong animosities stirred up during a peasants' revolt. Another very useful way of doing POV analysis is to consider the type of document. For example, if it is a diary entry, you can argue that it is likely to reflect the true views of the author as it was not expected to be read by anyone else. Or if it is a diary entry written by a political leader, you can query if it might not reflect the full truth because a politician might reasonably expect that her diary might be part of the public record or read by biographers. A government document might reflect the particular interests of government officials, seeking to either protect or enhance their positions. A speech or a newspaper article has an intended audience, but it might be heard or read by others, the unintended audience, who might understand the intent differently.

Sometimes a document clearly reflects the class or nationalist position of its author. A letter written by someone identified as a humanist might reflect humanist values with references to ancient authors or with enthusiasm for education. An aristocrat would express typical views of his class if he wrote disdainfully of the peasants or described merchants as upstarts, but he would be contradicting the views of his class if he lauded the peasants or merchants. A landowner typically defends agricultural interests over mercantile ones. A Calvinist would typically be appalled by dancing or displays of Catholic devotion. Similar analysis could be easily applied to national identity, political affiliation, or position in society.

What is the point of asking students to do POV analysis? Historians do research by finding and examining documents, and in each case, they too have to evaluate the reliability of documents or how much they represent the views of various subgroups in society. Teachers of history want to know that students have learned to think like historians. A document is not the whole historical truth; it is a particular document written at a particular time by a particular person or persons for a particular purpose in a particular manner.

For examples of POV analysis, look at the explanations for the DBQs on the diagnostic and practice tests.

OTHER DBQ ESSAY-WRITING TIPS

Do not repeat the historical background. Each DBQ begins with a question, followed by a paragraph called historical background, which is designed to give you key information you need to understand and analyze the documents. Do not repeat the historical background. You may use or refer to it, of course, but do not waste your time repeating it. The readers already know it well.

Do not refer to documents by number. Always, always, always, refer to documents by name, author, or content, never by number alone. It is all right for you to use the numbers if it will help you keep count—put them in parentheses—but be sure to have some specific identification, typically the author or the title. Never say "Document 1 says." It is not the document that speaks; the author of the document does.

Do not be colloquial. If the author of a document has a common nickname, do not use it and do not refer to historic figures by their first names alone. For example, it is Queen Elizabeth not Queen Bess, it is Lenin not Vladimir, it is Churchill not Winnie.

Do not feel compelled to use every document. If there is a document you cannot figure out, skip it. An essay can earn a 9 using most but not all of the documents. But remember: *There are no intentionally misleading or trick documents*; every document can be used.

In summation, what you need to do minimally in your DBQ essay is have a thesis statement, use a majority of the documents, divide them into three groups, and give three POV analyses. Set this chant, *T, 3G, 3P,* in your mind to help you remember. As you read the documents for the first time during the AP Exam, mark up the examination booklet, making notes as to possible groupings and POV analyses, and begin to formulate your thesis. Now that you are ready to earn a 6, remember that if you can do more than the basic core points—use more documents, make more POV analyses, form more groups, compose a stronger and more comprehensive thesis—you will earn a high score of 7, 8, or 9.

Be sure to examine the DBQs, the essays, and the scoring guidelines available to you on the College Board website for students, www.collegeboard.com/testing.

THE FREE-RESPONSE QUESTION ESSAYS

The FRQs demand some similar but also some different skills. The answers here reflect your knowledge and understanding in addition to your skills. Be sure to select the question in each group that you know best. And remember to select one question from each group; if you select two from the same group, the second essay does not count at all.

To write a good essay,

1. *Formulate a clear thesis statement.* Take a position on the question and express it in the thesis statement. Many questions are worded in such a way as to encourage a thesis, as in *evaluate* or *analyze*, but you should have a thesis statement even if the question does

not seem to ask for one, as when the question word is *explain* or *discuss*, for example.

2. *Answer all parts of the question.* Most questions have at least two elements, such as political and economic, or Spain and France, or seventeenth and nineteenth centuries. It may be that you know more about one part of the question than about another, but *be sure to discuss all parts of the question, even if unevenly.*

3. If it is a comparative question, remember to draw *both* similarities and differences, even if you stress one more than the other.

4. Develop several arguments, usually although not necessarily in separate paragraphs, and *use specific evidence* to support them. Vague generalizations or broad statements on their own will not do you much good; try to have at least one but preferably several specific facts, dates, or names for each argument. The best essays are filled with lots and lots of evidence, accompanied by good analysis.

5. *Be well organized.* Although essays are not scored on their writing per se, it is typical that a good essay is a well-organized one. If you know the five-paragraph essay format, use it: an introductory paragraph with thesis statement, argument one with supporting evidence in paragraph two, argument two with supporting evidence in paragraph three, argument three with supporting evidence in paragraph four, and a conclusion in paragraph five. The very best essays will acknowledge a counterargument to the thesis and give reasons why it is less valid than your thesis.

6. *Avoid making major errors.* Small mistakes of dates or people's names are not taken all that seriously, and even an essay earning a 9 need not be perfect, but many, many small errors and certainly major errors leading to erroneous conclusions will keep your score down.

7. *Watch your time.* If you have written the DBQ in 45 minutes, you will have an hour for the two FRQs. You want to write both essays, even if they are unbalanced in length or detail. Try to use only a half hour for the first FRQ so you will have time to write the second.

SAMPLE ESSAYS

Question (from AP Exam 1997): Focusing on the period before 1600, describe and analyze the cultural and economic interactions between Europe and the Western Hemisphere as a result of the Spanish and Portuguese exploration and settlement.

STUDENT ANSWER (with many thanks to my student who let me use it)

Before the turn of the sixteenth century, Europe, especially Spain and Portugal, had already left its mark on the Western Hemisphere. And, the New World had left its mark on Europe as well. The interaction, which is known as the Columbian Exchange, had a dramatic effect on both Europe and the Western Hemisphere. However, the drastic cultural changes affected the Western Hemisphere more, while Europe experienced more of the economic changes.

In Latin America, after much of the conquest by the Europeans was finished by the mid-sixteenth century, religious missionaries attempted to convert the locals. The missionaries succeeded because of the "opportunities" that were given to the natives. The natives were taught how to read, write, and speak Spanish, and they were given residence in towns created for the sake of the missionaries. Also, when the use of Native Americans as slaves began to become obsolete due to the deaths of many natives, the Spanish and Portuguese began to import Africans to the New World. Culturally, this affected Latin Americans because of the mix of Europeans, Native Americans, Africans, and mestizos. This mix of different peoples gave Latin Americans a less rigid attitude concerning race and racial differences. In Europe, cultural change occurred somewhat in the exchange of goods back to Europe. For example, the potato became a staple crop for the poor in Europe and eventually led to cultures that revolved very much around the harvesting and use of potatoes such as Ireland and Germany.

In Europe, the economic gains during this period were tremendous. The harvesting of sugar by Native Americans at first and then by Africans in Brazil and the Caribbean led to astounding profits for Portugal and Spain. Going back to potatoes and the poor, potatoes had a big affect on economics in Europe as well. Since potatoes grew easily and grew well in cold climates, poor people lived longer. When more people live, there are more people who work and more people to sell goods to. Also, the silver and gold mines that were found not only had the obvious effect of making European countries richer, but in the case of trading with China, silver became more valuable than ever. And with the silver in Bolivian and Peruvian mines plentiful, Spain was able to prosper greatly. In Latin America, the obvious change in economic interaction was the use of slavery, which put wealth in the hands of Europeans who lived in Latin America. Also, wives of colonists in Latin America had a chance to get lucky if their rich husbands died unexpectedly in the unpredictable violent world in the Western Hemisphere.

The cultural effects of Spanish and Portuguese exploration were greater in Latin America, while the economic effects were greater in Europe. There were more than a few exceptions, such as the reaffirmation of European attitudes of superiority and ranching in South America, but in the sixteenth century and before, this was the extent of cultural and economic change in Europe and the Western Hemisphere.

STRENGTHS OF THIS ESSAY

1. A clear thesis in the opening paragraph, repeated in the final paragraph

2. Well-organized

3. Use of some specific evidence

WEAKNESSES OF THIS ESSAY

1. Leaves out some of the crucial developments in both Europe and Latin America, especially the encomienda system in the colonies and the price revolution in Europe. Spain's siglo d'oro is hinted at but not mentioned specifically. Only one element of the Columbian exchange—the potato—is discussed; what is left out is the importation into Latin America of animals—horses, pigs, sheep, and so on—from Europe and of other crops—such as maize (corn)—into Europe and those–such as wheat and sugar—that went to Latin America. Many aspects of cultural impact are also ignored.

2. Much of the analysis refers to developments after 1600, particularly the racial mixing in Latin America and attitudes of greater tolerance, and the impact of the potato on Germany and Ireland.

SCORE: 5. This essay has some good points but too little that addresses the period under question. Let us rewrite this same essay to turn it into an essay earning an 8 or 9. In bold face, you will find my corrections and additions.

REVISED ANSWER

Before the **end** of the sixteenth century, Europe, especially Spain and Portugal, had already left its mark on the Western Hemisphere. And the New World had left its mark on Europe as well. The interaction, which is known as the Columbian Exchange, had a dramatic effect on both Europe and the Western Hemisphere. However, the drastic cultural changes affected the Western Hemisphere more, while Europe experienced more of the economic changes.

In Latin America, **soon after** the conquest by the Europeans **began in the late fifteenth and early** sixteenth centur**ies,** religious missionaries attempted to convert the locals. The missionaries succeeded because of the "opportunities" that were given to the natives. The natives were taught how to read, write, and speak Spanish, and they were given residence in towns created for the sake of the missionaries. **Christianity replaced the indigenous religions, although over time a syncretism of the two was forged. The conversion en masse to Christianity brought the entire apparatus of the church structure to the New World, from cathedrals to charitable institutions and schools to the**

Inquisition. Also, when the use of Native Americas as slaves began to become obsolete due to the deaths of many natives, the Spanish and Portuguese began to import Africans to the New World. Culturally, this affected Latin Americans because of the mix of Europeans, Native Americans, Africans, mestizos **(the offspring of Europeans and natives), and mulattoes (the offspring of Africans and whites).** This mix of different peoples **would give** Latin America a less rigid attitude concerning race and racial differences. In Europe, cultural change occurred somewhat in the exchange of goods back to Europe. For example, the potato **later** became a staple crop for the poor in Europe and eventually led to cultures that revolved very much around the harvesting and use of potatoes such as Ireland and Germany. **Europeans had many reactions to the encounter with the natives in the New World; some, perhaps most, took the primitive lifestyle of the natives as confirmation of their own superiority, while others were impressed by the dignity and high state of civilization of the natives. Bartolomé de Las Casas, the Dominican missionary who came to the New World in the early sixteenth century, praised the Indians he met and argued that they could be converted to Christianity but that they were too superior to be forced into slavery. He lamented the brutal treatment of the natives by the Spaniards. European intellectuals such as Thomas More wondered if the New World offered examples of earthy paradises; it is not accident that he placed his Utopia there. The discovery of the New World created a new cosmology for Europeans.**

In Europe, the economic gains during this period were tremendous. The harvesting of sugar by Native Americans at first and then by Africans in Brazil and the Caribbean led to astounding profits for Portugal and Spain. Going back to potatoes and the poor, potatoes had a big effect on economics in Europe as well, **beginning well after 1600 in the mid-eighteenth century. Other crops also transformed the European diet, such as maize and later on chocolate and tobacco.**

A much bigger impact came from the massive importation of silver and gold. Silver and gold mines that were found not only had the obvious effect of making European countries richer, but in the case of trading with China, silver became more valuable than ever. **Silver was how the Chinese wanted to be paid, so the increased amount available encouraged trade with China. Originally** the silver in Bolivian and Peruvian mines was plentiful, and Spain was able to prosper greatly. **The crown particularly benefited because of the *quinto*, but most of the gold and silver went out of Spain to various parts of Europe. The sudden wealth of Spain produced what it not accidentally called its siglo d'oro, its golden age. But Spain made inefficient use of its new wealth, in terms of building or supporting native industries; this led to serious financial difficulties, so much so that the king, Philip II, repudiated the royal debt in 1596. Nevertheless, the new mining**

industries prompted technological improvements and the growth of the shipbuilding industries.

A second and more widespread impact of the silver and gold rush was the price revolution. After centuries of more or less stable prices, prices in Europe began to inflate, only a few percentage points a year but enough to have significant impact. Merchants benefited, but the standard of living of workers and peasants went down. The price revolution helped fuel the growth of commercial capitalism.

In Latin America, **the first change in the economic situation as a result of the Spanish conquest was the encomienda system, a type of forced labor placed on the Native Americans, which ended their traditional economic arrangements and put them in the all-too-often rough hands of the Spaniards. The brutality of this system, combined with the awful impact of diseases unknown to the natives, led to a horrific loss of life, 30 to 40 percent in general and in some places even more.** An obvious change in economic interaction was the use of slavery that put wealth in the hands of Europeans who lived in Latin America. **New crops introduced from Europe transformed the economies of the Spanish and Portuguese colonies, none more so than sugar, which the Portuguese had first cultivated in the Azores. They quickly established large-scale sugar cane plantations and sugar-producing factories in Brazil. Slaves were brought first to the New World from Africa in 1518 by Portugal to use on such plantations. Other new crops included wheat and rice. A third impact on the Spanish and Portuguese colonies came from the introduction of animals hitherto unknown in the New World, particularly horses, swine, and cattle. The latter would become the basis of the Argentinean beef industry.**

While the economic consequences of the Columbian Exchange were great in both Europe and the Western Hemisphere, the cultural impact of Spanish and Portuguese were greater in Latin America **than the other way around**. There were more than a few exceptions, such as the reaffirmation of European attitudes of superiority, **and over time the cultural impact of the Americas on Europe would be great,** but in the sixteenth century and before, this was **still somewhat limited, in contrast to the great** economic changes in **both** Europe and the Western Hemisphere.

A Diagnostic Test

AP EUROPEAN HISTORY EXAMINATION
SECTION I: Multiple-Choice Questions
Time—55 minutes
Number of questions—80

Directions Each of the questions or incomplete statements below is followed by five suggested answers or completions. For each question, select the best response in each case.

1. Which of the following was not true of the Black Plague (Black Death)?
   A) Almost one-third of Europeans died.
   B) Eastern Europe escaped the disease.
   C) The disease was spread in part due to trade routes.
   D) Laborers could demand higher wages.
   E) Europe experienced a general rise in prices.

2. The Hundred Years' War
   A) was fought continuously for one hundred years.
   B) was won by England.
   C) led to the canonization of Joan of Arc, so that she could retire.
   D) caused countries to recognize the need for standing armies.
   E) caused the decline of nationalism.

3. The Babylonian Captivity and the Great Schism
   A) deepened faith in the Catholic Church.
   B) caused people to question the church.
   C) improved papal prestige.
   D) caused countries to battle over religion.
   E) prolonged the era of the Middle Ages.

4. Uprisings such as the jacquerie occurred in the fourteenth century due to all of the following except
   A) class clash.
   B) taxation.
   C) religious differences.
   D) frustration with the nobility.
   E) defeat in war.

5. Which of the following contained bitter criticism of the Catholic Church?
   A) Dante's *Divine Comedy*
   B) Chaucer's *Canterbury Tales*
   C) Villon's *Grand Testament*
   D) *Dalimil Chronicle*
   E) Pisan's *Book of Three Virtues*

6. The Italian city-states during the Renaissance
   A) were oligarchies.
   B) were able to prevent corruption because the leaders were educated.
   C) created cooperative economic units.
   D) prevented the French from invading.
   E) were wealthy but not interested in culture.

GO ON TO NEXT PAGE

7. A Renaissance man
   A) attempted to specialize so that he could become an expert.
   B) was increasingly secular.
   C) emphasized modesty and using his talents for God.
   D) avoided the study of Latin classics.
   E) avoided pleasures of the senses.

8. Which of the following is *not* true of Italian Renaissance art?
   A) It studied classical subjects.
   B) It reflected significant use of perspective.
   C) It was rejected by the guilds.
   D) Artists signed their works.
   E) The Catholic Church was a major patron.

9. Humanists
   A) promoted education for the elite.
   B) departed from Castiglione's *The Courtier.*
   C) avoided a study of classical literature as outdated.
   D) allowed upper-class women to be educated but never established schools for girls.
   E) concentrated on humanitarian efforts.

10. The role of women during the Renaissance included all of the following *except*
    A) slavery.
    B) jobs such as making sails, managing businesses, weaving, and midwifing.
    C) some political and legal activity for upper-class women.
    D) running their husband's establishments.
    E) overseeing servants and entertaining.

11. Machiavelli's *The Prince*
    A) reflects a pessimistic view of man.
    B) was written to praise Italy's success during the Renaissance.
    C) emphasizes civic virtue and morality.
    D) was embraced by successful monarchs in sixteenth-century Europe.
    E) was adopted by Lorenzo de' Medici.

12. Henry VII's Court of Star Chamber
    A) reflected an enlightened view of the monarch's role.
    B) reduced the power of the nobles through intimidation.
    C) conducted foreign policy.
    D) resulted in peasants' uprisings.
    E) eliminated torture.

13. During the fifteenth century, Spain
    A) joined five key provinces.
    B) gained power over the Catholic Church and the aristocracy.
    C) failed in the reconquista.
    D) eliminated resentment against the Jews.
    E) ended the medieval practice of the Inquisition.

14. Until the beginning of the sixteenth century, criticism of the Catholic Church was focused primarily on
    A) relics and transubstantiation.
    B) the desire to allow priests to marry.
    C) immorality and ignorance among the clergy.
    D) overly spiritual bishops.
    E) refusal of the church to allow divorce.

15. Martin Luther
    A) sought to create a new church as an alternative to corrupt Catholic practices.
    B) joined forces with Calvin to spread Protestantism.
    C) supported the peasants in their major revolt in 1525.
    D) hoped to reform Catholic theology as well as corrupt practices.
    E) was burned at the stake.

16. The impact of the Protestant Reformation included all of the following *except*
    A) reform of practices within the Catholic Church.
    B) division among Protestants.
    C) religious wars.
    D) continued fragmentation of the Holy Roman Empire.
    E) increased social mobility for the peasants.

17. John Calvin's theology emphasized
    A) salvation by faith alone.
    B) morality and hard work.
    C) free will in terms of salvation.
    D) cooperation with the Anabaptists.
    E) spiritual warfare against the Catholic Church.

18. Henry VIII broke from the Catholic Church because of
    A) serious doubts about Catholic theology.
    B) his concerns about succession.
    C) his desire to protect Protestants in England.
    D) influence from his first wife.
    E) his political designs on Spain.

19. The Council of Trent
    A) affirmed Catholic theology as it had been for the preceding 1,500 years.
    B) brought about reconciliation with the Protestants.
    C) limited the number of saints to be honored.
    D) separated itself from the influence of international politics.
    E) allowed couples to exchange marriage vows without witnesses.

20. The series of civil wars in France during the sixteenth century ended because of
    A) success by the Catholics.
    B) a moderate policy by King Henry IV.
    C) exile of the Huguenots.
    D) invasion by the Spanish Habsburgs.
    E) peace-making efforts by the pope.

21. Western expansion in the sixteenth century included involvement in the Muslim area currently known as
    A) China.
    (B) Indonesia.
    (C) Central America.
    (D) South Africa.
    (E) Canada.

22. All of the following technological improvements contributed to sixteenth-century exploration *except*
    A) the astrolabe.
    B) better sails.
    C) the magnetic compass.
    D) the caravel.
    E) galleys.

23. Baroque art and music were
    A) solely religious.
    B) ornate and dramatic.
    C) based on classicism.
    D) favored in Protestant countries.
    E) a reaction against the Catholic Church.

24. Louis XIV was
    A) a believer in the divine right of kings.
    B) a politique.
    C) the victor in the Thirty Years' War.
    D) a leader who accomplished a lot during his short reign.
    E) a monarch who made peace with the Protestants in his country.

25. Mercantilism is associated with all of the following *except*
    A) Colbert.
    B) colonies.
    C) government subsidies.
    D) tariffs.
    E) a command economy.

26. A major reason for the decline of Spain during the seventeenth century was
    A) its treatment of the Amerindians in South America.
    B) inflation.
    C) civil war between the monarchy and Parliament.
    D) colonial revolts.
    E) friction between the monarchy and the aristocracy.

27. The English Civil War was caused by problems with
    A) peasants.
    B) Catholics.
    C) Puritans and Parliament.
    D) succession to the throne.
    E) the threat of foreign invasion.

28. The seventeenth-century Netherlands was
    A) monarchical.
    B) republican.
    C) theocratic.
    D) totalitarian.
    E) aristocratic.

GO ON TO NEXT PAGE

29. The Thirty Years' War
    A) devastated central Europe.
    B) provided additional territory to the Catholic Church.
    C) was based solely on religious differences.
    D) contributed to the unification of Germany.
    E) strengthened the new monarchies.

30. Peter the Great's policies resulted in
    A) less nationalism.
    B) increased westernization.
    C) strengthening the Orthodox church.
    D) creation of a group of loyal boyars.
    E) loss of a major war.

31. Which of the following did *not* contribute to the development of the scientific revolution?
    A) Renaissance attitudes
    B) Better instruments
    C) The Enlightenment
    D) The medieval university tradition
    E) The need to solve navigational problems

32. The Enlightenment
    A) appealed to peasants and the urban poor as well as to intellectuals.
    B) rejected the scientific revolution as too mechanical.
    C) was profoundly secular.
    D) attempted to reform the church.
    E) emphasized the university movement.

33. Whose policies were most strongly influenced by Enlightenment thought?
    A) Peter the Great
    B) Louis XIV
    C) William and Mary
    D) Catherine the Great
    E) Louis XVI

34. The enclosure movement contributed to the agricultural revolution because
    A) the peasants supported it.
    B) it consolidated land.
    C) it allowed the government to control more land.
    D) it preserved the monasteries.
    E) it led to the end of tariffs.

35. The agricultural revolution promoted the growth of population in Europe during the
    A) fifteenth century.
    B) sixteenth century.
    C) seventeenth century.
    D) eighteenth century.
    E) nineteenth century.

36. The Atlantic slave trade
    A) was a major reason for commercial success for Europe and North America.
    B) declined after the American Revolution.
    C) contributed to widespread economic improvement in Africa.
    D) was not formally opposed until the U.S. Civil War.
    E) and slavery had been abolished in Europe by the middle of the nineteenth century.

37. Adam Smith
    A) wrote persuasively against Marx and Marxism.
    B) was considered an economic liberal.
    C) did not favor any government involvement in the economy.
    D) believed in a command economy.
    E) was a mercantilist.

38. Until the late eighteenth century, women
    A) married late and immediately began bearing children.
    B) married early but waited to begin bearing children.
    C) married when the family could provide a sufficient dowry.
    D) lived with their extended families, even after marriage.
    E) were encouraged to date before settling into an arranged marriage.

39. Which of the following was true in the eighteenth century?
    A) Peasants ate less food in 1700 than in 1500.
    B) Small traders and master craftsmen had a more varied diet than peasants.
    C) The poor of northern Europe ate better than the poor of southern Europe.
    D) The urban poor did not have ready access to vegetables.
    E) Milk, in small quantities, was a staple in most homes.

40. Shortly after the storming of the Bastille in Paris, in July 1789,
    A) the Terror began.
    B) Austria invaded France, hoping to help the monarchy.
    C) the National Assembly abolished noble privileges.
    D) the king was beheaded.
    E) the revolutionaries fought among themselves.

41. Napoleon's expansion in Europe resulted in all of the following *except*
    A) nationalism in Spain and Germany.
    B) unity and order in France.
    C) Russian victory.
    D) French power over the Catholic Church.
    E) more rights for women.

42. Malthus and Ricardo
    A) predicted a better standard of living as a result of the Industrial Revolution.
    B) predicted that population would outgrow food sources as a result of the Industrial Revolution.
    C) influenced the Parliament in Britain to pass the Reform Bill of 1832.
    D) created railroad monopolies.
    E) stimulated inventions in the textile industry.

43. Put these countries in order of their economic power in the *early* nineteenth century on the basis of numbers of factories, cities, roads, canals, and trade.
    I. Great Britain
    II. France
    III. Germany
    IV. Russia
    A) I, II, III, and IV
    B) III, I, II, and IV
    C) III, II, IV, and I
    D) I, IV, III, and II
    E) II, I, III, and IV

44. Which of the following benefited most from the second Industrial Revolution?
    A) Peasants
    B) The urban lower class
    C) The middle class
    D) American anarchists
    E) Impressionist artists

45. In 1848 revolutions occurred in many European countries. Which of the following countries did *not* experience such revolutions, primarily because it made some political accommodations?
    A) Britain
    B) Italy
    C) France
    D) Austria
    E) Germany

46. Which of the following was labeled the Sick Man of Europe?
    A) Austria
    B) France
    C) Turkey
    D) Britain
    E) Poland

47. Who said, "The great questions of our day cannot be resolved by speeches and majority votes—that was the great mistake of 1848–1849—but by blood and iron."
    A) Winston Churchill
    B) Otto von Bismarck
    C) Karl Marx
    D) Count Camillo di Cavour
    E) Adolf Hitler

GO ON TO NEXT PAGE

48. The Boers
    A) were Dutch Calvinists.
    B) aligned with the British in South Africa.
    C) were defeated by the Zulus.
    D) encouraged British control of the diamond mines.
    E) decided to leave South Africa after the Boer War.

49. On January 13, 1898, Emile Zola's "J'Accuse," an open letter to the president of France, directly denounced the military and implicitly denounced
    A) anti-Semitism.
    B) Aryans.
    C) French Jerusalem.
    D) the Rothschilds.
    E) Zionists.

50. The first Industrial Revolution during the early nineteenth century involved which industry and country?
    A) Silk / France
    B) Textiles / Britain
    C) Coal / Germany
    D) Steel / United States
    E) Manufacturing / Japan

51. The growth of railroads created all of the following effects *except*:
    A) allowing factories to be built in more locations.
    (B) creating new jobs and sparking production.
    (C) enabling the development of planned cities, with railroad stations at the center.
    (D) providing a boost to agriculture.
    (E) marking the dawn of mobility of the masses.

52. The enclosure movement in Britain had all of the following effects *except*
    A) the rapid growth of cities.
    B) new large landowners experimenting with agricultural innovations.
    C) a dramatic decline in Europe's population.
    D) an increased labor force for new industries.
    E) forcing many small landowners off of their land.

53. The most common occupation for women in the late nineteenth century was
    A) teacher.
    B) nurse.
    C) factory worker.
    D) domestic servant.
    E) doctor.

54. Japan responded to nineteenth-century Western industrialization in all of the following ways *except*
    A) with imperialism.
    B) with a "select and adopt" policy.
    C) by accepting laissez-faire economics.
    D) by building up its military.
    E) with a policy of "Opening the country to drive out the barbarians."

55. By the late nineteenth century most social welfare in Europe included all of the following *except*:
    A) public works.
    B) compulsory education.
    C) improved sanitation.
    D) safety standards.
    E) women's suffrage.

56. Which of the following was introduced during the late nineteenth century?
    A) Methodism
    B) Laissez-faire economics
    C) Machiavellian politics
    D) Existentialism
    E) Social Darwinism

57. Who was considered the Father of Psychology?
    A) Nietzsche
    B) Freud
    C) Darwin
    D) Jung
    E) James

58. All of the following made political statements through their art in the eighteenth or early nineteenth century *except*
    A) Constable.
    B) Goya.
    C) David.
    D) Delacroix.
    E) Hogarth.

59. Romanticism in the nineteenth century is best described as
   A) an indirect protest against the inadequacy of social conditions.
   B) a school of painting that studied the effects of light and dark.
   C) an artistic emphasis on feeling, emotion, and imagination.
   D) secular art with careful attention to reason.
   E) genre painting.

60. Who discovered and studied bacteria that cause disease in man and animals?
   A) Robert Koch
   B) Joseph Lister
   C) William Harvey
   D) Louis Pasteur
   E) Antoine Lavoisier

61. The causes of World War I included all of the following *except*
   A) alliances.
   B) propaganda.
   C) intellectual influences.
   D) nationalism.
   E) the arms race.

62. The most representative symbol of World War I warfare was
   A) trench warfare.
   B) the atomic bomb.
   C) the Luftwaffe.
   D) night bombing.
   E) the Maginot line.

63. The social impact of World War I on women included all of the following *except*
   A) more focus on the home while the men were at war.
   B) women were more visible.
   C) women worked in industry, offices, and transportation.
   D) several countries granted women suffrage shortly after the war.
   E) some women bobbed their hair, shortened their skirts, and smoked.

64. Russia's involvement in World War I
   A) ended when winter defeated the enemy.
   B) ended when Lenin signed a treaty and withdrew from the war.
   C) contributed to the success of the Allies.
   D) included submarines as well as infantry.
   E) inspired support for the tsar.

65. Causes of the Russian Revolution included all of the following *except*
   A) social mobility.
   B) weak leadership.
   C) desperation for food.
   D) an inspired revolutionary leader.
   E) war losses.

66. Lenin was all of the following *except*
   A) Marxist.
   B) opposed to Russian involvement in World War I.
   C) supportive of the Provisional Government.
   D) not in Russia when the revolution broke out.
   E) supported by the majority of the Duma.

67. Lenin's victory in the Russian Revolution was followed by all of the following *except*
   A) civil war.
   B) war communism.
   C) Cheka.
   D) worldwide revolution.
   E) foreign involvement that fought against Lenin's Reds.

68. Which of the following is *not* considered a realist?
   A) Henry James
   B) James Joyce
   C) Gustave Flaubert
   D) Charles Dickens
   E) Fyodor Dostoevsky

GO ON TO NEXT PAGE

69. Who wrote the following?
"Take up the white man's Burden—
Send forth the best ye breed—
Go bind your sons to exile
To serve your captives' need. . . ."
A) Anton Chekhov
B) Rudyard Kipling
C) George Bernard Shaw
D) Emile Zola
E) David Livingston

70. The Treaty of Versailles
A) ensured peace in Europe through the League of Nations.
B) allowed Germany and Russia to participate as a conciliatory measure.
C) insisted that Germany pay for the war.
D) created a French buffer state to protect against Germany.
E) gave Germany's colonies their independence.

71. During the early 1920s both France and Germany experienced all of the following *except*
A) rapid rebuilding of the areas destroyed by war.
B) communists and socialists battling for control.
C) strong business interests being represented in government.
D) lack of confidence in the economy of the country.
E) a trend toward conservative leadership.

72. The Great Depression prompted all of the following *except*
A) the New Deal in the United States.
B) the rise of Hitler in Germany.
C) the Popular Front in France.
D) Britain experiencing the highest unemployment in Europe.
E) The "middle way" in Scandinavia.

73. Which of the following Soviet policies was *least* totalitarian?
A) NEP
B) Collectivization
C) Five Year Plans
D) Stalin's purges
E) Social realism in art

74. During World War II, the Axis Powers conquered all of the following *except*
A) the Philippines.
B) the Soviet Union.
C) France.
D) the eastern coast of China.
E) eastern Europe.

75. Which of the following was *not* part of the Soviet cold war policies?
A) The Berlin wall
B) Satellite countries
C) Decolonization
D) The Brezhnev Doctrine
E) The response to the Hungarian Revolution in 1956

76. After World War II western European demographic trends could be described as
A) the baby boom followed by a decline in birth rates after 1952.
B) the baby boom of an average of four children per family until the 1980s.
C) small families so that children could experience more material benefits.
D) fewer marriages due to high unemployment.
E) women continuing to work in heavy industry and thus postponing marriage.

77. Which of the following are most closely associated with the twentieth-century feminist movement?
A) Riefenstahl and Cavendish
B) De Beauvoir and Friedan
C) De Stael and Geoffrin
D) Wollstonecraft and Mill
E) Stanton and Mott

78. Which of the following was *not* an indication that Soviet communism was weakening?
    A) The Polish Solidarity movement
    B) *Glasnost*
    C) *Perestroika*
    D) The invasion of Afghanistan
    E) A reduction of Soviet arms buildup

79. The revolutions of 1989 resulted in all of the following *except*
    A) the prevention of the breakup of Yugoslavia.
    B) the Velvet Revolution in Czechoslovakia, which ended communism there.
    C) the reunification of East and West Germany.
    D) Gorbachev's reforms facing difficulties.
    E) the end of the cold war.

80. Which of the following is *not* associated with the European Union?
    A) The Maastricht Treaty
    B) The euro replacing the currency of individual countries
    C) Immigration issues
    D) The European Economic Community
    E) The European Union standing army

STOP
END OF SECTION I

IF YOU FINISH BEFORE TIME IS CALLED, YOU MAY CHECK YOUR WORK ON THIS SECTION. DO NOT GO ON TO SECTION II UNTIL YOU ARE TOLD TO DO SO.

SECTION II: Free-Response Essays

Part A
Suggested writing time—45 minutes
Percent of Section II score—45

Directions The following question is based on the accompanying Documents 1–12. The documents have been edited for the purpose of this exercise. Write your answer on the tinted pages of the Section II free-response booklet.

This question is designed to test your ability to work with and understand historical documents.

Write an essay that

- Provides an appropriate, explicitly stated thesis that directly addresses all parts of the question and does *not* simply restate the question
- Discusses a majority of the documents individually and specifically
- Demonstrates understanding of the basic meaning of a majority of the documents
- Supports the thesis with appropriate interpretation of a majority of the documents
- Analyzes the documents by explicitly grouping them in at least three appropriate ways
- Takes into account both the sources of the documents and the authors' point of view

You may refer to relevant historical information not mentioned in the documents.

1. Analyze the various reactions to and views about the execution of Charles I.

   Historical Background: The Stuarts, who took over the throne of England on the death of Elizabeth I in 1603, believed in the divine right of kings and were sympathetic to Catholicism. Charles I attempted to rule without Parliament from 1629 to 1640, but a Scottish threat forced him to call it into session. Many Parliamentarians had become radical Protestants who sought to "purify" the Church of England created by the English Reformation. Civil war broke out between the supporters of the king and the supporters of Parliament. Parliament's forces, led by Oliver Cromwell, won. Parliament appointed a court that put the captured king on trial for treason and ordered his execution on January 30, 1649. The regicide was highly controversial and not supported by all of the radicals. A commonwealth (or republic) was declared, but in 1660 the monarchy was restored with the executed king's son, Charles II, on the throne. In 1688, the more liberal members of Parliament, the Whigs, joined with the conservatives, the Tories, to exclude his son James II from the throne and offer it to William of Orange and his wife Mary jointly. This peaceful Glorious Revolution established the sovereignty of Parliament.

Document 1

The Trial of Charles I, various eyewitnesses to the conclusion to the trial, published 1650.

Source: Norton Topics on line: From *King Charls his Tryal at the High Court of Justice* (London, 1650); John Nalson, *A True Copy of the Journal of the High Court of Justice for the Tryal of K. Charles* (London, 1684); and John Rushworth, *Historical Collections,* 8 vols. (London, 1721–22), Vol. 7. Printed in *The Trial of Charles I: A Documentary History,* David Lagomarsino and Charles T. Wood, editors, © 1989 by the Trustees of Dartmouth College, by permission of University Press of New England. 1649. Available at www.wwnorton.com/college/english/nael/17century/topic_3/trial.htm.

Now, . . . this court is in judgment and conscience satisfied that he (the said Charles Stuart) is guilty of levying war against the said Parliament and people, and [of] maintaining and continuing the same, for which . . . he stands accused. And by the general course of his government, counsels, and practices, before and since this Parliament began (which have been and are notorious and public, and the effects whereof remain abundantly upon record), this court is fully satisfied in their judgments and consciences that he hath been and is guilty of the wicked designs and endeavors in the said charge set forth, and that the said war hath been levied, maintained, and continued by him as aforesaid . . . and that he hath been and is the occasioner, author, and continuer of the said unnatural, cruel, and bloody wars, and therein guilty of High Treason and of the murders, rapines, burnings, spoils, desolations, damage, and mischief to this nation acted and committed in the said war and occasioned thereby. For all which treasons and crimes this court doth adjudge that he, the said Charles Stuart, as a tyrant, traitor, murderer, and public enemy to the good people of this nation, shall be put to death by the severing of his head from his body.

Document 2

Anonymous, KING CHARLS, HIS SPEECH Made upon the SCAFFOLD At Whitehall-Gate Immediately before his Execution On Tuesday the 30 of Jan. 1649 With a Relation of the maner of his going to Execution Published by Special Authority. London: Printed by Peter Cole, at the sign of the Printing-Press in Cornhill, near the Royal Exchange, 1649.

Source: Project Canterbury n.d. King Charls His Speech, available at www.anglicanhistory.org/charles/charles1.html; "The Execution of Charles I, 1649," EyeWitness to History, www.eyewitnesstohistory.com (2003).

"[As for the people,] truly I desire their liberty and freedom as much as anybody whomsoever; but I must tell you that their liberty and freedom consist in having of government. . . . It is not for having share in government, sirs; that is nothing pertaining to them; a subject and a sovereign are clear different things. . . . I tell you (and I pray God it be not laid to your charge) that I am the martyr of the people. . . . And to the executioner he said, 'I shall say but very short prayers, and when I thrust out my hands. . . .' The bishop: 'You are exchanged from a temporal to an eternal crown,—a good exchange.' After a very short pause, his Majesty stretching forth his hands, the, executioner at one blow severed his head from his body; which, being held up and showed to the people, was with his body put into a coffin covered with black velvet and carried into his lodging. His blood was taken up by divers persons for different ends: by some as trophies of their villainy; by others as relics of a martyr; and in some had had the same effect, by the blessing of God, which was often found in his sacred touch when living."

Document 3

Unknown artist, German engraving of the execution of Charles I, 1649.

Source: British Library Images online. Available at http://www.imagesonline.bl.uk/results.asp?image=064720&imagex=1&searchnum=2.

Document 4

John Milton, poet, Puritan pamphleteer, The Tenure of Kings and Magistrates, 1650, title page.

Source: www.constitution.org/milton/tenure_kings.htm.

PROVING THAT If IS LAWFUL, AND HATH BEEN HELD SO THROUGH ALL AGES, FOR ANY, WHO HAVE THE POWER, TO CALL TO ACCOUNT A TYRANT, OR WICKED KING; AND, AFTER DUE CONVICTION, TO DEPOSE, AND PUT HIM TO DEATH; IF THE ORDINARY MAGISTRATE HAVE NEGLECTED, OR DENIED TO DO IT. AND THAT THEY, WHO OF LATE SO MUCH BLAME DEPOSING, ARE THE MEN THAT DID IT THEMSELVES.

Document 5

Mary Bayly, reported in "A Letter Sent into France to the Lord Duke of Buckingham His Grace: of a Great Miracle wrought by a piece of a Handkerchief dipped in His Majesty's Blood. The Truth whereof, he himself saw, and is ready to depose it, and doth believe will be attested by 500 others, if occasion requires," imprinted in the year 1649.

Source: Project Canterbury. Available at www.anglicanhistory.org/charles/letter.html.

This my Daughter about a year and a half after her birth was troubled with a swelling under her Chin . . . both her eyes and lips were extremely ill, the swelling in her neck still continuing, and at last she was absolutely blind in her right eye for twelve months, . . . that she could scarce discern the light of a Candle; some telling me that it was the King's Evil, others doubting of it; I never sought for remedy by a touch from the hand of His Sacred Majesty while He was living; the Saturday after his death, [a] Journey-man gave me a little piece of a Handkerchief that was dipped in the King's blood, and then returning home . . . whereupon I stroked my Daughters eyes, and the swelling under her chin with it, . . . ; whereupon . . . it hath helped her, and she is now perfectly recovered, as you see, in her eyes, and the swelling under her chin is almost gone, the color of her flesh is recovered, and the pain totally gone: with this [s]mall piece of a Handkerchief was all this done, which many have desired of me; but, although I am but a poor woman, and of mean condition, I protest I will not sell it for forty pounds.

Document 6

A declaration of the most Christian King, Louis the XIII, King of France and Navarre, 1649.

Source: The National Archives. Available at www.learningcurve.gov.uk/civilwar/g5/cs1/s5.

At length, with kisses and greetings beginning their betrayal, they invited his Majesty to a personal treaty. To show his passionate desire for peace, he bent over backwards, going beyond all former rulers in generous concessions [giving in and making promises]. Yet even when he had given in beyond their hope and expectation, and surrendered his most unquestionable rights and privileges into their hands, with hate as relentless as the grave, deep and bottomless as hell, they abruptly broke off. By force of arms they dragged him to court. Subordinates took it upon themselves to judge their king. They called him to an account, he who owed an account to none but God alone. They disrespectfully criticized him with the unjust shame of tyrant, traitor and murderer. Having behaved with scorn and contempt, after a short time, in triumph they took him to the scaffold. Making his sorrow worse, they had prepared the scaffold at the entrance to his royal palace. In the sight of his subjects they committed a most brutal murder upon his sacred person, by severing his royal head from his body, by the hands of the common hangman.

GO ON TO NEXT PAGE

Document 7

Abraham Bosse, French engraver and artist, Huguenot, front piece to *Leviathan* by Thomas Hobbes, 1651. Hobbes was a mathematician, philosopher, and tutor to Charles II in France.

Source: Answers.Com. Available at www.answers.com/topic/abraham-bosse.

Document 8

Diary of Samuel Pepys, Member of Parliament and Naval administrator under King James II, and member of the Royal Society, diary entry. He attended the execution of Charles I; at that time, he supported it enthusiastically.

Source:

Thursday 30 January 1661/62

Fast-day for the murdering of the late King. I went to church, and Mr. Mills made a good sermon upon David's words, "Who can lay his hands upon the Lord's Anointed and be guiltless?" So home and to dinner, and employed all the afternoon in my chamber, setting things and papers to rights, which pleased me very well, and I think I shall begin to take pleasure in being at home and minding my business. I pray God I may.

Document 9

Lucy Hutchinson, Puritan poet and translator; and wife of John Hutchinson, close adviser to Oliver Cromwell and signer of the King's death warrant. Memoirs of the Life of Colonel Hutchinson, 1664.

Source: Norton topics on line: Norton Anthology English Literature. Available at http://www2.wwnorton.com/college/english/nael/17century/topic_3/colonel.htm.

. . . so this king [Charles I] was a worse encroacher upon the civil and spiritual liberties of his people by far than his father. He married a papist, a French lady, of a haughty spirit, and a great wit and beauty. . . . By this means the court was replenished with papists, and many who hoped to advance themselves by the change, turned to that religion. All the papists in the kingdom were favored, and . . . the puritans were more than ever discountenanced and persecuted, insomuch that many of them chose to abandon their native country, and leave their dearest relations, to retire into any foreign soil or plantation, where they might, amidst all outward inconveniences, enjoy the free exercise of God's worship. Such as could not flee were tormented in the bishops' courts, fined, whipped, pilloried, imprisoned, and suffered to enjoy no rest, so that death was better than life to them . . . yet was not the king satisfied till the whole land was reduced to perfect slavery.

The example of the French king was propounded to him, and he thought himself no monarch so long as his will was confined to the bounds of any law; but knowing that the people of England were not pliable to an arbitrary rule, he plotted to subdue them to his yoke. . . . He was the most obstinate person in his self-will that ever was, and so bent upon being an absolute, uncontrollable sovereign, that he was resolved either to be such a king or none. . . . But above all these the king had another instigator of his own violent purpose, more powerful than all the rest, and that was the queen . . . let them remember that the felicity of [Queen Elizabeth]'s reign was the effect of her submission to her masculine and wise counselors.

GO ON TO NEXT PAGE

Document 10

Engraving, Execution of John Jones and other regicides, October 1660.

Source: www.spartacus.schoolnet.co.uk/STUregicides.htm.

Document 11

White Kennet, Bishop of Peterborough, A Complete History of England, 2d edition, 1719.

Source: Freida H. Blackwell and Jay Losey, "The Execution of Charles I: History and Perspectives." Available at www.web.archive.org.

It must be dreadfully remembered, that the cruel Powers did suspect that the King would not submit his Head to the Block; and therefore to bring him down by Violence to it; they had prepared Hooks and Staples . . . to haul him as a Victim to the Slaughter . . . by the Example of his Savoir, he resisted not, he disappointed their Wit, and yielded to their Malice.

Document 12

Laurence Echard, Whig historian, The History of England, 3d edition, 1720.

Source: Freida H. Blackwell and Jay Losey, "The Execution of Charles I: History and Perspectives." Available at www.web.archive.org.

His head was at one blow severed from his Body. . . . None of the kings of England ever left the world with more open marks of sorrow and affection. The venerable Archbishop Usher, from a Window, swooned at the sight of the fatal blow, as at a prodigy too great for Heaven to permit, or the Earth to behold: And as the rumor of his death spread throughout the Kingdom, women miscarried, many of both sexes fell into palpitations, swoonings and melancholy, and some, with sudden consternations, expired.

End of Part A

GO ON TO NEXT PAGE

SECTION II, Part B
Suggested planning and writing time—35 minutes
Percent of Section II score—27 ½

DIRECTIONS You are to answer *one* question from the three questions below. Make your selection carefully, choosing the question that you are best prepared to answer thoroughly in the time permitted. You should spend 5 minutes organizing or outlining your answer. Write your answer to the question on the lined paper of the Section II free-response booklet, making sure to indicate the question you are answering by writing the appropriate question number at the top of each page.

Write an essay that

- Has a relevant thesis
- Addresses all parts of the question
- Supports the thesis with specific evidence
- Is well organized

2. To what degree and in what ways was the Reformation an outgrowth of the Italian Renaissance?

3. Describe how the revolution in physics in the twentieth century undermined the revolution in physics in the seventeenth century.

4. "In the seventeenth century, the French kings tamed the aristocracy, while in England, the aristocracy tamed the king." Evaluate the historical accuracy of this statement.

End of Part B

SECTION II, Part C
Suggested planning and writing time—35 minutes
Percent of Section II score—27 ½

DIRECTIONS You are to answer *one* question from the three questions below. Make your selection carefully, choosing the question that you are best prepared to answer thoroughly in the time permitted. You should spend 5 minutes organizing or outlining your answer. Write you answer to the question on the lined paper of the Section II free-response booklet, making sure to indicate the question you are answering by writing the appropriate question number at the top of each page.

Write an essay that

- Has a relevant thesis
- Addresses all parts of the question
- Supports the thesis with specific evidence
- Is well organized

5. Compare European colonialism in the early modern period and in the late nineteenth century.
6. How did artists and writers react to the Industrial Revolution in the nineteenth century? Be sure to discuss at least three specific works.
7. Account for the differences in the treatment of the defeated power at the Congress of Vienna and at the Congress of Versailles.

END OF EXAMINATION

ANSWERS FOR SECTION I

MULTIPLE-CHOICE ANSWER KEY

1. B	15. D	29. A	43. A	57. B	71. A
2. D	16. E	30. B	44. C	58. A	72. D
3. B	17. B	31. C	45. A	59. C	73. A
4. C	18. B	32. C	46. C	60. D	74. B
5. A	19. A	33. D	47. B	61. C	75. C
6. A	20. B	34. B	48. A	62. A	76. A
7. B	21. B	35. D	49. A	63. A	77. B
8. C	22. E	36. A	50. B	64. B	78. D
9. D	23. B	37. B	51. C	65. A	79. A
10. C	24. A	38. A	52. C	66. C	80. E
11. A	25. E	39. A	53. D	67. D	
12. B	26. B	40. C	54. C	68. B	
13. B	27. C	41. E	55. E	69. B	
14. C	28. B	42. B	56. E	70. C	

SCORING The multiple-choice section counts for 50 percent of your examination grade.

EXPLANATIONS FOR THE MULTIPLE-CHOICE ANSWERS

1. **ANSWER: (B)** The plague spread through central and eastern Europe, although some areas were not as heavily affected. (McKay, *A History of Western Society*, 8th ed., pp. 385–386/9th ed. p. 377)

2. **ANSWER: (D)** One reason the war lasted for such a long time was that the monarchs did not have standing armies, but could only request their vassals send knights for short periods of time to fight the battles. The strong central government, whether in the form of Parliament or monarch, could raise taxes to pay for the army. (McKay, *A History of Western Society*, 8th ed., pp. 388–389/9th ed., pp. 381–383)

3. **ANSWER: (B)** The arguments and division within the Catholic Church created a lack of credibility in an institution that had had tremendous influence for 1,300 years. (McKay, *A History of Western Society*, 8th ed., pp. 393–394/9th ed., pp. 387–388)

4. **ANSWER: (C)** Peasants blamed the nobility for their miserable lives, including taxation, chaos in the countryside, and defeat in war. Although they sometimes resented church taxes, they did not revolt for religious reasons. (McKay, *A History of Western Society*, 8th ed., p. 401/9th ed., pp. 390–392)

5. **ANSWER: (A)** Although a Christian work, Dante's poem includes bitter criticism of the Catholic Church. (McKay, *A History of Western Society*, 8th ed., pp. 405–407/9th ed., pp. 399–401)

6. **ANSWER: (A)** Given the economic strength of the city-states in Renaissance Italy, it is not surprising that the government would be ruled by the rich and well educated. (McKay, *A History of Western Society,* 8th ed., pp. 415–418/9th ed., pp. 409–410)

7. **ANSWER: (B)** A Renaissance man was admired for his multiple talents, individualism, and confidence, not necessarily for his devotion to religion. (McKay, *A History of Western Society,* 8th ed., pp. 420–421/9th ed., pp. 412–416)

8. **ANSWER: (C)** Renaissance art was commissioned and supported by secular groups such as noble families, guilds, and merchants. (McKay, *A History of Western Society,* 8th ed., p. 422/9th ed., pp. 421–422)

9. **ANSWER: (D)** Although education was increasingly important to humanists, they thought that the focus of women's education should be on religion and morals. (McKay, *A History of Western Society,* 8th ed., p. 428/9th ed., p. 414)

10. **ANSWER: (C)** Humanists believed that women should focus on activities in the home. (McKay, *A History of Western Society,* 8th ed., p. 432/9th ed., p. 433)

11. **ANSWER: (A)** Machiavelli's observation of human behavior during the intensely competitive era of the Renaissance led him to view man as inherently capable of evil. He praised Italy's past glory but wanted to change the politics in Renaissance Italy. (McKay, *A History of Western Society,* 8th ed., p. 429/9th ed., p. 416)

12. **ANSWER: (B)** Henry VII had a significant distrust of the nobility, in part due to the bitter struggle against his competition in the War of the Roses, so he used the Court of Star Chamber to rein in potential enemies. (McKay, *A History of Western Society,* 8th ed., p. 442/9th ed., p. 435)

13. **ANSWER: (B)** Ferdinand and Isabella reduced the influence of the nobility by appointing mostly middle-class men to government positions and by persuading the pope to allow them to appoint bishops. (McKay, *A History of Western Society,* 8th ed., p. 443/9th ed., p. 436)

14. **ANSWER: (C)** Criticism of the Catholic Church did not begin with Martin Luther, but his actions created the catalyst for the Protestant Reformation. (McKay, *A History of Western Society,* 8th ed., p. 454/9th ed., pp. 446–447)

15. **ANSWER: (D)** Luther was a conscientious priest, monk, and theology professor, who wanted to stimulate reform within the Catholic Church. (McKay, *A History of Western Society,* 8th ed., pp. 457–459/9th ed., pp. 446–449)

16. **ANSWER: (E)** Luther initially sympathized with the plight of the peasants, but was dismayed at the Peasants' Revolt in 1525, preferring to focus on religious, not social reform. (McKay, *A History of Western Society,* 8th ed., pp. 461–463/9th ed., pp. 450–451)

17. **ANSWER: (B)** Calvin upheld most of Luther's ideas, but the implications of his theory of *predestination* were that Christians should reflect their

beliefs in the morality and hard work evident in their lives. (McKay, *A History of Western Society*, 8th ed., pp. 470–472/9th ed., pp. 463–465)

18. **ANSWER: (B)** Similar to many monarchs, Henry VIII was very concerned about having a son to continue the dynasty. Since the pope would not grant him a divorce, he broke with the church and created the Anglican Church so that he could divorce and marry Anne Boleyn. (McKay, *A History of Western Society*, 8th ed., p. 475/9th ed., p. 465)

19. **ANSWER: (A)** The Catholics reconsidered both theology and practice in a series of meetings entitled the Council of Trent. Although they bolstered the discipline of the clergy, the church maintained all of its former theological doctrines. (McKay, *A History of Western Society*, 8th ed., pp. 479–480/9th ed., pp. 467–469)

20. **ANSWER: (B)** Henry IV, a politique, was willing to forgo his Protestant faith and become Catholic in order to spare France further religious war. He issued the Edict of Nantes, giving Protestants freedom to worship. (McKay, *A History of Western Society*, 8th ed., pp. 492–493/9th ed., pp. 472–473)

21. **ANSWER: (B)** Muslims dominated Indian Ocean trade before the arrival of the western European explorers, and the area known as Indonesia had valuable spices. (McKay, *A History of Western Society*, 8th ed., pp. 504–505/9th ed., pp. 484–485)

22. **ANSWER: (E)** Galleys were ships propelled by manpower and could not withstand the force of the wind and waves faced by explorers. They were replaced by the smaller and more maneuverable caravels. (McKay, *A History of Western Society*, 8th ed., pp. 505–506/9th ed., pp. 493–494)

23. **ANSWER: (B)** The Baroque style emphasized religious themes, in part as a reaction to the Protestant Reformation, and was very dramatic and emotional in order to rekindle faith. (McKay, *A History of Western Society*, 8th ed., pp. 523–524/9th ed., pp. 539–540)

24. **ANSWER: (A)** Absolutism, the creation of a strong central government, developed in response to peasants' revolts and the need for stronger armies to defend the country. Louis XIV intentionally created a strong government, not only to preserve France but to glorify himself and his country. (McKay, *A History of Western Society*, 8th ed., pp. 537–539/9th ed., pp. 540–541)

25. **ANSWER: (E)** Although both mercantilism and a command economy are under the guidance of the government, only the command economy allows the government to control every aspect of the economy, including retention of the profits. (McKay, *A History of Western Society*, 8th ed., p. 540/9th ed., pp. 532–533)

26. **ANSWER: (B)** The tremendous influx of silver from South America created inflation, which, coupled with royal expenditures and a lack of middle class, produced an economic crisis and the subsequent decline of Spain. (McKay, *A History of Western Society*, 8th ed., pp. 544–545/9th ed., pp. 534–535)

27. **ANSWER: (C)** Stuart monarchs James I and Charles I insisted on imposing their views of divine right monarchy and Anglican beliefs in an environment of Puritan influence and the desire for Parliamentary power. The Stuart insistence led to the English civil war. (McKay, *A History of Western Society,* 8th ed., p. 550/9th ed., pp. 544–546)

28. **ANSWER: (B)** The Netherlands was neither absolutist nor parliamentary, but rather was led by middle-class republican merchants and financiers. (McKay, *A History of Western Society,* 8th ed., p. 556/9th ed., pp. 549–550)

29. **ANSWER: (A)** The Thirty Years' War destroyed one-third of the urban population and two-fifths of the rural population, devastating the countryside. (McKay, *A History of Western Society,* 8th ed., pp. 498–500/9th ed., pp. 562–565)

30. **ANSWER: (B)** Peter's goal was to bring Russia out of isolation by expanding trade and providing the benefits of westernization. (McKay, *A History of Western Society,* 8th ed., pp. 581–585/9th ed., pp. 576–580)

31. **ANSWER: (C)** The Enlightenment followed the scientific revolution and was influenced by the attitude of experimentation during the scientific revolution. (McKay, *A History of Western Society,* 8th ed., p. 602/9th ed., pp. 598)

32. **ANSWER: (C)** Although many Enlightenment thinkers were deists and believed in God, their philosophies were focused on the nature of man and rationalism. (McKay, *A History of Western Society,* 8th ed., p. 605/9th ed., pp. 598–599)

33. **ANSWER: (D)** Catherine was admired by the philosophes, and exchanged considerable correspondence with Voltaire. Although many of her practices were unenlightened, she represented sympathy for the ideas and consideration of them. (McKay, *A History of Western Society,* 8th ed., p. 618/9th ed., pp. 610–613)

34. **ANSWER: (B)** Even though the consolidation of small farms into larger fields was more efficient, it was met with resistance by both poor peasants and noble landowners. (McKay, *A History of Western Society,* 8th ed., p. 635/9th ed., pp. 634–636)

35. **ANSWER: (D)** Population growth was relatively slow before the eighteenth century, in part due to war and disease, but the improvements during the agricultural revolution contributed to more food for the populace. (McKay, *A History of Western Society,* 8th ed., p. 637/9th ed., p. 626)

36. **ANSWER: (A)** Slavery enabled European investors in the Caribbean to profit from the sugar production and North Americans to profit from tobacco plantations. (McKay, *A History of Western Society,* 8th ed., pp. 650–651/9th ed., pp. 641–643)

37. **ANSWER: (B)** Smith argued against what he viewed as the confining policies of government involvement in trade in the prevailing economic philosophy of mercantilism. However, he believed that the government

should provide infrastructure and defense. (McKay, *A History of Western Society,* 8th ed., p. 655/9th ed., pp. 647–648)

38. **ANSWER: (A)** A common misconception is that couples married young, but records confirm that they waited until their late twenties, when they could afford to live away from their parents. (McKay, *A History of Western Society,* 8th ed., pp. 662–663/9th ed., pp. 653–654)

39. **ANSWER: (A)** As the population grew, so did inflation, which meant that the poorest people could not afford much to eat. Game laws also deprived people of shooting or trapping animals on the land they rented from the nobles. (McKay, *A History of Western Society,* 8th ed., p. 672/9th ed., pp. 663–664)

40. **ANSWER: (C)** When peasants in the countryside began ransacking chateaux during the Great Fear, the nobles agreed to eliminate many of the taxes and oppressive policies the nobles had forced on the peasants. (McKay, *A History of Western Society,* 8th ed., p. 703/9th ed., pp. 690–691)

41. **ANSWER: (E)** Although women had been involved in the French Revolution, they had not gained official political rights. Napoleon wanted a stronger role for men and reduced the economic and social power of women. (McKay, *A History of Western Society,* 8th ed., p. 714/9th ed., p. 705)

42. **ANSWER: (B)** The dramatic growth of the population caused some economists to predict that wages would sink and the standard of living would decrease. Their predictions proved to be false. (McKay, *A History of Western Society,* 8th ed., pp. 734–735/9th ed., pp. 725–727)

43. **ANSWER: (A)** Britain was the first to industrialize, focusing on the textile industry. Russia, still isolated and lacking a foundation in education and the Enlightenment, did not industrialize until the turn of the twentieth century. (McKay, *A History of Western Society,* 8th ed., p. 736/9th ed., p. 728)

44. **ANSWER: (C)** Middle class Europeans were wealthy and enjoyed the good life. The top 1 to 2 percent had servants, invested in art, and traveled extensively throughout Europe. (McKay, *A History of Western Society,* 8th ed., p. 796/9th ed., pp. 788–789)

45. **ANSWER: (A)** Britain had a history of some democracy and was the first to introduce reform legislation. (McKay, *A History of Western Society,* 8th ed., pp. 772–775/9th ed., p. 763)

46. **ANSWER: (C)** Although Napoleon III brought on a series of disasters, France retained enough vitality to remain one of the five great powers of the 1800s. (McKay, *A History of Western Society,* 8th ed., pp. 824–826/9th ed., pp. 816–818)

47. **ANSWER: (B)** The Iron Chancellor, whose statements foreshadowed Hitler, preferred force to parliamentary procedures. (McKay, *A History of Western Society,* 8th ed., p. 830/9th ed., pp. 821–822)

48. **ANSWER: (A)** They were Dutch Calvinists who fought against the British and lost. (McKay, *A History of Western Society*, 8th ed., p. 869/9th ed., p. 859)

49. **ANSWER: (A)** Outraged, Zola accused France's General Staff of falsifying evidence to keep Alfred Dreyfus in prison and letting the guilty person go. For this Anatole France called Zola the Conscience of Man, but he was still accused of libel and had to leave France to avoid imprisonment. (McKay, *A History of Western Society*, 8th ed., pp. 842–843/9th ed., pp. 834–835)

50. **ANSWER: (B)** The cotton textile industry in Britain was the first to undergo mechanization; automatic machinery increased production. (McKay, *A History of Western Society*, 8th ed., p. 727/9th ed., p. 719)

51. **ANSWER: (C)** Many new jobs emerged. Millions of workers were involved in the construction of the railroads (miners, iron workers, those who built the railroads, and those who ran them) and in the growth of industry they produced. McKay, *A History of Western Society*, 8th ed., p. 732/9th ed., pp. 726–728)

52. **ANSWER: (C)** Although some British small farmers left the country, the increased food production resulting from the enclosure movement contributed to a rise in population. (McKay, *A History of Western Society*, 8th ed., p. 633/9th ed., pp. 624–625)

53. **ANSWER: (D)** Thousands of immigrant women, especially from Ireland and Scandinavia, found work in middle- and upper-class homes. (McKay, *A History of Western Society*, 8th ed., pp. 802–803/9th ed., pp. 791–794)

54. **ANSWER: (C)** Unlike the West, Japan's government was very much involved in developing its industries. (McKay, *A History of Western Society*, 8th ed., pp. 879–882/9th ed., pp. 870–872)

55. **ANSWER: (E)** Women did not earn the vote until after World War I. (McKay, *A History of Western Society*, 8th ed., pp. 838–839/9th ed., pp. 831–832)

56. **ANSWER: (E)** Sociologists applied Darwin's theories to their observations about society. (McKay, *A History of Western Society*, 8th ed., p. 815/9th ed., p. 807)

57. **ANSWER: (B)** Freud developed the theory that adult problems could be traced to childhood experiences. (McKay, *A History of Western Society*, 8th ed., p. 811/9th ed., p. 804)

58. **ANSWER: (A)** John Constable (1776–1837) painted misty, dreamy idealizations of rural life. (McKay, *A History of Western Society*, 8th ed., p. 766/9th ed., p. 758)

59. **ANSWER: (C)** The word *romanticism* derives from the romances of the Middle Ages, which were imbued with the ideals and emotions of chivalry. (McKay, *A History of Western Society*, 8th ed., p. 766/9th ed., p. 758)

60. **ANSWER: (D)** Pasteur also discovered that disease could be prevented by purifying foods. (McKay, *A History of Western Society,* 8th ed., p. 792/9th ed., p. 783)

61. **ANSWER: (C)** At the end of the century some intellectuals were concerned about the values of European society, but their ideas did not contribute to the causes of World War I. (McKay, *A History of Western Society,* 8th ed., pp. 888–891/9th ed., pp. 880–883)

62. **ANSWER: (A)** The horrors of World War I centered on the uncertainty of the trenches, where soldiers lived day and night and never knew when mortars, poison gas, or enemy attacks might strike. (McKay, *A History of Western Society,* 8th ed., p. 895/9th ed., pp. 887–888)

63. **ANSWER: (A)** Although the women's role in the home continued, it was also necessary for women to take the jobs of men who were fighting in the war. (McKay, *A History of Western Society,* 8th ed., pp. 900–901/9th ed., pp. 890–892)

64. **ANSWER: (B)** One strong persuasive strategy was that Lenin promised to withdraw Russia from World War I due to the vast loss of lives and deteriorating morale. He fulfilled his promise and signed a treaty with Germany. (McKay, *A History of Western Society,* 8th ed., pp. 906–908/9th ed., pp. 896–898)

65. **ANSWER: (A)** The lack of social mobility, as well as extensive starvation, poverty, and the losses in World War I, caused the Russian Revolution. (McKay, *A History of Western Society,* 8th ed., pp. 904–906/9th ed., pp. 895–896)

66. **ANSWER: (C)** Lenin gained popularity by opposing the Provisional Government, criticizing it for remaining in the war and not addressing the desperate starvation of the people. (McKay, *A History of Western Society,* 8th ed., pp. 906–908/9th ed., pp. 896–898)

67. **ANSWER: (D)** The Russian Revolution was not copied by other countries, although China became Communist some thirty years later. (McKay, *A History of Western Society,* 8th ed., pp. 906–908/9th ed., pp. 896–898)

68. **ANSWER: (B)** Joyce, an early-twentieth-century author, revolutionized structure and form by developing stream of consciousness writing. His style pushed language to what some consider its most extreme limits. Some of his books are very difficult to understand. (McKay, *A History of Western Society,* 8th ed., p. 929/9th ed., p. 920)

69. **ANSWER: (B)** A British author, born in India, Kipling held a romantic view of imperialism and a condescending view of the natives. After his death, public rancor against his belief in the privileges of the empire damaged his literary reputation. This was temporary, however, and his works are even now widely known. Many children read his *Jungle Book.* (McKay, *A History of Western Society,* 8th ed., p. 876/9th ed., p. 867)

70. **ANSWER: (C)** Although the causes of World War I were complex, Germany was clearly the aggressor, and the Allies, led by France, insisted

that Germany pay reparations. (McKay, *A History of Western Society*, 8th ed., p. 913/9th ed., pp. 902–903)

71. **ANSWER: (A)** Only France experienced destruction of its land because the war was fought there. (McKay, *A History of Western Society*, 8th ed., p. 940/9th ed., p. 932)

72. **ANSWER: (D)** Britain remained relatively stable after World War I. Germany suffered economic woes due to its losses during the war and its reparation payments. (McKay, *A History of Western Society*, 8th ed., p. 938/9th ed., pp. 929–930)

73. **ANSWER: (A)** Lenin's New Economic Policy was the least totalitarian policy because it allowed some capitalistic characteristics, such as private profit. (McKay, *A History of Western Society*, 8th ed., pp. 957–958/9th ed., pp. 949–950)

74. **ANSWER: (B)** Germany invaded Russia, but Russian resistance and the bitter winter defeated the Germans. (McKay, *A History of Western Society*, 8th ed., pp. 975, 980–981, 982/9th ed., pp. 966, 972–974)

75. **ANSWER: (C)** Decolonization, the process of colonies gaining independence, was unrelated to the cold war. However, the newly freed colonies did become targets for the two superpowers in terms of attempts to gain allies through economic contributions. (McKay, *A History of Western Society*, 8th ed., pp. 999–1001/9th ed., pp. 989–993)

76. **ANSWER: (A)** Although there was a slight increase in family size after World War II, in general the birth rate has declined in Europe since the 1960s. Currently some countries are offering tax benefits to couples who have more than one child. (McKay, *A History of Western Society*, 8th ed., p. 1011/9th ed., p. 1002)

77. **ANSWER: (B)** Simone de Beauvoir wrote *The Second Sex* and Betty Friedan wrote *The Feminine Mystique*, raising consciousness about women's rights. (McKay, *A History of Western Society*, 8th ed., pp. 1017–1018/9th ed., pp. 1017–1018)

78. **ANSWER: (D)** Taking advantage of detente, the Soviet Union invaded Afghanistan in 1979. The other answers were causes of the fall of communism. (McKay, *A History of Western Society*, 8th ed., pp. 1031–1033/9th ed., pp. 1020–1022)

79. **ANSWER: (A)** When communism ended in Yugoslavia, underlying ethnic tensions escalated. (McKay, *A History of Western Society*, 8th ed., pp. 1047–1048/9th ed., pp. 1037–1039)

80. **ANSWER: (E)** The European Union focuses on economic and political unity. It has no plans to supplement the United Nations and NATO military forces. (McKay, *A History of Western Society*, 8th ed., pp. 1048–1050/9th ed., pp. 1039–1041)

ANSWERS FOR SECTION II

PART A RESPONSE

AP European History DBQ essays are scored on the core-scoring method. Each specific instruction before the DBQ question itself refers to a core point. Once you earn all core points, you can earn additional points for doing those tasks well or for effectively bringing in outside information. For more discussion on core scoring, see the introductory chapter.

Thesis: To earn a point for thesis, it must be specific and refer to documents.

Example of a thesis statement that would *not* earn a point:

> People always get upset when there are terrible executions. Although it often happens during revolutions, as in the case of Russia too, afterward people usually regret it.

Why is this not acceptable? It doesn't refer to or come out of the documents, so while it is a valid statement in and of itself, it is not a good thesis for a DB.

Example of a thesis statement that would be acceptable:

> There were many reactions to the execution of Charles I. While the Puritans supported it, others at the time and later on came to see it as cruel and unnecessary.

Use of documents: If you fail to get a point for thesis, you also can't get a point for using documents in support of your thesis.

Uses a majority of documents: In this case, seven must be used. If you use only six, you cannot earn this point. You get one point for using seven, even if you make mistakes on one or two of them. Don't list documents together (e.g., Documents 3, 5, and 7); you must discuss them individually.

INTERPRETS DOCUMENTS CORRECTLY: You are allowed to make only one major error, which is defined as an interpretation that leads you to an erroneous conclusion or an erroneous grouping. A major error, for example, would be to describe John Milton as an opponent of the execution of the king.

GROUPS: You must have three groups of documents. A group must have two documents in it, discussed specifically. Don't list documents together (e.g., Documents 3, 5, and 7); you must discuss them individually and show how each belongs in the group you have made.

POV: Point-of-view analysis. This is a crucial core point, one that some students don't do or do poorly. Such analysis shows that you understand that a document is written by a particular person at a particular time for a particular purpose and may not be the whole truth. The documents summary above includes POV analysis that you could make for most documents. It's important to think about the reliability of the document (for example, how accurate can an engraving be if made by a foreigner who presumably was not an eyewitness?) or about how a person's position in society or political views could color what he or she writes (for example, Lucy Hutchinson's description of Charles I is probably biased because her husband signed his death warrant).

PART B RESPONSES

2. *To what degree and in what ways was the Reformation an outgrowth of the Italian Renaissance?*

To address this essay, you need to think about what elements the Renaissance and the Reformation share and in which they differ. The question asks you to make an evaluation as well as to demonstrate your knowledge of the two periods.

Ways the Renaissance influenced the Reformation: Secularism fostered by the Renaissance was reinforced by Protestantism. Although primarily religious, the Protestants argued that one must do God's work in this world rather than abandon it. They rejected celibacy in favor of marriage and family, and accepted worldly work as a calling from God. The individualistic spirit of the Renaissance was acknowledged by the Reformation's insistence on each individual's ability to read and interpret Scripture. Renaissance humanism made the work of Christian textual analysis and editing possible. The nationalism spawned in the Renaissance period was acknowledged by the establishment of national churches.

Ways in which the Renaissance did not foster the Reformation: The Renaissance was profoundly interested in antiquity, which the Reformation ignored. This included the republican and homoerotic values of ancient Greece and Rome. The Italian humanists explored various aspects of paganism (Pico) while northern humanists (More and Erasmus), although critical of the church, remained faithful to the notion of a universal church. The Renaissance exalted the arts, and the graphic arts conveyed the values of proportion, realism, and imitation of nature including the nude body. The Protestants generally rejected visual representation or elaborate architecture, seeing art as potentially dangerous or distracting rather than fundamental and liberating.

3. *Describe how the revolution in physics in the twentieth century undermined the revolution in physics in the seventeenth century.*

This question involves description across the centuries. Be sure you have some knowledge of both periods before you select this one.

In the seventeenth century, the work of Galileo, Kepler, and Newton, among others, proved the Copernican heliocentric hypothesis through observation with the telescope, experiment, and mathematics. They overthrew Ptolemaic cosmology and Aristotelian physics. The Earth was displaced from the center of the solar system; the Moon, Earth, and the Sun were not perfect spheres; and the planetary orbits were elliptical, not circular. Newton's universal law of gravity demonstrated that the heavens and the earth followed the same laws. Galileo developed the law of inertia. The universe imagined by the seventeenth-century physicists was limited, predictable, and subject to universal scientific laws.

In the twentieth century, this cosmology was overturned because of new understandings on both atomic and astronomical levels. Max Planck and others developed quantum physics to describe uneven energies of protons and electrons; matter and energy were no longer distinct. Einstein's theory of special relativity disputed the idea that observable matter is not fixed; he also argued that space was curved and that time was a dimension. New subatomic particles were continuously being discovered. Heisenberg developed the uncertainty principle asserting that it was impossible to exactly predict the location and movement of electrons. The universe was infinite, uncertain, based on unstable building blocks, complex, and knowable only with highly abstract mathematics.

4. *"In the seventeenth century, the French kings tamed the aristocracy, while in England, the aristocracy tamed the king." Evaluate the historical accuracy of this statement.*

Essentially this question refers to the English Revolution and absolutism in France. Again, you'll need to know both subjects to answer this question well. You should not assume that the statement must be valid, if you have evidence to the contrary. A superior essay will answer this not with a yes-or-no response but with a measured answer carefully delineating the degrees of accuracy, noting, for example, that Louis XIV won the cooperation of the nobility more than he browbeat them into submission.

Kings Louis XIII and XIV established French absolutism in the seventeenth century. With the guidance of his chief minister, Cardinal Richelieu, Louis XIII attacked the independence of the nobility. Neither king called the Estates General. Intendants were sent to the countryside to impose royal control over local politics. The nobility reacted to Louis XIII's attempts at centralization of power with a revolt called the Fronde. Louis XIV worked assiduously to diminish the power of the nobility. He built the extraordinary palace at Versailles to impress the nobles and turn them into courtiers. He spied on the nobles and used bourgeois men for important positions rather than nobles. He also sold the bourgeoisie titles of nobility; this brought down the prestige of those titles. Although the nobility remained wealthy, they lost prestige and power under Louis XIV.

In England, on the other hand, the lower aristocracy, the gentry, worked with the other classes to insist on their rights when Charles I attempted to rule on his own. They fought and won a civil war with the royalists and executed Charles I, the first monarch to be so treated in Europe. After a complex and convoluted conflict and a short-lived republic, England became a constitutional monarchy in the Glorious Revolution of 1688. The nobility of England were willing to tax themselves as long as Parliament, in which they sat in great numbers in both houses, had a voice in government expenditures. They retained their political power in Parliament and as advisers to the king in the cabinet system.

Part C Responses

5. *Compare European colonialism in the early modern period and in the late nineteenth century.*

- To answer this question well, you should discuss several similarities and differences.
- Similarities: In both periods, Europeans were motivated by religious missionary zeal, by economic motives, and by the desire for national glory. In both periods, colonies were seen as crucial for national prestige as well as necessary for naval reasons.

- Differences: In the early period, Europeans rarely penetrated into the interior of a colony, building mostly coastal settlements. In Asia and Africa, they showed some respect for native rulers. Their impact there tended to be limited to those with whom they came into contact, but in the New World, the European conquest thoroughly transformed those societies. Economically, Europeans were mostly interested in raw materials, slaves, and agricultural produce. By the nineteenth century, Europeans had lost most of their colonies in the New World but colonized virtually all of Africa and most of Asia. They penetrated to the interior of their colonies because of medical and technological shipping advances and had vast military superiority, which allowed them to take over politically through either direct or indirect rule. They built infrastructure and imposed European educational and value systems. Economically, rubber, oil, and other products needed for their industrial economies were important.

6. *How did artists and writers react to the Industrial Revolution in the nineteenth century? Be sure to discuss at least three specific works.*

- Many AP examinations have questions about literature or art. In answering such questions, it's crucial not to discuss the art only as art but to look for its historical importance and meaning.
- In this case, the two movements that most reacted to the Industrial Revolution in the early nineteenth century were realism and romanticism.
- Realism: Realist artists and writers sought to depict the lives and conditions of ordinary people. Writers: Dickens, *Hard Times*; Zola, *Germinal*; Flaubert, *Madame Bovary*; and George Eliot, *Middlemarch*; among many others. Artists: Daniel McDonald, *The Discovery of the Potato Blight*, and Ford Maddox Brown, *Work*.
- Romanticism: Romantic writers sought escape from the industrial, urban landscape, focusing instead on nature and the mysterious. They glorified pre-industrial times, particularly the Middle Ages, although some artists were fascinated by trains and railroad stations. Writers: Walter Scott, *Ivanhoe*; William Wordsworth, poems like "Daffodils"; Victor Hugo, *The Hunchback of Notre Dame*; and Mary Shelley, *Frankenstein*. Artists: J. W. Turner, and Delacroix, *Liberty Leading the People, Massacre at Chios*.

7. *Account for the differences in the treatment of the defeated power at the Congress of Vienna and at the Congress of Versailles.*

- This question asks you to describe the treatment of the defeated power at each conference, to compare the two treatments, and explain the differences.
- Congress of Vienna: The defeated power was France.
- Treatment: France was invited to the conference, and its representative, Talleyrand, played a big part in the negotiations. France got off relatively lightly, losing little land and being welcomed back into the family of nations.
- Explanation: The great powers of Europe had definitively defeated Napoleon and he had abdicated, although he returned and had to be defeated again, and was sent far off again into exile. The monarchy was restored, according to the principles of legitimacy and conservatism of the conference.
- Paris Peace Conference, Versailles: The defeated power was Germany.

- Treatment: Germany was not invited to the conference and did not participate in the negotiations. The peace was harsh, with Germany losing some land and its colonies and being saddled with reparations and a severely restricted military. The Kaiser abdicated, and a republic was declared.
- Explanation: The war ended with an armistice, not a victory. The war had been horribly costly in terms of human life as well as financially, and four years of terrible war had been accompanied by strongly nationalistic, anti-German propaganda. All this left France and Britain suspicious of German power, seeking vengeance.

Calculating Your Score on the Diagnostic Test

The following is based on the 2002 AP World History Examination, which is the only released examination at this time.

Scoring the Multiple-Choice Section

Use the following formula to calculate your raw score on the multiple-choice section of the exam:

[_______ − (1/4 × _________)] × 0.8571 = __________

number correct (out of 70) — number wrong (do not round) — weighted Section I score

Scoring the Free-Response Section

Use the following formula to calculate your raw score on the free-response section of the exam:

Part A ________ × 2.2222 = ___________
(out of 9) (do not round)

Part B ________ × 2.2222 = ___________
(out of 9) (do not round)

Part C ________ × 2.2222 = ___________
(out of 9) (do not round)

Sum = ___________
weighted Section II score
(do not round)

Your Composite Score

__________ + __________ = ___________

weighted Section I score — weighted Section II score — composite score (round to nearest whole number)

Once you have calculated your composite score, see where it falls in the Composite Score Range below. *Remember that your composite score is only an estimate of your performance on the College Board exam.*

AP GRADES BY SCORE RANGE

Composite Score Range	AP Grade
78–120	5
62–77	4
43–61	3
27–42	2
0–26	1

Part II

A Review of AP European History

12

The Crisis of the Later Middle Ages, 1300–1450

The fourteenth century, which can be considered both the end of the Middle Ages and the beginning of the early modern era, was a pivotal era that saw both horrific disasters and significant changes in economic and social structure and in people's ideas. Societal tensions were reflected in changing attitudes toward the dominant religious institution in Europe, the Catholic Church; the growth of "fur-collar" crime; concerns over gender relations and sexuality; and a new ethnic consciousness. The period from 1300 to 1450 laid the groundwork for modern Europe. In a time much preoccupied with death, European life was reshaped and reborn.

Key Concepts

- Europe experienced climate change and an epidemic of extraordinary swiftness and devastation in which about half of the population of Europe died within a few years. The horrendous loss of population had a significant and long-lasting impact.
- England and France forged their identities as states in the Hundred Years' War, which they fought intermittently between 1337 and 1453. What began as a feudal war helped midwife the formation of two powerful and territorially integrated states.
- After the high-point of its power in the thirteenth century, the Catholic Church faced challenges in the fourteenth century. Kings sought greater influence over the clergy, theologians rejected many of the church's positions, and others challenged the legitimacy of its power. The Babylonian Captivity, during which the popes resided in Avignon, France, for nearly seventy years, and the Great Schism, during which there were two or three competing popes for the next more than forty years, significantly damaged the prestige of the church.

- The late Middle Ages witnessed a great deal of social change, particularly in the growing cities. Guilds tightened their memberships, gender roles became more stratified, and there were many peasant and urban revolts. A pattern of late marriage led to prostitution, homosexuality, and other sexual issues that became a matter of public concern.

CLIMATE CHANGE AND FAMINE

Natural and human records have led historical geographers to conclude that the period from 1300 to 1450 was a "little Ice Age" in which the climate became colder and wetter after three centuries of relative warmth. Crops were destroyed by the cold and storms as frequently as one year in four; this led to scarcity. A great famine occurred from 1315 to 1322, weakening those people who were not already dying of starvation (about one-third of the population of Burgundy died) and thus further reducing productivity.

Epidemics reduced the population of both humans and animals still more. In some areas, homesteads were abandoned; vagabonds were everywhere. As marriages were delayed, the population declined even further. Decline in demand from a smaller population increased urban unemployment.

Governments were ineffective in the face of these difficulties, although they did try to control speculation, establish price controls, and acquire grain from abroad. Although long-distance trade was fostered, particularly when the Italians improved sailing ships and opened up new routes, famine relief was difficult to achieve. Popular discontent was vented on the rich, on speculators, on Jews, and on lepers.

International ships spread disease-carrying rats and insects. The Black Death, originating from China and arriving on Genoese ships in 1347, was a combination of bubonic plague spread by fleas on rats and spread by air in a pneumonic form. The Black Death spread quickly and devastatingly throughout Europe, giving between a third and a half of the population a very unpleasant death. It was particularly devastating in the cities where sanitary conditions were very poor, and it recurred with some regularity until 1721. There were some attempts to prevent it by quarantine, improving sanitation, eradicating the "poisons" in the air, and treating the disease with lancing and bloodletting. Vivid descriptions, like those written by Boccaccio in *The Decameron* shortly after the onset of the Black Death, reveal attempts to prevent the spread of the disease and a rudimentary if not inaccurate understanding of how it spread. There were some hospitals in major cities, mostly established by merchants, but they provided shelter and compassion more than treatment.

Some blamed Jews for the plague, and thousands of Jews were murdered in mob violence. Others blamed human sinfulness, seeing the plague as a punishment from God. Many priests stayed with the ill to minister to them; the clergy had a terribly high death rate. In some places, the loss of clergy led bishops to permit lay administration of the sacraments.

AP Tip

The Black Death led many to question their faith. This, as well as the occasional administration of the sacraments by laymen, had consequences during the Reformation.

The economic consequences of the Black Death are much disputed. Aristocratic, or seigniorial, prosperity was disrupted, but only temporarily. In Florence, guilds accepted many new members, bringing "new men" to the fore. There was a general inflation in Europe, and the shortage of labor led to a brief rise in real wages, although laws like the English Statute of Laborers sought to prevent this. In general, the standard of living in towns went up, and per capita wealth increased. Peasants, too, had greater mobility.

AP Tip

The shortage of labor after the Black Death meant urban workers and peasants could negotiate better terms for themselves, a relatively rare situation in European history. When economic conditions began to improve and population stabilized, employers and nobles tried to revert to lower wages and higher manorial obligations. They succeeded only in part.

Psychologically, many people became deeply pessimistic. Some became pleasure seekers, while others turned to religion. Ascetics, pilgrims, and flagellants sought to do penance for humankind's sins. The Dance of Death was a frequent motif in art.

This period also saw the foundation of many European universities, including universities in Prague and Florence, and several of the colleges at Oxford and Cambridge. Student bodies in medieval universities tended to become more national rather than international as had been characteristic of earlier university life when students traveled from university to university, from city to city, seeking the most prominent scholars.

THE HUNDRED YEARS' WAR

From 1337 to 1453, England and France fought over English feudal claims to the French throne. During the 116 years of intermittent war, England won every important battle, except the last one, and each country forged its identity as a nation-state while establishing fundamental institutions of government.

AP Tip

Typically, the AP exam has few multiple-choice questions on specific battles; its focus is on the causes and consequences of war. It is wise not to skim over wars.

Causes

The conflict was first focused on Aquitaine, a valuable area that the English crown had inherited in the twelfth century but the French king wished to absorb. When the Capetian dynasty died out in 1328, the French nobles, in order to exclude the English king Edward III from his royal claim in France (his mother was the sister of the last Capetian king), voted to exclude women and their sons in general from the French throne, a provision that stayed in force until 1789, and to pass the crown to Philip VI of the Valois line. Those French nobles seeking to weaken the French monarchy supported Edward, so the English-French war was also a civil war. Another issue was economic competition over the rich Flemish wool-producing towns, with the Flemish aristocracy tied to the French while its merchant class supported the English. The war offered many opportunities for honor, advancement, and wealth for enthusiastic nobles.

Importance

Public opinion was manipulated on both sides of the Channel, each country sensationalizing the evils of the other and enjoining the clergy to support their king. The fostering of mutual hatred helped nationalism grow in each country.

The war was militarily important. It ended both medieval tactics and chivalric rules of war. England won most of the battles, the famous ones being Crécy in 1346, Poitiers in 1356, and Agincourt in 1415, by using artillery for the first time and the longbow, which unhorsed knights in armor and proved superior to the crossbow. The effective use of cannon meant stone castles became obsolete while the expense of artillery enhanced the power of national governments.

Nevertheless, the French won the war, largely because of the nationalistic fervor stimulated by Joan of Arc. A simple peasant girl who saved the French monarchy, she later became one of the two patron saints of France. When she was sixteen, she heard voices urging her to help the dauphin (uncrowned king) expel the British. She went to court and was able to swiftly convince him to allow her to accompany an army to relieve the siege of Orléans. Her leadership inspired the French soldiers; ten days later, the English withdrew, and ten days after that, Charles was crowned. Joan was captured by the Burgundians, who sold her to their English allies. The English tried and executed her for witchcraft and heresy because she had cut her hair, wore men's clothes, and claimed to hear directly from God. The war itself ended in 1453. The English possessions in France were reduced to Calais.

AP Tip

Although the AP exam focuses on events after 1450, the consequences of the Hundred Years' War are important. The war shows the validity of Yogi Berra's statement "It ain't over till it's over," as the English won every important battle of the war except the last one. The war is also a wonderful example of how sometimes it is better to lose: If England had won the war and held onto its French territories, its development as a nation-state would have been hindered. As it was, by losing everything in France except Calais, English nationalism and the sense of identity of England with a distinct culture and a defined space on its "blessed isle" was much enhanced.

CONSEQUENCES

The death toll from the Hundred Years' War was huge, in contrast to medieval wars. The economies of France and the Low Countries, the areas where the war was fought, were devastated. In England, the costs of the war were stunning, although initially the plunder the soldiers brought back added to the wealth of their households. The government raised taxes on wool, making it harder to sell abroad and thus hurting the economy.

In England, the war fostered the development of Parliament, as Edward III's constant need for money for the war forced him to call Parliament into session thirty-seven out of the fifty years of his reign. In other countries in Europe, representative assemblies were losing their role as kings centralized their power. But in England, the Commons—consisting of knights and wealthy burghers—separated out from the Lords and won the right to approve all nonfeudal levies in 1341, ensuring their power of the purse. England was also unusual in that it had one Parliament for the whole country, while elsewhere, regional or provincial assemblies dominated. England's path toward constitutional monarchy advanced greatly during the Hundred Years' War.

> **AP Tip**
>
> One of the most important stories in European history is England's early creation and successful operation of a limited monarchy for nearly 800 years. The origins of English constitutionalism lie in the Magna Carta and the development of Parliament during the Hundred Years' War. The Magna Carta, which the barons of England forced King John to sign in 1215, is arguably the single most important document in establishing limitations on royal power. It restricted the judicial powers of the king, protecting the barons, clergy, and burghers (wealthy townsmen) from arbitrary arrest or cruel punishment and granting trial by jury. It also required the "common consent of the realm" for the levying of new taxes. During the Hundred Years' War, when the king needed ever more funds, he was forced to get that common consent; this made Parliament more powerful. Although the Magna Carta was a feudal document, the rights it guaranteed to the ruling elites were extended over the centuries to all royal subjects.

CHALLENGES TO THE CHURCH

The Catholic Church faced a number of challenges during these tempestuous centuries: inadequate and conflicted leadership, which put it under the domination of powerful states; a demand from within for restructuring of the church from a papal hierarchy to councils made up from the clergy; and the growth of lay piety and mysticism.

The Babylonian Captivity is the name commonly used to describe the period from 1309 to 1376 when the popes resided in Avignon, under the domination of the French king, rather than in Rome. There the popes focused their attention on internal administrative reforms. The luxurious nature of the Avignon court fueled discontent, while Rome and the Papal States suffered from the absence of the popes. After nearly seventy years, the papacy returned to Rome, only to be caught up in nationalistic disputes over who should be pope. Two popes were elected, one an Italian (Urban VI) in Rome, the other a cousin of the King of France (Clement VII) in Avignon, with the various European states supporting one or the other according to their political interests. One result of this Great Schism was an effort to reform the essentially monarchical organization of the church by sharing power with church councils representative of all Christians. The intellectual underpinning of the conciliar movement was the writing of Marsiglio of Padua whose *Defensor Pacis* of 1324 led to his excommunication. Marsiglio also argued that the church must be subordinate to the state and that it had no right to own property.

Another powerful intellectual challenge to the church was laid down by John Wyclif whose ideas would reappear in the work of Martin Luther. He argued that the only source of Christian doctrine and practice should be the Scriptures, which should be read in the vernacular by the laity. Therefore, he declared, common religious practices like the veneration of saints and pilgrimages, as well as common church practices like simony (buying or selling of church office or preferment), pluralism (holding several offices, or benefices, at the same time), absenteeism (holding an office but living in another place), and even property ownership were all illegitimate.

AP Tip

Pilgrimages and the veneration of saints were also an important part of the urban economy, since pilgrimages fostered trade and the founding of towns along their routes.

Wyclif's ideas spread widely, and his supporters, called Lollards, were many. The English peasants used his ideas to justify their revolt in 1381, around the time the first English translation of the Bible was made. Women appreciated the Lollard support for women preachers. The Lollards had their greatest impact in the fifteenth century in Bohemia where the Czech priest John Hus, preaching at the university in his native language, not Latin, promoted Wyclif's ideas. Hus was himself not a radical, never challenging the fundamental legitimacy of the church or of the doctrine of transubstantiation, which asserts that a miracle occurs during the Eucharist and the wine and bread become literally the blood and body of Christ. But he did denounce abuses and argue for Scripture to be accepted, along with tradition and conscience, as the basis of church authority, and for both laity and clergy to receive both the wine and the bread at communion, in contrast to the practice of the day. His ideas were adopted by many Bohemians, particularly in the large city of Prague, for social, political, and economic reasons as well as religious ones. Czech nobles found them useful in their drive for independence from their Habsburg, German-speaking overlords. In 1415, at the Council of Constance, Hus was tried, found guilty, and executed for heresy, a decision publicly criticized in a petition signed by hundreds of Czech nobles. The nobles and the people joined together in an armed rebellion against the Habsburgs called the Hussite Wars.

AP Tip

The stories of Wyclif and Hus reveal the degree to which religious reform was tied to politics. They said much of what Martin Luther would articulate a century later, but the opposition had too much power, and their supporters were too weak to bring about reform. That would not be true in Luther's time.

The Council of Constance, called by the Holy Roman Emperor Sigismund, was one of several called to end the Great Schism, and this time it was ended with the election of Martin V as pope. Although several more councils were held, the conciliar movement was over; the papacy had won.

Lay Piety

The disorder and disunity in the Church, coupled with disputes among the various mendicant orders (especially the Franciscans and Dominicans), the disappointing performance of some priests, or the absence of priests (the Black Death made it hard to replace all those who had died), brought the laity, the ordinary members of the church, into a more prominent role as managers of ecclesiastical properties. Many formed confraternities, voluntary associations of like-minded individuals, to do charitable or spiritual work.

Economic and Social Change

One reflection of social turmoil was the widespread peasants' revolts throughout Europe in the fourteenth and fifteenth centuries, beginning with a revolt in Flanders in the 1320s over taxes and fees. Similar issues, prompted by the financial demands of the Hundred Years' War, led to a major jacquerie in France in 1358. Such revolts usually involved venting frustration through arson and pillage of aristocratic estates, and sometimes murder and rape. Often, the peasants were joined by the urban poor and even parish priests. The Peasants' Revolt in England in 1381 was a similar reaction against the attempt to return wages to pre–Black Death levels and reflected the rising expectations of increasingly prosperous working classes as well as their resentment over aristocratic privilege and the collection of a head tax on adult males. Most revolts were crushed with ferocious force. Nevertheless, enough time without serfdom passed for it to disappear from England within a hundred years.

In the areas of Europe where urbanization had reached significant proportions, peasants' revolts were often accompanied by urban revolts as well. In Florence, one of only five European cities with over 100,000 people in the fourteenth century, poor workers known as *ciompi* demanded political rights. This particular revolt reflected a new form of capitalist production. While still hand manufacturers, guild masters now often ran shops that employed others to do only one or two steps of the manufacturing process of a larger enterprise, instead of running shops that did all the steps of the manufacturing process. This offered wonderful opportunities for some artisans but lowered the social and economic status of most.

AP Tip

It is important to understand the guild system as an early form of European capitalism. In the typical medieval city, the various trades, manufactures, and services were each organized into craft guilds, one for bakers; another for notaries, a third for wool manufacturers, another for wood merchants, and so on. The guilds organized production, ensured quality by insisting on specified standards for materials and craftsmanship, provided training from apprentice to journeyman (skilled day worker) to master, who showed his or her expertise by creating a masterpiece. They also ensured that all masters would have enough work by limiting the hours of operation and setting minimum wages and prices. Competition was encouraged more with other cities than within the city. Guilds were also social service agencies, taking care of the widows and children of the masters. In some cities, such as Florence, they dominated the government and formed guild republics.

In the fourteenth century, guild masters increasingly restricted the membership of the guilds, thus freezing out ambitious journeymen, who were skilled workers. In response, the journeymen tried to organize their own guilds to protect both their standard of living and the honor or prestige that separated them from unskilled workers. It was these journeymen who rose up in 1378 in Florence, seeking recognition so that they could participate in the republican government, which was restricted to guild masters.

GENDER AND SEXUALITY

In medieval cities, women had often worked in the shops and sometimes became masters. In the fourteenth century the participation of women was increasingly restricted. Women were excluded from the guilds and had no access to political power; nor were they welcomed in the journeymen guilds.

There were also significant changes in women's marital patterns in the late fourteenth century, which some historians argue helped create urban unrest. The typical pattern in Italy was that women married in their teens or early twenties; in northwestern Europe (England, Germany, France, and Scandinavia), however, noble and wealthy women married in their mid- to late twenties—an unusually late age of marriage for southern Europe—indicating that women tended to be more independent of their husbands and also to have fewer children.

Men too were typically older at marriage. Many in Italy did not marry until the age of thirty, and others married in their mid-twenties, as journeymen and university students were often forbidden from marrying. This European late marriage pattern for men left many unmarried men living in cities, which helped foster a riotous atmosphere. Many cities established brothels to fill the needs of these young men, with rules for the prostitutes and their customers; this was deemed justified, in part to prevent homosexuality. Although prostitution was legal, the women who provided this legal service had marginal rights and low social prestige.

Nevertheless, rape and sexual harassment were frequent, with female servants being particularly vulnerable. Although officially a capital offense, the actual penalties were light (except in cases of rape of a young girl of marriageable age) especially in contrast to the severe penalties for sodomy, mutilation, and forgery.

Same-sex relations also were part of medieval urban life, and in this period, they began to be considered crimes against nature, and sodomy (sexual acts not leading to procreation) became a capital offense. It is hard to estimate how common homosexuality was. In Elizabethan England, there were only six trials for sodomy while in Florence, some 17,000 men over the course of seventy years were brought before the Office of the Night, created in the early fifteenth century to root out sodomy. Men of all classes and all professions participated in homoerotic relationships.

Fur-Collar Crime

Nobles in western Europe suffered from idleness after the end of the Hundred Years' War and from inflation that made it hard to keep up their lavish lifestyles on fixed incomes. Many resorted to crime, named after the fur collars that only they were allowed to wear, mostly involving extortion and stealing from the poor and weak, and kidnapping high clergy and nobles for ransom. Like modern-day white-collar criminals, members of organized crime, and even terrorists, they corrupted the judicial processes with bribery and intimidation. The tales of Robin Hood expressed the desire for retributive justice and the resentment of the victims of fur-collar crime.

Ethnic Tensions and Restrictions

There was a great deal of movement of people during the twelfth and thirteenth centuries, particularly urbanization and colonization of frontier regions like Ireland by the English; Poland, Bohemia, and Hungary by the Germans; and parts of Spain by the French. These permanent migrants spoke different languages from the local rural population and were protected under the laws of their original countries, as were conquered peoples like the Muslims in Spain during the Reconquista. Such legal pluralism was ubiquitous except in Ireland where the English established their laws over the Irish, who were not considered free because of their Irish blood and were granted few rights and even less access to legal recourse.

Ethnic tensions intensified with the economic crises of the fourteenth century. Blood counted more and more in the competition for important clerical positions in Ireland and Poland, where the English and Germans, respectively, publicly denigrated the natives. In the Baltic and Slavic lands, German preachers of monastic orders were seen as agents of cultural colonization and German-speaking elites in towns restricted membership in guilds on ethnic grounds. In Bohemia, Czech nationalism grew in response; a Czech-only friary was established in 1333, and for the first time, a book—a history of Bohemia—was written in the Czech language.

Legislation prohibiting sexual relations and intermarriage among groups was passed. Purity of ethnic background became required for public office in many places in laws such as Ireland's Statute of Kilkenny, 1336. Writers focused on the issue, using words like *gens* ("race" or "clan") or *natio* ("species" or "kind") to describe people who differed by culture and language, and also by blood. Religious beliefs were conflated into blood inheritance as well, particularly in Spain, where purity of blood became crucial and Christians tried show they had no Jewish or Muslim ancestors. The laws similarly forbade mixtures of noble and common blood. This concept of blood would later morph into modern racism.

LITERACY AND VERNACULAR LITERATURE

One positive outgrowth of the growing sense of ethnic identity was the growth of vernacular literature, which in the fourteenth century began to challenge the primacy of Latin as the language of writing. Dante's *Divine Comedy* and Chaucer's *Canterbury Tales*, the first written toward the beginning and the latter toward the end of the fourteenth century, played important parts in creating national languages and national identity. *The Divine Comedy*, written in poetic triplets in 100 cantos, imagines the journey of Dante, guided by the Roman poet Virgil, through hell, purgatory, and heaven. Filled with contemporary figures, it is a masterful commentary on social and religious issues and reflects both medieval intense religiosity and nascent modern materialism and secular ambition. Chaucer's collection of stories of pilgrims on their way to Canterbury depicts the earthy, sensual, and even materialistic values and behaviors of a wide variety of English people of that time.

Literacy increased among laypeople in the fourteenth century, as reflected in wills and in the wide variety of texts prevalent, from manuals on etiquette to historical and philosophical works. The number of schools for boys increased dramatically as more and more laymen took positions in governments formerly held by clerics. Girls were sent to convent schools, although often they were taught to read but not to write. Trade and commerce too demanded literate workers, so that even before the printing press came into being, a literary culture had been created. Christine de Pizan (ca. 1365–1430), a well-educated widow around the French court, reflected this literary culture, since she could support herself (the first woman writer to do so) by writing a wide variety of works, from biographies of kings to her most famous work countering negative views of women in society, *The City of Ladies*, 1404.

Literacy was particularly high in the Italian city-states, which, although devastated by the Black Death, retained their economic vitality and primacy. As the fourteenth century was coming to an end, writers and artists in these vibrant and wealthy communities began to articulate a new set of values and to create new artistic forms, leading to what they themselves called a renaissance.

Multiple-Choice Questions

1. One consequence of the high death rate of priests and monks during the Black Death was that
   (A) the church began to require communion only once a year.
   (B) women were, for two decades, allowed to become priests.
   (C) occasionally laymen would be allowed to give the sacraments to the dying.
   (D) the church became impoverished.
   (E) priests were imported from the Byzantine Empire.

2. Which factor did not lead to a decline in population in the fourteenth century?
   (A) People postponed getting married until they were older.
   (B) Malnutrition made people more vulnerable to diseases.
   (C) People usually shared beds at home and in hospitals as well.
   (D) Abandonment of homesteads reduced agricultural production.
   (E) Isolation and quarantine were used.

3. Which groups did not benefit economically from the plague?
   (A) Men seeking admission to guilds
   (B) Rich farmers who could buy out their poorer neighbors
   (C) Speculators
   (D) Aristocratic landowners dependent on rents
   (E) Wage earners

4. A major cause of the Hundred Years' War for the French was that
   (A) the nobles were divided in their support for Philip VI.
   (B) a woman had become ruler of France for the first time.
   (C) the French were urged to go to war by wealthy Flemish merchants.
   (D) the King of France claimed the throne of England.
   (E) the Valois dynasty ended and the Capetian dynasty began.

5. Which was not an English victory?
   (A) Crécy
   (B) Agincourt
   (C) Orléans
   (D) Poitiers
   (E) Normandy

6. Which is not a reason for the popularity of the Hundred Years' War in England?
   (A) It gave many opportunities to acquire wealth and plunder.
   (B) Anti-French propaganda was spread by the king's officials.
   (C) The church called it a crusade against infidels.
   (D) Military victories enhanced nationalistic sentiments.
   (E) The war was believed to be just and honorable.

7. Joan of Arc became the second patron saint of France because she
   (A) was a martyr for the Christian faith.
   (B) saved the French monarchy.
   (C) was an early advocate of equality for woman.
   (D) had been tried and executed for heresy and witchcraft.
   (E) had been publicly thanked by Charles VII.

8. The impact of the Hundred Years' War on representative assemblies was that
   (A) both French and English assemblies were strengthened.
   (B) neither French nor English assemblies were strengthened.
   (C) the French but not the English assembly was strengthened.
   (D) the English but not the French assembly was strengthened.
   (E) representative assemblies everywhere in Europe were getting stronger, so that the Hundred Years' War's impact was relatively small.

9. The Babylonian Captivity and the Great Schism both demonstrate the
   (A) vulnerability of the papacy to increasingly powerful monarchies.
   (B) spread of heretical ideas.
   (C) growth of lay piety.
   (D) success of the conciliar movement.
   (E) influence of the Italian people on the selection of the popes.

10. Wyclif's and Marsiglio of Padua's criticisms of the church
    (A) were similar in that both advocated that the authority of the church be with church councils.
    (B) differed in that Marsiglio focused on theological issues while Wyclif focused on church abuses.
    (C) led to both men's excommunication.
    (D) had little immediate impact.
    (E) differed in that Marsiglio focused on political and administrative issues while Wyclif focused on theological issues.

11. Thomas à Kempis, author of the *Imitation of Christ,* and Bridget of Sweden are both representative of
    (A) the conciliar movement.
    (B) the growth of lay piety and mysticism in the fourteenth and fifteenth centuries.
    (C) disillusionment with Christianity as a religion.
    (D) the impact of religious figures on the Hundred Years' War.
    (E) the impact of the Black Death in the fourteenth century.

12. The English Peasants' Revolt of 1381 reflected the
    (A) deteriorating conditions of the peasants.
    (B) overwhelming success of Statute of Laborers of 1351.
    (C) rising expectations of the peasants.
    (D) widespread support for the head tax.
    (E) lack of common interests between urban workers and peasants.

13. Gender roles in the fourteenth and fifteenth centuries changed in that
    (A) women for the first time were granted membership in the guilds.
    (B) many women married late in their twenties in northwestern Europe.
    (C) prostitution was outlawed and severely punished.
    (D) there were many prosecutions and severe punishment for rape.
    (E) homosexuality rarely came to the attention of pubic authorities.

14. Ireland was treated differently from other conquered areas in Europe in that
    (A) religious toleration was established.
    (B) laws protecting minorities elsewhere were not put in place.
    (C) notions of ethnic purity were seen as irrelevant.
    (D) intermarriage was tolerated between the English and the Irish.
    (E) the English living in Ireland were encouraged to learn and speak Irish.

15. John Hus, Dante Alighieri, and Geoffrey Chaucer were all
    (A) religious reformers.
    (B) advocates for the Catholic Church.
    (C) well-known poets.
    (D) residents of England.
    (E) forgers of national identity.

Free-Response Questions

1. Describe the social and economic consequences of the Black Death.

2. Discuss the challenges faced by the Catholic Church in the fourteenth and fifteenth centuries.

ANSWERS

MULTIPLE-CHOICE QUESTIONS

1. ANSWER (C) The church made no major revisions in its rules (thereby eliminating options A and B), but laymen were given the right to perform extreme unction (last rites) in special circumstances. The church remained the largest single landowner. Priests could not be imported from Byzantium as Orthodoxy was practiced there; the Catholic and Orthodox churches had no official contact. (McKay, *A History of Western Society,* 8th ed., p. 386/9th ed., p. 379)

2. ANSWER (E) Quarantine and isolation were somewhat effective in reducing the spread of the plague. (McKay, *A History of Western Society,* 8th ed., pp. 384–385 /9th ed., pp. 377–378)

3. ANSWER (D) Wage earners and guild members had more bargaining power because of the decimation of guild membership. Aristocrats faced inflation, had lost much of their workforce, and could not increase rents. (McKay, *A History of Western Society,* 8th ed., pp. 386–387/9th ed., pp. 379–380)

4. ANSWER (A) The end of the Capetian dynasty in 1328 was the immediate cause of the war, in that the French nobility refused to give the crown to the sister of the last Capetian king or to her son, Edward III of England, who later claimed the throne of France. Many French nobles did not support the French king but instead supported Edward III during the war because of their resistance to royal centralization. The Flemish merchants supported the English because of their need for English wool. (McKay, *A History of Western Society,* 8th ed., p. 386/9th ed., pp. 381–382)

5. ANSWER (C) The British won all the major battles of the war except for the siege of Orléans, at which they were forced to withdraw because the French troops were inspired to victory by Joan of Arc. The war lasted another 20 years. (McKay, *A History of Western Society,* 8th ed., pp. 389–390/9th ed., pp. 383–385)

6. ANSWER (C) The clergy were exhorted by the monarchy to preach patriotism, but as both states were Catholic, there was no religious element to the war. Most of the English resented the injustice of the French denial of Edward III's claim to their throne. The war offered opportunities for men of all classes. (McKay, *A History of Western Society,* 8th ed., pp. 388–389/9th ed., pp. 382–383, 386)

7. ANSWER (B) Through the intensity of her convictions and her inspiring leadership, Joan was able to rally the French troops to force the British to retreat from Orléans; this allowed Charles VII to be crowned king and restored French morale and pride. The war would probably have ended quite differently without her role. Although she was, of course, intensely religious and from peasant stock, it was her patriotism that mattered to nationalists. Charles VII ungratefully did not protest her trial by English ecclesiastical authorities. (McKay, *A History of Western Society,* 8th ed., pp. 390, 392/9th ed., p. 385)

8. ANSWER (D) Throughout Europe, representative assemblies were getting weaker as monarchs became stronger, and that was true for France. But in England, which was unusual in that it had only one national assembly (not the plethora of provincial assemblies that existed throughout the continent), the king was forced to call the assembly, Parliament, into session often in order to obtain increased funding for the war effort, and Parliament became well established. (McKay, *A History of Western Society,* 8th ed., pp. 392–393/9th ed., pp. 396–397)

9. ANSWER (A) During the Babylonian Captivity and the Great Schism, the French monarchs exerted substantial control over the papacy. The conciliar movement was an unsuccessful effort to reform church administration. Lay piety did grow in this period but as a result of the decline in the prestige of the church, not as its cause. The Roman

elites, but not the Italian people, did have a great say in the selection of the pope in 1378. (McKay, *A History of Western Society,* 8th ed., pp. 393–395/9th ed., pp. 387–389)

10. ANSWER (E) Marsiglio was mostly concerned about the church's relationship with society, arguing that the church should be under the authority of the state, while Wyclif argued that Christian practice and theology should be determined by the Scriptures. Marsiglio was excommunicated, but Wyclif was protected by the isolation of England. Wyclif's ideas had a huge impact, particularly in Bohemia where they were spread by John Hus. (McKay, *A History of Western Society,* 8th ed., pp. 394, 397/9th ed., pp. 388, 391)

11. ANSWER (B) Bridget of Sweden was a fourteenth-century mystic, and Thomas à Kempis the most prominent fifteenth-century author of texts expressing lay piety, particularly the ideas of the Brethren and Sisters of the Common Life. (McKay, *A History of Western Society,* 8th ed., pp. 455–456/9th ed., p. 389)

12. ANSWER (C) Most historians argue that peasants were better off for the century after the Black Death than ever before. Since the Statute of Laborers had failed to uniformly roll back wages or limit social mobility, peasants expected a better future and were angry at attempts like the head tax to increase their taxes. Protests by urban workers over similar issues merged with the peasants' unrest. (McKay, *A History of Western Society,* 8th ed., pp. 401–403/9th ed., pp. 390, 392)

13. ANSWER (B) There were important changes in the late medieval period in gender roles. Women who had played important roles in the guild system in the Middle Ages became excluded in the fourteenth century. Women married later in northwestern Europe. Since men too were marrying later, towns provided brothels and supervised prostitutes. The penalties for rape were usually lighter than those for theft, and there were few prosecutions for this crime. Homosexuality was a matter of concern to city governments, some of which set up commissions to investigate and prosecute cases of sodomy. (McKay, *A History of Western Society,* 8th ed., pp. 396, 398/9th ed., pp. 393–396)

14. ANSWER (B) Ireland suffered worse than any other area in its treatment by its conquerors. Elsewhere, conquered minorities or foreigners had some legal rights. Religious toleration was not needed, since both English and Irish were Catholic at that time. The Statute of Kilkenny in 1366 expressly forbade intermarriage of Irish and English and insisted that English people living in Ireland speak only English. Ireland was similar to many places such as Spain where purity of blood became more and more important. (McKay, *A History of Western Society,* 8th ed., pp. 403–405/9th ed., p. 397)

15. ANSWER (E) John Hus's promotion of Wyclif's ideas found a welcome reception among nationalistic Bohemians, while Dante's and Chaucer's literary works were crucial for establishing the form of the national languages and for helping create a sense of national identity. Dante and Chaucer held positions in government, but neither was directly engaged in church reform movements; Hus was a professor of theology. (McKay, *A History of Western Society,* 8th ed., pp. 397, 405–406/9th ed., pp. 391, 399–401)

FREE-RESPONSE QUESTIONS

1. The essay should address the question asked, so do not waste valuable time writing about extraneous materials or describing the Black Death itself, how it came to Europe, how it spread, and what type of disease it was. You can certainly discuss the population loss as that is relevant to the question.
   - The terrible loss in population had important consequences for the survivors. Real wages went up, a relatively rare phenomenon, for workers in cities, and peasants were able to negotiate a reduction in their manorial obligations since the lords needed a labor force. This meant a rise in prices as well, which hurt the lords who were dependent on traditionally fixed rents.
   - The guild masters responded by tightening admission to the guilds. Women, who had been allowed to become masters on occasion (usually when their husbands died) in the earlier medieval period, found themselves excluded from the guilds, both as masters and even as skilled workers. The opportunities for journeymen became more limited; in response they tried to form their own guilds and occasionally rioted, as the *ciompi* did in Florence.
   - Governments tried to return wages and manorial dues to what they had been before the Black Death. Such legislation, like the English Statute of Laborers, was met with resistance and often violence.
   - Ethnic tensions also increased in the face of the Black Death. During the epidemic, it was common for Jews to be blamed; many were murdered. Concepts of ethnicity or nationality that were in the blood began to shape legislation.

2. The church faced major political and theological challenges in the fourteenth century.
   - Politically the church faced two challenges. During the Babylonian Captivity, when the French kings dominated the papal court and moved it to Avignon for almost seventy years, Rome and the Papal States were neglected and the prestige of the papacy suffered. When the popes returned to Rome in 1376, there were two competing popes, one selected by cardinals loyal to France, the other by the Roman elite. This Great Schism, when there were two popes, lasted until the election of Martin V as pope some forty years later. This schism also damaged papal prestige.
   - Theologically the church faced two significant challenges. The first, by the Italian Marsiglio of Padua, challenged the legitimacy of the church as an institution, arguing that it should own no property and be under the authority of the state. The second was from the Englishman John Wyclif, who asserted that religious authority for a Christian was

Scriptures and that Christianity should permit only practices sanctioned in Scripture. Therefore, pilgrimages and veneration of saints, as well as corrupt practices like absenteeism and pluralism, were all illegitimate. Wyclif's ideas spread widely and were advocated by the English peasants in their revolt of 1381 and by Czech nationalists in Bohemia. The church tried and executed the leading Czech dissident, John Hus.

Lay people also challenged the church by emphasizing inner spirituality and simple lifestyles. The Brethren and Sisters of the Common Life became a highly popular lay order, and Thomas à Kempis's *The Imitation of Christ* became a bestseller. The laity were asserting their right to determine their own spiritual lives; although they were not breaking with the church, their pious lives and their membership in a religious order that they themselves had created made the institutional church less important.

13

European Society in the Age of the Renaissance, 1350–1550

The Renaissance specifically refers to the cultural, literary, and intellectual movement that many historians would argue created modern Europe. It started in Italian city-states run by merchant oligarchies that fostered the development of the new values of secularism and individualism and furthered the importance of the middle class. As the movement spread outside of Italy, it encompassed more religious or nationalistic elements. During the same period, nation-states with powerful monarchies were forged in Spain, England, and France.

Key Concepts

- The Renaissance was the new literary and artistic culture that first emerged in Italy and then spread gradually and at different times and in different ways throughout western and central Europe.
- The rebirth of ancient Greek and Roman artistic and literary styles, languages, and values was at the heart of the Italian Renaissance. The revival of classical texts and the educational curriculum based on them was called humanism. The Renaissance rested on new political and social structures forged in quasi-independent city-states in Italy, called *communes,* which were dominated by wealthy merchants who became the patrons of artists and scholars. Individualism and secularism developed as new societal values.

These city-states competed and went to war with each other; their disunity left them vulnerable to unified nation-states like France and Spain. The most influential writers were Castiglione and Machiavelli. In northern Europe, Christian humanism developed with a special focus on ethics and religion. Two major northern humanists were Thomas More and Desiderius Erasmus.

- Renaissance artists adopted many elements from antiquity, from Roman arches to motifs and themes in painting. Perspective and realism allowed them to imitate nature. Communal bodies, wealthy merchants, and the church were important patrons.
- The invention of movable type and the printing press in the mid-fifteenth century allowed for the quick and relatively inexpensive dissemination of new ideas, fostered literacy, and made the Renaissance an international movement.
- In Spain, France, and England, effective monarchs were successful in creating centralized nation-states.

AP Tip

As you read through this chapter, keep in mind the way the cultural movement of the Renaissance and the new values it spawned intersected with changes in political, social, and religious ideas in the next centuries and the way it changed as it moved from country to country. Many FRQs on the AP exams have asked students to answer questions using their knowledge of the Renaissance as a starting point—for example, its influence on later developments or comparison of it with other artistic movements.

Economic and Political Developments that Provided the Setting for the Renaissance

Northern Italian cities, particularly Venice, Milan, and Genoa, had emerged in the twelfth century as economic powerhouses, based on extensive foreign trade and the advances made in shipbuilding by Venetians and Genoese. The Renaissance itself was born in an inland city, Florence, whose wealth derived from its bankers, who had become the bankers for the papacy in the thirteenth century and had extensive networks throughout Europe. The bankers invested their profits in Florentine manufacturing, particularly wool and silk, and in selling this high-quality merchandise. Florentine prosperity helped it survive several economic crises and the horrific Black Death in the mid-fourteenth century.

Florence was organized, as were most Italian city-states, as a commune, an association of free men who over time won independence from local nobles and efficiently managed their cities, building city walls, levying taxes, and regulating trade and business. Powerful local oligarchies, often made up of noble and merchant families interwoven by marriage, wrote constitutions and called their communes republics. The ordinary people, the *popolo*, were generally excluded from citizenship and disenfranchised, even after temporarily successful revolts, as the oligarchies brought in military leaders (*condottieri*) or handed the government over to one man (a *signor*). There was not a huge difference between those states that were ruled by *signori* and those that retained their republican constitutions; a small number of men held real power in either case, and luxurious courts were the centers of cultural life in both. These courts became the models for later monarchs outside of Italy.

THE BALANCE OF POWER AMONG THE ITALIAN CITY-STATES

The city-state was the focus of loyalty and political passion in the Renaissance period on the Italian peninsula. The five strong states were Florence, Venice, Milan, the Papal States, and Naples. The first three were republics, although by the fifteenth century, powerful families—the Sforza in Milan and the Medici in Florence—had come to dominate. Naples was a kingdom, which passed to the House of Aragon in 1435, while the Papal States were ruled by the pope in his temporal authority. These five states competed furiously with each other and sought to dominate smaller states. They invented modern diplomacy with permanent resident ambassadors and the concept of the balance of power to prevent the hegemony of any one state. A French invasion in 1494 began a long period in which ununified Italy became the battleground for the ambitions of kings and emperors, often terribly damaging the Italian states (for example, the sack of Rome by Charles V in 1527). In Florence, the fear of foreign invasion gave credence to the predictions of the fiery, antisecular preacher Savonarola, who ruled the city for a brief period until he was executed in 1498.

AP Tip

The term *city-state* means a city that governs itself and usually controls the surrounding countryside in order to guarantee the food supply to the city. Italian city-states took advantage of the long-standing conflict between the Holy Roman Empire and the papacy to assert their independence. Even though the actual franchise in city-state republican governments was very limited, the men who created the republics were aware that they were dong something unusual for their time and articulated new ideas about government.

INTELLECTUAL CHANGE

The harbinger of intellectual change was Petrarch, a fourteenth-century poet who articulated a vision of his own time separated from the previous period, which he identified as dark and gloomy. Humanism, derived from the term *studia humanitates*, meaning "liberal studies," refers in its Renaissance usage to the study of Latin and eventually Greek classics and in its broader sense to an emphasis on the abilities and achievements of humans. The study of the Latin classics had continued throughout the medieval period, but it was largely religious in orientation. Renaissance humanists sought to revive classical Latin, as opposed to medieval or Church Latin, and the art of rhetoric, elegant written and oral communication, and emulate the lively dialogues of the ancient Platonic Academy.

Renaissance humanists searched for validation of their notions of human greatness and perfectibility. The 1486 essay, *On the Dignity of Man,* by Pico della Mirandola, asserted man's inherent and unlimited potential for greatness, reflecting the influence of Greek thought, particularly Plato's, which was enthusiastically embraced in the fifteenth century. Individualism and individual ambition were hallmarks of Renaissance humanism, as they were of political and economic life. In many of the Italian city-states, ambitious men became wealthy or took power and established new dynasties through individual initiative. Individuals such as Leon Battista Alberti or Leonardo da Vinci encapsulated the ideal of the Renaissance man, *uomo universale,* the multitalented and highly creative individual who would be successful at many different tasks. The goldsmith and sculptor Benvenuto Cellini called himself a genius (and beautiful, too) in his *Autobiography.*

AP Tip

Renaissance individualism is easily seen in the new literary genre of autobiography and the new artistic genre of the portrait—a useful point to make in essays. We know relatively little about how medieval leaders looked—even for Columbus, who did live during the Renaissance, there is no portrait done from life—but we can see the faces of many Renaissance men and women, some famous like the Medicis or Raphael and some unknown to us by name.

EDUCATION

New educational curricula and values were at the heart of the Renaissance. Humanists argued for the validity of the secular world and the need for education to prepare students for success in it by training their "highest gifts" while at the same time providing a firm moral foundation. Education was not only for private benefit but also for the public weal; city-states needed individuals trained to speak and write well and to argue persuasively. Humanists such as Paul Vergerio opened schools teaching Latin and Greek grammar and historical, ethical, and philosophical texts. Over time this curriculum would become the basis of advanced education for most Europeans of the middle and upper classes.

However, most humanists excluded women from this educational vision. No schools for girls were created. Humanists wrote a good deal on this issue. Rhetoric, Bruni said, is the proper study for men, while women should study morals and religion. In his treatise *On the Family,* the humanist and architect Leon Battista Alberti argued that women should be strictly limited to household responsibilities. Nevertheless, some women, mostly from the upper classes, did acquire a humanist education and wrote humanist texts. The general exclusion of women from both humanism and the arts raises the question of whether there was a Renaissance for women.

The most influential educational text was Baldassare Castiglione's *The Courtier,* 1528, which articulated an ideal for aristocratic men and women, and was read all over Europe. A proper gentleman should have a broad academic background and be physically skilled as well; he should be able to recite Latin poetry, compose a sonnet, wrestle, solve a mathematical problem, dance, and so forth. A lady should develop her artistic talents, but be modest and beautiful as well. In other words, individuals should develop their knowledge of and talent in all spheres of human endeavor. This notion of universal competence revived a classical ideal, and stands in sharp contrast to medieval ideals stressing religiosity and conformity.

POLITICAL THOUGHT

Perhaps the single most widely read and most discussed text of the Renaissance is Niccolò Machiavelli's *The Prince,* written in 1513. Machiavelli was an excellent scholar of history and had been intimately involved in the politics of the Florentine republic as a diplomat and local official. An analysis written for *signori,* or princes, on how to achieve and hold power, *The Prince* argued for amoral and at times ruthless manipulation of people, whom Machiavelli saw as generally selfish and inconstant. The ruler should be both a fox in his cleverness and a lion in his fierceness. *The Prince* is considered by many to be the first work of modern political science, in that it sought to analyze what people did rather than what they ought to do, identifying politics as a distinct discipline with its own laws.

SECULAR SPIRIT

The Prince perfectly embodies the Renaissance value of secularism, holding this world, rather than the next, in highest regard. Secularism was enthusiastically adopted by new wealthy elites who patronized the arts and sought more pleasurable lives. Few people challenged the basic tenets of Christianity, and religious feelings remained strong, but the emphasis of values changed.

For example, the humanist Lorenzo Valla, in his treatise *On Pleasure,* exalted sensual pleasures. Valla was an important humanist and the father of modern historical criticism because he used his knowledge of Latin to unmask an eighth-century papal forgery known as the Donation of Constantine which had justified the temporal authority of the popes. Other humanists wrote secular tales portraying the rascality, sensuality, and wit of ordinary people, the most famous of which is Boccaccio's *Decameron* (see Chapter 12, p. 378). The popes, too, relished worldly pleasures, decorating the Vatican with stupendous works of art and spending huge sums on commissioning the best artists of the day, such as Michelangelo, who built the dome of St. Peter's and painted the ceiling and altar wall of the Sistine Chapel.

CHRISTIAN HUMANISM

As the Renaissance moved north in the fifteenth century, its emphasis began to shift. Students from England, Holland, France, and Germany had flocked to Italy for the new learning and brought it home. There the focus of humanist inquiry turned toward Christian texts and ethnical concerns. Northern humanists sought to reconcile classical and Christian virtues and stressed the value of reason and human intellect.

The two most famous northern humanists were Thomas More (chancellor of the Tudor king Henry VIII), who wrote a revolutionary text, *Utopia,* imagining an ideal egalitarian socialistic community where everyone works, receives a solid classical education, disdains gold and silver, and eschews war. It is greed and private property that, according to More, ruin society.

Desiderius Erasmus was a friend of More's and was the better known of the two. He became the first international scholar of the Renaissance, famed for his knowledge of Greek. He too wrote a treatise of advice to a prince urging the study of the classics, and the renowned *In Praise of Folly* which satirized worldly wisdom. These two works crystallize his stress on education as the key to reform and his advocacy of an inner Christianity. He used his knowledge of Greek to prepare a new edition of the Greek New Testament and argued for the translation of scripture into vernacular languages.

The Printed Word

In the mid-fifteenth century, Johann Gutenberg and several other German craftsmen invented movable type, with individual letters cast in metal that could be used time after time. Adopting principles of wood stamp manufacturing and Chinese block printing, they used movable type to meet the growing demand for books from an ever-increasingly literate population. Paper technology also developed to replace the much more expensive vellum and parchment with the less expensive paper product. The printing press spread quickly with some 110 cities having presses within three decades. It transformed both public and private life, providing more plentiful and cheaper books and standardized texts, offering new forms of identity, and stimulating literacy. Although the first printed books were religious, soon broadsides and books on all types of subjects were being printed and easily sold, from romances, pornography, and manuals to scholarly, medical, and legal texts. Some were even illustrated. The gap between literate and illiterate people narrowed as the first read to the latter from these printed works.

Art and the Artist

Art is probably the most admired and well-known aspect of the Renaissance. During the fifteenth and sixteenth centuries, called the *quattrocento* and the *cinquecento* in Italian, artists transformed painting, sculpture, and architecture, initially in Florence but then spreading throughout Europe.

How Did Changes in Art both Reflect and Shape New Ideas?

Patronage in early Renaissance Florence was given by guilds and religious confraternities, which commissioned such works as Brunelleschi's dome for the Florentine Cathedral, called *Il Duomo*;

Ghiberti's baptistery doors; and Michelangelo's *David*. Later on, the patrons were wealthy merchants, bankers, *signori*, or oligarchs such as the Medici, who glorified themselves and their positions in society through expenditures of vast sums for the arts. Such expenditures reveal changing patterns of consumption for the wealthier classes, who in medieval times had spent their monies on arms and armaments for knights and now bought art and hired mercenaries to fulfill their military needs. More and more household goods were purchased to decorate urban palaces. Elaborately decorated private chapels, first in churches and then within the palaces themselves, became the center of wealthy families' religious lives.

SUBJECTS AND STYLES

While much of Renaissance art was religious, it was often placed in a secular context, with historical figures depicted in contemporary dress or used to highlight new attitudes. Artistic forms and content shifted. New genres like portrait painting, with a mixture of realism and idealized landscapes, reflected the secular, humanist values of wealthy families. Patrons had themselves put into the artworks they commissioned. Giotto, a Florentine painter of the early fourteenth century, spearheaded realism; in the next century, Piero della Francesca and Andrea Mantegna developed the technique of perspective, which provided three dimensionality in two-dimensional painting. Masaccio, who died in 1428, revolutionized painting in his short life by emphasizing the narrative element of painting and brilliantly using light and dark. Toward the end of the century, Leonardo da Vinci painted (although never quite finished) the *Last Supper*, famous for its remarkable portrayal of tensions between Christ and his disciples. Over the course of the fifteenth century, the subjects of artworks became more and more secular, and the ubiquity of classical motifs, figures, and themes reflected the impact of literary humanism.

In sculpture, Donatello revived the classical figure and the classical nude—freestanding, balanced, and emotionally expressive. Brunelleschi performed the same function for architecture, designing the Foundling Hospital as the first truly Renaissance building, with rounded, Roman-style arches and successfully building the first dome, *Il Duomo*, since antiquity, remarkable for both its engineering and its gracefulness. Artists studied ancient sculptures and reliefs.

In northern Europe, art, as humanist studies, tended to be more religious. Flemish painters like Rogier van der Weyden and Jan van Eyck, painting around the same time as Masaccio, demonstrated the Flemish love of detail, realism, and focus on the human personality. Their paintings, such as van Eyck's renowned portrait of *Giovanni Arnolfini and his Bride*, were much admired in Italy.

By the beginning of the sixteenth century, the center of art had moved from Florence to Rome, where the Florentines Michelangelo and Raphael were commissioned for works that are counted among their greatest masterpieces. Michelangelo's Sistine Chapel, Pietà, and dome of St. Peter's, and Raphael's fresco paintings, such as the *School of Athens*, are among the most famous works of the entire Renaissance. Venice too became an important center for art, with Titian its most prolific and famous artist. Titian and other painters of the later sixteenth century developed the artistic style known as mannerism in which figures and their musculature were often exaggerated and colors were heightened to intensify emotionality.

Leonardo da Vinci is considered by many to be one of the greatest geniuses in history, if not the greatest, the very model of the Renaissance man. His paintings—the *Mona Lisa* and the *Last Supper*—have fascinated scholars and the public alike for centuries. He was an impassioned scholar, deeply interested in optics and anatomy, drawing everything he could see or imagine, including plans for inventions which would only be realized centuries later, such as the helicopter and tank. He designed weapons, fortresses, and water systems for the Sforza duke of Milan, experimented with perspective and new materials for paintings, and kept extensive notebooks on everything.

AP Tip

Michelangelo's *David,* the most famous sculpture of the Renaissance, is often considered an expression of Platonic idealism. Both this sculpture and Pico's work in philosophy exalt man in all his glory. The *David,* commissioned for the town hall, also expressed civic pride.

Patronage and Creativity

Almost all Renaissance art was produced on commission and on demand from patrons. Many paid their artists very well, and some artists, like Leonardo da Vinci, earned huge sums. The social status of artists changed from medieval craftsmen to highly honored individuals who were often seen as geniuses and on occasion called divine, as Michelangelo was praised by more than one contemporary. Artists themselves boasted of their creative powers, as did Cellini in his introduction to his *Autobiography,* and Renaissance artists, unlike their medieval predecessors, typically signed their works. Giorgio Vasari, Italy's first historian of contemporary art, filled his *Lives of the Most Eminent Italian Painters, Sculptors, and Architects* with high praise for the achievements of individual artists. Vasari, an artist himself, was also the director of a Medici-funded artistic academy. The academy formalized the training of artists, which previously had taken place in the workshops of established artists.

As was the case with humanism, the validation and public acclaim of artists was gendered, with no known female architects, one female sculptor, and several women painters who were all marginalized in the discussion of art. The arts where women excelled, embroidery for example, were regarded as minor and only decorative, even though embroidery, too, reflected Renaissance artistic values and motifs. The few women painters known in their day were typically daughters of artists or of nobles, and while they were given some training, they were not allowed to study or paint the male nude or learn the art of fresco. The seventeenth-century painter Artemisia Gentileschi painted numerous biblical and mythological heroines, such as the Jewish heroines Esther and Judith.

Also typically excluded from full societal acceptance as artists were men from a common or artisan background, as happened in humanist circles as well. In this sense, the gap between the educated and artistic elite and the uneducated masses grew in the Renaissance.

AP Tip

The life and work of Artemesia Gentileschi show the intersection of gender issues and art particularly well. She was the daughter of a well-known artist, Orazio Gentileschi, who encouraged and trained her, and she ended up having quite a successful career. She was the center of a famous trial, in which she accused her art teacher of rape and was herself treated badly. There is a recent feature film about her that is not reliable in its interpretation.

SOCIAL HIERARCHIES

Social hierarchies are the social structure of society, the nature and positions of the social classes and other subgroups, and social mobility, both real and imagined. They reflect the economic and political organization of a society. Ideas about social hierarchies can have a substantial impact on people's lives.

RACE

Renaissance ideas about race grew out of the notions of ethnic purity and bloodlines discussed in Chapter 12. Culture and blood together defined what made a person belong to one group, called either *gens* or "people," or *natio* or "nation," and not another; sometimes the word *race* was used interchangeably with *people* or *nation*. The notion of race, however, was not physical, that is, of criteria such as hair type or color, as much as it was socially constructed, that is, of criteria such as dress. Modern biological notions of race began in the eighteenth century, but Renaissance people did see skin color as a distinction, woven in with ethnic and religious identities.

In the fifteenth century, a sizable number of slaves from Africa came into Europe, brought in at first around 1530 by Portuguese explorers, with about 5,000 sold each year. Blacks made up 3 percent of the population of Portugal and 10 percent of the population of its cities, and there were large numbers of mixed-race individuals as well. There were many, unidentified in number, throughout Europe, some free and some slave. Black servants were highly desirable: they were a sign of wealth. This is why so many Italians included black servants in their portraits. Blacks were prized as objects of curiosity and as entertainers; others were employed in business tasks, supplementing the labor force. Europeans knew little, until the Age of Exploration, about Africans, relying on biblical texts and ancient accounts. The color black was associated with evil and sin as God was identified with light, but also with religious purity—monks often wore black robes—and with mourners, who are blessed by Christ.

CLASS

Modern notions of class derive from the work of nineteenth-century theorists. Medieval notions classified people in three orders, or estates, according to function: those who prayed, the clergy; those who fought, the nobility; and everyone else, including laborers and merchants. This was the way some provincial assemblies were organized as well, as in France. Status in the second category, that of nobility, was inherited and brought some exemptions from taxation, and other privileges. The period of the Renaissance transformed this medieval triptych of inherited status by creating a new hierarchy based on wealth, particularly in cities. Many merchants not only were very wealthy but also held political power. These two hierarchies—of order and of wealth—intertwined, although the clergy and nobility always held high status, regardless of wealth. Many merchants were anxious to ape noble lifestyles and to marry into noble families, or even, in some cases, to buy titles of nobility. Considerations of honor also played a role in social hierarchies, as some weapons and tactics and some urban occupations were considered honorable, and others clearly not. In urban environments, there was a lively mixture and interchange among members of different orders and classes. Merchants were often wealthier than the resident nobles and sought to restrict entrance into their privileged group by passing dress and behavior codes, called sumptuary laws, making visible distinctions between groups and restricting access to town citizenship. This was also a way to identify members of minority groups like Jews.

GENDER

The concept of gender as a changeable cultural construction more than a biological determinant is a twentieth-century creation. During the Renaissance, although this word was not in use, scholars and popular writers began what became known as the *querelle des femmes*, the debate about women's nature and women's roles, which lasted for centuries. While some writers categorized women as scheming and devious, others wrote treatises praising exemplary women, as Boccaccio wrote, for being like men or explaining, as Christine de Pizan delineated, why there had been so few great women in the past. Popular interest in the issue was reflected in the large number of books and broadsides about women's roles, virtues, and vices. Gender roles were articulated for men as well; for example, unmarried men lost political rights in Venice. Many expressed fears that disruption in the subordinate position of women would be destabilizing for society. Popular culture supported traditional gender roles and ridiculed those who broke them.

The debate over women's roles intensified because of the very public role several women rulers or women regents played. These women rulers, particularly Elizabeth I of England and Isabella of Spain, took care to demonstrate qualities identified as masculine—bravery, stamina, wisdom, and duty—traits that male rulers also made a point to emphasize.

POLITICS AND THE STATE IN THE RENAISSANCE (CA. 1450–1521)

Many modern political institutions had their origin in the High Middle Ages, the twelfth and thirteenth centuries, such as representative assemblies, bureaucracies, and juries. Up to the fifteenth century, monarchs were generally too weak to dominate the aristocracy. That began to change when monarchs applied the ideas of Renaissance political thinkers and enforced their power and sovereignty, taming the nobles by reducing their political power and their use of violence.

AP Tip

This change in the power of the nobles was made possible by changes in military technology. Artillery and the longbow, first used by the English in the Hundred Years' War, followed by early forms of the rifle, were all wielded by commoners, making knights useless on the battlefield and their castles easily penetrable. Since monarchs no longer depended on the nobles to fight, the nobles lost their raison d'être, although they soon became the officer corps of the royal armies.

FRANCE

Left depopulated and economically devastated by the Hundred Years' War, France under Charles VII, the dauphin crowned king through the efforts of Joan of Arc, recovered. Charles brought the dissident Burgundians into his fold, gave the middle classes greater influence in the royal council, and established two taxes as the main source of royal income, the *gabelle* (salt tax) and the *taille* (land tax). He and his successors established Gallican liberties, asserting their rights over the French church, first in the Pragmatic Sanction of Bourges in 1438 and then in the Concordat of Bologna in 1516, which confirmed the king's right to select bishops and abbots in France. Charles VII's son Louis XI (known as the Spider King) focused on economic issues, funding new industries such as silk weaving and entering into commercial treaties with other states. He used the funds he derived from taxes on these endeavors to improve his army, and with that, took control over most of Burgundy and also stopped fur-collar crime.

ENGLAND

Once the Hundred Years' War was over, the English aristocracy broke into factions and fought each other in the War of the Roses, which created disorder and hurt the economy. The Yorkist side initially defeated the Lancastrians and began to restore strong monarchical rule and repress the power of the nobility. The important kings here were Edward IV, his brother Richard III, and Henry Tudor (a Lancastrian), who established the Tudor dynasty, which ruled until the death of Elizabeth I in 1603.

AP Tip

Richard III was the title character of a Shakespeare play that repeated the accusation that Richard murdered the two sons of his brother. This remains a subject of debate. Josephine Tey's *The Daughter of Time* is a modern mystery novel that exculpates Richard. Considering both works is an excellent way to understand POV (point-of-view analysis) needed for the APEH DBQ.

During the Hundred Years' War, Parliament had grown in power, as noted in Chapter 12. Edward IV and later the Tudors generally got around their obligation to call Parliament when new taxes were to be levied by following a cautious foreign policy. Henry VII made the royal council, some dozen men, many of them gentry (lower landowning class) and lawyers, the center of royal authority. It had an offshoot, the Star Chamber, which tried persons, usually aristocrats, accused of undermining or challenging royal authority. Torture and secrecy were used, against the traditions established by the Magna Carta and common law. The monarchs also used justices of the peace, usually landowners, to run local government. The Tudors promoted prosperity through the maintenance of order and pro-commerce policies which benefited the important cloth and shipbuilding industries. Henry VII also secured peaceful relations with Ireland, through military action, and Scotland, through marriage.

Spain

Spain remained quite powerful even though ununified in the fifteenth and sixteenth centuries, both politically and culturally. Two large kingdoms, Castile and Aragon, dominated their less powerful neighbors. When the rulers of Castile and Aragon married in 1469, they did not create a unified state; rather each of the many separate kingdoms had their own parliaments (called *corteses*), courts, laws, and even coinage. Ferdinand of Aragon and Isabella of Castille shared a common foreign policy and jointly warred to defeat the last remaining Muslim kingdom of Granada, finishing the task in 1492. They restricted aristocratic power through the use of *hermandades*, town councils, which were so successful in repressing violence that they were able to be disbanded in 1498, and with a restructured royal council in which the now-excluded great magnates were replaced with middle-class lawyers. They used the church to dominate the political landscape as well, winning the right to appoint the bishops of Spain and its New World colonies, and funding their armies with income from ecclesiastical estates.

After the success of the *Reconquista*, Spain became increasingly concerned with the Jewish and Muslim minorities. Although Jews had supported royal power, much resentment against them had grown in the later Middle Ages, culminating in several brutal incidents of violence in 1331, 1355, and 1391. Many Jews converted after the latter wave of widespread mob violence. Called New Christians or *conversos*, some held high positions in the church and in the government as well as in business, law, and medicine. Although a small percentage of the population (less than 3 percent), New Christians and Jews were highly influential. Many, including the monarchs, were suspicious of the New Christians; in 1480, with papal authorization, Ferdinand and Isabella established the Inquisition in Spain to ferret out those whose conversion may have been insincere. When most of the *conversos* rejected such claims, purity of the blood became the new standard for true Christians. Anti-Semitism thus acquired a racial component. Noble status required purity of blood; Jewish blood was seen as a threat to Spain as a nation. The Inquisition, which routinely used torture to extract confessions, became a tool for political unification. After the defeat of Granada in 1492, Ferdinand and Isabella expelled all practicing Jews from Spain; some 150,000 fled while another 50,000 or so converted. Similar treatment began to be applied to Muslims as well, many of whom were forcibly baptized. They, too, would be expelled from Spain, although not for another century.

AP Tip

A common misconception is that the Inquisition tried and persecuted Jews. As an ecclesiastical court, it had no authority over Jews or Muslims, only those who were members of the church. While most of the victims of the Inquisition were *conversos*, they were persecuted as Christians, not as Jews, although it was their Jewish origin that made them suspect. The Inquisitors claimed and probably believed that they were protecting the accused's immortal soul by forcing confession through torture. The loss of most of the Jewish and Muslim population of Spain deprived it of people with expertise in agriculture, business, and scholarship. This had harmful consequences for Spain after its *siglo d'oro* was over.

Ferdinand and Isabella made an important marriage alliance when they wed their daughter Joanna to Philip, the Habsburg heir to the Holy Roman Empire. The child of this marriage, Charles V, ruled vast lands from 1519 to 1556, and his son Philip II unified Portugal and Spain in 1580.

Multiple-Choice Questions

1. Renaissance Florence derived most of its wealth from
   (A) international trade.
   (B) banking.
   (C) highly productive agricultural estates.
   (D) silk manufacturing.
   (E) its services to the Holy Roman Emperor.

2. In the typical northern Italian commune,
   (A) people owned property in common.
   (B) the entire male adult population had the franchise; women did not.
   (C) nobles ruled as princes.
   (D) the ruling families had similar interests and rarely fought each other.
   (E) merchant oligarchies held power.

3. Renaissance Italians used permanent resident ambassadors as diplomats in order to
   (A) unify their responses to the threat of French invasion.
   (B) help the papacy.
   (C) create alliances and preserve a balance of power.
   (D) deal with the Ottoman threat.
   (E) prevent the kingdom of Naples from being taken over by the king of Aragon.

4. Renaissance humanists were different from their medieval counterparts in that
   (A) medieval humanists did not read the classics.
   (B) Renaissance humanists did not read Christian texts from antiquity.
   (C) Renaissance humanists exalted the dignity of man, while medieval humanists exalted the dignity of God.
   (D) Renaissance humanists rejected Christianity in favor of paganism, while medieval humanists rejected paganism in favor of Christianity.
   (E) Renaissance humanists rarely wrote about political matters, while medieval humanists were focused on political issues.

5. Which would be *least* likely to be studied in a humanist school?
   (A) History
   (B) Philosophy
   (C) Grammar
   (D) Rhetoric
   (E) Theology

6. Which Renaissance text best exemplifies the Renaissance ideal of the multitalented, well-trained individual?
   (A) Castiglione's *The Courtier*
   (B) More's *Utopia*
   (C) Machiavelli's *The Prince*
   (D) Erasmus's *In Praise of Folly*
   (E) Boccaccio's *Decameron*

7. Machiavelli differed from medieval political theorists in that he wrote about
   (A) the morality of the prince.
   (B) the importance for a prince to win over the masses.
   (C) how political life operates, not how it should be.
   (D) the importance for the prince to come to terms with the church.
   (E) how the prince must engage in immoral behavior.

8. The Christian humanism of Erasmus led him to
   (A) reject the idea that the Bible should be translated into the vernacular.
   (B) make a new edition of the Greek New Testament.
   (C) call for strict adherence to the rules of the church.
   (D) reject the Catholic Church wholeheartedly.
   (E) insist that the Latin Bible was the only legitimate one.

9. Which statement is most accurate about the invention of the modern printing press?
   (A) It created a demand for books that had not existed before.
   (B) The European discovery of paper proved Europeans' technological superiority.
   (C) It spread slowly and only had a real impact in the sixteenth century.
   (D) It led to government censorship and often to the arrest of printers.
   (E) The gap between oral and written cultures grew.

10. Over the course of the fifteenth century, artistic patronage
    (A) came mostly from private wealthy patrons
    (B) came mostly from corporate bodies like guilds and governments.
    (C) shifted from private patronage to corporate bodies.
    (D) shifted from corporate bodies to private patronage.
    (E) came almost entirely from the popes.

11. The admiration given to artists that developed in the Renaissance reflected all of the following social trends *except*
    (A) the growing stress on individualism.
    (B) new ways of earning social prestige.
    (C) the hierarchy of wealth created in Renaissance cities.
    (D) humanistic respect for human potential.
    (E) the importance of the sumptuary laws passed by urban communes.

12. Northern Renaissance art differed from its Italian counterparts in that
    (A) it was less religious.
    (B) its architecture was little influenced by Italian Renaissance architecture.
    (C) it was less detailed.
    (D) it was more religious.
    (E) its paintings rarely used perspective.

13. Women during the Renaissance were
    (A) generally excluded from artistic and literary circles.
    (B) accepted as humanists but not as artists.
    (C) accepted as artists but not as humanists.
    (D) rarely discussed in educational texts.
    (E) important for their roles as patrons of major artworks.

14. Blacks in Renaissance Europe
    (A) were extremely rare.
    (B) were used for both slave and wage labor.
    (C) had been imported into Portugal from Africa but were isolated there.
    (D) were almost always employed as entertainers.
    (E) were vilified since black was always seen as a negative color.

15. The monarchs of England, France, and Spain all used which of the following in their efforts to centralize power and forge national unity?
    (A) The Inquisition
    (B) Royal councils with many middle-class members
    (C) Parliaments, or representative bodies
    (D) Citizens' councils empowered to curtail the nobility
    (E) Encouragement of warfare among nobles

Free-Response Questions

1. Machiavelli suggested that princes needed to be both foxes and lions, both clever and fierce. To what degree and in what ways were the kings of France, Spain, and England foxes and lions during the fifteenth and early sixteenth centuries?

2. What characteristics of Italian cities in the fifteenth century created an environment that fostered the development of Renaissance culture?

ANSWERS

MULTIPLE-CHOICE QUESTIONS

1. ANSWER (B) Because the Florentine bankers were tax collectors for the papacy, their dominance of banking was ensured throughout Europe, providing enormous sources of wealth. They were bankers to the king of England, rather than to the Holy Roman Emperor. While Florentines did manufacture silk, it was a relatively small part of their economy. (McKay, *A History of Western Society*, 8th ed., p. 414/9th ed., p. 408)

2. ANSWER (E) Most of the city-states were ruled by merchant oligarchies, although some were ruled by one man who came from a powerful family. Most such families competed furiously with each other. The nobles generally played a secondary role in these communes. In no commune did more than a small percentage of the men have political rights; most ordinary people were completely excluded from power. Option A is a twentieth-century definition of commune, not the one used in the Italian Renaissance. (McKay, *A History of Western Society*, 8th ed., pp. 415–416/9th ed., pp. 409–410)

3. **ANSWER (C)** The endlessly feuding city-states used ambassadors to help forge alliances and prevent any one state from dominating the peninsula. They were unable to unify and prevent French invasion. There was little threat from the Ottomans, and Naples passed peacefully to Aragon in the middle of the fifteenth century. (McKay, *A History of Western Society*, 8th ed., pp. 416–419/9th ed., pp. 410)

4. **ANSWER (C)** A humanist by Renaissance definition is someone who reads the classics. Scholars did so in the medieval period as well, but in the Renaissance, new stress was placed on human achievement, dignity, and individualism. Renaissance humanists were Christians who sought to reconcile pagan learning with Christian faith and with their contemporary world. They wrote a great deal about political matters. (McKay, *A History of Western Society*, 8th ed., pp. 420–421/9th ed., pp. 412–413)

5. **ANSWER (E)** Greek and Latin grammar, rhetoric, history, and philosophy were the fundamentals of humanist education. Theology itself was of little interest to most humanists. (McKay, *A History of Western Society*, 8th ed., pp. 428–429/9th ed., pp. 414–415)

6. **ANSWER (A)** Castiglione's book became like a bible in the training of the ideal gentlemen, who could write and recite poetry, fight well, dance, play music, and speak eloquently. *Utopia* imagined a semisocialistic ideal state; *The Prince* focused almost exclusively on the political talents needed by a prince; *In Praise of Folly* satirized human pretensions; and *The Decameron* is a book of tales revealing the hearty sensuality and acquisitiveness of ordinary life. (McKay, *A History of Western Society*, 8th ed., pp. 421, 428–429, 439/9th ed., pp. 414–415)

7. **ANSWER (C)** Machiavelli argued not for immorality or morality in the behavior of the prince but for a realistic assessment of human fickleness and self-interest and a consequent focus on what works, not what ought to work. It is his lack of concern for the moral standing of the prince that led to accusations of amorality or immorality in his work. (McKay, *A History of Western Society*, 8th ed., p. 429/9th ed., p. 415)

8. **ANSWER (B)** Erasmus, the most renowned of the northern European intellectuals in the sixteenth century, used his humanistic knowledge of Latin and Greek to create a new, critical edition of the New Testament. At the same time, he called for the widespread reading of the Bible by ordinary people and therefore its translation into many languages. While he focused on inner spirituality, he never rejected the Catholic Church outright. (McKay, *A History of Western Society*, 8th ed., p. 439/9th ed., pp. 417–418)

9. **ANSWER (D)** The printing press, which included a whole variety of inventions and technologies, spread quickly throughout Europe as it was better able to meet the growing demand for books than earlier techniques such as hand copying and block printing. Books were printed on paper, a discovery of the Chinese brought to Europe by Arabs. Governments and churches quickly made up lists of prohibited

books and often attacked printers and their presses. (McKay, *A History of Western Society*, 8th ed., pp. 429–430/9th ed., pp. 418–421)

10. ANSWER (D) The early Renaissance artistic masterpieces, such as Brunelleschi's dome for the Florentine cathedral, were commissioned by guilds or oligarchic governments. After the middle of the century, private patrons such as the Medicis played more and more of a prominent role. The popes became prominent patrons in the sixteenth century. (McKay, *A History of Western Society*, 8th ed., pp. 422–426/9th ed., pp. 421–422)

11. ANSWER (E) Sumptuary laws were dress codes delineating class lines and had nothing to do with the arts. Renaissance artists had high prestige and were often very well paid, even wealthy, so their rise in social status reflects the social mobility in Renaissance cities created by wealth as well as the articulation of human potentiality by humanists. (McKay, *A History of Western Society*, 8th ed., pp. 425–426/9th ed., pp. 425–426, 431–432)

12. ANSWER (D) Northern art during the Renaissance tended to be more religious and more detailed. Artists used the innovations from Italy of perspective in painting but not its new architectural principles. (McKay, *A History of Western Society*, 8th ed., pp. 440–441/9th ed., pp. 424–425)

13. ANSWER (A) Women interested in the arts or humanism were rarely accepted by those circles, although a few women wrote or painted. Women also rarely were patrons in their own right. But there was much discussion about their roles and education in literature in what became known as *les querelles des femmes*. (McKay, *A History of Western Society*, 8th ed., pp. 428–429, 432–434/9th ed., pp. 414–415, 426–428, 432–434)

14. ANSWER (B) Beginning in the fifteenth century, there were substantial numbers of African blacks in European cities and courts, both slave and free. Some worked as entertainers, but others were treasured servants, maids, and dockworkers. Europeans had ambivalent notions about blackness: it was the color of demons but also the color worn by monks and mourners. (McKay, *A History of Western Society*, 8th ed., pp. 436–438/9th ed., pp. 429–431)

15. ANSWER (B) Royal councils with middle-class members were effective tools for dominating the aristocracies. The Inquisition and citizens' councils were used only in Spain in the fifteenth century. All the monarchs tried to avoid calling representative bodies as they were strongholds of aristocratic power. The monarchs sought to curb aristocratic violence and become guarantors of law and order. (McKay, *A History of Western Society*, 8th ed., pp. 441–447/9th ed., pp. 434–439)

FREE-RESPONSE QUESTIONS

1. This question asks not only what those monarchs did but which of those deeds showed cleverness or careful planning and which showed fierceness or strength. All the monarchs sought to enhance their own

power by curtailing that of the aristocracies. To achieve this goal, they needed to find ways other than the aristocratic assemblies of financing their governments, manning their armies, and creating an effective administrative structure.

- Using cleverness as foxes: They enhanced their revenue to strengthen their armies by creating new taxes, like the *gabelle* and *taille* in France. They developed the role of royal councils, staffed with middle-class lawyers, to outmaneuver the aristocratic assemblies. Both of these were shrewd actions. In Spain and France, the kings negotiated with the papacy to allow them to appoint their own bishops, effectively taking control over the national church. The Pragmatic Sanction of Bourges and the Concordat of Bologna confirmed Gallican liberties.
- The kings of Spain and France made effective and important marriages that enhanced the royal domains. The daughter of the king of Spain married into the Habsburg Holy Roman Empire; France acquired Brittany; and England allied with Scotland through marriage.
- Using force as lions: With their armies, the kings conquered new territories, Burgundy for France and Granada for Spain, or subdued rebellions, Ireland for England. Charles VII created the first permanent standing army in France. The monarchs used violence and the threat of violence against people who were seen as threats; in England the king had the Star Chamber, in Spain, the Inquisition. The English kings also used justices of the peace to run local governments.

2. Renaissance culture—humanism, new artistic styles and values, and new educational system—was intimately and necessarily connected to the Italian cities. Italian cities prospered early from trade and wool manufacturing and became wealthy, growing in size and influence. They were able to act independently of both the pope and the Holy Roman Emperor and establish communal governments. While some states, like Milan, became despotisms, Florence was a guild republic.

- Communal governments and powerful guilds were important patrons of early Renaissance architects, painters, and sculptors, from Masaccio to Michelangelo. Merchants and bankers became wealthy and had disposable income to spend, which they used as patrons of the arts and humanities. Wealthy merchants and oligarchs developed a new hierarchy of wealth for social status, thus fostering secularism and individualism. The opportunities for individuals to become wealthy and rise in social class paralleled the humanist sense of man's potentiality, which was reflected in the noticeable rise in the status of artists. Political thinkers used examples from ancient Greece and Rome to justify and explore their republican city-states; this required an educated political class.

14

REFORMATION AND RELIGIOUS WARS, 1500–1600

The unity of the western Christian world, separated from the Orthodoxy prominent in eastern Europe, was permanently broken by the Protestant Reformation in the sixteenth century. Initiated in the Germanic states, Protestantism spread successfully to most parts of northern Europe but met resistance in France, Spain, and the Italian states.

AP Tip

Almost every AP exam includes an essay question on the Reformation or the Counter-Reformation. While sometimes those questions deal primarily with religious issues, more often they deal with social, economic, or political factors.

KEY CONCEPTS

- Martin Luther, articulating many of the same ideas as Wyclif had two centuries earlier, publicly challenged both the practices and the theology of the Catholic Church when he posted his *95 Theses* in 1517. Protected by several German princes, Luther escaped persecution and launched a new church, based on the premises of *sola Scriptura* ("only by Scripture"), justification by faith alone, and the priesthood of all believers.

- Luther's reformed church stimulated other reformers: John Calvin, who focused even more on the importance of predestination, found enthusiastic support, first in Geneva and later in England and Holland. The Tudor king Henry VIII established the Church of England, the Anglican Church, independent of Rome but largely for political reasons.
- The Catholic Church removed some of the abuses that had cost it support but at the same time went on the offensive, theologically, with confirmation of the key elements of the Catholic faith, such as the seven sacraments, and new religious orders to combat Protestantism. Of these, the Jesuit order would prove most successful in Europe and abroad.
- Most western European countries were fraught with religious tensions that erupted into civil war. In France, Catholicism won out, although toleration for Protestants was granted in the Edict of Nantes in 1598. Religious issues were a major factor in the revolt of the Dutch provinces against their Spanish overlord, Philip II.

THE CENTRAL IDEAS OF THE REFORMERS AND THEIR APPEAL TO DIFFERENT SOCIAL GROUPS

THE CHRISTIAN CHURCH IN THE EARLY SIXTEENTH CENTURY

Most western Europeans remained deeply religious as the sixteenth century began. At the same time, following the long history of criticisms of the church and reforms within it, the Babylonian Captivity and the Great Schism had damaged the church's prestige. Christian humanists had called for reform and an end to corrupt practices like simony (buying or selling of church offices), absenteeism (holding an office but living in another place), and pluralism (holding more than one benefice, or office). Anticlericalism, opposition to the clergy— both priests and monks—for their ignorance and immorality and resentment over their privileges, was widespread. Many of the clergy had concubines, were on occasion (or often) publicly drunk, or gambled, and many were only minimally literate. All of these situations led the people to a common sense of neglect or abuse, although many of the situations were not new.

It was the response to these situations by a monk and professor of theology at the University of Wittenberg that was to have enormous consequences. Martin Luther struggled first with his miner father's ambitions for him, and then with deep anxiety over sin and God's forgiveness. His studies led him to challenge the Catholic notion of the importance of good works (attending church, taking communions, and so forth) as necessary for salvation. Salvation comes from faith, which is a gift from God, and from faith come good works and charitable acts. God's word is revealed only in the Scriptures.

AP Tip

The intensely personal nature of Luther's spiritual agony inspired a new subfield in historical studies called psychohistory, which analyzes the impact of personal psychodynamics on important historical figures. A classic text in this field is *Young Man Luther* by Erik Erikson, which used Freudian psychoanalysis to explain Luther's theology and actions.

The particular issue that sparked Luther into action was the selling of indulgences by the Dominican monk Johann Tetzel, which was authorized by Pope Leo X to pay for St. Peter's in Rome with permission for the archbishop, who was in debt, to keep a portion of the proceeds. Indulgences promised forgiveness for sins or time off in purgatory, where sinners not condemned to hell for all eternity make amends after death to earn their place in heaven. Indulgences were a long-standing and well-established tradition, granted to Crusaders and sold to an eager public. Tetzel was a particularly successful salesman. Luther challenged the whole concept of indulgences on theological grounds in his famous *95 Theses on the Power of Indulgences*, supposedly posted on the door of the court church at Wittenberg on October 31, 1517 (Halloween). When *95 Theses* was translated into German shortly thereafter, its ideas spread widely. Two years later, Luther denied the legitimacy of papal authority or the church councils in a debate with a church representative, after which he was threatened with excommunication. The Holy Roman Emperor Charles V called an assembly of the estates of the empire, the Diet of Worms, to force Luther into obedience. But Luther refused to withdraw his views, claiming to be bound only by the Scriptures.

AP Tip

Modern Catholicism is quite different from the Catholicism that was practiced in Luther's time, and many Christian students do not know the theological details of the churches to which their families belong. Be sure you understand what the theological disputes were all about. While the details varied, the basic disagreement was over the relationship of man and God and the role the organized church plays in man's salvation.

PROTESTANT THOUGHT

Luther's followers began to be called Protestants, from the *protest* of some German princes in 1529, as the name began to be applied to all anti-Catholic dissidents.

A second important Protestant thinker was Ulrich Zwingli, a Swiss Erasmian humanist, based in Zurich, who also insisted on *sola Scriptura* and attacked indulgences, monasticism, clerical celibacy, and the Mass.

Both Luther and Zwingli argued that only faith, and not faith combined with good works, determined salvation, which is granted by God alone, and that each individual must interpret the Bible for him- or herself. Because Scripture was the only authority, only two sacraments, baptism and the Eucharist (or Holy Communion), are legitimate. The church, according to Protestants, is not a clerical, hierarchical institution with the pope as its head but the community of all Christians, all of whom are equal in status, whether commoner or cleric, whether married or celibate. Protestants rejected clerical celibacy and in fact promoted the value of marriage. Zwingli and Luther disagreed about what happens in the Eucharist. Catholics believe in the doctrine of transubstantiation, the actual transformation of the wine and wafer into the blood and body of Christ. Luther believed in the doctrine of the *Real Presence,* which holds that Jesus is present in the wine and wafer during the Eucharist but the elements remain physically unchanged, and although Christ's presence is Real, it is not physical. Luther's concept is known as the doctrine of consubstantiation. Zwingli argued that the Eucharist was only a memorial. The Eucharist was a divisive issue among Protestants.

AP Tip

The doctrine of transubstantiation asserts that a miracle occurs each time the Mass is performed. It is so that they can perform this miracle that priests must be pure in thought and deed, and therefore cannot marry or live ordinary lives. When the Protestants renounced this doctrine, they removed the distinctive function of Catholic priests. All Protestant clergy can marry and have children, and except in the Anglican version, are called ministers, not priests.

ART IN THE REFORMATION

Artists served both the Catholic and Protestant causes to propagate their version of Christianity. Lucas Cranach the Elder, a close friend of Luther's, painted a number of Old Testament scenes, as Protestants enthusiastically embraced the Hebrew Bible as well as the New Testament. Vasari painted the St. Bartholomew's Day Massacre for the pope. Protestants and Catholics also disagreed about the function of art. Catholics affirmed that the likenesses of Christ, the saints, and Mary would promote piety and deserved veneration. The Catholic Reformation developed the Baroque form of art with its drama and intense emotionality to proselytize their faith (see pp. 452–453). Protestants took their lead from the second commandment forbidding graven images. Some like Zwingli believed that art and music were unnecessary and interfered with true faith, while Luther saw the usefulness of art spreading the message of faith and himself composed a number of hymns. John Calvin, another major Protestant theologian (see pp. 463–465), insisted on stark simplicity in his churches; such churches were empty of decoration. His laws forbidding dance and theater also dampened artistic production.

AP Tip

Several essay questions have used images of Protestant and Catholic churches or religious objects like chalices as the starting point of a comparison question. Look at an art book or visit local churches to get a sense of the differing concepts of church decoration and artistic styles.

THE APPEAL OF PROTESTANT IDEAS

Luther's ideas spread quickly through printed broadsides with vicious caricatures of the pope and indulgences, serious theological texts, and Luther's own translation of the Bible into German, as well as through preaching. Luther's hymns, such as "A Mighty Fortress Is Our God"; psalms; and two catechisms helped people learn and remember Protestant doctrine. Luther's excellent translation of the Bible helped make his German dialect the standard version of the language.

People from all varieties of classes and occupations were drawn to Protestantism. Humanists and educated people had been calling for many of the reforms that the Protestants promulgated and were attracted by their insistence on everyone's reading the Scriptures. Many priests and monks became Protestant preachers, and some nuns left their convents. The status of women improved when Protestants argued that marriage was the true Christian life. Urban dwellers and peasants saw their status raised by the doctrine of the priesthood of all believers. Protestant leaders worked closely with city governments, which increased their revenues as they could tax the Protestant clergy.

Luther was also protected by the ruler of the state in which he lived, the elector of Saxony. Protestants argued that Christians were obliged to obey their secular rulers, who were urged to reform the church. While many people converted to Protestantism, states became Protestant when their ruler or city council became so, sometimes against the wishes of the population. The kingdom of Denmark-Norway was the first to become Lutheran, although in parts of Norway the people had to be forced to accept Lutheranism. Sweden too became Lutheran.

THE RADICAL REFORMATION

While Lutherans created a national church, where the ruler held authority over the church except in matters of faith, other Protestants sought to establish voluntary communities of believers, making even greater breaks with the past, for which reason they are called radicals. Anabaptists repudiated infant baptism. Others argued for a literal interpretation of the Bible. Some were pacifists and refused to swear oaths, such as the Quakers in Britain in the seventeenth century. Others argued for communal ownership of property. Congregationalists in Britain and the New England colonies insisted on democratic organization. Some groups were fiercely doctrinaire; others advocated religious toleration. The radicals were persecuted by mainstream Protestants and Catholics alike. Both shared an opposition to the separation of church and state, which they saw as secularizing society.

AP Tip

All revolutions, it seems, prompt small extremist groups. Most of the Protestant radicals were persecuted or even killed, but some groups like the Quakers in England and the Mennonites or the Amish in Czech Moravia found a haven in the American colonies, particularly New England and Pennsylvania.

The German Peasants' War

Peasants' revolts were common in the fourteenth and fifteenth centuries, but the conditions of the peasants grew worse as the sixteenth century began. Crop failures in 1523 and 1524 aggravated this deteriorating situation. The next year peasants in Swabia, a small region in southern Germany, drew up Twelve Articles, which condemned both lay and ecclesiastical lords for seizing common lands and imposing new rents, taxes, and services on peasants. At first Luther joined them in criticizing the lords, but when massive revolts broke out with great violence, with the crowds shouting Protestant slogans, Luther turned against the mob, as the title of his tract *Against the Murderous, Thieving Hordes of the Peasants* indicates, and strongly condemned the peasants for taking religious freedom to mean social freedom and urged the nobles to suppress the peasants. Over 75,000 were killed in that process.

AP Tip

This incident is a good one for demonstrating Luther's relationship with the state. Luther was a fierce advocate of the individual's freedom to interpret Scripture, but he argued, also on the basis of Scripture, that in their political lives, people must obey the state. In this sense one can see Luther as both a revolutionary and a conservative. Insisting on obedience to rulers certainly earned him strong support from them and made Lutheranism not only an acceptable change for them but even a desirable one.

The Reformation and Marriage

Both Luther and Zwingli married and had children, as did most other Protestant leaders, demonstrating their abandonment of celibacy as a Christian ideal. Their wives created new roles for themselves as the wives of pastors, obedient to their husbands and modeling virtue. Scripture justified marriage. While Protestants, as did Catholics, believed that women were to be subject to their men, they argued for spiritual equality and reciprocity in marriage. Often Protestant couples had double wedding portraits commissioned, as did Luther and his wife. Women were to obey cheerfully; men were to be kind unless their wives needed physical coercion to be obedient. Catholics believe that marriage is a sacrament, and therefore dissolution or divorce is impossible. For Protestants, marriage is a contract between a man and a woman, so divorce is permissible, although it remained relatively rare. Protestants argued that marriage was the remedy for lust and condemned prostitution, closing the city-sponsored brothels and harshly condemning women who sold themselves for sex. This is in distinct contrast to Catholic cities like Florence, which taxed their prostitutes and gave them a certain freedom of movement. The abolition of nunneries, which generally accompanied Protestantism, removed an arena where medieval women had been able to achieve some prominence and power. Marriage became the only option for women.

THE REFORMATION AND GERMAN POLITICS

The fact that Protestantism was born within the Holy Roman Empire is part of the reason for its success. The Holy Roman Emperor, elected by seven princes and archbishops, was titular ruler of hundreds of large and small states, but had little real power himself. The Habsburgs, rulers of Austria and since the fourteenth century of the Holy Roman Empire, married well; for example, Mary of Burgundy brought under Habsburg rule Burgundy and the Netherlands and some lesser lands along with the permanent enmity of the French; her son married the daughter of Ferdinand and Isabella, bringing Spain, southern Italy, and the New World to the Habsburgs. All of these territories, about half of Europe, were inherited by Charles V, who was committed to maintaining the power and the unity of Catholicism. It was at the Diet of Worms called by Charles that Luther declared his independence.

THE POLITICAL IMPACT OF THE REFORMATION

At this time, religious practice was public, determined by the ruler. Few in the sixteenth century could imagine religious toleration or freedom of religion. Therefore the Protestant Reformation inevitably became tied up with political issues. Anticlericalism and fury over papal taxes sometimes merged with nationalism, which Luther, for one, promoted with his translation of the Bible into German and with his opposition of "us Germans" against the papacy. Some German princes were attracted by the economic possibilities offered by Protestantism in that they could legally confiscate the lands and monasteries of the church. Such princes saw Protestantism as a way to enhance their power and their independence from the Catholic emperor.

Charles V and Catholic forces battled Protestant forces, first in several Swiss cantons—Zwingli himself dying in battle in 1531. There the result was that each canton could choose its religion; this would be the solution found twenty-five years later after much warfare. The Protestants defined their doctrine in the Augsburg Confession which they presented to the emperor at a diet in that city in 1530. Charles rejected their statement of faith and threatened them; in response, they formed a military alliance. There followed some dozen years of political maneuvering amid other military actions, including an Ottoman siege of Vienna in 1529, and constant Habsburg-Valois rivalry. Outright war began in 1546, ending nine years later with the Peace of Augsburg, which codified a victory for the Protestants. It officially recognized Lutheranism and allowed each ruler to choose Catholicism or Lutheranism for his territory, but granted no religious freedom to dissidents. Germany tended to divide geographically on religious lines, with the north Protestant and the south Catholic. Charles recognized that this treaty meant the failure of his dream of keeping the empire unified and Catholic, and he abdicated the next year, dividing his empire between his son Philip II, who got Spain and the Netherlands, and his brother Ferdinand I, who received the imperial crown.

The Spread of the Protestant Reformation

By the 1520s Protestant ideas had spread to England, France, and eastern Europe. In England and Ireland, the juncture of political and religious issues was acute. The Tudor king Henry VIII sought to annul his marriage to Catherine of Aragon, another daughter of Ferdinand and Isabella, who had not produced a male heir. Such an annulment was quite common, but the pope was under pressure from Catherine's uncle, Charles V, and refused. Henry had Parliament enact the separation of the Church of England, with himself as its head, from the Catholic Church. The humanist Thomas More, author of *Utopia,* and several others refused to accept the Act of Supremacy and were beheaded. The king retained many elements of Catholicism but dissolved the monasteries and confiscated the monastic lands, selling them off to the upper classes, who were thereafter more bound to the Tudors. Managing those estates required the development of a government bureaucracy; Henry's chief minister, Thomas Cromwell, reorganized the bureaucracy's structure and improved its efficiency.

Henry married not one but five more times, producing only one male heir, Edward VI, but two daughters—Mary Tudor and Elizabeth I—both of whom became queen. There was a large rebellion in the north called the Pilgrimage of Grace in 1536, but it ended relatively quickly. Edward VI, who ruled only six years, oversaw the production, under Archbishop Thomas Cranmer, of the *Book of Common Prayer,* the standard service of the Church of England. But the Catholic cause was reinvigorated by the short but controversial rule of Mary Tudor, who restored Catholicism and alienated the people by burning Protestants at the stake and marrying Philip II of Spain. When Mary died, Elizabeth became queen. She sought to ensure religious stability by restoring the Church of England and following a middle path between those who wanted Catholicism and some radical Protestants, called Puritans, who wanted to eliminate all its remnants. This compromise, sometimes called the Elizabethan Settlement, required outward conformity, while the Thirty-nine Articles of 1563 articulated the basic tenets of the Church of England. Services were given in the vernacular and the clergy allowed to marry, but the hierarchical structure of the church was preserved.

Loyalty to the Catholic Church remained strong in Ireland, although the Irish Parliament, which represented only English landlords and the area known as the Pale that the English ruled directly, established the Church of Ireland. This only intensified the already strained ethnic tensions (see Chapter 12). When Irish Catholics resisted, they were harshly repressed and their church pushed underground.

CALVINISM

Calvin had an even greater influence than Luther on the future course of history, both by his theological writings and by his role as magistrate in Geneva. Calvin, as articulated in his *Institutes of the Christian Religion*, 1536, believed that God is omnipotent and absolutely sovereign. Men and women are weak and incapable of earning their own salvation. God predetermines who is saved and who is condemned, predestining people to heaven or hell. But instead of leading to pessimism, the doctrine of predestination led to the firm conviction by Calvinists that they were among the elect, as the saved were called. The elect in Geneva were inspired by Calvin's eloquence and his mastery of Scripture to enforce morality not only on themselves but on the entire population. In fact, the Geneva Consistory, laity and pastors, kept watch over the residents of Geneva, punishing not only religious lapses and dissent but also activities like dancing, drinking, and gambling. Michael Servetus, a Spanish humanist who denied the Trinity, was arrested when he came to Geneva, tried, and burned at the stake. Reformers and refugees flocked to Geneva; going home, they became the Presbyterians of Scotland and the Huguenots of France. The Puritans of England and America were also Calvinists. Calvinism's notion that God calls the elect to a calling dignified all labor and encouraged an activist approach to life.

AP Tip

More than one hundred years ago, the German sociologist Max Weber wrote a short book, *The Protestant Ethic and the Spirit of Capitalism*, which argued for an intimate connection between the rise of commercial capitalism and Protestantism. The Calvinist calling encouraged the traits of hard work, saving, and frugality, which made the growth of capitalism possible. Those countries that became Calvinist—England in the mid-seventeenth century, Scotland, and Holland, particularly—saw great economic success in the seventeenth and eighteenth centuries. Although many historians have challenged the Weber thesis, it has led to much fruitful analysis.

THE REFORMATION IN SCOTLAND

Calvinism found a ready audience in Scotland, with a weak monarchy, King James V and his daughter Mary Queen of Scots, staunch Catholics, and fractious nobles. John Knox worked with Calvin in Geneva and brought his doctrines home to restore the Scottish church. Reform-minded barons in the Scottish Parliament, similar in their beliefs to English Puritans, established the Presbyterian Church of Scotland as a national church.

AP Tip

While many Scots became Calvinist, others had sympathy for Catholicism. This was important in British history when the son of Mary Queen of Scots, who had been executed for treason by Elizabeth I, became King James I of England in 1603. The Stuart sympathy for Catholicism prompted the English Revolution of the mid-seventeenth century.

The Reformation in Eastern Europe

Ethnic factors proved to be the ultimate determinants of religion in eastern Europe, where the populations were heterogeneous. In Bohemia, the Hussite Church was both an early form of Protestantism and a nationalist movement (see Chapter 12). In the 1520s and 1530s, Lutheranism spread quickly among Bohemians, many of whom shared German ancestry, and most of whom were opposed to Habsburg rule. The Catholic Reformation had some success here, but in the next century the religious issue would spark the Thirty Years' War.

The huge, sparsely populated and mostly agricultural Grand Duchy of Lithuania had a great diversity of population—Germans, Italians, Tartars, Jews, Poles—plus the native population of the Baltic states, now Estonia, Latvia, and Lithuania. Italian Renaissance humanism had influenced Polish arts and literature. Luther's ideas spread to the German-speaking Baltic towns, but the Polish king banned his writings. Calvin's ideas spread to the Polish nobility, however, but the Calvinist ideas' influence proved short-lived, as the Counter-Reformation, led by the Jesuits, was successful in restoring Catholicism to Poland.

In Hungary, students who had flocked to Wittenberg to hear Luther helped spread Lutheranism in the Hungarian capital, where it was briefly welcomed, only to be declared anathema by the Hungarian Diet in 1523. Three years later, the Ottoman sultan Suleiman the Magnificent defeated the Hungarians at Mohács, killing their king, many nobles, and some 16,000 soldiers. Hungary was left divided into three parts, one ruled by the Ottomans, one by the Habsburgs, and the third by an Ottoman puppet. In response, many of the Hungarian nobles, or magnates, accepted Lutheranism. Perhaps 85 percent of the population became Protestant. Catholicism was restored when Hungary was conquered by the Habsburgs in 1699.

The Catholic Reformation

The Catholic Church was able to defend itself against Protestantism after the initial shock, preventing its spread after about 1540, except in the Netherlands, by a combination of interior reform and energetic Counter-Reformation activities. Paul III was the great reforming pope, turning the papal court into a center of reform, not its enemy. He improved the education of the clergy; banned pluralism, simony, and absenteeism; and established new religious orders to preach to the laity. The Holy Office, established in 1542, also known as the Roman Inquisition, was a committee of six cardinals with judicial authority over all Catholics and charged with the eradication of heresy; it had good success in the Papal States but not much elsewhere. An *Index of Prohibited Books* was a tool used by the Holy Office to enforce religious conformity. Paul called the Council of Trent, 1545 to 1563, inviting Lutherans and Calvinists in the hope of reconciliation, although that proved impossible. International politics and the political concerns of Charles V and the French kings impinged on the religious debates. The council met the Protestant challenge with doctrinal reaffirmation but changes in church practice. The council reconfirmed the basic tenets of Catholicism, including the seven sacraments and transubstantiation. At the same time, the church tightened its rules and its supervision of the clergy, established seminaries for the training of priests, and expanded preaching to the laity. The Protestant assertion that marriage was not a sacrament was specifically rejected by a decree banning private marital unions and requiring that marital unions be performed by priests.

New Religious Orders

One of these new orders was influenced by perhaps the most famous Catholic visionary of the sixteenth century, Teresa of Ávila, immortalized in a Baroque statue by Bernini. She was made a saint and the first woman to be called a doctor of the Church. A descendant of a New Christian, she became a Carmelite nun and a mystic. She founded some fourteen new convents with the principles of egalitarianism, obedience, poverty, and isolation; traveled widely; wrote numerous books; and urged women to take an active part in evangelical work.

Another woman, Angela Merici, founded the Ursuline order in order to educate women and thereby combat heresy. The Council of Trent had sought to keep nuns enclosed and to restrict their roles, but when the church recognized the order in 1565, Ursulines spread quickly. These two women demonstrate the influence Catholic women could have and their crucial role in the success of the Counter-Reformation.

AP Tip

The importance of Teresa of Ávila and Angela Merici demonstrates that religion remained a path for women to achieve significant power along with mysticism and love for the saints. While we know about a number of Protestant women, they tended to play a more subservient role.

The Society of Jesus, founded by Ignatius Loyola, was particularly important in limiting the spread of Protestantism by stressing the spiritual needs of the people rather than theological doctrines. The Jesuits played a major role in converting the natives of the New World, bringing Christianity to Japan and China, and in establishing schools with humanistic curricula throughout Europe. In a way, Jesuits were quite modern, ready to go where the need was greatest. The order was highly centralized, almost military in its organization (soldiers of Christ), and under the direct authority of the pope. The Jesuits became hugely successful, highly influential, and very popular, even succeeding in converting some Protestants back to Catholicism. Along with the Ursulines for women, education became an important tool of the Counter-Reformation.

Religious Violence

The Treaty of Cateau-Cambrésis ended the Habsburg-Valois wars, but the promised peace was undercut by religious violence, especially in France and the Netherlands. Both Catholics and Protestants were uncompromising and used violence as much as preaching to advance their cause, and both persecuted people identified as witches.

In France, the monarchy had won control over the church in France by the Concordat of Bologna, making Catholicism its state religion and giving the king no reason to rebel against Rome. Calvinism made sizable inroads among the artisans and middle classes, particularly as Calvin wrote in French. Most of the Huguenots (French Calvinists) lived in cities, making up about 10 percent of the population and perhaps half of the nobility who sought greater independence from the crown. Protestants and Catholics clashed bitterly in France, with Protestants attacking Catholic religious images in a form of popular iconoclasm and with each side often attacking the other during religious ceremonies. The St. Bartholomew's Day massacre, on the occasion of a religious marriage of the king's sister to the Protestant Henry of Navarre, led to the killing of thousands of Huguenots, an event that sparked a fifteen-year civil war. What saved France was a small group of politiques, practical men who sought to restore order to France by resolving the religious conflict by seeking a moderate path between the extremes. They sought toleration for the Huguenots. After Henry of Navarre became King Henry IV, he eventually renounced Protestantism, making the apocryphal remark "Paris is worth the Mass," and became a Catholic. He then issued the Edict of Nantes in 1598 giving the Huguenots freedom to practice their faith.

AP Tip

The term *politique* is applied to rulers like Elizabeth I as well. She, like Henry IV, put national interest over religious issues, stability and moderation over ideology.

The Netherlands under Charles V

In the Netherlands, too, religion and politics intertwined. The seventeen provinces of the Low Countries, the Netherlands, were each self-governing and prosperous through trade and industry. During the rule of Charles V in the first half of the sixteenth century, Protestantism made limited inroads, but under his son Philip II, religious tensions intensified, especially as the merchants and financial and urban workers became fairly militant Calvinists. When Spanish authorities tried to suppress Calvinist worship and raise taxes, riots spread, leading Philip to decide on a policy of pacification through force. The ruthless duke of Alva persecuted dissidents, setting up his own tribunal, nicknamed the Council of Blood, in addition to using the Inquisition. Ten years of civil war ensued, after which the ten southern provinces were controlled by the Spanish while the seven northern provinces, all Protestant controlled, signed the Union of Utrecht in 1581 and declared their independence. The Dutch were led by William of Nassau, also known as William the Silent (assassinated in 1584) and got much-needed help from Protestant England. Spain's failed attempt to invade England in the 1588 disaster of the Spanish Armada weakened Spain enough that by 1609, Spain agreed to a truce and recognized the independence of the United Provinces.

THE GREAT EUROPEAN WITCH HUNT

Large-scale persecution of witches began in the 1480s but intensified after the 1560s, when both Protestant and Catholic civil authorities persecuted witches. Witches were not primarily seen as heretics but as consorters with the devil, an additional demonological element from premodern notions of magic. Some 100,000 to 200,000 witches were tried and about a third executed in hugely popular spectacles. Most of them were women. Partially this reflected misogyny, the association of women with the demonic and with nature, and the weakness of women's position in societies. Women were closely involved with rearing children, health care, taking care of animals, and preparing food, and it was these activities that were the source of many accusations. Sexuality and gender roles thus played an important part. Inquisitorial methods and legal procedures were used; this meant the accused had a harder time proving innocence and faced torture. Sometimes groups were rounded up; this led to witch panics. Interestingly enough, the most famous inquisitions in Europe, such as the one in Spain, engaged relatively little in witchcraft persecution, since they were skeptical of the accusations. Gradually such skepticism spread and led to the gradual end of the persecutions. Historians have long debated the causes and the meaning of the witchcraft persecutions, and even the reasons why they abated.

AP Tip

Among the elements of the witchcraft craze debated by historians are the degree to which it revealed the survival of pagan ideas, the importance of economic motives in removing large numbers of women property holders from communities, the way it was used to reinforce religious ideals, and its relationship to the scientific revolution, which was beginning at the same time. Students often compare it to the Salem witch trials, but the European witch craze lasted longer, involved many thousands more victims, and included both Catholic and Protestant persecution.

Multiple-Choice Questions

1. Pluralism and absenteeism
   (A) resulted in the depriving of the sacraments to parishioners.
   (B) occurred because so many bishops had concubines.
   (C) caused nationalistic resentments.
   (D) resulted in the widespread illiteracy of the priesthood.
   (E) were part of church doctrine as well as practice.

2. Martin Luther demonstrated Protestant attitudes in his personal life when he
   (A) remained committed to the monastic life.
   (B) became a minister but remained celibate.
   (C) insisted on the right to be a professor without being a monk.
   (D) married a woman who had also once taken monastic vows.
   (E) raised his daughter to become a Lutheran minister.

3. The selling of indulgences bothered Luther so much because
   (A) it was another example of corruption in the church.
   (B) Tetzel had no legal authority in the church.
   (C) Tetzel was charging too much money.
   (D) he believed that there was no need to raise money for St. Peter's Basilica in Rome.
   (E) it implied a limitation on the power of God to determine salvation and give penance.

4. At The Diet of Worms, Luther
   (A) refused to speak.
   (B) recanted to save his life.
   (C) was treated the same way Jan Hus had been at the Council of Constance.
   (D) asserted that he was bound only by the Scriptures and conscience.
   (E) attacked Calvinist ideas.

5. Zwingli and Luther disagreed mostly about
   I. the nature of the Eucharist.
   II. justification by faith alone.
   III. the importance of the Scriptures.
   IV. clerical marriage.
   V. art and music in the church.
   (A) I and IV
   (B) II, III, and IV
   (C) IV and V
   (D) I and V
   (E) All of the above

6. Ultimately the factor that determined the spread of Lutheranism was
   (A) Luther's translation of the Bible.
   (B) the popularity of antipapal broadsides.
   (C) Luther's hymns like "A Mighty Fortress Is Our God."
   (D) the Council of Trent.
   (E) decisions made by princes or rulers to adopt or reject Protestantism.

7. Protestant radicals like the Anabaptists were
   (A) protected by Luther but attacked by Zwingli.
   (B) attacked by both Protestants and Catholics.
   (C) protected by Protestants but attacked by Catholics.
   (D) attacked by Protestants but given safe haven by Catholics.
   (E) generally ignored and left alone.

8. The significance of the German Peasants' War of 1525 was that it
   (A) was prompted by a drop in prices due to overproduction.
   (B) led Luther to call for absolute obedience to the state.
   (C) was inspired by Anabaptist ideas.
   (D) alienated the nobles from the Lutherans.
   (E) ended with the peasantry becoming conservative.

9. As a result of the Reformation and the Counter-Reformation,
   (A) clandestine unions became less acceptable.
   (B) convents for women were abolished in both Catholic and Protestant states.
   (C) brothels were closed in Catholic cities but tolerated in Protestant cities.
   (D) witches ceased to be tried and executed.
   (E) women came to be considered the equals of men.

10. Which territory did Charles V *not* rule?
   (A) Burgundy
   (B) Spain
   (C) The Netherlands
   (D) Hungary
   (E) Sicily

11. The Peace of Augsburg
   (A) was a victory for Charles V.
   (B) gave rulers of member states of the Holy Roman Empire the right to choose whichever religion they wanted.
   (C) gave rulers of member states of the Holy Roman Empire the right to choose Catholicism or Lutheranism as their state religion.
   (D) gave religious toleration to Lutherans but not to Anabaptists.
   (E) led to a new war over religion within a decade.

12. The English Reformation was
    (A) hugely popular with the English people.
    (B) inspired by Calvin's ideas.
    (C) initially more political and economic than religious.
    (D) supported by humanists like Thomas More.
    (E) instrumental in bringing England into alliance with Wittenberg against France.

13. Which factor best explains why Calvinism had greater international impact than Lutheranism did?
    (A) It spread to Scotland.
    (B) The concept of the calling proved to be dynamic.
    (C) The Geneva Consistory was noted for its fairness and moderation.
    (D) The doctrine of predestination created a deep sense of pessimism.
    (E) Lutheranism spread only in Germany.

14. The Catholic Reformation involved all of the following *except*
    (A) Baroque art to stimulate spiritual emotionality.
    (B) improving the education of the clergy.
    (C) banning absenteeism and pluralism.
    (D) reducing the number of sacraments from eight to seven.
    (E) new monastic orders.

15. The common thread between their religious wars resulting in France remaining Catholic and the Netherlands becoming Protestant was
    (A) England's involvement.
    (B) the military victory of the Catholic and Protestant sides, respectively.
    (C) the decisions made by *politiques.*
    (D) Spain's involvement.
    (E) national interests.

Free-Response Questions

1. What are the differing views concerning the roles of women held by Catholics and Protestants? What do these views reveal about the impact of theology on gender roles?
2. Select two states in which there was substantial conflict between Protestants and Catholics in sixteenth-century Europe, and analyze the role national politics played in those domestic struggles.

ANSWERS

MULTIPLE-CHOICE QUESTIONS

1. **ANSWER (C)** Concubinage and illiteracy were all too common, but were not directly related to the fact that so many high churchmen held more than one position, usually in different cities or even countries,

which led them to be absent most of the time from their duties in each of them. When these churchmen were part of the papal curia and held positions abroad, resentment included nationalistic sentiments as well. Usually, low-level priests fulfilled the spiritual duties of those positions. (McKay, *A History of Western Society*, 8th ed., pp. 454–455/9th ed., p. 446)

2. **ANSWER (D)** Both Luther and his wife had taken religious vows and left their orders to marry. (McKay, *A History of Western Society*, 8th ed., pp. 463, 466/9th ed., pp. 446–447, 457)

3. **ANSWER (E)** The issue of indulgences was primarily theological, in that Luther could find no justification for it in Scripture and it implied that humans could determine their own destiny, rather than God. The notion that one could buy time off one's penitential service in purgatory was also challenged because there is no mention of purgatory in Scripture, only heaven and hell. (McKay, *A History of Western Society*, 8th ed., pp. 458–459/9th ed., pp. 447–449)

4. **ANSWER (D)** Luther was ordered to recant, but refused, saying that he was bound only by the Scriptures and conscience. Unlike Jan Hus, he escaped punishment. Calvin was still a child in 1521. (McKay, *A History of Western Society*, 8th ed., pp. 458–459/9th ed., pp. 448–449)

5. **ANSWER (D)** Protestants generally agreed on most issues, but did disagree about the meaning of the Eucharist. Luther argued for the Real Presence of Jesus during communion, while Zwingli asserted it was only a memorial. They also disagreed about the legitimacy of having artistic representations in the church, with Luther seeing their value and Zwingli insisting on relying solely on God's words. (McKay, *A History of Western Society*, 8th ed., pp. 458–461/9th ed., pp. 449–453)

6. **ANSWER (E)** Although A, B, and C all helped spread Protestant ideas, it was only when rulers decided to adopt Protestantism that it was accepted and territories became Protestant. The Council of Trent was where the Catholic Reformation was formed, confirming Catholic doctrine but making important reforms. (McKay, *A History of Western Society*, 8th ed., pp. 462–466/9th ed., pp. 450–451)

7. **ANSWER (B)** Protestants and Catholics alike thought the radicals would bring dangerous secularization because they advocated separation of church and state; on this issue, they held common views. (McKay, *A History of Western Society*, 8th ed., pp.472–473/9th ed., pp. 451–454)

8. **ANSWER (B)** Although initially supportive of the peasants who adopted his religious ideas to protest their social and economic grievances, Luther quickly turned against them, saying that freedom was in the realm of faith, not disobedience to the state. This pleased the nobles and the rulers, of course. The revolt was prompted by several years of crop failures, not by Anabaptism, which had not yet developed. Many peasants turned to the radical sects after the failure of the revolt. (McKay, *A History of Western Society*, 8th ed., pp. 461–462/9th ed., pp. 454–455)

9. **ANSWER (A)** As part of the Catholic Reformation, marriage rules were tightened and secret marriages discouraged. Protestants closed brothels. Both Protestants and Catholics avidly persecuted witches after the 1560s. Neither saw women as equal. (McKay, *A History of Western Society* 8th ed., p. 480/9th ed., pp. 455–457, 469, 475–477)

10. **ANSWER (D)** Charles V inherited all of those territories except Hungary, which was lost to the Ottomans in 1526 at the Battle of Mohács and retaken by the Habsburgs only in 1699. (McKay, *A History of Western Society*, 8th ed., pp. 466–467, 476–477/9th ed., pp. 458, 465–466)

11. **ANSWER (C)** The Peace of Augsburg gave Germanic rulers the right to choose Protestantism or Catholicism for their states. No religious toleration was given to any group. Charles V abdicated after the treaty was signed, his dream lost. A new religious war was fought but only in the seventeenth century. (McKay, *A History of Western Society*, 8th ed., p. 470/9th ed., pp. 458–461)

12. **ANSWER (C)** Henry VIII initiated the Reformation to establish a national church under his control, which would allow him to divorce his wife and marry another woman to have a male heir. These were political reasons. In addition, he confiscated church lands and monasteries, which brought revenue to the national coffers. There was a large rebellion against the religious change called the Pilgrimage of Grace in 1536. (McKay, *A History of Western Society*, 8th ed., pp. 473–475/9th ed., pp, 461–463)

13. **ANSWER (B)** The concept of the calling sanctified work and attracted the hard-working bourgeoisie of France, England, and the American colonies, as well as elsewhere in Europe. Lutheranism spread to Scandinavia as well as within the Holy Roman Empire. Calvinists believed that they were predestined for salvation, so they were, generally speaking, personally optimistic. Calvinism did spread to Scotland, but it was more important that it spread to Holland. (McKay, *A History of Western Society*, 8th ed., p. 472/9th ed., pp. 464–465)

14. **ANSWER (D)** The Catholic Church reformed itself in a variety of ways but not by changing its theology. The Council of Trent confirmed the seven sacraments and other key Catholic tenets. New orders like the Jesuits and Ursulines helped the Church hold back the Protestant tide. (McKay, *A History of Western Society*, 8th ed., pp. 477–483/9th ed., pp. 466–472)

15. **ANSWER (E)** Dutch nationalism was a strong element in the Protestant cause there. French national interest ultimately led the Protestant victor in France, Henry of Navarre, to change to Catholicism; he was a politique. But the Dutch leaders were not so indifferent concerning matters of religion. Neither England nor Spain was involved in the French civil war in a major way. (McKay, *A History of Western Society*, 8th ed., pp. 490–497/9th ed., pp. 472–475)

FREE-RESPONSE QUESTIONS

1. This is a typical social history question. It asks you to discuss a mainstream topic but from a side view. It is important to address the question as asked; this is not a place to discuss the general differences between Catholicism and Protestantism, unless you are relating it to the gender issue.

- Both Protestants and Catholics saw women as subservient to men and limited to the household. Neither gave women an official role in the structure or administration of the church or in the Mass.
- Catholic women could achieve important positions as the heads of convents or founders of monastic orders. Angela Merici, founder of the Ursuline order during the Counter-Reformation, played a significant role in the education of women. Catholic women also achieved renown and status for their religiosity. Joan of Arc was allowed to inspire the French army to victory over the English because of her religious convictions; she later became a patron saint of France. Teresa of Ávila was famous for her mystical visions as well as for her writings, whose importance were acknowledged when she was made a doctor of the Church. The ideal life for a Catholic was a monastic one, away from the world, celibate, and devoted to religious work, so unmarried women who were cloistered were often highly regarded.
- Protestant women had different status issues. Protestants generally banned monasticism because it is not found in Scripture; instead they argued that to do God's work, one must live in this world, in secular society. Women lost opportunities for status and power when convents disappeared; unmarried women lost a place to live as well as a career path. Protestants also removed the special status of priests by denying transubstantiation. All believers were equal. The minister's role was to lead the congregation, not to act as an intermediary between man and God. This meant that ministers married and had children. Women gained new importance for their particular roles as wives of pastors and in general in their management of the household. They were encouraged to become literate so they could read the Bible and properly raise their children. Marriage began to be seen as more of an equal partnership. Martin Luther and his wife, like many other Protestant couples, had double portraits commissioned, reflecting this new spirit. Marriage was not a sacrament to Protestants, so divorce was permitted. This meant that an unpleasant or abusive relationship could be ended, thus providing greater protection for women.

2. Although the question does not ask you to make direct comparisons, a superior essay will draw conclusions that show similarities and differences between the two states.

- In England, the need for a male heir led Henry VIII of England to ask for an annulment; when the pope denied it in obedience to Charles V, the nephew of Henry's wife, Henry used the Protestant movement to break away from Rome, establishing the Church of England under royal control. For Protestants, divorce became legal; Henry used this right twice. Henry was able to use the confiscated monastic holdings to garner strong support for the Tudor dynasty. Mary Tudor's attempt to restore Catholicism was compromised by her marriage to Philip II of Spain, which sparked nationalistic as well as religious resentment. Elizabeth I acted as a politique to settle the religious matters, restore stability, and encourage national economic development. England defended the Protestant cause as part of its great competition with Habsburg Spain, helping the Dutch to become independent of Spain.

- In France, the kings had won control over the church in the Pragmatic Sanction of Bourges and the Concordat of Bologna. Because the kings appointed their own bishops, they had no great need to break away from Rome; Catholicism had already become a national church in practice. Protestantism appealed to all classes in France, particularly the nobles who sought relief from the centralizing Valois kings, and the middle classes who sought to reduce their taxes and control their economic decisions in the towns where they lived. Both groups saw Protestantism as a way to resist the monarchy. The war between Protestants and Catholics in France ended when the politique Henry of Navarre, the leader of the Protestant forces, converted to Catholicism in order to win acceptance by still-Catholic Paris, and issued the Edict of Nantes, which gave Protestants freedom of worship and rights in their towns.
- The Holy Roman Empire, this decentralized conglomeration of more than 300 states, was loosely ruled by the emperor, by this time always a Habsburg. Many princes sought more independence from him, and Protestantism gave them a way. Luther's survival after the Diet of Worms was dependent on the protection he got from the elector of Saxony. Protestantism allowed princes to establish national churches over which they were the ultimate authority in their states, and also benefited them economically from the expropriation of church lands and monasteries. Charles V fought to hold his empire together and to keep it Catholic. The Peace of Augsburg, settling the religious wars of the sixteenth century, allowed each prince to choose either Catholicism or Lutheranism for his state, thus enhancing his power and weakening that of the emperor.
- In Spain, the monarchs too had won control over the appointment of bishops in their kingdom, and so had no need to break away from Rome. Religion came to be tied to national unity; the monarchs sought religious uniformity for nationalistic reasons. The Inquisition, which sought to ferret out insincere conversions within the formerly Jewish and Muslim population, also persecuted heretics. Protestantism had little chance to gain a foothold in Spain.
- In the Netherlands, many of the Dutch became followers of Calvinism. The seventeen provinces of the Low Countries resented being ruled by the Spanish both as foreigners and as Catholics. When the Spanish attempted to eradicate Calvinist worship, violence erupted. Philip II sent the duke of Alva who imposed a harsh persecution on Calvinists. Resentment over Spanish taxes added fuel to the religious issue. Civil war ended with the division of the Low Countries into two groups: ten provinces accepted Spanish rule; the other seven signed the Union of Utrecht and declared their independence from Spain, which they won in 1609 after a long and bitter struggle.

15

EUROPEAN EXPLORATION AND CONQUEST, 1450–1650

The Age of Exploration led to extraordinary changes in world history and the transformation of world trade networks. The mutual impact of the encounter of the New and Old Worlds had significant effects on the European economy, social and political institutions, and cultural life. It is important to master the various motives for exploration and conquest, the changing positions of the European states on the Atlantic that were so heavily involved, and the consequences of the encounter of the Old and New Worlds.

KEY CONCEPTS

- From ancient to medieval times, there was a widespread and thriving network of global trade among East Asia, Southeast Asia, the Mediterranean, the Middle East, and Africa. This network was transformed by the intrusion of new groups of Europeans. The Portuguese and the Dutch competed first with Muslim merchants and then with each other in Asia. They joined the British and French in the exploration and colonization of the Americas.
- Europeans had a variety of motives as well as certain technological advantages that prompted the expansion of their trade in Asia and their exploration of the New World. "Gold, God, and Glory" were not only motivators of exploration, but also led Europeans to colonize in ways that fostered economic development and Christianization.
- Among the consequences of the encounter of the Old World with the New was a rapid and thorough decimation of the native populations, the transformation of their economic and religious

lives, and an enormous expansion of the already existing African slave trade. The Columbian exchange of peoples, crops, and animals led to radical changes in agriculture and diets, as well as in values and technology. As gold and silver infused the European economy, inflation benefited the middle classes while hurting the poor and those on fixed incomes. The increasing wealth of the middle class was an important change in the social structure. Intellectual life saw the introduction of new ideas like skepticism and cultural relativism as well as new forms of racism.

WORLD TRADE BEFORE THE AGE OF EXPLORATION

AP Tip

For those of you interested in world history, the first section of this chapter is very rich with a detailed exploration of centers of wealth and trade around the globe. Although most of this material would not appear on an AP European history exam, it is important to understand it for background and the long-term legacy of colonialism. Pay particular attention to those sections that deal with Europe.

Ever since China under the Han dynasty and the Roman Empire developed trade with each other, there was a global economic network, with the Indian Ocean and the Silk Road as key foci on sea and land respectively, and with Malacca in Malaysia as the epicenter. Chinese silks and porcelains; Indian jewels; peppers, cloves, and textiles; and African slaves, gold, and ivory were the chief commodities. Europeans played a relatively small role in this trade, having little that was desirable to what were then more technologically advanced civilizations. China, India, Ottoman Turkey, Safavid Persia, and Mameluke Egypt held dominant roles until the European ascendancy, so that by and large the international trading system was multinational and multicultural, with relatively few incidents of monopolization or ethnic violence but with stiff competition and many shifting alliances.

Europeans experienced a surge in population and a growth in the demand for Asian goods, particularly spices, after about 1000 C.E. This began a process that by around 1550 led to European domination of what had become a truly global trade network.

Europeans sought to compete in the Asian trade, which was heavily dominated by Muslims. Religious factors were one prompt, compounded by the Ottoman conquest in 1453 of Constantinople, the center of Orthodox Christianity and the largest city in Europe, and the subsequent expansion of the Ottomans into the Balkans and eastern Mediterranean. The Ottomans twice besieged Vienna, in the heart of Europe, the first time in 1529, marking the height of their expansion and the second in 1683, marking their decline. Europeans particularly fantasized about Africa, where the legendary and fictitious Christian king Prester John was believed to rule.

Venice and Genoa dominated the Mediterranean and Asian trade routes for Europe, particularly in slaves and luxury goods like silks and spices, during the medieval period. Venice became very wealthy and even more powerful in the late fourteenth century, with its excellent navy maintained by its efficient city-state merchant oligarchy. Venice and Genoa began to lose their dominance of trade markets to the Ottomans on the one side and to the Portuguese and the Dutch on the other. Genoese and Venetians played an important role in the exploration of the New World and in the management of commercial enterprises like sugar plantations.

The declining fortunes of Genoa and Venice and of the traditional trans-Asian trade led ultimately to the transfer of economic energy to new European players, especially to the Iberians and the Dutch, both on the Atlantic rather than on the Mediterranean.

CAUSES OF EUROPEAN EXPLORATION

Europe had recuperated from the Black Death in terms of population and economic life by the mid-fifteenth century. Population growth fueled the growing demand for spices and luxury goods, for new sources of gold and silver to pay for those goods, and for new routes to bypass the now Ottoman-held Istanbul and give Europeans direct access to Asian goods. Spices had medicinal as well as culinary uses.

Christian fervor was stimulated by the victory over the last Muslim kingdom in Spain in 1492. Religious zeal to take the Asian trade out of Muslim hands and to convert non-Christians there and in the newly discovered Americas brought religious motives into play along with commercial ones.

Glory, too, was an important motivator. The urge to do things no one had done before, whether conquest or adventure, reflected the Renaissance curiosity and thirst for knowledge. Interest in natural history, geography, and cosmology was promoted by the publication of numerous books, some quasi-scientific and others more imaginary.

The lack of opportunity at home often motivated individual explorers or conquerors, particularly in Spain where opportunities shrank after the Reconquista (the re-establishment of Christian control of Spain) as the nobles monopolized government positions and the great merchants dominated trade. Similarly, poverty and lack of opportunity motivated many a poor man to take to the seas although conditions on ships were horrendous. The increasingly centralized European nation-states emerging in the fifteenth and sixteenth centuries provided the finances and the maritime and military power for exploration and conquest.

Technological advances borrowed from the East, such as the caravel, which replaced the galley ship, navigational tools like the astrolabe and the magnetic compass, and new military weapons like cannons, made the voyages of exploration and conquest possible. More accurate geographical knowledge became possible with the early fifteenth-century recovery of Ptolemy's *Geography*, although ironically enough, its inaccuracies encouraged the notion that sailing west from Europe to reach Asia was viable. Historians debate the importance of technology in making the voyages possible, with some stressing the importance of knowledge and technology developed in the existing trade networks involving China and the Indian Ocean, while others argue that technological advances were a result, not a cause, of exploration.

EUROPEAN OVERSEAS EMPIRES

PORTUGAL Portugal was a poor nation until the fifteenth century. Its fortunes were made by its seafaring on the Atlantic Ocean.

Prince Henry (1394–1460), dubbed the Navigator, encouraged early voyages of exploration along the west coast of Africa. In 1415 the Portuguese conquered the Arab city of Ceuta in Morocco and thus initiated the period of European exploration and colonization. Thereafter Henry led Portugal to the establishment of settlements in Madeira and the Azores (islands in the Atlantic about 950 miles from the Iberian Peninsula) and their first commercial colony in Mauritania in northwestern Africa. In 1487 Bartholomew Diaz rounded the Cape of Good Hope, and ten years later Vasco da Gama did the same and went onward to the port of Calicut in India, returning home laden with spices and textiles and making evident the value of the sea route via the cape to India. Portugal established trading posts in India shortly thereafter, engaging in violent conflict with the rulers of the port cities that it took over. Alfonso de Albuquerque, Portuguese governor of India, attacked Malacca, Goa, and other entrepôts (trading centers) and laid the foundation of the Portuguese empire in Asia. Annual convoys brought Asian goods to Lisbon and wealth to Portugal.

Pedro Alvares Cabral, en route to India, sighted the coast of Brazil in 1500 and claimed it for Portugal. Brazil, rich in mineral resources and lucrative sugar plantations worked by some 2 million African slaves, became the most important Portuguese colony.

SPAIN Spain's overseas empire was initiated by the voyages of Christopher Columbus (1451–1506), a Genoese who sailed for Isabella and Ferdinand of Spain.

Ever since the 1992 celebration of the 500th anniversary, the quincentenary, of his discovery of the New World, Columbus has become a subject of great controversy. Long considered a hero, he has now been criticized for his enslavement and murderous mistreatment of native peoples. Instead of a discovery, historians now speak of an encounter with enormous consequences for both sides.

Columbus was emblematic of the long-standing Genoese devotion to international trade and their attempts at circumventing other states' similar interests, whether Venice, Portugal, or the Ottoman Empire. Highly knowledgeable and well experienced in seafaring, Columbus was also a deeply religious Christian, who shared its then-contemporary missionary agenda. Columbus's letters and writings on his expeditions reveal his expectation of finding Japan, China, and India; his Christian zeal; and his materialistic interests. Columbus's early reports to the Spanish monarchs were enthusiastic on all counts: that natives would convert easily and could equally as easily be enslaved and that there were great stores of gold and silver. He remained convinced until his dying day that he had reached Asia, never quite realizing the extraordinary impact on world history of what he had done.

Columbus established the model of conquest and colonization rather than of an exchange with equals as first envisioned by Marco

Polo during his visit to Mongol China. On his second voyage, Columbus enslaved the population of Hispaniola and set up a system of forced labor, the forerunner of the encomienda system. Columbus's ineptitude as governor led to royal control over the conquered territories.

Columbus's letters were quickly published, translated, and widely disseminated, as was the work of other explorers. It was a 1503 letter of Amerigo Vespucci, a Florentine, that first described the existence of the New World, which was thereafter named after him.

The Treaty of Tordesillas in 1494 made by Pope Alexander VI divided the New World into Spanish and Portuguese empires, giving Spain everything to the west and Portugal everything to the east, including Brazil, of an imaginary line 370 leagues west of the Cape Verde Islands.

When gold and silver were not found in the Caribbean, Charles V, king of Spain and Holy Roman Emperor, commissioned further voyages. In 1522, Ferdinand Magellan's ships were the first to circumnavigate the globe, finding the route to Asia via the Atlantic in a horrific three-year voyage involving disasters at sea, starvation, mutinies, and the death of Magellan himself in the Philippines. Demonstrating the vastness of the Pacific, the voyage revolutionized European consciousness and led Spain to abandon its effort to compete with Portugal for the Asian spice trade.

In 1519–1520, Hernando Cortés conquered, with relatively few men but with horses, cannons, and some fortuitous elements beyond his control (dissension within the Aztec empire, a demoralized population, and a weakened leadership), the highly sophisticated Aztec Empire in Mexico, with its large and wealthy cities. Its king Montezuma and his advisers made decisions that were logical for their culture but that paved the way for Spanish victory.

Francisco Pizarro made an even more amazing conquest of the huge and prosperous Incan Empire in Peru, known for its remarkable engineering and construction. It too faced internal dissension at the time of the Spanish arrival in 1532. Pizarro captured and executed the Incan ruler Atauhualpa, but it took until the 1570s for the Spanish to establish firm control.

Some 200,000 Spaniards immigrated to the New World colonies in the sixteenth century. Originally soldiers or drifters, they established large agricultural or ranching estates inland, sugar plantations in the coastal tropics, and silver mines in Bolivia (Potosí) and Mexico. Labor was provided by the encomienda system, a form of forced labor, akin to slavery, of the Amerindians. The brutal exploitation of the native populations, combined with their exposure to European diseases like smallpox to which the Amerindians in their long isolation from the rest of the world had developed no resistance and the transfer of productive land from food to export crops, led to their rapid and staggering decline in population. Brutal violence, famously lamented by the Franciscan missionary Bartolomé de Las Casas, led to the death of thousands. Las Casas argued that the Amerindians were good people and should have rights. Charles V abolished the worst abuses of the encomienda system in response to Las Casas's vivid denunciation.

Christian missionaries accompanied the conquistadores and settlers, converting most of the population and introducing European ways.

HOLLAND The Dutch dominated the world maritime trade in the second half of the seventeenth century from Amsterdam, the financial center of Europe since the sixteenth century. In 1602 they established the Dutch East India Company, and within a few decades it had taken over from the Portuguese in Ceylon and acquired the very valuable spice-producing islands of the Indonesian archipelago, giving the Dutch the monopoly on the highly profitable Asian spice trade. They also made inroads into Spanish trade in the New World and briefly had a colony in what would become New York in 1664.

FRANCE AND BRITAIN French and English explorations were less dramatic. A Genoese who became known by the English name John Cabot explored Newfoundland and New England for the British. Jacques Cartier explored Quebec, which became the site of France's first permanent New World settlement in 1608.

THE IMPACT OF THE ENCOUNTER WITH THE NEW WORLD

International trade became truly global for the first time in human history, bridging both hemispheres. The Columbian exchange of peoples, foodstuffs, diseases, animals, and ideas created a global network of trade between Africa, Europe, Asia, and North and South America.

The Amerindian population was devastated by disease, murder, and brutal working conditions, in what has been called the quickest destruction of an aboriginal population ever.

As the European demand for sugar grew, the demand for slave labor grew. The histories of sugar and slavery are deeply intertwined. While slavery has been the basis of many economies, including ancient Greece and Rome, the ever-increasing demand for sugar transformed the medieval slave trade, which had been dominated by Venice and involved mostly white people from the Balkans, Anatolia, and southern Russia, a trade virtually ended in any case by the Ottoman conquest. Italians played crucial roles both in the slave trade and in providing the capital and resources for Portuguese sugar plantations.

Slavery in the New World began shortly after the arrival of the Europeans. The first Portuguese bought West African slaves from local kings and dealers and brought them to the New World. The slave trade was taken over in the seventeenth century by the Dutch and later by the English. By 1790, the proportion of black to white populations in the United States was about 1 to 5; in Brazil, it was about 2 to 3.

The Age of Exploration led to the Colombian exchange, an earth-transforming movement of peoples, animals, and plants. Wheat, grapes for wine, olive trees for oil, sugar plants, rice, and bananas were among the important crops brought by the Spaniards to the New World, while horses, cattle, sheep, dogs, pigs, chickens, and goats were also introduced. In return, Europeans brought back maize (corn), white potatoes, beans, squash, pumpkins, avocados, and tomatoes. Maize and later the potato became crucial basic foods for Europeans.

Silver was more important than gold in transforming the economies of Europe and in providing the basis for Spain's *siglo d'oro* (golden century) and its widespread influence in the sixteenth century. The Spanish economy, however, suffered during this time. The loss of the skilled labor and trading expertise of the expelled Muslim and Jewish populations made it harder to meet the increasing demands for goods from the colonies and from the rising population at home. Prices spiraled, but not directly because of the importation of Peruvian silver, which reached its peak after the greatest increase in prices. The price revolution, as this period of inflation is known, placed unexpected demands on government finances; the Spanish king Philip II repudiated the royal debt several times. The price revolution spread throughout Europe, hurting those on fixed incomes and the poor but helping those in debt, such as many traders and merchants. The chief source of worldwide demand for silver was China, which insisted on its use for trade and taxes.

The new global economy, linking all continents except Australia, was dominated first by the Portuguese, then by the Spanish, and then by the Dutch, each of whom built far-flung empires. The Portuguese traded in spices and sugar produced in their own colonies and in a wide variety of goods produced in China or acquired from the colonies of other European states, especially West African slaves and Bolivian silver. The Spanish established a land empire in the New World, but their Pacific empire, particularly the Philippines, was seaborne, bringing Chinese silk to their colonies in the New World. A worldwide commercial boom from about 1570 to 1630 made many traders and capitalists wealthy.

The Dutch became dominant in seaborne trade in the latter half of the seventeenth century. Their wealth was built largely on spices; the Dutch East India Company went after Portuguese interests in Asia and established direct control over the Spice Islands, as Indonesia was then called.

Spain's global empire radiated from the many territories inherited by the Holy Roman Emperor Charles V—the Low Countries, Spain, Austria, and the overseas colonies. Charles's son Philip II inherited Spain and the overseas territories. Philip, who was widely traveled and adept at international relations, was a fervent Catholic opposed to the religious toleration that was a hallmark of the Dutch lands he ruled. He fought against the advancing Ottoman Turks and promoted Catholic interests in England by supporting conspiratorial efforts of Mary Queen of Scots against Elizabeth I, who was helping the Dutch, fellow Protestants, in their revolt against Spain. Philip, on the encouragement of the pope, organized an armada to invade England, which met with a disastrous defeat in 1588. Although a dramatic event, its consequences were limited since Spain rebuilt its navy and the war with England went on. It was, however, an enormous boost to English nationalism. The attempt to impose religious uniformity by force had failed, and in a bit more than twenty years, in 1609, the Spanish recognized the independence of the Republic of the United Provinces, as the seven states led by Holland were called.

CHANGES IN ATTITUDES AND BELIEFS

The period of exploration and conquest, which also witnessed intense religious conflicts in so many European states, was one of enormous intellectual and artistic ferment. New ideas, artistic forms, and genres responded to the ongoing economic, religious, and social transformations.

European ideas about race originated in attitudes toward Africans. These in turn were influenced by Christian theological writings and by medieval Arab sources whose disparagement of Africans for their physical features, their heathen religions, and what was seen as cultural primitiveness were bolstered by the many accounts about Africa written by European slavers and travelers in the sixteenth and seventeenth centuries. These prejudices were used to justify slavery and the imposition of Christianity, and in turn, slavery reinforced notions of African inferiority.

The life of Juan de Pareja, a Spanish mulatto, reveals some aspects of racial issues in seventeenth-century Europe. He became a slave of the great artist Diego Velasquez, who painted an impressive portrait of his talented assistant and later freed him. De Pareja traveled widely after winning his freedom and became a well-known painter of portraits and religious scenes.

The variety of peoples encountered by Europeans created doubt in many European minds about absolute truth. Skepticism and cultural relativism were expressed by a number of writers from Las Casas to Michel de Montaigne. A new literary genre, the essay, was created in the sixteenth century, particularly by Montaigne, a wealthy judge of bourgeois origin, who wrote with an intellectual openness and a passion for reason that was new in its articulation.

Elizabethan literature—written during the reign of Elizabeth I (1558–1603)—included the poetry of Philip Sidney and Edmund Spenser and the plays of Christopher Marlowe and William Shakespeare, who reflected both Renaissance values of individualism and humanism and growing English nationalism. Shakespeare's history plays were written in the decade after the defeat of the Spanish Armada, while his last play, *The Tempest*, was an exploration of colonialism.

The high point of Jacobean literature—written during the reign of James I (1603–1625)—was the King James Bible, also called the Authorized Version, a new translation prompted by Protestant commitment for lay people to read the Scriptures in the vernacular.

AP Tip

Many AP questions ask you to make evaluations or comparisons. In such essays, be sure you take a position, develop a thesis, and defend it with evidence, not just answer the question with a listing of the important facts involved.

Multiple-Choice Questions

1. Which city was *least* important in medieval trade?
   (A) Malacca
   (B) Venice
   (C) Rome
   (D) Constantinople
   (E) Genoa

2. What impact did the Reconquista have on Spain's exploration and conquest?
   (A) It encouraged the Spaniards to immediately attack the Ottoman Empire.
   (B) It meant that there were fewer opportunities for ambitious young men within Spain.
   (C) The conquest of Granada was accompanied by anti-Muslim riots.
   (D) Spain acquired huge sums of money to fund Columbus's voyages.
   (E) Many of the conquered Spanish Muslims acted as navigators and pilots.

3. How did technology and better information fuel the explorations?
   (A) Ptolemy's *Geography* gave a reasonably accurate estimate of the distance from Europe to Asia.
   (B) The recent European invention of the astrolabe made possible sea navigation.
   (C) The lateen sail made it possible to sail into the wind.
   (D) The astrolabe allowed sailors to calculate their latitude.
   (E) Cannons proved useful in almost every climate and condition.

4. Which is *not* true about Columbus's voyages of exploration?
   (A) His decision not to sail north to look for the Great Khan was based on his interest in finding gold.
   (B) He believed the Indians would convert easily to Christianity.
   (C) He established effective control as the governor of Hispaniola.
   (D) He traveled with letters to the Great Khan from Ferdinand and Isabella.
   (E) He enslaved the Indians under his control.

5. Which factor *least* explains the Spanish conquest of the Incan and Aztec empires?
   (A) The fierceness and military expertise of the Spanish soldiers
   (B) The internal dissensions within each of the empires
   (C) The auguries and religious legends that led the rulers to see the Spaniards as possible gods
   (D) The effectiveness of cannons and muskets
   (E) The cultural values and attitudes of the Mexicans and Peruvians

6. The life story of Juan de Pareja reveals
   (A) how brutal European slavery was.
   (B) how race was the ultimate determinant of his destiny.
   (C) that in the seventeenth century Europeans owned slaves born in Europe.
   (D) that black painters had a very difficult time getting commissions.
   (E) that slavery was illegal within Spain by the seventeenth century.

7. For Spain, the most important consequence of Magellan's voyage was that
   (A) it led to the immediate conquest and colonization of the Philippines.
   (B) Spain became discouraged from competing with Portugal for the Asian spice trade.
   (C) Spain focused more on the Asian trade rather than on the New World for the next half-century.
   (D) Magellan returned to the strait south of Chile that bears his name to improve the passage to Asia via the Atlantic.
   (E) Portugal ceded Goa to Spain.

8. The importance of the defeat of the Spanish Armada in 1588 was that
   (A) Spain's navy never recuperated.
   (B) England invaded the northern Spanish coast.
   (C) Mary Queen of Scots was executed for treason.
   (D) Ultimately the Dutch won their independence from Spain.
   (E) Philip abdicated in favor of his son Don Carlos.

9. The term *encomienda* refers to the
   (A) system of forced labor for the Amerindians.
   (B) sugar plantation system in the Caribbean islands.
   (C) outright enslavement of the Amerindians.
   (D) establishment of churches for the Amerindians with services in their languages.
   (E) use of African slaves as laborers.

10. The one social group who were clearly beneficiaries of the price revolution were the
    (A) poor.
    (B) merchants.
    (C) monarchs.
    (D) clergy.
    (E) landlords.

11. Which did *not* travel from the Old World to the New?
    (A) Horses
    (B) Pigs
    (C) Wheat
    (D) Corn
    (E) Dogs

12. The importance of sugar for the world economy was its
    (A) impact on agriculture in Spain.
    (B) transformation of the economy of Mexico.
    (C) role in encouraging the African slave trade.
    (D) role in the increase in the demand for silver.
    (E) usefulness in exchange for Chinese silks.

13. Montaigne was noted for his essays expressing
    (A) religious zeal.
    (B) nationalism in France.
    (C) new reasons for supporting the monarchy.
    (D) skepticism.
    (E) racist views of the native populations of the New World.

14. A masterpiece of Jacobean literature is
    (A) *Romeo and Juliet.*
    (B) *The Fairie Queene.*
    (C) the Authorized Version of the Bible.
    (D) Montaigne's essays.
    (E) Christopher Marlowe's *The Jew of Malta.*

15. In the document at the end of the chapter, "Columbus Describes His First Voyage," Columbus depicts how
    (A) frustrated he is over having found only two islands.
    (B) rich the gold mines on Hispaniola are.
    (C) the native men are naked but the women cover their breasts.
    (D) fierce the natives were when he first met them.
    (E) stupid the natives are.

Free-Response Questions

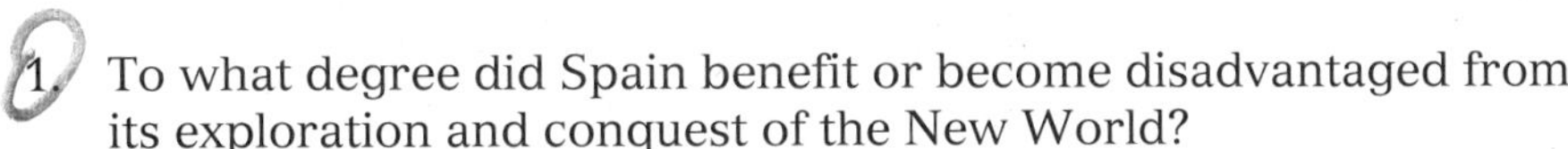

1. To what degree did Spain benefit or become disadvantaged from its exploration and conquest of the New World?

2. Discuss the various motives that prompted the exploration and colonization of the New World, and evaluate their relative importance.

ANSWERS

MULTIPLE-CHOICE QUESTIONS

1. ANSWER (C) Rome was an unimportant city, economically speaking, in the Middle Ages. (McKay, *A History of Western Society,* not discussed in 8th ed./9th ed., pp. 484, 488, 490–491)

2. ANSWER (B) The Reconquista was a period of movement and opportunity for Spanish Christians. After their victory, the social structure solidified and became more restrictive. None of the other options are accurate. (McKay, *A History of Western Society,* 8th ed., p. 506/9th ed., p. 493)

3. **ANSWER (C)** Ptolemy was wrong in his estimates of the distance to Asia. The ancient Greeks invented the astrolabe, which could be used to estimate latitude. Cannons were unreliable in the tropics. (McKay, *A History of Western Society*, 8th ed., pp. 505–506/9th ed., pp. 493–495)

4. **ANSWER (C)** Columbus was a poor ruler; there was a revolt on the island, and Columbus and his brother were brought back to Spain in chains. (McKay, *A History of Western Society*, 8th ed., pp. 507–509/9th ed., pp. 498–499)

5. **ANSWER (A)** All the other factors were discussed in the text. As the number of Spanish soldiers was small, they could have been easily overcome if the other factors had not given them the advantage. (McKay, *A History of Western Society*, 8th ed., p. 510 but not discussed in detail/9th ed., pp.501–504)

6. **ANSWER (C)** As C and E contradict each other, one of these must be wrong. Slavery was not abolished in Europe until the nineteenth century, although it played a small role in the economy for centuries. Although most slaves were imported, some were born in Europe. Race was generally not a factor in slavery in Europe, since traditionally most slaves there were white. (McKay, *A History of Western Society*, 8th ed., p. 517/9th ed., p. 507)

7. **ANSWER (B)** The Philippines were indeed colonized by Spain but not until the 1560s. Magellan died there. Portugal kept hold of Goa through most of the twentieth century. Spain recognized that, with the size of the Pacific, they could not compete with the well-established Portuguese. (McKay, *A History of Western Society*, 8th ed., p. 509/9th ed., pp. 500–501)

8. **ANSWER (D)** The English, having defeated the armada, continued to aid the Dutch, who won their independence in 1609. Mary Queen of Scots was executed before the invasion. Don Carlos died while Philip was king. Spain quickly rebuilt its navy. (McKay, *A History of Western Society*, 8th ed., pp. 496–497/9th ed., pp. 512–513)

9. **ANSWER (A)** The encomienda system was the first system of forced labor in the New World, a legalized form of enslavement of the native population, many of whom died from overwork and brutal treatment. (McKay, *A History of Western Society*, not discussed in 8th ed./9th ed., p. 504)

10. **ANSWER (B)** During periods of inflation, the people who benefit are those who are in debt, which in this case would be merchants who often borrow money to conduct business. Those who suffer are those on a fixed income, like the clergy and the landlords. The monarchs had to pay more for services and soldiers, and the poor had to pay more for food; neither had an easy time increasing their income to pay for these increases in necessary costs. (McKay, *A History of Western Society*, 8th ed., pp. 510–511/9th ed., pp. 509–510)

11. **ANSWER (D)** Corn was one of the most important gifts of the New World to the Old in the Columbian exchange. (McKay, *A History of Western Society*, 8th ed., pp. 511–512/9th ed., pp. 508–509)

12. ANSWER (C) Sugar plantations required a substantial labor force, which could not be filled by the decimated native American populations; African slaves were imported to fill that need. Sugar was not planted in most of Mexico or in Spain. (McKay, *A History of Western Society*, 8th ed., p. 516 but not discussed in detail/ 9th ed., pp. 505, 508)

13. ANSWER (D) Montaigne is noted for his skepticism, personal contemplation, and rationalism. He wrote an expressly nonracist essay and espoused religious toleration. Generally, he stayed away from politics. (McKay, A History of Western Society, 8th ed., pp. 519–520/9th ed., p. 514)

14. ANSWER (D) A, B, and E are all Elizabethan. Montaigne wrote in the sixteenth century, whereas *Jacobean* refers to the early seventeenth century. (McKay, *A History of Western Society*, 8th ed., pp. 520–522/9th ed., p. 516)

15. ANSWER (B) Columbus makes false claims to have found gold in Hispaniola. He claims to have found many islands and describes San Salvador and Cuba as well as Hispaniola. He describes the natives as highly intelligent, naked, and timid. (McKay, *A History of Western Society*, 8th ed., pp. 526–527/9th ed., pp. 518–519)

FREE-RESPONSE QUESTIONS

1. This question asks you to evaluate the positive and negative aspects of Spain's colonization of the New World. Be sure to discuss some elements from both sides.
   - Benefits
     - Increase in prestige and power so that Spain became competitive with other European powers
     - Great wealth that fueled its greatest artistic period
     - Many opportunities for Spaniards of all classes who couldn't find them at home in Spain
     - Fulfillment of Spain's Christian mission
   - Disadvantages
     - Price revolution and inflation, increase in royal expenditures, instability of royal finances, and repudiation of royal debt
     - Overextension of the monarch's ability to promote Catholicism (conflict with British, Dutch, and Ottomans)
     - Difficulties in fulfilling economic demands because of expulsion of traditional trading populations (Jews and Muslims); discouragement of need to modernize economy or promote manufacturing

2. "Gold, God, and Glory" summarizes the motivations. For this question, you need to argue for one being more important than the other two.
   - Gold: primary motive. Evidence: Columbus was promised 10 percent of all material wealth he took for Spain. Columbus changed route from going north to the hoped-for court of

Genghis Khan to a southern route where gold was promised. The *encomienda* system was established to turn Amerindians into forced laborers. The chief reasons for the voyages were a search for new trading routes after the cutoff of trade with the East, including the slave trade after the Ottoman conquest of Constantinople. The native populations were treated with disdain and brutality; for example, Cortés deceived and murdered the Aztec ruler to obtain huge stores of Mexican gold, and laborers panning for gold or mining silver were cruelly treated. The African slave trade began soon after the first contact with the New World and provided huge profits for European traders, as did the sugar plantations where the slaves worked.

- God: Columbus was a deeply religious man, believed God promoted his voyages, and delighted in the possible conversion of natives. Missionaries were among the earliest settlers. Most of the native population converted to Christianity. The Muslim dominance of world trade was a major reason for the search for new trading routes. However, these motives were as much, if not more than, commercial as religious.
- Glory: The motive of glory reflects the Renaissance values of individualism and fame seeking. Renaissance humanism and interest in technology and geography, combined with individual egoism, encouraged men to become explorers, conquerors, and settlers. After the Age of Exploration began, a desire for national glory, prestige, and power fueled further explorations and expansion of empires. However, the desire for glory was also intertwined with and promoted by commercial interests.

16

Absolutism and Constitutionalism in Western Europe, 1589–1715

The sixteenth through the eighteenth centuries witnessed two contrary developments in western Europe: constitutional governments in England and Holland, and absolutist governments in France and Spain. The growing power of the wealthy commercial classes in England, Holland, and France helped the kings challenge the traditional prerogatives of the nobility. In Spain, the nobles retained their political and economic roles as economic decline and political malaise set in. The establishment of constitutional governments was the beginning of what would prove to be a worldwide revolution toward popular sovereignty.

Key Concepts

- The seventeenth century was a period of economic stagnation, population decline, and constant warfare. As armies grew in size, governments required more revenues and better administration to collect and spend them. Both constitutional and absolutist governments created new sources of revenues and modern state bureaucracies.
- The Bourbon kings Louis XIII and XIV created an absolute monarchy in France by taking power away from the nobility. In Spain, absolutism had less success because of economic difficulties.

- Absolute monarchies fostered culture and the arts as part of the royal aggrandizement of power. Baroque music, art, architecture, theater, and literature all received substantial royal patronage.
- In constitutional governments or monarchies, the monarchs accept that their power and authority are limited by constitutions or legal documents. England achieved constitutional government after a tumultuous revolution, the execution of a king, and the establishment of a short-lived republic, followed by the restoration of the monarchy, which eventually became constitutional.

The Seventeenth-Century Crisis and Rebuilding

The European population and economy stagnated in the seventeenth century, partly because of climatic changes and partly because of constant religious warfare. Economic life was still largely rural and focused around the small peasant village where the wealthier landowning peasants employed the landless poor. Many people were land starved, barely surviving at the subsistence level, with a diet based on bread and with meat eating saved for special events. In the seventeenth century, a little Ice Age shortened the growing season and made this precarious existence even more so, with recurrent famines that weakened the population and made it vulnerable to the still active plague. Industry also stagnated, so prices rose and unemployment increased in most places, although the Netherlands flourished. Men and women rioted for food and just prices.

At the same time, both absolute and constitutional monarchs placed more demands on people, raising taxes to expand their armies and centralizing political power. The seventeenth century saw the establishment of government monopoly over justice and the use of force, and the elimination of private armies and nongovernment courts, whether aristocratic or ecclesiastical. Centralization was made more difficult by inadequate and slow transportation networks, limited information, small bureaucracies, and cultural and linguistic barriers. Both types of monarchs sought to rein in the nobles who had traditional powers, prerogatives, and prestige, and to dominate other challengers to royal centralization like the church, guilds, and towns. Previously, historians said that the absolute monarchs like Louis XIV tamed the nobles, but new research shows that they made many compromises with them, co-opting rather than controlling them. Similarly, the nobles retained substantial power in the constitutional states of England and Holland.

There were many revolts in seventeenth-century Europe. For example, in 1640 Philip IV of Spain faced revolts in many of the lands he inherited—the Netherlands, Portugal, Sicily, and Catalonia—many of them over high bread prices but some over dreams of more egalitarian republics. During the reign of Louis XIV France also had many revolts in which royal officials were often beaten to death. Royal authority was limited enough that rebels had some leverage until the end of the century when the monarchies grew more powerful.

Warfare and the Growth of Army Size

Both constitutional and absolute rulers needed to expand their sources of revenues to fund the new type of armies. In constitutional states, parliaments could use such royal needs for military funding to negotiate limitations on royal power. Direct taxes were collected and managed by full-time bureaucrats, who were culled from the middle classes in France and from the nobility in Spain and eastern Europe. In most countries, standing armies, in peacetime as well as wartime, were recruited and became substantially larger, more nationalistic, and more professional than medieval or mercenary armies. The French, for example, nearly tripled the size of their army over the course of the seventeenth century and had it commanded by nobles who purchased their commissions and outfitted the men they led into battle, often at the cost of their lives. The French paved the way to huge armies, and other states soon followed. Britain, however, focused on building its navy rather than its land forces.

ABSOLUTISM IN FRANCE AND SPAIN

Absolute monarchs claimed sole legislative and executive rights, asserting that they need not share political power with any aristocratic assembly or court, or with any other institution in society. Such claims were justified by either religious or secular theory. The religious theory, known as divine right (developed by Bishop Bossuet at the Versailles court), asserted that God selected the king to rule and the king was answerable only to God. Thomas Hobbes articulated the most important secular theory in defense of absolutism when he wrote *Leviathan* shortly after the execution of King Charles I. Hobbes argued that only a strong, centralized power could prevent the violence and disorder that the selfish nature of man would otherwise create. A powerful monarch was needed to protect man from himself. Both theories asserted that only absolute power would allow the king to fulfill his obligation to ensure law and order.

AP Tip

Students sometime see absolutism as synonymous with dictatorship, which was an all-too-common phenomenon in the twentieth century. But the words have quite different meanings in the seventeenth and eighteenth century when however absolute, no monarch could be called a dictator. They were legitimate hereditary monarchs who sought to rule without any institutional constraints, but they did not have the power or control that twentieth-century dictators had. Absolute monarchs were establishing political traditions that their progeny would inherit; modern dictatorships rarely outlived their founders.

FRANCE: HENRY IV, SULLY, AND RICHELIEU

Henry IV, king of Navarre, won the religious war in France in 1589. The leader of Protestant forces, he converted to Catholicism for reasons of state (see Chapter 14, p. 473) and issued the Edict of Nantes, which provided religious toleration for the Huguenots (French Protestants). A much beloved king, he sought to restore prosperity and order. He built roads and canals, kept the peace, lowered taxes by creating a new tax on royal officials (the *paulette*), and reorganized the collection of indirect taxes. After his assassination in 1610, the government was run by his widow, Marie de' Medici, who acted as regent for the future Louis XIII, and by her chosen adviser, Cardinal Richelieu, who ably served as first minister. Richelieu created many of the institutions of French absolutism, all with the aim of reducing the influence of the nobles and the independence of the towns. Intendants, royal officials, were sent out to each province to monitor matters for the king and supervise the local nobility. Almost all intendants belonged to a new type of nobility, the *noblesse de la robe* (nobles of the robe), who earned or bought their titles of nobility for service to the crown. Richelieu also went after the powerful fortified Protestant towns, such as La Rochelle, which lost its municipal government and its Huguenot focus when he reinstated the Catholic liturgy.

For Richelieu, religion was not the primary concern, as became easily apparent when France supported the Protestants in the Thirty Years' War. Such policies were justified by *raison d'état,* reasons of state, which, he argued, made them acceptable to God. Cardinal Mazarin, his successor as chief minister, continued his policies, but Mazarin's attempts at raising taxes to pay for a war with Spain brought about a widespread, five-year revolt called the Fronde, led by nobles of the robe, upset over attempts to cut the salaries of judges, and nobles of the sword (*noblesse de l'epée*), opposed to the centralizing efforts of the king. The Fronde was also supported by the people of Paris. Disorder was widespread, ending only when Louis XIV declared he would rule in his own person. The Fronde taught Louis that compromise with the nobility was necessary and taught the French that without a strong monarch, peace and order would be impossible; all would agree that rebellion was to be avoided.

Louis XIV

> **AP Tip**
>
> One characteristic of many of the absolute monarchs was their longevity. Louis XIV inherited the throne at the age of five, was crowned at the age of twenty-three, and ruled until he died at the age of seventy-seven. Frederick William of Prussia ruled for forty years; Peter the Great of Russia for thirty-six (see Chapter 17). Their long rules gave them many years to create the political institutions they needed to achieve their goals.

Louis sat on the throne longer than any other European monarch (1643–1715) and had the time, the wherewithal, and the energy to fulfill his ambitions as an absolute monarch. Imbibing the doctrine of divine right of kings from Cardinal Mazarin, Louis took the job of king seriously, ruling without a chief adviser and taking a personal hand in almost all aspects of government administration. Portraits he commissioned emphasized not only his glory but also his vigor (see chapter frontispiece, p. 522). He relied on councilors of state and intendants mostly from the upper middle class or men who had been recently ennobled. They served at his pleasure but did not share power. He prevented the grandees, the old nobility, from having their say by never calling the Estates General into session; instead, he relied on a network of spies and informers and opened private letters to gather information. To foster national unity, he eliminated the religious toleration granted by Henry IV and revoked the Edict of Nantes in 1685. This led many Huguenots to leave France, but it was a hugely popular decision among the rest of the population.

AP Tip

Many of the Huguenots who left France after 1685 went to the Netherlands or to England, where they energetically opposed French absolutism and in the next century authored or published many of the Enlightenment texts that advocated constitutionalism and individual rights for France. In this way, the revocation of the Edict of Nantes ultimately undermined the French monarchy.

Although excluding the nobles from direct access to political power, Louis offered them a marvelously grand lifestyle at the gorgeous, huge palace he built for himself some eight miles away from Paris at Versailles. The excerpt from the memoirs of the Duc de Saint-Simon (see Listening to the Past, pp. 556–557) reveals how Louis cleverly manipulated the nobles at Versailles.

To strengthen the economy and enrich the middle classes on whom he was dependent, Louis XIV employed the economic policy of mercantilism, which seeks to regulate economic activities for the benefit of the state. Seventeenth-century mercantilism was based on the idea that the measure of a nation's wealth was the amount of gold and silver bullion it had. To increase those reserves, exports were encouraged and imports discouraged through the imposition of protectionist tariffs, which raised the cost of imports, and the expansion of local industry through subsidies and monopolies. The financial genius Jean-Baptiste Colbert was appointed by Louis to manage the administration of the economy. Colbert encouraged the establishment of new textile industries and the importation of foreign craftsmen to work them. He subsidized the shipbuilding industry and created a merchant marine to take French goods abroad. He sought to expand France's international empire with the foundation of the East India Company and with the exploration and settlement of Quebec and Louisiana.

Colbert improved the efficiency of tax collection but could not crack the fundamental inequities of the French system, in which nobles and many bourgeois were exempt from the direct taxes on property. The burden of taxes fell unfairly on the least wealthy. In addition, France continued to use tax farming, a form of privatized tax collection, which reduced the revenues coming into the king while not reducing the tax burden on the people at all.

Louis's Wars

Louis kept France at war for more than half the years of his reign with the aim of expanding France to its natural borders in order to protect it from invasion. Louvois, his secretary of war, increased the size of the army and its ability to conscript and dragoon soldiers. Soldiers were given uniforms and standardized weapons, trained professionally, and promoted along hierarchical lines. Louis acquired some important towns in the north, the Franche-Comté in the east, Strasbourg in Alsace, and the province of Lorraine after extensive wars with Holland, the Holy Roman Empire, and Spain. Later wars brought few rewards, although other states saw them as attempts at hegemony and organized coalitions against France. Constant warfare put terrific pressure on public finances; ministers after Colbert raised taxes and sold titles and offices. The tax burden on commoners grew, and their economic position became more precarious when poor harvests led to sudden increases in the price of wheat. Perhaps 2 million people died of starvation in 1693 and 1694. Louis's last major military adventure was the War of the Spanish Succession in which he claimed the throne of Spain for his grandson when Spain's king died childless in 1700. This violated previous treaties, so England, the Netherlands, Austria, and Prussia organized an alliance against what they perceived as a threat to the balance of power. When the war ended in 1713, the Peace of Utrecht gave the Bourbons the throne of Spain but with the understanding that the crowns of Spain and France would never be united. France lost territories in the New World to England, which also acquired Gibraltar, Minorca, and the control of the African slave trade (the *asiento*) from Spain. Austria gained the former Spanish Netherlands (Belgium). The treaty, which reflected the vitality of the idea of balance of power, signaled the decline of Spain as well as the rise of England.

Absolutist Spain

Spain had become an absolutist state in the sixteenth century, with a permanent professional bureaucracy, a standing army, religious uniformity, and national taxes. With its gold and silver bullion from its New World colonies, Spain (which annexed Portugal in 1580) was able to play a dominant role in Europe.

By the seventeenth century, Spain began to lose her dominant role. When in 1609, Philip III expelled all the converted Muslims (known as Moriscos) from Spain, Spain lost some 300,000 people, who, like the already expelled Jews, were largely skilled workers and merchants. Revenues from the colonies declined when the colonies began to develop their own industries, in spite of mercantilist policies restricting them, and the English and the Dutch began to trade with them. Spain's gold and silver mines began to go dry while royal expenditures were growing apace. The kings of Spain took a fifth of all the precious metals of the New World, the quinto, so as the production of the mines fell, so did the quinto. The financial difficulties of the crown led it to declare bankruptcy about every ten to twenty years and to devalue the currency, which cost it its credit standing. Population decline, agricultural difficulties because of high rents, intellectual and psychological malaise, and the failure to invest in domestic industry, all added to Spain's decline in status by the end of the War of the Spanish Succession. Perhaps the most important cause of this decline was the lack of a sizable middle class and a general attitude of disdain toward money-making and hard work, particularly among the nobles and those seeking high social status. The relatively small number of businessmen faced constant obstacles, including the inflation of the price revolution, which made it harder for Spanish goods to compete. The aristocracy retained both their wealth and their power.

The kings of Spain were not up to the task of reforming their kingdom. They seemed overwhelmed with pessimism and passivity, even fatalism. Philip IV relied on Count Olivares, an able administrator but committed to the imperial tradition of military glory and militant Catholicism. Spain's unfruitful wars with France ended in 1659 with Spain giving up valuable territories to France in the Treaty of the Pyrenees. There were domestic problems as well, with substantial revolts in 1640 from Catalonia (where Barcelona is) and Portugal, with the latter regaining independence. The elite looked with suspicion on foreign ideas that might have benefited Spain, such as mercantilist legislation to promote domestic industry and the scientific revolution. Miguel de Cervantes' masterpiece, *Don Quixote,* delineates the illusions and delusions of the title character, who might be said to represent much of Spain.

AP Tip

Spain's decline at the end of its golden age is an example of the often destructive nature of sudden enormous wealth, in which short-term benefits and lack of foresight undermine the viability of the state. A number of oil-producing states in the twentieth century have experienced a similar phenomenon.

In its colonies in the New World, Spain continued the system of four viceroyalties set up in the sixteenth century, each ruled by an imperial governor with an advisory board called the audiencia. Emulating France, the Bourbon king Charles III introduced the intendant system in the late eighteenth century. Portugal's Brazil became the world's largest producer of sugar in the eighteenth century, with a highly mixed society of natives, Europeans, and African blacks.

THE CULTURE OF ABSOLUTISM

Absolute monarchs encouraged the arts as a way of enhancing their power. Baroque artists like Rubens were commissioned to glorify the monarchs and their family members. The Baroque style, which had flourished first as part of the Counter-Reformation, was dramatic, colorful, emotional, and often monumental in size. Rubens (1577–1640), probably the most famous Baroque artist and much admired for his melodramatic portraits and his sensuous nudes, was hugely successful, working for both the Bourbons of France and the Habsburgs of Austria. Baroque art and architecture were particularly popular in Catholic countries such as Bavaria, Poland, Austria, and Spain, while Baroque music saw its apogee under Johann Sebastian Bach in Protestant Germany.

Grandiose architecture became the norm once Louis XIV set the model by building Versailles, a hugely impressive, gold-and-marble-studded complex that housed both the home of the royal family and the administration of government. Room after room, some 6,400 of them, decorated with luxuries, and extensive formal gardens filled with classical statues underlined the rightfulness of the king's rule. Designed to inspire awe in both French nobles and foreign visitors, the palace served the king's political purposes. The nobles, required to spend part of the year there, became caught up in court etiquette and intrigue, competing for the favor of serving the king, whether attending to him personally or winning important commissions or positions. Their extravagant spending led them to become more and more dependent on the king's bounties. Women played an important role in this patronage system, using their rank and family connections to navigate among competing factions and to negotiate for influence at court. Madame de Maintenon, Louis XIV's mistress, had extraordinary power.

The standardization of language and the patronage of writers also served state purposes. Richelieu had established the French Academy in 1635, which to this day determines what is correct usage in the French language. It created the first standard dictionary of French. In the late seventeenth century, the academicians sought to emulate antiquity in style. French classicists such as Racine sought to restore balance and discipline after what they perceived were the excesses of the Baroque style. Racine wrote tragic dramas based on stories of moral conflict from ancient Greece and Rome, often, as in his famous *Phèdre,* with woman heroines. Music and dance were also encouraged at Versailles. The composers Jean-Baptiste Lully (ballets and operas), François Couperin (harpsichord and organ works), and Charpentier (religious music), all received royal patronage. Louis XIV loved the theater and subsidized the plays of Racine and of Molière, a witty satirist of bourgeois hypocrisy, pretensions, and foibles.

Under Louis's patronage, the arts flourished and added to the international prestige of France, which became so high that French became the international language of culture and diplomacy throughout European courts and, over time, even the language of scholarship. To be cosmopolitan and sophisticated anywhere in Europe meant to speak French and to know and appreciate the culture at Versailles.

AP Tip

This remained true until the twentieth century when English began to replace French as the international language. French cultural dominance would have important political consequences in countries like Russia where the aristocracy often knew French better than their national language. France's cultural position in the seventeenth century is analogous to American culture's worldwide impact now.

CONSTITUTIONALISM

England and Holland forged a different path in the seventeenth century, establishing constitutional governments in which the power of the monarchs was limited and the rights of individuals affirmed by law. Unlike that of the United States, the constitutions of England and Holland were not single written documents but accrued traditions and legal precedents acknowledged as binding by monarch and people alike. In a constitutional state, in one form or another, it is the people or the electorate (however that is defined) who are sovereign, not the monarch. In the seventeenth and eighteenth centuries, the franchise was severely limited, so the number of voters remained small; nevertheless, the legislatures they voted for had ultimate political authority.

ENGLAND

Constitutionalism was achieved in England through revolution, civil war, and, ultimately, peaceful resolution. England had had a well-established parliamentary tradition (see Chapter 12), which the Tudors had carefully avoided offending. When Elizabeth I died without an heir, the crown passed to her cousin James I of the Stuart line of Scotland. James was intrigued by the divine right of kings being implemented in France and argued its validity in an essay, "The Trew Law of Free Monarchy," and directly before Parliament, which took offense at his notion of royal prerogatives. Englishmen early on perceived a threat to due process of law and their property rights from Stuart absolutist ideas. James I's son, Charles I, also tried to act as an absolute monarch. He did not call Parliament into session for eleven years, financing his expenditures by levies, such as "ship money," not legislated by Parliament. In 1640, however, he was forced to call Parliament into session, and thus began the English revolution.

Members of Parliament had become, during the reign of the Tudors, a much wealthier, more socially mobile group, due to the Protestant confiscation of monastic lands, commerce with the colonies, and enclosure of common lands, which allowed landowners to cultivate land capitalistically. A new class, the gentry, made up in part of wealthy merchants and manufacturers who bought estates in the country, came into prominence. The gentry, like the traditional nobility, were willing to pay taxes but insisted on some say over how the money was spent in return. Religious issues were also important in fomenting hostility between king and Parliament. Henry VIII's Act of Supremacy had made the king the head of the Anglican Church. Puritans, influenced by Calvin and wishing to purify the Church of England of its Catholic remnants, such as bishops, increasingly populated Parliament. Calvinism's emphasis on hard work, thrift, and modesty of pleasures suited the hardworking capitalist classes of England, whether in town or country, and these became the values of many if not most Parliamentarians. Charles I's sympathies toward Catholicism seemed confirmed by his marriage to a French Catholic and by his support of Archbishop Laud, who sought nationwide uniformity of practice. When Laud insisted on the use of a new Anglican prayer book, *The Book of Common Prayer*, in Scotland, the Scottish Presbyterians rebelled. It was the need to obtain the funds to put down this rebellion that forced Charles to call Parliament into session.

After a brief "Short Parliament," the Long Parliament (it sat with long interruptions, from 1640 to 1660) rejected Charles's requests and instead passed the Triennial Act, requiring him to call Parliament into session every three years. It also impeached Archbishop Laud. When Parliament refused to give Charles funds for an army to put down a new rebellion, this time from Catholic Ireland, Charles went north to raise an army of nobles and mercenaries. Parliament had its own army, later called the New Model Army, and by 1642 civil war broke out between the Cavaliers, the monarchists, and the Roundheads, the Parliamentarians, to decide which was sovereign, king or Parliament. The New Model Army, led by Oliver Cromwell, captured the king in 1647. Cromwell purged the Parliament of moderates. The remaining Rump Parliament put Charles on trial for treason and had him beheaded on January 30, 1649. This radical act, the first of its kind in Europe, ended the monarchy. A commonwealth—or republic—was established, but in practice it was Cromwell and the army that ruled. According to its constitution of 1653, executive power was invested in a lord protector, Cromwell in this case, with triennial parliaments having sole power of the purse. However, Cromwell tore this constitution up and set up a military dictatorship instead. Religious toleration, except for Catholics, was accompanied by Calvinist theocratic practices like the closing of theaters and the banning of sports.

Cromwell sent his army to Ireland to crush the Drogheda rebellion of the Catholics, and crush it they did with ferocious brutality; perhaps as many as 600,000 people were killed or exiled. Catholicism was banned in Ireland, and English and Scottish settlers were given land confiscated from Catholics. Economically, Cromwell was a mercantilist, enforcing a Navigation Act that required all English goods be transported on English ships, winning a short war against England's economic rival Holland, and welcoming back after four centuries Jewish immigrants because of their skills. The story of Glückel of Hameln (see Individuals in Society, p. 551) is an example of the enterprising business activities of many Jews.

When Cromwell died in 1658 and his son was not the measure of his father, the English sought a return to civilian rule and the end of military government. Charles II, the son of the executed king, was restored to power, as was the Anglican Church and the traditional systems of local government. Parliament, now strongly monarchist and Anglican, passed a strict law called the Test Act, enforcing religious conformity and denying Catholics and many other non-Anglicans the right to vote or hold office, teach, attend university, or assemble for meetings, although in practice the English were reluctant to enforce such laws. Charles II appointed five members of Parliament—the Cabal—to advise him and act as liaisons. This was the forerunner of the contemporary cabinet system, which acts on the principle that ministers are responsible to Parliament. But money problems continued to beset the king. When Parliament did not vote him sufficient funds, Charles made a secret treaty with the king of France. Louis would give him substantial funds if the laws against Catholics were removed and if Charles would himself convert. When this treaty became publicly known, an anti-Catholic fervor swept

England, which intensified when Charles's Catholic brother became King James II in 1685. James disregarded the Test Act in his appointments and seemingly was reviving Stuart absolutist claims. When James issued a Declaration of Indulgence, granting religious freedom to all, and shortly thereafter, his Catholic wife gave birth to a son and heir, Parliament offered the crown to his daughter by his first marriage, Mary, a Protestant married to William of Orange, the stadtholder of Holland. In 1688, James fled; the next year, William and Mary were crowned. By accepting the crown from Parliament, they acknowledged that sovereignty was shared, that kings ruled with the consent of the governed. This principle was enshrined in the Bill of Rights of 1689, which established Parliament's legislative authority, the independence of the judiciary, and the rights of individual subjects. No standing army was allowed in peacetime to prevent either military government or royal abuse.

AP Tip

Some historians, notably Crane Brinton, have used the English Revolution to create a model of revolutions, beginning with a reform stage in which most people see the need for political change, civil war (and often foreign wars as well), radicalization of the revolution with major divisions among the revolutionaries over values and class interests, leading to violence and repression, followed by one-man rule and ultimately by restoration. This pattern fits the French and Russian revolutions as well. It is useful to break down the narrative of revolutions in such a way, although it does lead one to the conclusion that revolutions are inevitably failures.

The intellectual underpinnings of the Glorious Revolution, 1688, and its Bill of Rights, 1689, were laid down by John Locke, who argued that it is the people who create governments to protect their lives, their liberties, and their property, which are their natural rights, and they have the right to change the government when it fails to do so. The right to rebellion is protection against tyranny. Locke saw a close connection between political rights and the ownership of property, and therefore limited the suffrage to property owners. Locke's ideas of natural rights had widespread appeal, and are particularly evident in the U.S. Declaration of Independence.

THE DUTCH REPUBLIC IN THE SEVENTEENTH CENTURY

In a great variety of ways, the Dutch Republic was unique among European states in the seventeenth century. Perhaps no other area saw such a flourishing of progressive ideas, capitalistic energy, and scientific and artistic achievement. While elsewhere on the continent monarchies ruled, the seven provinces remained fiercely republican. While elsewhere religious toleration was limited, if it existed at all, people of all religions were welcomed in the Dutch Republic and free to practice their faith. While many nations were forging unified, centralized nation-states, the Dutch states, which earned their independence from Spain in 1609, remained a loose confederation of seven independent and strong states, each with its own provincial assembly or estate. They unified in a States General on foreign policy issues, where they also appointed a chief executive for each province, the stadtholder. The sons of William the Silent of the House of Orange, who had led the independence movement, became the stadtholder in all seven provinces. It was the Dutch stadtholder William, husband to Mary, who became king of England in 1689 in the Glorious Revolution. Holland, because of its extraordinary wealth, was the dominant state of the seven.

Dutch capitalistic success was certainly connected, either as a cause or a result, with the Calvinist work ethic and also with the concerted efforts of city councils to create good business climates. The city councils made sure that their granaries were full, so that famine was completely avoided and food prices stayed stable. The City Council of Amsterdam guaranteed the deposits at the Bank of Amsterdam, thus attracting a great deal of foreign capital. The Dutch merchant marine, the largest in Europe (some 16,000 ships), not only carried the huge herring catches each year but also charged the lowest rates in Europe for shipping. With these ships the Dutch were able to buy in bulk entire wheat crops in Poland, for example, and then sell the goods in Amsterdam and transport them on their own ships. The Dutch successfully expanded their sphere of business beyond Europe when they founded the Dutch East India Company in 1602 and the Dutch West India Company in 1621. They established important trading posts and settlements in South Africa (Capetown), Ceylon, and Malacca, among others. The Dutch lived better than virtually everyone else in Europe in the seventeenth century as a result of their enormous success as merchants and traders. This was even true for ordinary people, who could afford to spend more on other types of food because of the low price of bread and comparatively high wages.

The Dutch began to fall on harder times due to increasing competition from France and England, both of which went to war with the United Provinces in the 1670s. By the end of the War of the Spanish Succession, which had drained Dutch resources, Dutch economic decline was under way.

Multiple-Choice Questions

1. Where were there *least* likely to be peasant uprisings or urban revolts in the seventeenth century?
   (A) France
   (B) Catalonia
   (C) Holland
   (D) England
   (E) Sicily

2. In terms of religion, Louis XIV adopted which idea from Spain?
   (A) Toleration for all religions
   (B) Uniformity and conformity
   (C) Toleration for Lutherans but not Calvinists
   (D) Toleration for Protestants but not Jews
   (E) Widespread use of the Inquisition

3. Spain's economic troubles increased in the seventeenth and eighteenth centuries when
   (A) it lost Gibraltar.
   (B) the colonies in the New World revolted.
   (C) England was given the quinto in the Peace of Utrecht in 1713.
   (D) the Dutch began to raid Spain's northern coasts.
   (E) the gold and silver mines in the Americas began to run dry.

4. The execution of Charles I
   (A) ended the Stuart line.
   (B) was voted for by the majority of the Long Parliament.
   (C) led France to send troops to defend his son, Charles II.
   (D) was approved by a Parliament purged of moderates.
   (E) was opposed by Oliver Cromwell, who argued that exile was sufficient.

5. France, England, and Holland all sought to expand which part of their economies in the seventeenth century?
   (A) Textile manufacturing
   (B) Transportation
   (C) Agriculture
   (D) Banking
   (E) Trade with central Europe

6. *Don Quixote* by Miguel de Cervantes is a useful historical source in that it shows
   (A) the military prowess of the Spanish nobility.
   (B) the role of the middle classes in Spain.
   (C) Spanish illusions about glory.
   (D) the impact of the New World colonies at home.
   (E) Spanish devotion to Catholicism.

7. The response of the Spanish kings to their economic difficulties in the seventeenth century was
   (A) generally passive and uninspired.
   (B) to reorganize the administrative structure of Spain.
   (C) to adopt mercantilist policies similar to France.
   (D) to insist on paying their debts, thus adding to their financial problems.
   (E) energetic and forward thinking although ultimately unsuccessful.

8. The Peace of Utrecht
   (A) put a Habsburg on the throne of Spain.
   (B) was a victory for Louis XIV in his claim to the throne of Spain.
   (C) gave France control over the former Spanish Netherlands.
   (D) ended French ambitions to combine the crowns of France and Spain.
   (E) upset the balance of power in Europe.

9. Bossuet and Hobbes both supported strong governments but differed in their reasons. While Bossuet argued for divine right of kings, Hobbes based his views on
   (A) man's selfish and aggressive nature.
   (B) Machiavellian ideas about the need for a prince to unify the nation.
   (C) More's ideal community in which the government carefully supervised the population.
   (D) a non-Christian idea of divine right.
   (E) the analogy of the brain's role in the body.

10. The English civil war was fundamentally fought over
    (A) Catholic demands for the right to freely practice their religion.
    (B) Puritan demands for the right to freely practice their religion.
    (C) whether Parliament or the king would have the power of the purse.
    (D) whether the House of Lords or the House of Commons should have ultimate authority.
    (E) whether Parliament or the king would appoint the head of the Anglican Church.

11. Which event prompted the Glorious Revolution?
    (A) Charles II's treaty with Louis XIV
    (B) James I's "The Trew Law of Monarchy"
    (C) The death of Oliver Cromwell
    (D) The birth to James II of a son and heir
    (E) The Declaration of Indulgence granted by James II

12. One important factor in creating Dutch prosperity in the seventeenth century was
    (A) their political unity.
    (B) their alliance with the British.
    (C) the active promotion of business by city councils.
    (D) important colonies in the New World.
    (E) the establishment of constitutional monarchy.

13. Baroque art and architecture appealed to the absolute monarchies because of its
    (A) focus on classical antiquity.
    (B) drama and monumental size.
    (C) intense religiosity.
    (D) simplicity and understatement.
    (E) rejection of the nude.

14. Historians have changed their views on Louis XIV's relationship with the nobility. They now say that he
    (A) emasculated the nobles.
    (B) severely diminished the wealth of the nobles.
    (C) cooperated with the nobles.
    (D) successfully replaced the nobles with the bourgeoisie as the dominant political class.
    (E) ignored the nobles.

15. Armies changed in the seventeenth century in all of the following ways *except* that
    (A) they became larger.
    (B) they became more professional.
    (C) most soldiers were mercenaries, as few countries had standing armies.
    (D) the death toll was high particularly for officers.
    (E) they became more expensive for kings to pay for.

Free-Response Questions

1. Analyze the methods used by Louis XIV to establish absolutism in France in the seventeenth century.

2. Discuss the concept of mercantilism, and show how it was put into practice in Holland, France, and England in the seventeenth century.

ANSWERS

MULTIPLE-CHOICE ANSWERS

1. ANSWER (C) Only in Holland were food prices generally stable; elsewhere famines and high taxes sparked revolts. (McKay, *A History of Western Society*, not treated in 8th ed./9th ed., pp. 527–528)

2. ANSWER (B) Having already expelled the Jews, the Spanish kings expelled the converted Muslims. With the widespread use of the Inquisition, Protestantism had no chance to take root. Louis revoked the Edict of Nantes in 1685, with the aim of creating religious uniformity in France. State power rather than the Inquisition was used to enforce it. (McKay, *A History of Western Society*, 8th ed., pp. 510, 541/9th ed., pp. 532–534)

3. ANSWER (E) Spain lost the important *asiento*, not the quinto, in the 1713 treaty, as well as Gibraltar, whose importance was more strategic and symbolic than economic. The colonies revolted but only in the nineteenth century. Spain's supplies of gold and silver, on which the economy was dependent, began to dwindle as the mines ran out. (McKay, *A History of Western Society*, 8th ed., pp. 544–545/9th ed., pp. 534–535)

4. **Answer (D)** Cromwell sought the king's execution and purged Parliament to avoid a negative vote. It was this Rump Parliament that approved the execution. France gave refuge to Charles II but sent no troops. Charles II was crowned king in 1660. (McKay, *A History of Western Society*, 8th ed., pp. 551–553/9th ed., pp. 546–547)

5. **Answer (B)** All three governments promoted shipbuilding and the merchant marine through legislation. The Dutch were less interested in textile manufacturing and agriculture and more interested in banking and shipping. Trade with central Europe at that time was not extensive or crucial for any of their economies. (McKay, *A History of Western Society*, 8th ed., pp. 540, 552, 558/9th ed., pp. 532, 546, 552)

6. **Answer (C)** Don Quixote, forever tilting at windmills, can be used to demonstrate the idealistic but impractical nature of seventeenth-century Spain. (McKay, *A History of Western Society*, 8th ed., p. 548/9th ed., pp. 537–538)

7. **Answer (A)** The kings of Spain in the seventeenth century lacked the will to reform and to lead Spain out of difficulties and were suspicious of ideas from other countries. They repudiated their debts several times in the late seventeenth and early eighteenth centuries. (McKay, *A History of Western Society*, 8th ed., pp. 545, 547/9th ed. pp. 535, 537)

8. **Answer (D)** The crown of Spain was given to a Bourbon but with the proviso that it could never be unified with the crown of France. The balance of power was restored when French ambitions were checked. Austria was given the Spanish Netherlands. (McKay, *A History of Western Society*, 8th ed., p. 544/9th ed., p. 534)

9. **Answer (A)** Hobbes argued that men formed governments to protect themselves from their own selfishness and aggression. Without powerful governments, those traits lead society into disorder and chaos. This was an important secular argument for monarchy. (McKay, *A History of Western Society*, 8th ed., p. 551/9th ed., pp. 528, 553)

10. **Answer (C)** The English civil war was fundamentally fought over Parliament's assertion of its right to control royal revenues and taxes, that is, its political power against Charles I's attempt to rule without it. Religious issues played a role in alienating Parliament from the king, and in sparking revolts in Scotland and Ireland, but the causes of the conflict demonstrate that the political, not the religious, issue was fundamental. (McKay, *A History of Western Society*, 8th ed., pp. 549–551/9th ed., pp. 543–546, 554)

11. **Answer (D)** Although Charles II's treaty with France and James II's Declaration of Indulgence rankled with most of the English, it was the birth of a male heir to James II and his Catholic wife that led Parliament to offer the crown to Mary, James's Protestant daughter. The death of Oliver Cromwell led to the Restoration of 1660, while James I died in 1625. (McKay, *A History of Western Society*, 8th ed., pp. 553–554/9th ed., p. 548)

12. ANSWER (C) The city councils, particularly of Amsterdam and Rotterdam, promoted prosperity by guaranteeing deposits in their banks, stabilizing food prices, and promoting the merchant marine. There was no unified government of the seven provinces that made up the Netherlands, each of which remained a republic. They had few important colonies in the New World and in fact lost New Amsterdam in 1664 to the English with whom they fought several wars in the seventeenth century. (McKay, *A History of Western Society*, 8th ed., pp. 555–559/9th ed., pp. 548–553)

13. ANSWER (B) The dramatic and monumental qualities of Baroque art appealed to the absolute monarchs because they could use them to impress and enhance their prestige. Rubens painted many nudes. French classicism did revive classical motifs but as a rejection of the Baroque. (McKay, *A History of Western Society*, 8th ed., pp. 523, 541/9th ed., pp. 539–542)

14. ANSWER (C) Whereas the older view was that Louis XIV tamed the nobles and weakened both their wealth and their power, the new view is that he cooperated with them as well as co-opted them. (McKay, *A History of Western Society*, 8th ed., pp. 537–538/9th ed., p. 532)

15. ANSWER (C) Armies became bigger, more professional, and more expensive. Nobles, who held to traditional ideals of honor, suffered high death tolls. Standing armies, that is, armies that exist in peacetime as well as wartime, were the norm everywhere except in England. (McKay, *A History of Western Society*, 8th ed., p. 532/9th ed., pp. 526–527)

FREE-RESPONSE ANSWERS

1. This is a mainstream, uncomplicated question asking you to demonstrate that you understand how Louis established absolutism in France. The more you can include in your essay, the higher the score. A superior essay will discuss the new work of historians showing that the nobility was not crushed or devalued by Louis XIV but that instead he cooperated with them. Among the methods you could discuss are the development of a theory of divine right (Bossuet); the building and use of Versailles to impress nobles and foreigners; the use of intendants and spies to control the nobles; the promotion of middle-class individuals to important roles in the state and sometimes to titles of nobility; the selling of noble titles, which reduced their value; the revocation of the Edict of Nantes and the enforcement of religious uniformity; not calling the Estates General even once in his long reign, thereby depriving the nobility of their political platform; creating an elaborate patronage system at Versailles; using art, architecture, and literature to enhance the prestige of the royal court; successfully expanding France's borders to their natural limits; expanding the army; creating a national language through the French Academy; and mercantilism, which increased the national wealth and improved the royal finances.

2. You need to show you understand both the concept of mercantilism and how it was applied by the three states. Again, the more specific evidence you include, the stronger the essay will be.
   - The concept of mercantilism was based on the notion that wealth is determined by the amount of bullion (gold and silver) in the state. The goal was to increase bullion reserves by decreasing imports and increasing exports, thus bringing gold and silver into the country. Governments carefully regulated the economy to achieve this goal.
   - Policies shared by all three states were the promotion of the merchant marine and shipbuilding industries and the expansion of international trade and acquisition of colonies.
   - France, under the leadership of Colbert, reduced domestic tariffs and raised protectionist tariffs to discourage imports. He promoted new industries, particularly in textiles, with state supervision and inspection to ensure quality and encouraged the immigration of skilled craftsmen from other countries, and the employment of women as well. He gave bonuses to shipbuilders and shipowners and set up a system of conscription and academies for the recruitment and training of sailors.
   - Holland founded the Dutch East India and West India companies in the early seventeenth century for trade and the establishment of outposts around the globe. Banks were supported by city councils, who guaranteed their deposits. The Dutch greatly expanded their merchant marine, which offered highly competitive rates and allowed for the shipment of the catch of their substantial fishing industry and for the purchase of commodities in bulk, which then could be resold at great profits. Religious toleration encouraged merchants from many nations to live or trade in Holland.
   - In England under Cromwell Parliament passed the Navigation Act of 1651, which required all English goods to be transported on English ships. Cromwell went to war with the Dutch and, as the Dutch did, allowed the immigration of Jews to England because of their success in business.

17

ABSOLUTISM IN CENTRAL AND EASTERN EUROPE TO 1740

Eastern Europe and much of central Europe diverged in significant ways from western Europe in the sixteenth and seventeenth centuries—differences that remain important to this day. Although economic and political changes in western Europe ultimately were providing ordinary people with greater personal freedom and opportunity, in eastern Europe serfdom not only was enduring but in fact was becoming more and more the bedrock of society. By and large, eastern European societies remained rural and agricultural, with a relatively small merchant class. These factors influenced the way absolutism developed in central and eastern Europe. Four powerful states emerged: Austria, Prussia, Russia, and the Ottoman Empire. While the monarchs in Austria and Prussia adopted western European models, the Russian and Ottoman rulers were seen by other Europeans as despotic and even fanatic. All four empires, which were frequently at war with each other, lasted until World War I.

AP Tip

The fact that these four autocratic states survived up until World War I without becoming constitutional monarchies had major consequences in the twentieth century. The Russian Revolution, Nazism, and World Wars I and II were outgrowths, directly or indirectly, of the institutions and traditions established in eastern Europe in the seventeenth and eighteenth centuries.

KEY CONCEPTS

- While serfdom was disappearing in the West, it reappeared and became more entrenched in the East. Peasants' uprisings sought relief from harsh conditions.
- The Thirty Years' War finally resolved religious conflicts in the Holy Roman Empire but delayed the unification of a German state for another 200 years. The war was devastating to both the German population and their economy.
- Prussia developed an absolutist government that was highly efficient and devoted to militaristic values. Both its effective administrative structure and its well-trained army would help it become the dominant state in central Europe.
- Austria under the Habsburgs developed into an absolutist state, conquered important territories such as Hungary from the Ottomans, and made Vienna a center of European culture.
- Russia developed into an absolute state under the Romanovs, the princes of Muscovy. The Russian tsars (emperors) expanded the territory under their control through conquest and warfare, and were closely associated with the Russian Orthodox Church. The most transformative tsar, Peter the Great, modernized and westernized Russia, expanded the empire, and built a splendid new capital city in the early eighteenth century.
- The Ottoman Empire was established in what is now Turkey when it defeated the last remnants of the Byzantine Empire in 1453 and took over Constantinople. Its emperor, the sultan, was both a secular and religious ruler as head of the Muslim community. The Ottomans conquered the Balkans, North Africa, and the Middle East, acquiring an empire filled with religious and ethnic minorities, who were given religious toleration and some legal rights.

AP Tip

While absolute monarchs in western and eastern Europe built similarly splendid palaces and had similar goals of aggrandizement of personal power, there were important and long-lasting differences in the social classes the monarchs used for this purpose. The merchant and manufacturing classes were given important roles in France, but were excluded from power, by and large, in the Austrian, Prussian, and Russian states, which all relied on their aristocracies instead.

WARFARE AND SOCIAL CHANGE IN CENTRAL AND EASTERN EUROPE

Unlike in western Europe, the elites of the states in central and eastern Europe regained control over the peasants and reimposed serfdom. In eastern Europe, as in western Europe, the period from 1000 to 1300 saw great economic growth, the rise of towns, and an increase in population. By 1300 serfdom had by and large disappeared throughout Europe, including in the East where people were enticed to do the hard work of clearing land east of the Elbe by offers of good terms in economic and personal freedom. When the Black Death hit Europe and population dropped precipitously, East and West diverged, with commoners winning in the West and landlords winning in the East. Peasants lost freedom of movement in Prussia and Russia, their land was taken away, and their labor obligations to the landlords increased, up to six days a week without pay. Because monarchies were weak, there was no royal justice to offset the landlords' control over the legal system.

This situation only grew worse after 1500 as permanent, hereditary serfdom became the legal norm in central and eastern Europe. Polish nobles, for example, were granted complete control—even the right to impose capital punishment—over their peasants in 1574. The development of estate agriculture (large plantations), prompted by the general rise in prices, made serfdom a valuable way to increase production and therefore profits. Much of the timber and wheat surpluses produced in the large German and Polish estates were shipped to the West.

AP Tip

There is a useful parallel here between Russia and the United States. Both developed large plantation agriculture, both used forms of unpaid labor (serfdom and chattel slavery), and both liberated that population in the 1860s (1863 and 1861, respectively, to be exact). This freeing up of their economies is part of the reason that both states rose to become major powers in the twentieth century.

However, it was political rather than economic factors that determined the reimposition of serfdom. In the East, frequent wars and disputed successions weakened royal power and gave nobles greater authority. Eastern monarchs generally benefited from serfdom themselves, and also agreed with the nobles about diminishing the power and influence of merchants in towns. Landlords eliminated the middleman and bypassed the towns by selling their goods directly to foreigners such as the Dutch.

THE THIRTY YEARS' WAR (1618–1648)

The Peace of Augsburg of 1555 temporarily solved the religious conflict in the Holy Roman Empire, but the spread of Calvinism, not protected by that treaty, as well as the changes in religions of several member states, stirred religious tensions again. Both Catholics and Lutherans felt they were being undermined; Catholics and Protestants each formed a league in the early seventeenth century. War began when Bohemian Protestants threw two of the representatives of their new Catholic king, Ferdinand of Styria, later Holy Roman Emperor, out the window of a Prague castle—the Defenestration of Prague—in

1618. The war was fought over religion, nationalistic goals of subject nationalities, and political centralization of power.

AP Tip

There were several Defenestrations of Prague, this one in 1618 and another in 1948 when Jan Masaryk fell or was thrown or jumped out of a window in protest against the establishment of a Soviet-dominated communist government in Czechoslovakia.

The Thirty Years' War can be discussed in four phases. The first, the Bohemian phase, was a civil war over both Bohemian religion and independence, ending with the defeat of Czech nationalism and Czech Protestantism at the Battle of White Mountain in 1620. In the second, the Danish phase, the Protestant king of Denmark aided the Protestant forces, but generally the Catholics did so well that the Holy Roman Emperor confidently reinstated Catholic rights in many places. The Catholic leader, the opportunistic Wallenstein, however, was a divisive figure. In the third, the Swedish phase, Gustavus Adolphus of Sweden, subsidized by Cardinal Richelieu of France, decisively won the day for Protestant forces and ended the Habsburg dream of uniting the German states under their authority. His battlefield death in 1632 led France to intervene directly on the Protestant side. The fourth, the French or international phase of the war, was a long and indecisive struggle with much wanton destruction on the German lands. The Peace of Westphalia, signed in 1648, awarded the Protestant side important victories, restricting the role of the papacy in the empire and confirming the Peace of Augsburg with rights extended to Calvinists. The princes of the Holy Roman Empire were confirmed in their power, thus preventing a centralized government from developing. Dutch and Swiss independence was confirmed, Sweden got some German territories, and France got Alsace.

The Thirty Years' War has the distinction of being Europe's most destructive war up to the twentieth century, with warfare, refugees, and disease causing the death of about one-third of the urban population and two-fifths of the peasants within the Holy Roman Empire. Agriculture, livestock, and commerce rapidly declined just as the price revolution, due to the influx of Spanish silver, was causing inflation. Nobles were able to expand their estates and enforce serfdom.

THE RISE OF AUSTRIA AND PRUSSIA

The Thirty Years' War and military threats from the Turks helped create absolutism in the East. Monarchs traded off political for economic power with the nobles: kings won the right to impose taxation without their consent to pay for permanent standing armies, in exchange for granting nobles virtually unlimited authority over their serfs. Absolute monarchs were particularly effective in Prussia.

In Austria the Habsburgs, after the exhausting and debilitating Thirty Years' War, recognized that the Holy Roman Empire would remain a disunified hodgepodge of states and turned their imperial attention toward securing and expanding their Austrian kingdom. In Bohemia, whose Protestant nobles had started the war, the Habsburgs imposed religious uniformity and diminished the Bohemian Estates, the center of noble power. After the defeat of the Bohemian Protestant nobles in 1620, Ferdinand III confiscated much of their land and distributed it, with titles, to loyal Catholics and foreign mercenaries. The largely new nobility in Bohemia was loyal to the Habsburgs. Their serfs worked for their lords from three days a week to in some cases almost every day; this system was called the *robot*. Ferdinand III also established a permanent standing army and improved the administration of the state.

In 1683 Leopold I forced the Ottomans to lift their siege of Vienna and pushed them out of Transylvania and the parts of Hungary that had been granted to the Ottomans after the Battle of Mohács in 1526. He built the lovely palace of Schönbrunn in Vienna to celebrate his victory. Like Versailles, Schönbrunn became the model for many other palaces. The Hungarian nobility had developed nationalistic ideals and in 1703, under Rákóczy, rebelled against their new overlords. Although the Habsburgs defeated the Rákóczy rebellion, they had to restore the nobles' privileges; this allowed Hungary to remain somewhat independent of Austrian rule. Over time and partially because of shared Catholicism, the Habsburgs were able to create a sense of loyalty and common identity among the Hungarian nobles, who voted them substantial funds for the royal army and began to speak German. The nobles prospered by transforming their expanding estates, manned by heavily burdened serfs, into capitalistic enterprises producing for the market.

AP Tip

Austria, Russia, and the Ottoman Empire, but not Prussia, developed into multiethnic, multireligious states in this period. As they expanded from their original heartlands, they conquered peoples of different faiths and nationalities. Each state handled its minorities differently—a factor that would ultimately determine the fate of each empire to a large degree.

Charles VI, who ruled from 1711 to 1740 and had no male heir, got agreement from the other powers for the Pragmatic Sanction, which proclaimed that the Habsburg possessions were never to be divided even if a woman were to inherit the throne, which his daughter Maria Theresa did on his death.

SEVENTEENTH-CENTURY PRUSSIA

The Hohenzollern family ruled both Prussia, a largely agricultural area along the Baltic Sea, now in Poland, and Brandenburg, a landlocked swampy area with Berlin at its center, where they held the title of elector of the Holy Roman Emperor. In 1618 the two states were united under the elector of Brandenburg, although it is usually referred to as Prussia. Prussia had two significant problems, lack of territorial integrity (Prussia, Brandenburg, and several small territories along the Rhine did not abut each other) and lack of natural borders, making it vulnerable to attack. It was the carefully crafted and ultimately successful solution to these two problems that bolstered absolutism in Prussia.

During the Thirty Years' War, Prussia was largely a victim, but ultimately the war strengthened the monarchy because it eroded the position of the Junkers, as the nobles in Prussia were called. Frederick William the Great Elector, whose forty-eight-year rule began in 1640, engaged in a successful constitutional battle with these nobles. Their traditional assemblies, the estates, had had final say over the levying of taxes, but within about a dozen years, the Estate of Prussia and the Diet of Brandenburg had each relinquished that power to the king in exchange for affirmation of their economic privileges and domination over their serfs. The Brandenburg Diet did not meet after 1652. Military threats from the Crimean Tatars who marauded in Russia and Prussia in the 1650s and the visible growth of the French army legitimized the king's plans to strengthen the army. When towns such as Königsberg tried to defend their traditional privileges, the nobles refused to come to their aid; instead the king used force to crush urban opposition. Frederick William also reorganized the tax collection system and created a highly efficient bureaucracy. Military preparedness, effective administration, and the elimination of institutions that could challenge royal power were hallmarks of Hohenzollern rule.

Frederick, the Great Elector's son, was granted the title king in Prussia in 1701 and became Frederick I. His son, Frederick William I, the Soldiers' King, proved to be the ablest of them all. He sought a strong army to make Prussia a state to be reckoned with. He tripled the size of his army, and trained and disciplined the troops to a degree not seen elsewhere, turning the army into the best prepared in Europe. He infused militaristic values throughout his kingdom so that hard work, devotion to duty, honesty, and obedience became Prussian ideals as Prussia became the Sparta of the North. Living modestly himself, he turned the Junkers into servants of the state by making them the officer class of the new army. While later rulers would use the army often and well, Prussia was almost always at peace under Frederick William I.

The Development of Russia and the Ottoman Empire

Both Russia and the Ottoman Empire were seen as foreign, even exotic, by other Europeans. Partially due to the 200-year-long occupation by the Mongols, Russia at the beginning of the seventeenth century had many traits similar to Asian empires, with despotic rulers and large but lightly populated landmasses, but by the middle of the next century was partially westernized. The Ottoman Empire offered a model of religious and cultural toleration rarely seen elsewhere in

Europe at that time, although Europeans saw its rulers, the sultans, as cruel despots.

The dynasty that created a centralized state in Russia were the rulers of Muscovy, who came to prominence when they overthrew the Mongols. The Golden Horde, as the Mongol army was known, ruled the eastern Slavs with brute force from the thirteenth to the fifteenth centuries. Alexander Nevsky, prince of Moscow in the thirteenth century, and his successors became able servants of the Mongols, who allowed them to keep their titles and government roles. Over time, they outmaneuvered their rivals and established a kingdom, under Ivan III, which reached almost to the Baltic from Moscow and Novgorod. Around 1480, Ivan III felt strong enough to refuse to acknowledge the Mongol khan as his ruler, declaring himself to be the sole source of political authority in Russia. By adopting Mongol administrative practices and aligning themselves with the Orthodox Church (Moscow was to be the "third Rome"), the princes of Moscow enhanced their claim to imperial power. The great nobles, called *boyars*, and the lesser gentry were allowed to keep their local power, and new titles for the officer corps were created.

Ivan IV, known as Ivan the Terrible, took the title of tsar (Caesar) and warred against the Mongols, defeating them in the 1550s. He added their lands to his realm, creating the foundation of the modern, multiethnic Russian empire. Ivan dominated the nobles by making them all serve the tsar in exchange for land. Frustrated by his unsuccessful war against Poland-Lithuania and angry over the unexpected death of his wife, Ivan instituted a reign of terror with special squads attacking his suspected enemies. Many victims were boyars, whose lands were confiscated and given to the service nobility, but peasants and servants were also killed. As peasants grew increasingly unhappy, some formed armed groups called Cossacks. Although probably demented, Ivan is also famous for having built the gorgeous gold-domed St. Basil's Cathedral in Moscow.

Ivan's death led not to peace but to a time of troubles when competing claimants to the throne struggled for power, a conflict complicated by the demands of the peasants for a reduction of taxes and obligations and a restoration of their liberties. A former slave led Cossack bands in attacks on nobles and government officials. This rebellion was crushed by the nobles, who in the end elected Michael Romanov as tsar in 1613. It was this dynasty that was overthrown in the Russian Revolution of 1917.

Michael and his successors were able to restore orderly government and expand his realm, taking over the Ukraine and Siberia. The Romanovs built up their army, using foreign experts paid for with the profits from the natural resources (fur and timber) of Siberia. But they could not suppress the social discontent. Cossacks under Stenka Razin attracted widespread support for a revolt in the 1670s in which they violently attacked their oppressors, but they were defeated in the end. Religious discontent also surfaced. The Orthodox Church broke into two hostile factions—the ecclesiastical hierarchy who supported Patriarch Nikon's effort to purify the church, and the Old Believers, largely common people who believed they were holding onto the true religion. The Old Believers were harshly persecuted; about 20,000 burned themselves alive rather than give in.

A description of Russia in the 1630s by the German Olearius (see "A Foreign Traveler in Russia," pp. 586–587) portrayed Russia as a primitive, perhaps bizarre land ruled by a despotic autocrat and filled with drunken, impoverished, and craven people suited only for slavery, although he did say they made brave soldiers and could be dangerous rebels. Strange practices, like saunas, churches without musical instruments, and secluded women among the nobility, added to the sense of Russia as exotic.

Perhaps the most extraordinary of the Romanovs was Peter the Great, a larger-than-life personality who put his mark indelibly on Russia. Peter sought to make Russia a great nation. As a young tsar, he traveled extensively throughout Europe and became determined to bring western technology and many of Europe's ways to Russia.

His reforms were sparked by a disastrous defeat at Narva in 1701 in Peter's war with Russia's main rival in the north, Sweden. Mandatory lifetime military or civil service for nobles was rewarded by titles in a new fourteen-tier ranking of nobility, and each noble was expected to work his way up the ranks. Infantrymen, mostly peasants, also served in the army for life. Five years of education away from home was required for every young nobleman. Peter welcomed talented foreigners, established schools and universities, and built factories and mines worked by forced labor of serfs to meet military needs. Social habits were also changed. Peter ordered the nobles to shave their beards and give up their caftans in favor of western-style men's clothing. Men and women were to attend parties together and were allowed to choose their own spouses. Unigeniture, inheritance only by the oldest child, was imposed. The gulf between the uneducated peasantry and the nobles, some reluctant but others enthusiastic about the new western ideas, grew. Peter's reign meant higher taxes and greater obligations for serfs.

Peter won the important battle of Potlava against the Swedes in 1709, and finally the long and difficult Great Northern War in 1721. Estonia and Latvia became part of the Russian empire. To demonstrate that Russia had taken over from Sweden as the dominant Baltic power, he built a strategic new capital at the mouth of the Neva River on formerly Swedish territory. The land was swampy, the climate damp, and the human cost of building high, but the new city, St. Petersburg, would be very impressive.

AP Tip

One might say that Peter outdid Louis XIV, Leopold I, and every other ruler and ambitious noble who built impressive palaces in the seventeenth century when he built himself a city. Like those palaces, it was designed to both impress visitors and to serve the political needs of the monarch. Expansiveness, spaciousness, rationality, and stunning designs were hallmarks of the architecture of the new city.

After building a fortress there to protect his new and growing navy, Peter planned out a modern, beautiful city modeled on the ones he had seen in western Europe, with canals, stone bridges, parks, street lighting, regulated height of buildings, and the like. He issued various imperial decrees to get the city built and force people to move to it. Huge numbers of peasants were drafted each summer to form building crews (without pay); some ran away and others died in the work. Nobles, merchants, and artisans were ordered to build houses for themselves in the new city and live in them, and also to pay for the embellishment of the city's infrastructure. By Peter's death in 1725, the city had many grand buildings and some 6,000 inhabitants. Development proceeded apace under Elizabeth, Peter's daughter, who made the Italian Rastrelli, the designer of the Winter Palace (now the Hermitage Museum), her chief architect. By the end of the century, some 300,000 people lived in the splendid city Peter built.

THE GROWTH OF THE OTTOMAN EMPIRE

If Russia was seen as a strange place, the Ottoman Empire seemed even more so to Europeans. The fall of Constantinople, strategically important and the last remnant of the Christian Byzantine Empire, to the Muslim Ottoman Turks in 1453 was considered a disaster by Europeans but a great triumph by the Ottomans. Originally Asiatic warriors, the Ottomans quickly conquered the Balkans, North Africa, and much of the Middle East, building one of the great empires of the day. Their greatest ruler was Süleyman the Magnificent, sultan from 1520 to 1566; it was he who defeated the Hungarians at Mohács in 1526.

There were a number of ways in which the Ottoman Empire was distinct from the Russian, Prussian, and Austrian. It had neither hereditary nobility nor private landed property. The janissaries, a slave corps made up of Christian boys taken as a "tax" from the Balkans every year and brought to Istanbul where they were trained and converted to Islam, became either high-level administrators or soldiers in the sultan's army. The women of the palace were isolated in the harem, and by tradition, the sultan procreated only with his concubines, each of whom was allowed to have only one male heir. Süleyman broke tradition when he married his concubine Hürrem, born a slave in the Polish kingdom, and allowed her not only to have six children but also gave her an important place at court. While she was an able diplomat and known for her charities, many Turks saw her as a manipulative social climber who undermined the sultanate (see "Individuals in Society," p. 583). After Süleyman, a sultan's wife began to be more important and palace life became more Europeanized. Government administration also became more European-like as it became more bureaucratic.

AP Tip

The janissary corps often strikes students as a strange idea, but one can see that it made sense to create a special group, far away from their homeland and their families, who would be loyal only to the sultan. In a multicultural state, it also helped, for a long time, to reduce competition for key positions. Later on, the janissaries grew so powerful that they had to be reined in by the sultan. While we can assume that families were unhappy to lose their sons, they often benefited from the wealth and power the sons obtained at the Ottoman court.

In one of their most significant differences from other European states, the Ottomans tolerated people of different faiths and nationalities and offered a haven to persecuted Jews, Muslims, and even Christians from Europe. They accepted Jews and Christians as "people of the book" who deserved respect and protection. Each of the religious—and a few of the national—communities, called a *millet*, had some autonomy and self-government under its own religious or secular leaders. Each millet paid taxes to the state and had its own courts, schools, and hospitals, free to observe their religious or national laws. Greeks, Jews, Armenians, and others lived in reasonable harmony and traded with each other throughout the empire and in and out of Europe. Even as an Islamic state with an influential religious elite and with the Sunni caliphate transferred from Cairo to Istanbul, the Ottoman Empire adopted a flexible Islamic legal code and respected preexisting local laws. Süleyman the Lawgiver began a process of legal centralization to standardize the law code for all Muslims in the Empire.

AP Tip

The millet system allowed for religious freedom in exchange for the payment of taxes that Muslims did not pay. In this way, the Ottomans did not demand conversion, although a number of people in the conquered territories did convert. For example, the Bosnians and Albanians are mostly Muslim to this day. This is quite the opposite of the practice in most European states, where conversion to the dominant religion was usually mandatory and nonconverts were persecuted.

The Ottomans also adopted many of the practices of the peoples they conquered: Byzantine tax systems, Arab spirituality, and Persian political structures. Such openness and the diversity of religions and cultures were important elements in the longevity of the Ottoman Empire. But the Ottomans suffered from many of the crises that beset other parts of Europe, such as peasants' rebellions and political conspiracies, in their case often by janissaries or ambitious courtiers.

They also began to suffer military defeats: they lost the naval battle of Lepanto to Philip II in 1571, and in 1683 had to abandon their siege of Vienna, losing Hungary on the way.

Multiple-Choice Questions

1. A comparison of serfdom in western Europe and eastern Europe would best be summarized as
   (A) in both, serfdom disappeared by 1500.
   (B) in neither had serfdom disappeared by 1500.
   (C) in eastern, but not in western Europe, serfdom was reinstated after 1500.
   (D) in western, but not in eastern Europe, serfdom was reinstated after 1500.
   (E) in both, serfdom had disappeared by 1300 but was reinstated after 1500.

2. During the Thirty Years' War, Prussia
   (A) played a prominent role in the defeat of the Habsburgs.
   (B) allied with the Habsburgs against the Swedes.
   (C) was militarily unimportant.
   (D) was defeated by Gustavus Adolphus at the Battle of Lützen.
   (E) stayed neutral.

3. At the end of the Thirty Years' War, the dominant power in northern Europe was
   (A) Denmark.
   (B) Sweden.
   (C) Prussia.
   (D) Pomerania.
   (E) Finland.

4. Eastern European landlords
   (A) continued to use traditional methods of production and selling.
   (B) paid very low wages to most of their labor force.
   (C) sold their goods to merchants in nearby towns.
   (D) bypassed local towns, selling their goods directly to foreign merchants.
   (E) produced very little surplus that could be sold.

5. After the end of the Peace of Westphalia, the Habsburgs
   (A) turned their attention eastward.
   (B) competed furiously with the Prussians for dominance in the Holy Roman Empire.
   (C) began to allow religious toleration in Bohemia and Hungary.
   (D) moved the capital from Vienna to Budapest.
   (E) crushed the Hungarian nobility.

6. Frederick William I of Prussia was able to build up the German army by
   (A) calling the diet into sessions annually to approve funds.
   (B) hiring well-trained foreign mercenaries.
   (C) expanding the army to become larger than France's.
   (D) opening the officer corps to men of talent, regardless of social class.
   (E) levying taxes without approval by the Prussian Diet.

7. The Prussian towns lost their traditional rights when
   (A) they became Calvinist.
   (B) the nobility refused to support their political claims.
   (C) they renounced them voluntarily.
   (D) the king bought their agreement with financial benefits.
   (E) they admitted Jews as permanent residents.

8. Frederick William I, the Soldiers' King, of Prussia
   (A) thought only soldiers could have militaristic values.
   (B) rarely went to war.
   (C) joined Russia in the Great Northern War.
   (D) built a lavish palace outside of Berlin.
   (E) was the first king of Prussia.

9. The princes of Moscow were able to make it the central state of Russia
   (A) after having been the servants of the Mongols.
   (B) because they had refused for two centuries to serve the Mongols.
   (C) after Ivan the Terrible killed off his opponents.
   (D) because they were blessed by the patriarch of Kiev.
   (E) after its princes moved there from St. Petersburg.

10. Peter the Great's main motive for westernizing Russia was
   (A) political.
   (B) economic.
   (C) military.
   (D) cultural.
   (E) architectural.

11. Which battle is correctly matched?
   (A) Poltava—Peter the Great defeated the Swedes.
   (B) White Mountain—Austria defeated the Ottoman Empire and got Hungary.
   (C) Mohács—The Habsburgs defeated Bohemia.
   (D) Narva—Ivan the Terrible defeated the Mongols.
   (E) Vienna—The Ottomans defeated the Habsburgs.

12. The discontent of Russian peasants under the tsars
   (A) rarely expressed itself in riots or uprisings.
   (B) increased because of rising expectations.
   (C) broke out in a revolt led by Stenka Razin.
   (D) usually was expressed by organized protests in the capital.
   (E) brought them into alliance with urban workers.

13. The slave corps, the janissaries, in the Ottoman Empire
    (A) were horribly treated because they were Christians.
    (B) rose to important positions as administrators and palace guards.
    (C) mostly came from Anatolia (now Turkey).
    (D) were employed as eunuchs in the harems.
    (E) were not allowed to convert to Islam.

14. Which did the Prussian state *not* share with the Ottoman, Russian, and Austrian Empires?
    (A) Absolute monarchs
    (B) Repressed peasantry
    (C) Territorial integrity
    (D) Territorially expansionist regimes
    (E) Great capital cities

15. The Pragmatic Sanction was designed to
    (A) allow a Spanish Habsburg to assume the throne in Austria when Charles VI died without an heir.
    (B) keep the Habsburg empire together.
    (C) prevent a woman from inheriting the throne.
    (D) prevent a Hohenzollern from becoming Holy Roman Emperor.
    (E) keep a Bourbon off the Spanish throne.

Free-Response Questions

1. Analyze the factors that led to the reimposition of serfdom in eastern Europe after 1500. Discuss specific developments in Russia and Austria, as well as general trends.
2. Compare the relationship between monarchs and the nobility in Austria, Prussia, and Russia.

ANSWERS

MULTIPLE-CHOICE QUESTIONS

1. **ANSWER (C)** Western and eastern Europe significantly diverge after 1500 with regard to serfdom, which is reimposed in the East but disappears in the West. (McKay, *A History of Western Society*, 8th ed., pp. 566–569/9th ed., pp. 560–561)

2. **ANSWER (C)** Prussia's rise to military prominence began under Frederick William, the Great Elector, who began to rule in 1640 as the Thirty Years' War was coming to an end. During the war, Prussia was mostly a battleground and a victim of destructive warfare. (McKay, *A History of Western Society*, 8th ed., pp. 573–574/9th ed., pp. 567–570)

3. **ANSWER (B)** Sweden did very well in the Thirty Years' War, winning some German territories, including Pomerania, at the Peace of Westphalia. It remained the dominant state along the Baltic until its

defeat by Russia in the Great Northern War. (McKay, *A History of Western Society*, 8th ed., pp. 498–499/9th ed., pp. 562–563)

4. **ANSWER (D)** Landlords in eastern Europe took control over their distribution of their goods. They sold them directly to foreign merchants, the Dutch for example, bypassing the local towns. The merchant class in eastern Europe remained small. (McKay, *A History of Western Society*, 8th ed., pp. 568–569/9th ed., pp. 560–561)

5. **ANSWER (A)** The Habsburgs conquered Hungary and Transylvania from the Ottomans in the late seventeenth century. There, they made compromises with the Hungarian nobility, allowing them to retain many of their privileges. In Bohemia and Hungary, Protestantism was harshly put down; both states became Catholic. (McKay, *A History of Western Society*, 8th ed., pp. 572–573/9th ed., pp. 565–567)

6. **ANSWER (E)** Prussia built a relatively small but tightly disciplined army, made up of Prussian subjects. It was over the issue of war funding that Frederick William was able to get the Prussian nobility to renounce their rights. They became the officer corps. He did not call the diet into session after 1652. (McKay, *A History of Western Society*, 8th ed., pp. 574–575/9th ed., pp. 567–571)

7. **ANSWER (B)** The key issue when the Prussian towns, such as Königsberg, sought to retain their traditional rights against the demands of the monarchy was the refusal of the nobles to support them. The nobles had already relinquished their political rights. Neither Calvinists nor Jews were issues at the time. The cities were crushed by force. (McKay, *A History of Western Society*, 8th ed., p. 575/9th ed., p. 571)

8. **ANSWER (B)** Frederick William I, the second king of Prussia (the first was his father, Frederick I), loved his soldiers so much that he did not want to waste them in war and so went to war rarely. Russia would not have wanted nor did it need Prussian help against the Swedes. Frederick William lived an austere, soldier's life and disdained luxury. (McKay, *A History of Western Society*, 8th ed., pp. 575–576/9th ed., pp. 571–572)

9. **ANSWER (A)** The princes of Moscow first served the Mongol overlords; only later did Ivan III refuse to pay obeisance to them. St. Petersburg had not yet been built, and Ivan the Terrible inherited the position of prince, although he was the first to take the title tsar. The important patriarch was in Moscow. (McKay, *A History of Western Society*, 8th ed., pp. 577–579/9th ed., pp. 572–574)

10. **ANSWER (C)** It was the need to modernize the army that primarily motivated Peter. To improve the army, he sought western technology, changed the way noble titles were awarded, and required the nobles to become educated and to symbolize their modernization by cutting off their beards and wearing western dress. For most of his reign, he was at war and substantially expanded the empire. (McKay, *A History of Western Society*, 8th ed., pp. 581–585/9th ed., pp. 576–578)

11. **ANSWER (A)** Peter the Great's important victory over the Swedes was at Poltava in 1709; he had lost to them seven years before at Nerva. Mohács was where the Ottomans took Hungary in 1526, losing it 150 years later when they lost the siege of Vienna. The battle of the White Mountain was the end of Bohemian hopes for independence in 1620. (McKay, *A History of Western Society*, 8th ed., pp. 569, 570, 584–585/9th ed., pp. 576–578)

12. **ANSWER (C)** Stenka Razin led a widespread revolt, which was ultimately put down; it was one of many. The conditions of the Russian peasants were getting worse and worse, so expectations were certainly not rising. There were very few urban workers with whom to make alliances. (McKay, *A History of Western Society*, 8th ed., pp. 581, 583/9th ed., p. 576)

13. **ANSWER (B)** The janissary corps was made up of slaves, which meant they had to be Christians as Muslims are not allowed to enslave other Muslims. Young men, taken mostly from the Balkans, were brought to Istanbul, raised as Muslims, and trained for government service. They rose to high positions in the military or civil administration. (McKay, *A History of Western Society*, 8th ed., pp. 571–572/9th ed., p. 582)

14. **ANSWER (C)** Prussia was the only one of the four that consisted of territories that were not contiguous. All four monarchs sought to expand their empire and establish firm control over their state, and they all embellished their capital cities. Prussia was also the only one that was not multiethnic. (McKay, *A History of Western Society*, 8th ed., pp. 573–574/9th ed., p. 567)

15. **ANSWER (B)** The chief goal of the Pragmatic Sanction was to prevent the breakup of the Habsburg empire when Charles VI died without a male heir; it allowed his daughter to inherit the Habsburg lands. It was not specifically designed to exclude the Hohenzollerns or to permit the Spanish Habsburgs from inheriting. (McKay, *A History of Western Society*, 8th ed., p. 573/9th ed., p. 567)

FREE-RESPONSE QUESTIONS

1. General trends: Population decline led to a need to guarantee a labor force; high food prices encouraged estate agriculture, so lords took more and more of the lands of the peasants and imposed heavy labor obligations; a relatively small urban population and small middle classes meant there were few alternatives to serfdom; and weak monarchies needed the cooperation of nobles; and their own lands were worked by unpaid labor.

- Prussia: By law, runaway peasants had to be returned to their lords. Frederick William the Great Elector allowed the nobility virtual freedom of action over their serfs in exchange for relinquishing political say in levying taxes. In 1653 peasants were tied to their lords in hereditary subjugation.
- Austria: Bohemian serfs were obligated by the *robot* system to work three to six days a week for their lord without pay.
- Russia: Serfs began to lose their freedom of movement in the late fifteenth century and lost it completely in 1603. In 1649 the tsar

lifted the statute of limitations on runaway serfs and gave lords unlimited authority over their serfs.

2. Similarities

- In all three states, the monarchs granted nobles virtually unrestricted rights over their serfs, thus guaranteeing wealth in exchange for political power.
- Nobles in all three states served as the officer corps of expanding armies.

Differences

- Russia: Ivan the Terrible required that all nobles serve the tsar in order to own land. He killed many *boyars* in his reign of terror and gave their lands to service nobles who got their titles in return for loyalty to him and military service. The nobles elected Michael Romanov as tsar in 1613 after a period of social disorder. Peter the Great created new rankings for nobles, the Twelve Ranks, rewarding service to the state with higher ranking. All nobles were expected to work their way up the rankings. Military service was for life. Some slots were given to middle-class servants of the state. Nobles were forced by the tsar to dress in European style, become educated, shave their beards, and build and live in fancy houses in his new capital, St. Petersburg.
- Prussia: Frederick William the Great Elector forced the nobles to relinquish their traditional political rights and did not call their representative assembly, the estates or diet, into session at all in the last thirty-six years of his rule. Nobles were given greater authority over their serfs instead. Junkers became the officer corps after Frederick William I threatened to destroy them.
- Austria: Hungarian nobles retained their privileges, allowing Hungary some autonomy after it was conquered and absorbed into the Austrian Empire. Many Protestant Bohemian nobles lost their lands after the Battle of White Mountain in 1620; their lands and titles were given to Catholics usually of German origin who were loyal to the throne.

18

TOWARD A NEW WORLDVIEW, 1540–1715

Over 200 years, scientists and intellectuals created a new worldview, transforming people's understanding of their universe and their place in it. They asked new questions and created new methods for answering those questions. During the scientific revolution, scientists replaced medieval reliance on authorities with experimentation, observation, and mathematical analysis, and arrived at a cosmology that lasted until the twentieth century. In the Enlightenment, intellectuals applied the same light of reason to society, creating the social sciences of economics, psychology, and political science, and advocating concepts of human rights and tolerance. The scientific revolution and the Enlightenment formed the basis of the thinking about the natural world and attitudes about society of modern western societies, and over time, they had spread to much of the rest of the world as well. In a nutshell, their chief characteristics are reason and rationalism, a belief in the possibility of human progress both materially and intellectually, a profound secularism, and a deep commitment to limited government and human liberty. Science and reason, the scientists and philosophes (philosophers) asserted, are the way to discover truth, and with truth, humankind can free itself of its chains. However, there is a dark side to these movements, suspiciousness of or even hostility to religious faith and a certain arrogance toward nature.

KEY CONCEPTS

- The scientific revolution, beginning around 1540, overturned Aristotelian physics and Ptolemaic astronomy. Copernicus advocated the heliocentric theory of the solar system, which was proven through observation and mathematics by Galileo, Kepler, and others. Governments established science societies. Newton discovered the universal law of gravitation.

- The Enlightenment philosophies, centered in France and fostered by conversations held at salons given by well-to-do women, used reason to examine their own societies and discover the scientific laws of human life. In order to allow reason to operate freely, they opposed censorship, religious or political persecution, and autocratic governments; individual rights and intellectual freedom were crucial for human advancement.
- Enlightened monarchs in Austria, Prussia, and Russia, to a lesser degree, reformed their societies according to the principles of the Enlightenment. Reforms included the banning of torture, reduction in the number of capital crimes, religious toleration, and reduction of mercantilist restrictions and the burdens of serfdom. These reforms had varying degrees of success.

THE SCIENTIFIC REVOLUTION

SCIENTIFIC THOUGHT IN 1500

The understanding of natural philosophy, as science was then called, before 1500 was based on the work of the great philosopher Aristotle, with the Ptolemaic system from the second century B.C.E., providing a mathematical explanation for the geocentric theory of the solar system. The natural philosophers of the sixteenth and seventeenth centuries did not see a divide between faith and reason; most of them were of the Christian faith, and many, such as Kepler and Newton, dabbled in occult sciences like alchemy. But they did ask new questions and, with the invention of the telescope, were able to come up with answers that could only be explained by the heliocentric theory proposed by Copernicus.

The Aristotelian cosmology postulated a motionless Earth around which revolved, in perfectly circular orbits, ten crystalline spheres holding and moving unchanging planets and heavens. Aristotle also argued that the earthly and heavenly spheres operated differently, with Earth having four elements while the heavens had a fifth "quintessence." Aristotelian astronomy and physics were held to be true for some 2,000 years, since they provided an explanation for observations and worked with Christian conceptions of the centrality of Earth in God's creation and therefore of humans in the great chain of beings. The church's affirmation of the Aristotelian view led it to criticize those scientists who rejected it.

COPERNICUS AND THE COPERNICAN HYPOTHESIS

The Polish monk Nicolaus Copernicus rejected the Ptolemaic system for its inaccuracies and its cumbersome structures on the basis that its imperfections meant that it could not have been God's creation. He adopted the idea of a heliocentric universe as a better explanation but never doubted Aristotle's crystalline spheres or circular motion. Cautious, he published his work, *On the Revolutions of the Heavenly Spheres,* only in the year of his death, 1543. His thesis postulated that Earth moved and not the stars, that Earth was one planet among others and not special, and that the universe was huge and unlimited by crystalline spheres. Where was God, asked critics attacking the Copernican hypothesis, particularly the Protestants such as Luther and Calvin, and after 1616 the Catholic Church, too. The Copernican thesis was supported by the appearance of a new bright star in 1572 and a comet in 1577 that challenged the Aristotelian notion of unchanging heavens.

FROM BRAHE TO GALILEO

The sixteenth century Danish astronomer Tycho Brahe built an advanced observatory where he made careful observations with the naked eye for twenty years, developing a huge collection of data that was important for later astronomers. He never adopted the Copernican system, although he made some modifications to the Ptolemaic system. His assistant, Johannes Kepler, a brilliant mathematician, originated the three laws of planetary motion showing that the planets' orbits are elliptical and their speeds vary. His mathematical calculations showed how the heliocentric theory worked in detail and invalidated the theories of Aristotle and Ptolemy for good.

The Florentine Galileo Galilei became a professor of mathematics at the University of Pisa in 1589. Galileo tested many Aristotelian ideas about the physics of motion and mechanics through experiments, formulating the law of inertia. This challenged Aristotle's idea that the natural state of matter was rest; instead, an object in motion naturally stays in motion unless stopped. When he applied the same methodology to the heavens, using the newly invented telescope, he discovered that Jupiter had moons; that Earth's moon had craters and the sun had sunspots—making both heavenly bodies imperfect; and that the Milky Way is made up of countless stars. All these discoveries offered indisputable support for the Copernican hypothesis.

What was most significant about Galileo's work was not the science itself but the independence of science or natural philosophy from philosophy and theology. Reliance on authorities, whether classical or religious, was replaced by the scientific method, relying on repeatable and reliable experiments and observations that could be expressed mathematically.

Galileo came under scrutiny by the papacy in 1624, which restricted what he could write. When he published his *Dialogue on the Two Chief Systems of the World* defending the Copernican cosmology some eight years later, he was arrested and put on trial by the Roman Inquisition. Unprotected by the Medici court in Florence where he had been employed, and threatened with torture, Galileo recanted and was placed under house arrest for the rest of his life.

AP Tip

The trial of Galileo is one of the best-known trials in European history. The papacy had not opposed the new science completely; they had hired an astronomer to come up with an improved calendar, the Gregorian calendar in use to this day. Nor was Galileo the first scientist put on trial; Giordano Bruno had been executed a few decades earlier. Galileo's trial and recantation, which almost certainly was not sincere, certainly negatively affected the growth of science in Italy. The papacy apologized for the trial and rehabilitated Galileo only in the twentieth century.

Newton

The brilliant English mathematician and scientist Isaac Newton brought the many threads of the revolutionary scientific work together to create a synthetic cosmology that would only be overturned by the new physics of Einstein and Heisenberg more than 200 years later. Newton's most important discovery was the law of universal gravitation that operates with mathematical precision throughout the universe. That there are mathematical laws of physics and astronomy that explain motion and mechanics on Earth as well as in the skies offered a cosmology of a rational universe explainable by science and mathematics. Newton's most famous work was his *Principia*, published in 1687.

Causes of the Scientific Revolution

- The transformation of medieval universities included the study of natural philosophy: mathematics, astronomy, and physics. Scientists like Galileo and Newton were university professors, working in a community of scholars.
- The Renaissance brought to light Greek mathematical texts, which helped improve European mathematics. Many Renaissance patrons supported scientists.
- Navigational needs, such as the calculation of latitude for long-distance travel, prompted technological advancements useful for sea travel and important scientific instruments as well: the telescope, pendulum clock, microscope, and air pump, among others.
    - The articulation of the scientific method was both a cause and a consequence of scientific work. Two thinkers, with quite different views, developed the scientific method of forming a hypothesis, testing the hypothesis with observation or experiment, and drawing conclusions and expressing them mathematically. Francis Bacon advocated experimental research and the inductive way of reasoning, meaning that general truths are drawn from many empirical facts. Empirical truths are ones that can be confirmed through the senses. Bacon also advocated the great social usefulness of science. René Descartes was a brilliant mathematician who developed analytic geometry,

bringing together algebra and geometry. In his vision of the way to do science, the first rule was to doubt everything, then to use deductive reasoning—going from the general to the specific, as one does in geometry. There were only two types of substances, matter and mind, or the physical and the spiritual. Cartesian dualism was highly influential for centuries.

AP Tip

Cartesian dualism liberated scientists to explore the physical world without having to be concerned about the world of the mind and spirituality. Religion and science were separate spheres and had little or nothing to do with each other. In this way, Descartes acted as a bridge from the seventeenth-century scientific revolution to the eighteenth century Enlightenment. Some commentators would argue that this was crucial for the foundation of western scientific and technological superiority. Cartesian dualism faced many challenges in the twentieth century.

- In religion, Protestantism may have fostered scientific thinking in that it made scientific work a matter of conscience and not of faith. Some Protestant countries like England, Denmark, and Holland quite typically, though not always, encouraged science and, with their interests in international trade, promoted technological innovation. The independence of science from religion was promoted during the English Revolution, in which Bacon had many followers.

SCIENCE AND SOCIETY

A new phenomenon came into being as a result of the scientific revolution: the international community of scientists, sharing common interests and connected through scientific journals and scientific societies. Kings set up academies of science in London (the Royal Society), Paris, and Berlin in the late seventeenth century to promote scientific endeavor and the dissemination of scientific work. Here scientific work was vetted through critical examination by other scientists. Governments also supported research by funding scientific work or building observatories.

Women were typically excluded from membership in scientific academies, and this remained true even at the beginning of the twentieth century. But women scientists found ways to be involved, typically in the type of scientific work that one can do on one's own. Maria Sibylla Merian, for example, went to study insects in Surinam, where she discovered a number of new species. Like several other women, she played an important role as a botanical and zoological illustrator. A few women in Italy became university professors in the seventeenth century, while others—Margaret Cavendish and Mary Astell, among others—in England wrote books on the philosophical debates engendered by scientific work. Nature itself was often described as a woman.

AP Tip

Women also were active astronomers, often collaborating with their husbands, though occasionally making discoveries of their own, as did Maria Winkelmann Kirsch. Medical research was hindered by male chauvinistic beliefs. Madame du Châtelet (see pp. 601–602) made the first French translation of Newton's *Principia*, annotated with her own commentary, thus making his ideas accessible to those who could not read Latin. She, like most of the women scientists, advocated equal access to education for women.

THE ENLIGHTENMENT

The intellectual movement known as the Enlightenment, succinctly delineated at that time in Immanuel Kant's essay "What Is Enlightenment?," was born out of the fruits of the scientific revolution and its liberation from traditional authorities. The Enlightenment itself was a diverse movement, across countries and disciplines, and across political lines. Three key ideas, however, were shared by virtually all Enlightenment thinkers, who are called philosophes.

- Rationalism: All truths must be arrived at through logical, critical thinking, and none should be accepted on faith or authority alone.
- Science: Scientific methods could be used to examine the human world as well as the natural world to discover the laws of human society as they had discovered the laws of the physical world.
- Progress: Humans could use scientific research to find ways to improve life and advance humanity. The golden age was not behind us in classical antiquity or the Garden of Eden but ahead of us.

THE EMERGENCE OF THE ENLIGHTENMENT

The Enlightenment began in the late seventeenth century and reached its culmination in the eighteenth century. It began when writers popularized the new science with books written for the general public. Fontenelle used the dialogue form in his *Conversations on the Plurality of Worlds* to explain the new astronomy. He also expressed skepticism about religion and attacked priests as reactionary in their thinking; he reflected new uncertainties about religious truth and the conformity in ideas demanded by church and state. Pierre Bayle articulated this skepticism from the safe refuge of Holland to which he had gone as a Huguenot (French Protestant). His *Religious and Critical Dictionary*, published in Holland in 1697 but written in French, argued that absolute certainty was impossible and showed the many mistaken ideas of the past, so that open-mindedness and toleration of others' ideas was required. This book was hugely influential and was the most popular book in eighteenth-century France. Europeans had begun to read travel accounts about Asia, Africa, and the Americas, and the great variety of human behaviors and beliefs they learned about encouraged the type of skepticism about absolute truth and morality that Bayle expressed.

John Locke, whose political theories were significant for the Glorious Revolution (see Chapter 16), also offered a highly influential new view of humanity in his *Essay Concerning Human Understanding*, 1690. At birth, the human mind is a *tabula rasa*, a blank slate or tablet. Humans are not born with preconceived ideas as Descartes had postulated or with original sin. Instead their blank slates are written on by society; children develop into what they are taught and learn from experience, so that they can be turned to good or to evil.

AP Tip

Locke's idea of a tabula rasa created the idea that humanity can be remade, and thus underlies the radical theories of communism and fascism, both of which sought to create a new man. It had a huge impact on education and child-rearing practices as well. Locke's belief in a tabula rasa underlay his commitment to popular sovereignty and republicanism outlined in Chapter 16; human beings are born inherently equal in their rights.

THE PHILOSOPHES AND THE PUBLIC

The philosophes proudly announced they were bringing the light of reason and knowledge to the world. The fact that we use a French word to describe this group of philosophers indicates the crucial role France played in the Enlightenment. French was the international language of the time. In addition, after the death of Louis XIV, his successors were less successful in limiting the outflow of new ideas and imposing religious or philosophical orthodoxy. Even with government censorship, France was a less repressive state than many in eastern Europe. Radical books were published abroad or spread in France in manuscript copy from hand to hand. Plays and novels were used as means of disseminating ideas that might be seen as too radical; satirical humor could express a dangerous idea. The philosophes also produced encyclopedias to spread knowledge around, the greatest of which was the seventeen-volume *Encyclopedia: The Rational Dictionary of the Sciences, the Arts, and the Crafts*, edited by Denis Diderot, a writer, and Jean le Rond d'Alembert, a mathematician. Based on the premise that knowledge and the use of reason would improve society and increase happiness, the *Encyclopedia* offered a cornucopia of factual information in hundreds of articles by dozens of authors and with hundreds of illustrations, covering virtually every aspect of life. Its criticisms of religious intolerance and government injustice and its exaltation of science were hugely influential in France, even though it was banned by the government after the publication of the first volume and placed on the church's index of forbidden books.

Several philosophes made important contributions to political theory. Baron de Montesquieu followed Fontenelle in using dialogue, this time between two imagined Persian travelers, to examine and satirize European society in his *Persian Letters,* 1721. The Persians mock the power women hold at court, part and parcel of the absolutist system that easily allowed a king's favorites undue influence. His most important work, *The Spirit of Laws,* was based on scientific exploration of political systems in various parts of the world and showed that climate, geography, and customs influenced the type of political system adopted by a particular society. To prevent abuses of power, Montesqueiu argued for the separation of, and balance of power among, the three branches of government: the legislative, the executive, and the judicial. There should be substantial power in the hands of the nobility to check the power of the king; in France, that meant the courts called parlements.

Voltaire was probably the most famous of all the philosophes, even during his lifetime. A prolific author and shrewd businessman, Voltaire lauded Newton, translated by his friend and companion Madame du Châtelet, as the apostle of reason. He was appointed royal historian in 1743, writing a work praising Louis XIV. As he knew from personal experience how arbitrary the justice system in France was, but lacked faith in the ability of commoners to govern themselves, he hoped for enlightened monarchs who would be both competent and just.

AP Tip

Voltaire's novel *Candide,* a satirical tale of the misadventures of an innocent in Europe and the New World, lampoons virtually all aspects of society, including pretentious intellectuals who argue that "all is for the best in this best of possible worlds." The novel was a best-seller in its time and continues to be popular.

The main objects of Voltaire's criticisms were the Catholic Church, especially Jesuits and theology in general; the intolerance and oppression they represented; and the fanaticism and savagery they often encouraged. Voltaire, like many other philosophes, believed in God as a creator, a clockmaker who makes the clock and then lets it run according to his laws. His *Philosophical Dictionary* (see the excerpt on pp. 618–619) criticized the terrible killings done in the name of religion and the hypocrisy of religious leaders in an imagined dialogue with Jesus.

AP Tip

Such a religious philosophy is called Deism. God created this world and gave man reason to understand it, but is neither involved directly in human affairs nor redeems mankind. Deists tended to support the separation of church and state and encouraged respect for other religions. Many of the founding fathers of the United States were deists.

Rousseau, who died the same year as Voltaire, offered quite a different political theory, one that was crucially important in the revolutions in France and Russia and was also the progenitor of Romanticism. He broke with his fellow philosophes in the 1750s when, instead of seeing reason as the key to liberation, he argued that it destroyed the individual by boxing in feeling and spontaneity. Similarly, children were basically good and were only harmed by becoming civilized. Women should not aspire to be sophisticated; their proper sphere was in the home, tending, and even breast feeding, their children themselves, in opposition to the then standard practice of employing other women, called wet nurses, to breast-feed the children.

Fiercely committed to individual freedom, Rousseau argued for popular sovereignty, an idea relatively new on the continent. The people hold sovereign power, and their common, long-term interests, which he called the general will, are absolute. How should the general will be made known? Not through representative democracy or the will of the majority, as Locke would recommend, because the majority may be wrong and in any case can be tyrannical toward the minority. Instead, the general will is likely to be made known to a minority, who then should have complete authority. It is this idea that later appealed to dictators and radicals.

URBAN CULTURE AND THE PUBLIC SPHERE

The ideas of the philosophes were spread in several ways. One was through an explosion of book production, both in the number of books printed and in their purchase by consumers. Some scholars have argued that a reading revolution was under way; whereas as before it was typically the patriarch of the household who read aloud to others, reading became more democratic, more widespread, and also private and silent. Lending libraries helped those too poor to buy their own books. Another important venue for the dissemination of ideas was the salon, social gatherings organized by wealthy women in Paris, such as Madame Geoffrin, where clever and free-ranging conversation was valued, and men and women of the middle and upper classes could meet and speak freely. Perhaps the influence of these women encouraged some of the philosophes to promote education for women. Madame Geoffrin was important for her support for the *Encyclopedia*, both financially and in welcoming its editors regularly in her home. These *salonnières* (hostesses of salons) also influenced artists towards the rococo, a highly florid and sentimental style. Coffeehouses, which had first appeared in the seventeenth century, served a function similar to the salon for more ordinary people. Salons, libraries, book clubs, and coffeehouses, all were parts of a public sphere that encouraged public discourse on the issues of the day. Although most philosophes disdained the common people, evidence shows that the common people were learning about the new ideas through inexpensive pamphlets, which were sometimes read out loud.

THE ENLIGHTENMENT OUTSIDE FRANCE

Enlightened thinkers were active in most parts of Europe, as well as in America. In England and Germany, they sought to reconcile science and faith. Scotland was brought into union with Britain in 1707 and quickly became a center of the Enlightenment. It had the first public school system in Europe. Two figures stand out from the eighteenth-century Scottish Enlightenment: the philosopher David Hume and the economist Adam Smith (see Chapter 19). David Hume saw the human mind as a bundle of impressions created by sensory experiences. Reason is limited to analyzing through scientific or mathematical investigation only those impressions; it cannot evaluate any other issue such as the existence of God. Adam Smith analyzed the law of supply and demand to argue against mercantilism and for free-enterprise capitalism.

In Germany, the outstanding Enlightenment thinker was Immanuel Kant, the greatest philosopher of his age, who argued for both freedom of the press and obedience to law, however unjust. His call, *Sapere Aude!* (Dare to Know!), became the motto of the Enlightenment.

Race and the Enlightenment

The scientific revolution and the Enlightenment, and the European experience of other civilizations and cultures as they traded around the world, radically changed the concept of race. Philosophes often used non-European cultures as foils for seeing their own. As scientists observed nature, some such as the Swedish botanist Carl von Linné believed it was organized hierarchically. Humans too were organized into hierarchies determined by race, now defined as biologically determined differences. Europeans began to define themselves as not only culturally superior but racially superior as well. Hume and Kant both popularized such ideas, describing other races as uncivilized, inferior, and degenerate. Although some intellectuals challenged such ideas, most philosophes shared racist views and used them to justify slavery and colonialism. Similarly, ideas about women's natural passivity and inferiority were considered scientific.

The Enlightenment and Absolutism

As noted above, most of the philosophes, with the rare exception of Rousseau, were not advocates of democracy; instead they argued that change could and would come only from the top. Benevolent or enlightened absolutism was the best means of improving society, and many rulers were indeed interested in the new ideas. Frederick the Great and Catherine the Great were both correspondents of Voltaire, who lived at Frederick's court for three years. Although many smaller states such as Denmark had successful enlightened monarchs, it was in Prussia, Austria, and Russia that Enlightenment ideas were put into practice, with varying degrees of success. There the monarchs spread the secular ideas of the Enlightenment and fostered the arts and education. Yet, all in all, the reforms were modest; the lives of the peasants in these states remained hard and got even harder in Russia. Historians now see the attempts of these rulers at reform as a continuation of the state-building efforts of their predecessors. Legal reforms and religious toleration can be seen as ways to make the people happier and more productive. The fact that the rulers instituted reforms from above only showed they retained absolutist ideas.

In Prussia, Frederick the Great was impassioned about the arts as a young man, much to the dismay of his militaristic father, Frederick William I. But when he became king in 1740, he broke the Pragmatic Sanction and invaded Austrian lands in order to take Silesia, an area rich in iron ore and coal. Although Maria Theresa ultimately won the War of the Austrian Succession, she had to cede Silesia to Prussia, which thereby doubled its population. Frederick also survived the attempt to cripple Prussia in the Seven Years' War, known as the French and Indian War in America, but only by the fluke of fate that suddenly Peter III, who admired Prussia, became tsar and called off the attack. In the wake of this near defeat, Frederick implemented some of the ideas of the Enlightenment. He promoted religious toleration and intellectual freedom and improved Prussia's schools. He simplified the law code, abolished torture of prisoners, and demanded impartial legal judgments. His officials were expected to be honest and hardworking, as Frederick was himself as the "first servant of the state." However, Frederick maintained the nobility in their privileges and in their domination over the serfs. He also would not extend religious toleration to Jews, in spite of the pleas of Moses Mendelssohn, a representative of the Jewish Enlightenment who sought to modernize Jewish thinking along Enlightenment principles. Mendelssohn argued that reason and faith, while different spheres, should strengthen each other rather than be antagonistic.

AP Tip

Mendelssohn and the Jewish Enlightenment initiated the modern era of Jewish life, in which Jews kept their faith and their practice but participated fully in the intellectual and cultural life of the society in which they lived. Intellectual Enlightenment in the eighteenth century would be joined by the lifting of restrictions beginning in the nineteenth century.

In Russia, Catherine the Great, born a German princess and impassioned about the Enlightenment, became tsar after deposing her husband Peter III, who was later murdered. She continued the westernization of Russia initiated by Peter the Great by importing art and artists and intellectuals to Russia. She sent letters to Voltaire and funds to Diderot. She set the model for the nobles by writing plays and engaging in witty conversation herself. Catherine attempted a number of domestic reforms: a unified law code (never quite finished), restriction of torture, limited religious toleration, educational improvement, and reform of local government. But a huge peasants' revolt led by Pugachev ended her intentions to reduce the burdens of serfdom. In fact, she gave the nobles absolute authority over their serfs in the late 1770s and extended serfdom to the Ukraine. She later exempted the nobles from taxation and state service.

Catherine followed in Peter the Great's footsteps by expanding Russia's territory and its international trade. Russia, Austria, and Prussia took advantage of the weak Polish monarchy, elected by the nobles, and cut Poland up among themselves three times in the late eighteenth century (1772, 1793, and 1795). As an independent state, Poland was wiped off the map of Europe.

> **AP Tip**
>
> In Poland, more than in any other European country, the aristocrats had kept their political power. The end result was a weak monarchy and ineffective decision making by the aristocratic assembly. The restoration of Poland was a major Allied goal in World War I, one of Wilson's Fourteen Points.

THE AUSTRIAN HABSBURGS

Joseph II, who ruled for only ten years, 1780 to 1790, initiated the most far-reaching reforms of any enlightened monarch. His mother, Maria Theresa, initiated reforms herself, limiting the role of the papacy in the kingdom, strengthening the central bureaucracy, and improving the tax system—even taxing the nobles—and reducing the power of the lords over their serfs and peasants. Joseph granted religious toleration and extended rights to both Protestants and Jews, and abolished serfdom, ordering that all labor obligations be remunerated with cash. These radical edicts were canceled when Joseph II died and his brother inherited the throne. This counterreform indicated how entrenched the old system was.

Over the next two centuries, Enlightenment values of reason, skepticism, and working toward societal improvement spread so that they are now the guiding principles of most European states and others around the globe. They have been challenged and continue to be so to this day. The promise of these ideals has not yet been fulfilled.

Multiple-Choice Questions

1. Before the scientific revolution, people seeking scientific information generally found it in
   (A) the Bible.
   (B) statements issued by the church.
   (C) the writings of Aristotle.
   (D) the writings of St. Thomas Aquinas.
   (E) Chinese texts.

2. Kepler's relationship to the Copernican thesis was to
   (A) prove it by using the telescope.
   (B) reject it as had his mentor Tycho Brahe.
   (C) challenge it because it did not include the harmony of the spheres.
   (D) provide mathematical proof for it.
   (E) denounce Galileo for denying the church.

3. Newton provided the theory to explain which of Galileo's observations?
   (A) That Jupiter has moons as Earth does
   (B) That the moon's surface is uneven and rough
   (C) That the Milky Way is filled with stars
   (D) That the moon is not perfectly spherical
   (E) That bodies have a uniform rate of acceleration

4. Cartesian dualism can best be described as the division between
   (A) truth and untruth.
   (B) science and humanities.
   (C) mind and matter.
   (D) right and wrong.
   (E) the heavens and the earth.

5. Which was *not* a cause of the scientific revolution?
   (A) The recovery of ancient mathematical texts during the Renaissance
   (B) The search for the physical location of the soul within the body
   (C) The patronage of princes and kings
   (D) New technology
   (E) The establishment of chairs in physics and mathematics at universities

6. Who first articulated the social usefulness of scientific knowledge?
   (A) Galileo
   (B) Bacon
   (C) Kepler
   (D) Newton
   (E) Margaret Cavendish

7. The chief difference between the scientific revolution and the Enlightenment is
   (A) the gender of the scientists, all male, and the philosophes, many female.
   (B) the country in which each began.
   (C) the focus of scientific inquiry.
   (D) the religions of the scientists and philosophes.
   (E) the attitude of the church.

8. Which philosophe believed in popular sovereignty?
   (A) Voltaire
   (B) Montesquieu
   (C) Rousseau
   (D) Fontenelle
   (E) Diderot

9. Descartes and Bayle would agree on the importance of
   (A) mathematics.
   (B) doubt.
   (C) empirical research.
   (D) believing in God.
   (E) constitutional monarchy.

10. Locke's concept of the tabula rasa was taken in the eighteenth century to mean that
    (A) humans were not born with original sin.
    (B) public education ought to be established for all children.
    (C) enlightened monarchy was the best form of government.
    (D) rebellion was a natural right.
    (E) parents could have little influence over their children.

11. Madame du Châtelet's importance in the Enlightenment was due to her role as
    (A) an important *salonnière*.
    (B) a correspondent of Catherine the Great.
    (C) mistress of Voltaire.
    (D) adviser to Peter the Great.
    (E) translator of Newton.

12. Which was a common practice of the Enlightened monarchs?
    (A) Abolition of serfdom
    (B) Religious toleration for Jews
    (C) Public education
    (D) Abolition of torture
    (E) Re-establishing legislative assemblies

13. Catherine the Great's effort at reforms came to a virtual end when
    (A) the nobles of Russia resisted.
    (B) Voltaire publicly criticized her, thus humiliating her.
    (C) the peasants rose in the Pugachev revolt.
    (D) Prussia declared war on Russia.
    (E) she was assassinated by a former lover.

14. Diderot's *Encyclopedia*
    (A) was published in its entirety in France.
    (B) democratized knowledge.
    (C) was read by a small number of people because it was so expensive.
    (D) had little technical information.
    (E) was published in part with funds from Frederick the Great.

15. The term *reading revolution* refers to
    (A) nearly universal literacy in the eighteenth century.
    (B) the new literacy of women.
    (C) the way reading became private and silent.
    (D) the great expansion in the number and variety of newspapers during the Enlightenment.
    (E) the public reading of the texts of the philosophes.

Free-Response Questions

1. To what degree and in what ways were ordinary people affected by the scientific revolution and the Enlightenment?

2. Evaluate the degree to which the political ideas of Rousseau and Montesquieu are representative of main thrusts of Enlightenment thought.

ANSWERS

MULTIPLE-CHOICE ANSWERS

1. ANSWER (C) Aristotle was the main source of information for more than 2,000 years because he had written on virtually every field of science. The Bible was not read very much except by Protestants and not for scientific information. The church and St. Thomas Aquinas, the great scholastic of the thirteenth century, were not focused on science. Chinese texts would have had much scientific information, but they were not available at that time. (McKay, *A History of Western Society*, 8th ed., p. 596/9th ed., pp. 590–591)

2. ANSWER (D) Although Kepler did have mystical tendencies, it was his three laws of planetary motion expressed mathematically that proved Copernicus's theory. Kepler was already dead when Galileo was tried by the Inquisition. His mentor, Tycho Brahe, never fully accepted Copernican theory, but Kepler did. (McKay, *A History of Western Society*, 8th ed., pp. 598–601/9th ed., p. 592)

3. ANSWER (E) While the other four observations were crucial for proving Copernican theory, it was Galileo's experiments with falling and moving bodies that could only be explained Newton's theory of universal gravitation. (McKay, *A History of Western Society*, 8th ed., pp. 598–601/9th ed., pp. 592–595)

4. ANSWER (C) Cartesian dualism postulates that mind is separate from matter. Man therefore is free to explore the physical world since such exploration cannot affect the spiritual world. (McKay, *A History of Western Society*, 8th ed., p. 603/9th ed., pp. 595–596)

5. ANSWER (B) When scientists and physicians began to do autopsies, a few did search for the soul, but this was not a major cause of the new science. Kings and princes played an important role by providing funds for observatories, as the king of Denmark did for Tycho Brahe. (McKay, *A History of Western Society*, 8th ed., pp. 598, 602–603/9th ed., pp. 592, 595)

6. ANSWER (B) Bacon's importance lay not only in his defense of empiricism and the experimental method but also in his claims that science would benefit society and improve people's lives. Galileo, Kepler, and Brahe were more interested in scientific work than in developing a theory of science. Margaret Cavendish wrote on the new philosophy but later in the century. (McKay, *A History of Western Society*, 8th ed., p. 603/9th ed., pp. 595–598)

7. ANSWER (C) The main difference is that in the seventeenth century, natural philosophers explored the physical world, while in the eighteenth century, they studied the human world. There is no consistent pattern of ethnicity, nationality, or religion; they are similar

only in that almost all of the public intellectual work was done by men. (McKay, *A History of Western Society*, 8th ed., p. 605/9th ed., pp. 597–598)

8. ANSWER (C) Only Rousseau advocated popular sovereignty; the others all supported enlightened monarchy as the best system. (McKay, *A History of Western Society*, 8th ed., pp. 611–612, 615/9th ed., pp. 41-42, 46-47)

9. ANSWER (B) Both Descartes and Bayle argued that one must begin an inquiry with doubt. Bayle was the leading skeptic of the Enlightenment. (McKay, *A History of Western Society*, 8th ed., pp. 603, 607/9th ed., pp. 607–609)

10. ANSWER (A) If children are born blank slates, there can be nothing like original sin: this was a major change in the understanding of the nature of humans. It meant that parents' influences were all-important. Public education would not be a popular idea for another hundred years. (McKay, *A History of Western Society*, 8th ed., p. 607/9th ed., p. 595–596, 599–600)

11. ANSWER (E) By translating Newton, she made his scientific work available to French readers across Europe and thereby encouraged the use of reason and rationalism. (McKay, *A History of Western Society*, 8th ed., p. 609/9th ed., pp. 601–602)

12. ANSWER (D) All the enlightened monarchs promoted legal reforms, although to varying degrees. Only Joseph II abolished serfdom and instituted religious toleration for Jews. (McKay, *A History of Western Society*, 8th ed., pp. 616, 619, 620/9th ed., pp. 610, 613–615)

13. ANSWER (C) When the peasants rose in rebellion under Pugachev, Catherine abandoned her reform efforts. The nobles' position was strengthened, not weakened, under Catherine. Voltaire never humiliated her in print. Catherine died a natural death. (McKay, *A History of Western Society*, 8th ed., pp. 612–613/9th ed., p. 613)

14. ANSWER (B) Diderot's efforts were underwritten by Catherine the Great, not Frederick. The *Dictionary* was a hugely popular work, published mostly abroad because of censorship. It was filled with technical knowledge and helped democratize knowledge, which was its aim. (McKay, *A History of Western Society*, 8th ed., pp. 598–601/9th ed., pp. 602–603, 612–613)

15. ANSWER (C) A greatly enlarged literate population began to read silently and privately, in contrast to the typical reading aloud by the head of the household in the evenings to his family and guests. (McKay, *A History of Western Society*, 8th ed., pp. 598–601/9th ed., pp. 604–605)

FREE-RESPONSE ANSWERS

1. Common people were affected in both positive and negative ways by the scientific revolution and the Enlightenment.

- Positive effects: There was a belief that human reason, given by God to all people, who are born with a tabula rasa, will underpin efforts to establish democratic forms of government. A few wealthy or talented individuals gained influence because of their intellect. The reading revolution empowered individual readers to learn and interpret on their own. The huge explosion in publishing and particularly the *Encyclopedia* encouraged literacy and empowered people without formal education. Libraries disseminated books to the poor. Coffeehouses provided venues for the discussion of new ideas. Legal reforms enacted by enlightened monarchs eliminated or reduced torture and the worst abuses of the traditional legal system. Enlightened monarchs also encouraged the education of the lower orders in order to have better trained soldiers and workers. The secular and skeptical spirit of both movements helped reduce the influence of religion and the church.
- Negative effects: The highest level of philosophical inquiry and discussion was reserved for the elites in salons run by wealthy women. Scientific classifications of the natural world led to classifications of the human world, providing justifications for racism and sexism. There was little improvement in working or living conditions; in Russia, the conditions of the serfs worsened under Catherine the Great. Women were excluded from scientific academies and were limited mostly to a supporting role during the Enlightenment.

2. While Montesquieu's ideas were typical in many ways of the Enlightenment, those of Rousseau were quite distinct.
   - Montesquieu represents the typical philosophe in his scientific examination of political systems. Creating a new social science, he argued that climate, geography, and other nonpolitical elements affect the political system. He was concerned to defend the rights of individuals and argued for a constitutional government to protect them, one in which the legislative, executive, and judicial powers are separated and can check each other. Such a system would prevent abuse of power by any of the branches of the government. Montesquieu was also typical in his belief that a strong aristocracy was necessary to prevent royal despotism. His *Persian Letters* was typical in that the philosophes used foreigners as foils to point out the deficiencies of the European system. Like many philosophes, he admired the English system. Montesquieu was a frequent visitor at the salons in Paris.
   - Rousseau on the other hand used the reasoning methods of the Enlightenment, but came to quite different conclusions. He argued that reason was a chain, not a liberator, and that it would be better to trust one's feelings and emotions. Civilization corrupted the innocence and basic goodness of humans. Politically, he was a believer in popular

sovereignty and radical democracy, in which a minority might know the long-term interests of the people—the general will—and would therefore have the right to absolute rule. This was the path to individual freedom. Majority rule was not a reliable protector of freedom. Rousseau lived in isolation from the other philosophes and was alienated from the world of the salons. He rejected the elitist attitudes and the belief in reason of the Enlightenment.

19

THE EXPANSION OF EUROPE IN THE EIGHTEENTH CENTURY

The eighteenth century saw enormous changes in the lives of ordinary people, with agricultural improvements and new patterns of manufacturing, a rapid rise in population, and increasing prosperity, particularly in the Atlantic countries involved in colonization and trade in Asia, Africa, and the Americas. These widespread economic changes set the stage for the Industrial Revolution and are comparable in their significance to the economic and social expansion in the eleventh and twelfth centuries that paved the way for the Renaissance.

KEY CONCEPTS

- An agricultural revolution, involving the enclosure of common lands, the use of new crops, and the application of scientific principles to agriculture, led to a great burst in agriculture productivity. England was at the forefront of these changes.
- The European population increased dramatically in the eighteenth century.
- Cloth manufacturing moved out of towns, where guilds held tight control, to the countryside, where spinning and weaving were done in peasant cottages. Guilds prospered in towns in the seventeenth and eighteenth centuries. Crucial changes in attitudes about work and the employment of children and women as wage workers marked an industrious revolution.
- Colonial markets provided ready consumers of European goods, benefiting manufacturing interests, both individuals and states. Europeans competed with each other for control over these colonial markets and adopted mercantilism to improve their

economies. The Atlantic states—particularly England, France, and Holland—grew wealthy and increasingly competitive with each other.

- Adam Smith developed a new economic theory called economic liberalism that opposed mercantilism for its hindrance of competition. His theory held that governments should limit themselves to a protective function and leave the economy free to operate. Such laissez-faire policies would promote social harmony and the general welfare.

Agriculture and the Land

Throughout Europe, agriculture remained the predominant part of the economy, with some 80 percent of the population of western Europe engaged in farming of one sort or another, a percentage that was even higher in eastern Europe. At the beginning of the eighteenth century, crop yields remained low, perhaps 5 or 6 bushels harvested for each bushel planted, and bad harvests occurred with depressing regularity, every eight or nine years. This made the people vulnerable to diseases like smallpox and influenza. During famines, the poor were driven to eat unhealthy foods like bark or grass. Most Europeans practiced the open-field system, developed in the Middle Ages, dividing large fields into strips, and continually faced exhaustion of the soil. In order to restore nitrates to the soil, one-half or one-third of the land had to be left fallow (unplanted) each year. Open fields, called the commons, were used by all as grazing lands for their animals and for gleaning.

In western Europe, but not in eastern Europe, peasants were not bound to the soil; they were free but burdened by high taxes, inadequate land, and unending poverty. They had limited options. Violence might win them an improvement of their condition, as happened during the French Revolution (see Chapter 21), but usually resulted in repression. What did bring improvement was new technology and ideas that eliminated leaving land fallow, automatically increasing production by a third or a half. This is what is meant by the term agricultural revolution, which had several components.

The first of these was crop rotation. The land that would in the past have been left fallow was planted with crops that restore nitrates to the soil—peas, beans, turnips, potatoes, clover, and grasses. Farmers experimented with different cycles of crop rotation and with different crops for different land. The resulting increased productivity meant that there was more feed for animals, and thus more animals, leading to more manure, and, with more manure, higher productivity. More sheep and cattle also meant more meat; more wheat meant more bread and porridge. The diet of the ordinary European improved.

A controversial aspect of the agricultural revolution was the enclosure movement, that is, the enclosure of the common lands originally used by everyone to graze their animals. Landowners who wanted to experiment with new methods and new crops sought to create larger fields and to fence them in. Smaller landowners, the vast majority of the peasants, were opposed to enclosure. They resisted enclosure more successfully in France and Germany than in England and the Netherlands.

AP Tip

Because such enclosures broke traditional rights, an act of Parliament was necessary in England to enclose the common fields in those cases where private initiatives would not suffice. For this reason, historians have a great deal of evidence about enclosure, which began in the early seventeenth century in England. The fact that the enclosure movement in Germany and France was much less extensive was a reason that farms there tended to remain small, and since larger farms generate greater surplus capital, industrialization did not begin there until the nineteenth century.

THE LEADERSHIP OF THE LOW COUNTRIES AND ENGLAND

Holland was probably the most advanced country in Europe at the beginning of the eighteenth century, with its well-established constitutional government, tradition of tolerance, and extraordinarily successful trading empires. It also had the lowest percentage of the population engaged in agriculture at that time, and quite sophisticated farmers, forced to be innovative because of the particular position of the Dutch lands, farmed dangerously close to sea level. Holland's urban population lived in the most crowded cities in Europe, providing a ready market for the farmers, who soon developed the commercial attitudes found among the Dutch urban residents. They drained swamps and marshes to put them under cultivation, and specialized in what they grew. Holland became the place where other European agriculturists could learn the most up-to-date techniques. Dutch experts helped drain English marshes and swamps in the seventeenth century and created some of the most fertile land in England.

England's Jethro Tull was an important agricultural innovator, advocating the use of horses over oxen in the pulling of ploughs, drilling equipment rather than hand sowing for seeding, and selective breeding of livestock. His empirical approach to farming reflected the rationalism of the Enlightenment. By the mid-eighteenth century when he died, English agriculture was well on its way to a fundamental transformation and an extraordinary increase in productivity. Most British farms were enclosed by the end of the eighteenth century, so that only a tiny minority of the English and Scots owned the vast majority of the land, which they used for market-oriented agriculture. Often the large landowners rented out land to farmers with middle-sized holdings, who used landless agricultural workers for their laborers. By 1870, British farmers were producing 300 percent more food than they had produced in 1700. It was because of such availability of foodstuffs that urbanization could proceed; this also gave the landless rural poor the chance to move to the cities to improve their lot. The landless worker in England was experiencing proletarianization, being turned into a laborer and wage-earner, to a degree not found elsewhere in Europe.

> **AP Tip**
>
> This is no doubt why it was easier to turn landless workers into factory workers and miners, a process that they resisted to a large degree in the early years. The extent of the agricultural revolution in England is one of the most important factors why the Industrial Revolution took place there.

The Beginning of the Population Explosion

The population grew in Europe beginning in the eighteenth century and did not stop for another 200 years. But before that, contrary to some popular misconceptions, population growth was slow and erratic. The population had dropped precipitously during the Black Death, allowing a better standard of living to those who survived, and it took about 200 years for it to return to pre-1348 levels. A population surge after 1500 was not matched by a surge in agriculture productivity, so high food prices, compounded by the price revolution caused by the infusion of gold and silver from the New World, led to a general decline in living standards. As a result, in the seventeenth century, population growth stagnated at the slow rate of 1 percent per year on average, higher in some areas like Russia and lower in France. Occasional higher birth rates were offset by demographic catastrophes like recurrent epidemics, war, and famines. For example, the population of the Germanic states dropped by about two-thirds during the Thirty Years' War (see Chapter 17). Plague continued to be a problem; during its last major outbreak at Marseilles in 1720, some 100,000 people died.

But in the eighteenth century, a distinctly new pattern of noticeable population growth appeared, in all regions and all types of societies. The basic cause was a marked decline in the death rates, rather than an increase in the birth rates, and Europe-wide improvements in public health measures. A number of factors led to the fall in death rates, some of which were promoted by governments.

- There was an almost mysterious disappearance of the plague. It may have resulted from more extensive use of quarantines.
- Inoculation against smallpox, through the efforts of Lady Montagu and Edward Jenner, was important for England although hardly used on the continent in the eighteenth century.
- Improvements in water supply and sewage systems and swamp drainage reduced diseases like typhoid and typhus in urban areas in western Europe and diminished the number of disease-carrying flies and mosquitoes.
- The building of roads and canals in western Europe expanded greatly, allowing for the easier circulation of foodstuffs from areas where there was plenty to areas in need.
- Warfare in the eighteenth century became less destructive and more gentlemanly.
- New crops, such as the potato from South America, grew well in European soils and provided more nutritious sustenance for the poor.

COTTAGE INDUSTRY

Until the Industrial Revolution of the nineteenth century, the most important industry worldwide and in Europe was the textile industry, mostly wool and linen. The changes in agricultural production and the rise in population meant insufficient land and unreliable employment for the many peasants, who found ways to supplement their meager incomes through textile production in what has been called the cottage industry or the putting-out system.

AP Tip

It also was sometimes called the domestic system because production occurred in the home. The term *putting out* comes from the fact that the capitalist put out, or gave out, the work to peasants.

In this form of capitalism, the merchants typically lent the tools of production—looms and spinning wheels—to peasants, brought the raw materials to them in their cottages, paid them by the piece rather than by the hour, and collected the finished work—thread or cloth—from them to sell in the market. There were many variations on this system, with the rural peasants working independently or collaboratively. Each step of the woolen cloth production process would typically be done by a different person and sometimes by different families. Families quite typically worked together, and sometimes they owned their own looms and spinning wheels. In addition to wool, other items were manufactured in this way: clocks, knives, and housewares, among others. For the capitalists, this system gave them the advantage of avoiding the restrictions of the guild system, which continued to dominate in towns and cities. Without the supervision of the guilds, the merchant capitalists could pay lower wages and also experiment with newer methods of production.

The cottage industry was particularly strong in England, which, as noted above, was also one of the most advanced in agriculture productivity. By 1500, the cottage industry produced half of England's textiles, and this proportion grew over time. In the eighteenth century, the cottage industry expanded throughout continental Europe.

Typically, rural workers lived in small, sparsely furnished one-room cottages. Where they participated in the putting-out system, the loom would dominate the cottage. Weaving was considered man's work, but the children and women would help out by preparing threads for weaving. In England, women performed the crucial job of spinning (ergo the term *spinster*), crucial in that it required the work of four or five spinners to provide enough thread for a single weaver. On the continent, however, men and women both spun.

The relationships between merchants and workers in the cottage system were rarely harmonious, with merchants doing whatever they could to keep down wages and often accusing workers of stealing the raw materials. Workers, particularly women whose wages were terribly low, earning perhaps one-quarter of what a male weaver or wool comber (one who cleaned the wool) earned, were suspicious of the merchant capitalists as well. Capitalists had a hard time controlling the laborers, whose timetable was still fundamentally determined by the agricultural calendar, so during planting and harvest time there would be a substantial drop in textile production, particularly of thread. The merchants bitterly complained about the lazy spinners and insisted on keeping wages low to encourage them to produce more. They won the right to punish workers for small infractions, such as gleaning (taking what was left over), which workers believed was their traditional right; peasants typically gleaned from the common lands.

Urban Guilds

Historians now argue that the high point of the guild system was not the Middle Ages but the seventeenth and eighteenth centuries. As towns expanded in size, so too did guilds in both number and size, sometimes because of government encouragement. Louis XIV's finance minister Colbert, for example, gave guilds special privileges and monopolies to promote the production of high-quality French goods.

Guilds aimed to provide a secure living for their members and therefore limited the number of shops in any craft or trade that could be opened, and restricted competition by maintaining quality standards. Guild membership, which gave the right to open a shop and hire workers, was tightly controlled, restricted to men, many with family connections, who demonstrated the quality of their work by creating a masterpiece. Guilds also served a variety of functions in addition to the production and selling of goods. They acted as educational institutions, training apprentices in their crafts, and as social centers and foci of group identity, marching proudly in communal processions with their corporate insignias.

The degree to which the guilds controlled the urban economies varied a great deal from place to place. In England, for example, national regulations often trumped guild regulations. In France, both guild and nonguild production was encouraged by the monarchy. Guilds were most powerful in Germany and lasted longer there than in either England or France, although as revealed in the document at the end of the chapter *Breakdown of the Guilds in Germany*, there too guilds had to make compromises with those who worked outside the guild system.

Historians have long debated the role of the guilds in Europe (see "Listening to the Past," pp. 650–651). Previously the general view was that the guilds impeded technological changes and the progression to modern capitalism by blocking the free movement of people and goods. When the bourgeoisie dominated France during the revolution in 1791, they abolished the guilds. Recently historians have argued that the guilds were remarkably flexible and vital in the eighteenth century, with guild masters adopting new production techniques and relying on guild standards to create trust with consumers. Over the seventeenth and eighteenth centuries, some guilds also opened their doors to women, particularly in dressmaking. Colbert created a new all-female guild for seamstresses in Paris or allowed them to join tailors' guilds. Similar changes happened in England and the

Netherlands; in many places, needlework training centers were created for women. Women workers also began to be hired in other guilds, even against traditional regulations, and in 1777, fourteen years before their abolition, all guilds in France were opened to women. Journeymen's associations often, however, upheld traditional values and methods of production. They resisted the proletarianization that would accompany mechanization of work.

The changes in rural and urban production were accompanied by new attitudes and values, which one historian has called the industrious revolution. People worked harder and restricted their leisure time. Particularly important was that women and children turned from unpaid work in the household and farm to paid work. Households could therefore produce more goods, earn more income, and participate more fully in the consumer economy. But there is much debate about this, particularly in terms of the impact on women, who typically worked long hours for very low wages at menial and tedious tasks, performing a crucial, dynamic role in the cottage industry. There's some evidence that this economic role gave them a greater say in household decision making and allowed them a few items of personal luxury. The industrious revolution paved the way for the Industrial Revolution (see Chapter 22), by creating households where all the members worked for wages and produced for the market. Only in the nineteenth century was the notion of the male as the breadwinner—making enough money to support the whole family and excluding women and children as workers—possible. Some commentators argue that a second industrious revolution is underway in the twenty-first century in the global economy, with poorly paid women once again crucial parts of the workforce.

BUILDING THE GLOBAL ECONOMY

World trade expanded enormously in the eighteenth century. In Europe, this trade was dominated above all by Great Britain (formed in 1707 when England and Scotland combined to form one kingdom), with France and Holland, and to a lesser extent, Spain and Portugal, also significant. It was clearly the Atlantic states in Europe that took most advantage of the rise in the global economy.

England's advanced position was due to its adoption of mercantilism in the seventeenth century (see Chapter 16). Mercantilist theory asserted that government involvement in the economy was necessary to augment the amount of gold in the country by decreasing imports and increasing exports. Governments encouraged industries with tax subsidies and the granting of monopolies. Mercantilists believed that such policies would benefit the business owners but also ordinary people, workers, seamen, and farmers. Both France under Louis XVI (Colbert) and England under the Stuarts and the Commonwealth were energetically mercantilist. Cromwell passed the first Navigation Act in 1651 requiring that virtually all goods coming into Scotland and England, whether from Europe or the colonies, be brought in by British ships, and this legislation was continued by the restored Stuart monarchs and, in fact, was on the books in Britain until 1786. Colonists were also required to buy almost all their goods from Britain.

The general goal of the Navigation Acts was to make Britain the dominant maritime power by strengthening the British shipping industry and outmaneuvering its competition. In the seventeenth century, Britain's chief competitor was Holland. The British went to war three times with the Dutch in the mid-seventeenth century; they took New Amsterdam from the Dutch in 1664, renaming it New York, and in general damaged Dutch shipping and trade. France then took over as Britain's chief rival, a more formidable one as it had advantages the Dutch did not: a large population; alliance with Spain, then Europe's strongest military power; substantial resources; and many highly regulated colonies. From the beginning of the eighteenth century until 1763, Britain and France engaged in a number of wars, which were ultimately won by the British. The first was the War of Spanish Succession, a threat to the balance of power in Europe. When France lost to a grand coalition, it ceded to Britain, in the Peace of Utrecht, important territories—Newfoundland, Nova Scotia, and Hudson Bay. Britain also won the highly valuable control of the West African slave trade, the *asiento*. Next was the War of Austrian Succession in which Britain helped Austria's Maria Theresa hold onto her throne, followed by the Seven Years' War, also known as the French and Indian War, fought both on the European and America continents. It was the latter war that was decisive. The British used their naval power to defeat the French forces under General Montcalm in Quebec. In the Treaty of Paris of 1763, which concluded the war, France ceded Quebec and its remaining possessions east of the Mississippi as well as its holdings in India to Britain. It also gave Louisiana to Spain, which had ceded Florida to Britain. By the end of the war, Britain reigned supreme on the seas and had established the basis for its empire in India and Canada, as well as a greatly expanded colony in what would shortly become the United States. The United States would forge an alliance with France reflecting continuing French-British rivalry. As these colonies grew in size and wealth, they were eager to buy Britain's manufactured goods. Although trade on the continent stagnated, partly because of the wars with France and the blockade of British goods later imposed by Napoleon, trade (mostly metal items like firearms, nails, axes, and chains and household goods like clocks and furniture) with Africa and the colonies boomed (see Chart 19.3 for a visual representation of the expansion of British trade). Such great success in exports demonstrated the usefulness of mercantilist policies and set the stage for industrial production in the next century. France, in spite of all its losses, retained highly valuable colonies in the West Indies that provided enormous wealth in the form of coffee, sugar, and slaves. Haiti, with some half a million slaves, became the leading producer of sugar and coffee in the world and the single most profitable colony in the entire New World. That wealth, held by merchants in Paris and Bordeaux, would later have political consequences, as they would demand a greater and direct voice in political decision making and work to establish constitutional government in France.

London became Europe's richest and largest city, its wealth generated by trade in manufactured goods, slaves, and sugar. The various images of London (see pp. 638–639) illustrate the transformation of London from a city of about 400,000 people before the Great Fire of 1666 to a rebuilt city—new brick buildings, crowded streets with wealthy and poor alike, and then expanding new areas in the West End with fine houses built around squares with gated parks, attracting both urban businessmen and professionals and the rural notables who would come to London for the social season.

LAND AND LABOR IN BRITISH AMERICA

While at home land ownership was highly concentrated in the hands of nobles and gentry, in the colonies British settlers had an easy time acquiring land and keeping the value of what they produced. This encouraged immigration to and population growth in the colonies and helped create a high standard of living. The demand for labor outstripped the supply; this spurred the growth of slavery. Slavery in the New World was introduced by the Spanish and Portuguese and enthusiastically adopted by the Dutch and the English for sugar plantations in the Caribbean in the seventeenth century. The English continued this pattern in the tobacco and later cotton plantations they established in the North American colonies. Typically, smaller white farmers tended to sell out and migrate, leaving a small number of large white landowners, such as the wealthy slave-owning planter class in Maryland and Virginia, surrounded by a large black population. By the time of American independence, some 20 percent of the entire U.S. population was black. Slavery was uncommon in New England as its economy was not based on plantation agriculture, but many merchants in the nonslave colonies benefited from supplying the plantations and from the slave trade itself.

THE ATLANTIC SLAVE TRADE

Throughout the eighteenth century, a key element in the expansion of Europe and the Atlantic economic system was the African slave trade, which reached its peak in the 1780s. More than half of the estimated 11.7 million Africans brought as slaves to the Americas were shipped in the eighteenth century, up to 80,000 a year. African slaves were vital for the success of the American economy, and the Atlantic trade was responsible for four-fifths of the commodities produced for sale in the Atlantic economy. The slaves produced crucial items like sugar and coffee and generated wealth for their owners, who then could purchase more of Europe's manufactured goods

After 1700, Britain took over the slave trade, and wars over domination of the trade became less frequent. Europeans now began to use shore trading, whereby they came to the shores of Africa and met local traders who would supply the slaves, as their main technique. The Africans got slaves through small-scale slave raiding, kidnapping, and the imposition of slavery rather than fines for small crimes. The price of slaves rose as demand increased, bringing large profits to some Africans. They used their new wealth to buy European arms for competitive wars fought for the acquisition of slaves, with mixed results. The kingdom of Dahomey in West Africa grew wealthy and strong, while previously stable kingdoms in the Congo were undermined by the slave trade. Relatively few of the blacks were brought to Europe, although there was the occasional personal or household slave. In Britain, but not in its colonies, a slave who ran away was supported by the law, so there were free and escaped blacks in London, some of whom intermarried with whites. After 1775, a movement to abolish the slave trade and end slavery began to grow in size and importance and became, perhaps, the first large-scale peaceful movement for social change in British history. In 1807 Parliament abolished the slave trade.

AP Tip

The U.S. Constitution of 1787 allowed for the importation of slaves until 1808, as a compromise between those opposed to slavery and the slave-holding states. Slavery was abolished in the British Empire in 1833 and in the French empire in 1848; it continued in Brazil until the 1880s. Slavery was an institution that was thousands of years old; this makes its abolition all the more remarkable.

The story of Olaudah Equiano, who wrote a popular autobiography in the eighteenth century, reveals many of the aspects of the slave trade. He was born in Nigeria in 1745, kidnapped at age eleven, experienced the harrowing middle passage journey to the Caribbean, and was taken by his owner to England, where he was educated, and where he also converted to Christianity. He was taken back to the Caribbean, disappointing his hope of freedom, and sold to a Philadelphia merchant who allowed him to trade on the side. Equiano became rich and bought his freedom at age twenty-one. He returned to London and became a leader of the local black community and an important voice in the antislavery campaign. He used his own experiences to denounce slavery and his Christian faith to argue for equal treatment of blacks.

Revival in Colonial Latin America

Spain recovered from its weakened position at the start of the eighteenth century and during the War of Spanish Succession, partly because of the capable leadership of Philip V, the Bourbon grandson of Louis XIV, who ruled with competence and energy until 1746. Spain enlarged its empire in the Americas with the acquisition of Louisiana from the French in 1763. The empire became more prosperous as silver mining, in particular, revived; Spanish America produced half of the world's silver. The local notables of Spanish origin, the Creoles, became wealthy consumers of European manufactured goods. They depended on the Native Americans for labor, first as slaves and then as a new type of serf in a system known as debt peonage, in which people worked to pay off debts that they were almost required to acquire. There were also many mestizos, people of mixed Spanish and Indian blood, who came to number about 30 percent of the population with the whites accounting for about 20 percent. In Mexico, the whites remained fascinated by issues of race, creating a new genre of painting called casta paintings, which portrayed the variety of racial mixtures.

TRADE AND EMPIRE IN ASIA

At the same time as the Europeans were competing for dominance in the New World, they were competing in Asia as well. In the sixteenth century, the Portuguese eclipsed the Venetians and were predominant until Dutch ships gave them more intense competition in the Asian trade. The Dutch were phenomenally successful traders, making huge profits on imports of pepper, clove, and nutmeg from the Spice Islands (now Indonesia). In 1602, the newly founded Dutch East India Company took aim at its Portuguese competition. It won the right from the Dutch States General to rule the territories it acquired, establishing a monopoly on the spice trade, and slowly took control over the whole archipelago, including the port of Jakarta in Java. Batavia, the Dutch name for Jakarta, became the center of Dutch operations in Asia, the entrepôt for the exchange of European manufactured goods for spices. Soon the Dutch expelled the Portuguese from Ceylon and similar areas.

The Dutch held sway in Asia for a hundred years or so but began to lose out to the British East India Company. They had also not diversified sufficiently, and suffered when the European market for spices declined. Britain focused on India, winning trade concessions from its Mughal emperor, engaging in local politics, and competing against the French. In 1763 at the end of the Seven Years' War, the French ceded their Indian territories to Britain. The next year, the British defeated the Mughal emperor; they kept him on the throne but in name only, giving real power to Robert Clive as governor general of Bengal. By the early nineteenth century, the British dominated most of the continent, the "jewel in the crown" of the British Empire.

ADAM SMITH AND ECONOMIC LIBERALISM

European empires were acquired and controlled through mercantilist policies, but over time, opposition to mercantilism was expressed both by British and Creole merchants complaining about the unfair privileges granted to the East India Company, and by intellectuals. Ultimately, this led to the creation of a new doctrine variously called laissez-faire, economic liberalism, or free enterprise. Its main progenitor was the Scottish Enlightenment philosopher, Adam Smith, whose path-making and hugely popular book, *The Wealth of Nations* (1776), may be said to have established the basis of modern capitalist economies. Free competition, Smith argued, is preferable to mercantilist monopolies because it offers the greatest benefits to the society as a whole, protecting the consumer and offering opportunities to individuals. Governments should limit themselves to three tasks: military self-defense, the maintenance of public order and justice, and public works, and not intervene in the economy. Smith argued that free enterprise would create social harmony and raise the standard of living for everyone. Smith was not an advocate of paying workers merely subsistence wages or of the division of labor that was part and parcel of industrialization, whose beginning he witnessed. Instead he argued that workers should be paid decently and be protected by the government.

AP Tip

As a philosophe, Smith searched for fundamental laws; the law of supply and demand, which he articulated, required free operation. Smith believed that if every businessperson, indeed if every person, pursued his or her "enlightened self-interest" in an atmosphere of free competition, it would produce the greatest quantity of goods at the highest quality and lowest prices. An "invisible hand" would act as a regulator if needed. Mercantilism protects the manufacturer, but the chief beneficiary of laissez-faire is the consumer. Although the United States and many other states claim their economies are laissez-faire, in fact government intervention in the economy never disappeared.

Multiple-Choice Questions

1. The term *industrious revolution* refers to
   (A) the industrial revolution in the countryside rather than in the cities.
   (B) household labor becoming market orientated and wage paid.
   (C) men working harder to support their households so that wives and children did not work.
   (D) the use of new tools in agricultural work.
   (E) the cottage industry in southern and southeastern Europe.

2. Which is the correct order in which states became dominant in world trade in Asia from the sixteenth to the eighteenth centuries?
   I. Britain
   II. France
   III. Holland
   IV. Portugal
   (A) III, IV, II, and I
   (B) I, III, IV, and II
   (C) IV, III, II, and I
   (D) II, IV, III, and I
   (E) IV, II, III, and I

3. The theory of economic liberalism, or laissez-faire capitalism, is concerned mostly about the needs of
   (A) manufacturers.
   (B) governments.
   (C) merchants.
   (D) consumers.
   (E) landlords.

4. The Navigation Acts helped Britain to become a great naval power by
   (A) requiring foreign goods be brought into Britain on British ships.
   (B) requiring that all slaves going to the Americas be transported on British ships.
   (C) creating Europe's first naval academy for the training of officers.
   (D) requiring the use of sailors from the American colonies.
   (E) arming British ships with the newest military technology.

5. Which was *not* an advantage of the cottage, or putting-out, system?
   (A) It allowed merchant capitalists to evade guild regulations.
   (B) It allowed households to increase their incomes.
   (C) It gave women greater say in household decisions.
   (D) Women began to earn almost the same as men.
   (E) It kept the family together as an economic unit.

6. The guild system in the seventeenth and eighteenth centuries
   (A) went into serious decline, never to recuperate.
   (B) expanded its control over manufacturing into the countryside.
   (C) flourished as never before.
   (D) was too rigid to adapt to new methods of production and new technology.
   (E) remained closed to women.

7. By the eighteenth century, which was the largest group in the population after the native Indians in Spanish America?
   (A) Recent immigrants from Spain
   (B) Creoles
   (C) Mestizos
   (D) Free blacks
   (E) Enslaved blacks

8. Spain's South American colonies were similar to Britian's New England in that
   (A) few Europeans settled there.
   (B) the economy was city based, not land based.
   (C) both already had some autonomy in the early eighteenth century.
   (D) the British were not allowed to trade there.
   (E) African slavery was relatively uncommon.

9. The single most important component of the agricultural revolution was the
   (A) ending of the practice of leaving the land fallow.
   (B) animal breeding.
   (C) use of the potato.
   (D) use of root crops.
   (E) enclosure movement.

10. The chief reason for the rise in population in the eighteenth century was the
    (A) rise in birth rates.
    (B) rise in illegitimacy.
    (C) decline in death rates.
    (D) improvements in medicine.
    (E) widespread use of the smallpox vaccine.

11. The enclosure movement in England
    (A) was opposed by Parliament.
    (B) led to the tight concentration of land ownership.
    (C) allowed many small and medium-sized farmers to prosper.
    (D) meant large fields were divided into strips.
    (E) had little impact on productivity.

12. The time span between the height of the slave trade and its abolition in Britain was about
    (A) thirty years.
    (B) fifty years.
    (C) one hundred years.
    (D) ten years.
    (E) one hundred and twenty years.

13. The impact of the slave trade on African states was
    (A) uniformly disastrous.
    (B) uniformly beneficial.
    (C) very little as slaving was mostly a coastal matter.
    (D) disastrous for the West Indian kingdom of Dahomey.
    (E) to encourage warfare among Africans.

14. By the Treaty of Paris in 1763,
    (A) England won the *asiento.*
    (B) France took possession of Louisiana.
    (C) Spain gave England its colonies in the Caribbean.
    (D) France ceded its territories in India to Britain.
    (E) France ceded Nova Scotia and Newfoundland to Britain.

15. By the end of the eighteenth century, London
    (A) had become the second largest city in Europe, behind Paris.
    (B) expanded with new townhouses surrounding squares in the West End.
    (C) abandoned its location on the Thames after the Great Fire.
    (D) became more industrial than commercial.
    (E) rebuilt the city as a series of circular rings.

Free-Response Questions

1. What were the chief characteristics of the agricultural revolution, and how did they develop in Britain in the eighteenth century?
2. Analyze the factors and developments that made England the dominant state in world trade in the eighteenth century.

ANSWERS

MULTIPLE-CHOICE QUESTIONS

1. ANSWER (B) The term refers to the transformation of household labor, particularly that of women and children, toward production for the market and being paid in wages in the cottage system. (McKay, *A History of Western Society*, not used in 8th ed. but the ideas are discussed on pp. 639–643/9th ed., pp. 633–634)

2. ANSWER (C) It is the British who end up on top in Asia at the end of the eighteenth century. (McKay, *A History of Western Society*, 8th ed., pp. 505, 644, 647/9th ed., pp. 644–647)

3. ANSWER (D) Mercantilism benefits manufacturers and merchants by protecting them from competition and providing them with guaranteed markets. Consumers, ordinary people who buy goods, would benefit the most from economically liberal policies. (McKay, *A History of Western Society*, 8th ed., pp. 654–656/9th ed., pp. 647–648)

4. ANSWER (A) With this requirement, the British shipbuilding and shipping industry boomed and outcompeted its nearest rival, the Dutch. (McKay, *A History of Western Society*, 8th ed., pp. 643–644/9th ed., pp. 634–635)

5. ANSWER (D) Women were terribly paid; their wages were a small fraction of what men earned. (McKay, *A History of Western Society*, 8th ed., pp. 639–643/9th ed., pp. 629–631)

6. ANSWER (C) The guilds found ways to incorporate new technology and methods of production, and some new guilds were formed, for example, of seamstresses. Historians now say the guilds' highpoint was the seventeenth and eighteenth centuries, not the High Middle Ages. (McKay, *A History of Western Society*, 8th ed., pp. 640, 658–659/9th ed., pp. 631–633, 650–651)

7. ANSWER (C) Mestizos were about 30 percent of the population, Creoles about 20 percent. The percentage of blacks was much smaller in the Spanish colonies. (McKay, *A History of Western Society*, 8th ed., pp. 652–654/9th ed., pp. 643–644)

8. ANSWER (E) In Argentina, Chile, and Peru, the most important Spanish colonies, most of the laborers were native people. There was relatively little African slavery there or in New England, where there was little plantation agriculture. (McKay, *A History of Western Society*, 8th ed., pp. 646–647, 652–654/9th ed., pp. 640–641, 643–644)

9. ANSWER (A) By ending the practice of leaving the land fallow, agricultural productivity went up substantially. Although enclosure and the other options also were important and helped make increased productivity possible, crop rotation and planting all fields every year were the definitive elements. (McKay, *A History of Western Society*, 8th ed., pp. 632–633/9th ed., pp.622–623)

10. **ANSWER (C)** Only in England was there inoculation against smallpox. There was relatively little rise in birthrates, and illegitimacy was not significant for population growth at that time. (McKay, *A History of Western Society*, 8th ed., pp. 637–639/9th ed., pp. 627–628)

11. **ANSWER (B)** The result of the enclosure movement in England was that smaller farmers sold out to larger ones, leading to concentration of ownership. Parliament passed many acts of enclosure. Enclosing the common fields helped increase productivity. (McKay, *A History of Western Society*, 8th ed., pp. 634–636/9th ed., pp. 622–625)

12. **ANSWER (A)** The height of the slave trade was the 1780s; it was abolished in 1807 in Britain. (McKay, *A History of Western Society*, 8th ed., pp. 651–652/9th ed., pp. 641–643)

13. **ANSWER (E)** Dahomey became wealthy, but in general the impact was to increase warfare in the competition to acquire slaves to sell to Europeans. (McKay, *A History of Western Society*, 8th ed., pp. 651–652/9th ed., pp. 642–643)

14. **ANSWER (D)** France gave up its outposts in India in the treaty that ended the Seven Years' War. Spain had ceded the *asiento* and France Nova Scotia at the Peace of Utrecht in 1713. Spain acquired, not ceded, Louisiana and did not cede its Caribbean colonies at that time. (McKay, *A History of Western Society*, 8th ed., p. 644/9th ed., p. 635)

15. **ANSWER (B)** London became the largest city in Europe. It rebuilt itself after the Great Fire of 1666, moving west with townhouses built around squares. (McKay, *A History of Western Society*, 8th ed., pp. 648–649/9th ed., pp. 638–641)

FREE-RESPONSE QUESTIONS

1. The agricultural revolution refers to changes in agricultural production techniques and organization, and the resulting huge increase in agriculture productivity.

- Its major elements were the enclosure movement, new crops, production for market rather than use, scientific agriculture such as animal husbandry, and ending the practice of leaving land fallow.
- The enclosure movement's goal was to enclose the common fields on agricultural lands that by tradition were open to the tenant farmers and laborers to graze their animals, glean firewood, and so on. It began in the seventeenth century and was nearly complete a century later. Enclosure allowed landowners to experiment with new crops and new production techniques. It resulted in an increase in the number of landless peasants and poor agricultural workers.
- New crops—potatoes, tomatoes, and so on—enriched the European diet and also provided ways to restore nitrates to the soil while at the same time producing crops like sunflowers, turnips, and so on.
- Use of such restorative crops and crop rotation eliminated the need for leaving land fallow. About one-third more land was under cultivation as a result of ending the practice of leaving land fallow.
- Selective breeding of animals and crops reflected scientific and empirical approaches.

2. English Navigation Acts of the seventeenth century created a strong shipbuilding and shipping industry. Successful early industries gave the English many manufactured goods to sell, from clocks to firearms. English mercantilist regulations guaranteed England's trading dominance in their colonies in the Americas.

- England defeated the Dutch in several wars in the seventeenth century and took over their colony in New York. The British East India Company undermined the Dutch position in Asia and won important trade concessions from the Mughal emperor in India in the early eighteenth century.
- As a result of its role in defeating France in the War of the Spanish Succession, Britain acquired the French colonies of Newfoundland, Nova Scotia, and Hudson Bay and the *asiento* from Spain, which gave it control over the slave trade in the New World.
- British naval domination was demonstrated during the Seven Years' War; the Treaty of Paris of 1763 that concluded it gave Britain the remaining French territories in Canada and east of the Mississippi, and India.

20

The Changing Life of the People

This chapter is devoted to social history, which is increasingly important in the AP program.

It analyzes how the lives of ordinary people changed in the seventeenth and eighteenth centuries—their living conditions, marriage patterns, child-rearing practices, educational opportunities, consumption of food and other commodities, medical practices, religion, and culture. Although research into such topics is particularly complicated because illiterate people typically leave few records and there are so many regional variations, historians feel more confident than ever before that they can understand the lives of ordinary people.

> **AP Tip**
>
> An emphasis on social history has become a vital part of the AP European history curriculum. Sometimes students tend to see social history as less serious or less important, but that would be a serious error in preparing for the AP exam, since the exam includes a substantial number of social history questions. The DBQ for the 2007 exam was a social history question on attitudes toward children.

Key Concepts

- Marriage and family patterns changed over the eighteenth century. From the seventeenth to the mid-eighteenth century, there was a high proportion of women who were pregnant at marriage but a low illegitimacy rate. Young couples rarely lived with extended families and had to be able to support a household to marry, so

Europeans tended to marry late, an unusual pattern in world history. After 1750, illegitimacy rates soared while fewer women were pregnant at marriage. The population grew dramatically.

- Children were often not breast-fed by their mothers, particularly in the aristocratic and middle classes, which added to the threats to their health from disease; a high percentage of children died before reaching adulthood. The Enlightenment encouraged women to breast-feed their own children and created a new concept of childhood as separate from adulthood. Severe discipline began to be replaced by more tenderness. Schools for children began to be established in the eighteenth century.
- A consumer culture began to develop in the eighteenth century for new food crops that originated in the Americas (sugar, chocolate) or Asia (tea, coffee) and for highly fashionable clothes available in shops. Households changed as more private and individualized spaces were created. Women were active as medical practitioners, especially as midwives. Smallpox disappeared from Europe because of the efforts of Lady Montagu and Edward Jenner.
- Religious revivals occurred in both Protestant (Pietism and Methodism) and Catholic (Jansenism) communities, which offered a more intensely personal religious experience to their followers. Recreational activities remained relatively unchanged in the countryside, but in towns, paid entertainers at public fairs and commercially organized spectator sports attracted people of all classes. Traveling circuses, horse races, bullfights, and cockfights were popular with the masses, and were considered vulgar by the upper classes.

MARRIAGE AND FAMILY LIFE

The family is the most fundamental organizing unit in any society. There are many misconceptions about European family life in this period. In fact, the European pattern is unique in the world at that time; this may have played an important role in the particular dynamism of European societies. Parish records indicate that the extended family was already a rare phenomenon by 1700. Young married couples usually established their own households instead of moving in with one of their parents. Almost certainly for this reason, people did not marry young in the seventeenth and eighteenth centuries: in some cases, they averaged twenty-five years of age, in others twenty-seven or twenty-eight at time of first marriage, and some never married at all. In other words, men and women had usually worked for about ten years and were fully formed adults by time of marriage. In some areas, another delay to marriage was that permission from local lords or government officials was needed to marry.

Typically, a young man would leave home as an apprentice, if he was lucky, or as an itinerant worker, who would be often unemployed if he was not apprenticed. Girls, too, left home but they had fewer opportunities, usually in traditional female occupations, although as the eighteenth century wore on, more opportunities for them arose if they were skilled. The likeliest out-of-the-home labor for girls was domestic service, where they worked hard and earned little, and often were the victim of unwanted sexual advances from their employers. Should a domestic servant become pregnant, she would be fired, with little recourse besides prostitution available to her. Such stories and the theme of the "fallen woman" were common in literature and painting. Boys too were abused, though usually with beatings.

Brothels had been tolerated or even established by cities in the late medieval period, but by the seventeenth century, they were declared illegal and closed. Nevertheless, unemployed women turned to the sex trade, in spite of the repression and the constant threat of venereal disease.

PREMARITAL SEX AND COMMUNITY CONTROLS

Illegitimacy was relatively low until 1750, perhaps one in twenty children or fewer, although about one-fifth to one-third of all children were conceived before marriage. The very low rates of illegitimacy and the relatively high percentage of pregnant brides leads to the conclusion that few couples who were not intending to marry engaged in premarital sexual intercourse. It also reflects strong community controls in traditional village life that could pressure young couples to marry. Community intervention in private life continued after marriage, with public rituals that humiliated or degraded people whose behavior, adultery or abusive treatment of a spouse, for example, was seen as inappropriate. Being forced to "ride stang" (backward on a donkey) was one such method of social control.

AP Tip

The 2000 DBQ on peasant rituals had several documents on such methods of social control. It is available online at the College Board website.

NEW PATTERNS OF MARRIAGE AND ILLEGITIMACY

The patterns described above began to change in the mid-eighteenth century. Illegitimacy rates soared from about 1750 to 1850, reaching more than one-quarter, even up to one-third, of all births. More young people were engaging in premarital sex, and fewer men were marrying women they had impregnated. There is much dispute over the causes for this change. Some historians argue that the growth of cottage industry meant income was no longer tied to land, so younger people could become independent and marry earlier, and more often for love than to fulfill parental needs. Cottage workers could now freely court as they saw fit. As both the illegitimate and legitimate populations grew, more and more young people moved to cities in search of economic opportunities or jobs, and such mobility further encouraged sexual freedom. Young girls, poorly paid as domestic or textile workers, still hoped for marriage, and often were enticed into sexual relationships with the promise of marriage, which sometimes could not be fulfilled because men's working lives were also insecure. The practice of "penny weddings" (guests providing cash gifts to pay for the wedding) in Scotland shows how hard it was for families to pay for the wedding on their own.

AP Tip

This pattern is quite similar to contemporary American practice; both reflect the inability of community controls to force marriage and enforce sexual conduct. Many commentators, then and now, see high rates of illegitimacy as signs of societal decline.

CHILDREN AND EDUCATION

In typical agrarian communities, women had six or more children, but many of these died in infancy or childhood from diseases or dehydration. Childbirth was also risky, with about 5 to 10 percent of women dying in childbirth. Lower-class women typically breast-fed their children for about two years, which improved the health of babies; breast feeding also acts as a natural, though unreliable, method of birth control as it sometimes reduces women's fertility and helps space children. Upper-class women rarely nursed their own children, hiring a wet nurse at home or sending the baby to a wet nurse in the countryside, usually for two years. Rural wet nursing was widespread, even though the wet nurses' own babies might suffer in the process. This was particularly common in northern France around Paris, where there was a government-supervised system of hiring rural wet nurses, although elsewhere in the late eighteenth century, upper-class women were beginning to nurse their own children. In Paris, only about 10 percent of the babies were nursed at home in the late eighteenth century. This was a centuries-old practice there, but it may also be related to economic difficulties; with wages low and prices high, more women worked outside the home. Even when upper-class women began to change toward breast feeding, poor women continued to use wet nurses until cow's milk could be sterilized and artificial nipples were invented in the nineteenth century. Infant mortality rates were high, and were higher in places where wet nurses were used more. In northern France, only about 45 percent of infants reached age ten; in England, where more nursing was done by mothers, the comparative rate was 70 percent.

AP Tip

One reason women had so many children was that many, typically two or three out of every five babies, would die before they reached adulthood. Only when medical care and sanitation improved did more babies survive to adulthood; at that point, family size began to shrink.

Pregnant women who couldn't afford to have a child had few options, since abortion was illegal and dangerous and probably rare. Infanticide was all too common; women sometimes smothered unwanted newborns or left them to die in the streets. Foundling hospitals existed in cities; in Paris, for example, about one-third of the babies were abandoned to them, many who were born to married couples who could not afford another child. The hospitals took in about 100,000 per year, although there were always more babies than they could take in. Foundling hospitals became a popular charity in the eighteenth century. But many children died in them; high death rates, with 50 to 90 percent of the babies dying in their first year in such hospitals, caused some contemporaries to call them "legalized infanticide."

The high infant mortality rates led some historians to conclude that eighteenth-century parents were not very emotionally attached to their children. Contemporaries certainly were aware of the problem and often wrote about it. While some earlier writers described indifference to babies (Michel de Montaigne, for example), others wrote with despair and sadness over the death of their children (Ben Jonson, for example).

Children were typically treated with severe discipline, as the phrase "spare the rod and spoil the child" indicates. Children were expected to be obedient and quiet. Later in the eighteenth century, new views of childhood—the idea that children live in a separate sphere from adults, should be held to different standards, and should be allowed to play and learn by playing—reflected the Enlightenment. Philosophes argued for better treatment of children in the hope that this would produce better adults and a better society. Children were no longer dressed in smaller versions of adult clothes, but allowed to wear distinct clothes that gave them greater freedom of movement. Rousseau was probably the most influential philosophe on children and their education, although he himself abandoned his five children to foundling hospitals. His novel *Emile* advocated breast feeding by mothers and natural dress and exercise in the fresh air for children and inspired many elite women to modify their mothering.

AP Tip

Rousseau is the forerunner of what is now called progressive education, which asserts that the best way to educate children is to have them follow their own interests and to stimulate their curiosity. Children, Rousseau said, should be given practical skills—crafts for boys and domestic skills for girls. Such gender bias was typical of most Enlightenment writers on education.

SCHOOLS AND POPULAR LITERATURE

Many boys and even more girls were illiterate, but over the course of the eighteenth century, more opportunities for education developed. Nobles and the well-to-do bourgeoisie often sent their children to Jesuit schools or colleges. Basic literacy, along with religion, was taught to boys and girls in schools beginning in the seventeenth century, reflecting increased concern by both Protestants and Catholics that young people be able to read. Prussia was the first state to make elementary education mandatory, in 1717, with the goals of helping Lutheran children read the Scriptures and of creating an educated population who could better serve the state. Other Protestant states followed suit, Scotland and England establishing their "charity schools." Among the Catholic states, only Habsburg Austria promoted elementary education in the eighteenth century.

As a result of such efforts, there was a remarkable increase in male literacy rates between 1600 and 1800, from around 20 percent to somewhere between 50 percent in England and 90 percent in Scotland. Women too were increasingly literate, although typically at a lower rate than men. The newly literate masses were reading "chapbooks," or short pamphlets, often on religious topics. The novel was a new literary genre in the eighteenth century, which some considered a feminine genre in that novels dealt so often with issues of love and family. A number of women became novelists, and many women were devoted letter writers. Popular literature included fantasy stories, romances (particularly medieval ones), crime stories, and what we would call fairy tales. Some scholars see these as purely escapist, but others argue that such tales were didactic and helped children to learn to navigate in the world. Other popular writing included practical manuals and almanacs, the latter crossing class lines and offering universal information across the board. Some popular literature printed in cheap pamphlets, newspapers, and broadsides brought translated and simplified versions of some of the ideas of the Enlightenment to a mass public. Thomas Paine's pamphlet *Common Sense* sold some 600,000 copies, largely to working people.

Food, Medicine, and New Consumption Habits

A consumer culture began to be created in Europe in the eighteenth century, particularly in the upper classes in Britain, but even in the lower ones. New consumer goods—whether ribbons for a girl's hair or coal stoves—encouraged individual self-expression. Households also changed; private spaces were built in homes to allow for some privacy where little had existed before. Rooms began to have defined functions and to be decorated with books and prints. People could afford to give each person an individual plate at the dining table, rather than the common dish of a century before.

Before the eighteenth century, the diet of ordinary people in northern Europe was almost entirely coarse dark bread or grains added to soup, supplemented by peas and beans, whether freshly picked or dried. Fruit was uncommon, and milk was used mostly to make cheese and butter. In 1700 commoners ate less meat than they had in 1500, partially because of high prices and partially because strict game laws limited their right to hunt. The poor in England and Holland ate better than elsewhere in Europe. The rich were distinctive in the huge quantities of meat and drink they consumed, in addition to the great variety of foods. Often they suffered from gout.

New foods cultivated in the eighteenth century and new methods of farming brought significant changes in food consumption. The potato, rich in both carbohydrates and vitamins, and more durable in harsh climates than other crops, became a staple in much of Europe. Other new crops were corn, squash, and tomatoes—all part of the Columbian Exchange with the New World. The greatest change in the diet of Europeans came from the importation of tea from Asia and sugar, tobacco, coffee, and chocolate from the New World. Tea, coffee, and sugar became so cheap—and they were so desirable as stimulants—that they became necessities in the diets of peoples of all classes. See Mercier's description of daily life in Paris in the 1780s (pp. 678–680), which shows the energizing effect of coffee for the working classes.

The eighteenth-century consumer revolution was not only a response to the increased supplies of goods; it was also created by capitalists who used market techniques to stimulate demand. Fashion merchants, rather than courtiers, began to dictate the style of aristocrats as prices for clothing went down, making shopping a favorite activity of the well-to-do. Women of all classes acquired both a greater number of garments and a greater diversity in the style and fabrics of garments and accessories. They began to outspend men to attire themselves, as men began to adopt plain dark clothes and gave up their magnificent, multicolored outfits of previous centuries. Europeans became increasingly dependent on the global economy as colonies fed their food and drink addictions and provided cottons and dyes for cheaper clothing. However, this consumer society was generally limited to northwestern Europe and North America and to the upper classes, mass consumption would have to wait until the Industrial Revolution of the next century.

MEDICAL PRACTITIONERS

The eighteenth century saw a large increase in the number of medical practitioners—physicians, surgeons, midwives, faith healers, and apothecaries (pharmacists)—and a change in their gender. Although women medicinal practitioners had been quite common before, they were now being increasingly excluded from medical practice. Women were generally denied admission to medical college, but were active as faith healers and midwives. Madame du Coudray (see the "Individuals in Society" section, p. 669) taught provincial women the art of midwifery through hands-on teaching and the use of the first life-size obstetrical model, which she created. She also wrote a well-received childbirth manual, even getting government support, and may have helped reduce infant mortality rates in France. Women midwives delivered the vast majority of babies, usually at home, and treated women's illnesses; although when forceps were invented, surgeon-physicians used their monopoly over the new instrument as a way to denigrate and exclude midwives. Faith healers, that is, people using religious practice to cure medical ailments, remained popular in the countryside. In towns, apothecaries concocted drugs, such as purgative medicines that were considered crucial to good health, from a wide variety of ingredients. They too were part of the new consumer society.

To become a physician required long years of hands-on training, so generally they (virtually all men) came from prosperous families. They practiced bloodletting, getting rid of the "bad blood" that they believed caused illnesses, though they began to realize its limitations and experimented with new methods. Surgeons separated themselves from their associations as barbers and butchers by performing useful roles on battlefields and amputating the many wounded limbs of soldiers. There was no anesthesia and no attention to sanitary conditions (germ theory would not be discovered until the mid-nineteenth century), so many died under the surgeon's knife or shortly thereafter from infection.

There were some real advances in medicine, most notably the conquest of smallpox, which had killed or scarred millions of Europeans. Lady Montagu brought back from the Ottoman Empire the idea of smallpox inoculation in the early eighteenth century. Its inadequacies—about one-fiftieth of patients died from Ottoman inoculation procedure—prompted Europeans to look for a safer method of combating the disease. Edward Jenner at the end of the century came up with the alterative method of inoculating people with cowpox. The horrible scourge of smallpox disappeared first in Europe and then slowly throughout the world.

Religion and Popular Culture

For most Europeans, the parish church was the center of both religious and social life. The clergy kept the records of births and deaths, educated the children, and organized the care of the destitute and orphans. The parish priest in Catholic areas and the pastor in Protestant areas acted as the intermediary between local people and the large ecclesiastical hierarchy that aimed to control religion, often in conjunction with the state. The Reformation had started out as a radical movement, but it too crushed dissidents like the Anabaptists and bureaucratized religious life.

Catholic monarchs increased control over the church as part of royal absolutism. For example, in Spain, no papal proclamation could be read in church without prior royal approval. The Jesuits, well educated themselves and successful preachers and educators of the Catholic elite, were seen as so loyal to the pope that they were expelled from France in 1763 by Louis XV and, under pressure from him and the king of Spain, were dissolved completely by the papacy in 1773 (the order was later restored). In Austria, Maria Theresa and Joseph II abolished monastic orders that were contemplative in nature rather than engaged in productive or practical work like teaching or nursing.

Protestants had transformed religious practice and architecture by removing all images and stained glass windows from churches and banning processions and pilgrimages. But by the seventeenth century, the Protestant movement had stagnated and become conformist. A new movement, called Pietism, which stressed personal, emotional religious experience and sought to implement the Lutheran ideal of the "priesthood of all believers" through mass education, study groups, and the reading of the Bible, grew in Germany. Pietism offered Christians the chance to be reborn. John Wesley, influenced by Pietism, catalyzed a popular religious revival in England by organizing a new club for students at Oxford University. His followers, who soon became known as Methodists, spread their impassioned and optimistic Christianity through revival meetings and energetic preaching. Wesley himself preached, often in open fields, some 40,000 sermons in the eighteenth century, asserting that all men and women could be saved. Many in England were ready for change because of resentment over favoritism in the Church of England, the impact of Enlightenment skepticism, and a shortage of churches in a period of population growth.

In Catholic countries, religion was flourishing, though elaborate Baroque decoration and popular pilgrimages and processions in celebration of the saints and of the life of Jesus were in stark contrast to religious practice in Protestant areas. The new movement analogous to Pietism within Catholicism was called Jansenism, which adopted many Calvinist concepts such as predestination and encouraged piety and spiritual devotion. It attracted many of the French intellectual elite but also the urban poor, who came together for rapturous religious worship. Louis XIV attacked a number of Jansenist centers. In the countryside, a number of pagan elements remained in Catholic practice, such as blessing farm animals or jumping over bonfires during Lent. Such activities generated condemnation from those who sought a purer Catholic church.

LEISURE AND RECREATION

Probably the most important popular celebration in Catholic countries was Carnival, a festive period of several days before the deprivations of Lent began. Dancing, drinking, and masquerading, as well as plays and processions, helped to temporarily upset the normal order of things and allowed people to vent their frustrations. Although literacy grew, popular culture remained largely oral, usually centered around the tavern or pub where people drank cheap beer and wine as well as gin. In towns and cities, there was a wider variety of amusements with paid entertainers in urban fairs and commercially organized spectator sports, from horse races to boxing matches and blood sports like bullfighting, bull baiting, and cockfighting. Elites, who previously had enjoyed such activities but now were educated on Enlightenment ideals, began to criticize these blood sports as primitive, disorderly, and vulgar.

Multiple-Choice Questions

1. What distinguished European marriage patterns from those in the rest of the world?
   (A) People married early and lived in extended families.
   (B) People married late and lived in extended families.
   (C) People married early and lived in nuclear families.
   (D) People married late and lived in nuclear families.
   (E) Men married late but to younger women, who moved in with their new husband's families.

2. European laws about prostitution in the early modern period
   (A) grew stricter in comparison to those of the medieval period.
   (B) effectively eliminated most brothels by the eighteenth century.
   (C) were so lax that prostitution flourished.
   (D) were stricter in Catholic areas than in Protestant areas.
   (E) were enforced in cases of male prostitution but not in cases of female prostitution.

3. The rapid rise in illegitimacy after 1750 was due to
   (A) the rising population.
   (B) the high death rate of men in war, leaving many women with a shortage of eligible partners.
   (C) a decline in community controls.
   (D) increasing restrictions on marriage.
   (E) Enlightenment attitudes about sex.

4. Cottage industry tended to
   (A) tie young people to their homes.
   (B) create ways to earn an income not tied to the land.
   (C) delay marriage because young people had to wait until they could inherit land before they could marry.
   (D) discourage marriage because land got so expensive.
   (E) flourish in areas where the land was of good quality.

5. Child care practices in Paris were different from many other parts of Europe in that women there
   (A) relatively rarely nursed their own babies.
   (B) usually used wet nurses in their own homes.
   (C) rejected wet nursing as unhealthy for the babies.
   (D) rarely abandoned their babies to foundling hospitals.
   (E) regularly committed infanticide.

6. The eighteenth-century phrase "spare the rod and spoil the child" reflects
   (A) Enlightenment attitudes toward children.
   (B) the ideas of Rousseau in *Emile*.
   (C) the idea that strict discipline prepares a child for a harsh world.
   (D) the impact of high infant mortality rates.
   (E) attitudes found in Spain but rarely in England.

7. The first state to establish compulsory education for male children was
   (A) England.
   (B) Holland.
   (C) Austria.
   (D) France.
   (E) Prussia.

8. Rising literacy among men and women in the eighteenth century was reflected in the
   (A) popularity of chapbooks that mostly dealt with practical subjects.
   (B) reading of almanacs by commoners, though rarely by the well-to-do.
   (C) new literary genre of the novel.
   (D) widespread reading of the works of the Enlightenment.
   (E) abandonment of fairy tales in favor of more serious reading.

9. The consumption of tea and sugar
   (A) was almost entirely limited to the working classes.
   (B) was replaced by the consumption of chocolate and coffee in the late eighteenth century.
   (C) was too expensive for most common people.
   (D) was generally done at work by workers but at home by the well-to-do.
   (E) declined noticeably at the end of the eighteenth century.

10. The midwife Madame du Coudray
   (A) spread knowledge of midwifery through teaching and books.
   (B) was arrested for practicing medicine without a license.
   (C) was considered socially unacceptable and never found a husband.
   (D) died in childbirth herself.
   (E) did little to improve infant mortality rates.

11. Which was *not* an aspect of the developing consumer culture of the late eighteenth century?
   (A) Cotton and other materials from the colonies expanded the size and diversity of wardrobes.
   (B) Men and women both followed the dictates of fashion merchants.
   (C) More household goods meant rooms were given specific functions.
   (D) Working women could acquire cheaper versions of fashionable attire.
   (E) Apothecaries advertised the miraculous curative powers of their medicine.

12. Medical practice in the eighteenth century
   (A) made little improvement in treating battlefield wounds.
   (B) generally removed women from the practice of midwifery, replacing them with physicians.
   (C) limited midwives to delivering babies, while physicians took over medical treatment of women.
   (D) began to eliminate smallpox after the idea of inoculation was brought from Turkey.
   (E) denounced the former practices of purging of the bowels and bloodletting.

13. Which exemplifies the weakness of the papacy against growing state power in the eighteenth century?
   (A) The dissolution of the Jesuit order
   (B) Protestant and Catholic attacks on Anabaptists
   (C) Joseph II's abolition of all monasteries in Austria
   (D) The state takeover of the charitable functions of the church
   (E) The banning of Carnival celebrations in France

14. Pietism, Methodism, and Jansenism all represented
    (A) religious reform movements in Catholic countries.
    (B) religious reform movements in Protestant countries.
    (C) the widespread need for a more personal and spiritual Christianity.
    (D) a rejection of Calvinist ideas.
    (E) movements that appealed to the educated elite.

15. Carnival helped release social tensions by allowing people for those few days to
    (A) bet on cockfighting.
    (B) drink gin.
    (C) dress up and play-act as their opposites.
    (D) go to urban fairs.
    (E) attend boxing matches.

Free-Response Questions

1. How did the lives of women change in the eighteenth century?

2. To what degree and for what reasons did the social gulf between the upper and lower classes grow in the eighteenth century?

ANSWERS

MULTIPLE-CHOICE ANSWERS

1. ANSWER (D) The combination of late marriage and nuclear families marks Europeans as distinct from virtually all other societies. Men and women were typically in their twenties when they married; they waited until they could afford to set up their own households. (McKay, *A History of Western Society*, 8th ed., p. 662/9th ed., pp. 653–654)

2. ANSWER (A) The repression of prostitution grew more severe after the sixteenth century in both Protestant and Catholic states, but it flourished nonetheless. Male prostitution was virtually unheard of at that time. (McKay, *A History of Western Society*, 8th ed., p. 664/9th ed., p. 655)

3. ANSWER (C) Before 1750, there were low rates of illegitimacy but high percentages of brides who were pregnant, showing that community controls effectively worked to pressure young people into marriage. This declined after 1750 for a variety of reasons. (McKay, *A History of Western Society*, 8th ed., pp. 664–666/9th ed., pp. 656–658)

4. ANSWER (B) Cottage industry gave a great deal of independence to young people, who could earn a living if they had space for a loom or a spinning wheel. It tended to develop in areas where the land was poor. (McKay, *A History of Western Society*, 8th ed., p. 665/9th ed., p. 657)

5. ANSWER (A) Only about 10 percent of babies in Paris in the eighteenth century were nursed at home. Infanticide happened less often in cities,

where there were many foundling hospitals, than in the countryside. (McKay, *A History of Western Society*, 8th ed., p. 667/9th ed., p. 658)

6. **ANSWER (C)** This famous phrase was written by the Englishman Daniel Defoe, representing the view that only harsh discipline prepares a child for life. The Enlightenment opposed such a view, arguing that children should be treated tenderly and as children, not adults, and encouraged in their natural curiosity. (McKay, *A History of Western Society*, 8th ed., pp. 668–669/9th ed., pp. 660–661)

7. **ANSWER (E)** France and England lagged behind Prussia and Scotland, although "charity schools" were set up by the Church of England. Austria did promote elementary education but after Prussia had made it compulsory in 1717. (McKay, *A History of Western Society*, 8th ed., p. 670/9th ed., p. 662)

8. **ANSWER (C)** Most ordinary people read religious chapbooks, fairy tales (which were collected and written down at that time), and novels but not the works of the Enlightenment. Everyone read the almanacs. (McKay, *A History of Western Society*, 8th ed., pp. 670–671/9th ed., pp. 662–663)

9. **ANSWER (D)** Prices of tea and sugar had gone down so much in the eighteenth century that ordinary people could afford them and became quite addicted. Workers needed the stimulation provided by tea, which they usually drank at work, while the well-to-do drank at home in leisurely rituals. Coffee and chocolate were also consumed but to a lesser degree in the eighteenth century. (McKay, *A History of Western Society*, 8th ed., pp. 674–675/9th ed., pp. 663–665)

10. **ANSWER (A)** A highly successful educator (and developer of the first model of women's reproductive system as an educational tool), Madame du Coudray may have reduced infant mortality in the eighteenth century. (McKay, *A History of Western Society*, 8th ed., p. 677/9th ed., p. 669)

11. **ANSWER (B)** By and large, the increased consumption of clothes was gendered, with women becoming more varied and elaborate in their attire and men adopting the simple dark suit by the end of the century. (McKay, *A History of Western Society*, not in the 8th ed./9th ed., p. 666)

12. **ANSWER (D)** Lady Montagu brought the idea of inoculation from Turkey, and Edward Jenner figured out a safe way to do it. While some attempts were made to restrict midwifery, most women went to midwives for medical help for themselves and their babies as well as for help in labor and delivery. Bloodletting and purging continued to be standard medical practice. (McKay, *A History of Western Society*, 8th ed., p. 679/9th ed., p. 670)

13. **ANSWER (A)** The state would take over much of the charitable role of the church but not for a century or two. Protestants and Catholics did join forces to attack Anabaptists, but not against the will of the pope. Joseph II abolished only some monasteries. The Jesuit order, with its close ties to the papacy and dominant role in education, came under attack; the pope gave in to pressure and dissolved the order in 1773 (it

was restored later). McKay, *A History of Western Society,* 8th ed., pp. 680–681/9th ed., pp. 671–672)

14. ANSWER (C) Pietists in Germany (Lutheran), Methodists in Anglican England, and Jansenists in Catholic France all sought a more personal, more intensely spiritual religious experience. The sects were popular with elites and commoners alike. Jansenism particularly was influenced by Calvinist ideas. (McKay, *A History of Western Society,* 8th ed., pp. 682–683/9th ed., pp. 672–675)

15. ANSWER (C) They could drink gin, attend urban fairs and boxing matches, and bet on cockfights all the time; only at Carnival was the world turned upside-down for a few days. (McKay, *A History of Western Society,* 8th ed., pp. 683–685 /9th ed., pp. 675–676)

FREE-RESPONSE ANSWERS

1. This is an open-ended question, which can include discussion of many aspects of women's lives. Develop a thesis that focuses on several factors, though it would make the essay stronger to discuss or at least mention other factors as well.
   - Factors affecting women can be categorized into work, sexual and parenting behavior, marriage patterns, consumption habits, and education. In the eighteenth century, more and more women were leaving home for work in towns, either as servants or in the textile industry. Rates of illegitimacy went up dramatically after 1750; this meant more women were engaging in premarital sexual activity and their men were not living up to promises of marriage. Such women lost their jobs if they had them and often became prostitutes. Women used wet nurses, particularly in Paris, rather than nurse their own children. A high percentage of women abandoned their babies to foundling hospitals. More and more women became literate, and some women were successful writers and also readers of the new literary genre of the novel. Women began to shop in fancy shops and rely on fashion merchants, who set the standard of style, and usually were more fashionably dressed than the men.
2. Although wealth had always divided the upper and lower classes, in the eighteenth century new elements were added to their differences, though in some areas the gap between the classes closed a bit.
   - Factors dividing the classes: The upper class grew to disdain blood sports, which they had once enjoyed. Upper-class women, under the influence of Enlightenment ideas, began to breast-feed their children and to treat them with tenderness, while lower-class women tended to continue to use wet nurses because of their own need to work. Poor women abandoned babies to foundling hospitals often set up by nobles and gentry as charities. The upper class read Enlightenment texts, whereas the lower classes read chapbooks. The well-to-do drank their tea at home while the poor drank it at work. The upper class had a rich diet

with plentiful meats while the diet of the poor remained carbohydrate based, first bread and later potatoes. Prostitutes were divided into two groups: poor women driven to it by lack of employment or marriage and often treated poorly, and wealthy courtesans who served well-to-do clients and were usually well treated.

- Factors lessening the divide between classes: Lower-class women had more possibilities to emulate the fashion of the upper class because of inexpensive imported cotton. Both classes enjoyed drinking beer, wine, and hard liquors, which became more available to the poor as prices dropped. The lower classes became more literate and increasingly participated in the exchange of ideas in coffeehouses and other public spaces. People of all classes enjoyed urban fairs and commercially produced entertainment. New religious movements like Pietism, Methodism, and Jansenism appealed to people of varied backgrounds.

21

THE REVOLUTION IN POLITICS, 1775–1815

For Europeans, the French Revolution was *the* revolution, the one most hated or the one most loved. Complex and complicated, reaching hitherto unseen levels of radicalism, it had widespread deep and long-lasting influences in Europe and around the globe.

> **AP Tip**
>
> Many courses in modern European history begin with the French Revolution. While some historians date the origins of modern Europe to the Enlightenment or the Industrial Revolution, there is no doubt that the forces of nationalism, ideologies and ideological warfare, and mass politics that define modern history were given great impetus by the French Revolution.

KEY CONCEPTS

- A revolutionary period began with the American Revolution of 1775, followed fourteen years later by the revolution in France, and shortly thereafter by a successful slave revolt in Haiti. Freedom and equality became publicly articulated ideals and were implemented to varying degrees.
- The short-term causes of the French Revolution of 1789 lay in the financial difficulties of the monarchy combined with the poor economic conditions of the peasants and working peoples. The long-term causes included the inability of the monarchy to reform the taxation system, the lack of political representation not only for

commoners but even for nobles, and the impact of the Enlightenment.

- The Estates General, called into session for the first time in 175 years, was quickly transformed into the National Assembly when the Third Estate swore the Tennis Court Oath and created a constitutional monarchy, with limited suffrage, which lasted until 1791.
- The refusal of the king to accept limited powers combined with the radicalization of the working classes of France led to the transfer of the government from a limited monarchy to a republic, the end of the monarchy, and the execution of the king. Radicals in the Committee of Public Safety were empowered to rule France and instituted a reign of terror in 1793–1794 against domestic enemies, while the country waged war with Austria. The new nationalistic army was ultimately successful at war, but reaction set in and a new government, the Directory, was established in 1795.
- The young military genius Napoleon, who conquered Italy for revolutionary France, staged a coup d'état in 1799 and three years later crowned himself emperor of France. He established a benevolent dictatorship at home, with political repression accompanied by widespread reforms establishing legal equality and freedom of opportunity. He conquered or made treaties with all of Europe except England in campaigns of stunning military brilliance, but was undone by resistance in Spain and a failed invasion of Russia. Napoleon was defeated and abdicated twice, in 1814 and finally in 1815.

AP Tip

It is helpful to keep in mind the stages of revolution outlined in an AP Tip for Chapter 16: reform, radicalization, civil war, foreign war, reaction, one-man dictatorship. Although the specifics are of course different, there are a number of similarities in the process of revolution in the English and the French cases, as will be true for the Russian Revolution of 1917 as well. The chronologies on pages 685, 699, and 704 will be helpful in keeping track of the many events and developments of the revolution and its aftermath.

Background to Revolution

The causes and path of the French Revolution are complex, varied, and international.

Legal Orders and Social Change

The Old Regime's social structure was enshrined legally in the system of estates, in which every French subject was classified into one of three estates: clergy, nobility, and everyone else. The clergy numbered about 100,000 and owned about 10 percent of the land on which it paid only a "voluntary gift" rather than taxes. It collected a church tax, the tithe, from landowners. The Second Estate numbered about 400,000, owned about 25 percent of the land, and retained traditional manorial rights, mostly small in and of themselves but irksome and burdensome to the peasants. The commoners—the Third Estate—were the most diverse group: wealthy bourgeoisie (merchants, financiers, lawyers, and officials), mostly poor peasants and agricultural workers, and artisans and unskilled day laborers in cities, often called sans culottes (without short pants). Historians have long discussed the French Revolution as a conflict between the bourgeoisie, growing in size and importance, and the aristocracy, between emergent capitalism and remnants of feudalism. Recent historians have questioned how extensive this conflict was, and instead have demonstrated that both aristocracy and bourgeoisie were fragmented and divided and that they shared common economic values of preferring wealth from land or government service. The nobility, the revisionists argue, was fluid and open to commoners, who bought titles or married into the nobility, and contained many liberals and reformers within their ranks who supported the Parlement of Paris. In either case, the Old Regime, in keeping the estates classification, had not made way for the emergent elite.

THE CRISIS OF POLITICAL LEGITIMACY

Louis XV, who inherited the throne from Louis XIV in 1715 and ruled until 1774, was incapable of maintaining his great-grandfather's absolutist path. He reinstated councils of state instead of ruling personally and restored the right of the parlements—the high courts—to evaluate royal edicts before they became law. The judges (or magistrates) in the parlements, usually nobles of the robe, inherited these positions and were unlikely to allow the basic reform needed for France's finances. That is, they were unlikely to allow the landed property of the nobles to be taxed. Louis XV—and his successor Louis XVI—contended with the parlements over taxation; each time the king tried to do something to solve his ever-pressing financial needs, the parlement refused to allow it. Wars created such a financial crisis that Louis XV tried to institute taxes. After the War of Austrian Succession, he decreed a 5 percent income tax; after the Seven Years' War, he tried an emergency tax. In both cases he was forced to retreat by the Parlement of Paris, which now claimed the right to approve new taxes. In 1768, Louis tried to replace the Parlement of Paris with more pliable bodies known as the Maupeou parlements, raising cries of royal absolutism. The king's private life, his extramarital relationships with the highly influential but low-born Madame du Pompadour and later with a common prostitute, Madame du Barry, damaged his reputation at court and in the public eye. Such a man could not rule by divine right (desacralization).

When the twenty-year-old Louis XVI became king, he relented on the Maupeou parlements. Similarly, he responded to complaints over the controller-general's (Turgot's) efforts to liberalize the economy by firing him.

THE IMPACT OF THE AMERICAN REVOLUTION

A third war brought the crisis to a head. The French supported the American colonists in their rebellion against Britain, which, like France, came out of the Seven Years' War in debt and quickly raised taxes. The colonists argued that since they were not represented in Parliament, they should not have to pay these new taxes or be subject to its laws. Their fury escalated as the British tried coercion, and in 1775 fighting broke out in Massachusetts and spread around the colonies. A declaration of independence in July 1776 justified the rebellion by listing the abuses of power of King George III and declared the equality of all people, their natural rights, and the right of people to change their governments.

AP Tip

The Declaration of Independence shows the direct influence of John Locke (see Chapter 16). Many Enlightenment ideas (see Chapter 18) inspired the Americans, and in turn, seeing them come to fruition inspired many Europeans.

French support included men (the Marquis de Lafayette, for one), military matériel, a formal alliance, and money. Spain and Holland joined the American side too, and Catherine the Great organized a league to protect neutral shipping rights. Britain relinquished its American colonies in 1783. The American victory surprised and delighted many Europeans, who saw it as a vindication of Lockean ideals of popular sovereignty and constitutional government. The hundreds of officers from France who helped in the American war came back to France inspired by these ideals.

Financial Crisis

But it was the American war's impact on finances that ultimately sparked the revolution in France. The king had financed the war by borrowing, so much so that by the 1780s, half of the government's budget went to pay off interest on that debt. Reluctant to cancel the debts, held mostly by Frenchmen, the king tried once again to raise taxes. To gain support, he called an assembly of notables, but it opposed the new tax insisting that the king call the Estates General into session. The king tried to decree new taxes, but met resistance from the Parlement of Paris, which was enthusiastically supported by the people. Without other recourse, the king agreed in the fall of 1788 for the Estates General to meet the following spring.

AP Tip

One might say that the nobility caused the Revolution, in their refusal to compromise on the tax issue. Because of their intransigence, they soon lost all traditional rights and privileges. It is useful to remember that the American slogan "no taxation without representation" is true, at least in democratic states, in reverse: "no representation without taxation."

REVOLUTION IN METROPOLE AND COLONY, 1789–1791

The last time the Estates General had been called was 1614, so the king's decision unleashed a fury of political discussion. As part of the tradition, people were asked to vote for representatives and to prepare petitions or lists of grievances for the government to examine. These reveal dissatisfaction with the church hierarchy and with the absolute monarchy. People expressed the desire for the Estates General to meet regularly and approve legislation, for economic liberalization, and for legal guarantees of civil liberties. This commonality of interests was undermined by conflict over how the Estates General should be organized—whether in the way it had been in 1614, with the three estates each having one vote and meeting separately to decide on that vote, or whether in a more democratic way, with the vote of each estate reflecting its proportion in the population. The Parlement of Paris ruled in favor of the former, which prompted much agitation. Abbé Sieyès wrote a widely distributed pamphlet, *What Is the Third Estate?*, in which he asserted that the Third Estate was France. The government's concession of increasing the number of representatives for the Third Estate was seen as meaningless, though as things fell out, it proved crucial.

When the Estates General met, it was immediately deadlocked since the Third Estate delegates insisted that the king require the delegates of the other two estates to sit together with them in a single body. On June 17, the Third Estate declared itself the National Assembly and was joined by a few members of the First Estate (clergymen). Three days later they swore the Tennis Court Oath not to disband until they had written a constitution for France. The king waffled, both ordering the three estates to sit together and bringing troops to Versailles with the idea of dissolving the Estates General.

AP Tip

In considering the causes of a revolution, it is worth considering the role of the monarch who is overthrown. Had Louis XVI acted at this point—or later on—with more resolution or firmness or, alternatively, made more sincere compromises, radical revolution might have been avoided.

THE REVOLT OF THE POOR AND THE OPPRESSED

As the crisis in Versailles was heating up, the common people in Paris took action. A bad harvest in 1788 had increased the price of bread so much that it cost half the wages of an ordinary laborer. Artisans lost their jobs, and small traders their businesses in the resulting economic depression, with unemployment probably reaching 25 percent in July 1789. The king's dismissal of his moderate finance minister and rumors about the king's troops stirred the people's anxieties. They began to seize arms to protect themselves from the king's troops; on July 14, they marched to the Bastille, a prison where they believed they could find weapons. The prison governor ordered his men to fire on the mob, killing ninety-eight. The people fought back, took the Bastille, and hacked the governor to death, taking his head, sticking it on a pike, and jubilantly parading it through the streets. The next day, a committee of citizens appointed the Marquis de Lafayette to command the city's armed forces. The king acquiesced, recalled the dismissed finance minister, and withdrew his troops; thus the National Assembly was saved. Meanwhile in the countryside, peasants spontaneously rose in rebellion against their lords in a movement called the Great Fear. They seized land, burned the records of their feudal obligations, refused to pay taxes, and in general, took possession of the countryside. In response, the nobles of France, on the night of August 4, 1789, renounced their traditional privileges and rights, one by one, abolishing all remnants of serfdom. The Old Regime died that night.

AP Tip

The actions of the common people proved crucial in the French Revolution whenever there was stalemate. Violence or the threat of violence pushed the Revolution forward at crucial moments. Therefore it is hard to discuss the leadership of the Revolution in a cohesive way. The class tensions that underlay the violence of 1789 to 1795 broke out again in 1830 and 1848.

A Limited Monarchy

In place of the Old Regime, a limited or constitutional monarchy was created, with individual liberties, equality before the law, and due process of law guaranteed in the Declaration of the Rights of Man and the Citizen of August 1789. Two months later, the women of Paris, frustrated over the deepening economic crisis, made worse by the loss of business from the many emigrating nobles, marched to Versailles to demand that the National Assembly meet their needs for more bread at lower prices. They also entered the royal apartments searching for the hated queen Marie Antoinette and murdering some guards on the way. They demanded that the royal family return to Paris, which they did in a procession in which they were mocked and vilified. The National Assembly followed and wrote a constitution accepted by the king in July 1790 in which he remained head of state but lost all lawmaking power to the legislature, elected by about 50 percent of the male population.

AP Tip

The revolutionaries had a tripartite slogan—*Liberté, Egalité, Fraternité*—shared by all classes in the beginning. But liberty, equality, and fraternity (brotherhood or nationalism) are often contradictory, and the different classes stressed different goals. This destroyed the early unity. The first stage of the Revolution focused on liberty, the second stage on equality and fraternity.

The new government made some important reforms: giving women more rights to file to divorce and to inherit property, and forcing fathers of illegitimate children to pay child support. But women were not given the vote. A *Declaration of the Rights of Woman and the Female Citizen* was written by Olympe de Gouges in 1791 (see pages 714–715) to demand equal rights for women, but to no avail. The National Assembly also reorganized France into eighty-three departments, still used today; standardized weights and measures; and banned guilds and workers' organizations as well as monopolies, thus implementing many of the ideals of the Enlightenment.

In terms of religion, the National Assembly was much more radical, giving religious freedom to Jews and Protestants, abolishing monasteries, and nationalizing church property, which was used to back its paper currency, the *assignats,* and to satisfy the land hunger of many peasants. Priests in this new national church were to be elected and to take a loyalty oath to the French government, not the papacy. This proved to be a highly divisive issue for France.

AP Tip

One might say that this legislation, called the Civil Constitution of the Clergy, was a major mistake, in that it alienated the peasantry, which already was quite satisfied with the results of the Revolution, and upset international defenders of Catholicism.

FOREIGN REACTIONS AND THE BEGINNING OF WAR

The startling events in France inspired strong reactions in England both by liberals who celebrated the victory of liberty over despotism and by conservatives, such as Edmund Burke. Burke defended inherited privileges as the best way to maintain stability; rapid and overwhelming reform would lead, he argued, to chaos and tyranny. Mary Wollstonecraft answered Burke's *Reflections on the Revolution in France* with her *Vindication of the Rights of Man,* both published in 1790, and then two years later, published *A Vindication of the Rights of Women.* This latter work, a foundational feminist tract, defended women's intelligence and called for education and equal rights in the public sphere of employment and even politics. It advanced many of the ideas expressed by Olympe de Gouges.

Meanwhile, the limited monarchy in France was unraveling. The king and queen tried to escape but were caught and brought back to Paris in June 1791. Their credibility was now seriously undermined. In 1791, implementing a new constitution, the National Assembly decided that none of their members could stand for reelection; the new Legislative Assembly, which convened in October 1791, was therefore made up of all new representatives, many quite young and some of them members of a radical club, the Jacobins. Elsewhere on the continent, kings and nobles who felt threatened by the events in France tried to intervene to protect the French monarchs. Austria and Prussia issued the Declaration of Pillnitz indicating their willingness to intervene in France, but instead of intimidating the revolutionaries in France, it enraged and strengthened them. Promising "a war of people against kings," in April 1792 France declared war on Austria. At first France did poorly. Prussia joined Austria and for a brief moment they might have taken Paris. Patriotism inspired volunteer armies to form, singing the "Marseillaise," which became the national anthem of France. In such a fraught environment, rumors of the king's treason brought a Parisian mob into action, which led the Legislative Assembly to arrest the king. A national convention, to be elected by universal manhood suffrage, was called to write a new constitution for a republic.

The Second Revolution

This period of radicalization of the revolution saw great violence in France, the establishment of a republic, and the intensification of war. In September 1792, crowds, furious over the treason of nobles plotting with the invaders, slaughtered about half the men and women in the prisons of Paris, and the newly elected National Convention declared France a republic. The republican government sought to make deep changes in France, creating a new calendar without saint's days and with new names (mostly drawn from nature) for the months and days, and used popular celebrations to replace the people's former love of Catholic festivals.

AP Tip

The political terminology of *left* and *right* comes out of the Revolution, originally referring to the arrangement of seats by political party in the Legislative Assembly. *Left* referred to radicals like the Jacobins, while the monarchists were on the right. In current political usage, *right wing* usually refers to reactionaries or conservatives, while *left wing* refers to socialists or communists. Generally the right is concerned with order and tradition, the left with social justice.

The Jacobins dominated the convention but divided into two groups over the issue of the king after he was found guilty of treason:

the Girondists, more moderate, and the Mountain, led by Robespierre, who advocated execution of the king. Citizen Louis Capet, as he was now called, was executed on January 21, 1793, by guillotine, a new invention designed to make execution more humane. The struggle between the two revolutionary groups intensified as each saw the other undoing the Revolution. As had happened before, it was the working people of Paris, the sans culottes, who ended the political stalemate. The sans culottes wore trousers; they were too poor to wear the breeches [the culottes] and stockings of the middle and upper classes. Economic conditions in Paris had deteriorated, and they demanded redress. The Mountain organized an uprising in which thirty-one Girondists were arrested for treason, leaving the Mountain in charge. The convention created a Committee of Public Safety and gave it dictatorial power to deal with division at home and the war abroad. Robespierre was one of the twelve members of the committee. They met the demands of the sans culottes, which would also serve the country's military needs. They established maximum prices of key products, particularly bread; rationed bread; and regulated its production. The government nationalized many small workshops to turn them toward war production and requisitioned materials and grain. This embryonic socialism would excite thinkers and activists in the next century but also terrify property owners.

AP Tip

At the beginning of the Revolution, all classes had agreed on the need for political reform. But in the second revolution, the sans culottes were fighting more for economic revolution, making demands that benefited the urban poor—maximum prices, government provision of employment—but which were against the interests of shopkeepers, manufacturers, merchants, and property owners. Class warfare thus became part of the French Revolution. Incidentally, the political importance of the sans culottes led to a fashion change; men of all classes began to wear long pants in the nineteenth century.

The developments in Paris upset moderates in provincial cities, like Lyons and Marseilles, and outraged more conservative areas, like the Vendée in western France. The Committee of Public Safety unleashed a reign of terror to crush opposition at home. About 300,000 men and women were arrested on suspicion of treason, called enemies of the nation, and tried by special courts without due process of law; some 40,000 were executed. People of all classes were executed. News of the Reign of Terror spread quickly abroad and alienated many previous supporters of the Revolution while confirming the worst fears of the conservatives.

AP Tip

It is often assumed that the victims of the terror were all aristocrats. In fact, the vast majority were commoners. Outside Paris, the commoners were resentful of the domination of Paris as well of much of the revolutionary legislation, while inside Paris, they were suspected of inadequate support for the Revolution. Most aristocrats were able to emigrate.

The French, in spite of all this turmoil, began to do well at war. They stopped the Prussians, took Nice, and by November 1792 had occupied the Austrian Netherlands (Belgium). They spread the ideals of the Revolution and abolished feudalism wherever they could, but since they fed themselves off the land, they were seen as invaders more than liberators. A month after the execution of the king, France declared war on Britain, Holland, and Spain, who joined the First Coalition of Austria and Prussia and routed the French in the Austrian Netherlands. By July 1794, the French once again had taken the Austrian Netherlands and the Rhineland. Their remarkable success revealed the efficacy of nationalistically inspired soldiers, the usefulness of a planned economy during war, and the value of suppression of dissent. The enthusiasm of these soldiers who attacked relentlessly at bayonet point proved what a potent force men fighting for their own country and for ideals they believed in could be. The bonds of common loyalty inspired a new type of commitment to the defense of the nation as war became an all-consuming effort of soldier and citizen alike. The Committee of Public Safety established conscription of all unmarried men, hugely expanding the size of this army so that it outnumbered those of their enemies by around four to one. Young men rose from the ranks to become generals, chosen for their abilities, not as before, because of noble blood. This is an example of the opportunities created by the Revolution for men of talent. One of these young men was Napoleon.

REVOLUTIONARY ASPIRATIONS AND REVOLUTION IN SAINT-DOMINGUE

Haiti was a highly important sugar-producing colony of France with about half a million slaves working for a small white population of French colonial officials, wealthy planters and merchants, artisans, and poor immigrants. Starting in the 1760s, rights granted in 1685 to free people of color were replaced by discriminatory laws. After the first French Revolution, Haitian slaves hoped for freedom, free blacks for the restoration of their rights, and the white elite for a representative government. The National Assembly, after initial reluctance, granted the requests of the free blacks. In 1791, a slave rebellion in Haiti was supported by the Spanish, next door in Santo Domingo, and the English, both at war against the French. The convention in Paris abolished slavery in the colonies in October 1793 and in all French territories a few months later. The French in Haiti held the Spanish and English off with the help of Toussaint L'Ouverture, a freed slave, who was named commander of Saint-Domingue. Napoleon reestablished slavery in the colonies and had L'Ouverture arrested and taken to France, where he died in 1803. The Haitians won independence the next year by defeating the French in battle. Their slave rebellion was the only successful one in history and an inspiration to liberation movements everywhere.

AP Tip

Although it may seem that Haiti is not relevant to European history, the issue of slavery was hotly contested in France during the Revolution, caught up in both economic and ideological issues. A movement to abolish slavery and the slave trade had grown in the eighteenth century. Britain abolished the slave trade in 1807, as did France in 1833.

THE THERMIDORIAN REACTION AND THE DIRECTORY 1794–1799

This new government, the Directory, came to power after the reaction known as Thermidor, named for the month of the revolutionary calendar in which it took place. It was July 1794 on our calendar. Robespierre's Reign of Terror had gone so far as to execute his former friend and colleague Danton and the radical social democrat Hébert, as well as many of their supporters. These executions alienated the sans culottes and many of the members of the convention, who shouted Robespierre down when he tried to address them, and had him arrested and executed the next day. The middle classes, mostly respectable lawyers, reasserted their authority, with the support of the provincial cities, the better-off peasants, and the bourgeoisie. The radical, socialistic economic program of the convention was abolished; this, combined with high inflation, put the working classes in a poor position. A last revolt in early 1795 was put down by the army; the urban poor would remain quiescent politically for the next thirty-five years.

The new constitution written by the now middle-class–dominated convention established an indirectly elected legislature, which picked a five-man executive called the Directory. The Directory pursued the war with France's enemies, which reduced unemployment at home and offered plunder to the conquering soldiers. Some people, particularly religious women in the provinces, were happy about the restoration of the church. The population showed their disgust at this war by voting for pacifist and monarchist deputies in the election of 1797. The Directory used the army to nullify the elections and rule dictatorially. This weak government was easily overturned in a coup d'état by one of its most successful generals, Napoleon Bonaparte.

THE NAPOLEONIC ERA, 1799–1815

Napoleon Bonaparte was a world-historic figure who changed the course of European history. An extraordinary general, he proved to be a shrewd politician at the same time. He made deep and long-lasting reforms in France, restoring order but enforcing key elements of the Revolution.

The son of impoverished nobles in Corsica, Napoleon became a committed revolutionary who rose up quickly in the new army, winning impressive victories in Italy in 1796 and 1797. He returned to France before his reputation was damaged by a disastrous failure in Egypt the next year. Abbé Sieyès, who had written *What Is the Third Estate?* ten years earlier, urged Napoleon to return to France to join in a coup d'état against the Directory, which he saw as too weak and too dominated by nobles. In November 1799, the successful coup declared Napoleon first consul. Next month, a plebiscite on the new government was overwhelmingly approved by the French people. Napoleon instituted a number of major reforms that gratified important groups in society. The middle classes were delighted when he created the Bank of France and by his Civil Code of 1804, which guaranteed property rights and equality of all male citizens before the law. Peasants who had acquired land during the Revolution were also pleased by these measures and by the restoration of Catholicism in France. His agreement with the pope, in the Concordat of 1801, guaranteed the rights of French Catholics to practice their faith but allowed the government to nominate the bishops and pay the clergy. Nobles were relieved when Napoleon offered amnesty to some 10,000 émigrés, aristocrats who had left France during the Revolution; they returned to high offices in his expanding bureaucracy as long as they swore a loyalty oath. Disillusioned revolutionaries were recruited as ministers, prefects, and mayors. Only a small number on the extreme left or the extreme right did not find a home in Napoleon's France.

AP Tip

Napoleon also widened educational opportunities for men of talent by creating lycées, schools to train the managerial elite, which were open to capable students of all classes.

Some groups lost out under Napoleon. Women lost rights that they had gained and were placed by the Napoleonic Code under the authority of their fathers or husbands. They could not sign contracts or have bank accounts in their own name. Fathers were given absolute authority over their wives and children.

AP Tip

Women lost the right to retain their dowries, which limited their options. Workers also lost out, as trade unions were banned. However, Napoleon fed the desire of the French for glory by creating the Legion of Honor to reward service to France.

Although one part of the tripartite revolutionary slogan—equality—was established, at least for men in terms of legal rights, with the Napoleonic Code, the goal of liberty shrank under Napoleon, even before he crowned himself emperor in 1804. (See David's painting of the coronation, p. 706.) Civil liberties—freedom of the press, speech, and assembly—were severely reduced. Newspapers were closed down; only four remained by 1811. There were no real elections, only several plebiscites in which the choices were limited to yes or no. A secret police under Fouché spied on thousands of citizens, and detained or sent to mental hospitals those suspected of subversion. When Napoleon abdicated in 1814, there were some 2,500 political prisoners.

It was the third part of the slogan that Napoleon did best—fraternity. Napoleon led French armies to one victory after another, until the Peninsula War and the Russian winter took their toll. In 1802, the Treaty of Amiens recognized French possession of Holland, the Austrian Netherlands, the west bank of the Rhine, and most of Italy. Napoleon aimed to weaken England, which in 1801 stood alone against him, and planned to invade England, only to take a terrible beating in October 1805 at the important Battle of Trafalgar, which crippled the French fleet. Napoleon turned his attention east, defeating the Austrians and Russians two months later at Austerlitz. In 1806, he abolished the Holy Roman Empire and many of the smaller German states and created the German Confederation of the Rhine. Later that year he defeated the Prussians at the Battle of Jena and signed the Treaty of Tilsit with Russia. Only Britain remained outside his orbit (see map 21.2, p. 710). To punish and weaken it, Napoleon imposed the Continental System, a prohibition of the importation of British goods by European countries in the Napoleonic orbit. It proved difficult to enforce, since British manufactured goods were highly desired, and it sparked greater resistance to Napoleon.

Napoleon's grand empire had three parts: France and adjacent territories; satellite states, like Italy and Spain, on whose thrones he placed members of his family; and the independent states, Austria, Russia, and Prussia, which had signed treaties with him. Wherever the French ruled, feudalism and serfdom were abolished and the ideals of the Revolution spread. But French demands for men and monies sparked nationalistic resistance, first in Spain where monarchists, nationalists, and Catholics fought back with guerrilla warfare (see Goya's engraving, p. 711). Britain sent help to them and countered the Continental System with a counterblockade and effective smuggling of goods, particularly their manufactured goods much in demand, into Europe. When Tsar Alexander I announced that he would no longer uphold the anti-British blockade, Napoleon organized a large-scale invasion of Russia. When he invaded in June 1812 with possibly the largest force up to that time in a single army (about two-thirds made up of draftees from satellite and allied states), he expected a quick victory. The Russians initially were forced to retreat, and abandoned Moscow in the face of Napoleon's advance. After five weeks there, the French army, without sufficient food or warm clothes, was forced to retreat, a huge disaster in which hundreds of thousands of men—more than half the army—died or were taken prisoner.

Napoleon refused to accept the offer of a smaller French empire, made by the Austrian foreign minister Metternich, and soon had to face a Fourth Coalition of Britain, Austria, Prussia, and Russia. Defeated, Napoleon abdicated in 1814 and went into exile on Elba, an island off the Italian coast. The Bourbon monarchy was restored but as a constitutional monarchy, with guarantees of civil liberties, though with a rather limited electorate. But the aged Louis XVIII had little appeal. Napoleon escaped from Elba and marched his way up to Paris, ruling again for one hundred days. But once again he was defeated by the allies at the Battle of Waterloo, and this time was sent into exile far away to St. Helena, an island off the coast of Africa. He died there in 1821.

AP Tip

Napoleon remains a highly controversial figure, with some seeing him as a benevolent monarch who brought stability and greatness to France and secured important gains of the Revolution, while others are more critical, seeing him as the first modern dictator, who made his ruthless disregard of civil liberties acceptable because of nationalism. He was and is both loved and hated in France. Even his death was controversial; there's some evidence that he was poisoned, but not clear by whom.

Multiple-Choice Questions

1. The chief problem facing the monarchy before 1789 was
   (A) constant, nearly yearly, peasant revolts.
   (B) near bankruptcy.
   (C) that the Estates General insisted on voting on taxes.
   (D) lack of an heir.
   (E) hostile relations with the church.

2. Choose the correct chronological order for the following events:
   I. American Revolution
   II. France becomes a republic
   III. France becomes a constitutional monarchy
   IV. Haitian independence
   V. Napoleon becomes first consul
   (A) I, III, II, IV, and V
   (B) I, III, II, V, and IV
   (C) III, I, II, IV, and V
   (D) I, II, III, IV, and V
   (E) I, III, V, II, and IV

3. When the Third Estate took the Tennis Court Oath, Louis XVI
   (A) remained steadfast in his opposition to their demands.
   (B) gave in immediately to their demands.
   (C) disbanded the National Assembly with his troops.
   (D) refused to respond in any way in order not to dignify them.
   (E) relented after the storming of the Bastille.

4. The constitution of the constitutional monarchy created in the first French Revolution
   (A) allowed for universal suffrage.
   (B) allowed for universal male suffrage.
   (C) was accepted by the king only with great reluctance.
   (D) led to the attempted coup d'état by Napoleon.
   (E) did very little to limit royal or noble power.

5. The phrase "law is an expression of the general will" from the *Declaration of the Rights of Man and the Citizen* shows the influence of
   (A) Locke.
   (B) Montesquieu.
   (C) Descartes.
   (D) Rousseau.
   (E) Wollstonecraft.

6. The Civil Constitution of the Clergy and Napoleon's concordat with the pope both
   (A) placed the clergy under direct supervision of the papacy.
   (B) alienated the mostly religious peasants.
   (C) restored expropriated lands to the church.
   (D) effectively put the French church under national authority.
   (E) allowed priests to marry.

7. During the first and second French revolutions, the economic agendas of different social classes dominated. Which were those classes in the first and then the second revolution, respectively?
   (A) Nobility, bourgeoisie
   (B) Sans culottes, bourgeoisie
   (C) Bourgeoisie, sans culottes
   (D) Bourgeoisie, nobility
   (E) Nobility, sans culottes

8. The Reign of Terror and Napoleon's regime shared which political practice?
   (A) Repression of nobles
   (B) Repression of free political thought
   (C) Use of the plebiscite
   (D) Dictatorship by one individual that only ended with foreign intervention
   (E) Government reliance on support from labor unions

9. Which statement about the war against Austria during the second revolution and the Reign of Terror is most accurate?
   (A) It went badly for France, which survived militarily only because the Reign of Terror ended.
   (B) The government relied on volunteers to man its army.
   (C) Many soldiers refused to fight because of their opposition to the Terror.
   (D) Robespierre proved to be a surprisingly effective general.
   (E) French soldiers fought well and conquered important territories for France.

10. Napoleon's Civil Code
   (A) gave women full equality including the vote.
   (B) gave women equality before the law but not the vote.
   (C) made women legally subservient to their husbands or fathers.
   (D) allowed women economic rights, like the signing of contracts, but not political rights.
   (E) gave legal equality to noble women but not to bourgeois women.

11. The economic policies of the Committee of Public Safety can best be summarized as
   (A) proletarian communism.
   (B) mercantilism.
   (C) free-enterprise capitalism.
   (D) embryonic socialism.
   (E) guild capitalism.

12. In terms of slavery in the French colonies, Napoleon
   (A) abolished it in his Civil Code.
   (B) effectively cancelled its abolition by the convention.
   (C) did nothing.
   (D) continued the policies of the convention.
   (E) temporarily restored it to Haiti, promising to abolish it in twenty years.

13. Napoleon's blockade of British goods
   (A) was broken officially when Tsar Alexander I refused to honor it.
   (B) led Britain to make a treaty with Napoleon in 1810.
   (C) devastated the English economy.
   (D) was hugely popular in that it promoted the sale of French goods.
   (E) was effective in preventing the smuggling of British goods into Europe.

14. The government that replaced Napoleon was a(n)
    (A) absolute monarchy under Louis XVII.
    (B) constitutional monarchy under Louis XVIII.
    (C) provisional government that was to write a new constitution for France.
    (D) puppet put in by the coalition that defeated France who had little legitimacy there.
    (E) commonwealth with Napoleon's son as president.

15. The chief effect of Napoleon's rule on the territories he conquered in Europe was
    (A) to stimulate nationalistic resistance.
    (B) a series of unsuccessful revolutions against their monarchs.
    (C) little, in that he did not impose any major reforms.
    (D) the stimulation of local industries.
    (E) permanent changes in the ruling families in Spain and Italy.

Free-Response Questions

1. Analyze the political, social, economic, and intellectual causes of the French Revolution.

2. To what degree did Napoleon betray the ideals of the French Revolution?

ANSWERS

MULTIPLE-CHOICE QUESTIONS

1. ANSWER (B) It was the financial crisis and the threat of bankruptcy that forced the king to call the Estates General into session in 1789 for the first time in 175 years. Although there had been occasional peasants' revolts, they were not annual or all that disturbing to the king. (McKay, *A History of Western Society*, 8th ed., p. 698–700/9th ed., p. 684–686)

2. ANSWER (B) See the chronology that puts these events in order. The outbreak of the Haitian uprising was in 1791, after the first French Revolution; Haiti won independence under Napoleon. (McKay, *A History of Western Society*, 8th ed., p. 709, 713/9th ed., p. 685, 699)

3. ANSWER (E) Louis was indecisive and unsure. He only accepted the National Assembly's legitimacy after the sans culottes took action at the Bastille. (McKay, *A History of Western Society*, 8th ed., p. 700–703 /9th ed., p. 689–690)

4. ANSWER (C) Only about half of the men had the vote. The nobility lost their legal distinction. Napoleon's coup was not until nearly a decade later. (McKay, *A History of Western Society*, 8th ed., p. 703–704/9th ed., p. 691–692)

5. **Answer (D)** The concept of the general will comes from Rousseau and is for him the basis of popular sovereignty. Olympe de Gouges also defined law as the expression of the general will in her *Declaration of the Rights of Woman and the Female Citizen*. (McKay, *A History of Western Society*, 8th ed., p. 612, 723/9th ed., p. 714, also Chap. 18, p. 608)

6. **Answer (D)** Both documents put the church under state authority. The latter pleased the peasants while they were alienated by the first. No changes were made in religious doctrine or practice in either case. Church lands were expropriated by the Civil Constitution of the Clergy. (McKay, *A History of Western Society*, 8th ed., p.704, 714/9th ed., p. 693, 705)

7. **Answer (C)** In the first revolution, the bourgeoisie held sway (ban on labor unions and guilds, guarantee of property rights) while legislation in the second revolution was opposed by the bourgeoisie but met the needs of the sans culottes (maximum prices, nationalization of workshops, stabilized price of bread). The economic position of the nobility was undermined with their loss of manorial rights and taxation privileges. (McKay, *A History of Western Society*, 8th ed., p. 704, 708/9th ed., p. 692–693, 697)

8. **Answer (B)** Both the Reign of Terror and Napoleon ruthlessly suppressed political dissent. Labor unions were banned by Napoleon; the Reign of Terror did not use plebiscites. While Robespierre dominated, he did not rule alone; he was part of a twelve-man Committee of Public Safety empowered by the convention to rule. (McKay, *A History of Western Society*, 8th ed., p. 710, 714/9th ed., p. 697–698, 705)

9. **Answer (E)** In spite of domestic turmoil, the French did well militarily and occupied the Rhineland and the Austrian Netherlands by 1794. They instituted the draft in 1793. Robespierre was not a general. (McKay, *A History of Western Society*, 8th ed., p.708, 710–711/9th ed., p. 697–700)

10. **Answer (C)** Women lost rights under Napoleon and no longer could sign contracts or open bank accounts in their own name. They certainly were not given the vote or legal equality. They were under the authority of fathers or husbands. (McKay, *A History of Western Society*, 8th ed., p. 714/9th ed., p. 705)

11. **Answer (D)** The Committee of Public Safety instituted a variety of measures that created a planned economy—maximum prices, rationing, nationalization of workshops, requisitioning of raw materials and grain—which was an early form of socialism. (McKay, *A History of Western Society*, 8th ed., p. 708/9th ed., p. 697)

12. **ANSWER (B)** The convention had abolished slavery in 1794 and that abolition was confirmed in the Constitution of 1795, but Napoleon announced that French laws would not apply in the colonies. This meant that slavery would be restored, and prompted fierce resistance in Haiti, which ultimately led to the defeat of the French army and Haitian independence. (McKay, *A History of Western Society*, not in 8th ed./9th ed., p.702, 707)

13. **ANSWER (A)** The demand for British manufactured goods was so great that Napoleon's blockade could not be enforced. Many goods were smuggled in through Helgoland. Alexander repudiated the blockade; this prompted the invasion of Russia. The British imposed a counterblockade, which hurt the French economy. (McKay, *A History of Western Society*, 8th ed., p. 717/9th ed., p. 705, 708)

14. **ANSWER (B)** Louis XVII died in prison and never ruled. Louis XVIII ruled as a constitutional monarch from 1814 to 1824. (McKay, *A History of Western Society*, 8th ed., p. 718/9th ed., p. 708, 711)

15. **ANSWER (A)** Nationalism was sparked in the conquered peoples because Napoleon typically imposed a ruler he chose, usually someone from his own family, and because he demanded men and money to pay for his wars. The attempt to blockade British goods also brought resentment among people dependent on imports from Britain. (McKay, *A History of Western Society*, 8th ed., p. 717/9th ed., p. 708)

FREE-RESPONSE QUESTIONS

1. The key task in this essay is to discuss the various causes of the Revolution with some analysis as to why each was a cause of revolution. In other words, it is not enough to describe conditions in France before the revolution; you must specifically indicate why each led to revolution. A superior essay will evaluate the relative importance of the various causes. Among the causes you might discuss—and you should write about at least three—are the following:
   - Noble privilege and political intransigence. By refusing to allow reform of the taxation system, the nobles set in motion the events that led to their loss of privilege. A sophisticated essay would describe the differences between the old nobility and the nobility of the robe, which generally was reform minded. The nobles were not a monolithic group; some were capitalists themselves, and many were progressive in their economic thinking.
   - Incompetence of the last king. Louis XVI gave in to pressure from the nobles and abolished the Maupeou parlements. He gave the Third Estate double the number of representatives but did not change the system of voting in the Estates General. He wavered back and forth between compromise and intransigence, right up to his attempted flight. He was indecisive and incompetent, and some believed his wife was decadent, which alienated many from the regime.

- American Revolution. The revolution in American hugely increased the financial difficulties of the king. Many soldiers who had fought for American independence returned home imbued with new ideas about popular sovereignty.
- Immediate economic crisis and bad harvests. The economic problems made the lives of the peasants and urban poor more insecure, which meant they were easily called to action and mob violence.
- The ideas of the Enlightenment. Particularly the ideas of John Locke and Rousseau, which were popularized by cheap publications, created a demand for responsive and reasonable government.
- The frustrations of the bourgeoisie. The bourgeoisie were now wealthy but still excluded from political power except in individual roles. They were also angry at the nobles because of their privileges, social pretensions, and disdain for the hard-working middle classes. The bourgeoisie created wealth for France, and they demanded a constitutional government in which individual liberties and legal equality would be guaranteed and in which they could wield significant power. A superior essay will discuss how the bourgeoisie had moved closer to the nobility in terms of values; both valued land ownership and the life of a gentleman. The bourgeoisie too were not monolithic. Some, wealthy merchants and government officials, were quite conservative and others, particularly some lawyers, were liberal or even leaning toward radicalism.

2. To answer this question well, you must first define the ideals of the French Revolution. This is not a yes-or-no question, but one where you are asked to make an evaluation. Because Napoleon's regime was ambivalent on this issue, you can make many different arguments, some of which are below.
   - Liberty: There was no political freedom in Napoleon's France with a secret police, arrest of dissenters, and censorship of the press. There were no real elections, only yes-or-no plebiscites. Napoleon took power in a coup d'état and later crowned himself emperor. Members of Napoleon's family were put on the thrones of many conquered states rather than giving those people choice. Economic policies guaranteed property rights and encouraged opportunity and economic development, thus promoting economic liberty.
   - Equality: Legal equality before the law was established for men. Women lost some rights, but it can be argued that as the revolutionary government did not extend the vote or equality to women either (although they had gained the right to support for their illegitimate children and lost it under Napoleon), he was continuing the pattern established in the Revolution. Army commanders came from common as well as noble origins, continuing the practice begun in the Revolution. Feudalism and serfdom

were abolished and the Napoleonic Code was enforced in countries conquered by Napoleon. But Napoleon reinstated slavery in the colonies, which had been abolished by the convention.

- Fraternity: A string of victories and conquests by the French army was a huge stimulus to French nationalism. Napoleon sought to reunify France after its revolutionary, divisive years by giving new honors for service to the state and signing the Concordat of 1801 with the pope, which reconciled the religious Catholics. He welcomed the émigré nobles back and gave them roles to play in his government. French influence spread throughout Europe in the wake of his armies.

22

THE REVOLUTION IN ENERGY AND INDUSTRY CA 1780–1860

Perhaps to an even greater degree than the French Revolution had transformed the political landscape, the Industrial Revolution transformed not only the material conditions of life but also the social fabric in both private and public spheres. Beginning in England around the 1780s and on the continent after 1815, it radically improved the standard of living of people of all classes and changed the class structure of society and the international balance of power after 1850, giving Europeans enormous advantages in warfare and technology.

KEY CONCEPTS

- The Industrial Revolution began in Britain, which had the capacity, the resources, and the capital to respond to increased demand with new technology and new ways of organizing production.
- Industrialization on the continent developed with significant involvement of government, a quite different pattern from the process in Britain. By the outbreak of World War I, industrialization had progressed to a significant degree in Germany, Belgium, and France but much less so in Italy, Russia, and Austria-Hungary.
- Class-consciousness in both middle and working classes rose as the industrial system created clearer demarcations in occupation and lifestyle. Workers began to form unions and advocate for political change.
- Urbanization and population growth accompanied industrialization. The living and working conditions of the laborers in the early decades were terrible. There was substantial debate about how to understand the new urban poverty, and some efforts were made to

improve those conditions. By around 1840, real wages were going up and the standard of living improved.

AP Tip

What does the term *Industrial Revolution* mean? Generally speaking, it refers to the replacement of animal and human power by harnessed forms of natural energy: steam, then later electricity and oil, and still later nuclear power. It encompasses the making of goods by machines in factories, replacing hand manufacturing in the home or in small workshops, and transporting goods by railroads and steam-powered ships rather than by horse-drawn carts and sailing ships, all leading to the mass consumption of goods. Generally, industrialization is accompanied by urbanization, the addition of new classes of industrialists and workers to the social structure, and after a while, a slow but steady rise in the general standard of living.

THE INDUSTRIAL REVOLUTION IN BRITAIN

England had a combination of unique factors that fostered industrialization as the solution to the economic needs of its rising population. Among these were

- Its huge colonial empire and its control of the slave trade (asiento) brought it great wealth and offered a guaranteed market for its manufactured goods. The British already had the navy to protect sea lanes for transporting these goods overseas. Colonies also provided an additional tax base.
- Canals, built largely after 1770, as well as plentiful rivers, offered manufacturers cheap means of selling their goods in the domestic market and suitable locations for expanding cities.
- British farmers were highly productive and innovative, so there was a plentiful and inexpensive food supply, leaving people with disposable income for the purchase of manufactured goods.
- Britain had long had a national bank to provide credit.
- After 1688, political life was relatively stable. The government intervened very little in the economy and did not discourage individual initiative.
- Britain had a mobile labor force of agricultural workers available to become industrial workers.
- Britain had substantial natural resources like coal and iron, so it was not dependent on imports.

The Industrial Revolution began in the textile industry, the most important sphere of manufacturing for centuries. It had been organized by the putting-out or cottage industry, in which the capitalist provided the tools and the raw materials to cottagers and paid them to spin thread and weave the cloth at home. But this system could not meet the increasing demands of both the colonial and domestic markets. Cotton provided the impetus for change, as it allowed for the use of new technology more than the traditional textiles of wool and linen, made from flax. Two early inventions increased production in cotton manufacturing. About 1754, James Hargreaves invented the spinning jenny, a machine for the production of multiple threads from one spinning wheel, with the women operators providing power by turning the wheel, and Richard Arkwright invented the water frame, which used waterpower to operate the spinning machines. Both multiplied the production of threads so much that the weavers (mostly male) could not keep up. The water frame could drive hundreds of spindles but spin only coarse thread. Samuel Crompton solved that problem by creating another method for the mass production of fine cotton thread, requiring much more power. This helped revolutionize the organization of production, leading to concentration of spinning in factories.

Increased cotton production was beneficial in many ways. Cloth was cheaper, so poor people could afford cotton outer clothing and, for the first time, underwear, called body linen. As demand for their work grew, weavers became the best-paid workers in England, which encouraged many laborers to go into this line of work, a situation which lasted until around 1800, when better designed machines put them out of business.

AP Tip

Ironically, it may have been Napoleon's blockade, which encouraged British trade with the southern American states, that, once the cotton gin was invented, reinforced the slave system there.

Crompton's thread-making machines and the new power loom invented by Edmund Cartwright in 1785 moved workers from the cottage to factories as the site of the new machines, the special skills they required of workers, and the need for adequate power sources made the cottage impracticable. Machine-equipped factories came into use in the 1770s and 1780s; it is these cotton mills that mark the beginning of the Industrial Revolution. Some of the new factories had as many as 1,000 workers, usually working under terrible conditions. The workers were often foundlings (abandoned orphans) who were apprenticed to the factory owners as young as ages five or six—both boys and girls—for some fourteen years. They were paid very little and worked fourteen hours a day, six days a week, and were controlled with strict and often brutal discipline. These near-slavery conditions prompted reformers to seek ways to reduce such exploitation in this, the largest industry in Britain.

The factories, in turn, increased the demand for power. Wind, water, plants, animals, and humans had been the main sources of energy for millennia; this was about to change forever, and the natural limitation on production would disappear. Britain had particular needs for new sources of energy, as it had become almost completely deforested; wood was used in homes but also processed into charcoal to mix with iron ore to produce pig iron. By 1640, coal had replaced wood in London's houses and breweries and manufacturing. Britain turned to its coal reserves and looked to expand the amount mined, and faced the problem that the deeper you go in a coal mine, the more water needs to be pumped out. It was to power these pumps that the steam engine was invented, by Thomas Savery and Thomas Newcomen, which used coal to produce steam to operate a pump. The early steam engines were inefficient, but James Watt in the 1760s figured out how to increase their efficiency. He found the capital, the skilled workers, the precision parts, and the factory he needed to manufacture the improved steam engine; within twenty years, it was a huge success, and modified for use in all sorts of industries, from textiles to the crushing of sugar cane. The iron industry was transformed. With the steam engine, heavy-duty rolling mills and a new way to mix coke, from charcoal, with iron called the puddling furnace (both invented by Henry Cort), Britain quadrupled its iron production in forty years and no longer needed to import iron from Russia. Iron became cheap and a linchpin of the industrial economy. The steam engine is the single most important invention of the Industrial Revolution, creating the possibility of abundance and reduced physical labor.

One immediate impact was on transportation. As early as 1800, "steamers on wheels" were in use in American cities. The need to move large amounts of coal stimulated the development of the effective locomotive (by George Stephenson) capable of pulling a heavy load. By 1830, the first proper locomotive, the Rocket, ran in the heart of industrial England, Liverpool to Manchester, and within twenty years, Britain was covered with railroad tracks. The railroad radically reduced the cost of shipping and made previously inaccessible markets easily available, thus bringing down prices and encouraging the growth of larger factories. Farmers and day laborers took jobs building the railroads, but usually moved to the cities instead of going home when the job was done. Railroads changed the way people understood time and saw themselves. A number of important artists—J. M. W. Turner and Claude Monet—were fascinated by the power of the trains and the majesty of train stations and railway bridges, and railway engineers become cultural icons.

By 1850, England had become the workshop of the world, making about half of the world's iron and cotton cloth and two-thirds of its coal. It went from producing about 2 percent of the world's industrial output in 1750 to 20 percent a hundred years later. The GNP quadrupled. The Great Exhibition of 1851 at the Crystal Palace, so called because it was made of glass and iron, demonstrated Britain's industrial exuberance.

Population also increased dramatically, more than doubling in eighty years and providing both laborers and consumers. Although historians see this as ultimately a positive outcome, at the time it was of much concern to observers. Thomas Malthus argued in 1798 in a famous essay that population grows geometrically while food supply grows arithmetically, meaning that poverty is inevitable unless there are "positive checks" to population growth such as war or epidemics or "prudential restraint" of young people. David Ricardo followed up on Malthus's work by articulating the iron law of wages which asserted that wages would always sink to subsistence level because of overpopulation. Although they were proven wrong in the long term, their insights seemed reasonable at the time.

AP Tip

The iron law of wages was an important advance in economic theory, in that it asserted that labor was a commodity responding to the laws of supply and demand. Overpopulation means that wages would inevitably remain low. If there should be population decline, an employer would pay higher wages, but then workers would have more children and wages would go down in the next generation. Malthus, Ricardo, and Adam Smith are considered *classical liberals* in the nineteenth-century sense of the term, in that they argued that government ought not to intervene in the economy and that merchants and manufacturers must be free to operate in their self-interest, which, in theory, would be the best interest of the nation as a whole. The terms *liberal* and *conservative* had quite different meanings in the nineteenth century than they do in the twentieth and twenty-first.

INDUSTRIALIZATION IN CONTINENTAL EUROPE

Industrialization spread inconsistently and incompletely across Europe. The Napoleonic wars interfered with the export of British technology and machinery to the continent. Belgium, rich in coal and iron, was the first nation to begin to industrialize in the nineteenth century, but in the 1830s, France and the United States slowly began to catch up. France industrialized relatively slowly, reaching to about half the degree Britain had by 1913. Germany made huge progress after unification in 1870. The least industrialized of the major countries in Europe by 1900 were Italy, Austria-Hungary, and Russia (see Table 22.1, p. 728). Most nations did not follow the British model; many lacked the free labor force or sources of capital for investment in railroads and factories, and all had to compete with Britain's advanced lead and domination of world markets. But the capitalists on the continent had the advantage that they did not need to invent industrial technology but could simply import it, and several states had governments strongly motivated to engineer industrialization from above.

Although the British made the export of both skilled laborers and machines illegal, numerous clever Englishmen went abroad to set up industrial enterprises, such as the Cockerills, who settled in Belgium and built ironworks and engine manufacturing plants. Other British workers worked for European entrepreneurs creating their own enterprises, such as Fritz Harkort, who built steam engines in the Ruhr Valley, Germany. Banks played a large role in continental industrialization. Two banks in Belgium became corporations with limited liability for individual investors, and similar banks were created in France, such as the Crédit Mobilier in Paris, and in Germany in the 1850s and 1860s, which helped mobilize huge funds for investments.

Government played a much larger role in industrialization on the continent than it had in Britain, promoting tariff protection to protect new industries, building roads and canals, and funding the building of railroads. It was the building of the railroads that was both the marker of industrialization and the spur to its expansion. In Prussia, the government guaranteed bonds issued by private companies building the railroads, so investors could put in substantial sums of money at little risk. Between 1850 and 1873 when there was a financial crash, France, Belgium, and Germany saw high rates of economic growth, between 5 to 10 percent per year. Active government support was encouraged by thinkers like Friedrich List, a German journalist who argued in his influential *National System of Political Economy* of 1841 that it would pay off in the reduction of poverty and the defense of the nation. List also supported the formation in 1834 of the *Zollverein*, a customs union of Germanic states removing trade barriers between them and letting them forge common economic polices with other nations. While Britain was going toward free trade—no tariffs or export duties—List expressed the continental trend toward economic nationalism.

Relations Between Capital and Labor

Both the middle classes and the working classes were transformed by the Industrial Revolution. To the merchants, traders, and workshop owners who had previously made up the middle class were added the new groups of factory and coal mine owners, railroad magnates, and the like. To the laboring classes of artisans and day laborers was added the new industrial working class, or the proletariat, as they were called by Karl Marx. People became aware of their class status, and this class-consciousness affected their understanding of the social problems around them and their reactions to the changes stimulated by the French Revolution. A new paradigm was created, whereby membership in social classes was determined by occupation and economic status, and classes had clearly conflicting interests. To some degree, class-consciousness fed itself; as people saw themselves as distinct, they acted on those perceptions.

The new industrialists often found themselves in precarious financial straits, which led them to search for new ways to cut production costs, including jobs and wages. They themselves came from varied backgrounds: wealthy merchant families, skilled artisans, and members of minority ethnic or religious groups (Quakers, Scots, and Jews). As the industrial system developed, there were fewer and fewer opportunities for new entrepreneurs to break into it, so that in Britain by the 1830s and by thirty years later in France and Germany, factory owners usually inherited, rather than created, their enterprises. Similarly, women who had earlier played an important role in many enterprises, as can been seen in the story of Elizabeth Strutt (see Individuals in Society, p. 735), now tended to be excluded from participation in the industrial business world. A new ideal of middle-class domesticity was created instead for these women.

The conditions of the new working class improved after 1850 but were harsh before then; almost from the beginning, there was controversy over these harsh conditions, over who was responsible for them, and what could be done about them. Early on, romantic writers, such as the poets William Blake and William Wordsworth, lamented the loss of the rural lifestyle and protested against the conditions of the urban poor. The Luddites were workers themselves, mostly artisans, who protested vehemently against machine manufacturing by destroying machines. As noted above, Malthus and Ricardo thought poverty could not be alleviated. Friedrich Engels, later a colleague of Marx, wrote passionately about the horrific *Conditions of the Working Class in England* after visiting Manchester and bluntly blamed the middle classes for their exploitation and mistreatment of the poor. Engels and Marx argued that the poverty of the urban workers was worse than the old forms of poverty in the countryside, because competition for jobs and demands on workers were relentless. However, some contemporaries believed that things were getting better for the workers. Andrew Ure described good conditions in cotton factories. Edwin Chadwick, a reformer and government official, asserted that the poor had more disposable income than they had had before.

AP Tip

Why is this issue so important? Two factors are particularly relevant. The spread of industrialization around the globe means that its impact on working peoples is still a considerable issue; and in Europe, workers were politicized by socialists and communists who denounced the capitalist, industrial system for its exploitation of workers. If workers were to be found not to have been so badly off, then socialist criticism would be undermined; if the evidence were to support their claims, then their political cause would be strengthened.

Recent scholarly studies have attempted to use statistics and new sources to evaluate the conditions of the working classes. Some of the earlier impressions, for example, that workers' purchasing power did not improve in the early years of industrialization, have been confirmed by statistical analysis, which shows that in fact living conditions and wages declined until 1820. The long war Britain fought with France was hard on the workers, but over time, they ate better and more varied food and in general experienced a rising standard of living, even though the typical laborer worked some fifty days more a year in 1830 than he had in 1750, with a typical workday of eleven hours. As for working conditions, it is clear that many cottage workers were not willing to work in the new cotton mills because of the monotony of that labor, which really meant keeping up with the machines. Cottage workers appreciated that they could work when they wanted to and stop when they chose, something not possible in the industrial factory. Many of the early factory workers were so poor that they lived in poorhouses, a type of industrial prison where they had to work for their lodging and food. As noted above, the difficulty in attracting a workforce is why abandoned children were used in the early days. In 1802 Parliament forbade the employment of pauper children. Former cottage workers came to work in the factories and coal mines, continuing their tradition of working as family units, with parents disciplining and working alongside their children. As long as they could work together, most parents did not object to the employment of their children, even at young ages. But many people were horrified by child labor, including some progressive industrialists like Robert Owen and Jedediah Strutt, who opposed the employment of children under ten. Parliament established a commission to investigate conditions in the mines and factories and heard many workers testify to their experiences as child workers. It passed legislation restricting abuse of children, notably the Factory Act of 1933, which limited the working hours of children from ages nine to eighteen and required children under nine to attend school. Thus the pattern of families working together was broken.

Another type of personal relationship continued in the early days of industrialization, that of the personal ties between employers and employees that had existed in rural communities. Much of the work in factories before 1840 was given to subcontractors who had well-established relationships with their work crews. This system also helped newcomers to cities find jobs, particularly the Irish who came over to England in large numbers in the early nineteenth century and found employment and lodging with fellow Irish people.

Changes in family work patterns had a major impact on women as well as on children. Factory work became gendered, as opportunities for women in the workforce shrank. The notion of "separate spheres" emerged, with women supposed to be at home and men the primary bread earners. Even working-class women were less likely to work full-time, unless their husbands were ill or absent. But even if a woman worked full-time, she wouldn't earn enough to be able to live on her own; women were paid substantially less than men for the same work and typically were given the poorer-paying jobs. Why this happened is much disputed by historians. Some see continuity of patriarchal patterns in craft unions; others point out the particular conditions of industrial work. Working by the clock is harder on mothers; women could not breast-feed or tend babies while they manned machines, and the long workday made it harder for women to fulfill their household duties of shopping, cooking, and cleaning. Employment in factories and mines had also brought young people of both sexes into easy intimacy in the workplace, which partially explains the explosion of illegitimate births, so older people sought to keep men and women apart at work. The commissioners who heard testimony (see Listening to the Past, pp. 744–745) about mine conditions—where heat led both men and women to work in relative undress—were shocked, assuming that such behavior encouraged debauchery, though in fact most of the women worked alongside family members who protected them. The Mines Act of 1842 prohibited women, as well as boys under ten, from working in the mines. Some women were happy about the change, as running the household placed quite sufficient demands on them and they knew full well the impact working in the mines and factories had on their health and the lives of their children.

The Early Labor Movement in Britain

It is important to remember that even with industrialization under full sway, half of British workers in 1850 still worked on the land, and many of the rest worked as household servants. Artisans continued to make things by hands in those industries where large-scale capitalistic investment and new technology were not necessary. While the iron mining and smelting were completely done in large-scale enterprises, artisans continued to forge iron into small goods until 1850 or so when new machines came into use. Workers of all types began to develop class-consciousness. In large factories, the workers had a growing sense of solidarity with other workers, partially because of their very numbers—perhaps a thousand—against the few owners and managers. In the small workshops, too, workers developed class-consciousness, especially after the repeal of acts protecting apprentices and artisans reduced their wages. Although the Combination Acts of 1799 had banned them, unions began to be organized, and anticapitalistic sentiments were expressed in both print, newspapers, and action, strikes and protests. Finally in 1824, the Combination Acts were repealed, and unions became legal if not fully accepted.

AP Tip

It was the laissez-faire liberals who encouraged the passing of the Combination Acts and other legislation freeing up the rules for the craft guilds, on the ground that unions and guilds restricted the free operation of the market. And it was the conservatives in Parliament who pushed for the Factory and Mines Act to protect workers and reduce the freedom of industrialists to operate their enterprises without any regulation.

Robert Owen, who had opposed the employment of young children, was a successful manufacturer who believed that workers would be more productive if treated well. His cooperative, socialistic societies (New Lanark in Scotland and New Harmony in Indiana in the United States) were experiments in new forms of organization of work and workers' lives. In 1834, he tried to create a national union of workers with the short-lived Grand National Consolidated Trades Union, though ultimately such a union did come into being. Some unions, like those of the skilled machinists, were successful in winning benefits for workers as they tended not to be very radical and therefore more easily accepted.

Many workers in the 1840s joined a reformist political movement called the Chartists, which proposed a six-point charter to establish political democracy; one demand was universal male suffrage. Others became involved in political movements to limit the workday and to lower bread prices by abolishing protectionist tariffs against foreign wheat. Thus the working classes were becoming more and more politically adept and more and more important.

Multiple-Choice Questions

1. Which was *not* discussed in the textbook as a reason why Britain was the first to industrialize?
   (A) Its good water transportation system
   (B) Its colonial empire
   (C) Its stable political system
   (D) Its Protestantism
   (E) Its productive agriculture
2. In the first factories, the workforce was predominately
   (A) women displaced from the cottage industry.
   (B) foundling apprentices.
   (C) unemployed agricultural day laborers.
   (D) young boys but not girls.
   (E) weavers.
3. Which inventor is *incorrectly* matched with his invention?
   (A) Cort—puddling furnace
   (B) Stephenson—locomotive
   (C) Watt—improved steam engine
   (D) Arkwright—spinning jenny
   (E) Newcomen—steam engine
4. England's energy crisis was a result mostly of
   (A) deforestation.
   (B) exhaustion of coal reserves.
   (C) lack of rivers to use for water power.
   (D) poor roads that hindered transport.
   (E) lack of iron.
5. Malthus and Ricardo would both agree that
   (A) one solution to poverty was to pay higher wages.
   (B) poverty was inevitable.
   (C) economic growth will end poverty in the long term.
   (D) the government must provide jobs when the private section cannot.
   (E) capitalism is an evil system.
6. Friedrich List in Germany
   (A) supported industrialization for nationalistic reasons.
   (B) rejected the idea of a *Zollverein* as a hindrance to economic progress.
   (C) warned against the dangers of Prussian industrialization.
   (D) claimed that free trade was the best path to prosperity.
   (E) argued that nationalism would get in the way of economic progress.

7. One significant difference in the process of industrialization in England and the continent was
   (A) banks were less important on the continent.
   (B) support for free trade was strong in Germany.
   (C) the English focused on luxury goods.
   (D) many governments actively promoted industrialization on the continent.
   (E) there was reluctance to use skilled workers from Britain on the continent because of nationalistic sentiments.

8. The industries that first propelled industrialization forward in England and in Germany and Belgium were
   (A) textiles in both countries.
   (B) textiles in Britain and railroads in Germany and Belgium.
   (C) iron production in Britain and textiles in Germany and Belgium.
   (D) textiles in Britain and armaments in Germany and Belgium.
   (E) shipbuilding in Britain and iron production in Germany and Belgium.

9. By 1850, industrial workers in the United Kingdom
   (A) were working fewer days than they had as agricultural laborers.
   (B) typically worked eight- to nine-hour days.
   (C) saw a rise in real wages.
   (D) had organized a powerful national union.
   (E) were the majority of the employed.

10. Women were forbidden from working in mines in legislation passed in 1842 because
    (A) it was believed that the conditions of the mines encouraged debauchery.
    (B) women went on strike in the mines.
    (C) they were seen as too physically weak to do such work.
    (D) it was such well-paid work that men argued it should be given to the breadwinners in the family.
    (E) women had to be paid for the days they were giving birth.

11. Artisans in craft workshops by the early nineteenth century
    (A) had disappeared because of competition from factory-produced goods.
    (B) developed a sense of solidarity with workers as the guilds became more competitive.
    (C) continued working in some fields like baking but not in others like iron mongering.
    (D) refused to join unions or labor groups.
    (E) opened up their leadership to women to infuse new blood.

12. The gendering of work and the idea of separate spheres
    (A) affected women of the working but not the middle classes.
    (B) affected women of the middle but not the working classes.
    (C) affected women in domestic service but not other workers.
    (D) affected both working- and middle-class women.
    (E) was restricted mostly to aristocratic women.

13. In the early days of the industrial revolution, child labor was
    (A) banned completely by legislation.
    (B) considered desirable by parents because it kept families together.
    (C) opposed by working-class parents who were, however, powerless to prevent it.
    (D) considered unnecessary and undesirable by most industrialists.
    (E) limited to abandoned or orphaned children.

14. The testimony of mine workers in the 1840s showed that
    (A) female workers were generally illiterate.
    (B) the coal owners were well aware of conditions in the mines.
    (C) girls were rarely used as hurriers, workers who move coal wagons underground.
    (D) girls usually did not start working in the mines until they were in their teens.
    (E) Sunday schools provided good religious instruction.

15. Which of the following praised the industrial system?
    (A) William Blake
    (B) Friedrich Engels
    (C) William Wordsworth
    (D) Andrew Ure
    (E) Robert Owen

Free-Response Questions

1. How did the Industrial Revolution transform family and gender relations?
2. In what ways did workers attempt to influence the industrial system in nineteenth-century Britain?

ANSWERS

MULTIPLE-CHOICE QUESTIONS

1. **ANSWER: (D)** Although Britain had been Protestant for about 200 years, its religion was not mentioned as a significant factor in its early industrialization. (McKay, *A History of Western Society*, 8th ed., p. 726/9th ed., pp. 718–719)

2. **ANSWER: (B)** Foundlings were apprenticed to factory owners and worked under harsh conditions. Because working conditions in the first factories were so terrible, few people were willing to work in them. (McKay, *A History of Western Society*, 8th ed., p. 729/9th ed., pp. 720–721)

3. **ANSWER: (D)** Arkwright invented the water frame; Hargreaves invented the spinning jenny. (McKay, *A History of Western Society*, 8th ed., pp. 728–732/9th ed., p. 720)

4. **ANSWER: (A)** The lack of forests led to a shortage of wood and therefore a shortage of charcoal for the making of iron. Iron is not a source of energy. The British had plenty of coal but needed pumps to get the water out as they dug deeper. (McKay, *A History of Western Society*, 8th ed., pp. 729–730/9th ed., p. 721)

5. **ANSWER: (B)** They both draw the same conclusion, for different reasons, that poverty is inevitable. (McKay, *A History of Western Society*, 8th ed., pp. 734–735/9th ed., p. 726)

6. **ANSWER: (A)** List was an economic nationalist. Only the British—and only some of them—were free traders in the nineteenth century. (McKay, *A History of Western Society*, 8th ed., pp. 739–740/9th ed., pp. 731–732)

7. **ANSWER: (D)** The role of the government was a significant difference in industrialization, in that it stayed out of the picture, by and large, in England, but was actively involved on the continent, protecting investments and building infrastructure. (McKay, *A History of Western Society*, 8th ed., pp. 737–738/9th ed., pp. 730–732)

8. **ANSWER: (B)** The Industrial Revolution began in the textile industry in Britain, but for Germany, it was the building of the railroads that prompted industrial growth in other sections, particularly iron. The industrial armaments industry was relatively small at this time. (McKay, *A History of Western Society*, 8th ed., pp. 727, 739/9th ed., pp. 719–721, 730)

9. **ANSWER: (C)** Industrial workers were still a minority of the workforce in 1800; agriculture and domestic service were the dominant areas for work. They worked more days than before and usually eleven hours a day, but real wages began to rise. (McKay, *A History of Western Society*, 8th ed., pp. 744–746/9th ed., pp. 736, 740)

10. **ANSWER: (A)** Because of the heat, men and women often worked nearly naked, and this, some observers argued, led to immorality. (McKay, *A History of Western Society*, 8th ed., pp. 747–748, 753/9th ed., pp. 739, 744–745)

11. **ANSWER: (B)** When the legislation protecting apprentices in the guilds was repealed, craft workers found themselves unprotected and facing competition that drove down their wages; this led them to greater class-consciousness. They continued to be active until the mid- to late-nineteenth century, still making iron goods, although with machine-made iron. (McKay, *A History of Western Society*, 8th ed., pp. 748–749/9th ed., p. 740)

12. **ANSWER: (D)** Middle- and working-class women were both affected by the gendering of work. Middle-class women were pushed out of managerial roles, and working-class women were restricted by law from certain types of labor. (McKay, *A History of Western Society*, 8th ed., pp. 747–748/9th ed., pp. 738–739)

13. **ANSWER: (B)** As families had worked together on the farm and in the cottage, parents continued that pattern in the early days of factory

work until child labor was limited by legislation in 1833; it was not banned completely until much later. (McKay, *A History of Western Society*, 8th ed., pp. 744–746/9th ed., pp. 737–738)

14. **ANSWER: (A)** Two girls whose testimony is reproduced in Chapter 22 said they did not know how to read or write. They all started working in the mines before they were ten, and all had been hurriers. One girl said she had never heard of Jesus. The testimony of the coal master showed he had little idea of the real conditions in the mines. (McKay, *A History of Western Society*, 8th ed., pp. 752–753/9th ed., pp. 744–745)

15. **ANSWER: (D)** Ure thought the conditions in cotton factories were pretty good. Blake and Wordsworth were romantics who opposed industrialization for its impact on both environment and people. Owen, although a manufacturer, formed socialistic communities and tried to form a national union. (McKay, *A History of Western Society*, 8th ed., pp. 742, 749/9th ed., pp. 734, 738, 741)

FREE-RESPONSE QUESTIONS

1. This question asks you to describe the impact of the Industrial Revolution on women and family relationships. It would be wise to separate the two, as the impact on them was not identical. In a social history question like this, specificity is particularly important so that you can show you are not relying on or making up generalizations.

- Impact on families: In the early industrial period, the impact was not great, as families continued to work together in factories, as they had on farms and in cottages. The father often acted as contractor for the family and parents disciplined their children. Child labor generally was welcomed by these families but opposed by reformers like Robert Owen. Parliament banned the employment of children under nine and limited the hours of older children in the Factory Act of 1833. The tradition of families working together ended because of this. Long working hours—eleven a day—and exhaustion from the physical work usually meant families had little time together once the Factory Act was passed.
- Impact on women: Middle-class women like Elizabeth Strutt worked alongside their husbands as managers of factories or as merchandisers of goods, but this began to change as the industrial system became established. Women were generally excluded from the world of business and expected to manage the household only. Similarly, for working women, the doctrine of separate spheres furthered the idea that women should stay home and tend the household and men should work outside the home. Originally, women were a large part of the industrial workforce. They did the same work as men in mines, though it impinged more on their physical health, and their smaller hands were particularly desirable in the textile factories. Reasons for gendering of work are debated, but some factors are the difficulties of being a mother on factory time and the intimate working conditions of men and women working together, which led to sexual intimacy in many cases. Legislation forbidding women from working in mines was passed in 1842.

2. Workers' attempts to influence the industrial system in nineteenth-century Britain changed over time.

- In the early period of industrialization, workers influenced the industrial system first by resisting it; Luddites destroyed machines, and cottage workers refused to work in factories. When they began to work in factories, they brought with them their traditional practices of working in family groups and maintaining strong and personal employer-employee relationships. The latter were maintained by the frequent use of subcontractors in the factories. The Irish particularly benefited from this in that they found compatriots to give them work and lodging. Families worked together, adults and children alike, until the Factory Act of 1833.
- Later, workers formed unions and went on strike for better wages and conditions, although it was against the law. Some, like the unions of machinists, were reasonably successful in winning improvements for their members. Pressure from workers led Parliament to repeal the Combination Acts. In the 1830s, Robert Owen led an unsuccessful attempt to create a national union. Workers joined the Chartist movement, demanding political democracy and organized politically to reduce the workday and end protectionist tariffs that kept cheap foreign wheat out of Britain. Workers also developed their own newspapers and worked for solidarity across the various occupations, including those of the skilled artisans.

23

IDEOLOGIES AND UPHEAVALS, 1815–1850

The thirty-five years after the defeat of Napoleon were tumultuous. The forces and changes unleashed by the Industrial and French Revolutions—the dual revolution as it was called by the noted historian Eric Hobsbawn—over time transformed the entire world and gave birth to both new intellectual understandings and new political movements. Ideologies, that is, sets of political ideals and theoretical interpretations that take root so firmly that political action of some sort or another follows, were unique creations of the early nineteenth century and remained powerfully in force for the next century and a half. The political settlement after Napoleon's defeat attempted to hold back change and impose a single ideology, but repression only led to violent outbursts virtually everywhere in Europe in 1848.

KEY CONCEPTS

- The profoundly conservative Congress of Vienna sought to reestablish the order that had existed before Napoleon. It restored the legitimate monarchs displaced by Napoleon's rule and, with a few exceptions, undid the changes he had made. The major powers formed alliances to uphold this order through military action and internal repression of nationalistic and liberal ideas.
- New and powerful ideologies were formed in the early nineteenth century: liberalism, nationalism, and socialism, the latter first in utopian varieties and then in Marxism.
- Romanticism was less an ideology than a movement with many threads, some romantics being conservative or even reactionary, others liberal and nationalistic. It appealed to many artists and writers, and was particularly profound in its influence on music.
- Great Britain underwent significant political change in 1832 when the Great Reform Bill redistributed the seats in Parliament and

expanded the suffrage. France became a constitutional monarchy after a revolution in 1830. Greece established a monarchy after its successful revolt against Ottoman rule.

- In one country after another, liberal or nationalistic revolutions took place in the spring of 1848, with almost all of them defeated within a few months. Few reforms lasted, and the failure to unite Germany as a constitutional state had enormous consequences later on.

THE PEACE SETTLEMENT

When the Grand Coalition defeated Napoleon in 1814, their leaders met in Vienna to redraw the map of Europe and to ensure peace by creating an effective balance of power. France's newly restored Bourbon monarchy was represented by the shrewd Talleyrand, Austria by the deeply conservative and powerful foreign minister Metternich, Prussia by its chancellor Prince Hardenberg, England by Lord Castlereagh, and Russia by Tsar Alexander I himself. Each of the four victorious powers gained valuable land: Prussia expanded in Saxony and the Rhineland, Austria won Lombardy and Venetia as well as Galicia in Poland, and Russia was to rule a restored small Polish kingdom. England kept what she had won outside of Europe during the wars. France lost relatively little territory, considering the twenty years of war in which it had embroiled Europe, nor was it originally required to pay war reparations. After Napoleon's One Hundred Days, France had to pay an indemnity and accept occupation for five years. The allies enlarged Holland, now a monarchy, and Prussia to ward off French expansionism. After the congress ended, the four victorious powers met periodically to enforce the peace settlement.

AP Tip

It's important to remember the Congress of Vienna when considering the Paris Peace Conference or the Versailles peace settlement made after World War I. Germany expected to be treated more or less as France had been in 1814; instead Germany was not invited to the peace conference and was given a draconian peace.

A more insidious effort to repress the ideas and energies unleashed by the dual revolution was undertaken by the three conservative states, Austria, Prussia and Russia, who formed the Holy Alliance in 1815. When liberals revolted in Spain and in Sicily in the early 1820s, a meeting of the Quadruple Alliance, now with France as a member, at Troppau made a commitment to defend autocratic regimes with military intervention if necessary. France sent troops to Spain, and Austria to Sicily, and they restored the monarchs that had been overthrown. The use of military force to repress revolutionary change, known as the Metternich system, generally was successful until 1848, although the American colonies of Spain did win independence in 1823, and Belgium became independent in 1830. In the German Confederation, which replaced the 300-odd member Holy Roman Empire and comprised Austria and Prussia and thirty-seven other states, Metternich imposed political repression with the infamous Carlsbad Decrees, which restricted freedom of assembly and the press and academic freedom in German universities.

Metternich, Austrian foreign minister from 1809 to 1848, was a brilliant diplomat and a fierce advocate of conservative values. Traditional classes, the nobility, and traditional values would conserve stability and protect against dangerous ideas like liberalism and nationalism, which, conservatives believed, led only to revolution, violence, disorder, and bloodshed. Nationalism in the form of national self-determination was particularly threatening to the multinational Austrian, Ottoman, and Russian empires. Metternich's empire was made up of numerous ethnic or national groups, dominated by his own, the Germans, who made up only about 25 percent of the population. The two other major national groups, the Hungarians (Magyars) and the Czechs (Bohemians), had already challenged German domination, and there were dozens of smaller groups of Slavic peoples plus Italians and Romanians in the empire. (Be sure to look at the map on p. 752). Should ethnic nationalism and its typical handmaiden, liberalism, come to the fore, as they did in 1848 and 1914, the Austrian Empire would be in serious danger. In fact, this is what caused World War I and ultimately the end of all three empires.

RADICAL IDEAS AND EARLY SOCIALISM

The ideologies created in the wake of the dual revolution challenged the conservative world order and its defense of hereditary monarchy, strong aristocracy, and established church. But these ideologies themselves were very different and often in opposition to each other.

AP Tip

It is important to recognize that these ideologies were not mutually exclusive. Many liberals were nationalists and many nationalists were liberals, although other nationalists were conservatives. Romanticism fed into nationalism in many ways; socialism was more isolated. Liberals and socialists often worked together to change governments but then came to loggerheads over the degree to which social legislation should dominate. As Marxian socialism abjured nationalism when it argued that class, not nationality, was the main determinant of identity, socialists tended not to be nationalists in the nineteenth century, although that was no longer true in the twentieth century. *The Communist Manifesto* ends with the internationalist cry "Working men of all countries, unite!"

LIBERALISM

Liberalism stresses freedom. It developed along two strands, which sometimes worked together and sometimes did not. One was political liberalism, seeking constitutional government, equality before the law, the expansion of suffrage, and civil liberties. Only Britain and France after 1815 had liberal governments. The second strand was economic liberalism, or laissez-faire capitalism, which defended the free market, opposed all hindrances to its operation whether unions or monopolies, rejected mercantilism, and demanded that governments leave the economy alone to operate on its own laws. The founder of this doctrine, known as classical liberalism, was Adam Smith, a Scottish Enlightenment philosopher, whose 1776 treatise, *The Wealth of Nations*, was the first major text in modern economics. Free competition, allowing the law of supply and demand to operate freely, would improve the standard of living for all, he said. (Malthus and Ricardo, discussed in Chapter 22, were also classical liberals.) Business groups enthusiastically adopted classical liberalism and were able to influence governments to ban labor unions. Usually these business groups supported political liberalism—expansion of the suffrage and written constitutions guaranteeing civil liberties—as a way to secure their economic interests, but they wanted to limit the suffrage to property holders. In response, some supporters of political freedom became radical democrats or republicans.

NATIONALISM

Nationalism also had several strands. One was cultural nationalism, which asserted that each ethnicity or nation, meaning people, has a distinct identity based on common language, food, dance, traditions, and often but not always religion. For an excellent example of nationalist feelings, read at the end of the chapter how the Czech nationalist Palacky expressed his love of his culture and his devotion to his people in his *Letter to the German National Assembly*. As this cultural identity was more often a dream than a reality in the early nineteenth century, early nationalists looked for ways to create it. Nationalists used emotionally laden symbols and ceremonies to make these imagined communities seem real, to create a sense of the nation, and to enhance the image of its nobility. After 1850 mass education would work for the same goal, as well as for economic goals like industrialization, which could be more easily advanced if people could use a common language.

AP Tip

The nineteenth century saw a great increase in interest in folk culture for nationalistic reasons. Nationalistic writers, like the Grimm brothers, Jacob and Wilhelm, often sought to collect folk legends, such as fairy tales, while nationalistic composers, like Frédéric Chopin, used folk songs in their compositions. In this manner, nationalism and romanticism intertwined. Popular novels also helped create a common literary language, which was typically codified in dictionaries.

Political nationalism, the second strand, also had two aspects. In already formed states, it meant patriotism, love of and commitment to country, and the drive to enhance the country's prestige and power. The more explosive form of nationalism developed where nation-states had not yet been formed. Nationalists demanded the right to form a state whose contours were determined by the nation—people sharing a common culture. This meant unification in the case of Italy and Germany, and independence for the subject nationalities under Austrian, Russian, or Ottoman rule. In those three empires, the two nationalisms collided, with Czechs, Hungarians, and Poles bridling under the national rule of their imperial overlords. Cultural nationalism became politicized by the 1848 revolutions. Many if not most nationalists were also political liberals, such as Mazzini, who saw individual liberty as intimately connected with the freedom of the nation and advocated a centralized democratic republic for Italy. But most nationalists also believed in the superiority of their people. The historian Jules Michelet, for example, claimed that his people, the French, were mankind's saviors. A follower of the eighteenth-century Italian philosopher Giambattista Battista Vico, who had argued that history was about societies and institutions, not great men, Michelet used his professional writing to spur French nationalism (see Individuals in Society, p. 769). He applauded Joan of Arc and the French Revolution as great moments of national revival, and in a widely read 1846 book called *The People*, exhorted the French to unify. Michelet is a good example of how the study of history influenced national development. In the twentieth century, nationalistic goals were achieved at the cost of political liberalism in many countries.

French Utopian Socialism

Socialism in France began after 1815 as industrialization spread and commentators sought to address its impact. Early socialists urged a planned economy, as France had had under the Convention, arguing that leaving control over the organization of the economy to the private sector was both exploitative and inefficient. Egalitarians, they urged either the abolition or restriction of private property; instead property should be owned communally or by the state in the name of the people. Only in this way could poverty be eliminated and a socially just society be created. French thinkers influenced workers who were beginning to show class-consciousness and political self-awareness.

Henri de Saint-Simon was an enthusiastic supporter of industrial development, but it must be used, he argued, for the improvement of all, including the poor. The economy ought to be controlled by a technologically sophisticated elite made up of scientists, engineers, and industrialists. Large-scale public works projects should be undertaken to improve the infrastructure and provide employment.

Charles Fourier took another approach. A fierce defender of freedom of choice, he opposed traditional marriage because it bound people together, often against their will. He established utopian communities, each with 1,620 people, where free love and voluntary unions were the norm. Many women were enthusiastic followers of Fourier, who was an early proponent of the total emancipation of women.

Louis Blanc fought for a new right, the right to work, the right to a job to be provided by the government when the private sector could not. Blanc advocated the establishment of workshops and factories by the government to achieve full employment.

AP Tip

Fourier's communities tended to be short-lived and were vilified by traditional moralists. In addition to free love, they were based on the idea that people should be able to choose a variety of different work tasks and not be bound to only one type of productive activity; the government of the community's responsibility was mostly to organize the schedule. Blanc's idea of the *right to work* should not be confused with how that term is usually used in contemporary America, where it means opposition to mandatory union membership; labor activists consider it to be anti-union and definitely not socialist. The right to work in its European definition—meaning the right to a job—will become a key part of the communist program in Soviet Russia. Saint-Simon was forward-thinking in his view that the most important people in society are not the nobles or clergy but the technocrats. The meritocracy he supported is now firmly in place in most Western societies.

Pierre Joseph Proudhon was not a utopian socialist but an anarchist who rejected the power of the state. Nevertheless, he articulated a profoundly socialist idea in his 1840 pamphlet *What Is Property?* His simply stated answer, "Property is theft," meaning that private wealth is always stolen from the workers who create it, led to the logical conclusion that it should be abolished.

The Birth of Marxian Socialism

Marxism was created by the joint efforts of two German intellectuals, Karl Marx and Friedrich Engels. Together they wrote the *Communist Manifesto* in 1848, in which they called for a revolution of the workers against the capitalist state and its replacement by socialism. Marxism is both a theoretical analysis of history and society and an impassioned call for political action.

As a historian and philosopher of history, Marx adapted ideas from two previous philosophers. From the classical liberal David Ricardo (see Chapter 22) he took the labor theory of value, which asserts that the value of any object is determined, with rare exceptions, by the labor that goes into producing it. Marx drew the conclusion, which Ricardo had not, that therefore all profit is based on exploitation as the workers create value but do not get it; instead it goes to the capitalist. From Georg Hegel, a major German philosopher, he took the theory of dialectics, which argues that change happens when an idea (the thesis) creates its opposite (the antithesis) and these two struggle with each other, ultimately forming a combination of the two (the synthesis), which becomes the new thesis. Society is ever moving forward to an ultimate end, which for Hegel was freedom. Marx rejected Hegel's stress on ideas and used the dialectic to analyze economic relations in society instead. Marx argued that history is not about the history of ideas but instead about class struggle, with two fundamental classes in any society opposing each other—the owners of the means of productions (farms, factories, etc.) and those who work for them; these are the thesis and antithesis, and in the struggle between them, social and economic change occurs. In feudal societies, the two classes were the nobles and the serfs; out of their struggle came the bourgeoisie, which played a crucial, revolutionary role when it created first the commercial and then the industrial economies. But now it has spawned its opposite, the proletariat or industrial working class, and just as surely as the bourgeoisie took over from the aristocracy, so too will the proletariat take over from the bourgeoisie. The victory of the proletariat is inevitable and when that happens, humanity as a whole and each individual will reach the highest level of development. This theoretical model was the basis for new historical analysis and for what some consider a new secular religion. Certainly it was an energizing call to action for workers and the occasional intellectual from the middle classes, like Marx and Engels themselves, who joined them.

AP Tip

The philosophical name of Marxism is dialectical materialism, dialectical referring to the process of change, and materialism referring to the fundamental importance of the economic relations of society. It is possible to find the theory of dialectical materialism useful as an analytical tool without accepting Marxist politics. Marxism has had a great impact on scholarship as well as in politics.

ROMANTICISM

Romanticism was a movement particularly strong in England and Germany from the 1770s through the 1840s, which both drew on and flowered into many threads. Generally rejecting Enlightenment rationalism and classicism, romantics also lamented the changes brought by the Industrial Revolution. The roots of the movement can be found in Rousseau, who exalted feeling over reason, and in the French Revolution, which contributed the idea that radical change was possible. In Germany, the movement was called *Sturm und Drang,* meaning "storm and stress," highlighting the intense emotionality of both thought and deed, which romantics believed was the essence of life.

Artists and young people were romanticism's greatest adherents. They were expected to live short but intense lives as unique individuals, breaking social rules and rejecting the materialism around them both in philosophy and society. Romantics were fascinated by the power and unpredictability of nature, which they saw as a source of spiritual power, and often went off to wild places to avoid the new cities, which they saw as evidence of the destructive nature of industrialization. Instead of either the modern or the classical world, they idealized the medieval period as an age of faith and chivalry. Many romantics became impassioned about history, whose dynamism demonstrated the true nature of the universe and served to stir national identity.

Romanticism flowered first in English literature in the late eighteenth and early nineteenth centuries. The poets John Keats, Percy Bysshe Shelley, William Wordsworth, Samuel Coleridge, and Lord

Byron and the novelist Walter Scott became the most famous group of British writers since Shakespeare. Wordsworth moved British poetry away from flowery language and formal conventions to simplicity and emotional expression of love of nature and the joys of solitude, as in his poem "Daffodils," which begins *I wandered lonely as a cloud* (pp. 759–760). Scott wrote historical novels about the Middle Ages of Scotland. In Germany, the most important writer was the great poet, novelist, and dramatist Johann Wolfgang von Goethe, who influenced legions of authors, including Scott, in his exploration of the individual hero. In France, there were numerous romantic writers inspired by Madame Germaine de Staël, an important writer in exile from Napoleon's France. Victor Hugo, author of *The Hunchback of Notre Dame,* was an advocate of political as well as personal freedom. George Sand, the pen name of a woman author of over eighty novels, was a flamboyant figure herself who left her husband and children, preferred to wear men's clothing, and had numerous love affairs known to her public. In Russia, the renowned poet Alexander Pushkin forged the modern Russian literary language. Many romantic writers were also nationalists, such as the brothers Grimm, previously mentioned, who collected German folk tales, songs, and proverbs. Goethe's beautiful German helped forge German national consciousness.

In music and art, romanticism lasted even longer as a movement. Painters used dramatic scenes, exotic subjects, and intense colors to stir the emotions. In France, the most important romantic artist was Eugene Delacroix, who painted Moroccan women but also many politicized works such as *Massacre at Chios,* which fueled support for the Greek war of independence against the Turks. In England, J. W. T. Turner and John Constable were fascinated by nature, Constable by rural landscapes, and Turner by turbulent seas and dramatic skies. Perhaps it was in music that romanticism achieved its broadest influence. Romantic composers expanded the size of the symphony orchestra and the range of musical forms. Compositions grew more emotional, more intense, and more pointed in their cultural or political messages. Chopin's Revolutionary Etude was meant not only to stir the listener's emotions but also to support the Polish cause. The venue of performance was transformed from court, church, and salon to concert halls, where great composer-pianists like Lizst performed before huge adoring crowds. The apogee of romantic composers was the iconic Ludwig van Beethoven, whose music was astounding in its ability to express and stir the noblest of emotions and whose life was the paradigm of the tortured genius.

AP Tip

It is an indication of how iconic Beethoven is that when the Berlin Wall came down in 1989, the music chosen for a concert conducted by the American Leonard Bernstein to celebrate this extraordinary event was Beethoven's Ninth Symphony. When they sang the "Ode to Joy" (based on a poem by Friedrich Schiller, one of the great German romantic poets) of the famous choral movement, the word *joy* was changed to freedom (from *Freude* to *Freiheit*).

CHALLENGES TO THE CONSERVATIVE ORDER IN GREECE, BRITAIN, AND FRANCE

The first revolution to succeed, after those in Spain and Sicily had been crushed by the forces of Metternich and his allies, was in Greece. Revolt against the Ottoman sultan broke out in 1821, led by Alexander Ypsilanti. Metternich and his fellow conservatives reacted as they had before, and refused to back Ypsilanti, but others, particularly in England and France, refused to follow suit, largely because of their attachment to the culture of ancient Greece. The romantic poet Lord Byron went to Greece to fight for its liberty and died there. Russians felt kindred to the Orthodox Greeks, and these three states sent their navies to force the Ottomans to grant Greece its independence; this ultimately happened in 1830. Russia took advantage of the situation to establish a protectorate in Romania, which had hitherto been under Ottoman rule.

In England, demands for change in the generally stable political system grew. The suffrage was very limited—about 8 percent of the population and the aristocracy still dominated in spite of all the economic changes in England. After 1815, under the leadership of the Tory party, conservative aristocrats grew increasingly repressive of liberal ideas. One hotly contested issue was the protectionist legislation called the Corn Laws (*corn* was the English word for wheat) designed to keep out cheap foreign wheat, which kept grain prices high at home and benefited the large landowners. In 1815, the aristocracy was able to pass even more stringent Corn Laws just as unemployment was rising in England, and the need for lower food prices greater. Protests were met with repression; the Tories temporarily revoked the rights to assemble and habeas corpus in 1817 and two years later used armed cavalry to break up a protest in Manchester. This incident, called the Battle of Peterloo after the field on which it took place, symbolized the intransigence of the conservatives. Liberal activists in Parliament, some of whom were aristocrats, and in the business elite formed the Whig party and were able to win some reforms in the 1820s, particularly civil rights for Catholics, more laissez-faire legislation, and limited imports of grain from abroad. In 1832, popular protests helped them convince the House of Lords to allow the passage of the Great Reform Bill, which altered British politics forever. It made the House of Commons more important than the House of Lords, expanded the suffrage to about 12 percent of the male population, and gave new seats in the House of Commons to the heavily populated industrial cities and removed "rotten boroughs," which had few residents and had been easily controlled by local nobles. Ordinary people pushed for greater democracy in the Chartist movement, with huge numbers signing petitions, only to see them rejected by the House of Commons. Workers also joined with manufacturers on the issue of imported grain in the Anti-Corn Law League, formed in 1839, which was able to win its case in Parliament when the failure of the Irish potato crop in 1846 created famine. The repeal of the Corn Laws in 1846 meant the victory of free trade (i.e., no protectionist tariffs or restrictions). The next year, the Tories, in an effort to woo the labor vote, passed the Ten

Hour Act limiting the working day for women and young people in factories.

THE POTATO FAMINE IN IRELAND

Conditions for the Irish farmers were very poor, made worse by the doubling of Ireland's population from 1780 to 1840 linked to the cultivation of the potato. In 1845 and then three times in the next few years, the potato crop disastrously failed because of blight, and starvation and terrible diseases became the order of the day. About one and a half million people died and another million fled the country. Ireland became the only country in Europe to lose population in the nineteenth century. The famine and massive emigration devastated Ireland. Those who had not left had to pay high rents and taxes, and faced eviction from their homes, in spite of the economic devastation, and resented the horribly inadequate governmental response to their plight. Anti-British feeling and Irish nationalism grew and blossomed into a movement for Irish independence within a few decades.

THE REVOLUTION OF 1830 IN FRANCE

In France, too, democratic forces were able to make a significant impact. When the Bourbons were restored in 1814, France became a constitutional monarchy, and Louis XVIII, by and large, resisted the forces of reaction, which sought to undo even this moderate change. The constitution limited the suffrage to "notable people," a tiny percentage of the male population, mostly aristocrats and wealthy businessmen and professionals, who varied a good deal in their political opinions. When Louis died, he was replaced by Charles X, who wished to return to the days of unlimited monarchy and would not uphold this compromise. He tried to win support through nationalism, conquering Algeria from the Ottomans in 1830, though with such brutality that native resistance continued until 1847. With victory in hand, Charles repudiated the Constitutional Charter of 1814, censored the press, and reduced the voting rights of the middle class. In "three glorious days" the Parisian artisans, supported by many other groups, brought down the government. Charles's cousin Louis Philippe was placed on the throne. Louis Philippe restored the Constitutional Charter of 1814, called himself the "king of the French people," and adopted the red, white, and blue colors of revolutionary France for the national flag. As the suffrage was extended only a little and the regime empowered the upper middle class to which it owed its existence, many of the 1830 revolutionaries felt frustrated and angry at the corrupt "bourgeois monarchy," indifferent to the social needs of the people and resistant to electoral reform.

AP Tip

The popular novel by Victor Hugo, *Les Misérables*, of which there are several film versions as well as a Broadway musical, takes place before and during the 1830 revolution in France. It illuminates many of the social issues in post-Napoleonic France.

THE REVOLUTIONS OF 1848

Those frustrations would burst forth in Paris in the spring of 1848, sparking revolutions in most European capitals except for England (where the Chartist petitions had just been presented to the House of Commons) and Russia. It was an extraordinary and unprecedented year in which governments were toppled, kings and ministers fled, all sorts of promises were made to the people, and what proved to be short-term changes were made. Nationalism, liberalism, socialism, romanticism, and economic crises all played a role, although in different ways and to varying degrees from country to country.

AP Tip

The revolutions of 1848 are complex and often confusing to students. It might help to make up a chart outlining the chief events and chief issues in each country. Make sure you have a clear understanding of the ideologies in the first part of the chapter, so you can make sense of the shifting alliances of the revolutions, particularly in France, Austria, and Prussia.

FRANCE Although not the first to revolt in 1848—that honor belongs to Naples—it was in France that the revolutionary turmoil across Europe began. Here the chief issues were liberalism and socialism. In February, artisans and unskilled laborers, furious over their lack of representation in government, set up barricades in the streets of Paris, and within two weeks, Louis Philippe had abdicated in favor of his grandson. But the Parisian revolutionaries would not accept any monarch and declared a provisional government that drafted a constitution for a democratic republic with universal male suffrage. All slaves in the French colonies were freed, the death penalty was abolished, and Parisian workers got the ten-hour day. But the revolutionaries were divided into those (workers and artisans mostly) who wanted more radical change in the form of socialism and those (mostly middle class) who wanted political but not social and economic change. Louis Blanc, the advocate of the right to work (see p. 771), and Albert, a worker, represented the former group in the provisional government, which set up national workshops to provide temporary relief for the unemployed in the form of public works projects. Large numbers of workers signed up. Yet in the first election under universal male suffrage in May, the French chose mostly moderates, both monarchist and republican, over radicals. One such moderate was the great historian and observer Alexis de Tocqueville, who described the general commitment to republicanism but opposition to socialism. When the newly elected government kicked out Blanc and soon thereafter dropped the national workshops, terrible street violence in Paris ensued. The "June Days" was a spontaneous uprising, with the artisans and the poor setting up barricades against the French army. Some 10,000 people died in the repression of the protests. In December, Louis Napoleon, the nephew of the late emperor, was elected by a huge majority; he created an authoritarian regime and restored order to France.

THE AUSTRIAN EMPIRE The chief issues in the Austrian Empire were nationalism and liberalism; the subject nationalities sought both independence from Austrian rule and liberal constitutions. The revolution began when Hungarian nationalists demanded autonomy and a constitution guaranteeing civil liberties and universal suffrage. Students and workers in Vienna and peasants in the countryside rose in rebellion, so much so that Metternich fled, and the emperor promised a constitution and in March abolished serfdom. Once again class and nationalistic divisions hindered the revolutionary efforts: peasants were content with their gains, the middle classes feared the socialism demanded by workers, the Hungarian nationalists alienated the Slavic minorities living in their part of the empire, and Czech nationalists combated German nationalists. The Austrian monarchy reasserted itself under the effective leadership of Archduchess Sophia, who convinced the emperor to abdicate in favor of her eighteen-year-old son, Franz Joseph. The loyal army crushed working-class radicals in Prague in June and in Vienna in October, and Russian troops sent by Tsar Nicholas I defeated the Hungarians and ended their revolt. Franz Joseph became emperor. He vetoed Palacky's proposal to create a "union of equals" that had been passed earlier by the constituent assembly in Austria, but saw nationalism in resurgence throughout his empire by the end of his reign in 1916.

PRUSSIA Again liberalism and nationalism initially combined but then collided. Prussian liberals seeking a constitutional monarchy were supported in March 1848 by artisans and factory workers who rose up against the king, Frederick William IV (see the illustration on p. 773), who then promised a liberal constitution. Here too the middle and working classes divided when the working classes demanded greater democracy with some hints of socialism. Prussian liberals had another dream: a unified German state, and to this end, a national assembly met in Frankfurt to write a constitution for a united Germany. Mostly middle-class professionals, the delegates had to wrangle with a conflict with Denmark over two bordering provinces populated mostly by Germans (Schleswig and Holstein) and called on the Prussian king to go to war with Denmark, which he did obligingly. But when they elected him emperor of a new German state with the liberal constitution they had written, Frederick William refused, saying he wouldn't take a "crown from the gutter." By then, he had taken back control of Berlin from the revolutionaries and reneged on his promise of a liberal constitution for Prussia. The attempt of the middle classes in Germany to create a unified state on constitutional principles failed; when Germany unified in 1870, it was as an autocracy.

AP Tip

The Frankfurt Assembly also had to wrestle with another difficult issue: whether the German state they were trying to create would include all German-speaking peoples (*grosse Deutschland*, "Big Germany") or would exclude the Austrians because their empire included so many non-Germans (*kleine Deutschland*, "Little Germany"). They ultimately opted for Kleine Deutschland, as did the Prussian-dominated state that came into being in 1870, but Hitler and the Nazis achieved grosse Deutschland when they absorbed Austria and Bohemia in 1938. The complicated nature of this issue is well revealed by Palacky's letter to the Frankfurt Assembly (see Listening to the Past, pp. 776–777) in which he refused to participate in the assembly because he feared that it would weaken the Austrian Empire and thus leave the weaker Slavic peoples vulnerable to the dream of "universal monarchy" held by the Russian tsars.

Ultimately, the revolutions of 1848 achieved relatively little. Authoritarian or autocratic rulers successfully repressed nationalistic and socialistic forces, though not forever, and made only minor modifications along liberal lines. There were some permanent changes: the abolition of serfdom and slavery and the establishment of universal male suffrage in France, and some acknowledgement of the legitimacy of constitutionalism in most other states.

Multiple-Choice Questions

1. The intellectual father of romanticism was
   (A) Voltaire.
   (B) Rousseau.
   (C) Mazzini.
   (D) Fourier.
   (E) Louis Blanc.

2. The romantics
   (A) saw themselves as the heirs of the Enlightenment.
   (B) were rarely involved in politics.
   (C) generally opposed nationalism.
   (D) disdained popular culture and music.
   (E) often wrote about medieval legends and heroes.

3. The Greeks were able to win their independence from the Ottoman Empire because
   (A) Austria supported their cause to weaken an old enemy.
   (B) Britain and France put pressure on the Ottoman Empire on behalf of the Greeks.
   (C) Russia agreed to stay neutral in the Greek-Ottoman conflict.
   (D) Prussia helped them in order to maintain the balance of power in the Balkans.
   (E) Romania, which was already independent, supported them.

4. The Congress of Vienna
   (A) punished France severely for forcing Europe into war for twenty years.
   (B) in order to keep things stable, kept the kings Napoleon had appointed on the throne.
   (C) awarded England important provinces on the European continent.
   (D) gave additional lands to Prussia.
   (E) restored Poland as a fully independent state.
5. The restored Bourbon king Louis XVIII
   (A) executed the revolutionaries who had executed Louis XVI.
   (B) tried to restore absolute monarchy.
   (C) helped preserve constitutional monarchy for France.
   (D) really had very little power.
   (E) modified the constitution to give all adult men the vote.
6. The chief demand in the 1830 revolution in France was for
   (A) greater political democracy.
   (B) national workshops.
   (C) the end of the war against Algerian rebels.
   (D) a republic.
   (E) the end of slavery in the French colonies.
7. In 1848, socialistic demands were most important in the revolutions in
   (A) England.
   (B) France.
   (C) Prussia.
   (D) Austria.
   (E) Hungary.
8. The repeal of the Corn Laws in Britain in 1846
   (A) was enacted by the Tories to help the landowning class.
   (B) reflected the changes in Parliament since the Great Reform Bill.
   (C) ended free trade.
   (D) was opposed by the working classes.
   (E) caused the famine in Ireland.
9. The Frankfurt Assembly failed because the delegates
   (A) could not agree on what to do about Schleswig-Holstein.
   (B) offered the crown to the king of Bavaria.
   (C) were not supported by the middle classes.
   (D) tried to write a constitution for Prussia.
   (E) failed to convince the king of Prussia to accept the crown.
10. The "June Days" in France in 1848 refers to
    (A) the election of Louis Napoleon.
    (B) fighting between workers and the army in Paris.
    (C) riots that took place when Louis Blanc was given a position in the Provisional Government.
    (D) fighting between liberals and monarchists in Paris.
    (E) the period when Louis Philippe abdicated.

11. The Hungarian Revolution of 1848 ended when
    (A) Metternich fled.
    (B) Franz Joseph became the new emperor.
    (C) Russian troops were sent to Budapest.
    (D) the Hungarians voluntarily rejoined the Austrian Empire to avoid further bloodshed.
    (E) the Austrian crown was given to a Hungarian for the first time.
12. The revolutions of 1848 in Berlin and Vienna were similar in that in both
    (A) the chief issue was nationalistic agitation by minorities.
    (B) both were crushed within two weeks.
    (C) nothing really happened.
    (D) the rulers promised liberal constitutions but then reneged on their promises.
    (E) the Russians helped defeat the revolutionaries.
13. Which is *not* a key point of Marxism?
    (A) Workers are inevitably exploited by their employers.
    (B) History is fundamentally about class struggle.
    (C) The proletariat can win over the bourgeoisie only with leaders who have been workers.
    (D) The value of any object is determined by the labor that went into making it.
    (E) The bourgeoisie has been a revolutionary class.
14. Which of the following would Marx and Engels agree with most in their views on economics?
    (A) Fourier
    (B) Proudhon
    (C) Saint-Simon
    (D) Michelet
    (E) George Sand
15. The Great Reform Bill of 1832
    (A) gave greater representation in the House of Commons to industrial cities.
    (B) made the House of Lords and the House of Commons equal.
    (C) expanded the suffrage to about the same percentage of adult men that had the vote in France.
    (D) was a victory for the Chartist movement.
    (E) eliminated aristocrats from any significant political role.

Free-Response Questions

1. "The revolutions of 1848 were more important in their failures than in their successes." Assess the validity of this statement by considering both short-term and long-term consequences.
2. Compare the changes in France and in England in the 1820s and 1830s. Be sure to discuss intellectual or cultural developments as well as political ones.

Answers

Multiple-Choice Questions

1. **Answer: (B)** Fourier and Blanc were socialists, not romantics. They, like Mazzini, were contemporaneous with romanticism. Voltaire defended the use of reason as the chief salvation of mankind. It was Rousseau, who had rejected reason in favor of emotionality and passion, who fathered romanticism. (McKay, *A History of Western Society*, 8th ed., p. 766/9th ed., p. 758)

2. **Answer: (E)** The romantics rejected the Enlightenment and longed for the Middle Ages in which they imagined, in novels like those of Walter Scott, heroes were brave and passions were unfurled. They were often wrapped up in politics and were fascinated by the popular culture of their nations. (McKay, *A History of Western Society*, 8th ed., pp. 766–770/9th ed., pp. 758–761)

3. **Answer: (B)** It was chiefly the British and French whose support helped the Greeks. Romania was not yet independent, and Prussia was hardly involved. Russia sent a navy but not troops. (McKay, *A History of Western Society*, 8th ed., pp. 770–772/9th ed., pp. 761–763)

4. **Answer: (D)** Poland was restored but only under Russian authority. France was treated quite leniently, even after the Hundred Days. England had not asked for nor was granted any lands on the continent; it was mostly interested in expanding its overseas empire. Prussia was given enlarged areas of the Rhineland. The congress was committed to the idea of legitimacy and restored the monarchs who had been on the throne before Napoleon, even when the people may have wanted a change. (McKay, *A History of Western Society*, 8th ed., pp. 757–759/9th ed., pp. 749–751)

5. **Answer: (C)** Louis XVIII appointed moderates as ministers and resisted the demands of the nobility to restore absolutism. As the suffrage was extremely limited, the king retained substantial power. (McKay, *A History of Western Society*, 8th ed., p. 776/9th ed., p. 767)

6. **Answer: (A)** The cause of the 1830 revolution was the attempt of Charles X to restore absolutism. The national workshops and the issue of slavery were important in 1848. (McKay, *A History of Western Society*, 8th ed., pp. 776–777/9th ed., pp. 767–768)

7. **Answer: (B)** Only in France was a specific socialist issue crucial—the national workshops. In Hungary, the chief issue was nationalism. In Prussia and Austria, workers took to the streets to support demands for liberal constitutions. England escaped revolution completely in 1848. (McKay, *A History of Western Society*, 8th ed., pp. 779–782/9th ed., pp. 770–774)

8. **Answer: (B)** The Great Reform Bill gave the liberal bourgeoisie much greater representation in the House of Commons, and it was they who enacted the repeal of the Corn Laws, much to the distress of the aristocracy. The working classes supported the repeal since it would

lower bread prices. It was passed in part to relieve conditions in Ireland. The repeal of the Corn Laws began a period of free trade. (McKay, *A History of Western Society*, 8th ed., pp. 772–775/9th ed., pp. 763–765)

9. **ANSWER: (E)** The mostly middle-class Frankfurt Assembly dealt effectively with the Schleswig-Holstein issue but failed to convince Frederick William IV to accept the constitution they wrote. (McKay, *A History of Western Society*, 8th ed., pp. 781–782/9th ed., pp. 773–774)

10. **ANSWER: (B)** During the "June Days," Parisian workers battled the French army and lost. This incident remains famous because of the intensity of violence, the large numbers of workers' lives lost, and the hostility between the classes it represented. (McKay, *A History of Western Society*, 8th ed., pp. 779–780/9th ed., p. 771)

11. **ANSWER: (C)** The Hungarian revolt was crushed by Russian troops aiding the Austrian emperor. The ascension of Franz Joseph calmed things down in Vienna but not in Budapest. (McKay, *A History of Western Society*, 8th ed., p. 780/9th ed., p. 772)

12. **ANSWER: (D)** The revolutionaries in the Austrian and Prussian kingdoms aimed at liberal constitutions. Both kings at first felt forced to grant the constitutions because of widespread popular protests, but they both reneged on those promises once they had taken back control of their capital cities. (McKay, *A History of Western Society*, 8th ed., pp. 780–782/9th ed., pp. 772–774)

13. **ANSWER: (C)** Marxists accept the labor theory of value and argue that all history is about class struggle. However, they believe that some individuals can rise above their own class backgrounds to play important roles in the revolution. (McKay, *A History of Western Society*, 8th ed., pp. 765–766/9th ed., pp. 757–758)

14. **ANSWER: (B)** Marx and Engels would most agree with Proudhon who, although an anarchist rather than a socialist, argued that private property is theft and has no legitimacy. George Sand was a romantic novelist, Jules Michelet was a nationalistic and liberal historian, Fourier focused on free love and had little interest in industrial society, and Saint-Simon defended the leadership of the technocratic elite, while Marx and Engels would want workers in control. (McKay, *A History of Western Society*, 8th ed., pp. 764–768/9th ed., pp. 756–760)

15. **ANSWER: (A)** The Great Reform Bill still limited the suffrage, although more British had the votes than the French. Its chief importance was it gave the industrial cities representation in the House of Commons. It was passed by the House of Lords only reluctantly, and meant that they lost significant power. Aristocrats remained important in both the Whig and Tory parties. (McKay, *A History of Western Society*, 8th ed., pp. 772–773/9th ed., pp. 763–765)

FREE-RESPONSE QUESTIONS

1. This is an evaluative question, asking you to use your knowledge of the revolutions to analyze the short-term and long-term consequences,

but you should focus more on the latter, as they reveal the lasting impact of the revolutions. The way the question is worded indicates that you can argue either way—that the successes of the revolutions were more important than the failures or the other way, which is where most of the evidence would point. Have clearly in mind what the goals of the revolutionaries were so you can articulate whether they achieved them.

- Successes were generally quite limited: universal male suffrage in France, abolition of slavery in the French colonies, abolition of serfdom in France, and a limited constitution in Prussia. Workers showed their power, even though they were crushed by the counter-revolution.
- Failures were significant in almost every country. In France, the short-lived republic was replaced by the authoritarian regime of Louis Napoleon. In the Austrian Empire, the nationalistic aspirations of Hungarians, Bohemians, and others were frustrated, but did not die out; instead they became even more important in the twentieth century. The failure of the Frankfurt Assembly to unify Germany as a liberal constitutional monarchy meant autocracy remained in force until 1918. It also meant that democracy had little chance to take root in Germany. More generally, the failure of the revolutionary groups—liberal bourgeoisie and socialistic-leaning workers—to work together after their initial success doomed their revolutions and showed that class antagonisms were deep. The conclusion drawn by many was that only forceful personalities and strong realists would be able to achieve results.

2. This question asks for the political, intellectual, and cultural similarities and differences in the changes in France and in England in the 1820s and 1830s.

- Similarities: Both developed into more liberal regimes, but in such a limited way that the demand for greater democracy continued. In both countries, as industrialization spread, the working classes organized themselves into political movements. Workers collaborated with the liberal bourgeoisie on specific issues—the Anti-Corn Law League in Britain and the 1830 revolution in France. Both groups were frustrated by the limited reforms they achieved in this period and became more active in the 1840s, with Chartism in Britain and violent protests in 1848 in France. In both, suffrage was very limited, with only about 12 percent of adult men enfranchised after 1832 in Britain and about 170,000 men out of a population of 30,000,000 getting the vote in France after the 1830 revolution. In both France and Britain, demands for universal male suffrage grew. In both countries, the bourgeoisie demonstrated their political power when they pushed through the Great Reform Bill in Britain and engineered the abdication of Charles X in France. Romanticism flowered in both countries, in literature—Hugo and Sand in France and Shelley, Keats, Scott, and Bryon in Britain—and in the visual arts—Turner in Britain and Delacroix in France.
- Differences: French intellectuals developed utopian socialist ideals—Fourier with his small communities and free love, Blanc articulating the right to work, and Saint-Simon demanding that the technocrats become the ruling elite. French and English workers did show growing class-consciousness, but British workers focused

on achieving greater political democracy in the Chartist movement. The liberal bourgeoisie in Britain generally supported the Whigs and became committed to free trade, which they achieved in 1846 with the repeal of the Corn Laws, limiting the importation of foreign wheat. The French bourgeoisie were still battling an entrenched aristocracy and an autocratic king in the 1820s. Some social reform legislation was passed by the Conservative Party in Britain, the Factory Acts, for example, showing the British aristocrats addressing the impact of the Industrial Revolution. French aristocrats were by and large trying to return to the lifestyles and privileges they had had before the French Revolution.

24

LIFE IN THE EMERGING URBAN SOCIETY IN THE NINETEENTH CENTURY

After the 1848 revolutions, Europe became a predominately urbanized society. The Industrial Revolution transformed Europe from a rural society based on agriculture and ruled by the aristocracy to an urban, industrial one dominated by the bourgeoisie.

KEY CONCEPTS

- Life in cities was awful for the working people at the beginning of the century, with overcrowded housing, rampant disease, and widespread poverty. Reformers created health services and were effective in getting governments to take action. After midcentury, conditions improved; real wages went up, sanitation and sewage systems were improved, new public transportation was instituted, and urban planning that razed slums and built new housing was begun.
- The two ever-more important social classes—the middle classes and the working classes—had many subgroups. The upper middle class aped the aristocracy, the middle middle class developed strong values and morality and were devoted to the home, and the lower middle class made sure that they were distinguished from the working classes, which were divided into skilled, semiskilled, and unskilled labor. The working classes tended to marry for love but live close to kin. Both groups of classes created cultural institutions, opera houses and concert halls for the middle classes, and music or vaudeville halls for the working classes.
- Family life stabilized after 1850 with illegitimacy rates and birth rates both dropping. "Separate spheres" characterized gender

relations in middle- and working-class homes. Devotion to children became more pronounced. Women had few legal rights and began to organize movements to fight for greater equality.

- Jean-Baptiste Lamarck and Charles Darwin in zoology and biology, Dmitri Mendeleev in chemistry, and Michael Faraday in electricity, all made major advances in scientific knowledge. Science became popular as it was applied in many useful ways. New social sciences—from Freudian theory in psychology to the positivism of Comte—were developed. Literature reflected the new spirit by turning to realism.

Taming the City

By the middle of the nineteenth century, real wages were increasing for the working classes of Europe, especially England. As a result, the intensely crowded early industrial cities began to change. Currently, a new historical evaluation of the impact of the Industrial Revolution focuses on the opportunities that became available for poor people, rather than their privations. Others still argue that the terrible quality of life, both physically and psychologically, in industrial cities outweighed the benefits of the increase in real wages.

AP Tip

The concept of real wages is often confusing to students. *Real wages* means the purchasing power of earned income, so sometimes when wages go up dramatically, real wages still go down because prices have also gone up more dramatically. The reverse can also be true. Real wages is an excellent way to figure out what were or are actual standards of living and to make sense of the great varieties of currencies. Generally, in the United States real wages have been going down the past few decades.

Industry and the Growth of Cities

Cities have been for centuries both centers of economic and intellectual activity and polluted and dangerously crowded pestholes. Diseases spread quickly so the population of native-born residents regularly declined only to be replenished with new immigrants. The terrible conditions in industrial cities were therefore not new, but they were revealed as never before. Industrialization made urban life attractive for employer and employee alike. As urbanization intensified, reformers sought to make cities safe and livable. British statistics on urbanization show how fast it spread: the number of people who lived in cities of more than 20,000 numbered less than 1.5 million in 1801, 6.5 million in 1851, and nearly 16 million forty years later. At that point, more than half of the British population lived in cities.

By the early nineteenth century, the United Kingdom had a large number of big cities, most of them terribly crowded, with many people living in too-small rooms with minimal comfort and inadequate sanitary conditions. Open sewers and woefully inadequate public toilet facilities frequently overflowed. There were few indoor bathrooms at this time for working people; instead 200 people might share the use of a single outhouse. The 1852 illustration "A Court for King Cholera" (p. 782) gives an idea of how poor living conditions were and how crowded and dirty the London streets were. As there was absolutely no public transportation at that time, people were forced to live in close quarters near their work. Recent immigrants to cities from the countryside had no expectation of anything better than a hovel since rural housing was equally inadequate.

Reformers, such as Edwin Chadwick, focused on the filth and unhealthy congestion of urban slums. Chadwick was a Benthamite, a follower of Jeremy Bentham, who developed the idea of the rational calculation of problems to achieve "the greatest good for the greatest number." Chadwick argued that disease and early death caused poverty, not the other way around, and developed his "sanitary idea" that cities should be cleaned up.

AP Tip

Bentham's philosophy is called utilitarianism, and has been a profound influence for nearly 200 years. It led to a new Poor Law in Britain in 1834, which encouraged the poor to work by putting them in workhouses when they didn't. The idea that social scientists can calculate the benefits or detriments of a proposal to society's overall well-being (Bentham developed the "hedonic calculus" to this end), and on this basis make government policy, has been especially strong in the United States.

Chadwick did extensive research that proved that disease was related to the lack of proper drainage, sewage facilities, and regular garbage collection, and made his findings known in a widely publicized report in 1842. After the cholera epidemic a few years later seemed to verify his arguments, Britain passed its first public health law, which created a national health board with the mandate to modernize sanitation facilities. Cheap iron pipes were installed to carry the sewage underground and away and to provide clean water. The public health movement spread quickly beyond Britain to the United States and to continental Europe. Within twenty years, real progress had been made, and death rates began to decline.

In the 1840s, there was still inadequate understanding of the causes of disease. The popular theory of the time, the miasmatic theory, asserted that disease was spread through bad fumes and odors. Soon doctors and public health officials were able to show that disease was spread by but not caused by filth. In the 1850s, Louis Pasteur, a French chemist, using a microscope, discovered germs, infinitesimal living organisms that carried disease. His solution, pasteurization, was to boil liquids such as milk or beer to kill off the germs. Some twenty years later, Robert Koch, a German doctor, cultured bacteria and demonstrated their life cycles; this allowed for the identification of the particular bacteria that caused particular diseases and the development of vaccines against them. The English surgeon Joseph Lister applied this new scientific knowledge in his surgeries, creating the antiseptic principle to treat wounds with chemical antibacterial agents. Soon that principle was extended to include not only wounds but also the physical environment in which they were treated; everything was to be cleansed and made antiseptic. Overall, the public health movement saved millions of lives and death rates dramatically declined after about 1880 in what has been called a "great silent revolution."

At the same time, although mostly for different reasons, urban planning—careful design of cities—was instituted, particularly by Napoleon III, who undertook a massive rebuilding of Paris. Under the leadership of Baron Haussmann, the old Paris, filled with deathly slums of horribly overcrowded narrow and dark streets (which were also easily controlled by crowds during revolutionary periods), disappeared. Most of medieval Paris was destroyed, replaced by new broad, straight boulevards, with two large parks and many small neighborhood parks and squares to provide open spaces. Sewage and water systems were also improved. New residential quarters were created on the outskirts, and everywhere new apartment buildings were built for people of varying wealth, with the poor in garrets at the top and the bourgeoisie in elegant apartments lower down (see the illustration on p. 785). Haussmann's success inspired city planners all over Europe; in Vienna and Cologne, for example, broad circular boulevards filled with theaters, office buildings, and museums, as well as middle-class housing, replaced torn-down walled fortifications. Zoning expropriation laws made such changes possible.

Along with reconstruction went the creation of public transportation systems on the new boulevards, making it possible for cities to expand and become less congested. Europeans adopted American innovations, first the horse-drawn streetcar in the 1870s, and then in the 1890s the much cheaper, faster and safer electric streetcar. Streetcar systems were built by private companies (as in London) or by city governments (as on the continent) and allowed ordinary people to travel further for work, shopping, entertainment, or school; to move to newer housing; and to travel to the countryside for weekend excursions. The use of public transport saw phenomenal increases between 1886 and 1910.

Rich and Poor and Those in Between

Urbanization and the changing nature of cities had a huge impact on social structure and on the lives of people of different classes. There was a general improvement in the standard of living for the average person when real wages doubled between 1850 and 1906. But poverty was not eliminated, nor was the gap between rich and poor substantially narrowed. Generally, the richest 5 percent of the population took a third (in Britain's case, 43 percent) of the national income, while the poorest 30 percent received less than a tenth of the national income. In addition, the wealthy paid virtually nothing in income taxes. Such inequity was particularly noticeable in Britain. While the gap between rich and poor was about the same as it had been before the Industrial Revolution, Marx's prediction of the disappearance of all other social classes into either the proletariat or the bourgeoisie did not happen, as new and diverse social groups and subclasses were created by the varieties of opportunities and employment of the industrial system.

The aristocracy, although small in number, remained wealthy, highly prestigious and influential, especially on the continent, where monarchies were the rule until the early twentieth century. They divided their time between grand country estates and splendid townhouses in the capital cities. Many intermarried with members of the wealthy middle classes and engaged in capitalistic exploitation of their own resources.

The middle classes made up about 20 percent of the population. The plural form, middle classes, is appropriate since there were many subgroups within the broad class. At the top was the upper middle class, made up of highly successful commercial, banking, and industrial families. They were drawn toward aristocratic lifestyles and no longer connected to their radical roots, bought or built country houses, and had private coaches and many servants. Together with the aristocracy, they made up about 5 percent of the overall population of England. The middle middle class, consisting of small industrialists and professionals—lawyers, physicians, engineers, and so on—was less wealthy but solid and comfortable. Engineering became a full-fledged profession, as did architecture, chemistry, accountancy, and the like. The managers of both government and private institutions like railroads, who were not themselves capitalists but had specialized knowledge and talents, also became members of the middle middle class.

The lower middle class consisted of the small shopkeepers, tiny manufacturers, and white-collar workers, typically office clerks, shop managers, and salesmen. The members of the lower middle class often did not have an income higher than that of skilled workers, but they were firmly committed to their middle class status and were forever seeking to move up in society. They made sure to sport markers of their middle class status, such as clean, soft hands or having at least one servant, to distinguish themselves from the proletarians, and they sought professional standing to increase their prestige. Teachers, nurses, and dentists, for example, achieved respectable middle class status in this period.

The middle classes shared many common cultural elements. They ate (especially meat) and drank well, spending as much as 25 percent of the income on food and drink and hosting lavish dinner parties on a regular basis. Middle-class wives supervised a bevy of servants since having domestic servants was one sure sign of success. Families lived in comfortable, well-appointed apartments. By 1900 or so, middle-class women had become passionate followers of fashion, shopping in the new department stores or hiring dressmakers, who now had sewing machines. Fabric and style were markers of social class, as middle-class women sought to emulate their "betters." The wearing of the constricting corset and bustle reflected societal expectations that women were to look attractive and proper rather than be productive workers. In the late nineteenth century, the English developed the tailored suit, a practical alternative adopted by the many women who began to work in offices in the 1890s. Education and culture were also important for the middle classes; they read novels, went to concert halls and to the opera, sent their children to good schools and on trips abroad, and gave them music lessons. Middle-class morality was strict, demanding discipline and industriousness, disdaining the idle and the criminal, and denouncing gambling, adultery, and intoxication as horrid vices to be extirpated.

The working classes also were subdivided on the basis of the level of skill required for their work. They made up about 80 percent of the population and were mostly urbanized by the turn of the twentieth century. Highly skilled workers like cabinetmakers or jewelers, masters of technology like railroad engineers and machinists, and managers like construction bosses and factory foremen became the labor aristocracy, earning the most money and having the highest prestige of any workers. Many skilled workers felt threatened by the ever-increasing technological improvements that made their skills obsolete. The upper working class adopted the puritanical middle-class morality and middle-class values like saving and personal ambition and sought to protect their social prestige. They enthusiastically endorsed the temperance movement organized in northern Europe in the nineteenth century.

The middle working class was made up of the many semiskilled workers, some in established crafts like carpentry or masonry and others working in factories. Below them were the huge numbers of unskilled workers, street vendors, and day laborers who performed the physical work of loading or unloading ships or the many menial tasks in the industrial system. They earned little and generally were divided by fierce competition for jobs and not organized into unions. In order to compensate for the inadequate incomes of their husbands, married working-class women often had to work in factories or at home using sewing machines to make ready-made clothes in a new version of the domestic system. The largest single group of unskilled workers was domestic servants, a growing sector of the economy in the nineteenth century, making up about 9 percent of the entire workforce in Great Britain. Mostly young and of rural origin, maids worked long hours at little pay and were often sexually exploited by their employers. But life was more exciting for them and marriage prospects brighter than in the countryside.

The working classes also had their own entertainment, with drinking the most popular leisure-time activity. As noted above, a temperance movement lamenting the impact of drinking on family and social life grew in response. Heavy drinking declined, replaced by social drinking in public houses (pubs and cafés), not only by male workers but also by couples. The presence of women in pubs certainly helped improve the behavior of men there. It was in such venues that workers organized themselves politically. Workers also enjoyed participation in sports and attending and betting on competitions, particularly racing and soccer. It was in fact the need to figure out racing forms that prompted many a worker to learn to read. Men and women of the working classes also frequented the hugely popular music halls and vaudeville theatres, their alternative to the institutions of middle-class culture, where broad humor and songs satirized the vicissitudes of family life.

There was a general decline in church attendance and donations throughout Europe in the late nineteenth century, more so in working-class neighborhoods than in middle-class ones. Most people continued to have their children baptized, but religion seems to have played a reduced role in their lives, especially as the established churches defined themselves as conservative and church construction did not keep pace with population growth in the cities. This general alienation of the working classes in Europe from the church, whether Protestant or Catholic, was not found in the United States, where churches thrived as foci of ethnic identity. In Europe that function was true generally only for minorities, such as the Irish Catholics in Protestant Britain and the Jews in Russia.

THE CHANGING FAMILY

During the eighteenth and early nineteenth centuries, family life had become quite destabilized with high rates of illegitimacy (reaching 40 to 50 percent of all births) and widespread premarital and extramarital sexual contact. Rates of illegitimacy varied from region to region but were usually higher in urbanized and industrialized areas and lower in religious communities in which premarital sex was sharply condemned. By the middle of the nineteenth century, illegitimacy rates declined, though not the percentage of pregnant brides, largely because more couples were able economically to get married before the baby arrived; gradually, the industrial working classes became more respectable. In general, family life stabilized after around 1850 as the home became more important for people of all social classes and attitudes toward women and children substantially changed. Romantic love rather than arranged marriage became the new ideal, particularly in the working classes where economic considerations were less relevant than they were to the bourgeoisie, for which marriage remained an important way to improve the family's social connections and economic prospects. Middle-class men often married late, after they had become established economically, and chose younger wives who had been under the careful supervision of their parents. This age gap was a quite common source of marital tensions.

Prostitution was widespread, with nearly a million prostitutes in Paris at the end of the nineteenth century. Men of all classes would visit them, although it was more common among the middle classes in spite of their official puritanical stance. The anonymous multivolume autobiography *My Secret Life* describes obsessive sexual adventures with prostitutes and reveals the dark side of nineteenth-century urban society where brutality, exploitation, and debauchery were rife. For the prostitutes, such work was prompted by poverty and was usually temporary, ending with marriage and family.

For working-class families, marriage did not outweigh kinship ties. Young couples usually lived in the same communities in which they had grown up and stayed close to parents and other relatives, who would be called on to help with crises. Government services for the poor barely existed, so people relied on their families for help, particularly in case of unexpected deaths to cover funeral expenses and take care of those left behind, and to aid in case of sickness or old age.

Gender roles, unlike kinship ties, changed dramatically in the second half of the nineteenth century. Husbands became the breadwinners and wives stayed home, managing the household and children. Thus, a new norm of separate spheres for men and women was created. Only in retail businesses did the older pattern of families working together continue, and generally only poor women whose husbands could not earn enough worked outside the home. In the context of separate spheres, women who needed or wanted to work faced even greater barriers than they had before, with hostility from embarrassed husbands and only poorly paid positions open to them. Married women also had few legal rights. An English or French wife had no independent legal identity and could not own property in her own right or keep her own earnings. Movements for equality for women began, mostly among middle-class women, in the nineteenth century. They used the arguments of Mary Wollstonecraft's *Vindication of the Rights of Woman* to campaign for equality of legal rights and access to education and employment, particularly for unmarried women and widows. Feminists achieved some victories, such as the 1882 law that granted English women full property rights, and opportunities for women for white-collar employment grew after 1880. Still it remained virtually impossible for women to matriculate at most universities or train to become doctors or lawyers. How difficult it was is demonstrated by the story of Franziska Tiburtius (see *Individuals in Society,* p. 801), who went to the only university to accept female medical students, the University of Zurich. Initially frustrated in her desire to practice legally, she ended up opening a clinic for female factory workers. She and her partner, also a woman doctor, were the only women doctors in Berlin for fifteen years.

AP Tip

An important voice on behalf of equality of women was John Stuart Mill, a nineteenth-century utilitarian philosopher who argued fiercely for individual rights and gender equality in his famous tract *On the Subjection of Women.*

Socialist-leaning or Marxist women argued, however, that women's equality could only be achieved through economic equality and that focusing on liberation of women was a diversion from the general goal of liberation for all proletarians. Within working-class families, women typically managed the money and made the major decisions about the children and about the household itself, even as they were expected to tend to the needs of their husbands. Running the household was full-time work, as there were few labor-saving devices and most working-class families couldn't afford servants; indeed many wives added to the family income through piecework or taking in boarders. The ideal of the warm, nurturing family home, a haven from the harsh world, was as powerful in working-class families as in those of the middle class. The phrase "Home, sweet home," first used in the 1870s, became almost a national anthem.

Married life also became stronger in the late nineteenth century, with couples more affectionate and more emotionally bound to each other. Married love, both mental and physical, was the key to human happiness, according to the hugely popular bestseller *Mr., Mrs., and Baby* by Gustave Droz. The fact that men and women went out together, whether to the concert hall or the pub, added to the satisfactions of domesticity.

Child-rearing practices changed in a similar way. As the death rates of babies declined, women made greater emotional commitments to their children, increasingly breastfeeding them personally rather than employing a wet-nurse. The abandonment of illegitimate children declined, and more parents began to limit the number of children they had. The birthrate declined noticeably, and family size shrank to about six in the 1890s and to about four in the 1920s. Dozens of books about child rearing and hygiene, like that of Droz, urged men to become involved fathers and children to be allowed freedom of movement. Middle-class parents were particularly keen on the success of their children; with a variety of contraceptive methods, they had fewer children but invested more in each of them. Sometimes that put enormous pressure on the children to succeed and on the parents themselves, as theories current at that time asserted that the fate of children was determined by what was going on at the moment of conception or by the youthful behaviors of the father. Stephan Zweig describes the utterly rigid control over children and parental enforcement of ignorance of anything sexual in their daughters, in the excerpt from his autobiography, *The World Yesterday,* (see Listening to the Past, p. 812). Working-class children, who went to work early, had greater opportunities to break free of such strict household rules and emotional control.

Psychologists also examined family relations. The father was usually seen as an outsider to the intense mother-child relationship, a man of affairs far removed from family affection whose main task was discipline. The destructive power of father-son relationships was a constant theme in late-nineteenth-century novels such as *The Brothers Karamazov* by Feodor Dostoevski and in new psychological theories. Sigmund Freud, a neurologist in Vienna, developed a theory of psychosexual development to explain the hysteria he saw so often in his patients. Hysteria is a physical condition, such as the inability to walk, without physical cause. Freud argued that the origin of hysteria and other emotional problems lay in experiences within the family during early childhood and developed the techniques of free association and psychoanalysis to allow his patients to uncover those memories and understand the cause of their problems. Human behavior, he argued, was dominated by completely unconscious feelings and needs, many of them sexual, and only by bringing them into consciousness could one achieve self-understanding. For example, in what Freud named the Oedipal complex, sons have unconscious but intense love and desire for their mothers and consequently hostile and competitive feelings for their fathers.

AP Tip

Few ideas have been as controversial as those of Freud, and few have had greater impact on academia, the arts, and family practices. Even though Freudian theory has been roundly criticized and discarded by many, its basic premises—that we have a powerful unconscious dominated by instincts; that childhood experiences affect our feelings, behaviors, and thoughts as adults; that the unconscious reveals itself in dreams and jokes; and that psychological therapy can help individuals—have become deeply engrained in western society. Psychoanalysis, a talking therapy created by Freud, became popular and inspired many other varieties of psychological help, which, by the mid-twentieth century, had become a normal part of middle-class life. Freudian terms like *ego* (self), *superego* (conscience), *id* (instinctual drives), *repression* (pushing into the unconscious), and *sublimation* (finding socially acceptable ways of fulfilling unconscious needs and desires) are commonly understood and used. Freud's articulation of women's sexuality helped liberate them from Victorian views, as Stephan Zweig suggests from the excerpt from his autobiography (see Listening to the Past, p. 812).

Science and Thought

Freud's theories are but one example of the enormously fertile European intellect of the late nineteenth and early twentieth centuries. Scientific knowledge and understanding changed profoundly, new social sciences offered entirely new ways of understanding society, and literary romanticism gave way to realism, as novels, serialized in newspapers as well as published in book form, were widely read.

Scientific achievements after the 1830s revolutionized thought but also were quickly transformed into practical applications. Louis Pasteur's germ theory brought immediate benefits through the pasteurization of milk products. Scientists discovered the fundamental laws of thermodynamics, such as the law of conservation of energy. The chemist Dmitri Mendeleev created the periodic table and codified the periodic law. German chemists took what was learned in organic chemistry about carbon and created entirely new industries such as textile dyes made from coal tar. Faraday's discoveries in electromagnetism in the 1830s and 1840s led to the first dynamo and set the stage for the development of the telegraph, electric car, and electric light. The chemical industry grew enormously and systematically did research and development to keep its place at the technical forefront. The practical application of science increased its prestige, and science and the philosophical implications of scientific thought became widely popular, with both lecturers and writers explaining the new science to the ordinary citizen. The Enlightenment's faith in human progress seemed to be verified by the improvements visible everywhere.

SOCIAL SCIENCE AND EVOLUTION

The social sciences came into their own as academic disciplines in the late nineteenth century. Applying the principles of science to huge sets of empirical data about societal practices and behaviors, social scientists developed new methodologies and theories to explain their data and went far beyond Enlightenment efforts to come up with all-encompassing theories. The work of Karl Marx falls into this category. So does that of his contemporary Auguste Comte, who initiated the discipline of sociology with his *System of Positive Philosophy*. Comte argued that intellectual life develops through stages: the theological or fictitious, the metaphysical or abstract, and finally, the positive or scientific. The use of the scientific method, or positivist method, would lead social scientists to discover the laws of human relations, just as science had discovered the laws of physical relations, and that would allow them to present these truths to as yet unenlightened citizens. Science was to be the new religion, and scientists its priests.

Like Comte, many intellectuals and scientists were fascinated by the concept of slow change or evolution. In geology, Charles Lyell established the principle of uniformitarianism, the idea that geological processes slowly formed the earth, not cataclysms like floods or earthquakes. Lamarck argued that all life forms had evolved slowly in adjustment to the environment, although he erred in understanding the process, in that he believed in the inheritance of acquired characteristics. Charles Darwin accepted Lamarck's basic premise but, on the basis of his many voyages to remote corners of the globe like the Galapagos, argued that accidental mutations gave certain members of a species certain advantages in their environment, so that they survived while others without these traits died out. Accepting Lyell's view that Earth was indeed very old and influenced by Malthus's arguments about the inevitable competition for existence caused by the discrepancy between population and resources, Darwin came to believe that all life forms had evolved from a common ancestor through the struggle for survival. By providing an explanation of how evolution proceeded, he fundamentally altered conceptions about human origin and development. His ideas had enormous influence on the social sciences and on political thinking as well. The secularist and evolutionary approach taken by Marx and Comte (although in different directions), both of whom dismissed religion as superstition, seemed validated by Darwinian theory. Darwinism was applied by thinkers such as Herbert Spencer to human society in a doctrine that came to be known as Social Darwinism. Spencer is the one who came up with the phrase "survival of the fittest." Social Darwinists believe humans are engaged in a fierce struggle for survival, that the poor are poor because they are unfit, and that unfit members of the species must be allowed to die out. Social Darwinism was particularly popular with the middle classes.

AP Tip

Darwin's seminal book, *The Origin of Species,* was published in 1859. He shocked his contemporaries even more with his *The Descent of Man,* which asserted that man too was a product of evolutionary process and descended from lower mammals, including the great apes. Religious people took this with great offense. It is striking, however, how quickly Darwinian theory was accepted by the mass of the population and tolerated by most religious establishments, especially in comparison to the time it took for the Copernican thesis to become accepted.

Realism in Literature

During the second half of nineteenth century, literary authors abandoned romanticism in favor of a realism that sought to depict life as it is. They used prose more often than poetry as their chosen medium and replaced romanticized stories of the past with objective reporting on social conditions, and replaced romantic fascination with the exotic with exploration of the quotidian, daily life lived by ordinary people. They put both the middle and working classes under their microscopes and described many aspects of life that had previously been taboo: adultery, slums, strikes, violence, and alcoholism. Instead of exalting individualism, the realists were social determinists; that is, they believed that heredity in conjunction with environment determined human behavior. Instead of judging human behavior, they sought to analyze it. The three great realistic authors in France were Balzac (*The Human Comedy*), Flaubert (*Madame Bovary*), and Zola (*Germinal*). Balzac's works were a huge panorama of bourgeois France; his single most famous novel, *Le Père Goriot,* describes how ambition and greed corrupt. Flaubert studied a frustrated, adulterous woman with great psychological insight while Zola portrayed the impact of the Industrial Revolution with a socialistic eye. In England, George Eliot (*Middlemarch: A Study of Provincial Life*) and Thomas Hardy (*The Return of the Native*) were the two most prominent realistic authors. George Eliot was the pen name of Mary Ann Evans, who put her insightful gaze on small-town life. Hardy, also a poet, was interested in how fate and bad luck affected individuals. In Russia, the masterful Leo Tolstoy wrote *War and Peace,* about the French invasion of Russia in 1812. In the United States, Theodore Dreiser depicted the social transformation of the United States in novels like *Sister Carrie.*

Multiple-Choice Questions

1. Which describes the relationship between illegitimacy rates and percentages of pregnant brides in the second half of the nineteenth century?
   (A) Both went down significantly.
   (B) Both went up significantly.
   (C) Illegitimacy rates went up while the percentage of pregnant brides shrank.
   (D) Illegitimacy rates when down while the percentage of pregnant brides stayed the same.
   (E) Both were about the same as they had been in the period from 1750 to 1850.

2. In the new apartment buildings built in Paris under Napoleon III,
   (A) people of different classes lived near each other but in separate buildings.
   (B) people of different classes lived in distinct neighborhoods identified by class.
   (C) people of different classes shared the same building with the poor living on the top floors.
   (D) only servants would live in the buildings where the bourgeoisie lived.
   (E) the higher up the apartment, the higher the social class of its inhabitants.

3. Which of the following were typical middle-class child-rearing practices in the late nineteenth century?
   I. Mothers breast-fed their children themselves.
   II. Children were given a great deal of personal freedom so they could learn responsibility.
   III. Children were given education and training for success.
   IV. Illegitimate children were typically abandoned to foundling hospitals.
   (A) II, III, and IV
   (B) I and III
   (C) III and IV
   (D) I, II, and III
   (E) I, III, and IV

4. The largest group of female unskilled laborers was employed in
   (A) factories.
   (B) mines.
   (C) domestic service.
   (D) street markets.
   (E) offices.

5. Which would *not* be members of the labor aristocracy?
   (A) Construction bosses
   (B) Factory foremen
   (C) Highly skilled artisans
   (D) Railway locomotive engineers
   (E) Wagon-driving teamsters

6. The women's movement in the nineteenth century focused mostly on obtaining for women
   (A) legal rights.
   (B) the vote.
   (C) the right to divorce.
   (D) equal pay for equal work.
   (E) the right to a medical abortion to end an unwanted pregnancy.
7. Chadwick's pioneering efforts in public health in England focused on
   (A) factory conditions.
   (B) sanitation and sewage systems.
   (C) addressing poverty first, which he believed caused ill health.
   (D) proving that the miasmatic theory was wrong.
   (E) building new housing.
8. Which was *not* a reason for Baron Haussmann's building of broad and straight boulevards in the city?
   (A) To justify the razing of old buildings and slums
   (B) To allow for the building of the Paris subway
   (C) To encourage the smoother and faster flow of traffic
   (D) To prevent revolutionaries from being able to barricade the streets of Paris
   (E) To provide impressive vistas for Parisians and visitors alike
9. Seventeen percent of the British population was urbanized in 1801. Which was the percentage of British people living in cities of 20,000 or more in the 1890s?
   (A) 35 percent
   (B) 54 percent
   (C) 28 percent
   (D) 75 percent
   (E) 67 percent
10. Lister's antiseptic principle was important in that
    (A) milk and beer were now pasteurized.
    (B) it predated Pasteur's discovery of germ theory.
    (C) wounds and medical facilities were disinfected regularly.
    (D) it led to the discovery of new vaccines against disease.
    (E) it proved the miasmatic theory.
11. Religious donations and church attendance
    (A) stayed about the same throughout the nineteenth century.
    (B) declined in the late nineteenth century, particularly among the working classes.
    (C) noticeably declined in the nineteenth century in the middle classes but not in the working classes.
    (D) increased in general as a response to the stresses of urbanization.
    (E) increased in the working classes but not in the middle classes.

12. Nineteenth-century prostitutes in London and Paris
    (A) were usually women who became prostitutes when they were young and remained so for their whole lives.
    (B) generally had working-class men as their clientele, as the middle classes were very moralistic.
    (C) were relatively few in number because of the easy availability of premarital sex.
    (D) generally married and had children after some years on the streets.
    (E) mostly worked in government-supervised brothels.

13. Darwin's chief contribution to science was
    (A) proving the old age of Earth.
    (B) describing the mechanisms of evolution through accidental mutation.
    (C) being the first to suggest the role of the environment in the changes of species.
    (D) his successful challenge to Malthusian ideas that there is always a struggle for existence.
    (E) providing the scientific proof of Comte's positivist philosophy.

14. Freud's theory of the Oedipal complex
    (A) reflected the emotionally intense nature of nineteenth-century middle-class family life.
    (B) argued that fathers feel a competition with their sons over the mother's love, which the sons do not reciprocate.
    (C) reflected widespread sexual abuse in nineteenth-century homes.
    (D) proved that marriage was a fraud.
    (E) was based on his extensive studies of the brain.

15. One major change in the world of science in the later nineteenth century was
    (A) science became so complex and abstract that the ordinary person had little interest in it.
    (B) scientists came to be seen as less important than poets and philosophers.
    (C) most scientific work involved applying already existing scientific knowledge rather than seeking general theories.
    (D) many scientists were employed by various industries in research and development.
    (E) important philosophers like Comte argued that science was an unreliable path to truth.

Free-Response Questions

1. Describe and explain the changes in family life in the late nineteenth century in the middle and working classes of Europe.

2. Analyze how the ideas of Freud and Darwin reflected social and intellectual developments of the nineteenth century.

Answers

Multiple-Choice Questions

1. **Answer: (D)** The percentage of brides who were pregnant at marriage stayed high. (McKay, *A History of Western Society,* 8th ed., pp. 805–806/9th ed., p. 798)

2. **Answer: (C)** The wealthy families lived on the first floor (American second floor), with poorer tenants on higher levels. Remember this is before the invention of the elevator. (McKay, *A History of Western Society,* 8th ed., p. 794/9th ed., p. 785)

3. **Answer: (B)** Children were carefully supervised by their parents or guardians. Fewer illegitimate children were born, and typically they were not abandoned to foundling hospitals. (McKay, *A History of Western Society,* 8th ed., pp. 810–811/9th ed., pp. 802–803)

4. **Answer: (C)** Domestic service took a large percentage, about 14 percent in 1911, of the workforce in the nineteenth century, particularly of young women. (McKay, *A History of Western Society,* 8th ed., pp. 802–803/9th ed., p. 794)

5. **Answer: (E)** Wagon drivers were considered unskilled laborers and low down on the status hierarchy. (McKay, *A History of Western Society,* 8th ed., pp. 799, 802/9th ed., p.791)

6. **Answer: (A)** Women had significantly fewer legal rights than men; for example, they could not own property in their own name or keep their earnings. Abortion, divorce, equal pay, and the vote all were the focus on women's movements in the twentieth century. (McKay, *A History of Western Society,* 8th ed., pp. 807–808/9th ed., pp. 799–800)

7. **Answer: (B)** Chadwick argued that disease and poor sanitation caused poverty, not the other way around. He fought for better sanitary facilities and sewage systems as a way to reduce disease and poverty. (McKay, *A History of Western Society,* 8th ed., pp. 790–791/9th ed., pp. 781–783)

8. **Answer: (B)** The Paris metro would not be built until the turn of the century. (McKay, *A History of Western Society,* 8th ed., p. 792/9th ed., p. 786)

9. **Answer: (B)** More than half of the British were urbanized by the end of the nineteenth century. Thirty-five percent was the percentage for 1851. (McKay, *A History of Western Society,* 8th ed., p. 788/9th ed., p. 780)

10. **Answer: (C)** Pasteur discovered germ theory and developed pasteurization in the 1850s; Lister worked in the 1880s. (McKay, *A History of Western Society,* 8th ed., pp. 805–806/9th ed., p. 783)

11. **ANSWER: (B)** Decline was particularly acute in the working classes. (McKay, *A History of Western Society*, 8th ed., pp. 804–805/9th ed., p. 797)

12. **ANSWER: (D)** Most prostitutes saw that work, like domestic service, as temporary and necessary because of lack of other opportunities. (McKay, *A History of Western Society*, 8th ed., pp. 806–807/9th ed., pp. 798–799)

13. **ANSWER: (B)** Lamarck suggested the role of the environment in evolution but had the process wrong. Darwin's explanation was verifiable scientifically. It was Lyell who proved the age of Earth. Darwin accepted Malthusian principles about scarcity. Comte wrote about the evolution of man's ideas, not of biological ideas. (McKay, *A History of Western Society*, 8th ed., pp. 814–815/9th ed., pp. 806–807)

14. **ANSWER: (A)** Freud saw the family as the focus of the individual's psychological needs, reflecting the importance of family to the nineteenth-century middle class. Freud was a neurologist but saw patients rather than studying the brain. He argued that boys unconsciously compete with their fathers for their mother's love, not the other way around. If widespread sexual abuse in middle-class homes was occurring, Freud did not know about it. Freud believed that marriage was a good way for people to achieve sexual and psychological satisfaction. (McKay, *A History of Western Society*, 8th ed., pp. 811–812/9th ed., p. 804)

15. **ANSWER: (D)** Particularly in the chemical industries, many scientists found good employment in new research and development labs. (McKay, *A History of Western Society*, 8th ed., p. 813/9th ed., p. 805)

FREE-RESPONSE QUESTIONS

1. Population growth was accomplished by a decline in death rates. As fewer children died young, parents limited the number of their offspring through the use of various contraceptive methods then available. Parents of all classes were more devoted to their children and more invested in preparing them for future success. Fewer illegitimate children were born, and fewer of these were abandoned.

- Gender roles in the family changed as separate spheres became the ideal and in many cases the practice, especially when real wages rose after 1850. This meant that the family was no longer an economically productive unit, except in working-class families where the husband could not support the family, and also in the retail business. Women were limited to household roles, such as supervision of servants, and had few legal rights.
- Religion became less important in working-class families, although they continued to baptize their children.
- Most working-class families continued to live close to kinship groups.
- The ideal of romantic love as the motivation for marriage, rather than finances or status that might be accrued through marriage, became current, generally more in the case of working-class than middle-class families.

- Married and unmarried couples went out together to pubs or music halls or concerts.
- Public transportation systems made it possible for many families to move to better housing and to have weekend excursions.

2. Both Freud and Darwin reflected new understandings of human biology and of the animal nature of man. Freud argued that people have instincts, just as animals do, while Darwin argued that humans participate in the struggle for existence and evolved in the same way that other animals do.

- Both Freud and Darwin sought and came up with wide-ranging theories that explained everything in their subject and believed that they were universally true.
- Freudian theory reflected the transformation of the family from an economic unit to one where the father was the breadwinner and away from the house most of the time, with the wife and children in an intense emotional relationship. The Oedipal complex suggests that boys unconsciously fall in love with their mother and see their father as their rival; it is through this resolution of the complex that the son learns about and accepts the rules of society and morality.
- Freudian theory is also a reaction against the strict and repressive middle-class morality of the late nineteenth century, which he saw as causing many psychological problems, particularly for his female patients. Middle-class puritanism made it harder for them to talk about their feelings and to recognize their needs.
- Darwinian theory is based firstly on Malthusian principles, in particular that as food supply never keeps pace with population growth, there is always competition for existence. It also was influenced by Lyell, whose geological work demonstrated that Earth was millions of years old, not thousands of years old as suggested by the Bible, and by Lamarck, who theorized that living beings evolve because of environmental suitability. Darwin's contribution was figuring out how the process of evolution works, because Lamarck's notion of the inheritance of acquired characteristics could not be confirmed scientifically. The general interest in evolution and the processes of change among intellectuals was reflected also in the work of Karl Marx and Auguste Comte.

25

The Age of Nationalism, 1850–1914

Although unsuccessful during the 1848 revolutions, nationalism became the dominant force in Europe and the United States in the second half of the nineteenth century and directly led to the cataclysm known as World War I. Nationalists were able to garner the energies produced by political liberalism, industrialization, urbanization, and the prosperous Atlantic trade, appealing to people across class lines and even political philosophies. Nationalism is sometimes liberal in its orientation, as it was under Giuseppe Mazzini or Jules Michelet, or it can be radical, as during the French Revolution, but it can also be associated with conservatism or dictatorship. Fascism and Nazism are extreme forms of nationalism, invented in the twentieth century, that combine radical change with a harkening back to an imagined glorious past.

Key Concepts

- Napoleon III modernized the economy of France but at the same time established an authoritarian government.
- The unification of Italy and of Germany had been achieved by 1871. In each case, a dominant and highly modernized state (Piedmont in Italy and Prussia in Germany) with a strong leader (Count Camillo Benso di Cavour in Italy and Otto von Bismarck in Germany) went to war with Austria (1859 and 1866 respectively) to generate enthusiasm and nationalistic sentiment, which prompted the independent states in Italy and Germany to voluntarily join together.
- Russia and the Ottoman Empire modernized but did so incompletely. Russia freed its serfs and began to industrialize but remained autocratic. The Ottoman sultan eliminated the antiquated Janissary Corps and modernized the legal system when the

reformist Tanzimat period began. However, it faced rising nationalism in the subject nationalities outside of Anatolia.

- The United States, divided regionally over the issue of slavery, survived a bloody four-year civil war, finding common ground thereafter in belief in its "manifest destiny."
- The nation-state after 1870 became the focus of strong nationalist sentiments. The suffrage expanded, and more and more people became invested in their nations. Each nation faced distinct challenges. The French managed to resolve their differences in their Third Republic after the bloody repression of the rebellious Paris Commune, but then the Dreyfus affair tore France apart. England expanded the suffrage, alternated governments between Conservatives and Liberals, and divided over the issue of home rule for Ireland. Germany attacked the Catholics and then the socialists, but instituted Europe's first social welfare legislation. The Austro-Hungarian Empire contended with the nationalistic demands of its many subject nationalities.
- Marxism offered the promise of an internationalist alternative to nationalism. Socialist parties grew, particularly in Germany, where the socialist party became the largest party by 1912. As the labor movement grew, socialists tended to become less radical and more moderate.

France Under Napoleon III

Like his uncle, Napoleon III combined nationalism with authoritarianism and conservatism in such a unique way that he served as a model for others. He had been overwhelmingly elected in December 1848 as president of France, partially because of his family name and partially because he promised protection against the socialist-leaning workers so visible in the 1848 Revolution. He did have a program, but it was not a democratic one. Parliament and political parties served narrow interests, he argued, but an authoritarian ruler would be free from corruption and able to rise above the special interests and serve all the people, provide jobs, and secure French prosperity. Louis Napoleon's disdain for democracy was made all too evident when he staged a coup d'état in December 1851 to dismiss the assembly that had not changed the constitution to allow him to run for a second term. He crushed protests against the coup with military force, and won 92 percent approval in a plebiscite and an even higher percentage a year later on whether he should be emperor for life.

Napoleon III was quite successful in his efforts to improve the economy. Railroads were built, new investment banks were chartered, and Paris was rebuilt and transformed, all of which provided a huge number of jobs. He also built housing for workers and in the 1860s gave them the right to form unions and to strike. He won impressive electoral victories, but over time lost support from frustrated liberals, to whom he made a number of concessions, giving the assembly more power and greater freedom to his opposition. In 1869, this opposition, a motley crew of monarchists, liberals, and republicans, polled nearly 45 percent of the vote, although his proposed new constitution won 80 percent of a plebiscite vote. Napoleon III had demonstrated how an authoritarian leader could win the approval of the vast majority of the population, but his regime came to an end when it was defeated in a war caused by the nationalistic efforts of the Germans to unify.

NATION BUILDING IN ITALY

Before 1848, there was little chance of unifying the fiercely independent states on the Italian peninsula, although this left Italian states vulnerable to takeover by the Great Powers, all of whom had unified much earlier. Austria ruled Lombardy and Venetia, and the pope ruled central Italy as a temporal (secular) monarch, while Bourbons ruled Naples and Sicily. By the early nineteenth century, various groups of nationalists sought to expel the foreigners and unify all of Italy under Italian rule. One group was republican, led by Mazzini who had established a democratic republic in Rome in 1848, during which time the pope had had to flee, with the result that the papacy was suspicious of Italian unification and indeed of liberal ideas. In 1864, Pope Pius IX issued the *Syllabus of Errors*, which denounced rationalism, liberalism, and socialism. A second group of nationalists, led by Vincenzo Gioberti, wanted a loose federation headed by the pope. Others looked for a strong state to take the lead in unification and found it in Sardinia-Piedmont, ruled by the House of Savoy.

In Sardinia-Piedmont, King Victor Emmanuel II retained the liberal constitution granted during the 1848 Revolution there, making it a real constitutional monarchy. He had a most able prime minister from 1850 to 1861, Cavour, an aristocrat who had made a substantial fortune in business. Cavour made Sardinia the model of the liberal constitutional state, by building highways and railroads and establishing civil liberties, and attracted much support. Cavour understood that he could not defeat Austria on his own and forged a secret alliance with Napoleon III. In a brief war in 1859, Franco-Sardinian forces defeated Austria, but Sardinia won only Lombardy because France pulled out. Meanwhile, several states in central Italy expelled their princes, and once Cavour gave France Savoy and Nice in exchange for its support, these states voted overwhelming to join Sardinia. Most of Italy was now unified in a constitutional monarchy under Victor Emmanuel of Sardinia-Piedmont, with Florence as the first capital.

AP Tip

The process of Italian unification was intimately connected with German unification. Venetia was granted to Sardinia-Piedmont as a reward for its role in the Austro-Prussian War in 1866. When Prussia went to war with France in 1870, France withdrew its troops, which had defended the pope for centuries, from Rome, and Rome was then easily annexed to Italy.

But Mazzini's republicanism had not died out. Giuseppe Garibaldi, a romantic adventurer and nationalist, organized an independent military force against Austria in 1859. Cavour encouraged him to liberate Naples and Sicily (known as the Kingdom of Two Sicilies), but discouraged his republicanism. Garibaldi invaded Sicily in 1860 with a thousand guerillas known as the Red Shirts, who quickly took Palermo and Naples, which then voted in a plebiscite to join Piedmont. In 1866 Venetia joined the new kingdom, and finally in 1870 Rome joined and replaced Florence as the capital. The new nation, in which suffrage was limited to property holders, struggled over a deep divide between the mostly agricultural south and the industrialized and cosmopolitan north.

AP Tip

Sicily and Naples had long been ruled by Spain. In terrain and values, there are many similarities between Spain and those parts of Italy, which makes them quite different from central and northern Italy. In addition, the Italian spoken there is quite distinct. These differences remain strong even to this day. In recent years, a political party advocating the division of Italy has had some electoral success.

It is also important to note that Rome was annexed to Italy against the wishes of the papacy, which withdrew into Vatican City in a hostile relationship to the new Italian state. Coincidentally, it was in that year, 1870, that the papacy articulated the doctrine of papal infallibility.

NATION BUILDING IN GERMANY

Earlier attempts to unify Germany, either from above or below, that is, from the rulers or the ruled, had failed, although the Zollverein, a customs union founded in 1834 of all the German states except Austria, had brought them into economic cooperation. The Zollverein, dominated by Prussia, was so successful that national unification under Prussian leadership won the support of business and commercial interests. The King of Prussia, William I, inspired by Piedmont's war against Austria in 1859 to strengthen his army, ran into conflict with the nonmilitaristic middle classes of Prussia over control over army finances. When parliament, with popular support, rejected the military budget in 1862, the king brought in Bismarck, a Junker (Prussian aristocrat) and master politician, to be his chief minister. An extraordinary and complex figure, Bismarck has been the object of intense interest as well as much vilification. Bismarck was a pragmatist, and his practical, fundamentally nonideological approach to problems led to solid and quick success. He was to dominate German politics for nearly thirty years.

AP Tip

There are a number of interesting similarities between Italian and German unification: both had strong leaders from advanced states, both fought against Austria to win their independence, with France also playing an important role, and both forged unity under the domination of a strong state but faced major dissensions and regional differences when they did unify.

Bismarck faced the constitutional impasse with a firm commitment to autocracy, saying in one of his most famous speeches that "blood and iron" and not parliamentary discussion would solve the problems of the day. The government would rule and collect taxes without parliamentary consent, Bismarck promised. The voters in Prussia did not approve; they continued to elect liberal representatives for the next four years. Bismarck used the issue of Schleswig-Holstein to win over parliament. By joining with Austria in a war against Denmark in 1864, and then two years later warring with Austria directly in the Seven Weeks' War, Bismarck demonstrated the value of blood and iron. Austria was defeated by the reorganized Prussian army and forced to cede Venetia to Italy and to agree to withdraw from German affairs, but was given otherwise easy terms by Bismarck. Most of the Protestant states joined the new North German Confederation with the king of Prussia at its head. The constitution had some liberal elements, with each state retaining its local government and the lower house elected by universal male suffrage, but the king controlled military and foreign affairs, and the chief minister was responsible only to the king. Bismarck used his military victory to win the approval previously denied by the parliament for the army funds collected by the government. Liberal representatives jumped at the chance to cooperate and, in a sense, voted themselves out of the power of the purse, a victory for militaristic values over liberal constitutionalism. Bismarck's program of war and industrial strength, militarism and industrialism, would reverberate in German history through the first half of the twentieth century.

The southern Catholic states had remained out of the North German Confederation. To win them over, Bismarck manipulated France into war in 1870. It was a quick and decisive victory for the Prussians who captured Napoleon III at the Battle of Sedan. In Paris, the people declared a republic and continued fighting for another five months but, facing starvation, were forced to surrender. The terms were harsh. France had to pay a huge indemnity and cede Alsace-Lorraine to Germany. King William I was declared Kaiser William I in the Hall of Mirrors at Versailles. The south German states joined the new unified Germany, and German nationalism soared. Germany had become a Great Power through Bismarck's methods, its military victories a source of enormous pride and validation for Germans. The new state, whose constitution was similar to that of the North German Confederation, had a parliament elected by universal male suffrage but also an authoritarian government that was not required to get parliamentary approval for military or foreign decisions,

AP Tip

One of the lessons Bismarck drew from the Franco-Prussian War was that war was destabilizing and should be avoided unless necessary and fought only if victory was assured. For that reason, in his eighteen years as chancellor of a united Germany, he avoided war—an irony given the great militarist he was.

Nation Building in the United States

The United States also had significant regional differences, an industrialized North using the free labor of many European immigrants, and a plantation-agriculture South dependent on slave labor to produce cotton for the thirsty northern and European markets. The debate over slavery grew more intense when the United States acquired large territories from Mexico after a war in 1848. A bloody four-year civil war was fought over slavery but also states' rights. It was particularly devastating in the South where it was mostly fought; many in the North prospered during the war years. During the war, the rise of large corporations, the Homestead Act of 1862 encouraging the settlement of the West, and the Thirteenth Amendment to the Constitution which abolished slavery, all marked the future of the United States. American nationalism, its "manifest destiny" to become first a continental power, then a world one, blossomed during and after the war.

The Modernization of Russia and the Ottoman Empire

Like the United States, Russia and the Ottoman Empire lagged behind western and central Europe at the beginning of the nineteenth century. By midcentury, Russia and the Ottoman Empire, both vast multinational states under absolutist rule, were facing significant challenges and the need to modernize their states and their armies in order to compete with the Great Powers of Europe. In both cases, the Crimean War, 1853 to 1856, fought over domination of the Balkan Peninsula, brought that need sharply into focus. Russia was defeated by the combined forces of France, Britain, Sardinia, and the Ottoman Empire, mostly because of its inadequate transportation system. Russia had failed to gain access to the Mediterranean from the Black Sea, and its industrial backwardness and desperate need for railroads and modern armaments became apparent.

Russia's population had grown rapidly in the nineteenth century, although the economy remained agrarian with very little industrialization. Agricultural estates were dependent on the unpaid labor of serfs who were little better off than U.S. slaves. Serfs could also be recruited into the army for a mandatory twenty-five years of service. Peasant discontent was intensified by the hardships of the Crimean War. Fearful of an outright rebellion, Tsar Alexander II liberated the serfs in 1861 (just two years before the Emancipation Proclamation in the United States) and granted them land for which, however, they had to pay. The land was given not to individuals but to village communities, which were responsible for the payments (known as redemption fees) for the land and taxes; this made them responsible for the land and restricted the freedom of choice of individual peasants. Similar halfway measures were used in creating new local assemblies, the zemstvos, elected by three classes—towns, peasant villages, and nobles. Liberal hopes that the zemstvos would become the model for a national assembly were disappointed. There were some successful reforms: equality before the law, some liberalization of education, and some reduction in restrictions on the Jewish population.

The government encouraged industrialization, particularly the building of railroads after 1860 (increasing tenfold by 1880) and of factories around Moscow and St. Petersburg. Industrialization brought benefits to Russia's military, which pleased the nationalists, but also the introduction of Marxian ideas. Originally, however, Russian radicals were not Marxists but anarchists who advocated the use of terrorism and assassination to bring down the government. When terrorists assassinated Alexander II, the new tsars, Alexander III (1881–1894) and Nicholas II (1894–1917) rejected reform, believing that the modest liberalizing reforms of Alexander II had only opened the door for radicalism. Political repression remained in force, but economic modernization proceeded apace, with state-sponsored industrialization under the leadership of Sergei Witte, the finance minister, who doubled Russia's railroad network, put up high protective tariffs, and put Russia on the gold standard. Witte encouraged foreigners to invest in Russia and to build factories and steel and coal mills, like the very modern ones built in Ukraine.

AP Tip

Anarchism is a political philosophy that argues that all governments are repressive, whether liberal, autocratic, or communist. It tended to be popular on the fringes of Europe, in Russia, Spain, and Italy particularly. In Russia, anarchists adopted the use of terrorism and assassination with the hope that by eliminating reformers or effective leaders, the system would collapse and people would be able to live freely in small, self-governing communities. For this reason, it was "good guys" who were the likely victims of terrorism, such as the reforming minister Stolypin, assassinated in 1911. Terrorists organized themselves into secret cells to avoid detection by the repressive secret police. Russian terrorists were socialist-minded, but the tactics they created have been adopted by other ideologues.

Nevertheless, Russia's modernization was still limited. Its military backwardness became all too apparent when it suffered a humiliating defeat by Japan in a war in 1904–1905. The defeat encouraged the many people hopeful for change: liberals seeking to turn Russia into a constitutional monarchy, radical Marxists organizing a still-illegal labor movement, non-Russian nationalities in the Russian empire wanting autonomy, and peasants resentful that they were still paying for the land they were given in 1861. These currents came together in the widespread 1905 Revolution **and** forced the tsarist government to make concessions. The revolution began on a day in January known as Bloody Sunday when a large crowd of peaceful protesters were massacred at the Winter Palace in St. Petersburg. Workers went out on strike, peasants and ethnic minorities rebelled, and secret political parties came out into the open, all culminating in a general strike in October, after which the tsar capitulated. His October Manifesto granted civil rights and promised a constitutional monarchy with a popularly elected parliament, known as the Duma.

> **AP Tip**
>
> A general strike is rare, as it involves everyone who works—from bus conductors and coal miners to shopkeepers—to go out on strike. It is a reflection of the degree of frustration felt by the majority of Russians that, without legal unions or political parties, they could organize and execute a successful general strike. It is also a sign of the power of the industrial working classes, many of whom had already become Marxists. As so much of Russian industrialization was state sponsored, workers were not just demanding legal protection but actually protesting against their employers.

The first Duma, elected by universal male suffrage, met in 1906, yet the new constitution of that year gave the tsar absolute veto power, limiting the Duma to debate. When disappointed liberals confronted the tsar, he dismissed the Duma and rewrote the constitution to restrict the electoral rights of workers and peasants. Some reforms were made; Stolypin ended the peasants' redemption payments and gave them the right to leave their villages. But the Russian political system remained autocratic, with the apparatus but not the reality of limited monarchy.

The Ottoman Empire began to lose out to the rising European states of Russia and Austria already in the eighteenth century, mostly because it relied on the Janissary Corps. The janissaries, taken from Christian homes in the Balkans as an annual tax and brought to Istanbul where they were converted to Islam and trained as soldiers and administrators, became high-ranking officials in the empire. In the 1820s, as the Ottoman Empire starting losing its European lands (Serbia got local autonomy in 1816 and Greece independence, and Algeria was taken by France in 1830), the Ottoman sultan Mahmud III destroyed the Janissary Corps and replaced it with a modern army. A more radical series of reforms called the Tanzimat were launched in 1839, with equality before the law for Muslims, Christians, and Jews; liberalization of commercial laws; Western education; and even secularism. The hope was that such reforms would make the Ottoman Empire more Western and win the loyalty of the non-Turkish subjects. But this goal eluded the reformers. Nationalism grew, and ironically, the new legal equality exacerbated, rather than reduced, religious conflict, especially as the European powers were constantly meddling. The Ottoman Empire relied on the Great Powers that supported it out of fear of the consequences of its collapse. In the 1830s, the European powers forced Muhammad Ali, the governor of Egypt who had taken Syrian and Iraq, to withdraw. Similarly, during the Crimean War, the Ottomans only won with French, British, and Sardinian support. The last sultan, Abdulhamid II (1876–1909), turned his back on liberalism and created a repressive regime with the support of Islamic conservatives. In 1908, the successful seizure of power of reform-seeking young officers and intellectuals known as Young Turks forced him to institute reforms. It was this group of young people that picked up the pieces after the defeat of the Ottoman Empire in World War I.

THE RESPONSIVE NATION-STATES, 1871–1914

After the unifications of Italy and Germany, most states in Europe experienced both the emergence of large-scale political parties and growing popular nationalism. As universal male suffrage became the norm, more people could vote, more legislation was passed on their behalf, and more people felt vested in their government. In most countries, a multiparty system was created, with parliamentary coalitions giving small parties significant leverage. Conservatives were able to manipulate the liberal or socialist masses by stirring their nationalism during international crises, which tended to foster aggressive foreign policies. Mass politics also allowed for radical political parties; some extremely nationalistic parties demonized the Jews as a way of winning popular support.

AP Tip

The typical European parliamentary system is quite different from the U.S. two-party system. In many European countries such as Britain (a constitutional monarchy) and Italy (a republic), the ministers who execute the laws and make up the cabinet (such as the minister of defense or of finance) are all members of Parliament who have been elected by their constituents. When an election is held, the party that wins the most seats forms the government; its members become the cabinet, and the head of the victorious party becomes the prime minister. If no party wins a majority, then the party winning the plurality, the most votes but not the majority of the votes, creates a coalition with other parties to form a majority of the seats in Parliament. In this way, a small party can negotiate for important concessions. Should the government not be able to pass a piece of major legislation, the government falls, and new elections are held. Such parliamentary systems, created in nineteenth-century Europe, can be unstable but also highly democratic.

THE GERMAN EMPIRE

The unified German state that came into being in 1871 was in fact a federal empire in which individual provinces could keep their traditional rulers, such as the kings of Bavaria. The national government was dominated by a chancellor who reported only to the kaiser (emperor) and by the Reichstag, the lower house of parliament elected by universal male suffrage. Bismarck, chancellor for nearly twenty years, tried to maintain control of the Reichstag even as he opposed liberalism. He first attacked the Catholic Church in what was called the Kulturkampf. When Catholics stayed loyal to their party, Bismarck abandoned that fight and won Catholic support when he enacted high tariffs against cheap U.S. grain, which pleased the small farmers of southern Germany, primarily Catholic, as well as the large landowners of his own Junker class. Bismarck then went after the socialists, whose growing strength alarmed him. In 1878, he convinced the Reichstag to outlaw the Social Democratic Party, the socialist party, which had the unintended effect of making it stronger. To outflank them, in the 1880s Bismarck instituted the most far-ranging social welfare measures of any state in Europe, including social security and national sickness and accident insurance. Protecting retired, injured, and sick workers was a way of creating positive feelings in them toward the German state. But the socialist movement and its party continued to grow, even though the new kaiser, William II, dismissed Bismarck, legalized their political activity, and passed more pro-worker measures. By 1912, the Social Democrats were the largest party in the Reichstag. By then they had become less radical and more reformist; nevertheless, the specter of radical revolution increasingly frightened conservatives and liberal capitalists alike.

AP Tip

Such social welfare legislation was adopted by other European states over the next few decades. The United States did not adopt these measures until the New Deal under Franklin Delano Roosevelt. Still to this day, the social welfare programs in most nations in Europe are extensive.

REPUBLICAN FRANCE

The Franco-Prussian War revived some of the old divisions in France. When the newly elected government of monarchists and conservatives accepted defeat and ceded Alsace and Lorraine, the Parisian republicans, who had created the Third Republic and defended France at great personal sacrifice, were furious. They declared that Paris was now under its own government, the Commune, but it was crushed by the assembly with terrible brutality; some 20,000 died.

AP Tip

Alsace and Lorraine have long been areas of contention. France was awarded them at the Peace of Westphalia. After losing them in 1870, France was committed to getting them back, which they did after World War I. The Germans took them back in 1940 when they defeated France at the beginning of World War II. At the end of that war, the territories were returned to France, where they are to this day.

The Third Republic was able, surprisingly, to bring the French people together. The right was divided, the left defeated, leaving the moderates secure. Under the leadership of the skilled Léon Gambetta, the republican majority in the National Assembly legalized trade unions, established free compulsory elementary schools for both boys and girls, and expanded secondary school education, an important step toward secularism in a Catholic country where the church had dominated education. The French empire also expanded.

By the early 1890s, a stable republic generally supported by the public had been achieved. But it was torn asunder by a legal case, the Dreyfus affair, which exposed underlying tensions. Dreyfus was a Jewish captain in the French army who was found guilty of treason, giving military information to Austria. The evidence against him had been trumped up by the army leadership. When Emile Zola, a realist novelist, took up the case, France split into two camps, those who supported the army—conservatives, anti-Semites, and most of the Catholic clergy—and those who defended Dreyfus—civil libertarians and republicans. Ultimately, Dreyfus was exonerated, but the case had rent France apart. In the early twentieth century, the government broke off all relations with the Catholic Church, ending the payment of clerical salaries by the state (begun during the French Revolution) and subsidies for Catholic schools. Once this consensus had been achieved, the only perceived threat to the stability of the Third Republic was the growing socialist movement.

GREAT BRITAIN AND IRELAND

Unlike most of the constitutional regimes that had multiparty systems, Britain's parliamentary system had evolved into a two-party system, the Conservatives, or Tories, and the Liberals. The Tories and Liberals alternated in office in the nineteenth century, each dominated by a towering figure: Benjamin Disraeli for the Tories and William Gladstone for the Liberals. In 1867 the Tories extended the suffrage in the Second Reform Bill to middle-class and better-paid workers hoping to expand the basis of Conservative support. Within two decades, the vote was given to almost every male but not to women—although women were fighting hard for the vote. Suffragists had had some limited success in the United States but less in Europe; by 1914, only Norway had granted the vote to women. In Britain, suffragists such as Emmeline Pankhurst became quite militant and engaged in numerous public demonstrations.

Aristocratic power lay in the House of Lords, which still held significant power, especially in its function as the highest court. When the Lords ruled against labor unions and voted against the People's Budget proposed by the Liberals to extend social welfare services in the early twentieth century, they were forced to back down. It was the last time the House of Lords seriously attempted to assert its power. Extensive social legislation—national health insurance, unemployment benefits, and old-age pensions—was passed under the Liberals, while taxes on the rich were raised to pay for the new programs.

Britain too had its defining issue: home rule for Ireland. Irish nationalism had grown in the wake of the terrible famine of the 1840s. Gladstone hoped to pacify the nationalists with home rule or self-government. The idea developed momentum, even after two defeats in Parliament, but the Irish Protestants, known as the Ulsterites because they lived mostly in the six Irish provinces to the north known as Ulster, vowed to resist home rule, refusing to be ruled by the Catholic Irish even though they were the majority of the population. Many Englishmen supported the Ulsterites, and the issue teetered back and forth, and was still unresolved at the outbreak of World War I.

AP Tip

The Irish rebelled in 1916, and all of Ireland except Ulster became independent a few years after the war. Tensions in Ireland lasted through the twentieth century, with Protestant Ulsterites fiercely adhering to the United Kingdom and Catholics in Ulster fighting for union with the Republic of Ireland. A great deal of blood has been shed in these two causes.

The Austro-Hungarian Empire

No nation in Europe faced as many problems with nationalism as did the Austro-Hungarian Empire, which was created in 1867 to pacify Hungarian nationalists in the wake of Austria's defeat in the Seven Weeks' War. The Dual Monarchy—one king wore both crowns—gave Hungary virtual independence and rule over some of the minorities in the Empire. In the Austrian half, ethnic Germans, speakers of German as their mother tongue, made up not quite half the population and felt threatened by the Slavs, especially the Poles and the Czechs. The language issue divided the governments, so often in the decade before World War I the ministers could not obtain a majority and ruled by decree. In the Hungarian part of the empire, the Hungarians insisted that their Magyar language be used in government and schools, creating huge resentment among the minorities of the region.

Jewish Emancipation and Modern Anti-Semitism

European Jews had been long under severe restrictions, but liberalism and revolutionary sentiment asserting the equality of all men argued against such discrimination. Jews were granted civil rights in France in 1791, and legal equality became more acceptable after the 1848 revolutions in Austria and Germany in which Jews played a significant role. The new constitution of Germany in 1871 gave Jews legal equality, although there were still some restrictions on government employment. Many Jews there and elsewhere responded gladly to the opportunities to succeed in professions previously denied to them such as medicine, journalism, academia, and the law, and expanded their businesses enterprises in retail, railroads, and finance. Most Jews joined the middle classes and became fervent patriots. But at the same time, anti-Semitism grew more virulent. Partially a reaction against liberalism and modernization, which had propelled the Jews forward, partially a response to competition offered by the newly emancipated Jews, and partially drawing on long-standing anti-Jewish traditions, modern anti-Semitism was distinguished from former versions in that the vilified group was the Jewish race, not the Jewish religion. Political parties were created with anti-Semitic platforms; the anti-Semitic party in Germany got just under 3 percent of the vote in elections in 1893, but won electoral victories for Mayor Karl Lueger in Vienna in the 1890s, providing useful lessons to the young Adolf Hitler (who lived in Vienna then).

AP Tip

Political anti-Semitism is a form of racism, in that being Jewish is not a religious choice but an inheritance of racial traits. Changing one's religion does not change one's race, an idea that limits the options of Jews in times of trouble. It is this racist form that was adopted by the Nazis. Racist ideas, sometimes combined with Social Darwinism, flourished in Europe at the turn of the century.

In response to his electoral victories and just before the Dreyfus Affair, an Austrian journalist in Paris, Theodor Herzl, delineated a new idea, Zionism, the creation of a Jewish homeland, a Jewish state to provide Jews with the same benefits and protection as nation-states provided for their citizens. Assimilation, Herzl argued, would ultimately not work. Zionism quickly took hold, with the First Zionist Congress meeting in 1897. Herzl worked tirelessly for the Zionist cause.

Anti-Semitism was most virulent, however, in Russia and eastern Europe. In Russia, some 4 million Jews remained mostly impoverished and were the occasional victims of mass attacks called pogroms, in which Jews were attacked and their property looted while the police watched. The government used pogroms to deflect the anger of the tsar's subjects. A series of pogroms in 1881–1882 and later in 1906 led some Jews to become Zionists and others to leave Russia for the United States. Nearly 3 million Jews left eastern Europe in the decades before World War I.

MARXISM AND THE SOCIALIST MOVEMENT

The chief alternative ideology to nationalism was Marxism, which proposed worldwide proletarian revolution. Socialist parties grew in virtually every European state in the late nineteenth century—something that made many wealthy conservatives nervous. In spite of Bismarck's social welfare program, the German Social Democratic Party saw phenomenal growth, becoming the largest party in the Reichstag by 1912. The Russian party, founded in 1883 in exile, and various socialist parties in France also grew though not as much. The excerpt from the autobiography of Adelheid Popp in Listening to the Past (McKay, *A History of Western Society*, 9th ed., pp. 844–845) shows how empowering it was to become a socialist. Socialists organized an international group, the Socialist International, in 1864 in London where Marx had settled after 1848. A second Socialist International functioned from 1889 to 1914, meeting every three years. Socialists even had their own holiday, May 1, celebrated everywhere as a one-day strike.

Socialist parties tended to become less radical and more moderate in their practices if not in their pronouncements. Workers too became more moderate, because of the right to vote, social welfare benefits, the rise in real wages and improvements in standards of living, and patriotism. Unions played a role in this process when they achieved legal status. They began to use less radical rhetoric and focused instead on winning wages and benefits, successfully using collective bargaining and the tool of the strike to make their power felt. Their membership skyrocketed as industrialization spread. Some socialists themselves began to turn away from radical revolution and adopted revisionism. Eduard Bernstein in Germany wrote an influential work, *Evolutionary Socialism,* which argued that since Marx's predictions had not come true, socialism needed to change and achieve its goals through electoral politics and unions. Revisionism was publicly criticized by orthodox Marxists and the Second International but won tacit acceptance by many socialists. This issue of gradual reform versus revolution divided the socialist movement, as did the varying degrees of Marxist influence in different countries. It was strong in Germany but weak in England where the Labour Party (which was formed at the turn of the century and soon succeeded the Liberal Party as the main opposition to the Conservative Party) was socialist but anti-Marxist, as well as in Spain and Italy where anarchism had many adherents. So, socialist movements, too, reflected nationalism.

Multiple-Choice Questions

1. Bismarck made his "blood and iron" speech as chancellor of Prussia in response to
   (A) the rise of socialism.
   (B) parliamentary resistance to his military budgets.
   (C) Austria's aggressive statements provoking the Seven Weeks' War.
   (D) efforts to form the North German Federation.
   (E) the resistance of Bavaria to joining a unified Germany.

2. Garibaldi and his guerilla army, the Red Shirts,
   (A) captured Rome.
   (B) demanded a constitutional monarchy under the king of Sicily.
   (C) conquered Sardinia.
   (D) refused to compromise their republican ideals with Cavour.
   (E) were defeated by the larger royal army.

3. In terms of their political systems, Sardinia-Piedmont and Prussia in the 1860s
   (A) were both constitutional monarchies.
   (B) were not constitutional monarchies.
   (C) were both ruled by incompetent kings.
   (D) differed in that Sardinia-Piedmont was a constitutional monarchy but Prussia was not.
   (E) differed in that Prussia was a constitutional monarchy but Sardinia-Piedmont was not.

4. Bismarck's attacks on the socialist movement and the ban on the Social Democratic Party
   (A) weakened the socialist movement in Germany permanently.
   (B) proved to be counterproductive.
   (C) gave rise to ultranationalistic parties.
   (D) spawned anti-Semitism in Germany.
   (E) led to the founding of the International to aid German socialists.

5. The Kulturkampf, Bismarck's attacks on the Catholic Church,
   (A) ended when he wooed Catholics with high protective tariffs.
   (B) alienated the Catholics from the new German state for decades.
   (C) was really part of an anti-French campaign.
   (D) led to an independence movement in Catholic states such as Bavaria.
   (E) was an attack on the authority of local princes and kings in the Catholic states.

6. An important consequence of the creation of Dual Monarchy of Austro-Hungary in 1867 was
   (A) smoother relationships with the subject nationalities in the empire.
   (B) that a weakened Habsburg dynasty retained its most important ethnic minority.
   (C) German language and culture were taught everywhere in the schools.
   (D) the king of Hungary replaced the Habsburgs as the Austro-Hungarian emperor.
   (E) Hungary ceased to have its own parliament but joined the one in Vienna.

7. Which of the states listed below faced nationalistic or independence movements of ethnic groups within their borders at the end of the nineteenth century and in the early twentieth century?
   I. Britain
   II. Germany
   III. Russia
   IV. The Ottoman Empire
   V. France
   (A) All of them
   (B) None of them
   (C) I, III, IV, and V
   (D) III, IV, and V
   (E) I, III, and IV

8. Bismarck's social welfare legislation was
   (A) rejected by western European states until the 1930s when the depression hit.
   (B) one factor that led many German socialists to adopt revisionism and reject revolution.
   (C) rejected by the conservatives of Germany.
   (D) achieved its goal of weaning the German workers away from socialism.
   (E) was opposed by liberals and socialists in France and Britain.

9. The Tanzimat reforms in the Ottoman Empire sought to
   (A) increase the power of the sultans.
   (B) reorganize the janissaries and make them the army officer corps.
   (C) westernize the government and army.
   (D) give legal privileges to Muslims over Christians and Jews.
   (E) turn the Ottoman Empire into a republic.

10. Political anti-Semitism, which developed at the end of the nineteenth century, was different from previous forms of anti-Semitism in that it
    (A) called for the murder of all Jews.
    (B) was strongest in Germany.
    (C) alienated Catholics from the church.
    (D) defined Jewishness as a race rather than a religion.
    (E) was highly unpopular.

11. Theodor Herzl's call for a Jewish state
    (A) was based on biblical prophecies.
    (B) reflects despair about the possibility of assimilation and true acceptance.
    (C) denounced the Arab takeover of the Holy Land.
    (D) was a response to recent pogroms in Russia.
    (E) won immediate support from Great Britain.

12. The conflict over the People's Budget in Britain
    (A) led to a loss in real power of the House of Lords.
    (B) pitted the Liberals who opposed it against the Conservatives who proposed it.
    (C) was about home rule for Ireland.
    (D) pitted the monarchy against the Liberals.
    (E) was a misnomer in that the budget called for a reduction in taxes for the rich.

13. Napoleon III's regime in France
    (A) would have been overthrown by revolution had it not been for the Franco-Prussian War.
    (B) was popular only with the middle classes.
    (C) became progressively more authoritarian.
    (D) combined economic success with authoritarian government.
    (E) resisted industrialization in an effort to preserve traditional French society.

14. Which was *not* one of the modernizing reforms of Alexander II in Russia?
    (A) Emancipation of the serfs
    (B) Establishment of zemstvos
    (C) Promotion of public education
    (D) Building of railroads and industrial factories
    (E) Establishment of the Duma

15. In the period after the assassination of Alexander II in 1881 up to the 1905 Revolution, Russia
    (A) was a constitutional monarchy.
    (B) strongly discouraged anti-Semitism and liberalized laws relating to Jews.
    (C) promoted industrialization with Western investment.
    (D) ended the redemption payments former serfs had to pay for the land they got on emancipation.
    (E) focused on internal development and avoided foreign entanglements.

Free-Response Questions

1. Compare the problems facing proponents of Italian and German unification and the processes by which they achieved their goal.

2. To what degree did Russia and the Ottoman Empire succeed in their modernization programs before World War I?

ANSWERS

MULTIPLE-CHOICE QUESTIONS

1. (B) The major issue confronting Bismarck as chancellor of Prussia was the power of the purse held by the Prussian parliament, which he effectively removed. (McKay, *A History of Western Society*, 8th ed., pp. 830–832/9th ed., p. 822)

2. (A) Naples and Sicily joined in 1860 after Garibaldi's Red Shirts defeated their Bourbon ruler. Garibaldi compromised with Cavour because of his intense patriotism and encouraged the people of Sicily to vote for union with Sardinia in plebiscites organized by Cavour. (McKay, *A History of Western Society*, 8th ed., pp. 826–829/9th ed., p. 821)

3. (D) Although Prussia had a parliament, it had little real power, and Bismarck was able to collect taxes without its consent. Piedmont became a constitutional monarchy during the 1848 Revolution. (McKay, *A History of Western Society*, 8th ed., pp. 827, 830/9th ed., pp. 818, 822)

4. (B) The ban only made the movement stronger. (McKay, *A History of Western Society*, 8th ed., pp. 840–841/9th ed., p. 833)

5. (A) The Catholics, newly joined to unified Germany, were seen as potentially more loyal to the pope than to the state. Bismarck attacked the church for eight years, but gave up when Catholics stayed loyal to their party. He wooed them with protective tariffs. (McKay, *A History of Western Society,* 8th ed., p. 840/9th ed., pp. 832–833)

6. (B) Austria felt compelled to appease Hungarian nationalists when its military weakness was revealed in the Seven Weeks' War. Hungary had its own parliament and imposed its language on the subject nationalities within its jurisdiction, thereby infuriating them. The Habsburg emperor became king of Hungary as well. (McKay, *A History of Western Society,* 8th ed., pp. 844–845/9th ed., pp. 836–837)

7. (E) Britain had the Irish problem, the Ottoman Empire was challenged by its subject peoples in North Africa and the Balkans, and there were uprisings among the subject nationalities in the 1905 Revolution in Russia. Germany and France faced no such problems. (McKay, *A History of Western Society,* 8th ed., pp. 837–838, 844 /9th ed., pp. 829–831, 835–836)

8. (B) The introduction of social welfare programs, along with the growing strength of unions and workers' political parties, led socialists like Eduard Bernstein to reject the need for revolution and advocate gradual evolutionary gain; this was called revisionism. The People's Budget, a Liberal Party program, created a variety of social welfare programs in England in the decade before the outbreak of World War I. Bismarck, who instituted them in Germany, was a conservative. His plan to wean the workers away from socialism failed as the Social Democratic Party became the largest in the Reichstag of 1912. (McKay, *A History of Western Society,* 8th ed., pp. 840–841, 844/9th ed., pp. 833, 835, 841)

9. (C) The Tanzimat sought to revitalize the Ottoman Empire by adopting many Western ideas. (McKay, *A History of Western Society,* not discussed in 8th ed./9th ed., pp. 830–831)

10. (D) It was the racial definition of Jews and its electoral success that marked nineteenth-century anti-Semitism, which was particularly strong in Austria but not in Germany at that time. People like Lueger called for the elimination of the Jews from public life but not their extermination. The Catholic Church was little involved in such movements. (McKay, *A History of Western Society,* 8th ed., p. 846/9th ed., pp. 837–838)

11. (B) Herzl was a secular Jew, not particularly religious. Lueger's election as mayor of Vienna on an anti-Semitic platform convinced Herzl that Jews would never be fully accepted unless they had a state of their own. Pogroms were happening in Russia during this time, and Jews were still under legal discrimination. Herzl lived in Vienna and Paris where Jews did not suffer from legal discrimination. Zionism did win some support from Britain but only twenty years later. (McKay, *A History of Western Society,* 8th ed., pp. 846–847/9th ed., pp. 838–839)

12. (A) The king supported the Liberals, who proposed the People's Budget, and forced the House of Lords to back down; this ended the

Lords' attempts to determine policy. The People's Budget was about social welfare legislation and raising taxes on the rich to pay for it. (McKay, *A History of Western Society*, 8th ed., pp. 843–844/9th ed., p. 835)

13. (D) Napoleon III encouraged industrialization and fostered prosperity, but as he legalized unions, he was popular with workers as well as many bourgeois. His government was authoritarian but made concessions to liberalism over time. (McKay, *A History of Western Society*, 8th ed., pp. 823–826/9th ed., pp. 817–818)

14. (E) The Duma was only reluctantly granted in the October Manifesto during the 1905 Revolution. (McKay, *A History of Western Society*, 8th ed., pp. 835–838/9th ed., p. 829)

15. (C) Redemption payments ended only after the 1905 Revolution. Russia never really became a constitutional monarchy. Anti-Semitic pogroms were fostered by the government to deflect popular resentment. Under the finance minister Witte, industrialization intensified with investments from abroad. (McKay, *A History of Western Society*, 8th cd., pp. 836–838/9th ed., pp. 828, 838)

FREE-RESPONSE QUESTIONS

1. This question calls for comparing both the similarities and difference of Italian and German unification.

- Similarities: Both were engineered by single strong, modernized and industrialized states (Sardinia-Piedmont and Prussia) under the exceptional leadership of royal appointees (Cavour and Bismarck). Both Sardinia-Piedmont and Prussia went to war with Austria (1859 and 1866). Both used France to achieve unification (Cavour's alliance with France in 1859 with Rome joining the new country when the French withdrew their troops in 1870 and the Franco-Prussian War of 1870). Both states had to contend with Catholic reluctance to join the new nation-states but were able to generate sufficient nationalistic sentiments to overcome that resistance.
- Differences: Sardinia-Piedmont was a constitutional monarchy, but Prussia an autocratic state where the Reichstag had limited power. Republican ideals and republicans, represented by Garibaldi, played an important role in bringing Naples, Sicily, and Rome into a unified Italy; no role was played by republicans in Germany. Germany unified as an empire in which individual states kept their princely rulers; Italy unified as a state under a single monarch. The German empire was declared at Versailles, accentuating the importance of military victory; the Italian capitals were first Florence and then Rome, each of whom had been republics, however briefly. Italy had limited suffrage, Germany universal manhood suffrage. Cavour died before final unification was achieved; Bismarck was chancellor of the unified Germany for another two decades.

2. In the period before World War I, both Russia and the Ottoman Empire had some moderate successes but significant failures in their modernization programs. Russian modernization attained more lasting success than Ottoman reform did.

- Russian successes: Industrialization was begun under Tsar Alexander II and continued under Tsar Nicholas II with the leadership of Witte in the early twentieth century. Railroads and factories were built and protective tariffs set to protect the new industries. The emancipation of serfs in 1861 allowed for some modernization of agriculture. Zemstvos were the beginning of local, autonomous governments. Some relaxation of censorship, restrictions on Jews, and educational policies created an intellectually freer atmosphere under Alexander II.
- Russian failures: The political repression of labor unions and workers' parties led to their radicalization; the emancipation of the serfs accompanied by peasant obligations to make redemption payments and limitations on personal freedom (not cancelled until 1906); increased political repression after 1881; and little or no accommodation of demands for liberalizing reforms in the political system led to the revolution of 1905. Even after the revolution, these accommodations, such as the Duma, were largely window dressing rather than real change. Zemstvos were still secondary to national bureaucrats and local nobles. Industrialization was not successful enough to provide Russia with a sufficiently modern army and weapons to win against Japan in 1904–1905.
- Ottoman successes: Modernization of the army and elimination of the Janissary Corps were accomplished by Mahmud III. The Tanzimat reforms established equality before the law for Jews, Muslims, and Christians; freedom of movement for goods and foreign merchants; and Western education and secularism.
- Ottoman failures: Its army was not strong enough to defend state interests, leading to reliance on the Great Powers, as in the case of Muhammad Ali's occupation of Syria and Iraq. This made the Ottomans vulnerable, however, to the imperialistic ambitions of those powers. The Ottoman Empire had already lost Greece and Algeria by 1830, and lost more and more Balkan territories in the course of the nineteenth century. Christian subjects within the Empire were not mollified by legal equality, which had the effect of making them more conscious of religious issues. Muslim conservatives reacted negatively to the Tanzimat reforms and supported the antiliberal sultan Abdulhamid who ruled until 1909. In 1908, a revolution brought the Young Turks to power and reforms were reinstated. But it was too late to preserve the Ottoman Empire, as World War I was looming.

26

THE WEST AND THE WORLD, 1815–1914

The profound changes in Europe—industrialization, urbanization, and modernization—spread throughout the world as Europe began its third and most dynamic period of expansion since its first, the Crusades, and its second, the overseas empires of the early modern period. Now with huge stores of manufactured goods to sell and the technical means to transport them all over the world, Europeans sought to guarantee their trading rights by political control over colonies in Asia, Africa, and the Middle East, either peacefully or through the use of force. European superiority in weapons and medicine made this "new imperialism" possible, and competition among the European powers made it seem necessary.

KEY CONCEPTS

- Industrialization widened the gap between the Western industrialized states and the rest of the world. World trade expanded enormously, due to new technologies like the steamship and the telegraph, and because Japan, China, and Egypt were forced, in one way or another, to become part of the world economy.
- Sixty million Europeans emigrated between 1815 and 1932, mostly going (although not necessarily permanently) to areas of previous European settlement, such as the United States, Australia, Canada, and Arctic Russia. This large-scale movement of people was one reason European expansion in the nineteenth century had such impact around the globe.
- The new imperialism of the decades before World War I differed from early colonization in that Europeans sought outright political control of their colonies. In the scramble for Africa in the 1880s and 1890s, virtually the entire continent of Africa was carved up, mostly

between the British and the French, with Italy, Belgium, and Germany also getting important colonies. Parts of Asia were also taken over by Europeans in this same time period—Indochina by the French, Indonesia by the Dutch, and central Asia by Russia. The causes of the new imperialism were economic, social, strategic, nationalistic, and Social Darwinian, and also altruistic when the goal was to spread the benefits of European civilization.

- Responses to imperialism in the non-Western lands varied. Traditionalists sought to preserve native culture and sometimes organized violent resistance. Westernizers recognized the technical, military, and scientific superiority of Europe and worked to adopt Western models and values. In India, a Western-educated native elite did most of the administrative and military work of imperial control; in Japan, the feudal state was abolished and the emperor restored, and Western-style political, economic, and educational institutions were adopted. In China, the Qing emperors lost prestige when they were unable to prevent Western penetration and were overthrown in a revolution in 1912 that established a republic.

INDUSTRIALIZATION AND THE WORLD ECONOMY

The revolutionary importance of the Industrial Revolution can be fully understood only in the context of its impact on the world economy and world history. The gap between the haves—the industrialized powers—and the have-nots—the not-yet-industrializing areas of the world, also sometimes called the Third World—grew enormously (see Figure 26.1). This inequality, which hardly existed before 1750, became institutionalized, deeply rooted, and long-lasting, with the gap in average income being about 25 to 1 in 1970. It is only with independence that the former colonies began to narrow the gap.

> **AP Tip**
>
> The term *Third World* originated during the cold war, when the Western states were considered the "first world" and the Soviet Union and its satellites the "second world." It refers to the countries in Africa, Asia, and Latin America still developing modern industrial economies.

There have been two major schools of interpretation about uneven economic development and all its consequences for living standards, health, and education. One school sees European wealth as stolen, in one form or another, from the exploited peoples of the Third World, while the other sees European expansion as a product of their scientific and technological advances, capitalistic business organization, and worldview. Both views have some merit. Britain's early superiority in industrial development certainly gave it the advantage, but it is also true that its control over crucial areas of the world economy even before the industrial revolution provided enormous wealth.

THE WORLD MARKET

In the nineteenth century, world trade grew in value to about twenty-five times what it had been in 1800, which is even greater in real terms since the prices of goods had dropped. Britain's already far-flung empire from Canada to India gave it the basis for expansion when the Industrial Revolution produced so many cheap goods that they could not be absorbed by the domestic market. Such political control served British economic interests. For example, Britain exported about 50 percent of its cotton textiles in 1820, with Europe buying about half of that and India only 6 percent. Thirty years later, India was buying 25 percent and Europe only 16 percent. Why? Europe could put up protectionist tariffs, but India, under British domination, couldn't. Britain, once the Corn Laws were repealed and free trade became the law, turned quickly into the world's emporium, buying and selling goods produced at home in Europe and in Africa, Asia, and Latin America. Britain's free trade stimulated economic development in the Third World, particularly in the exploitation of resources for export to Europe.

What made the growth of trade possible?

- Railroads were built all over the world, connecting inland mines and plantations with coastal seaports, reducing transportation costs, and expanding business opportunities.
- Steel-hulled steamships replaced wooden sailing ships around 1860 and greatly reduced the cost of transportation of goods and people. Steamships easily could travel around the world bringing goods and picking up goods a dozen times in one trip, and also could go upriver, allowing Europeans to penetrate to the interior of colonies and trading countries to a degree not seen before. New port faculties made loading and unloading goods more efficient.
- Raw materials needed for industrial production—jute, hemp, and rubber, among many others—added to traditional foodstuffs like tea, coffee, and sugar, increased the number and variety of international trade goods.
- The Suez Canal connecting the Red Sea and the Mediterranean and the Panama Canal connecting the Atlantic and Pacific Oceans in Central America, built in the 1860s and 1870s, respectively, made sea trade much faster and cheaper.
- Transoceanic telegraphic cables sped up communications to an extraordinary degree, whether orders for goods or prices or just useful information.
- Enormous investments were made overseas by Europeans, particularly the Germans, the French, and the British, flush with capital from their own industries. Most investment went to other industrial countries, particularly the United States and industrial countries in Latin America, Australia, and Europe. White settlers in many of the developing but sparsely populated areas in these countries, such as the Argentine or American plains, benefited easily at the expense of native peoples.
- China and Japan were opened, against their will, to trade. Both societies had tried to keep foreigners out. The Chinese had little interest in Western goods, exporting more than they imported, and

limiting foreign merchants to Canton. But the British found a product that the Chinese people (although not the government) wanted—opium grown in India—and forced the Qing emperor through a series of wars to allow its importation and to sign the Treaty of Nanking, which ceded Hong Kong to the British in 1842. Nearly two decades later, British and French troops occupied Beijing and won all sorts of trading concessions and legal privileges. Japan was opened to the West in 1853 when the U.S. Commodore Perry steamed into Edo (Tokyo) Harbor and threatened to bombard the capital unless the emperor granted trading privileges; he did, albeit reluctantly.

AP Tip

Europeans acquired spheres of influence in China that allowed them certain monopolistic trading privileges and legal protection, including extraterritorial rights, by which a European accused of a crime in the sphere of influence was tried under European law in a European court, not under Chinese law in a Chinese court. Europeans could act with greater impunity because of extraterritoriality. Naturally, it was resented by local residents. It was a sign of imperial weakness that this right had been granted.

Egypt too became an even greater part of the world market than it had been before. It had already experienced modernization in the first half of the nineteenth century, under Muhammad Ali, the Ottoman governor, who welcomed European businessmen and engineers to Alexandria and made Egypt virtually independent of Ottoman rule. Muhammad Ali turned Egyptian agriculture toward production for export and transformed free peasants into tenant farmers. His grandson Ismail became khedive (prince) and continued these westernizing trends, promoting the export of cotton, building irrigation projects, and remodeling Cairo. But he was forced to cede control of his pet project, the Suez Canal, to Britain when he found himself in debt to Europeans. The British took control over Egyptian finances, which prompted nationalist riots; Britain crushed the nationalists and occupied all of Egypt in 1882, not to withdraw their troops until 1956. The British experience in Egypt created a new model for control over a non-Western state: politically indirect rule combined with military occupation, plus bringing the benefits of Western civilization.

THE GREAT MIGRATION

One reason the expansion of Europe in the nineteenth century had such huge impact was that about 60 million Europeans migrated, bringing their culture and ideas with them. The European population continued to increase, more than doubling in the nineteenth century, so much so that by the time of World War I, Europeans totaled some 38 percent of the world population. At that time, African and Asian population growth was moderate. After 1900 European and African and Asian population rates would reverse as the European population growth rate began to decline. The explosive growth in Europe's population in the nineteenth century led to land hunger and fewer opportunities at home; many thought opportunities could be found abroad. Most of the migrants came from areas like southern Italy and Russia, where population had boomed but industrialization had not yet expanded enough to provide sufficient employment. About a third of the entire group, some 20 million, came from the British Isles, particularly Ireland. The migrants went mostly to areas where there were already substantial number of Europeans and a good deal of available land—the United States, Australia, Canada, Siberia, New Zealand, and Latin America. The greatest number—some 11 million—left in the decade before World War I, but national groups varied a great deal, with the Irish leaving in the 1840s and 1850s, the Germans leaving in the 1850s (after the failure of the 1848 revolutions) and again in the 1880s (just before industrialization had grown the economy), and the Italians around the turn of the century. The United States took the largest number of immigrants but less than half of the total, with Argentina, Canada, Australia, Brazil, and Arctic Russia taking large numbers.

Most of the migrants were small farmers and skilled artisans, not usually impoverished masses, mostly young, and typically unmarried. For some it was a way to escape the narrow strictures of village life, though usually immigrants settled where there were others from their village or province. Many settled first in other European countries before going farther abroad, and a not insignificant number returned home after some years away—perhaps half of those who went to Argentina and a third of those who went to the United States. This rate varied a great deal, usually depending on the availability of land. Eastern European Jews and the Irish rarely returned for this reason. Many Italians, mostly land-hungry peasants, called themselves swallows, and spent the harvest season in Argentina but returned to Italy for spring planting.

There was also a large-scale emigration of some 3 million people from Asia, particularly from China, Japan, India, and the Philippines. Mostly poor, they went as indentured laborers to plantations or mines in Latin America, Africa, Hawaii, and Australia, often replacing black laborers. For example, hundreds of thousands of Chinese laborers went to Cuba and Peru. Generally, though, Asians fled agricultural or mining work in their new countries in favor of trade or retail; this sometimes put them into competition with recent European migrants. Americans and Australians both passed discriminatory laws against Asian migrants in the 1880s, preferring a policy of "whites only" settlement. Such areas got the greatest benefit from the great migration: By 1913, Americans, Canadians, and Australians had higher average incomes than the British.

WESTERN IMPERIALISM, 1880–1914

The three decades before World War I saw the highpoint of European migration and expansionism. European states—particularly France and Britain, and belatedly and to a lesser extent Italy and Germany—competed to create political empires with valuable colonies in Asia and Africa. This was a significant change from the earlier forms of expansion, which created trading outposts around the globe but left their governments intact, at least on the surface. The new imperialism instead sought to establish political control, either directly or indirectly, to secure exclusive access to markets and raw materials. Aggressive foreign policies to plant the flag and take control here and there increased tensions among the European powers and led to wars or near-wars with non-Europeans.

The scramble for Africa of the 1880s and 1890s was the single most remarkable development in the new imperialism. Only a small part of Africa had been colonized by 1850. Portugal had held Mozambique and Angola since the Age of Exploration. The French took Algeria in 1830. The Dutch settled in South Africa in the seventeenth century.

The story of South Africa has some unique elements, but it also reveals the impact of industrialization on colonization. After the British won the Dutch Cape Colony during the Napoleonic wars, Dutch farmers escaped British control by making the Great Trek of 1835 east. In spite of their mutual hostility, the two groups of European whites wrested control of most of South Africa from the Xhosa and Zulu and other Bantu peoples. The Dutch in the Transvaal, where they had settled after the Great Trek, now called Afrikaners or Boers, declared their independence and battled British forces. But when diamond mines were discovered in Kimberly—diamonds are prized for their industrial uses—and gold in the Transvaal the British insisted on taking full political control of the colony. The conflict with the Dutch settlers opened into full-scale war at the end of the century. The South African War, also known as the Boer War, was bitterly fought from 1899–1902 and won by the British but at great cost. In 1910, the Union of South Africa came into being as a self-governing colony. Over time the Afrikaners were able to wrest back political control from the English settlers and severely restricted the rights of the majority black population.

AP Tip

The conflict between the Dutch and the English had several causes. Originally the Dutch in South Africa were mostly farmers, dependent on slave labor and indentured servitude, while the British were largely merchants. As Britain had abolished the slave trade in 1807, its rule over the Dutch farmers would adversely affect their farms. That was one reason for the Great Trek. These differences would continue on for the next century, with Afrikaners putting apartheid into place in 1948 over the opposition of many white South Africans of English origin.

Within two decades, from 1880 to 1900 or so, Europeans took over the rest of Africa, dividing up the entire continent with the exception of two states, Ethiopia and Liberia, which remained outside their orbit (see Map 26.2). The rules for the takeover were laid down at the 1885 Berlin Conference called by Otto von Bismarck to avoid conflicting claims among the Europeans that might lead to war and to prevent any one power from dominating Africa. The Germans had quite suddenly joined in the scramble and taken over Togo, the Cameroons, and colonies on the west and east coasts. "Effective occupation" was the agreed-on standard, meaning a European power had to do more than plant a flag and claim a colony; it had to actually control the land. The British aimed for a Cape-to-Cairo empire, and under the brilliant businessman (founder of the De Beers Mining Co.) and enthusiastic imperialist Cecil Rhodes, established protectorates in the 1890s over Bechuanaland and Rhodesia. The Cape Colony was theirs (Rhodes was its prime minister from 1890 to 1896), and so was Cairo after the 1882 occupation. They pushed into the Sudan, only to find themselves defeated by fiercely independent Muslim Sudanese at Khartoum in 1885. The British returned to the Sudan in 1898 but now had machine guns, with which they easily defeated the Sudanese at Omdurman. The death tolls reveal how effective the new weapon was: some 11,000 Sudanese but only 28 Britons died. This pattern would be repeated over and over again.

AP Tip

Originally, conservatives like Benjamin Disraeli and Bismarck opposed imperialism as unnecessary, burdensome, and potentially dangerous. By 1900, most conservatives, such as Winston Churchill, who enthusiastically participated in the South African War, had changed their minds on the issue.

The French, under Prime Minister Ferry, had also been expanding southward and eastward from Algeria and from their old ports in Senegal. Most of West Africa came under their rule. In 1898, their eastward expansion was stopped when they met up with British forces at Fashoda in the Sudan. Only French withdrawal prevented what seemed likely to be an outbreak of armed conflict.

Of all the European colonies in Africa, none was as notorious as the Congo, the personal colony of the king of Belgium, Leopold. It was Leopold's early intervention in Africa that prompted the scramble for Africa. First established by the British/American explorer and journalist Henry Stanley, who won trade concessions for Leopold from African chiefs, Leopold's personal rule was confirmed by the Berlin Conference. It was famous for its brutality. Perhaps some 10 million Congolese were killed or maimed by the colonists, who punished them severely, cutting off hands and feet if they didn't meet their quotas for rubber. Only in 1908 was Leopold forced by an international conference to give up his personal control and hand the Congo over to the Belgian government.

In Asia, too, the Europeans scrambled for colonies and put them under their political control.

By the 1850s, the English had already won trade concessions from the Chinese as had the Americans from Japan. The Dutch brought most of Indonesia under their rule; the French took Indochina. Russia expanded into the southern Caucasus and central Asia and established a sphere of influence in China. The first outright colony of the United States was the Philippines, won in the Spanish-American War of 1898 and held only after defeating strong resistance from Philippine nationalists. The United States issued the Open Door Policy in order to join the other Western powers in trading with China.

AP Tip

Russia's expansionist interests in the east brought it into conflict with Japan, which had similar interests. This was the cause of the Russo-Japanese War discussed in Chapter 25.

Causes of the New Imperialism

Because of the importance of the new imperialism in world history, its causes have been hotly debated. The dispute is not so much over the facts or the general causes such as economic motives but over their relative importance and the relationship between the causes and the impact on the native populations. Among the main causes were

Economic motives Great Britain was losing its industrial lead to France, Germany, and the United States. This made it value its old colonies like India all the more and seek to secure markets and sources of raw materials in new colonies. Before 1914 the economic gains from imperialism were relatively small, as the people of the newly colonized areas were too poor to buy European goods and many investments saw small returns.

Political and diplomatic factors Colonies came to be seen as crucial for the prestige of the state and national security and required to provide strategic ports and coal refueling stations for the larger and larger navies. No nation, it was said by the German nationalist historian Treitschke, could be great without colonies.

Ideological factors Social Darwinism combined with racism postulated competition among the white peoples for survival and their rightful exploitation of "inferior" races, blacks and Asians.

Technological factors European technological and military superiority made imperialist expansion possible and in fact relatively easy. The machine gun, quinine—which provided protection against malaria—the steamship, and the telegraph, all allowed the Europeans to safely go where it had been previously too dangerous and to monitor and respond quickly to developments in the colonies.

Domestic factors Domestic tensions and internal problems seemed less important because of successful imperialistic ventures and nationalistic pride. Propagandists on behalf of imperialism argued it benefited not only the capitalists and the merchants but also the ordinary workers in that it provided jobs and cheap raw materials that kept down the cost of manufactured goods for them to enjoy. Tabloid journalism, called the yellow press in the United States, promoted nationalism and the notion that imperialism was a necessity, not a choice.

Special interest groups, shippers and shipbuilders, settlers, missionaries, humanitarians, military men, and colonial officials, all of whom had powerful personal motives, fostered imperialism.

Altruistic motives Most Europeans and Americans believed that they had a mission to civilize the "barbarian" peoples of the world, the "white man's burden," as Rudyard Kipling articulated in a poem by that name exhorting the United States to take on the Philippines as a colony. Imperialism would bring the benefits of modern medicine, education, political democracy, and Christianity—the glories of

Western civilization—to the primitive peoples of the world, whose standard of living would noticeably increase and whose barbaric practices and tribal warfare could be ended. Christian missionary work was highly successful in Africa but much less so in Asia.

AP Tip

Europeans banned or discouraged practices that they thought morally repugnant, often involving the treatment of women: female circumcision, the practice of suttee (also called *sati,* the self-immolation of widows) in India, and foot binding in China.

CRITICS OF IMPERIALISM

As imperialism grew so did criticisms of it. The British economist Hobson in his 1902 work *Imperialism* delineated the classic Marxist analysis. Imperialism was motivated by the need of the rich to invest their excess capital, but in fact damaged the home country, whose taxpayers bore the brunt of the costs, as well as the natives of the colonies. Workers were being manipulated into nationalism and diverted from the class struggle while domestic reform and the need to reduce the gap between rich and poor was delayed. While Hobson's economic arguments were not generally accepted, his moral outrage about the blatant hypocrisy and complete contradiction between what Europeans valued for themselves and what they imposed on the natives stimulated much opposition to imperialism. A satire of Kipling's *White Man's Burden* by British member of Parliament Labouchère called *The Brown Man's Burden* indicted imperialism as racist, exploitative, and brutal. Also in 1902, Joseph Conrad's novel *The Heart of Darkness* showed the corrupting influence of imperialism. In this way, European critics provided the ideological basis for independence and liberation movements.

AP Tip

The debate over imperialism had an important impact on domestic politics in both the nineteenth and twentieth centuries, particularly in Britain and France. It became a litmus test issue between the left, generally opposed, and the right, generally in favor, during the period when the states were pursuing their colonies and later on during decolonization and when many of the former colonial subjects were moving to their imperial overlord state to live.

RESPONSES TO WESTERN IMPERIALISM

There was a wide variety of responses to European imperialism. In all cases, it displaced native political leadership and profoundly changed traditional societies. Christianity and secularism each in its own way disturbed values, religion, and ways of life.

AP Tip

Another important transformation came from the introduction of the "cash nexus," the relationship between employer and employee in a modern industrial society being entirely based on the exchange of services for cash. In many traditional societies, particularly in Africa, community, family, and personal connections were what were important; the cash nexus undermined such ties. The impact on Africans was also greater in terms of religion, as Christian missions made little headway in Asia but successfully converted millions of Africans.

The ways the natives responded can be used to categorize them into four broad groups.

- The resistors, who periodically attempted violent resistance but could not succeed against European military technology, as was evident at the battle of Omdurman in the Sudan. This group tended to fade away in the face of their military inferiority.
- The traditionalists, who determined to preserve native cultural traditions.
- The westernizers or modernizers, who recognized that Europeans were more advanced and argued their political, economic, and educational systems ought to be adopted. Typically native elites were sent to the home country for education and served in the colonial service. Later on, they became the leaders of nationalist movements, rejecting foreign rule as an insult to their dignity and using European ideas of liberalism and self-determination, often combined with Marxian anti-imperialism, against the Europeans. Nationalism, that European invention, would ultimately destroy the European empires.
- The conformers, who tolerated European rule, however unenthusiastically, not seeing all that much difference between it and what they were used to under native elites. They were the vast majority of the population, but their acceptance was thin, and they easily became supporters of liberation movements.

INDIA In India, the "jewel in the crown" of the British Empire, British influence ran deep, perhaps deeper than in any other colony, because India was ruled directly after the defeat of the Great Rebellion of 1857–1858. The British called it the Sepoy or Indian Mutiny because it was waged by native soldiers called sepoys, both Hindu and Muslim, in the British army in northern and central India and was put down by Indian troops loyal to the British. Thereafter, India was ruled directly by the House of Commons, administered by a small number of British bureaucrats, only about 3,500 officials ruling a population of 300 million. They were competent but snobbish about the Indians. Typically, they lived in separate communities with their British wives, some of whom tried to improve the lives of the Indians, particularly through education. The British introduced important reforms—modern secondary education with English as the language of instruction, high-level government jobs for educated Indians, a large railroad network, and improvements in agriculture such as irrigation canals and expanded tea plantations. While life for the vast majority of Indians did not improve much, it did for the educated elite. British rule unified the country, put it under the rule of law, and provided it with a modern economy, communications system, and political structure and a common language. Nevertheless, this elite became anti-imperialistic and nationalistic, largely because of racially discriminatory laws and British refusal to allow equal social relations, which contradicted their avowed commitment to liberal ideals. In 1885, the mostly Hindu Indian National Congress was formed, originally demanding equality and self-government but by 1907 calling for complete independence.

AP Tip

In 1877, Queen Victoria was crowned Empress of India, a moment of great celebration for British imperialists. It was a sign of India's importance to the British Empire. India's economy was transformed by British rule; whereas before Indians grew cotton and made their cloth, under British rule, raw cotton was exported from India, made into cloth in Britain, and sold to the Indians.

JAPAN Japan's response to the forced penetration of the Americans in 1853 was unique. When Perry steamed into Edo Harbor, Japan was still a feudal society with a titular emperor but really ruled by a shogun, the chief warlord and hereditary military governor who relied on a class of warriors, similar to medieval knights in Europe, known as samurai. The samurai tried to resist the foreigners and defend the shogunate with assassinations and terrorist acts for a few years, only to be roundly crushed by a combined fleet of U.S., British, Dutch, and French warships. In 1867, a different kind of samurai revolution, known as the Meiji Restoration, eliminated the shogunate and restored the emperor to real power in an effort to establish an effective government. Their solution, to be colloquial for a moment, was "if you can't beat them, join them," that is, to drop their antiforeign stance and in fact to adopt Western practices and modernize Japan so that it could compete on the world stage. The Meiji reformers created a strong unified state with social and legal equality and freedom of movement, and a free-enterprise capitalistic economy with the government building railroads and modern factories. They used Western military ideas of conscription and a professional officer corps in building up a modern navy and army, which showed its effectiveness early in 1877 when it repressed a rebellion of the former feudal elite. They embraced Western science and technology, sent their sons abroad for education, and brought in well-paid foreign experts. The political system they established was closer to the German than to the American, with an authoritarian government and limited powers for the legislature.

Japan soon showed how well it had learned the lessons of the West. It defeated China in a war in 1894–1895, took Taiwan (Formosa), attacked Russia in 1904 and defeated it in 1905 (the first Asian power to defeat a European state in centuries), and annexed Korea in 1910. Japan's successes inspired patriots in China and Vietnam.

CHINA In China, the imperial state did not long survive its acceptance of British penetration after its defeat in the Opium Wars of the 1840s. Appearing near collapse in 1860, the Qing dynasty revived enough to last for another half-century, with effective leadership that crushed a huge rebellion in the 1850s known as the Tai Ping rebellion. The empress dowager Tzu Hsi successfully made some modern reforms, using talented Westerners to improve the bureaucracy and increase tax revenues, until the war with Japan revealed China's weakness. That embarrassing defeat in the 1890s led to a wave of intrusions from the Western powers, with France, Russia, and Germany each winning important trade concessions and dominating recognized spheres of influence. In 1898, the government tried to improve matters with a program of one hundred days of reform, but to little avail. The United States hoped to preserve Chinese sovereignty and force the other powers to grant equal trading rights to all in the sphere of influence through its Open Door Policy, proclaimed in 1899. Traditionalists tried to get rid of the foreigners themselves, particularly the Christians, both missionaries and Chinese converts, in the so-called Boxer Rebellion of 1900 to 1903, named after one of the many secret antiforeign societies. The rebellion was brutally crushed by the imperialists, who occupied and plundered Beijing. When the empress dowager died in 1908, revolutionary sentiments grew, and in 1912, Dr. Sun Yat-sen successfully led a revolution that replaced the two-thousand-year-old Chinese empire with a republic.

Multiple-Choice Questions

1. Most of the European migrants of the late nineteenth century left Europe because of
   (A) political repression.
   (B) land hunger.
   (C) low wages in factories.
   (D) abject poverty.
   (E) lack of old-age pensions.

2. Which pattern of migration is described accurately?
   (A) Italians mostly left in the 1860s, just before unification was completed.
   (B) About one-half of migrants to Canada returned to their original countries.
   (C) Very few of the migrants to the United States returned to their original countries.
   (D) Germans emigrated in large numbers in the 1850s and again in the 1880s.
   (E) Many Irish considered themselves swallows, who were only temporarily abroad.

3. Modernization in Egypt
   (A) began after the French completed the Suez Canal.
   (B) was well underway before the arrival of the Europeans.
   (C) was opposed by Muhammad Ali and other Egyptian political leaders.
   (D) included land reform, giving most Egyptian peasants their own land.
   (E) reflected Tanzimat reforms in Istanbul.

4. China and Japan began to trade with the Europeans in the nineteenth century
   (A) because of the efforts of the Dutch and British East India Companies.
   (B) when British investors offered the governments a percentage of the profits.
   (C) only after the Suez Canal was completed.
   (D) after the British and Americans demonstrated their military superiority.
   (E) when the opium trade was banned and they needed new trading partners.

5. The economic expansion of Europe abroad had which of the following consequences in the nineteenth century?
   (A) Significant improvements in the standard of living throughout the Third World
   (B) The industrialization of Africa
   (C) The takeover of oil-producing Middle Eastern states
   (D) The creation of a world economy for the first time
   (E) A significant gap in average income between Europeans and non-Europeans

6. The battles of Khartoum and Omdurman in the Sudan showed that
   (A) native soldiers could defeat the Europeans.
   (B) there was no chance for natives to effectively resist Europeans.
   (C) European's technology was the decisive factor in their ability to take control over Africa.
   (D) the principles established at the Berlin Conference ended up meaning very little.
   (E) the French were willing to withdraw to avoid war with the British.

7. Which of the following countries had the *smallest* role in the scramble for Africa?
   (A) Portugal
   (B) Italy
   (C) Belgium
   (D) France
   (E) Germany

8. Before 1914, economic benefits of the new imperialism were
   (A) quite limited.
   (B) enormous profits in the investments in the colonies.
   (C) so meager that several small colonies were abandoned.
   (D) substantial for investors and workers at home alike.
   (E) much more important than the political benefits.

9. The main argument of Treitschke and other nationalists in favor of having colonies was that they
   (A) provide jobs for workers.
   (B) bring the benefits of civilization to native populations.
   (C) spread Christianity.
   (D) offer profitable return on investments.
   (E) demonstrate the strength and virility of the nation.

10. The ideology expressed in Kipling's poem *The White Man's Burden*
    (A) described natives as dignified and culturally equal to the Europeans.
    (B) helped the United States decide to take over rather than liberate the Philippines in 1898.
    (C) lamented British imperialism.
    (D) argued that imperialism benefits the white people in the home country.
    (E) showed how grateful the native populations were for Western education and medicine.

11. Hobson criticized imperialism in his important 1902 book mostly
    (A) for its contradiction of Christian principles.
    (B) for diverting attention from the need for domestic reform.
    (C) for its obvious racism.
    (D) because the great benefits to English workers came at the expense of non-Western workers.
    (E) because imperialism in fact brought virtually no benefits to the peoples of the colonies.

12. Japan responded to Western imperialism in the late nineteenth century
    (A) with large-scale peasants' rebellions.
    (B) by transforming the shogun into an emperor.
    (C) by making the samurai class its new officer corps.
    (D) by becoming an imperialistic power itself.
    (E) by establishing a limited monarchy with a strong legislature.

13. In China, which of the following led the Boxer Rebellion?
    (A) Secret societies of anti-Christian traditionalists
    (B) Westernizers
    (C) Radical republicans led by Dr. Sun Yat-sen
    (D) Japanese-trained secret societies
    (E) Groups supported by the Western imperialists to overthrow the empress

14. The Indian National Congress formed in 1885 took its inspiration mostly from
    (A) Hindu mythology.
    (B) Marxian anti-imperialism.
    (C) Western ideals of liberalism.
    (D) the long tradition of princely rule in Indian states.
    (E) Muslim ideals of equality before God.

15. The vast majority of the people in the colonies ruled by Europeans
    (A) enthusiastically welcomed European rule for the benefits it brought.
    (B) continuously engaged in passive resistance.
    (C) continuously engaged in open resistance.
    (D) held onto traditional ways, refusing to attend Christian or European schools.
    (E) unenthusiastically accepted European rule.

Free-Response Questions

1. Analyze the ways the British took over and ruled various colonies in Africa and Asia. Be sure to discuss one colony on each continent in detail.
2. Describe three of the motives for European imperialism and discuss the criticisms made of each motive by European opponents of imperialism.

ANSWERS

MULTIPLE-CHOICE QUESTIONS

1. **ANSWER: (B)** Most left because with overpopulation and tightly controlled land ownership, there were few opportunities to acquire sufficient land or obtain good employment. (McKay, *A History of Western Society*, 8th ed., pp. 863–865/9th ed., pp. 856–858)

2. **ANSWER: (D)** It was the Italians who considered themselves swallows; they left mostly in the decade before World War I. About a third of the migrants to the United States returned to their homelands. The Germans left Europe in the 1850s and 1880s. (McKay, *A History of Western Society*, 8th ed., p. 866/9th ed., pp. 855–858)

3. **ANSWER: (B)** Muhammad Ali promoted modernization in Egypt, some eighty years before the Tanzimat reforms. Europeans were invited to Egypt as a result of his policies; they benefited from them but did not initiate them. Most peasants became tenant farmers as a result. (McKay, *A History of Western Society*, 8th ed., pp. 861–863/9th ed., pp. 853–854)

4. **ANSWER: (D)** China and Japan were both forced to trade with the West in the 1840s and 1850s. (McKay, *A History of Western Society*, 8th ed., pp. 858–861/9th ed., pp. 850–853)

5. **ANSWER: (E)** While in 1750 the income gap between Europeans and non-Europeans was narrow, it had grown enormously by 1900. The standard of living in most Third World countries would only improve after independence in the twentieth century. A world economy had already come into being in the Age of Exploration. Africa was exploited for its natural resources, rather than factory labor. (McKay, *A History of Western Society*, 8th ed., p. 856/9th ed., p. 848)

6. **ANSWER: (C)** The British lost to the Sudanese at Khartoum but won at Omdurman with the use of the machine gun. The French withdrew at Fashoda. (McKay, *A History of Western Society,* 8th ed., pp. 870, 872/9th ed., p. 862)

7. **ANSWER: (B)** Portugal held onto its colonies from the Age of Exploration (Mozambique and Angola), but did not add to its African empire during the Scramble for Africa period. Italy took Libya and attempted to take Ethiopia. (McKay, *A History of Western Society,* 8th ed., pp. 869–872/9th ed., p. 860)

8. **ANSWER: (A)** Although there were several economic motives for the new imperialism, its benefits were relatively limited before 1914, both in terms of return on investment and in terms of selling European goods, as the people in the colonies were still too poor to be consumers. (McKay, *A History of Western Society,* 8th ed., p. 873/9th ed., p. 865)

9. **ANSWER: (E)** While all of these are arguments that were made in favor of imperialism, the last one is the nationalist argument. (McKay, *A History of Western Society,* 8th ed., p. 873/9th ed., pp. 865–866)

10. **ANSWER: (B)** For Kipling, imperialism was a moral obligation on Westerners to bring the benefits of Western civilization to people who would barely be appreciative. (McKay, *A History of Western Society,* 8th ed., p. 876/9th ed., p. 867)

11. **ANSWER: (B)** Hobson denied that British workers or Britain as a whole benefited from imperialism; only special interests, and particularly the capitalist class, benefited. His arguments were largely economic, since he himself was an economist. (McKay, *A History of Western Society,* 8th ed., p. 876/9th ed., p. 867)

12. **ANSWER: (D)** Japan adopted Western ways so well that within thirty years it became an imperialistic state itself, taking over Formosa and Korea. (McKay, *A History of Western Society,* 8th ed., pp. 878–880/9th ed., pp. 870–872)

13. **ANSWER: (A)** The Boxer Rebellion was anti-Western, anti-imperialist, and anti-Christian, led by traditionalists organized into secret societies. (McKay, *A History of Western Society,* 8th ed., p. 882/9th ed., p. 872)

14. **ANSWER: (C)** The leadership of the Indian National Congress was Western-educated and used European liberalism to criticize British rule in India. (McKay, *A History of Western Society,* 8th ed., p. 879/9th ed., p. 870)

15. **ANSWER: (E)** Most people in the colonies accepted European rule, but unenthusiastically. They quickly supported strong liberation leaders later on. (McKay, *A History of Western Society,* 8th ed., p. 877/9th ed., p. 868)

FREE-RESPONSE QUESTIONS

1. This essay should begin with a general statement about British methods of acquiring and of ruling colonies. The textbook describes four British colonies in some detail; pick Egypt or South Africa and India or China.

- Egypt: Egypt had been making substantial progress toward modernization under Muhammad Ali and his grandson Ismail, who ran up huge debts to the Europeans. Britain took control of Egyptian finances in the 1860s to make sure European bondholders would be repaid. Britain was anxious to make sure it controlled the Suez Canal, which shortened the sea route to India substantially. When nationalists rebelled in 1882, Britain occupied Egypt and kept troops there until 1956. As the local ruler was allowed to remain, Britain ruled indirectly.
- South Africa: Britain acquired the Cape Colony as part of the settlement after the Napoleonic wars. They, and the Dutch settlers who had come in the seventeenth century, took over most of South Africa from the various Bantu peoples who lived there. When gold and diamonds were discovered in the eastern part of South Africa, to which the Dutch had fled after the arrival of the English, Britain insisted on full political control. British entrepreneurs, such as Cecil Rhodes, were making millions from these mines. The British won a brutal three-year war with the Dutch settlers in 1902, and in 1910 established the Union of South Africa, which, like Canada and Australia (also colonies dominated by white settlers), was given local autonomy.
- India: Britain acquired France's trading outposts in India as a result of its victory in the Seven Years' War. Originally, Britain's interests in India were represented by its East India Company, which acted as a virtual government. Over the next fifty years or so, it negotiated with the various princes and defeated the last Mughal emperor. In 1857 and 1858, Hindu and Muslim soldiers in the British army mutinied in what was known as the Great Rebellion. After its defeat, Britain ruled India directly. The House of Commons passed legislation for India and appointed a viceroy to administer the colony. Direct rule brought many benefits to the Indian elite—education in England and secure positions in Indian Colonial Service. India's economy was developed and a national railroad system built. But the British practiced social segregation and legal discrimination, which prompted the nationalists to organize the Indian National Congress in 1885.
- China: Britain had long been frustrated by the resistance of the Chinese to British manufactured goods and by Chinese imperial rules limiting foreign merchants to the city of Canton. It fought and won several wars with the Chinese to force them to allow Britain to sell opium from its colony India. The Chinese emperor also had to cede Hong Kong to Britain in 1842, which the British ruled directly. In their spheres of influence, the British were dominant but officially the Chinese emperor still ruled, although the British acquired the right of extraterritoriality in its sphere of influence in China, which meant that British subjects accused of crimes there were tried by British courts under British law.

2. This question asks for a description of three motives for European imperialism and a criticism of each.

- *Economic motives* Imperial control would secure access to markets and raw materials and bring profits from investments in developing infrastructure (railroads, etc.). It would also reduce the prices of goods and provide employment and economic benefits for workers. Critics said that for most of the nineteenth century, people in the colonies were too poor to buy European goods, that raw materials were extracted at the cost of great suffering, and that instead of bringing economic benefits to the home economy, imperialism was detrimental in that the taxpayers had to pay for the imperial armies and navies. Critics, such as Hobson, argued that only a very small percentage of the population, the cash-rich capitalists who needed places to invest their surplus capital, benefited from imperialism.
- *Political motives* Nationalists argued that imperialism was necessary for the prestige of their country and for strategic ports for trade and in case of war. Critics challenged this view on the basis that imperialist competition fostered aggressive foreign policies that might lead to unnecessary war. Critics also asserted that imperialism was a way for the ruling elite to avoid the discussion of domestic problems and of the need to reduce the gap between rich and poor at home.
- *Altruistic motives* Some people, like Rudyard Kipling, argued that imperialism was a moral obligation for Europeans, who owed it to the "primitive" peoples of the world to bring them the benefits of Western civilization—medicine, education, political democracy, science, and technology. Christian missionaries believed they were saving the souls of the heathen when they converted them, which they did mostly through the establishment of Christian schools. Critics argued that such imposition of Western culture was destructive of native cultures, religions, and languages and presumed a superiority that was not always valid.
- *Social Darwinian motives* Social Darwinists believed that the European states were engaged in a fierce struggle for survival and that colonies were important for victory. Racists argued that imperialism was justified because of the inferiority of the African and Asian races. Critics opposed both Social Darwinism and racism as lacking any scientific basis and said that they were prejudices justifying less lofty-sounding goals.

27

The Great Break: War and Revolution, 1914–1919

At the beginning of the twentieth century, European civilization reached its high point. Europeans controlled most of Africa and large parts of Asia, standards of living had improved, and everywhere were visible signs of progress. There had been no European general war for nearly 100 years. Yet in 1914 Europeans began what would turn out to be a four-year slaughter, destroying millions and millions of lives, and bringing down four long-standing European empires in the process: the Russian, Ottoman, Austro-Hungarian, and German. In Russia, two revolutions in 1917 within six months of each other toppled the tsar and established the world's first communist dictatorship. A compromise set of peace treaties disappointed many in Europe and the Middle East. Appropriately called the Great War, World War I and the peace that settled it mark a turning point not only for Europe but also for world history.

Key Concepts

- What might have been a localized conflict over competing nationalistic sentiments in Serbia and Austria became a world war because of a complicated alliance system. Xenophobia, nationalism, imperialistic competition, and militarism created a hostile atmosphere that led quickly to war once tensions in the Balkans provided the spark. The machine gun gave the advantage to defense and was, more than any other weapon, responsible for the huge death tolls of this war.
- World War I was the first total war involving every segment of society, including civilians. Governments rationed food, controlled

the economy, and waged massive propaganda campaigns to keep up civilian spirits. Women took on many of the jobs men had had and earned sufficient credibility to be given the vote virtually everywhere in Europe and in the United States after the war.

- The war intensified the discontent long felt in Russia about the tsarist regime. In March 1917, the tsar was forced to abdicate, and a provisional government was created to write a new constitution. Six months later, the Bolsheviks under Vladimir Lenin's leadership took power and founded the first communist regime anywhere in the world.
- The peace settlement set the stage for many of the later conflicts of the twentieth century. Germany was not invited to the peace conference and was given a punitive peace, losing relatively little territory but forced to pay huge reparations and accept blame for the war. Poland, Hungary, Czechoslovakia, and Yugoslavia came into being. A mandate system for the former German and Ottoman colonies was established, although self-determination was declared a goal of the peace treaties; many people in Europe and in the colonies were disappointed.

BEFORE THE WAR: THE ALLIANCE SYSTEM

THE BISMARCKIAN SYSTEM

After the Franco-Prussian War, Bismarck said Germany was satisfied and aimed to keep the peace. France, he knew, would try to win back its honor and Alsace-Lorraine but would only be able to do so with allies. Bismarck maneuvered to keep possible allies away from France and to forge a series of alliances for Germany to protect it in case of war. He also sought to maintain a balance between Russia and Austria to prevent war over the territories of the decaying Ottoman Empire, the "sick man of Europe."

The first of Bismarck's alliances, the 1873 Three Emperors' League of Russia, Germany, and Austria, was formed to forestall radical and nationalistic movements. Bismarck played peacemaker after the Russo-Ottoman War of 1877–1878 at the Congress of Berlin; this infuriated the Russians. That led to the second of his alliances, the Dual Alliance between Germany and Austria the next year, a defensive military alliance, which Italy joined in 1882, making it the Triple Alliance. Bismarck made sure to maintain good relations with both of France's possible allies: Britain by not advocating German imperialism in Africa, and Russia by negotiating the 1897 Reinsurance Treaty, in which Russia and Germany promised neutrality in case the other was attacked. Such a treaty assuaged Russian anxieties and kept them from allying with France.

THE RIVAL BLOCS

The Bismarckian system was successful as long as he was around to maintain it but collapsed when he was dismissed by Kaiser William II in 1890. The kaiser refused to renew the Reinsurance Treaty, providing the perfect opportunity for France to offer friendship, loans, and arms to Russia. In 1894 Russia and France became military allies.

With the other five great powers involved in one alliance or another, Britain was increasingly isolated. Ethnic connections between Germany and Britain (which had been conquered by the Angles and Saxons, two Germanic tribes, in the sixth century) were undermined by economic competition as Germany industrialized and by aggressive acts of the kaiser. Particularly irksome to the British was the kaiser's plan to expand Germany's navy, which he claimed was needed to defend its colonies. This announcement coincided with the South African War, which took the British longer than expected to win and engendered widespread anti-British feelings. As a result, Britain recognized the need for alliances. It got on better terms with the United States, signed a treaty with Japan in 1902, and agreed to an entente in 1904 with France to peacefully resolve all colonial disputes between them. When Germany tried to break up this entente by calling an international conference at Algeciras about the French colony of Morocco, France and Britain only drew closer. Russia and Britain created separate spheres of influence in Persia and Central Asia and signed an entente in 1907. Tensions between the two blocs intensified when Germany announced it would build a fleet of powerful battleships, forcing Britain to do the same, and so divert funds from the People's Budget. Germany began to see itself as encircled by enemies. Nationalistic journalists fed the growing atmosphere of hostility and suspicion in Germany.

AP Tip

An entente is not a formal alliance that binds its members by the terms of a treaty, but an understanding. During the war, the Entente powers became known as the Allies, while the members of the Triple Alliance at war with them became known as the Central Powers.

THE OUTBREAK OF WAR

The crisis that led to the outbreak of general war came out of a series of conflicts in the Balkans, an area hotly contested by Russia and Austria as the Ottoman Empire weakened. The Russo-Turkish War of 1877–1878 was Russia's attempt to help the nationalistic movements of fellow Slavs under Ottoman rule. Serbia and Romania won independence, part of Bulgaria was given local autonomy, and Bosnia and Herzegovina (provinces that would later form part of Yugoslavia) were given to Austria to govern. But the Ottoman Empire, supported by the Great Powers out of fear of its total collapse, survived and retained some important territories.

AP Tip

To understand the Balkans, it is important to know its geography. Russia had long had ambitions in the region because it had no direct sea access to the Mediterranean from the Black Sea and had to go through the Ottoman-controlled Dardanelles. Serbia when it became independent in 1878 was landlocked, without access to the sea. It coveted Bosnia and Herzegovina on its northern edge or Albania on the southern. In addition, there was a religious factor: Serbs, Greeks, Bulgarians, and Russians are all Orthodox Christians, while Croatians are Catholics and most Bosnians and Albanians are Muslims. Russia saw itself as the protector of the Slavs in general and of the Orthodox Serbs in particular.

Serbia, however, sought additional territories and reacted with great fury when Austria annexed outright the provinces of Bosnia and Herzegovina in 1908, where there were many Serbs, as well as Croatians and Muslims. Serbia went to war twice, first in 1912 along with Greece and Bulgaria against the Ottoman Empire and again in 1913 against Bulgaria over the spoils of the first Balkan War. Austria, afraid of a strong Serbia, insisted that Albania be created as an independent state in 1913, although Serbia expected that it would get it, having been victorious in the Balkan wars. Austria feared a successful Serbian nationalist movement that might serve as a model for its subject nationalities.

This is the background to the incident that sparked the war: the assassination of the Archduke Francis Ferdinand, heir to the Austrian throne, and his wife when they visited Sarajevo in Bosnia in June 1914. The assassin was a Serbian nationalist, Gavrilo Princip, living in Bosnia, a member of the Black Hand, a secret Serbian nationalist organization. The assassination was not an official act of the Serbian government, but the Austrians believed that Serbia was directly implicated and in July, some three weeks later, issued a severe ultimatum. When Serbia equivocated, Austria declared war on Serbia on July 28.

This might have simply been the third Balkan War, but soon it broadened out to include almost all of Europe. Why? One reason was that Austria felt free to act as it wanted to with Serbia because it had guaranteed support from Germany. Another was that each country's war plans led it to act precipitously. Russia's huge size required it to mobilize early if it were to have an effective army, so in defense of Serbia, Tsar Nicholas II ordered full mobilization on July 29, which was taken by Germany as a declaration of war. The German General Staff had long expected a two-front war, in view of the Franco-Russian Entente, and had planned to defeat France quickly in order to fight the enemy it thought would be stronger. To get to Paris as expeditiously as possible, Germany on August 3 invaded Belgium, whose neutrality had been guaranteed by an 1839 treaty. Germany had hoped Britain would stay out of the war, but the invasion of Belgium sparked Britain to declare war on Germany the next day.

The causes of World War I have been debated for decades. If it had not been such a lengthy and devastating debacle, the determination of the cause would not have been so important, but as the war dragged on and the cost both in financial and human terms grew exponentially, the belligerents had to assign blame. Germany was judged by many to be ultimately responsible for goading Austria into action and for invading Belgium, for aspiring to be a great world power and acting on its frustrations with the Triple Entente. Perhaps the general cause of the war was the failure of all the other great powers to accept the new status of Germany.

Another interpretation argues that the war was prompted by German conservatives to prevent the socialists from taking power. Two years before the outbreak of war, the Social Democratic Party had become the largest party in the Reichstag. Nationalism would, it was hoped, deflect the workers from socialism. Similarly, domestic concerns in England with the tensions in Ireland, and in Russia, still recovering from the 1905 revolution, may have encouraged the choice for war. Ruling elites gambled that war would bring unity, forgetting that war often brings with it social revolution and political change.

AP Tip

The language of virility, as applied to states, used to foster nationalism also promoted militarism, the notion that states—and individuals—can prove themselves only in the test of war, that war is the height of human activity bringing glory to the individual and nation alike, and that peace, and extended peace, debilitate both. Such sentiments were widely held before World War I.

Nationalism was certainly a crucial factor. It pitted Slavs against Germans, encouraged the arms race, and weakened internationalism. When war broke out in August 1914, crowds enthusiastically rallied in the streets and in country after country young men lined up to volunteer to right the wrong their country had received. They all thought that the war would be over by Christmas, that it would be a war of heroic fighting, rapid movement, decisive battles, and clear victories.

THE WAR ITSELF

Those expectations of a short and glorious war all proved mistaken. The war lasted over four years without a clear victory and with few decisive battles. Instead of a war of movement, it was a war fought in trenches; instead of heroic deaths, men were killed by machine guns, poison gas, or shrapnel.

AP Tip

Ironically, the war plans of both the Germans and the French proved flawed. The German Schlieffen Plan was based on the assumption that Russia would prove the greater enemy. A quick victory over France, for which an invasion through Belgium was most expeditious, would allow Germany to pit its major forces against Russia. When war broke out, Russia was easily defeated in August 1914, while a quick victory over France proved elusive. The French war plans called for the repossession of Alsace and Lorraine; if the French had won, they would have had to leave substantial forces there and would not have been able to defend Paris so effectively against the advancing German troops.

STALEMATE AND SLAUGHTER

German expectations of quick victory over France were soundly disappointed. The Belgians fought hard, the British landed troops, and the French attacked the advancing Germans at the Marne River, even using taxis to bring Parisians to the front. The German advance was stopped, but the Germans were not defeated. Both sides dug in, digging trenches that soon extended over 1,000 miles of the western front, from northern France to the Swiss frontier. From each trench, protected by barbed wire and mines, daily barrages of artillery were launched, and regularly one side or the over would go "over the top" only to be mowed down by the other's machine guns. In case of victory, the trenches would move several hundred yards. The death tolls were enormous, beyond any war in the past. At the Battle of the Somme in 1916, the British and French gained 125 square miles at the cost of 600,000 of their own men and half a million Germans. Dozens of battles had similar high tolls of dead and wounded—an entire generation of young men, some 20 million, either dead or wounded. Such a terrible war generated some of the most poignant poems and novels ever written, the classic being Erich Maria Remarque's novel, *All Quiet on the Western Front* (1929).

AP Tip

World War I saw the introduction of new weapons—the airplane, submarine, tank, and poison gas—that changed the face of war forever. Airplanes were mostly used for reconnaissance in World War I, and tanks were not all that effective on the artillery-scarred landscape on the western front, but they revealed their military potential; they played key roles in World War II. Submarine warfare, used by the Germans to break the naval blockade, ended long-standing naval traditions that gave ship captains the opportunity to surrender and save their men before their ships were sunk. Poison gas brought immense suffering to soldiers; gas masks became part of standard equipment.

The eastern front saw more movement. Russia was quickly defeated at two battles in the first month of the war by German troops under the command of Ludendorff and Hindenburg. Russia lost 2.5 million men dead, wounded, or taken as prisoners.

AP Tip

Ludendorff and Hindenburg become de facto rulers of Germany during the war. They each played an important role in bringing Hitler to power.

The number of belligerents expanded. Italy, erstwhile member of the Triple Alliance, had stayed neutral at the outbreak of the war, but in 1915 joined the Triple Entente, the Allies. The Ottoman Empire joined Austria-Hungary and Germany in October 1914, as did Bulgaria the following September. The continuation of Russo-Ottoman conflict complicated the situation for Armenians, one of the Christian minorities living in eastern Anatolia, whose 1909 rebellion had been brutally repressed by the Turks. In 1915, some Armenians welcomed the Russian armies. In response the Ottoman government ordered that they be forcibly moved out of their homeland in what came to be seen as an act of genocide. Somewhere between half a million and a million and a half Armenians were murdered, starved to death, or died from disease.

AP Tip

The Turkish government has continuously rejected the accusation of genocide. Nearly a hundred years later, the issue continues to haunt Turkey as the denial of genocide has complicated its chances of admission to the European Union.

The British hoped to take the Ottoman Empire out of the war. First it tried a direct attack on the Dardanelles and Constantinople in 1915, which was entirely unsuccessful. Then they went after the Ottoman Empire from within. They urged the Arabs to revolt from their Ottoman overlords, promising independence on victory. Hussein ibn-Ali led the Arabs in revolt in 1917, aided the next year by the charismatic British officer T. E. Lawrence, known as Lawrence of Arabia. In the territory that became Iraq, the British occupied Basra in 1914 and Baghdad in 1917. They went into Syria in 1918, with a triumphal entry led by Hussein's son Faisal. The Arabs rejoiced at their freedom from Ottoman rule and many expected that soon they would be unified in one large state.

AP Tip

The 1915 invasion, known as the Battle of Gallipoli, was fought mostly by ANZAC troops, that is, men from Australia and New Zealand, which were still part of the British Empire. Planned by Churchill, it was an utter failure and a bloodbath. Australian nationalism began with Gallipoli. So many people from the colonies fought on the battlefields of Europe in World War I that its impact was truly global.

In 1917, the British also tried to woo the Jewish residents in the Ottoman Empire and win the support of British and other European Jews with the Balfour Declaration, promising a homeland for the Jews in Palestine, although Jews were only about 11 percent of the population in Palestine. Some British thought a Zionist state would help them keep control over the Suez Canal. At the same time, the British had already negotiated a secret deal with the French in the Sykes-Picot Treaty to divide the former Ottoman Middle Eastern lands between themselves, with Britain getting Iraq, Jordan, and Palestine and France getting Syria and Lebanon. Much of the tension in the Middle East since then derives from the promises made during World War I and not honored in the peace settlement.

In Africa and Asia, colonized peoples generally supported the war effort of the imperial overlords, disappointing German hopes. About a million of them served in British and French armies and helped seize German colonies. Japan, Britain's ally since 1902, took over German colonies in China and in the Pacific; this infuriated the Chinese.

The tide of war was turned, to a large degree, by the entry of the United States into the war in 1917. At the outset of the war, Britain and France had set up a naval blockade around Germany, prohibiting any neutral ship from bringing goods to Germany. The Germans retaliated with their new weapon, the submarine, which changed the rules of naval warfare. When the British passenger liner *Lusitania* was sunk in 1915 and some 1,000 people died, the U.S. president Wilson protested, and the Germans renounced unrestricted submarine warfare. But in 1917, the Germans resumed it, hoping to starve Britain into submission before the United States could get troops to Europe. The United States entered the war in April 1917; the German gambit had failed.

AP Tip

American public opinion was also stirred by the Zimmermann telegram of January 1917, a German diplomatic telegram intercepted by the British, which suggested an alliance between Germany and Mexico by which Mexico could regain the lands it had lost in the 1840s.

THE HOME FRONT

World War I was a total war, involving every aspect of the economy, every social class, and every civilian. Initially virtually everyone supported the war, even many socialists. In fact, the support of the working classes was crucial for the war effort. But as the war continued longer than originally anticipated, governments took more control over their societies to make sure of continued popular support and guarantee sufficient men and materials for war.

Economically, laissez-faire capitalism, to the degree to which it was practiced, was abandoned in favor of the planned economy, in which the government decided what was to be produced, who would produce it, and how it would be produced and instituted rationing, wage and price controls, and limitations of workers' rights. Successful state involvement in the economy strengthened the socialist cause after the war as state socialism came to be seen as a real option.

In Germany, Walter Rathenau ran the War Raw Materials Board, which not only rationed raw materials and foodstuffs and created a recycling program but also oversaw the making of synthetic goods. German chemists made synthetic rubber, synthetic nitrates for explosives, and even synthetic coffee. However, Germany did not tax the well-to-do sufficiently during the war, so inflation, black markets, and deficit spending caused problems. By 1917, Generals Paul von Hindenburg and Erich Ludendorff had taken charge of the government. They required all men between seventeen and sixty to work and encouraged female employment. But times were hard in Germany toward the end of the war, with most people eating only about 1,000 calories per day and many near starvation.

Britain was in a better position than Germany because of its prosperous empire and its imports from the United States. There, too, a Ministry of Munitions was established to organize private industry for the war and control wage and prices. By 1916, when David Lloyd George became prime minister, Britain was well on its way to a planned economy.

AP Tip

Another element of increased government control was the severe limitation and in some cases suspension of civil liberties in most of the belligerent states, including England and France. The British, who had relied on a volunteer army up to then, also began to conscript soldiers in 1916.

THE SOCIAL IMPACT

- Labor unions grew in importance and prestige because of their loyalty and cooperation with the government. They effectively participated in policymaking councils in the war governments.
- Women took jobs in industry, transportation, and offices, becoming visible in the public sphere as never before. They also worked at the front as nurses and ambulance drivers. Women were

given the vote right after the war in Britain, Germany, Austria, and the United States. In addition, because of fabric shortages, women's skirts were shortened, never to come down again; women also bobbed their hair and smoked cigarettes in public. The modern woman had been born.

- Class distinctions lessened both at the front and at home. The aristocratic officers died at the same rate as their commoner soldiers, though fewer labor aristocrats were sent to the front because they were so valuable. The gap between rich and poor narrowed, with a noticeable improvement in the lives of the poorest third of the population, and social equality grew. Generally, wartime meant full employment as well as a communal experience of hard times.
- Governments on both sides sought to manipulate public opinion through censorship of the press and propaganda (see the posters on pp. 887 and 891). Exaggerating the horrors of the other side was one way to inflame feelings and bolster support for the war.

AP Tip

Such massive and effective propaganda campaigns made the peacemaking process more complicated as they helped foster hatred and demands for a harsh peace.

- Irish nationalists took advantage of Britain's preoccupation with war and organized the Easter Rebellion of 1916. Although crushed within a week, it reflected class as well as nationalistic issues.
- Antiwar sentiment grew. Vera Brittain represents the disillusionment with the war after initial enthusiasm, which she later described in an autobiography, *Testament of Youth* (see Individuals in Society, p. 893). By 1916, demonstrations against the war and over inadequate food supplies became more frequent. The communist Karl Liebknecht led such a demonstration in Berlin in 1916. At the front, too, disillusionment with the war was expressed in the May 1917 mutiny in the French forces, which led to a change in command at the front as General Philippe Pétain took over, and at home with the new premier Georges Clemenceau and a promise of an end to grand offensives. Clemenceau put protesters and journalists in jail and ruled dictatorially. In Austria in 1916, the chief minister was assassinated, the long-serving (since 1848) emperor Franz Joseph died, and Czech and Yugoslav leaders demanded autonomy. In Germany, too, unity was breaking down, with socialists calling for a compromise peace and some 200,000 workers striking for a week in early 1917.
- The British blockade proved very effective. Without the ability to import foodstuffs by sea and limited to what the four states could produce domestically, the people in Germany and Austria began to starve. Bread rations periodically were reduced, finally reaching minimal levels.

THE RUSSIAN REVOLUTION

While Austria and Germany were shaken by the war and their regimes made more vulnerable, it was in Russia that revolution toppled the regime, and in such a way that it was to become a major turning point in world history.

CAUSES OF THE RUSSIAN REVOLUTION

- In spite of early and widespread enthusiasm for war and a strong sense of unity and nationalism, Russia saw early defeat at the hands of the Germans in August 1914. Terrible losses, more than 2 million casualties, were blamed on the tsarist regime's incompetence, sending, for example, large numbers of soldiers to the front without rifles. The home front mobilized more efficiently, with the Duma and the zemstvos coordinating local defense and economic life.
- The tsar, still an autocratic ruler, took personal charge of the war in order to maintain supreme power, rather than sharing power with or relying on the Duma. In 1915 a wide-ranging progressive bloc in the Duma called for a constitutional government, but the tsar responded by dismissing the Duma.
- The tsar went to the front to lead the armies, leaving his German-born wife and her adviser, the notorious monk Rasputin, in charge at home, to the disgust of the populace. Rasputin earned his place at court by his ability to control the bleeding of the tsar's only son, heir to the throne, a hemophiliac. Aristocrats murdered Rasputin at the end of 1916.
- Food shortages in the cities further depressed morale.

THE FIRST RUSSIAN REVOLUTION

In 1917, on March 8, International Women's Day, women marched for bread in Petrograd (St. Petersburg), and the protests quickly spread to factories and throughout the city. Military discipline broke when the soldiers refused to fire on the protesters and joined them instead. Within a few days, the Duma declared a provisional government and the tsar abdicated.

THE PROVISIONAL GOVERNMENT

The new government was welcomed everywhere and by all classes with the hope it would manage the war better and provide better wages and food for those at home. From being one of the most oppressed states in Europe, Russia became one of the freest. The provisional government enacted equality before the law, civil liberties, and the legalization of unions. Yet it was profoundly moderate. A moderate socialist, Alexander Kerensky, became prime minister in July, but he continued Russia's war effort and refused to allow land reform. The Provisional Government's chief nemesis was the Petrograd **Soviet**, or Council of Workers and Soldiers' Deputies, forged during the Revolution of 1905, which organized mass meetings of thousands of workers and acted like an alternative government. Its Order No. 1 established democracy in the army; officers were to be elected by their men, and thus army discipline collapsed in the summer of 1917. Huge numbers of soldiers simply walked away from the front to be home in their village to protect their land and grab more as peasants were on a rampage to seize lands. The soldiers were voting with their feet against the Provisional Government.

THE BOLSHEVIKS

Lenin, in Switzerland, had modified Marxian ideology in several important ways. He insisted that (1) the revolution could be achieved only through violence and not by revisionist, evolutionary methods; (2) revolution could happen in countries only partially industrialized and in many ways still feudal and medieval, like Russia; and (3) leadership was necessary to achieve revolution, since depending on the working classes themselves is unreliable. The Communist Party should be small, tightly disciplined, and under the control of committed intellectuals and full-time revolutionaries who would brook no compromise and would not be satisfied with short-term gains. People committed to this version of Marxism took the name Bolsheviks to distinguish themselves from the *Mensheviks* who wanted a more democratic, open party with mass membership.

AP Tip

Bolshevik means "majority," *Menshevik* "minority." The terms derive from a fissure of the Russian Social Democratic Party at its meeting in 1903. In actuality, the Bolsheviks barely had a majority of support at that time, and the Mensheviks were the key players in the 1905 revolution.

The Bolsheviks had never supported the war, seeing it as an imperialistic, capitalistic waste of workers' lives. Lenin and a band of followers were allowed to travel through Germany and return to Russia in April 1917, with the Germans hoping that he would pull Russia out of the war. Rejecting cooperation with reformist parties, Lenin immediately went about wooing the Petrograd Soviet with slogans like "All Power to the Soviet." An early attempt to seize power in July failed miserably, as did an attempted coup from the right under General Lavr Kornilov. Bolshevik party membership grew sixfold in a few months and became the majority in the Soviet.

THE SECOND RUSSIAN REVOLUTION

Leon Trotsky, a brilliant orator and thinker, organized the Petrograd Soviet to seize power. On the night of November 6, 1917, the Bolsheviks seized government buildings and communications centers and declared Lenin the head of a new government in which Soviets would have all the power. This coup d'état created a Communist one-party state that was to last more than seventy years.

The Bolsheviks not only seized power; they held on to it. How? They took advantage of the spontaneous peasant revolution redistributing the lands of aristocrats and the church that had begun in the summer of 1917 by giving the peasants the land they had taken. Urban workers were similarly given control of the factories in which they worked. Lenin immediately sued for peace, giving in to tough demands from the Germans for Poland, Finland, Lithuania, and the like, relinquishing about a third of Russia's population in the Treaty of Brest-Litovsk, signed in March 1918. When the planned elections for a Constituent Assembly to write a new constitution for Russia led to the victory for the Social Revolutionaries, the party of the peasants, Lenin ordered his soldiers to forcibly disband the assembly. A one-party state with dictatorial powers was under way.

> **AP Tip**
>
> The Social Revolutionaries rejected Marxism as Western and sought a Slavic socialism, with the village councils as the owners of cooperative farms. They were clearly the choice of the people in the one free election held in Russia before 1989. Lenin rejected the results of any election held in a bourgeois state as inherently fraudulent.

A two-year civil war ensued, between the Communists, known as the Reds, and a coalition of widely divergent opponents from monarchists to democratic socialists and ethnic nationalists, known as the Whites. By 1920, the Reds defeated the Whites and then took back the areas like the Ukraine that had broken away. Why did they win? First, because the Whites lacked unity, and secondly, because Trotsky, as war commissar, organized a well-run and disciplined army with conscripted soldiers. Thirdly, war communism, an economic program with the forced requisitioning of foodstuffs from peasants, nationalization of banks and industries, rationing, and mandatory labor, successfully fed the Red Army and fulfilled Bolshevik promises. Fourthly the Cheka, the secret police, effectively ferreted out and executed many of the enemies of the new regime; the tsar and his family were secretly executed. Lastly, the intervention of British, American, and Japanese troops on behalf of the Whites, while insufficient to turn the tide, stirred nationalistic fervor in favor of the Reds, winning them the support of even some tsarist military officers.

THE PEACE SETTLEMENT

THE WAR'S END AND REVOLUTION

With Russia out of the picture, and facing near starvation and internal war-weariness, the Germans under their dictatorial leaders Ludendorff and Hindenburg decided in the spring of 1918 on one last major offensive against France, but were defeated by the Allies, whose tired troops were considerably replenished by fresh and well-supplied Americans. The second Battle of the Marne in July 1918 effectively ended the war. As the Allies were advancing, Ludendorff cleverly maneuvered the kaiser into appointing a more liberal government to sue for peace in October. A month later, on November 3, angry mobs of workers and soldiers inspired by a mutiny in Kiel and by the Bolshevik Revolution formed revolutionary committees; on the same day Austria-Hungary surrendered. The kaiser abdicated, and on November 9 a German republic was declared. Two days later, on the eleventh hour of the eleventh day of the eleventh month, the armistice went into effect and the war was over.

In Austria, the Habsburg Empire came to an end. Hungarian and Czech nationalists proclaimed republics, and Austria, too, became one. Serbia united the southern Slavs into Yugoslavia. In Germany, the liberals and moderate socialists who established the republic formed an effective government that was able to defeat challenges from the more extreme left, partly because the socialists in Germany were already revisionists, moderates who favored a gradualist approach, partly because they were more nationalistic than internationalist, and partly because the workers and peasants were less radical. They did not emulate Russia's Provisional Government, which had also been led by moderates. By accepting the armistice and ending the fighting, the German army remained intact. The socialist leaders used the army to crush an attempt to seize power by Karl Liebknecht, who had just formed Germany's Communist Party, and by Rosa Luxembourg; the socialist leaders tolerated their murder by the army leaders.

The Treaty of Versailles

In January 1919, the peace conference to negotiate a settlement began, with great optimism that war in Europe could be ended for good. The U.S. president Woodrow Wilson's war aims, the Fourteen Points, articulated in January 1918, called for disarmament, self-determination, open treaties, freedom of the seas, and a League of Nations to prevent future war. These set the idealistic tone. But quite quickly, the different concerns of the European powers brought them into conflict. France wanted revenge and a permanently weakened Germany. England wanted to punish Germany with a harsh peace and have Germany pay for the war. So Germany, in spite of the promise of a nonpunitive peace in the Fourteen Points, was not invited to the conference; the treaty terms were dictated, not negotiated. So decisions were made by Clemenceau for France, Lloyd George for England, and Wilson, with other representatives present (not Russia, which was busy fighting its civil war) but playing a small role.

The compromise solution satisfied no one fully, certainly not Germany, who, it must be remembered, had not surrendered, only signed an armistice. The chief provisions of the treaties were

- Germany's colonies were given to France, Britain, and Japan. Alsace and Lorraine, taken by Germany in 1870, were returned to France. Parts of eastern Germany were ceded to Poland. The German army was limited to 100,000. Germany was forbidden from building military fortifications in the Rhineland on the border with France.
- Germany and her allies accepted responsibility for starting the war (Article 231) and therefore had to pay reparations to Britain and France for the civilian damages in the war. The amount was not set in the treaty.
- Poland was recreated, with former German and Russian territory. Danzig, a predominantly German city, was made a self-governing city under the League of Nations.

AP Tip

A corridor was created in Poland to provide it with access to the sea. This meant that Germany was separated from East Prussia, with Poland in between; it had lost its territorial integrity. When World War II began, the first goal of the Germans was to restore that integrity and take back the land ceded to Poland. Germany was also forbidden to have an air force and submarines, and its navy was limited to six battleships.

- Austria-Hungary lost the most territory, with Poland, Czechoslovakia, Hungary, and Yugoslavia formed as independent states out of its former lands. Hungary lost Transylvania to Romania.
- Italy got some but not all of Italian lands in the former Austrian empire.
- Promises made to both Jews and Arabs during the war were not kept, keenly disappointing Faisal, who came to the peace conference to plead for the Arab cause. Instead, the deal cut in the secret treaty between France and Britain was kept, under the guise of mandates of the League of Nations. Only the state of Hejaz (later Saudi Arabia), ruled by Faisal's father Hussein, was given independence.
- The League of Nations was created, with a weak executive and no army, as a forum for negotiation of disputes and with the promise of collective action against aggression. The league also supervised the mandates (former colonies given to the winners) and independent cities like Danzig.
- The Ottoman Empire was dismembered. Britain, France, Greece, and Italy were all given pieces of the empire and took over parts of Anatolia itself.

REACTIONS TO THE PEACE TREATY

- German representatives were presented with the completed treaty and protested fiercely but to no avail. As the Allied blockade was ongoing and the Germans starving, they had no other option but to sign, in the Hall of Mirrors at the palace in Versailles, exactly where the German Empire had been declared.
- The U.S. Senate refused to ratify the treaty when Wilson returned home. Republicans rejected it because the League of Nations might require the United States to participate in collective action. The United States turned its back on Europe and entered a period of isolationism.
- When Arab hopes for independent states were disappointed, their leaders met in Damascus 1919 and presented their views, protesting the mandate system to a fact-finding mission sent by President Wilson (see Listening to the Past, pp. 910–911). They strongly opposed Zionism, but promised full rights to their resident Jews and demanded independence for Syria (including Lebanon and Palestine) and Mesopotamia (Iraq). They met again when the British mandate in Palestine formally incorporated the promises made in the Balfour Declaration for support for a Jewish homeland

there. The Syrian National Congress declared independence in 1920, with Faisal as king; Iraq too was declared an independent kingdom. French and British troops took Damascus in 1920, forced Faisal to flee, and put down an uprising in Iraq. The mandates stayed intact under their rule.

- The Turks rebounded from the near deathblow of the treaty with a strong leader, Mustafa Kemal, known as Atatürk, the hero of Gallipoli. He organized a Turkish military force and defeated the British and French forces. Turkey was recognized in a formal treaty a few years later with territorial integrity in Anatolia, although it had lost its Arab territories. Atatürk was "father of the Turks" in more ways than military: He created an authoritarian republic, separated mosque and state, established a secular educational system, and banned the veil.

AP Tip

Almost everyone was disappointed in the treaties. The rise of fascism and Nazism and World War II all directly relate to those frustrations. In this sense, World War II was a continuation of World War I. In the Middle East, the mess made by the Allies is a huge part of the violence and disorder there to this day.

Multiple-Choice Questions

1. The tensions in the Balkans were intensified just before 1914 when Albania
   (A) was given to Serbia.
   (B) became part of Bosnia and Herzegovina.
   (C) was taken back by the Ottoman Empire in the second Balkan War.
   (D) was given to Bulgaria.
   (E) became independent because of Austrian insistence.

2. Germany is often blamed for starting the war because it
   (A) mobilized first.
   (B) gave unconditional support to Austria-Hungary.
   (C) invaded Belgium even before Serbia responded to Austria's ultimatum.
   (D) declared war on Britain first.
   (E) sent its troops with the Austrian army into Serbia.

3. The initial response to the outbreak of war was
   (A) votes against funding for the war by socialists in France and Britain.
   (B) enthusiasm in Germany, Austria, and Russia but less in Britain and France.
   (C) huge numbers of men volunteered to fight in every country.
   (D) pacifists staged many demonstrations.
   (E) British women like Vera Brittain tried to convince their men not to enlist.

4. The two Battles of the Marne were similar in that they both
   (A) brought French troops near the German border.
   (B) were clear French victories with the German army surrendering.
   (C) stopped German advances.
   (D) were dependent on British forces for victory.
   (E) were fought in Belgium right over the French border.

5. The weapon that provided defense in trench warfare was
   (A) the tank.
   (B) artillery.
   (C) poison gas.
   (D) the machine gun.
   (E) barbed wire.

6. The United States entered the war mostly because of the
   (A) sinking of the *Lusitania*.
   (B) invasion of Belgium.
   (C) German resumption of submarine warfare.
   (D) Treaty of Brest-Litovsk giving the Germans too many advantages.
   (E) Fourteen Points.

7. On the home front, labor unions
   (A) were severely restricted by law.
   (B) proved their loyalty.
   (C) sent their leadership to the front to show patriotism.
   (D) went on strike often to win better wages.
   (E) dissolved because of the new planned economy.

8. During the war, the Russian tsar
   (A) proved his competence by managing the war well.
   (B) lost credibility when Rasputin became adviser to the Tsar's wife.
   (C) left the management of the war to his General Staff.
   (D) used the Duma to generate support for the war.
   (E) retained the personal loyalty of the army.

9. The Provisional Government's big mistake was to
   (A) continue the war.
   (B) accept the Bolsheviks into its cabinet.
   (C) appoint General Kornilov as chief minister.
   (D) try to write a constitution for Russia.
   (E) sign the Treaty of Brest-Litovsk.

10. The saying "The soldiers voted with their feet" refers to
   (A) the assassination of Rasputin.
   (B) their enthusiasm when the tsar visited the front.
   (C) the impact of Order No. 1.
   (D) the protests on March 8, 1917.
   (E) their march to the front in August 1914.

11. The best description for the two Russian revolutions in 1917 is
    (A) both were coup d'états.
    (B) neither was a coup d'état.
    (C) the first was a coup d'état, the second a mass insurrection.
    (D) the first was a mass insurrection, the second a coup d'état.
    (E) both were mass insurrections.

12. Which was *not* a reason for the victory of the Reds in the Russian civil war?
    (A) The Whites were not unified.
    (B) The Red Army was well organized.
    (C) American, British, and Japanese troops aided them.
    (D) Political opponents were arrested or executed.
    (E) War communism made sure the Red Army was fed.

13. Which *contradicted* the principle of self-determination in the Versailles treaties?
    (A) The re-creation of Poland
    (B) Making Danzig into an international city under the League of Nations
    (C) The mandate system
    (D) The creation of Yugoslavia
    (E) The return of Alsace and Lorraine to France

14. Which was able to rewrite the peace treaties in its favor?
    (A) Turkey
    (B) Greece
    (C) Germany
    (D) Austria
    (E) Syria

15. Germany and Austria, as a result of the war, were similar in that both
    (A) lost about half their former landmass.
    (B) became constitutional monarchies.
    (C) nearly had their own Bolshevik revolutions.
    (D) had revolutions that turned them into democratic republics.
    (E) faced war crimes trials.

Free-Response Questions

1. Describe how Leninism revised Marxism, and analyze how that helped the Bolsheviks to take power in Russia.

2. Analyze how the causes and the course of World War I affected the negotiations at the Versailles Peace Conference.

ANSWERS

MULTIPLE-CHOICE QUESTIONS

1. **ANSWER: (E)** Serbia desperately wanted to expand, and Bosnia and Herzegovina had already been annexed by Austria. Serbia thought it

had the right to Albania because of its victories in the Balkan wars. (McKay, *A History of Western Society*, 8th ed., pp. 891–892/9th ed., p. 883)

2. **ANSWER: (B)** Russia mobilized first. Britain declared war on Germany after it invaded Belgium, which occurred a few days after the outbreak of war between Austria and Serbia. Some commentators feel that Austria-Hungary would not have been so bold with Serbia without Germany's unconditional support. (McKay, *A History of Western Society*, 8th ed., p. 893/9th ed., pp. 883–884)

3. **ANSWER: (C)** Everywhere there was enthusiasm for the war. Vera Brittain was enthusiastic for war in the beginning but then became deeply disillusioned. (McKay, *A History of Western Society*, 8th ed., pp. 900, 903/9th ed., pp. 887, 893)

4. **ANSWER: (C)** They stopped the first German advance in August-September 1914 and the last German offensive in 1918. (McKay, *A History of Western Society*, 8th ed., pp. 895, 911/9th ed., pp. 887, 901)

5. **ANSWER: (D)** It was the machine gun that created the high death rates when troops went over the top. (McKay, *A History of Western Society*, 8th ed., p. 895/9th ed., p. 887)

6. **ANSWER: (C)** The Fourteen Points were enunciated some eight months after U.S. entry into the war when Germany resumed unrestricted submarine warfare. The Lusitania was sunk in 1915, two years before U.S. entry. (McKay, *A History of Western Society*, 8th ed., pp. 899–900, 912/9th ed., pp. 890, 902)

7. **ANSWER: (B)** Labor unions earned a great deal of prestige because of their loyalty during the war. (McKay, *A History of Western Society*, 8th ed., p. 901/9th ed., p. 892)

8. **ANSWER: (B)** When the tsar went to the front to oversee the war, over which he took general charge, his wife and Rasputin were in charge of the palace; this cost him a lot of credibility, as did his incompetent management of the war. He tended to ignore the Duma. (McKay, *A History of Western Society*, 8th ed., pp. 904–905/9th ed., pp. 895–896)

9. **ANSWER: (A)** It was the Bolshevik regime that signed the Treaty of Brest-Litovsk, and the Constituent Assembly was elected to write a constitution. Neither the Bolsheviks nor Kornilov was invited into the Provisional Government. (McKay, *A History of Western Society*, 8th ed., p. 906/9th ed., pp. 896, 899)

10. **ANSWER: (C)** Order No. 1 weakened discipline so much that the soldiers felt free to walk away from the front. (McKay, *A History of Western Society*, 8th ed., p. 906/9th ed., p. 896)

11. **ANSWER: (D)** The first revolution resulted from widespread protests; the Bolshevik revolution was a coup d'état executed by the Petrograd Soviet under the Bolsheviks. (McKay, *A History of Western Society*, 8th ed., pp. 905–908/9th ed., pp. 898–899)

12. **ANSWER: (C)** The foreigners intervened on behalf of the Whites, to little avail. (McKay, *A History of Western Society,* 8th ed., pp. 909–910/9th ed., pp. 900–901)

13. **ANSWER: (C)** In the mandate system, former colonies were given to European powers and not allowed a choice. (McKay, *A History of Western Society,* 8th ed., p. 914/9th ed., pp. 903, 905–906)

14. **ANSWER: (A)** Only Turkey under Atatürk was able to rewrite the treaty it had been given. (McKay, *A History of Western Society,* not in 8th ed./9th ed., pp. 906–907)

15. **ANSWER: (D)** Both the kaiser and the Habsburg emperor were forced to abdicate by revolutionary outbursts. (McKay, *A History of Western Society,* 8th ed., pp. 911–912/9th ed., pp. 901–902)

FREE-RESPONSE QUESTIONS

1. To address this question, you must first articulate the key ideas of Marxism and then show how Lenin changed them. Then you must connect those changes to actual events. This question requires you to discuss both political theory and its realization in political developments.

- Lenin revised Marxism in three ways. First, while Marxism argued that revolution could occur only when industrialization had created a large enough proletariat to take power, Lenin argued that revolution could occur in a state that was still largely agricultural and feudal and where the proletariat was small. Peasants could join the proletariat to make a revolutionary mass. Therefore, society could skip the bourgeois, industrial stage before a revolution. Secondly, revisionist Marxism had come to believe that socialism could happen in an evolutionary process, rather than revolution. Lenin insisted that sudden, violent revolution was necessary, that evolutionary socialism would lead to compromise and piecemeal trade union negotiations, not socialism. Thirdly, revolution could succeed only if it was led by a small group of full-time communist revolutionaries, completely committed to the cause. Communists should reject revisionism and the Menshevik idea of creating a broad-based party with nonrevolutionary groups.
- These ideas helped the Bolsheviks take power. The idea that revolution was possible in backward Russia was rejected by the other Marxist party, the Mensheviks, because it contradicted Marxist theory. The Bolsheviks, however, understood that the enraged peasants together with small numbers of well-organized workers could make the revolution. Order No. 1 fomented revolution because it allowed the peasants to walk away from the front, thus depriving the tsarist regime of its military base. The peasants in the summer of 1917 were grabbing whatever land they could in anticipation of the Bolsheviks who would redistribute the land. The Bolsheviks had already formed a small party while in exile in Switzerland; when Lenin returned to Russia in April 1917, they rejected compromise with the Provisional Government. Allowing a bourgeois state to take hold would, according to Leninist theory, unnecessarily delay the revolution and therefore the easing of the suffering of peasants and workers. Once they had won a majority in

the Petrograd Soviet, they were easily able to stage a coup d'état and with relatively few people take power in November 1917. During the civil war, Lenin's model of top-down control, in contrast to Menshevik democratic principles, made the Bolsheviks effective. Lenin's willingness to use violence for political purposes was demonstrated when he used Bolshevik troops to disband the Constituent Assembly, which had a Social Revolutionary, not a Bolshevik, majority.

2. For this essay, you must connect the causes of the war and developments during the war to the peace settlement. Do not simply discuss the causes of the war or the peace settlement without drawing connections between the two.

- One cause of the war was tensions and competition over colonial claims, particularly in Africa. The Moroccan crisis of 1905 was an incident between Germany and France that spurred hostilities. Another source of tension in Europe before the war was the competition between Austria-Hungary and Russia over Ottoman territories in the Balkans. France and Britain coveted its Arab lands; for Britain it was a way to secure control over the Suez Canal, and both states were interested in trade in the eastern Mediterranean as well as in oil. During negotiations at Versailles, Britain and France made sure that they took the territories they wanted, in spite of promises during the war and the principle of self determination. Britain took East and West Africa and France got Cameroon from Germany. They also divided the former Ottoman Arab areas, with France getting Syria and Lebanon and Britain getting Palestine, Iraq, and Jordan. At the conference, Britain and France created the mandate system, where their rule over colonies was officially authorized by the League of Nations and theoretically temporary.
- Germany's invasion of Belgium, in violation of the 1839 neutrality treaty, as well as its alliance with and support of Austria-Hungary in its conflict with Serbia, was sufficient reason for Britain and France to assign to Germany the blame for starting the war. Once that responsibility was assigned, it was, they felt, logical and just that Germany had to pay for the costs of the war. Therefore, war reparations were put into the treaty. This was an important issue particularly for Britain, as the length of the war had meant skyrocketing financial costs. Lloyd George had won election in 1916 with the promise that Germany would pay for the war.
- The terrible loss of human lives had direct impact on peace negotiations. France felt vulnerable to Germany because of its smaller population. Since most of the war on the western front was fought in France and Belgium, France came into the negotiations wanting revenge and a permanently weakened Germany as well as a buffer state between it and Germany. Wilson and Lloyd George were able to reduce these demands to a smaller Germany with a small army, a few battleships, and no air force; a demilitarized Rhineland; and the return of Alsace and Lorraine to France. A buffer state between Germany and Russia was made with the re-creation of Poland.
- Wilson had articulated war aims for the United States in his Fourteen Points in January 1918, and these were the focus of U.S.

interests in the peace negotiations. Among these points was the League of Nations, an international body to prevent future wars. In order to get the agreement of the doubting Clemenceau and Lloyd George for the league, Wilson did not insist on the application of some of his other points, particularly self-determination.

- The length of the war, more than four years, and its nature as a total war involving civilians had meant that each nation launched propaganda campaigns to keep civilian spirits up and committed to the war. Over time, such propaganda, combined with censorship of the press, meant that hatred between the belligerents grew to such a degree that only a harsh peace would suffice to satisfy the hostile emotions of the populace. Therefore, the relatively equitable way that France was treated after the Napoleonic wars was not possible in 1918; instead Germany was not invited to the peace conference, nor was consideration given to the fact that it had changed its government to a republic.

28

THE AGE OF ANXIETY, CA 1900–1940

In addition to political, social, and military transformations underway during World War I, there were also significant intellectual and artistic changes that reflected the common feelings of anxiety, continual crisis, and the search for meaning. Britain, France, and Germany restored domestic and international stability after a crisis in 1923, leading to a short period of optimism ended by social dislocation and even despair when the depression hit Europe in 1930. Governments tried to solve the economic and social problems caused by deflation and mass unemployment.

KEY CONCEPTS

- In philosophy, physics, and psychology, new ways of thinking about the universe and about man's nature upset the secure Newtonian, Enlightenment worldview. Einsteinian relativity, quantum mechanics, and Heisenberg's uncertainty principle revealed an infinite but less predictable universe. Freudian psychology highlighted the irrational nature of humankind. Philosophers from Friedrich Nietzsche to Henri-Louis Bergson doubted the value of reason. The existentialists argued that humans had to create meaning for themselves.
- Literature, art, and music all reflected new ways of thinking and feeling. *Modernism*, a general term implying experimentation and new modes of expression, dominated the arts. Novels used the stream-of-consciousness technique to convey the inner person. In architecture, functionalism ended ornamentation in building. Expressionism, cubism, Dadaism, and abstractionism replaced representation in painting and sculpture while atonality replaced romanticism in music.

- Movies and radio transformed popular culture, providing new forms of entertainment and escape for the masses as well as new tools for governments, democratic and dictatorial, to manipulate public opinion.
- Political leaders searched for peace and stability after a tense Franco-German confrontation over reparations in 1923. The Locarno and the Kellogg-Briand Pacts inspired optimism as the former enemies of World War I accepted their mutual borders and agreed to avoid war as an instrument of state policy. Germany, Britain, and France each faced internal dissension but maintained their democratic forms of government.
- The Great Depression, which began in the United States mostly because of speculation in the stock market, hit Europe hard, causing high employment, deflation, and loss of productivity. Governments varied in their effectiveness in dealing with the crisis; the Swedes were the most successful.

UNCERTAINTY IN MODERN THOUGHT

Many of the new ideas had been actually developed before World War I, but their impact on the population as a whole was felt only after the war, leaving many to abandon or revise the rational world view created by the scientific revolution and the Enlightenment, and by the belief in progress created by the Industrial Revolution and the expansion of individual rights in the nineteenth century.

Writers, artists, and philosophers began to develop new ideas and values in the 1880s that challenged the optimistic belief in progress and human rationality. The horrors of World War I confirmed for many those doubts about human reason. The French poet Paul Valéry expressed commonly held forebodings of the crisis of the mind filled with fear, anxiety, darkness, and doubt. There were many important new thinkers.

- Nietzsche, a German classical philologist, wrote highly influential philosophical texts challenging the fundamental notions of Western civilization, including Christianity, which he described as a slave morality. He attacked rationalism and conventional morality as repressive of man's inner greatness and creative spirit, and said God was already dead and the only hope was to find individual meaning through personal liberation and exaltation of the individual spirit.

AP Tip

Nietzsche (1844–1900) created the concept of the superman who would not be bound by traditional notions of good and evil, and would impose his "will to power" on weaker individuals. Although in many ways Nietzsche was isolated by his radical criticisms, his frequent aphorisms rather than formal philosophical prose, and illness, he had widespread influence. Many of his anti-equalitarian ideas were enthusiastically adopted by the Nazis.

- Bergson, a French philosopher, argued that experience and intuition were as important as reason as ways to understand reality. Poetry and religion offer better access to the truth.
- Georges Sorel, a French socialist, regarded Marxism as unproven and unworkable. Instead, socialism could be achieved only through the use of the general strike—in which all workers go out on strike at the same time—which would be a massive blow against capitalism. The new state would have to be tightly controlled from the top by a revolutionary elite.

AP Tip

Sorel's theory was called syndicalism, after the French word for a confederation of unions. In Spain and Italy, it was combined with anarchism and became an important movement called anarcho-syndicalism.

- Ludwig Wittgenstein, a German philosopher, developed logical empiricism, also known as logical positivism, a revolution in philosophy that rejected its traditional concerns and argued instead that all philosophical thinking was really about language, so that discussions about God, freedom, morality, or truth were meaningless. Logical empiricism sharply narrowed the field of discourse for philosophy.
- Jean-Paul Sartre, a French philosopher, was one of the founders of existentialism, a philosophy that presumes in some of its forms that there is no God and therefore no externally defined meaning for mankind. People are left with the choice of despair and meaninglessness, or the creation of meaning for themselves through action, by becoming engaged with the issues of the day and facing them with courage and commitment. Other important existentialists were Martin Heidegger and Karl Jaspers, both Germans, and the Algerian-born Frenchman Albert Camus. All four of these writers had enormous influence after World War II.

AP Tip

Sartre and Camus demonstrated how to create personal meaning by being active in the anti-Nazi resistance during World War II. Camus's *The Myth of Sisyphus* is a lucid and readily approachable existentialist essay, and his novel *The Stranger* is often read in French classes.

- Søren Kierkegaard, a nineteenth-century Danish philosopher, sometimes called a Christian existentialist, was rediscovered in the early twentieth century. He disagreed with much in formal religion but saw man as sinful and desperately needing to make a personal and total commitment to God in order to find faith and forgiveness. Another Protestant philosopher, Karl Barth, similarly argued for emotional acceptance of revelation.
- Gabriel Marcel and Jacques Maritain, both French, represented Catholic existentialism, arguing that the Catholic Church offered a

way out of the conundrums of the modern world. They were also ecumenical, denouncing anti-Semitism and promoting dialogue with non-Catholics. Many poets and novelists turned toward Catholicism, particularly the Englishmen Evelyn Waugh and Graham Greene. Important non-Catholics also found themselves attracted back to their religions.

THE NEW PHYSICS

Scientific progress in the nineteenth century had added Darwinian evolution, explaining how life and man came to be, to the scientific surety of Newtonian physics and created a comprehensive scientific worldview. The early twentieth century saw this scientific synthesis broken up, particularly in physics. Atoms were discovered to be made of even smaller particles that emit energy unevenly, matter and energy were no longer considered distinct, and observations were now known not to be absolute but relative to the position of the observer. Many scientists were involved in the major breakthroughs.

- Marie Curie, Polish-born but living in France, discovered radium, thereby making X-rays possible. She and her husband, Pierre, also determined that radium emits subatomic particles.
- Max Planck, a German physicist, showed that subatomic particles emit energy unevenly in little spurts he called quanta, thereby founding quantum mechanics.
- Albert Einstein, a physicist who was born in Germany but later immigrated to the United States, developed the special theory of relativity, by which calculations of phenomena have to include the position of observers; this meant that reality could not be objective, except for the speed of light, which is unchanging. Einstein also postulated an infinite universe, as opposed to Newton's closed one, and proved that matter and energy are interchangeable.
- Ernest Rutherford, a British physicist, showed in 1919 that the atom could be split, releasing enormous energy. The neutron was one of subatomic participles identified subsequently; its ability to create chain reactions of amazing force would be important for the making of the atomic bomb.
- Werner Heisenberg, a German physicist, in 1927 formulated the uncertainty principle which showed that it was impossible to ascertain the exact location of any electron and therefore equally impossible to predict its behavior. The universe, it seems, was unpredictable and uncertain.

FREUDIAN PSYCHOLOGY

Similarly disturbing discoveries were made by Sigmund Freud (see also Chapter 24), a Viennese physician and neurologist who identified the unconscious mind and made it comprehensible scientifically, whereas previously the world of the unconscious had belonged to mystics and poets. Freud delineated three competing psychological elements in the unconscious mind: the id, demanding gratification of pleasure-seeking instincts of aggression and sexuality; the superego, demanding obedience to internalized societal rules and demands; and the ego, the rationalizing self that negotiates between the other two, seeking to satisfy both. When these powerful unconscious drives are unrecognized, unbridled aggression or sexual perversion results; on the other hand, repression of unconscious feelings leads to fears, guilt, and misery. After the war, it was this latter idea that took hold, promoting personal liberation, sexual experimentation, and a loosening of strict Victorian morality.

AP Tip

Freudian theory incorporated some of the elements of the new science. Darwinian notions of natural instincts for competition and aggression underlay the idea that humans have an innate aggressive instinct, which Freud called Thanatos and located in the id. It provided an explanation of what was seen as the irrationality, even madness, of the continuous sending of large numbers of men to their death for little purpose during World War I. In his postwar *Civilization and Its Discontents,* Freud argued that the best that humans could hope for was a modicum of happiness and that most men, and most societies, would be overcome by irrational drives. He created the talking therapy of psychoanalysis to help patients uncover their childhood memories and understand how conflicts between id, ego, and superego unconsciously affect adult behavior and feelings. His work prompted the development of other psychological theories and widespread interest in various forms of psychotherapy.

TWENTIETH-CENTURY LITERATURE

Literature also reflected the uncertainty of the post–World War I world. Novelists created new genres and new techniques, as the nineteenth-century novel with its passion for realism now seemed inadequate. The new novels and poems explored the inner world of the individual with his or her complex desires, memories, and fantasies. Many, such as Woolf, Joyce, and Faulkner, used the stream-of-consciousness technique in which the author does not organize a character's thoughts and ideas into some coherent structure, but instead lets them appear as randomly as they come up in real life. There were many important novelists.

- Marcel Proust, a Parisian who lived most of his adult life in seclusion, wrote *Remembrance of Things Past,* a detailed examination of childhood and youth.
- Virginia Woolf, a British writer at the center of the literary circle known as the Bloomsbury group, wrote the 1922 novel *Jacob's Room* as well as several important feminist works.
- William Faulkner, an American who explored the psyche of southerners, wrote *The Sound and the Fury,* telling part of the story through the eyes of an "idiot."
- James Joyce, an Irishman who lived in Trieste, Zürich, and Paris, wrote the most emblematic novel of the early twentieth century, *Ulysses,* a long work that accounts the thoughts and deeds of one ordinary man on one day of his life in Dublin. Joyce was also very innovative in his writing, abandoning narrative structure and

conventional grammar, using foreign words, memories, sensations, and bits of knowledge in what is at first reading a confusing array.

- T. S. Eliot, an American who lived in London, reflected in his poem *The Wasteland,* 1922, the sense of desolation after the war.
- Franz Kafka, a German-speaking Jew living in Prague, crystallized the despair of the period in his novels *The Castle* and *The Trial,* both from the 1920s, in which inexplicable forces crush the individual.
- George Orwell, an Englishman who fought on behalf of the republic during the Spanish Civil War, wrote in 1949 the definitive anti-utopian novel, *1984,* which predicted a totalitarian world run by a dictator, called Big Brother, who uses psychological manipulation and modern technology to terrorize and crush the individual.
- Oswald Spengler, although a German philosopher and not a novelist, wrote a bestseller that had an impact similar to the fictional works of these authors. His *Decline of the West,* written in 1918, predicted the imminent collapse of European civilization.

Modern Art and Music

As in literature, the visual and musical arts reflected the new cultural attitudes of the postwar period. Modernism involved experimentation as artists searched for new means of expression, which were often disturbing and strange.

Architecture and Design

Architecture was radically transformed by a new concept called functionalism by which the aesthetic preference for the design of buildings was based on usefulness, rather than ornamentation. Architects worked with engineers and designers, eliminating ornamentation in favor of clean lines.

The innovating architects were the Frenchman Charles-Edouard Le Corbusier, the Americans Louis Sullivan and Frank Lloyd Wright, and the Germans Walter Gropius (see the photograph of his shoe factory on p. 922) and Mies van der Rohe. In Germany, a new interdisciplinary school, the Bauhaus, applied the principles of modernism to other visual arts, household objects, theatrical design, and the traditional crafts of weaving and printing. The Bauhaus had enormous influence in Europe and the United States.

Painting

In the late nineteenth century, impressionists like Claude Monet, Pierre-Auguste Renoir, and Camille Pissarro dominated the arts in France. Even before World War I, modernists revolted against impressionism, either through postimpressionism, expressionism, or abstraction. Much art became nonrepresentational, particularly after 1905, as artists sought to represent psychological truths and emotionality of the inner self, just as authors had. Three nineteenth-century artists were particularly important. Vincent van Gogh, a remarkable painter, used new techniques and vivid colors to illuminate his inner intensity, initiating the expressionist movement before he died in 1890. Paul Gauguin, who abandoned his bourgeois Parisian life to live and paint in Tahiti, exalted the primitive and exotic and visualized them expressionistically. Paul Cézanne, who was fascinated by form and shape, over time moved from three dimensionality to two dimensionality and influenced much of the later direction of twentieth-century art.

The twentieth century saw even more innovations. Henri Matisse was part of a movement known as the *fauves* who used striking colors and moving lines, while Pablo Picasso was one of the founders of *cubism*. Cubism moved further away from representational art by breaking artistic subjects into overlapping planes, geometric shapes, and zigzagging lines. In his long life, Picasso achieved enormous fame and became the model of the modern artist—incessantly innovative, productive, politically engaged, and highly individualistic. His most famous works are *Les Demoiselles d'Avignon*, 1907; *Three Musicians*, 1921; and *Guernica*, 1937, perhaps the most powerful antiwar twentieth-century painting (see Images in Society, pp. 924–925). Wassily Kandinsky developed abstractionism, in which the painter uses colors and forms to convey his particular vision but not to represent real objects.

By the outbreak of World War I, an international artistic culture based on modernism, expressionism, and abstractionism had come into being. During and after World War I, these artistic movements were complemented by new ones. Dadaism, which was also a literary movement, rejected any and all artistic standards and encouraged outrageous and intentionally meaningless work. Surrealists were fascinated by the inner world of dreams, symbols, and fantasies, and these became the subjects of their artistic works. Surrealist artists like Salvador Dali painted watches that melt and impossible landscapes.

MODERN MUSIC

Painting and music followed parallel paths, as composers became expressionists as well, abandoning the romanticism that dominated nineteenth-century music. Igor Stravinsky's ballet music *The Rite of Spring* had intense rhythms and dissonant tonality while on the stage dancers erotically reenacted primitive fertility rites. The ballet nearly caused a riot when it was first performed in 1913. After the war, expressionism in music, opera, and ballet attracted innovative artists. *Wozzeck*, an opera by Alban Berg, is a thoroughly modernist work in both story, a Kafkaesque tale of an ordinary soldier with a miserable life, and music, half-spoken, half-sung, and atonal, meaning that it lacked a key around which musical harmonies are formed. It sounded harsh and dissonant to most ears used to nineteenth-century music. Arnold Schönberg in Vienna created the twelve-tone scale, in which all notes were equal, without a key, formed in mathematical patterns he called tone rows that were barely discernible to most listeners. Atonal and twelve-tone music found little popularity with concertgoers, though they became more acceptable after World War II.

MOVIES AND RADIO

Two new media, which were developed before the war but which came into their own afterward, profoundly altered the arts and popular entertainment. The masses were not thrilled by the new visual and musical styles, but they were by the radio and the movies, which soon replaced local, traditional cultural venues. The movies, at first silent and short motion pictures, were first created in the 1890s and were shown for the first time in a movie theatre in 1902. Full-length movies, such as *Quo Vadis* and *Birth of the Nation,* were produced in New York and later Hollywood before World War I. During the war, the United States began to dominate the film industry. Hollywood stars became hugely popular, with fan clubs and fan magazines. Comedy, originally of the slapstick variety such as that by Mack Sennett, developed into thoughtful and witty satire with artists like Charlie Chaplin. In the 1920s, the film industry in Germany became the center of the avant-garde with expressionist films such as *The Cabinet of Dr. Caligari,* 1919. By the 1930s, movies had become part of the lives of most Europeans and Americans, with the average person going to the movies about twice a week. Musical comedies, particularly, offered a wonderful escape during the hard times of the Great Depression.

Radio was made possible by two earlier inventions: Marconi's transatlantic wireless communication, 1901, and the vacuum tube that allowed the transmission of sound, 1904. In 1920, the first radio broadcast, of the soprano Nellie Melba, was heard all over Europe. National broadcasting networks were established in most major countries, under state ownership in England, the BBC, and in most of Europe, and privately in the United States. Radio became popular and influential very quickly, with some three-fourths of all German and British households owning one by the late 1930s. Radio was entertainment but also a powerful tool for propaganda in the hands of dictators like Hitler and Mussolini as well as democratic leaders like Roosevelt and Churchill. Movies too served as propaganda weapons. Vladimir Lenin encouraged the Russian film industry and its leading light, Sergei Eisenstein, whose film *Potemkin* is a cinematic as well as propaganda masterpiece. Hitler also made effective use of the German film industry. His favorite filmmaker, Leni Riefenstahl, made extraordinarily powerful propaganda films like *Triumph of the Will,* which portrayed Nazi Party rallies in Nuremberg with exhilarating cinematography, and *Olympiad,* which glorified the German athleticism in the Berlin Olympics of 1936.

AP Tip

The new artistic, literary, and musical movements had important political consequences when they became part of a culture war in the 1920s and 1930s during which they were fiercely denounced by fascists and Nazis, who defined them as degenerate, and defended by progressives. Many of the modernist artists, architects, filmmakers, and writers were forced into exile during the Nazi period.

THE SEARCH FOR PEACE AND POLITICAL STABILITY

The decades after the end of World War I were fraught with instability and anxiety politically and economically as well as intellectually and artistically. There was hardly a stable country in Europe, and international relations were tense, although a brief period of optimism began with the signing of the Locarno Pact in 1925.

GERMANY

The Germans, by and large, hated the Versailles Peace Treaty dictated to them. But it had not broken them. France and Britain quite soon disagreed about the treaty, with France insisting on strict enforcement of its provisions, especially those on the payment of massive reparations, while Britain, which valued Germany as a trading partner and hoped for its quick economic recovery, had second thoughts. The British economist John Maynard Keynes denounced the treaty for its treatment of Germany and argued that German impoverishment would hurt the economy of the entire continent. His 1919 tract, *Economic Consequences of the Peace*, stirred the British sense of guilt and influenced their turn away from the punitive treaty. Nevertheless, the Allied reparations committee met and in 1921 set the reparations bill to the equivalent of $33 billion, which the Germans had to pay or face the threat of foreign occupation of the Ruhr Valley, their industrial heartland. After their first installment in 1921, a bad year of inflation and assassinations led them to suspend payments and ask for a suspension of three years. The British were willing to accept the compromise but not the French, who sent troops into the Ruhr. The Germans responded with passive resistance under the instructions of the government and stopped working the coal mines and steel mills. In response, the French sealed off those areas to force Germans to work or face starvation. The German economy was paralyzed, and the resultant hyperinflation, as the government printed more and more money to pay the bills, destroyed the savings of many a middle-class family. Those who lost everything reacted with fury at the foreigners, the government, and big business but also blamed the Jews, the workers, and the communists. Finally the situation was saved when Gustav Stresemann took the reins of government, called off the passive resistance, and agreed to pay reparations after a reconsideration to which the French agreed (see the various interpretations about Stresemann in Individuals in Society, p. 931). The moderates won out in both countries, and a terrible crisis was prevented from becoming an all-out disaster.

International relations also went through transitions in the 1920s. France searched for new allies, now that the United States had adopted isolationism and Russia was communist. In 1921, it signed a mutual defense treaty with Poland and worked closely with the Little Entente of Yugoslavia, Romania, and Czechoslovakia. After the conflict between France and Germany abated, a period of optimism began. A reorganization of reparations under the Dawes Plan reduced the annual payments of the Germans and offered them loans from the United States to rebuild their economy. The United States had a vested interest in German recovery, since only that way would the loans they had made to Britain and France during the war be repaid. Germany returned to prosperity with remarkable speed and was able to pay about $1.3 billion of its reparation bills by 1928. In 1925, Germany and France, along with other European states, signed the Treaty of Locarno, accepting the borders created by the Treaty of Versailles, with Britain and Italy as guarantors of the peace. Germany made similar agreements with Poland and Czechoslovakia, which were promised protection by France if Germany invaded, and also joined the League of Nations. A new optimism, the spirit of Locarno, was widely felt, so much so that fifteen nations including the United States signed the Kellogg-Briand Pact in 1928, which denounced war as an instrument of national policy and promised peaceful resolution of disputes.

Hope in Democratic Government

The German republic survived these economic and international crises of the early 1920s. There were political crises as well, which the democratic republic survived reasonably well in the 1920s. One of these, highly significantly for the future, was an attempted coup d'état in Bavaria in 1923 by an extremely nationalist, anti-Semitic, and tiny party. Its leader, the then unknown Adolf Hitler, came to public attention during his trial and with the publication in 1924 of his political statement, *Mein Kampf.* Soon, the Nazi Party was known nationally, although not taken very seriously; it won only twelve seats in the Reichstag in the 1928 election. It was only when the depression hit Germany badly that their percentage of the vote substantially increased.

AP Tip

Erich Ludendorff of World War I fame marched with Hitler in this attempted coup, commonly called the Beer Hall Putsch, giving Hitler some credibility. Hitler served only nine months in jail for his attempted treason.

Germany was dominated by moderate businessmen, like Stresemann, and functioned effectively as a democracy with regular elections, although Communists, who were elected to local governments, noisily attacked their archenemies, the Social Democrats, the moderate, anti-Bolshevik socialists.

AP Tip

In every Western country, the socialist movement divided over the Bolshevik revolution. Socialists who did not support the idea of one-party dictatorship took the name Socialist or Social Democrat, while those who supported the Bolsheviks were called Communists, on Lenin's insistence. Socialists and Communists frequently attacked each other, so while the left grew in size, particularly during the depression, it was a severely divided movement.

In France, the political situation was similar, with moderates dominating the government and battling Communists and Socialists. France rebuilt quickly after the war and solved the problem of the inflation that resulted by raising taxes and slashing spending. France was particularly attractive to artists, who ventured to Paris from all over Europe and the United States. The expatriate American writer

Gertrude Stein held court in Paris for a large American colony of writers and artists.

In Britain, the adjustment after the war was made more difficult because of high unemployment. In June 1921, about 23 percent of the labor force was out of work, and the rest of the 1920s saw about half that percentage unemployed. This was expensive for the government, which paid unemployment benefits and provided subsidized housing and medical care. The Labour Party, made up of revisionist, moderate socialists, slowly replaced the Liberal Party, and under Ramsey MacDonald governed Britain in 1924 and 1929. Its rise helped maintain the greater social equality achieved during the war and ensured social harmony, though there was a major coal strike in 1926 that developed into a general strike, albeit unsuccessful. The Conservatives, then led by Baldwin, generally were willing to compromise. The issue that had divided Britain so much before the war, Ireland, was resolved at least temporarily when in 1922 the Irish Republic was created, excluding the northern provinces, which remained part of Great Britain.

THE GREAT DEPRESSION

The economic crisis that began in the United States in 1929 and in Europe in 1930 was greater in intensity and duration that any previous one. It lasted for years, caused enormous suffering because of massive unemployment and failed farms, and was not lifted until the outbreak of World War II in 1939; only with the economic demands of World War II did unemployment disappear. It had enormous consequences just about everywhere but most of all in Germany, where it was the single largest factor in the rise of the Nazis to power (see Chapter 29).

***THE ECONOMIC CRISIS:* WHAT CAUSED THE GREAT DEPRESSION?** American prosperity in the 1920s was based on stock market speculation and increasing inequalities in income between rich and poor. Money flowed into the stock market and out of investment in production (factories, farms, etc.), but that money was largely borrowed as investors bought on margin, which meant that they needed to put little down in actual cash, borrowing the rest from their stockbrokers. Such a system fueled the stock market and created the illusion of wealth, but when prices began to drop in the fall of 1929, the margins were called in and investors had to sell to pay off their debts. This led to a selling craze and a precipitous collapse in the prices of stocks. The result was deflation; as people lost money when their investments lost value, they had less to spend, and the prices of goods began to spiral downward. When they got low enough, factory owners ceased production, unemployment spread, and prices declined further as workers earned too little to buy goods.

The American crisis triggered one in Europe. Americans had made substantial loans to Europeans, particularly in Germany, and when they had to pay their debts, they demanded repayment and withdrew funds from their European investments. As borrowing money to keep businesses afloat became harder as a result in Europe, a downward spiral began and quickly intensified. The largest bank in Austria failed in 1931.

Gold flowed back to the United States, and world prices dropped everywhere, as businessmen tried to sell off goods, both agricultural and industrial, to earn cash. It is estimated that the drop of the output of world goods was 38 percent.

Government responses to the crisis tended to make it worse. Britain, for example, went off the gold standard, dropping the value of its currency in the hope of making its goods more exportable. But as other nations including the United States did the same, this didn't work. The United States tried to protect its manufacturing sector by raising protectionist tariffs, which didn't help to stabilize the world economy. Governments almost everywhere cut their spending instead of using deficit spending to stimulate the economies, as had been advocated by John Maynard Keynes.

MASS UNEMPLOYMENT Britain, which had a high unemployment of around 12 percent in the 1920s, saw it go up to nearly 20 percent. In the United States unemployment went from 5 percent in the 1920s to nearly 33 percent. Mass unemployment created many problems: increases in poverty even with the provision of some meager government aid, ill health, both mental and physical, and hopelessness and despair in millions of homes. Birthrates fell dramatically as people postponed marriage.

THE *NEW DEAL* IN THE UNITED STATES The depression hit the United States hard precisely because it had had such a prosperous 1920s. In 1933, the new president, Franklin Delano Roosevelt, used his landslide victory to make major changes in the U.S. system but kept it capitalistic. He abandoned the gold standard, devalued the currency, and passed legislation to raise prices by limiting production. The government put thousands on thousands of people to work by employing them in public works projects under the Works Progress Administration (WPA) and in general took on the role of providing for the welfare of Americans, thus breaking long traditions. The New Deal included some Bismarckian provisions, such as social security, unemployment benefits, and the right to organize unions, which doubled union membership. The New Deal was only partially successful, with some 7 million people still out of work in 1937.

THE SCANDINAVIAN RESPONSE TO THE DEPRESSION This was the most successful response of any Western state. In Sweden and Norway, the Social Democrats had become the largest party after World War I and had instituted substantial welfare programs for workers and peasants. Scandinavian socialism had particularities based on cultural traditions of cooperative enterprise. Sweden pioneered in the use of large-scale deficits to fund public works and keep the economy going. Instead of cutting spending, they increased social welfare benefits, which meant high taxes on the rich and a large bureaucracy. But this middle way between socialism and capitalism was generally accepted in the area.

RECOVERY IN BRITAIN AND FRANCE Britain faced the depression first with a Labour and then with a Conservative government, both following orthodox economic theory, which was relatively successful, in part because it focused on the national economy rather than the international market. While the old industries of coal and iron in the north declined, new industries in the south, such as automobile manufacturing, boomed. In general, Britain was better off in the 1930s than it had been in the 1920s. The excerpt from George Orwell's 1937 novel, *The Road to Wigan Pier,* describes the psychological impact of unemployment on less prosperous areas and the ironical ability of the British poor to own a radio even as they faced starvation.

In France, the depression had less impact because the country had remained more agricultural than in Britain or Germany. But it did hit, with decline visible until 1935, partially because of a lack of consistent government policy: there were frequent changes of government as one coalition cabinet after another fell (five in 1933 alone). A French fascist movement grew so strong that it attempted to take over the republic in 1934, and the communist movement also grew. To prevent the right from taking power, communists, socialist, and radicals (who were actually moderates), formed an alliance called the Popular Front, which won the election of 1936. The Socialists, led by Léon Blum, became the largest party in France, and they attempted to solve the problems caused by the depression with pro-union and pro-worker legislation—the forty-hour work and paid vacations—but the resulting inflation raised fears among conservatives. Blum was forced to resign as France divided into hostile factions over the Spanish Civil War, with the communists demanding intervention on the side of the republic and conservatives and fascists supporting Franco. France continued to lack effective leadership to face its domestic problems and the growing threats from Nazi Germany.

Multiple-Choice Questions

1. When Germany announced that it could not make reparations payments in early 1923
   (A) England and France strongly protested but did nothing.
   (B) France and England occupied the Ruhr to force Germany to pay.
   (C) England but not France occupied the Ruhr to force Germany to pay.
   (D) France but not England occupied the Ruhr to force Germany to pay.
   (E) France and England agreed to negotiate a different payment schedule.

2. Which artist is most closely associated with the development of Cubism?
   (A) Van Gogh
   (B) Kandinsky
   (C) Picasso
   (D) Matisse
   (E) Gauguin

3. The Bauhaus stood out from other artistic movements in that it was
   (A) interdisciplinary and included the crafts.
   (B) politically conservative.
   (C) an international movement.
   (D) led by women artists.

(E) a patron of the new composers who often had hard times getting commissions.

4. Atonal or twelve-tone music was often hard to listen to because it
   (A) was not sung but only spoken.
   (B) used new instruments unfamiliar to most concertgoers.
   (C) was played usually without a conductor, as musicians rejected the traditional hierarchy.
   (D) lacked a dominant key to organize the musical notes.
   (E) was randomized so much that a listener could never hear the same piece twice.

5. The influence of Freudian theory on literature can best be seen in
   (A) Joyce's use of language in *Ulysses.*
   (B) Faulkner's use of an "idiot" as the narrator in *The Sound in the Fury.*
   (C) Woolf's stream-of-consciousness writing in *Jacob's Room.*
   (D) T. S. Eliot's desolate tone in *The Wasteland.*
   (E) Franz Kafka's nightmarish plot in *The Trial.*

6. The impact of logical empiricism (logical positivism) on philosophy was to make it
   (A) very optimistic about human progress.
   (B) more mathematical.
   (C) more focused on religion than it had been in the nineteenth century.
   (D) more metaphysical, exploring the major questions of human existence.
   (E) smaller in the scope of its inquiry.

7. Nietzsche, Sorel, and Bergson shared a belief in which of the following ideas?
   (A) Marxism
   (B) The limitations of reason in guiding human destiny
   (C) The superiority of scientific thinking over philosophical musings
   (D) Freudian theory
   (E) The slave morality of Christianity

8. The 1929 stock market crash in the United States caused the depression in Europe because
   (A) Europeans had heavily invested in the U.S. stock market.
   (B) inflation in the United States caused a rapid rise in prices in Europe.
   (C) U.S. banks demanded repayment of their postwar loans to Europeans to pay off their own debts.
   (D) U.S. banks demanded full repayment of their World War I loans to European states.
   (E) the U.S. government immediately set up protectionist tariffs to keep out European goods.

9. Which best characterizes the response to the depression in Europe?
   (A) The heads of state called a conference to coordinate the recovery.
   (B) Each country tried to solve its problems alone.
   (C) Germany and France, in the spirit of Locarno, worked closely together.
   (D) The Popular Front government in France coordinated with the Labour government in Britain.
   (E) The finance ministers in Europe agreed it was important to stay on the gold standard.

10. According to the description in the textbook, which was the most effective program in dealing with the depression?
   (A) Scandinavia's use of deficit spending to finance public works
   (B) Roosevelt's New Deal
   (C) France's pro-worker legislation under the Popular Front after 1936
   (D) Britain's adherence to orthodox economic theory
   (E) France's early response before 1935

11. Gustav Stresemann ended the crisis in the Ruhr in 1923
   (A) because, as a socialist, he opposed war.
   (B) by announcing the resumption of reparations payments and ending the resistance.
   (C) by threatening France with war.
   (D) by offering to sign the Locarno Pact.
   (E) after convincing the British prime minister to intervene.

12. The Locarno Pact was important because it
   (A) outlawed war.
   (B) provided French with a secure alliance with the Little Entente.
   (C) ended the possibility of French-German war over their borders.
   (D) renegotiated the German reparations payment schedule.
   (E) ended the French occupation of the Ruhr.

13. Which physicist is correctly matched with his contributions to science in the 1930s?
   (A) Max Planck—demonstrated that energy is emitted in quanta, uneven spurts
   (B) Albert Einstein—demonstrated that the atom could be split
   (C) Ernest Rutherford—formulated the uncertainty principle
   (D) Marie Curie—showed that matter and energy are interchangeable
   (E) Werner Heisenberg—discovered that radium emits subatomic participles

14. Which statement most accurately characterizes Britain in the 1920s?
   (A) The Irish problem remained unresolved and a thorn in the side of the government.
   (B) The British recovered quickly after the war economically.

(C) The Labour Party, although moderate, was seen as too socialistic and could not win any election.
(D) Unemployment remained high throughout the decade.
(E) The labor unions maintained their wartime record of social harmony in that there were no major strikes or very little labor unrest until the depression hit.

15. France and Germany faced which similar domestic issue in the 1920s and the 1930s?
(A) Large numbers of expatriate Americans in the capital cities creating their own subculture
(B) Lack of competent leadership
(C) The election of Popular Front governments
(D) Attempts by fascist movements to take power
(E) Poor recovery from the war

Free-Response Questions

1. Analyze the impact of the reparations issue on German political and economic developments and foreign relations in the 1920s.

2. Describe the chief features of the new physics and psychology in the early twentieth century, and analyze its impact on literature and the arts. Discuss two art forms specifically.

ANSWERS

MULTIPLE-CHOICE QUESTIONS

1. (D) England strongly protested French military occupation of the Ruhr. (McKay, *A History of Western Society,* 8th ed., p. 938/9th ed., p. 920)

2. (C) Picasso's 1907 *Les Demoiselles d'Avignon* was a major breakthrough of cubism. (McKay, *A History of Western Society,* 8th ed., pp. 932, 934/9th ed., pp. 924–926)

3. (A) The Bauhaus included weavers, printers, and other craftspeople in its artistic school, unlike most of the other movements. (McKay, *A History of Western Society,* 8th ed., p. 930/9th ed., pp. 921–922)

4. (D) Atonality was difficult because it lacked a key, so it sounded dissonant to most people. *Wozzeck* was half-sung and half-spoken. Most orchestras retained their conductors and used traditional instruments. (McKay, *A History of Western Society,* 8th ed., p. 933/9th ed., p. 926)

5. (A) Stream of consciousness is meant to replicate in literature the outpouring from the unconscious that might happen on a psychoanalyst's couch. (McKay, *A History of Western Society,* 8th ed., p. 929/9th ed., p. 920)

6. (E) Logical empiricism argued that language was the only meaningful subject for discourse and analysis in philosophy, not religion or metaphysics, thus sharply reducing the scope of inquiry. (McKay, *A History of Western Society*, 8th ed., pp. 924–925/9th ed., p. 916)

7. (B) They all reject reason, but for different reasons. For Nietzsche, reason is a chain preventing human greatness; Sorel argued for action using the general strike rather than reason to achieve socialism; and Bergson suggested that experience and intuition were as good if not better than reason as guide to understanding. (McKay, *A History of Western Society*, 8th ed., p. 924/9th ed., pp. 915–916)

8. (C) The depression led to deflation, not inflation. U.S. investors pulled their money out of Europe, and U.S. banks insisted on repayment of the loans they had made to Europeans in the heady days of the 1920s in order to pay off their debts after their margins were called in. The United States did establish protectionist tariffs, but it was the flow of gold reserves out of Europe to the United States that damaged the European economies initially. (McKay, *A History of Western Society*, 8th ed., p.942 /9th ed., pp. 933, 935)

9. (B) There was very little coordination among the states, each trying to solve the problem alone. Most states went off the gold standard. (McKay, *A History of Western Society*, 8th ed., pp. 942, 944 /9th ed., p. 935)

10. (A) The Scandinavians did better than anyone else, with Britain a close second. Neither of the French efforts worked well, and while the New Deal had some success, unemployment was still massive in 1937. (McKay, *A History of Western Society*, 8th ed., pp. 946–947/9th ed., pp. 937–938)

11. (B) Stresemann was a fervent nationalist, not a socialist. Locarno was two years after the end of the crisis. German willingness to compromise ended the crisis, not British intervention. (McKay, *A History of Western Society*, 8th ed., pp. 938–939, 941/9th ed., pp. 930–931)

12. (C) In the Locarno Pact, France and Germany accepted their borders as established by the Versailles Treaty. The Ruhr crisis had been over for two years when it was negotiated. The Kellogg-Briand Pact outlawed war. France was tied to the Little Entente but not by formal treaty. (McKay, *A History of Western Society*, 8th ed., pp. 938–939/9th ed., pp. 929–930)

13. (A) Max Planck founded quantum mechanics, Curie discovered radium, Heisenberg formulated the uncertainty principle, and Rutherford first split the atom. Einstein showed matter and energy are interchangeable. (McKay, *A History of Western Society*, 8th ed., pp. 826–827/9th ed., pp. 920–921)

14. (D) There was a major general strike in 1926. The Labour Party was elected to power twice, in 1924 and 1929. Unemployment stayed around 12 percent throughout the decade. Ireland, except Ulster, was

given its independence in 1922. (McKay, *A History of Western Society*, 8th ed., pp. 940, 942/9th ed., pp. 932–933)

15. (D) France recovered from the war remarkably well, as did Germany after 1923. There was a large American expatriate community in Paris but not so much in Berlin in the 1920s. A Popular Front government was elected in France but not in Germany. Both faced fascist attempts at taking power: Hitler's attempted coup in 1923 and fascist streets riots in Paris in 1934. (McKay, *A History of Western Society*, 8th ed., pp. 939–940, 947/9th ed., pp. 930, 932, 939)

FREE-RESPONSE QUESTIONS

1. Impact of the reparations issue on German domestic affairs and foreign relations in the 1920s developed over time.

- Germany was assessed the equivalent of $33 billion by an Allied commission in 1921. They made an initial payment, but asked for a three-year moratorium the next year. France insisted on German compliance and occupied the industrial Ruhr Valley. The German government ordered the people to resist passively by not working in the coalmines and steel mills. France retaliated by closing off the border to prevent the importation of foodstuffs. The German economy was paralyzed, and to pay its bills, the government printed more and more money, leading to rapid inflation that wiped out the savings of many middle-class families. Many Germans felt betrayed and vented their anger on the government and big business but also on Jews and communists. In 1923, Hitler and a small band of anti-Semitic extreme nationalists attempted a coup d'état. Hitler wrote *Mein Kampf* and became nationally known while he was in prison for this treason.
- Germany stabilized when Stresemann ran the government between 1923 and 1929; he ended the passive resistance in the Ruhr and got the French to agree to a renegotiation of the reparations. A new currency was created which restored confidence. The United States helped with the Dawes Plan, which reduced the annual amount due, and lent Germany money so that its economy could recover and it could make the reparation payments. Stresemann also ended tensions with his neighbors by signing the Locarno Pact and having Germany join the League of Nations. Germany ended up paying off about a third of its reparations bill by 1928. Politically, moderates like Stresemann who supported parliamentary government dominated Germany; the Weimar Republic was gaining the support of the German people in the late 1920s. The Nazi Party was on the fringe, winning only twelve seats in the 1928 election.
- Nevertheless, Communists on the left attacked the Social Democrats, who were the largest party, and divided the working classes into political factions.
- When the stock market crashed, the U.S. banks demanded repayment on their loans and investors pulled out their funds. The German economy was hit badly by the depression. Germany's unemployment rate was one of the highest in Europe.

2. This question asks for the chief features of the new physics and psychology in the early twentieth century, and then their impact on literature and the arts.

- The chief features of the new physics stressed the behavior of invisible subatomic particles (discovered by Marie Curie) that emit energy in uneven spurts called quanta (Max Planck), which can be split releasing enormous energy (Ernest Rutherford) and whose behavior is unpredictable (Heisenberg). Albert Einstein disputed the notion that data from scientific observations is absolute, showing that the position of the observer has to be included in the calculations. The fixed, predictable Newtonian universe was no longer.
- The psychology of Freud also depended on invisible units, in this case instinctual drives in the unconscious mind, which dominate the id and influence adult behavior and feelings. It was important to understand the unconscious mind, which reveals itself in dreams and in seemingly random thoughts.
- Literature reflected the importance Freud gave to the unconscious by incorporating dreams and fantasies and using stream-of-consciousness techniques to emulate what happens on the psychoanalyst's couch. The inner self, not the narrative, was the important part of the story. Proust wrote a detailed exploration of his daily life and his childhood, and Woolf, Faulkner, and Joyce used stream of consciousness in their novels.
- Music reflected the sense of the Heisenberg principle of the unpredictability of the basic elements of nature, Curie's subatomic participles, and Einstein's principle of relativity. The twelve-stone scale and atonality removed the key that provided predictable relationships among notes and implied equality among the notes rather than the dominance of one in a key. Modern music, such as the opera *Wozzeck* by Berg, seemed to have no pattern and no predictability.
- Painting also reflected the new understandings. Surrealists painted dreams and images from the unconscious that often contradicted reality. Abstractionists like Kandinsky and expressionists like van Gogh painted the inner mind of the artist, not visual reality. Cubists like Picasso broke people and objects into planes and shapes and presented them from various angles in the same painting. Dadaists rejected the notion of meaning at all and applauded meaninglessness.

29

DICTATORSHIPS AND THE SECOND WORLD WAR, 1919–1945

During the 1920s and 1930s, the general crisis in Europe led to the waning of democracy, replaced in one country after another by authoritarian or fascist dictatorships and surviving only in Britain, France, Scandinavia, the Netherlands, and Switzerland. Fascism was a new political system created first in Italy. The idea spread throughout Europe, but in its Nazi form, it reached its apogee in Germany. Fascism was totalitarian, as was Stalinism in communist Russia. Both governments sought to control both the public and the private sphere and ruled with particular brutality but also with particular effectiveness. Both regimes led to the death of millions of civilians, in German death camps and Russian slave-labor camps.

KEY CONCEPTS

- Authoritarian governments took power in many states, particularly in eastern and central Europe. They sought to impose tight control over society and reassert traditional values and traditional sources of authority such as the church and the military.
- In the Soviet Union, Joseph Stalin imposed a brutal dictatorship, which industrialized Russia quickly.
- In Italy, Benito Mussolini developed an extreme form of militaristic nationalism, fascism, and became prime minister in 1922, establishing a fascist dictatorship over the course of the next few years.
- In Germany, Adolf Hitler added anti-Semitism to fascism to create Nazism. When Hitler was appointed chancellor in 1933, the Nazis quickly eradiated democracy and established a powerful Nazi state.

- World War II was begun, after several years of British and French appeasement of German demands, by the German invasion of Poland. By 1940, Britain stood alone against Germany. The United States and the Soviet Union were each attacked in 1941 and joined the war. Japan built a large puppet empire in Asia. Most of the decisive battles of the war in both Asia and Europe took place in 1942 and 1943. By the time the war ended in 1945, May in Europe and August in Asia, more than 50 million people, civilians as well as soldiers, had died.

AUTHORITARIAN STATES

CONSERVATIVE AUTHORITARIANISM

Conservative authoritarian leaders sought to prevent social change that would threaten traditional power elites. Like Catherine the Great and Metternich in the eighteenth and nineteenth centuries, they relied on their bureaucracies and armies, repressed political discussion, and persecuted dissidents. But they had little interest in the private lives of their subjects; as long as people did not actively oppose the government, they had a certain freedom. After World War I, Spain and Portugal and virtually all the states in eastern Europe, with the important exception of Czechoslovakia, became authoritarian dictatorships. Most of these states had had weak democratic traditions, and such dictatorships appealed to nationalists, militarists, aristocrats, and landlords trying to prevent land reform.

RADICAL TOTALITARIAN DICTATORSHIPS

Both authoritarian and totalitarian regimes rejected the entire liberal agenda of democracy, parliamentary governments, and civil liberties. But while the conservative authoritarian governments sought to maintain the status quo, radical totalitarian dictatorships sought to make profound changes in society and to create a radical new man. They took control over all aspects of public life and legislated private life as well. They generated huge support and extraordinary effort from their subjects.

- The origins of totalitarianism, which in either right-wing or left-wing versions emerged in the 1920s and 1930s, have been a topic of scholarly debate. Some see them in the waging of total war during World War I and in Vladimir Lenin's establishment of a one-party, minority dictatorship in Russia. Other analysts stress the use of modern technology and communications and the highly developed apparatus of the state to control every aspect of life. Still others focus on the glorification of violence, the absolute commitment to the cause, and the sense of constant, *permanent revolution*. Although there are many similarities, Nazi Germany and Soviet Russia were profoundly different because of their ideologies. In Stalin's Russia, private property, but not personal property, and the middle classes were eliminated. In Nazi Germany, both private property and the middle classes thrived but were turned toward achieving extreme nationalistic goals.

AP Tip

One element common to all forms of totalitarian dictatorships is the cult of the leader, whose image is everywhere and who is treated with the devotion and obedience given to a godhead. Typically, radical totalitarian states such as Nazi Germany do not survive the death of the leader for very long. A second common element in totalitarian states is the demand that citizens cede to the state personal loyalties that previously had been apportioned to family, community, and church. The state is all-powerful.

In the 1930s, Marxists and liberals passionately opposed the fascists' denunciation of liberal values. Marxists condemned fascism's efforts to mobilize a mass movement in opposition to socialism. In the 1950s comparative studies of fascist movements delineated common elements of glorification of war and violence, nationalistic expansionism, antisocialism, a charismatic leader, and support by capitalists and landowners. In recent years, historians have emphasized not the commonalities but the distinctive forms of fascism in each country, especially to explain why fascists came to power in Italy and Germany.

STALIN'S SOVIET UNION

The Bolsheviks won the two-year civil war, but Russia was in ruins. Both agriculture and industry had been devastated, and the worst famine in generations loomed in 1921, leading to peasant riots and naval mutinies. In response, Lenin instituted the New Economic Policy (NEP), which allowed a compromise with some elements of capitalism. Peasants were allowed to sell their surpluses at market prices, and small traders and manufacturers reopened for business, while major industries, banks, and utilities remained under governmental control. NEP brought Russia back to economic strength, with both industrial and agricultural production nearing or surpassing prewar levels. During the period of NEP, censorship also lightened, and Russian artists, like the abstractionist artist Malevich (see p. 950), were freely innovative.

Lenin died in 1924, leading to a power struggle between Leon Trotsky, his right-hand man and the inspiring and effective commander of the Red Army during the civil war, and Stalin, the party secretary who effectively used his position to garner support, although Lenin had warned against him. Stalin advocated "socialism in one country" as the way to make Marxism work in Russia in contrast to Trotsky's idea of permanent revolution, which insisted on socialist internationalism. Stalin's denunciation of NEP appealed to orthodox Bolsheviks, and with their support, he achieved supreme power by 1927. He soon ousted Trotsky and suppressed Trotsky's followers, ready to launch his own revolution from the top.

THE FIVE-YEAR PLANS

Stalin sought to industrialize Russia quickly, and to do so, he instituted the first of several Five-Year Plans in 1927. Each set high targets for heavy industry and agriculture production, the latter to be achieved by collectivization, in order to prevent a return to capitalism and help Russia catch up economically and militarily with the hostile West. Stalin's 1931 speech in Listening to the Past highlights his urgency to end Russian backwardness and vulnerability.

AP Tip

NEP had created a class of wealthier peasants who did well in its liberalized agricultural system. Collectivization was a way to eliminate this capitalistic and conservative group, as well as to create large farms that, in theory, would be more efficient in their use of machinery and animals and in their organization of labor. Family farms that are too small are rarely highly productive.

Collectivization was a way for Russia to generate the capital needed for industrialization. The peasants, who had—with the land reform of the revolution—finally acquired the land they had long sought, fiercely resisted it. Peasants killed their animals rather than let them be collectivized; about half of all livestock were killed between 1929 and 1933. The more prosperous peasants, the kulaks, were designated a dangerous group who, Stalin said, had to be "liquidated as a class." The term *kulak* itself became an insult. Stalin sent millions of men, women, and children to forced labor camps, where conditions were so harsh (see photograph on p. 951) that many died. The liquidation was particularly fierce toward Ukrainians, also vilified as reactionary nationalists. In 1932, the government refused to reduce the high quotas for grain deliveries even during a human-made famine; it is estimated that some 6 million Ukrainians died.

AP Tip

Some historians consider this treatment of the Ukrainians an act of genocide in that it targeted a specific nationality. The economic argument for continuing to export the grain abroad was that it was the only way for Russia to earn hard cash to pay for industrial development, since during the depression in Europe, there was nothing else the Russians could sell.

Collectivization was a success in that the vast majority of peasants lived on collective farms. But peasants continued to resist this "second serfdom" and forced the government to make compromises and allow families to have plots on which to grow their own food. These family plots produced nearly a quarter of all Soviet produce; in general collective farms did not do very well.

The industrial goals of the Five Year Plans, however, had spectacular results, achieving the most rapid growth of any industrializing country. Massive urbanization accompanied the expansion of heavy industry. But the workers paid the price; about a third of the net income was reinvested, and consumer goods were much less developed and often of poor quality. Industrial cities were built, some in western Siberia and often with foreign engineers, including some Americans. Labor unions lost most of their power to the government, which determined where workers worked and lived.

AP Tip

One reason why Marxism was so attractive to newly independent states seeking rapid industrialization after World War II was that the Soviet Union modeled how a nation could move quickly from being backward to modern and powerful—and do so without utter dependency on foreign capital.

LIFE AND CULTURE IN SOVIET SOCIETY

Stalinism was a radical form of Marxism expecting to create a new type of human being, as well as an economically and militarily strong Russia. The system Stalin created lasted for some fifty years. In the 1930s, the standard of living did not improve, as there were few consumer goods to purchase, and real wages grew slowly. Most people lived on a poor diet of black bread, though vodka was plentiful, resided in poorly built and crowded housing, and had shabby clothes. But workers had guaranteed jobs and were given pensions, free medical care, free education, and free day-care centers. There were many opportunities for advancement as managers and engineers. Egalitarianism was replaced by a new class system, with unskilled workers paid poorly and the managerial elite, whether industrial or political, paid well and having privileges.

Women's lives were radically transformed, perhaps more than any other single group. Women were given full equal rights after the November Revolution, including divorce and abortion, and were encouraged to be free sexually and work outside the home, as in fact they had to do because wages were too low for a man to support a family alone. Some women did hard physical work on farms, in factories, and in construction, while others pursued higher education and quite a few became doctors (about 75 percent of Russian doctors were women) and engineers.

AP Tip

One reason why Russian women were so necessary in the work force was the terrible loss of manpower during both world wars.

Art and culture were similarly changed. Socialist realism, stylized art that glorified the workers, Russia, and the Communist Party (see p. 953) turned art, literature, film, and music into agents of propaganda, with successful artists invited into the Soviet elite. Radio and newspapers became tools for indoctrination. Stalin's image was everywhere.

STALINIST TERROR AND THE GREAT PURGES

The Stalinist transformation of Russia was accompanied by persecution, imprisonment, or death of millions of Soviet citizens. A reign of terror was launched in 1934 after the assassination of Sergey Kirov, one of Stalin's closest associates. The first victims were Old Bolsheviks, comrades of Lenin during the revolution. One after another, they were arrested, accused of treason, and put on trial publicly, after which most were executed. Their images were even edited out of photographs and paintings. Lower party officials, intellectuals, army officers, and many ordinary citizens were similarly arrested, often in secret, and condemned to labor camps. While the numbers are not known exactly, at least 8 million people were executed or never returned from labor camps. The Communist Party replenished itself with 1.5 million new members, mostly upwardly mobile technocrats of worker origin. Stalin's purges sent clear warnings to people not to dissent or challenge the regime and encouraged loyalty to the party. But was the perceived threat real? Imagined or real enemies seem to be inherent to totalitarian states. On the other hand, many in the population seem to have shared Stalin's fears and, in a sort of mass hysteria or witch-hunt, enthusiastically collaborated with the mass terror.

MUSSOLINI AND FASCISM IN ITALY

Italian fascism was a combination of revolutionary nationalism and conservatism. The Italian constitutional monarchy created in 1870 became more liberal after World War I with universal manhood suffrage. Much of southern Italy was still poor and agricultural, and the Catholic Church remained a potent force, especially after 1921 when a powerful Catholic party emerged. Before the war, the elite ran Italy largely for their own benefit. The Italian Socialist party was strong, and the only one in Europe that had opposed World War I. The war proved disappointing on many fronts. Italy joined the Allies for territorial reasons but was disheartened by what they received in the peace settlement. Workers and peasants, inspired by the Russian Revolution and frustrated by inadequate progress after the war, began a series of strikes. In this volatile situation, support for parliamentary democracy was thin.

AP Tip

Italy had joined the Allied side in the war after signing the secret Treaty of London in 1915, which promised the Italians they would receive the *irredenta,* border areas where Italians lived in the Austrian Empire, on Allied victory. In the peace settlement, Italy did receive some but not all of those territories. Many Italians felt disappointed and angry about this.

Mussolini was originally a Socialist newspaper editor but he broke with the party over the issue of the war. After the war, he and some fellow veterans formed a band of fascists. Their program, developed over a couple of years, was a combination of extreme nationalism and a new type of anti-Marxist socialism promising benefits to workers but an end to class strife and the restoration of order and Italian greatness.

AP Tip

The fasces, a bundle of rods with an axe, was a symbol of the Roman Empire. The Italian fascists promised to restore Italy to the greatness it once had had. Fascism appealed originally to many veterans who had enjoyed the comradeship and intensity of the previous war.

The fascist private militia, called the Blackshirts, destroyed Socialist Party newspapers and union halls and had the especially nasty habit of forcing their enemies to drink castor oil. They created enough chaos so that in 1922, when the Blackshirts staged a March on Rome, Mussolini presented himself as the defender of law and order and was appointed prime minister by King Victor Emmanuel III. The fascist seizure of power was completely legal.

THE REGIME IN ACTION

While many of the Blackshirts hoped for a revolution, Mussolini's conservative and middle-class supporters were mostly concerned about preventing a Bolshevik-style revolution. An electoral law giving the party that won the plurality two-thirds of the seats in the Chamber of Deputies gave the fascists the parliamentary majority in 1924. When the Blackshirts killed the Socialist leader Giacomo Matteotti and calls for their dissolution abounded, Mussolini responded with severe repression, government by decree, strict censorship of the media, a one-party state, the end of independent labor unions, and fixed elections. A youth movement was created to indoctrinate the young. Mussolini's slogan "Everything in the state, nothing outside the state, nothing against the state," represented the fascist, totalitarian ideal.

AP Tip

Fascism tried to end class warfare by creating a corporate state in which each industry was run by a board with representatives of workers, employers, and government. In theory the three elements would work together; in practice, the workers lost out. There were no strikes, however.

Italian fascism was never fully totalitarian. Italy was never a very thorough police state, and relatively few political prisoners were condemned to death. The old power structure was not replaced as it was in Russia or Germany but remained in control. The Lateran Agreement of 1929 negotiated a settlement with the papacy after nearly sixty years of hostile relations between church and state. The Vatican was recognized as an independent state and given financial aid in return for support for Mussolini's government. Under fascism, women lost the right to divorce and were expected to stay home and breed. Restrictive laws limiting women's access to higher-paying jobs, and curtailing the rights of Jews, were passed in 1938.

> **AP Tip**
>
> The king remained on the throne, although completely ineffectual, throughout the entire fascist period. When World War II ended, Italy became a republic.

HITLER AND NAZISM IN GERMANY

Nazism was the most extreme and most disturbing form of fascism, going way beyond the Italian fascism in its thorough takeover of society and its mobilization of the economy for war. It was distinguished by its virulent, vicious anti-Semitism and its aggressive expansionism. It had many complex roots, and there were many reasons for its achievement of power. Among these were the following:

- The dynamic leadership of Hitler, an Austrian high school dropout who soaked up political anti-Semitism, anti-Slav racism, antiliberalism, and anticapitalism from Karl Lueger (see Chapter 25) and other German nationalists in Vienna before the war. Racism and anti-Semitism became the key elements in Hitler's ideology. Hitler served with relish in the Bavarian army in World War I, and afterward joined the tiny German Workers' Party in Munich. He soon turned it into a significant political force through the successful use of the mass rally and other methods of mass propaganda.
- Anti-Semitism was a useful tool to attack both communism and large-scale capitalism in one fell swoop; Marx and Trotsky's Jewish origins and the financial success of some Jews gave credence to the so-called international Jewish conspiracy as the single scapegoat for Germany's and Austria's ills, including the defeat in the war and the Versailles Treaty. Hitler's deep racism against Jews and Slavs appeared on virtually every page of his best-selling *Mein Kampf* and justified his promises of conquering "living space" for Germans.
- National Socialism rejected free-market capitalism as hurting ordinary people and promised government action on their behalf, and at the same time relentlessly criticized Marxism and Bolshevism for their egalitarianism and internationalism. This combination of anticapitalism and nationalism appealed greatly to the lower-middle-class shopkeepers, office workers, and peasants who feared both economic dislocation and Bolshevism.
- Hitler's denunciation of the Weimar Republic for its liberalism and for its "treason" in signing the Treaty of Versailles fell on mostly deaf ears when Germany had recovered from the difficulties of the immediate postwar period. When the depression hit Germany hard (see Chapter 28), his criticisms gained credibility, and his self-appointment as the leader, führer, who should have unlimited power to solve Germany's problems, seemed to offer a way out of the morass. In 1932, when the unemployment rate in Germany

reached a horrific 43 percent, the Nazis became the largest party in the Reichstag.

- Hitler was a master propagandist who used simple slogans over and over again to whip up support. Nazism offered a sense of belonging, excitement, and optimism in dark times, particularly to the young. It was largely a movement led and populated by young people; almost 40 percent of the Nazi Party members were under thirty in 1931.
- The government of the Weimar Republic effectively broke down in 1930, unable to deal with the depression, with Chancellor Heinrich Brüning and President Paul von Hindenburg (of World War I fame) ruling by decree but making bad decisions and hurting the government's credibility.
- The left was disunited, with Social Democrats and Communists battling each other and underestimating the threat from the extreme right.
- Hitler was a clever politician, making alliances in 1932 with conservatives in the army and big business. They were convinced that they could control him if he were appointed chancellor, which President Hindenburg did on January 30, 1933.

THE NAZI STATE AND SOCIETY

> **AP Tip**
>
> The Nazis called their state the Third Reich, or the third German government, the first being the Holy Roman Empire established by Otto I and the second the Kaiserreich established by Bismarck. The Weimar Republic, seen by the Nazis as treasonous, was not counted.

THE GOVERNMENT Unlike Mussolini, Hitler quickly established a totalitarian dictatorship. When the Reichstag building caught on fire shortly after his appointment as chancellor, Hitler blamed the communists. Hindenburg was persuaded to severely restrict civil liberties, and the Reichstag passed the Enabling Act in March 1933, which gave Hitler dictatorial powers. All independent organizations and other political parties were banned; Germany became a one-party state. Nazi Party members took over government bureaucracies, where they were under the Party's direct control in various Nazi organizations. The Nazi government was often inefficient with overlapping jurisdictions and bureaucratic rivalries.

THE ECONOMY Strikes were forbidden, and independent labor unions were abolished, replaced by the Nazi Labor Front. The Nazi government initiated huge public works projects—highways, stadiums, and public housing—to provide jobs and appointed a conservative banker to restore credit. In 1936, Germany began to rearm and prepare for war; this reduced unemployment so successfully that there was a shortage of workers by 1938. The standard of living for most people grew modestly, business profits grew as well, and opportunities abounded.

Civil Liberties and Artistic Freedom Both were ruthlessly repressed. Books written by Jews, socialists, and democrats were burned. There was censorship of the press and publishing, control over school and university curricula, and prohibitions of modern art, architecture, and music. The Gestapo, the Nazi political police, effectively ferreted out, arrested, and interned in concentration camps perceived enemies of the regime. Tens of thousands of opponents, initially communists and socialists on the left but later leaders of the Protestant and Catholic churches, were interned, and many were executed.

The Army Soldiers took an oath of personal loyalty to Hitler. The leadership of the Nazi equivalent of fascist Blackshirts, the S.A., also called the Brownshirts or Stormtroopers, was eliminated in a purge in 1934 (the Night of the Long Knives) because their demands for real revolution threatened Hitler's conservative supporters. The SS, an elite force, originally Hitler's personal guard, grew in importance under the leadership of Heinrich Himmler, and, with the Gestapo, were the enforcers of the totalitarian dictatorship.

Jews The Jews began to lose their rights almost immediately. By 1934, most Jewish professionals had lost their jobs and rights. The Nuremberg Laws of 1935 deprived them of German citizenship. Many German Jews emigrated, and even more left after the pogrom called *Kristallnacht,* in November 1938, destroyed Jewish religious and personal property and put many Jewish men into concentration camps. Other groups singled out for persecution were Slavs, Gypsies, Jehovah's Witnesses, communists, and homosexuals.

The Society Hitler had promised a social revolution, and to some degree the commonness of purpose felt by many Germans and the Nazi movement's empowering of the young, rootless, and poorly educated narrowed the division between classes. Studies have shown that in fact there was little real social leveling during the Nazi years. "Inferior" members of the German race, such as the deformed, the mentally ill, and the mentally retarded, were killed off in the late 1930s to "purify the race."

Hitler Hitler's popularity grew because of the Nazi success in lowering unemployment and because his triumphs in foreign policy confirmed the sense of superiority felt by German nationalists.

Aggression and Appeasements, 1933–1939

Underlying the Nazi domestic program was the goal of German territorial expansion, legitimized by notions of racial superiority, particularly to acquire living space (*lebensraum*) in the east. This Nazi goal was achieved in the 1930s through a series of carefully managed steps.

- Germany withdrew from the League of Nations in October 1933.
- Germany established a general military draft, instituted rearmament, and in March 1935 declared null and void those provisions of the Treaty of Versailles that limited the German armed forces. France, Italy, and Britain protested the German rearmament but took no action.

- Britain's primary goal was to avoid war and to assuage feelings of guilt over what had become to be seen as the unfair Treaty of Versailles. Many conservatives in Britain were more concerned about Soviet Russia than they were about Nazi Germany. Britain therefore followed a policy of appeasement, giving in to Hitler's demands, until September 1939.
- Germany was no longer isolated after 1935. In that year, Britain signed a naval agreement with Germany, and when Mussolini attacked Ethiopia, Germany supported Italy. In 1936, Italy and Germany signed the Axis Pact, soon to be joined by Japan. Germany intervened in the Spanish Civil War on the side of the rebels, supporting Franco with arms and air strikes. The republican government was given support only by the Soviet Union and fell to Franco in 1939.
- In 1936, Hitler remilitarized the Rhineland in direct opposition to the Treaty of Versailles. Britain refused to act, and France would not act alone.
- Hitler planned to incorporate Austria and German-speaking parts of Czechoslovakia, the Sudentenland, into Germany. In March 1938, under the threat of invasion, the Austrian chancellor put Austrian Nazis in charge of the government; the German armies marched into Vienna unopposed. *Anschluss,* the union of Germany and Austria forbidden by the Treaty of Versailles, was accomplished without violence. When later that year Hitler demanded the Sudetenland, Czechoslovakia, the only democratic state in central or eastern Europe at that time, was abandoned by its French ally and by the British, who at the famous conference in Munich, ceded the Sudentenland to Hitler. Joseph Chamberlain, the British prime minister who negotiated the deal, returned home saying he had achieved "peace in our time."
- Although Hitler had promised that the Sudentenland was the end of his ambitions, in March 1939 he occupied the rest of Czechoslovakia. Nazi aggression now seemed real to Britain and France, who announced they would defend Poland.
- Soviet Russia and Nazi Germany signed a mutual nonaggression treaty in August 1939, with a secret protocol to divide up Poland and the Baltic states.
- Secure on his eastern front and discounting the western states as hopelessly weak, Hitler ordered the German invasion of Poland on September 1, 1939. Two days later, Britain and France declared war on Germany; World War II had begun.

WORLD WAR II

For the first three years of the war, the Germans had unending success on the battlefield using tactics known as blitzkrieg, or lightning war, which involved first air strikes to weaken defenses, then invasion with overwhelming numbers of tanks and soldiers brought in by truck. Poland was defeated in four weeks in the fall of 1939 and was divvied up between Germany and Russia. In the spring of 1940, Denmark, Norway, Holland, and Belgium fell quickly to German forces. British forces retreated to Dunkirk but were evacuated through extraordinary efforts of civilians and the army alike. France fell in a few weeks in May 1940. The Germans divided France into two parts, the north under German occupation directed from Paris, and the south, where a puppet, nominally independent, regime in Vichy was headed by the World War I hero Marshall Philippe Pétain. From June 1940 to June 1941, the only nation at war with Germany was Britain. Hitler's plans to invade Britain were frustrated when Britain won the air Battle of Britain, although Germany relentlessly bombed British military and civilian targets. The combination of civilian determination, stirred by the oratory of the new prime minister Winston Churchill, the quick retooling of the economy for aircraft production, and the fighting spirit of the Royal Air Force, saved Britain from defeat and invasion.

Germany turned its attention eastward in the spring of 1941, first to the Balkans and then on June 22, 1941, to the Soviet Union—an invasion that broke the nonaggression pact. Initially successful with penetration of the Soviet Union along a 1,000-mile front and surrounding the city of Leningrad, the German advance was stopped by the bitter winter of 1941–1942.

The New Order

The Germans ruled from the western coast of Europe all the way to deep inside the Soviet Union in 1942 and established the New Order to fulfill their racial and imperialistic goals. Nordic peoples, racially close to the Germans, received preferential treatment, while Slavic peoples in the east were considered subhumans whose only purpose was to be slave laborers to serve the "master race." Slavic lands were turned over to Germans, and Slavs, as well as Gypsies, Jehovah's Witnesses, and Jews, were intensely exploited and put to work for Germans under the harsh and all too effective supervision of the SS. Should laborers die from their awful conditions, so much the better for the master race.

The Holocaust

A special place in this vast German empire was held for the Jews, whose physical extermination had been articulated as an early Nazi goal. When Germans occupied Poland and other eastern lands, they began to work toward this goal by moving all Jews into ghettoes or slave-labor camps. In 1941, extermination began in earnest, first by shooting Jews and burying them in mass graves and then by building a series of extermination camps to use modern technology to achieve the "final solution" to the "Jewish question."

AP Tip

The goal was to make Germany *judenrein*, "free of Jews." The dehumanizing treatment of the German Jews led about half of them to leave Germany before the war. When Germany occupied eastern Europe, the number of Jews under its command jumped to 11 million. With such huge numbers and ongoing war preventing movement of peoples, only murder could achieve the goal of making the Germanic empire *judenrein*. The plans for the execution of the final solution were laid at the Wannsee Conference in January 1942.

Jews were deported from the ghettoes in systematic liquidations, packed into cattle cars, and sent on trains to extermination camps. Once there many people were put immediately to death in gas chambers that looked like communal showers and held up to 200 people. The corpses were then burned in crematoria. Others were put to work in slave-labor camps where many died of disease and starvation. The daily brutality and complex moral choices in the lives of this group were vividly documented by the works of Primo Levi (see Individuals in Society). German efficiency was able to kill up to 12,000 people per day in Auschwitz-Birkenau. Some 6 million Jews were killed by the end of the war in 1945.

Historians have long debated how to explain this enormous crime. Originally, blame was placed squarely on the Nazi leadership. Recent scholarship has emphasized the willing participation of large numbers of ordinary Germans in the Holocaust, and its passive acceptance by millions of others. A controversial recent book by Daniel Goldhagen called the Germans Hitler's "willing executioners" and detailed the widespread anti-Semitism of the Germans and others in the occupied territories. Scholars are now focusing on how ordinary people, fed by Nazi propaganda, under peer pressure, and inoculated by the brutality of the war, became willing participants in mass murder or at least indifferent to the criminal mistreatment of so many of their former neighbors.

AP Tip

The Holocaust remains an issue of intense interest and endless debate. Why did Germany and Austria, home to many emancipated and previously accepted Jews, become centers of political anti-Semitism? What was the impact of the Holocaust on the German war effort? Could more Jews have been saved, and how? What was the response of Britain and the United States, and what could or should they have done? How could physicians who take the Hippocratic oath of "do no harm" conduct horrible experiments on humans and select people to live or die in the extermination camps? What could the Jews have done to save themselves? The list of questions goes on and on; they are worthy of further study, especially as there are neo-Nazis who deny the Holocaust took place at all and have substantial funds to promote their views on seemingly objective websites (so be careful when you're surfing the Internet!).

Japan's Empire in Asia

Japan by the 1930s was dominated by ultranationalists who touted Japan's mission in Asia and demanded absolute obedience to the emperor. Japan invaded China in 1937 but was unable to defeat either the Nationalists or the Communists. They took advantage of the European war by attacking European colonies in Asia, aiming to guarantee their supplies of oil and scrap metal. Japan invaded Indochina in 1941 and threatened Dutch Indonesia, resulting in increased tensions with the United States, which punished Japanese aggression by cutting off the sale of U.S. oil, dramatically reducing Japan's oil supply. Expecting a war with the United States at some point, Japan made a preemptive strike against the U.S. fleet at Pearl Harbor in Hawaii on December 7, 1941. The United States immediately declared war on Japan, and Hitler declared war on the United States.

Initially the Japanese successfully attacked European and U.S. colonies in Southeast Asia, claiming to be liberators, and created a vast empire, which they called the East Asian Co-Prosperity Sphere. While they had promised independence, Japanese military commanders ruled the newly "liberated" colonies, often with great cruelty. The colonies' standard of living declined as Japan used their resources and population for the war effort, since Japan itself lacked sufficient resources and labor supplies.

The Grand Alliance

The enemies of the Axis powers—Britain, Russia, and the United States—were brought together by chance and did not share a common ideology or goals. Both the United States and the Soviet Union were brought into the war by unexpected attacks. The United States and Britain agreed to Churchill's strategy to win the war in Europe first, and then attack Japan with an all-out effort, as well as plan the eventual peace, only after the defeat of Germany. They committed to fight until the unconditional surrender of Germany and Japan, which nullified German attempts to break apart the Grand Alliance but also meant that fighting would continue to the bitter end

The United States had exceptional industrial might, outproducing its enemies and indeed the rest of the world by 1943 when it produced 100,000 aircraft, for example. Britain's industries, totally mobilized for war, were less important to Allied victory, but Britain played a crucial role as the strategic center for the Allied war on the continent. The Soviet Union had extraordinary strengths. It moved its industrial plant and a large percentage of its population east of the Urals out of the path of German armies. Effective if tardy mobilization for war, Russian nationalism, and the sacrifices of its people underlay the ultimate success of the Great Patriotic War of the Fatherland. Anti-German resistance, which was dominated by communists virtually everywhere in Europe, aided the Grand Alliance.

THE WAR IN EUROPE, 1942–1945

1942 proved to be the turning point of the war. The Germans renewed their offensive in Russia in the spring of 1942, going after the southern city of Stalingrad. There, in November, the Soviet forces counterattacked and trapped the German forces, killing two-thirds and accepting the surrender of the remaining troops. Hitler, who had refused to permit a retreat, was dealt a catastrophic defeat, and soon the Soviet forces were on the offensive. In May 1942, the Germans suffered an important defeat at El Alamein in North Africa, which allowed Allied forces to land in Morocco and Algeria and drive the Germans from North Africa by the spring of 1943. From there, the Allies invaded Sicily and began the march to Berlin. The Italians deposed Mussolini and surrendered to the Allies, which German forces would not permit. German armies took over Rome and northern Italy, forcing the Allies to battle their way north in what proved to be bitter and destructive fighting. Germany fought back against the turning tide by intense mobilization for war and by using millions of prisoners of war and slave laborers to triple production. Hitler survived a German officers' attempt to assassinate him in July 1944.

AP Tip

Some of the origins of the cold war lay in the way World War II was waged. The striking discrepancy between the military death tolls of the Soviet Union and the United States—Soviet losses were ten times American losses—and the issue of the second front helped feed Soviet suspicions of the United States. Eisenhower's slow pace in leading the Allied forces east to Berlin allowed the Russians to liberate Berlin and set the stage for cold war conflicts there.

On June 6, 1944, the largest naval force in history invaded German-held France, landing some 2 million men on Normandy's beaches, who began to free Europe from the Nazi yoke. British and U.S. forces liberated western Europe and entered Germany in March 1945, while the Red Army liberated Poland, Rumania, Hungary, and Yugoslavia; in

April 1945 the Allied armies met at the Elbe river. Hitler committed suicide at the end of that month, and on May 7 Germany surrendered.

THE WAR IN THE PACIFIC, 1942–1945

The war in the Pacific was determined largely, also in 1942, by great naval battles: Coral Sea in May, which ended the Japanese threat to Australia, Midway the next month, in which the Americans destroyed enough of the Japanese fleet to establish naval equity with them, and Guadalcanal, which the Americans took after heavy fighting in August. In 1943, the United States and its ally Australia began island hopping to defeat Japan, with saturation bombing followed by manned invasion. The Asian war was brutal, filled with mutual hatred and racism and atrocities committed by both sides. The U.S. forces, for example, rarely took prisoners.

In 1944, the Battle of Leyte Gulf, the greatest battle in naval history, was a major victory for the United States, but the Japanese continued to fight with determination and bravery. Two bloody battles, Iwo Jima and Okinawa, in February and June 1945, led U.S. commanders to believe that an invasion of Japan proper would cost a million U.S. lives. On August 6, 1945, the United States dropped its newly developed atomic bombs on Hiroshima and three days later on Nagasaki, killing and maiming hundreds of thousands in a single moment. The Japanese surrendered on August 14, 1945.

Multiple-Choice Questions

1. What was the primary difference between authoritarian and radical totalitarian states?
   (A) Antiliberalism
   (B) Importance given to the military
   (C) Absence of parliamentary democracy
   (D) Privacy and control of family life
   (E) Strength of centralized government

2. The only democratic state in eastern and central Europe in the 1930s was
   (A) Yugoslavia.
   (B) Hungary.
   (C) Poland.
   (D) Bulgaria.
   (E) Czechoslovakia.

3. Fascism's attitude toward socialism was
   (A) complete rejection.
   (B) to replace Marxist socialism with new types of programs for workers.
   (C) that socialism could only be achieved slowly and voluntarily.
   (D) anticommunist but pro-union.
   (E) to merge with socialist parties to create a powerful new party.

4. In both Germany's and Italy's cases, fascists came to power
   (A) because they threatened to use violence.
   (B) because they won parliamentary majorities.
   (C) because they had won parliamentary pluralities.
   (D) completely constitutionally.
   (E) because they were appointed.

5. Mussolini and Hitler shared which aspect of their pasts before taking power?
   (A) Both had been socialists in their youth.
   (B) Both had become fierce patriots of their native countries.
   (C) Both had fought in World War I.
   (D) Both had become anti-Semitic in their youth.
   (E) Both were very poor as children.

6. The Fascist Party in Italy held the majority of the seats in the Chamber of Deputies after
   (A) winning a majority in the election of 1924.
   (B) passage of an electoral reform bill.
   (C) expelling the representatives of the Socialist Party.
   (D) the establishment of the one-party state and fixed elections.
   (E) the death of Matteotti.

7. Stalin's general industrial goals in the Five-Year Plans were
   (A) never met.
   (B) about as successful as collectivized agriculture.
   (C) remarkably successful.
   (D) successful but only marginally so.
   (E) undermined by the depression in Europe.

8. One goal of the collectivization of agriculture in the Soviet Union was to
   (A) equalize the landholdings of the peasant.
   (B) provide employment for unemployed urbanites.
   (C) use the land for industrial production.
   (D) remove the kulak class.
   (E) remove peasants from land with substantial mineral resources needed by the state.

9. Nazi economic policies
   (A) were no more successful than the Weimar government's policies in dealing with the depression.
   (B) were hardly different from those of the British and French governments of the early 1930s.
   (C) relied on private initiatives to restore production and employment.
   (D) were successful because they managed to win over the labor union leadership.
   (E) created huge state public works projects.

10. The tide of war definitively turned against the Germans when
    (A) Hitler refused to let his army retreat from Stalingrad in 1942.
    (B) D-Day began in 1944.
    (C) the Allied armies met at the Elbe in 1945.
    (D) the Holocaust took much of German army personnel to execute.
    (E) Italy surrendered to the Allies in 1943.

11. Recent historical scholarship on the Holocaust focuses on the responsibility of
    (A) the Nazi leadership.
    (B) the members of the Nazi Party.
    (C) the Poles.
    (D) ordinary German citizens.
    (E) the Allies.

12. The Nazi state and the Italian fascist state differed in the degree to which they
    (A) were opposed to democracy.
    (B) replaced traditional elites and government bureaucrats with party members.
    (C) stressed nationalism.
    (D) allowed communists and socialists to publicize their views.
    (E) idolized their leaders.

13. Japan's chief motive in establishing the Asian Co-Prosperity Sphere was to
    (A) ensure supplies of oil and other raw materials.
    (B) prove Japanese military superiority.
    (C) provide living space for its large population.
    (D) back the nationalists against the communists in China.
    (E) take Australia.

14. The single most important factor in the rise of the Nazi Party to political power was
    (A) Hitler's brilliant political leadership.
    (B) the example of Italy.
    (C) the collapse of the Weimar government.
    (D) the depression.
    (E) President Hindenburg's adoption of Nazism.

15. The mistaken judgment behind British appeasement at Munich was first clearly demonstrated when Germany
    (A) united with Austria.
    (B) occupied Czechoslovakia.
    (C) remilitarized the Rhineland.
    (D) instituted the draft.
    (E) withdrew from the League of Nations.

Free-Response Questions

1. Compare the goals and practices of Nazi Germany and Stalinist Russia in the 1930s. How did these help prepare for war?

2. How did the political decisions made during the war influence the military course of World War II?

ANSWERS

MULTIPLE-CHOICE QUESTIONS

1. (D) Totalitarian states intruded into private and family life while authoritarian states didn't bother to. The latter were mostly interested in maintaining the status quo, while the former sought to remake society. (McKay, *A History of Western Society*, 8th ed., pp. 954–955/9th ed., pp. 946–949)

2. (E) Conservative dictators took over everywhere in eastern Europe except Czechoslovakia. (McKay, *A History of Western Society*, 8th ed., p. 951/9th ed., p. 946)

3. (B) Fascism was profoundly anticommunist and anti-union and sought to replace socialism with a different type of socialism that would provide benefits for workers and replace unions with state-run workers' organizations. (McKay, *A History of Western Society*, 8th ed., pp. 964–966/9th ed., pp. 955–956)

4. (D) Both Hitler and Mussolini were appointed to their positions, chancellor and prime minister, respectively, Hitler by President Hindenburg and Mussolini by the king of Italy. In both cases, their parties did not have a majority, but their appointments were fully constitutional. (McKay, *A History of Western Society*, 8th ed., pp. 964–965, 967–969/9th ed., pp. 956, 960)

5. (C) Both Hitler and Mussolini did military service at the front in World War I. Hitler despised his native Austria and left it. He was never a socialist. Mussolini was not particularly anti-Semitic. (McKay, *A History of Western Society*, 8th ed., pp. 964, 966–967/9th ed., pp. 955, 957–958)

6. (B) The Chamber of Deputies passed legislation shortly after Mussolini became prime minister that would give a two-thirds majority of the seats to the party that won the plurality. The deputies voted for it because they did not think that the small Fascist Party had much of a chance. (McKay, *A History of Western Society*, 8th ed., p. 965/9th ed., p. 956)

7. (C) Unlike in agriculture, industrial development was stupendous under the Five-Year Plan. (McKay, *A History of Western Society*, 8th ed., p. 961/9th ed., pp. 950–952)

8. (D) The political goal of collectivization was to eliminate the kulaks, whom Stalin saw as capitalistic and conservative. The collectivized lands were by and large used for agriculture, not industry. During this period, there was massive urbanization as well. (McKay, *A History of Western Society*, 8th ed., pp. 959–960/9th ed., pp. 951–952)

9. (E) The Nazi government generated jobs with large-scale public works projects and later with rearmament. (McKay, *A History of Western Society*, 8th ed., p. 970/9th ed., p. 961)

10. (A) By not allowing his army to retreat, some 300,000 German soldiers were lost and the Soviets gained the initiative. (McKay, *A History of Western Society*, 8th ed., p. 981/9th ed., p. 973)

11. (D) Whereas earlier research focused on the Nazi leadership's responsibility, recent scholarship has focused on the acceptance of the Holocaust by ordinary German citizens. (McKay, *A History of Western Society*, 8th ed., p. 980/9th ed., pp. 969–970)

12. (B) The fascist revolution in Italy was less deep and thoroughgoing than the one in Germany. (McKay, *A History of Western Society*, 8th ed., pp. 966, 969–970/9th ed., pp. 956–957, 960–962)

13. (A) Japan lacks natural resources like oil. (McKay, *A History of Western Society*, not in the 8th ed./9th ed., p. 970)

14. (D) It was because of the high unemployment caused by the depression that the Nazi Party grew in votes and membership; before that, it had been a relatively small party. (McKay, *A History of Western Society*, 8th ed., p. 967/9th ed., pp. 958–960)

15. (B) It was only when the Germans occupied what remained of Czechoslovakia in March 1939 that the proponents of appeasement realized that Hitler was not going to be satisfied with Austria and the Sudentenland. (McKay, *A History of Western Society*, 8th ed., p. 973/9th ed., p. 965)

Free-Response Questions

1. This question asks for the similarities and differences in the goals and practices of Nazi Germany and Stalinist Russian in the 1930s and how they helped prepare for war:

- *Similarities*: Both totalitarian regimes were one-party states with the goal of thorough societal transformation. No civil liberties or freedom of the press were allowed; the government relied on constant propaganda to mobilize the population and the arrest and persecution of political enemies to prevent opposition. Millions of civilians were imprisoned or murdered in both states. Both of the governments' economic goal, to expand industry, was to be achieved by state intervention. In both states, the leader was treated as a godlike figure.
- *Differences*: Ideological goals were profoundly different. Communism believed it was achieving equality and social justice that would be models for international change, while Nazism sought an unequal order with privileges for the racially pure elite at the expense of peoples like the Slavs and Jews, who were

considered inferior. Nazi ideology called for German expansion into the east and glorified violence; communist ideology under Stalin focused on "socialism in one country." German ideology particularly targeted Jews, while the Soviet Union promised equal treatment of peoples of all ethnic backgrounds. Economically, although the German government intervened in the economy, it relied on capitalism and was allied with the middle and upper classes. Its economic policies successfully pulled Germany out of the depression. In the Soviet Union, the Communists crushed those classes and expropriated their property; there was virtually no private economy. Stalin pursued rapid and extensive industrialization with Five-Year Plans and forced collectivization of agriculture.

- Preparation for war: Through their economic policies during the 1930s, both states were prepared for war, with strong industries and government planning. Both states had built effective propaganda machines and achieved notable successes that stirred the patriotism of their peoples.

2. The political decisions of both sides in World War II impacted the military course and outcomes of the war.

- Roosevelt and Churchill decided at the beginning of the war that the war in Europe would have priority over the war in Asia and that both Japan and Germany would have to surrender unconditionally. This meant that no separate treaties would be signed and became particularly important when the Soviet Union joined the Grand Alliance in 1941. The demand for unconditional surrender meant that the fighting would go on until that end. The Germans fought intensely until the suicide of Hitler in April 1945. The Japanese fought with such determination and courage, in spite of intensive aerial bombing of their cities, that the U.S. president Harry Truman ordered, following the military judgment of the U.S. commanders in the Pacific, the atomic bombing of two Japanese cities.
- Hitler refused to allow the German army at Stalingrad to retreat, thereby leading to disastrous defeat, in which hundreds of thousands of German soldiers were either killed or taken prisoner. It was the first major defeat of the previously invincible German army in World War II. The German government also pursued its ideological goal of the extermination of the Jews from 1942 to 1944, the crucial years in which it needed all the resources of the state to wage war as the Allies were on the advance.

30

Cold War Conflicts and Social Transformations, 1945–1985

Europe recovered remarkably quickly from the devastation of World War II. Strong economies and thriving democracies in western and central Europe sharply contrasted with political repression and economic stagnation in eastern Europe. With Europe weakened by war, the two dominant world powers, the United States and the Soviet Union, engaged in a fierce ideological, economic, political, and cultural struggle called the cold war. In the late 1960s and 1970s, Europe underwent another series of domestic crises, with political stability and social harmony disrupted by conflicting views over the U.S. war in Vietnam, economic slowdowns, and changing gender roles.

Key Concepts

- The cold war affected Europe profoundly, particularly Berlin, which became the focal point of Soviet-American tensions. By the 1950s, most European countries were committed to one side or the other, either in NATO or in the Warsaw Pact.
- European economic and political recovery was accompanied by the abandonment of imperialism, as European powers gave independence to their colonies in Africa and Asia.
- De-Stalinization in the Soviet Union, beginning in the 1950s, reduced political and cultural repression and allowed for improvements in the Soviet standard of living. The Soviet Union used force in Poland and Hungary to prevent liberalization there. Détente between the Soviet Union and the United States in the 1980s reduced international tensions.

- The women's movement and the youth movement of the 1960s initiated major social and cultural changes in Europe.
- After 1968, a period of stagnation set in. While feminists and leftists continued to challenge the existing order, conservatism dominated in the late 1970s and 1980s, when there was high unemployment, inflation, and energy prices. The Common Market expanded to become the European Union.

THE DIVISION OF EUROPE

THE ORIGINS OF THE COLD WAR

As the German threat abated, the Allies divided into opposing camps, England and the United States on one side and the Soviet Union on the other. Decisions made during the war paved the way for the cold war. There was little discussion until the Teheran Conference in late 1943 about the organization of postwar Europe. Churchill urged an Allied invasion of the Balkans to attack Germany through its satellite states rather than directly, but Roosevelt and Stalin agreed on a frontal attack in France. The result of this important decision was that the Soviet Union liberated eastern Europe. By the time of the Yalta Conference in 1945, Soviet troops occupied Poland, Bulgaria, Hungary, Romania, and parts of Yugoslavia and Czechoslovakia, while U.S. troops had yet to cross the Rhine or be close to defeating Japan. The Allies agreed that Germany and its capital Berlin would both be divided into four zones of occupation and would pay reparations to the Soviet Union, which in turn would join the Pacific war, and that eastern European governments were to be elected freely but also be pro-Soviet. But the presence of Soviet troops led to early communist domination. Stalin refused Truman's demands for free elections at the postvictory Potsdam Conference in July 1945.

WEST VERSUS EAST

American and Soviet interests diverged as the war was coming to an end. The Soviet Union insisted on military security from Germany, which had invaded twice in thirty years, and with its troops on the ground, the U.S.S.R. was able to secure a buffer zone of states under its domination in Eastern Europe. The United States, belatedly outraged over Soviet claims for its spoils of war, could do little militarily but did what it could economically and politically: In 1945, the United States cut off all aid to the Soviet Union and announced it would not recognize any of these governments as legitimate. Churchill's lamentation in a famous speech in late 1946 over the "iron curtain" dividing the European continent was reiterated by U.S. leaders denouncing Soviet aggression and communist repression. The Soviet Union responded with equally fervid ideological denunciations of U.S. imperialism and capitalistic exploitation.

In the late 1940s and 1950s, Europe was the center of this epic struggle between two great world powers and opposing systems. Civil wars in Greece and Turkey were seen by Americans as crucial tests of the U.S. ability to "contain" Soviet expansionism. The Truman Doctrine, enunciated by the U.S. president in 1947 with Greece and Turkey in mind, announced U.S. military and economic aid to those resisting communism. The Marshall Plan fought communism by providing generous U.S. funds for the rebuilding of Europe. Stalin refused Marshall Plan aid for eastern Europe and tightened the Soviet Union's grip on its satellite states. Particularly dramatic were two events in 1948: the imposition of a one-party state in Czechoslovakia and the cutting off of traffic through the Soviet zone of occupied Germany to West Berlin. The United States responded with an impressive Berlin Air Lift, with hundreds of planes flying over Soviet-controlled air space for nearly a year to supply the beleaguered city, after which the Soviets relented. In 1949, the United States formed the North Atlantic Treaty Organization (NATO) as a defensive military alliance; six years later, the Soviet Union countered by forming the Warsaw Pact.

AP Tip

The general policy of the United States was containment, first publicly articulated by George F. Kennan. The goal was to prevent the further spread of communism, but at the same time, it accepted the legitimacy of the existing communist states. Containment defined U.S. foreign policy through the Vietnam War.

Asia was where the cold war became "hot." Initially it was Korea, divided after the war into a northern zone under Soviet domination and a southern zone under U.S. domination, that became the battleground; later it would be Vietnam. North Korean troops invaded South Korea in 1950; a U.S.-led United Nations force countered. China, communist since 1949, entered the war when United Nations forces began to prevail, leading to three years of indecisive warfare and ultimately, in 1953, a negotiated settlement that confirmed the division of Korea, a stalemate that continues to this day.

THE WESTERN RENAISSANCE, 1945–1968

Western Europe emerged from the war economically devastated, militarily weak, flooded with refugees and displaced persons, and facing rising nationalism in its colonies. Yet it recovered remarkably well and remarkably quickly. How?

THE POSTWAR CHALLENGE

Western Europeans established constitutional governments to replace wartime regimes, with republics created in France (the Fourth), Italy, and West Germany and constitutional monarchies restored in Belgium, Norway, and Holland. All the governments faced severe economic problems like inflation, black marketeering, shortages, and the loss of much of their industrial plants to wartime bombing. In Germany, conditions varied little in the four zones of occupation with refugees everywhere and the economy near collapse. In England, the Labour Party replaced the Conservatives, but in West Germany, Italy, and France, Christian Democrats won decisive electoral victories. In West Germany, formally separated from East Germany in 1949 as the

Federal Republic of Germany, the Christian Democrat chancellor Konrad Adenauer began a generation of their political dominance. These parties and progressive Catholics in Italy and France were anticommunist and antiauthoritarian, with leaders with antifascist credentials who advocated mutual cooperation rather than nationalism. That they were successful against domestic communists and socialists who emerged from the war with great prestige and credibility because of their consistent antifascism was due to their adoption of the social welfare programs advocated by the left, as well as the U.S. Marshall Plan. Throughout the continent, socialist ideas, such as nationalization of major industries, public housing, national health insurance, and family allowances, became the norm, and many of these exist to this day. England followed this trend and became a welfare state, France created a mixed economy, and Germany retained its extensive social welfare system while instituting free-market capitalism. The United States through its Marshall Plan and NATO provided economic support and a protective military umbrella. By 1948, the economic turnaround was palpable. For nearly two decades, western Europe experienced unprecedented economic growth, stimulated by the use of Keynesian deficit spending and the exponential growth of consumer demands.

Toward European Unity

The cooperative spirit of the Christian Democrats saw fruition in first tentative and then substantial steps toward European unity, which they believed was the only way Europe would be able to restore its leadership in world affairs and prevent another European war. First attempts in 1948—the Organization of European Economic Cooperation (OEEC) and the Council of Europe—were limited by the British refusal to give them any real power, dooming hopes for the creation of a European parliament. Economic cooperation was seen as a better route to union. In 1952, two French statesmen, Jean Monnet and Robert Schuman, organized six states—France, Belgium, West Germany, Italy, Luxembourg, and the Netherlands—into the European Steel and Coal Community. A single steel and coal market, with no tariffs or quotas, was rapidly realized. In 1957, these six states signed the Treaty of Rome that created the European Economic Community, known as the Common Market, to form an economic union with free movement of peoples and goods, without tariffs or visas, and common policies. The Common Market was a huge success and soon began to rival the United States as an economic unit.

AP Tip

French-German rapprochement has been the key to European peace and stability in the sixty years since World War II. It has proven a firm and enduring commitment on the part of both nations, in spite of disagreements and clashing personalities.

In the 1960s, however, nationalism reared up in France. Disturbed by its terrible war in Algeria, the French had turned to the hero of World War II, General Charles de Gaulle, and in 1958 established the

Fifth Republic with greater presidential powers. As president for eleven years, de Gaulle withdrew French forces from NATO, developed an independent nuclear force, and blocked further unifying proposals of the Common Market.

DECOLONIZATION IN EAST ASIA

After World War II, the combination of the rising nationalism of Asian and African peoples and European weakness led to the independence of most of the European colonies and the end of European imperialism. It was a major turning away from the previous 500 years of European history, which had been based on an enormous power differential and on the European belief in their moral and spiritual superiority. European arrogance had withered in the face of the bloodbath of the war. European anti-imperialists and colonial elites educated in the mother country used European ideas to defeat European imperialism.

In India, substantial opposition to British rule had emerged even before World War I and was energized by the leadership of Mahatma Gandhi, the inspiring advocate of pacifism, who used civil disobedience and noncooperation to great effect in the decades between the wars, and won a new constitution for India in 1935. Britain decided on partition to resolve the conflicting demands of the Muslim and Hindu populations and granted independence to India and Pakistan in 1947.

In China, the nationalist movement divided into two factions, the Nationalists, or Guomindang, under Chiang Kai-shek, and the Communists under Mao Zedong. In 1945, civil war broke out, with the United States and the Soviet Union supporting opposing factions. The Communists won in 1949 and established a one-party state, with labor camps, five-year plans to promote industrialization, and collectivization of agriculture. Other foreign influences were eliminated.

Most of the rest of Asia also threw off the foreign yoke. Japanese occupation during the war had bred well-organized nationalistic movements that turned their attention to their imperial overlords once Japan had been defeated. The Philippines won its independence from the United States in 1946, and Sri Lanka and Burma won theirs from Britain in 1948; they all more or less followed the constitutional model of India. In Indonesia and Indochina, communists played important roles in winning independence. The Indonesians fiercely and successfully fought Dutch attempts to restore their control in 1949. The Vietnamese, led by the communist nationalist Ho Chi Minh, fought the French, decisively defeating them in 1954. The United States prevented the creation of another communist state when Vietnam was divided into two states, which later led to civil war and the U.S. military involvement on behalf of the anticommunist South Vietnamese government.

AP Tip

Just as Lenin had revised Marxism, Mao revised Leninism. He advocated peasant communism, in which peasants and rural values are privileged. He was profoundly anti-Western and made revolutionary changes in Chinese family life, culture, and gender roles. In Europe, only Albania adopted the Maoist version of Marxism.

DECOLONIZATION IN THE MIDDLE EAST AND AFRICA

In the Middle East, France and Britain held their colonies as mandates of the League of Nations. The French gave up Syria and Lebanon in 1944, and in 1947, after violent confrontations between Zionist and Arab residents of Palestine as well as attacks on the British, Britain decided to withdraw from Palestine. The newly created United Nations drew up a partition plan dividing Palestine into a Jewish state and an Arab one. The Arabs rejected the partition and attacked Israel, which had become a haven for displaced Holocaust survivors since it had come into being in 1948. The Israelis won, and nearly a million Arabs left or were expelled. Since then, the region has suffered four more wars and an endless cycle of clashes between Palestinians and Israelis.

AP Tip

The United Nations was another focal point of cold war tensions complicated by the visible indication of the growing importance of newly independent states. Three of the five permanent seats on the Security Council were held by European states: France, the United Kingdom, and the Soviet Union.

Defeat in 1948 in Palestine spurred Arab nationalism. Egyptian nationalists led by Gamal Abdel Nasser ended the pro-Western monarchy in 1952 and, four years later, nationalized the Suez Canal. The British, French, and Israelis joined military forces against Egypt and won, but were forced by the United States and the Soviet Union to relinquish their gains. The Egyptian victory, visibly demonstrated when British troops left Egypt after more than seventy years, encouraged the Algerians to revolt against the French. However, in Algeria there was a substantial French population that opposed independence. A bloody and dirty civil war ended only when de Gaulle accepted Algerian independence in 1962.

Elsewhere in Africa, most colonies became independent without much violence and typically with some formal association with either Britain or France. European countries had substantial economic and cultural ties with the newly independent African states, which led critics to argue that they had replaced colonialism with neocolonialism to maintain Western economic domination, much as the United States had in Latin American states after their independence.

THE UNITED STATES'S CIVIL RIGHTS REVOLUTION

The United States experienced an economic boom after the war and slowly began to confront its most crucial social issue, the segregation of and discrimination against its African American population. In 1954, the Supreme Court ruled that "separate but equal" was no longer acceptable in educational faculties, and little by little, under the pressure of the civil rights movement led by the eloquent Martin Luther King Jr., that principle was applied to most facets of society. After 1964, under the presidency of Democrat Lyndon Johnson, legislation was passed to guarantee voting and employment rights to African Americans and to implement a war on poverty to reduce economic inequality by the adoption of some of the social welfare programs already in place in Europe.

SOVIET EASTERN EUROPE, 1945–1968

Stalin lived for another eight years after the end of the war, only to disappoint the hopes of many Russians that their heroism in the Great Patriotic War would bring greater democracy. Instead, rigid dictatorship; forced labor camps, in which many Soviet POWs were interned when they came home; and tight authoritarianism controlled cultural, political, and economic life. Artists and composers were denounced, Jews were targeted, and five-year plans, with their emphasis on heavy industry at the expense of consumer goods, were reinstituted.

While many elements of the 1930s reappeared for the Russians, they were new to the citizens of the eastern European states liberated by Soviet forces. Those states became one-party dictatorships under the leadership of local Communists supported by the Red Army and the secret police; civil liberties, freedom of worship, and the middle classes soon disappeared as private property was nationalized. Only Yugoslavia, where there were no Soviet troops, remained outside the Soviet orbit. Its war hero, Tito, successfully stood up to Stalin in 1948; until its dissolution over ethnic tensions in the 1980s, Yugoslavia was unique, a communist state independent of the Soviet Union. On occasion, it had limited Western support.

REFORM AND DE-STALINIZATION, 1953–1964

When Stalin died in 1953, his successors reformed his system. They restricted the powers of the secret police and closed many of the forced-labor camps. Nikita Khrushchev, a reformer, became premier and publicly denounced Stalinism and revealed Stalin's crimes and brutalities in a crucial speech before the Party Congress in 1956, initiating the process of de-Stalinization, or liberalization. The party was opened to new members; some focus on the production of consumer goods began as government controls on industry were lessened. Intellectuals responded enthusiastically, with novelists such as Boris Pasternak (*Doctor Zhivago*) and Aleksander Solzhenitsyn (*One Day in the Life of Ivan Denisovich*) publishing, although not always inside the Soviet Union, novels indicting Stalinism.

Khrushchev initially moved Soviet foreign policy in Europe toward "peaceful coexistence" with the West. Cold war tensions relaxed in

Europe as the Soviets allowed Austria, which had also been under four-part occupation, to become independent, albeit neutral. But liberalization was not tolerated in the Soviet satellites. Mass support for change led to more liberal and more autonomous governments in both Poland and Hungary in 1956. Khrushchev toppled the Polish reformers and sent troops to crush the Hungarian revolution; Hungarian hopes for help from the United States were disappointed. In the late 1950s and 1960s, Khrushchev's policies became more confrontational. Khrushchev rattled his saber in Berlin in 1958, only to back down, and in 1961 suddenly ordered the East Germans to build a wall to divide East from West Berlin. The Soviet Union became an active supporter of nationalist movements outside of Europe. In 1962, Khrushchev ordered nuclear missiles to be placed in newly communist Cuba, only to be forced to withdraw them by the naval blockade and resolute diplomacy of the U.S. president John Kennedy.

The End of Reform

Khrushchev lost the support of the party leadership, disturbed by these foreign policy fiascos and threatened by his domestic reforms. They replaced him in 1964 with Leonid Brezhnev, who brought back, albeit partially, some of the elements of Stalinism. Attempting to restore Soviet military might, the government, although more cautious in foreign policy, began a massive buildup of arms.

The Soviet satellites had not lost their appetite for liberalization. In 1968, a liberal communist, Alexander Dubček, became the new leader of Czechoslovakia and initially enthusiastically embraced democratic reforms to bring about "socialism with a human face." The Soviet leadership and their allies in other eastern European states feared their destabilizing effects, and in August 1968, amassed a large force to occupy Czechoslovakia and quickly restored the one-party state. The Brezhnev Doctrine affirmed the right of the Soviet Union to intervene in the internal affairs of the satellite socialist states. The Soviet Union maintained firm control until the 1980s, when Poland successfully challenged Soviet rule and the reformer Mikhail Gorbachev took the reins of power in the Soviet Union.

AP Tip

The crushing of the Hungarian Revolution and the Czech "Prague Spring" were highly disillusioning for many communists in western Europe (and the United States as well), many of whom created a new form of communism, Euro-communism, which sought to move Europe toward socialism democratically. Many Hungarian and Czech intellectuals fled to the West.

The Soviet Union to 1985

Many things improved in the Soviet Union under Brezhnev. The cult of personality associated with Stalinism disappeared, and the secret police were less powerful. A new focus on consumer goods brought a slow but steady increase in the standard of living, and ambitious and successful individuals found they had access to privileges like special shops and travel abroad. The communist leadership emphasized the glorious victory of the Great Patriotic War and Russian nationalistic desires to retain the non-Russian parts of the Soviet Union. But cultural dictatorship remained in force. Dissidents were blacklisted, removed from good jobs, or exiled to the east, and occasionally (like Solzhenitsyn) expelled.

As urbanization and economic modernization proceeded apace, technocratic elites increased in size and influence. Educational opportunities expanded hugely after the war, and the better educated began to address the problems of Soviet society, although in officially apolitical ways. This large, well-educated, urbanized elite was ready to make changes by the 1980s.

AP Tip

The Brezhnev period also was the period of détente, a reduction of tensions between the United States and the Soviet Union, which involved cultural exchanges as well as arms reduction treaties.

POSTWAR SOCIAL TRANSFORMATION, 1945–1968

SCIENCE AND TECHNOLOGY

The war had made science an adjunct of policy and strategy, and practical inventions like radar by scientists had a huge impact on the war. The development of the atom bomb by the nuclear physicists working on the U.S.-sponsored Manhattan Project led directly to Japan's surrender. Although nuclear weapons were used only twice, they became the core of the arms race between the Soviet Union and the United States. Big science became the new paradigm as theoretical and applied researchers were employed in large-scale private or public bureaucracies. Cold war military needs occupied more than 25 percent of U.S. and Soviet scientists, who invented new missile systems, rockets, nuclear submarines, and spy satellites. The competition of the big science states culminated in the space race. In 1957, the Soviet Union was the first state to put a satellite, Sputnik, into orbit and a man into orbit four years later. The United States countered with a push toward the moon; in 1969, the first human, an American, walked on the moon. European scientists were so attracted by the opportunities of big science in the United States that there was a noticeable brain drain in Europe. But Europe as a whole began to invest in its own big science facilities. The supersonic airplane, the Concorde, reflects that investment.

The scientific community became larger, ever more competitive, and increasingly specialized; this expanded both basic knowledge and applications of many subdisciplincs. One example of this was the discovery of the double helix, the mechanism for genetic transmission, one of the most important discoveries of all time.

The Changing Class Structure

With the European economic miracle of the 1950s and 1960s, social mobility increased in Europe so much that traditional class barriers were severely blurred. The middle class was transformed, with the manager or technocrat working in huge corporations replacing the small property holder, small entrepreneur, or self-employed professional that had dominated in the nineteenth century. Family connections and inherited property became less important, as the new managerial class welcomed capable individuals from all classes into its ranks. The lower classes also changed, with farmers becoming an ever-smaller percentage of the population, and many industrial workers becoming better educated and moving into white-collar (service or office) jobs. The industrial working class began to decline.

The leveling of the social classes was also a result of government social welfare programs, paid for by higher tax rates on the wealthy. As the standard of living rose, poorer people could afford what had been luxuries for the rich in previous times. For example, the number of cars in Europe increased ninefold between 1948 and 1965. A "gadget revolution" was promoted by the willingness of people to accumulate debt; in previous generations savings had been necessary to pay for illness and old age. Europeans generally had month-long or longer vacations and began to travel widely and often, with packaged tours and resorts offering reasonable rates to millions of leisure-seeking middle- and working-class families.

New Roles for Women

Certainly the emancipation of women in the twentieth century is one of its most important historical developments. It resulted from the combination of changing economic patterns and a new women's consciousness. In the 1950s and 1960s women married early and had large families in the postwar baby boom, but by the end of those decades, birthrates began a permanent decline and European population stabilized, growing only with immigration. As family size decreased, women became freer of household duties earlier (see Figure 30.1 for a chart illustrating the connection between birthrates and women's employment). Women entered the workforce in momentous numbers (which itself tended to reduce the birthrate) and adopted new roles. Whereas women had always worked at home, middle-class women as well as poor women now worked outside the house for pay. The strong demand for labor in the postwar economic boom offered women managerial or lower-level white-collar jobs, and many became educated and aspired to higher positions. This women's revolution went furthest in communist Russia and Eastern Europe, where about 50 percent of the labor force was women.

Many women faced discrimination in wages and promotion, and even in securing full-time work, without which divorced women with children faced poverty. These injustices sparked movements against sexism and discrimination, with powerful voices in each country giving broad support. The European writer who articulated feminism was Simone de Beauvoir, a novelist, philosopher, and companion of the great existentialist philosopher, Jean-Paul Sartre. Her influential work, *The Second Sex,* published in 1949, outlined the conditions that limited women's freedom, and she urged women to become creative and self-assertive. Betty Friedan's *The Feminist Mystique,* 1963, sparked the U.S. women's rights movement. European women focused on personal status legislation, such as the right to divorce in Catholic countries. By the late 1980s, women in Italy had won the rights to divorce and for abortion. In 1979 a woman, Margaret Thatcher, was elected head of a major European state for the first time. The success of the women's movement energized other groups subject to discrimination, such as homosexuals and people with disabilities.

YOUTH AND THE COUNTERCULTURE

The high birthrate in the immediate decade after World War II, economic prosperity, and a more open class structure led to an unusually high proportion of the population that was young and the creation of a distinct youth culture and rebellious counterculture. In the late 1950s, the U.S. "beat" movement of poets and writers challenged the complacency of the "silent generation." By the 1960s, the youth culture was defined by radical politics (particularly in opposition to the Vietnam War), the rejection of conventional morality, and the assertion of the freedom to choose one's own values and lifestyles (sexual freedom, communal living, or use of hallucinogenic drugs), and art and music.

AP Tip

Culturally, the youth movement was defined above all by its music, rock 'n roll, whose icons, from Elvis Presley in the 1950s to Bob Dylan and the Beatles in the 1960s, had worldwide influence. American cultural domination was of concern to many European intellectuals.

The American youth culture became a worldwide movement because of the ease of international travel and communication. The young had money to spend because economic prosperity meant plentiful jobs, and with their great purchasing power, they created their own consumer goods and influenced the entire society. Students in the United States and around the world protested against the Vietnam War and, idealistically and perhaps romantically, rejected Western values as overly materialistic and conformist, often embracing those of newly forged countries like China and Cuba.

In Europe, students were also agitated by problems in the educational system. Originally highly elitist in comparison to the United States where five times as many students attended university, European students became more democratic by 1960. The universities were not prepared for the huge increase in the number of students, so classes were crowded, competition was intense, and many students felt the education was inadequate. These tensions exploded most particularly in West Germany and France. In 1968 in Paris, students occupied buildings and fought with police. They won the support of many workers, and a general strike spontaneously occurred, only to bring the stiff resistance of the government of conservative Charles de

Gaulle, who sent troops toward Paris. When he called for new elections, he was overwhelmingly reelected.

AP Tip

The 1968 Paris "insurrection," as it is sometimes called, divided France. The radicals challenged not only the de Gaulle regime but also the traditional Marxist left. To some degree, it was part of a long historical tradition for Paris to be out of sync with the rest of France. The counterculture movement in Europe and the United States, while generally nonviolent, also spawned radicalized groups that engaged in attacks on government buildings and officials.

Conflict and Challenge in the Late Cold War, 1968–1985

The United States and Vietnam

The Vietnam War was the defining issue of the 1960s, bringing the ideology of containment into question and the Western alliance into disunity. Some saw it as a product of the cold war, others rejected it as a form of U.S. imperialism or neocolonialism. The United States had prevented the spread of communism to South Korea in 1950 to 1953 and sought to do the same after the division of Vietnam in 1956 by backing the anticommunist regime in the south. In the mid-1960s, President Johnson escalated U.S. involvement to support the South Vietnamese government with half a million soldiers and intense bombing of communist North Vietnam, sparking an antiwar movement opposed to U.S. intervention in what protesters saw as a civil war. Richard Nixon, a Republican elected in 1968, intensified the bombing but suspended the draft and reduced U.S. forces in response to growing antiwar sentiment. He initiated a rapprochement with China and in 1973 negotiated an agreement with North Vietnam to withdraw U.S. troops. Revelations of illegal means used to win reelection, commonly known at the Watergate scandal, led to Nixon's resignation in 1974. The next year, Vietnam was unified as a communist state.

Détente or Cold War?

Détente was initiated in Europe by Willy Brandt, the socialist chancellor of West Germany, who sought to establish a new, less confrontational foreign policy. Its basic premise was that the postwar settlement and boundaries ought to be accepted to encourage cordial relations. He flew to Poland in 1970 to sign a historic treaty of reconciliation, apologized for German crimes during the war, and opened direct negotiations with East Germany. Optimism underlay the Helsinki Accords of 1975, signed by thirty-five nations to guarantee human rights and political freedom for their citizens. Hopes for peaceful coexistence faded when these guarantees were ignored by Brezhnev, and U.S. president Ronald Reagan initiated a massive buildup against what he called the "evil empire." A swing toward conservatism helped revitalize the Atlantic Alliance, which had shown its disunity when the Soviet Union invaded Afghanistan in 1980 and U.S. president Carter's call for economic sanctions found support only in Britain.

THE TROUBLED ECONOMY

After some twenty years of prosperity, the European economy experienced inflation and stagnation in the 1970s. This was sparked by the U.S. abandonment of the gold standard and fixed rates of exchange and compounded by the sudden and sharp increase in the cost of oil when the Organization of Petroleum Exporting Countries (OPEC) put an embargo on oil shipments to the United States after the Arab-Israeli war of 1973. Unemployment rose and living standards declined, making this economic crisis the worst since the 1930s. Crude oil prices rose again when Islamic fundamentalists toppled the U.S.-supported shah of Iran in 1979. By 1985, unemployment was the highest in Europe it had been since the depression. The misery index, which calculates inflation and unemployment rates (see Figure 30.2), reveals that western Europe was having a much harder time than the United States or Japan. Yet the Common Market continued to grow, with an additional six nations, including Britain, joining in the 1980s.

SOCIETY IN A TIME OF ECONOMIC UNCERTAINTY

The psychological and attitudinal impact of the long economic crisis was great as people lost jobs and sometimes homes; some suffered mental breakdowns. Pessimism and calls for realism abounded. Nevertheless, the welfare system provided a cushion for most people, so that political democracy remained stable. Demands on government programs meant a great increase in government spending, which led to budget deficits and inflation. By the late 1970s austerity programs were put in place to reduce government spending, and marked a turn toward conservatism, paralleling the shift in foreign policy. Margaret Thatcher became prime minister of Great Britain in 1979 (see Individuals in Society, p. 1013) and in her eleven years in office reduced the role of government, replaced much of the welfare system with free-market policies including privatization of industries, reduced the power of unions, and increased the number of property owners in Britain. Reagan pursued many similar programs in the United States but kept government spending high with his military buildup, which made the budget deficit soar. France, however, attempted a different path when the socialist François Mitterrand was elected president in 1981. He nationalized industries and increased government spending, but two years later had to implement austerity measures. The computer industry, which blossomed in the 1990s, opened up new venues for employment and encouraged small entrepreneurial ventures.

A new political movement was born out of the economic crisis. Environmentalists formed Green parties to eliminate wasteful uses of energy and combat pollution; in Germany, they had some electoral success. Private lives were also changed by the economic difficulties. Many people became committed to a simpler, healthier lifestyle. Men and women postponed marriage as young people became anxious about securing their careers. Economic difficulties prompted even more women to work outside the home to support their families.

Multiple-Choice Questions

1. The Truman Doctrine and Brezhnev Doctrine both
   (A) promised that the great powers would support the civil rights of all Europeans.
   (B) promised that the great powers would act militarily only in cooperation with their allies.
   (C) claimed that great powers have the right to intervene in the domestic affairs of smaller countries.
   (D) focused on the rights of the great powers in occupied Germany and Austria.
   (E) were enunciated initially in relationship to civil war in Turkey and Greece.

2. Britain differed from other western European states in the early years after World War II in that
   (A) it rejected the welfare state.
   (B) it established an independent nuclear force.
   (C) it was the only monarchy left.
   (D) the governing party was socialist leaning.
   (E) it refused at first to join NATO.

3. The Christian Democrats in western Europe in the 1950s
   (A) resisted adopting social welfare programs.
   (B) initiated the Common Market.
   (C) uniformly rejected the idea of a mixed economy.
   (D) reduced the size of government.
   (E) supported the Hungarian Revolution.

4. The women's movement was prompted largely by
   (A) the economic roles women had played during World War II.
   (B) the visible presence of women at the front as nurses and drivers.
   (C) the general granting of the rights of divorce and abortion.
   (D) the high death tolls of the war, particularly in Britain and France.
   (E) declining birthrates.

5. Détente was initiated by the
   (A) West German chancellor Willy Brandt.
   (B) British prime minister Margaret Thatcher.
   (C) U.S. president Ronald Reagan.
   (D) Soviet premier Nikita Khrushchev.
   (E) French president Charles de Gaulle.

6. When the United States announced the Marshall Plan,
   (A) it offered aid only to noncommunist states.
   (B) only NATO members were allowed to get aid.
   (C) the Soviet Union refused to allow its satellites to get aid.
   (D) the Communist Party had become the largest party in Italy.
   (E) the civil wars in Greece and Turkey had already ended.

7. The origins of the cold war are most directly found in
   (A) the long-standing hostility between the United States and the Soviet Union.
   (B) the decision to defeat Germany by a direct attack on the Balkans.
   (C) Churchill's "iron curtain" speech.
   (D) lack of planning for postwar Europe.
   (E) the military strategy adopted by the United States and the Soviet Union at Teheran.

8. European economic recovery after the war was stimulated by the Marshall Plan and by
   (A) the use of Keynesian deficit spending by European governments.
   (B) careful attention to balancing the budget.
   (C) going off the gold standard.
   (D) military spending to restore the armed forces to prewar strength.
   (E) reducing military expenditures by giving independence to African colonies in the 1950s.

9. The chief domestic issue prompting French student protests in the 1960s was
   (A) overly restrictive admission policies to universities.
   (B) lack of jobs.
   (C) discrimination against women.
   (D) overcrowded and inadequate universities.
   (E) French military involvement in the Vietnam War.

10. Most western European nations responded to the economic crisis of the 1970s and 1980s
    (A) with increased deficit spending.
    (B) with an arms buildup to provide employment.
    (C) by returning to the gold standard.
    (D) with austerity programs.
    (E) by maintaining social welfare programs to help the unemployed.

11. In terms of domestic policy, Brezhnev
    (A) expanded Khrushchev's de-Stalinization program.
    (B) turned the economy away from heavy industry to consumer goods.
    (C) partially re-Stalinized Russia.
    (D) reduced military spending.
    (E) gave greater autonomy to the non-Russian minorities in the Soviet Union.

12. Decolonization in Indochina and Indonesia was different from that in India in that
    (A) the United Nations supervised their transition to independence.
    (B) they had to fight militarily against their imperial overlords to achieve independence.
    (C) they got military aid from newly communist China.
    (D) their independence was granted more than a decade after India's.
    (E) the United States aided their independence movements.

13. European unity
    (A) was successful first politically, then economically.
    (B) was enthusiastically endorsed by Charles de Gaulle.
    (C) began with Belgium and Holland over the objections of Germany.
    (D) involved creating an independent nuclear force under European control.
    (E) developed with the halfhearted participation of Britain.

14. Big science meant scientists
    (A) were focused on applying scientific work to consumer goods.
    (B) had so much prestige after World War II that they could operate without much government involvement.
    (C) became increasingly involved in military-related research in large corporations.
    (D) insisted on having a say in the political uses of their scientific advancements.
    (E) typically in the Soviet Union but rarely in the United States worked in government bureaucracies.

15. Dubček's establishment of "socialism with a human face" in Czechoslovakia
    (A) was militarily and economically supported by the United States as part of the Truman Doctrine.
    (B) received the same treatment as the Hungarian Revolution by the Soviet Union.
    (C) proved to be a sham in that little change was really made.
    (D) sparked a similar movement in Poland.
    (E) led to the building of the Berlin Wall.

Free-Response Questions

1. Discuss the changing attitudes toward liberalization in the Soviet Union from 1945 to 1985.

2. Discuss the economic problems faced by western Europeans from the end of World War II until 1985, and analyze the success or failure of governments to deal with those problems.

Answers

Multiple-Choice Questions

1. **Answer: (C)** While on opposing sides, both doctrines allowed the two states to send military aid, even troops, to states where movements to destabilize the regime, either communist or liberal, occurred. (McKay, *A History of Western Society*, 8th ed., pp. 992, 1007/9th ed., pp. 984, 997)

2. **Answer: (D)** In Germany, Italy, and France, Christian Democrats dominated the political scene, while in Britain, the Labour Party defeated the Conservatives in 1945. Holland, Belgium, and Norway

were monarchies; Italy became a republic. (McKay, *A History of Western Society*, 8th ed., p. 995/9th ed., pp. 987, 989)

3. **ANSWER: (B)** France and Germany under their Christian Democratic leaders forged European economic cooperation. France created a mixed economy, and all adopted social welfare programs. (McKay, *A History of Western Society*, 8th ed., pp. 995–997/9th ed., pp.987, 989)

4. **ANSWER: (E)** The rights to divorce and for abortion were results of the women's movement, not its cause. With declining birthrates, women were freer to enter the workforce. (McKay, *A History of Western Society*, 8th ed., p. 1011/9th ed., pp.1002–1004, 1009–1010)

5. **ANSWER: (A)** Brandt made a trip to Poland in 1970 and opened relations with East Germany. (McKay, *A History of Western Society*, 8th ed., p. 1016/9th ed., p. 1008)

6. **ANSWER: (C)** The Communists were never the largest party in Italy, nor were the conflicts in Turkey and Greece over when the Marshall Plan was announced. The United States offered aid to all European nations, but Stalin refused it for eastern Europe. (McKay, *A History of Western Society*, 8th ed., p. 992/9th ed., pp. 984–987)

7. **ANSWER: (E)** At Teheran, they decided to defeat Germany through a direct attack on France, which meant that only the Soviet Union liberated eastern Europe. (McKay, *A History of Western Society*, 8th ed., p. 991/9th ed., pp. 982–983)

8. **ANSWER: (A)** Most European governments adopted Keynesian, or deficit, spending in the immediate postwar period to stimulate the economy. (McKay, *A History of Western Society*, 8th ed., p. 996/9th ed., p. 987)

9. **ANSWER: (D)** It was the sudden expansion of unprepared universities that infuriated the students already upset over the U.S. war. (McKay, *A History of Western Society*, 8th ed., pp. 1013–1014/9th ed., pp. 1004–1006)

10. **ANSWER: (D)** Inflation, as well as stagnation and high unemployment and energy costs, marked this economic downturn. England, Germany, and France, after trying another approach initially, cut their budgets by reducing social welfare spending and other expenses. (McKay, *A History of Western Society*, 8th ed., p. 1020/9th ed., pp. 1011–1012)

11. **ANSWER: (C)** Brezhnev turned back from the partial liberalization under Khrushchev with cultural repression and authoritarian control. (McKay, *A History of Western Society*, 8th ed., p. 1006/9th ed., pp. 997–998)

12. **ANSWER: (B)** Indonesia had to fight the Dutch, Indochina the French. They achieved independence without help from either China or the United States within a decade of India's independence in the mid-1950s. (McKay, *A History of Western Society*, 8th ed., pp. 999–1000/9th ed., p. 992)

13. **ANSWER: (E)** Britain limited the initial efforts at political unification and participated but not completely in the economic unity. (McKay, *A History of Western Society*, 8th ed., p. 997/9th ed., p. 989)

14. **ANSWER: (C)** Scientists in both the United States and the Soviet Union worked in large bureaucracies and often on military projects. (McKay, *A History of Western Society*, 8th ed., p. 1008/9th ed., pp. 999–1000)

15. **ANSWER: (B)** Both the 1956 Hungarian Revolution and the 1968 "Prague Spring" were crushed by the invasion of Soviet and Warsaw Pact forces in order to prevent the spread of similar movements. (McKay, *A History of Western Society*, 8th ed., pp. 1006–1007/9th ed., pp. 997–998)

FREE-RESPONSE QUESTIONS

1. Soviet attitudes toward liberalization after World War II changed over time.

- After the end of the war, Stalinist policies—centralized planning of the economy, focus on heavy industry, forced labor camps, and political and cultural repression—were reimposed on the people of the Soviet Union, disappointing the hopes of some for liberalization. Some returning Soviet POWs were interned in forced labor camps. Stalin died in 1953.
- In 1956, the new premier Khrushchev initiated a program of de-Stalinization with a speech at the Party Congress denouncing Stalin's crimes. Some labor camps were closed, more open political discussion was allowed, and artists were given greater freedom.
- However, in the Soviet satellites, liberal governments put in place through mass movements in Poland and Hungary were crushed by Soviet tanks.
- After several foreign policy fiascos by Khrushchev, including the Cuban Missile Crisis, the party leadership replaced him with Brezhnev, who partially re-Stalinized the Soviet Union. Writers and composers were held under tighter control, and one important dissident, Solzhenitsyn, was expelled.
- In foreign policy, the Brezhnev Doctrine, which officially asserted the right of the Soviet Union to intervene in the domestic affairs of its satellite states, was a clear indication that liberalization would not be tolerated. The Brezhnev Doctrine was dramatically used against the "socialism with a human face" government of Dubček in Czechoslovakia in 1968.
- Improvements in the standard of living, partially produced by a turn toward consumer goods and expansion of educational opportunities, began to produce a class of highly educated and prosperous technocrats, who would ultimately push for liberalization.

2. Economic problems of western Europeans after World War II and the success or failure of attempts to deal with them also changed over time.

- In the early postwar period, western Europeans faced a number of serious economic problems: the need to rebuild infrastructure and factories, transitioning from wartime to peacetime production, inflation, shortages, and resulting black marketeering. These states were helped by the enormous infusion of funds from the United States as part of its Marshall Plan to rebuild Europe quickly.

- Western European states expanded already existing social welfare programs in the postwar period.
- The Labour government of the United Kingdom, elected shortly after the end of the war, nationalized major industries and banks. France, now in its Fourth Republic, established a mixed economy, with elements of both socialism and capitalism. France and West Germany, which elected its first postwar government in 1949, were both run by Christian Democrats. Germany retained its extensive social welfare system while reintroducing free-market capitalism.
- Western European states recovered quickly, reaching prosperity within a few years after the end of the war. Germany, France, Italy, and three small states organized the Common Market, which ended tariffs among the members, first on steel and coal, and later expanding to other commodities, and helped create a European economic revival to compete with the United States. Overall, economic policies in the three major states of western Europe were highly successful.
- In the 1970s and 1980s, western European states suffered economic decline, with high energy costs, stagnation, and high unemployment figures. Britain and Germany instituted austerity measures. Britain, under Prime Minister Thatcher, elected in 1979, privatized previously nationalized industries, reduced the influence of trade unions, shrank the welfare state, and reinvigorated the economy by encouraging unbridled free-market capitalism. France initially attempted to address the crisis with a socialist program under President Mitterrand, but a few years later adapted austerity measures too. By 1985, all these policies were only marginally effective as the western European economy remained troubled by high unemployment and stagnation.

31

Revolution, Rebuilding, and New Challenges, 1985 to the Present

Much to the surprise of most people in the West, almost overnight between 1989 and 1991, the communist system in eastern Europe collapsed, the Soviet Union disappeared, and the cold war ended. Democracy seemed to have won the day, and for a brief period, optimism for a world of peace, prosperity, and unity abounded. Those hopes were disappointed by the reappearance of ethnic hostilities leading to terrible civil wars and mass murders, high unemployment, and difficult transitions from command to market economies. New issues arose, the most difficult of which was the integration of Muslim immigrants into predominantly Christian Europe. The drive toward European unity remained strong as the European Community added new members, became the European Union, and created a common currency.

Key Concepts

- The Solidarity movement successfully challenged the communist system in Poland, paving the way for similar developments elsewhere in eastern Europe.
- The Soviet Union began to reform itself under the leadership of Mikhail Gorbachev, but the movement for change developed such momentum that within a few years, the Communist Party had lost control of the Soviet Union. Many republics broke away to become independent states. The economy became capitalistic, and a constitutional system was created to replace the communist government, although by the early twenty-first century, Russia had veered back toward authoritarianism.

- Germany reunified in 1991 and faced difficulties in incorporating the former communist East Germany into its capitalistic and democratic system.
- Resurgent nationalism broke apart Czechoslovakia and Yugoslavia, the former peacefully, and the latter in a series of brutal wars.
- The European Union welcomed many of the former communist states as members. A common currency, the euro, was created, as economic integration, although not political unity, intensified.
- Most western and central European states faced population decline and aging populations. Large-scale immigration from the Middle East and Africa exacerbated ethnic and religious tensions.
- The relations between the West and the Islamic world deteriorated. Two wars in Iraq, the rise of Islamic fundamentalism and radical terrorism, and the continuing Israeli-Palestinian conflict increased tensions worldwide and complicated domestic relations in Europe.

THE DECLINE OF COMMUNISM IN EASTERN EUROPE

The Brezhnev Doctrine, the assertion of the right of the Soviet Union to intervene in the domestic affairs of its satellite states first applied to Czechoslovakia in 1968, highlighted the strict authoritarianism and re-Stalinization of the Soviet system in the 1970s and 1980s, which doomed efforts at reform, both at home and in the satellites. A reform movement in Poland in the early 1980s that grew out of the dockyards in Gdansk, the former Danzig, was crushed by a still-powerful Soviet system. Communism in Poland had never deeply transformed society as it had in many other countries, in that most land remained in private hands and the Catholic Church remained a powerful institution. Protests in the 1950s and 1970s failed to move the government to make changes that would allow the economy to thrive; in fact, economic conditions grew worse. A new reform movement was prompted by the enthusiastically received visit in 1979 of the new pope, John Paul II, a former Polish cardinal.

In 1980, dockyard workers in Gdansk began a strike, demanding the rights to form free unions and to free speech, the release of political prisoners, and economic reforms. Instead of crushing the strike, the Polish government gave in to the demands of the workers in the Gdansk Agreement. The strikers organized a free and democratic trade union called Solidarity, which was endorsed by intellectuals and the church and which quickly grew to 9.5 million members, becoming the union of the nation. Cultural freedom and civil liberties abounded, as the communist government feared attempting to repress such a massive movement. Solidarity refused to promote violent revolution out of fear of Warsaw Pact intervention. Its charismatic leader, Lech Walesa, adopted a moderate stance, which, combined with a worsening economy, led to a loss of support for Solidarity. The communists regained their monopoly on political power when, in December 1981, the government declared martial law and declared Solidarity illegal. But the movement continued to flourish as an underground organization and the Poles retained the cultural and intellectual freedom they had won.

Solidarity's popularity encouraged change in the Soviet Union, which was facing a number of economic and social problems, not the least of which was a pervasive apathy in the masses produced by decades of party and state bureaucratic control. In 1985, Mikhail Gorbachev took the reins in the Soviet Union as general secretary of the Communist Party and de facto head of state and initiated a series of reforms known commonly as *glasnost* ("openness") and *perestroika* ("restructuring"), in order to bring the Soviet Union up to the technological and living standards of the West. The goal was to save the Soviet system by modernizing it. A key component of this program was better relations with the West in order to reduce military expenditures, so Gorbachev withdrew Soviet forces from Afghanistan and negotiated with the United States for the elimination of all intermediate land-based missiles in Europe and other arms reductions. Domestically, the program encouraged a greater emphasis on consumer goods, efforts against corruption and incompetence in the bureaucracies, and measures against Russia's age-old problem of alcoholism. Perestroika allowed for market pricing on some goods, the loosening of government control over production, and the establishment of consumer-oriented cooperatives. These reforms were too limited and too timid to improve the economy, but they would pave the way for the later undoing of the Soviet economic system.

Glasnost on the other hand was much more successful. Elimination of censorship led to a huge burst in literature and theatrical productions openly criticizing the Soviet system and denouncing Stalinist terror, enthusiastically received by an intellectually thirsty public. Political democratization led to the holding of the first free elections since 1917. In the resulting Congress of People's Deputies, the Communists remained the dominant party but dissidents also held seats, and their voices were heard loud and clear in the much-watched televised congressional proceedings. A new political and intellectual culture was quickly born.

These reforms inspired nationalist demands for independence by the non-Russian member states of the Soviet Union. Gorbachev made the crucial decision to abandon the Brezhnev Doctrine and allow such movements, as well as reformist movements in Poland and Germany, to flourish. But Gorbachev could not control the pace of change, and in 1989, a veritable revolutionary tide spread throughout eastern Europe which swept the Communists out of power virtually everywhere.

AP Tip

There was much debate over how to explain the sudden collapse of communism in the Soviet Union. Republican Americans like to give credit to Ronald Reagan, who labeled the Soviet Union the "evil empire" and proposed massive new military systems, raising the ante for the Soviet regime. Others point to the inherent difficulties of a command economy in a country as large as the Soviet Union and long-standing Soviet problems in agriculture and industry, to the impact of the Soviet Union's losing war in Afghanistan, which cost the government both credibility and popularity, or to the exhausting resistance in the satellite states. Some commentators, like Francis Fukuyama, author of *The End of History* (1992), jubilantly proclaimed the worldwide victory of democracy.

THE COLLAPSE OF COMMUNISM IN EASTERN EUROPE

POLAND

Once again, Solidarity in Poland paved the way. As economic conditions in Poland continued to worsen in the 1980s, Solidarity was able to negotiate itself out of the underground. It was legalized in early 1989 as part of an agreement announcing free elections for a minority of seats in the Polish parliament. This agreement was designed to protect the communist regime, but in the election Solidarity won most of those seats with overwhelming majorities while the Communists failed to win a majority of the seats. Lech Walesa carefully wooed two minor noncommunist parties to create a majority for Solidarity and became prime minister. The new government treaded cautiously at first in politics while eliminating the secret police and the former Soviet leadership, but in the economic sphere, initiated radical changes, adopting shock therapy to make a clear break with the past and bring capitalism to Poland quickly.

AP Tip

Shock therapy was the proposal of Professor Jeffrey Sachs of the United States and other neoconservative economists. Poland's transformation was unusual in that it was guided by the ideas of foreigners. Underpinning shock therapy was the assumption that the transition to capitalism would be relatively easy. This proved not to be the case in many countries.

HUNGARY

Hungary soon followed suit. The Hungarians too had tried to liberate themselves only to be crushed by Warsaw Pact tanks in 1956, although the communist leader János Kádár had liberalized the system economically in exchange for political control. The Communist Party leaders replaced him in 1988 and the next year called for free elections and welcomed Western investment, thinking incorrectly they would now be seen as reformers and win the election. They also opened their borders to East Germany on one side and to Austria on the other; this allowed East Germans fleeing the hard-line regime there to gain easy access to Austria or West Germany. The flight of tens of thousands of Germans, barred in Berlin from the West by the Wall, sparked anticommunist resistance in East Germany, led by intellectuals, environmentalists, and Protestant ministers. Huge demonstrations demanded a democratic if still-socialist society. In response to the growing crisis, the East German government opened the Wall in November 1989; it was torn down by the jubilant West and East Berliners stone by stone. The communist regime found itself replaced by a reform government.

CZECHOSLOVAKIA

In Czechoslovakia, the transition from communism to democracy was so peaceful and stress-free that it was called the Velvet Revolution. Students and intellectuals like the playwright Václav Havel led huge demonstrations, which quickly resulted in first a power-sharing agreement and then soon in the resignation of the communist government. Havel became president at the end of 1989.

AP Tip

It was the repudiation of the Brezhnev Doctrine by Gorbachev, when he withdrew Soviet troops from East Germany and the satellite states, that allowed for the success of the reformers. The widespread joy over the 1989 revolutions was about democracy and capitalism, but it was also about national self-determination.

ROMANIA

But in Romania, the transition was bloody and violent, even though the authoritarian Communist dictator Nicolae Ceauşescu had asserted independence from the Soviet Union in foreign policy. Faced with demonstrations, he ordered his security forces to fire on the protesters; this sparked an armed resistance. Ceauşescu and his wife were captured and executed, and a coalition government was formed.

ALBANIA

In all of communist eastern Europe, only Albania did not experience thorough-going change at this time. Albania had eschewed Marxist-Leninism in favor of Maoism, the peasant-focused communism of China, and had gone its own way for several decades.

THE DISINTEGRATION OF THE SOVIET UNION

In the elections of 1990, the Communist Party was soundly defeated; anticommunists, nationalists or democrats, won clear victories in most major cities. In Lithuania, openly nationalist candidates were elected both as president and to parliament, and they soon declared Lithuania independent. Gorbachev refused to recognize the new government but also refused to send in Soviet troops; instead he proposed a new constitution for the Soviet Union that would formally democratize the political system. Gorbachev became the first president of the Soviet Union, elected by a majority of congressional deputies, but he lost support when he refused to allow an election by universal suffrage, to the benefit of his rival Boris Yeltsin who had been elected leader of the parliament of the Russian Federation. Yeltsin announced his intention to declare Russia's independence from the Soviet Union, winning the support of Russian nationalists as well as proponents of democracy. Gorbachev tried to create a loose confederation to replace the Soviet Union, but six republics refused to join it as nationalism proved too strong.

AP Tip

It is useful to remember that *U.S.S.R.* stood for the Union of Soviet Socialist Republics. According to its theoretically liberal constitution, the individual republics were voluntary members of the Soviet Union. Russia was the largest of the fifteen members states both in population and size, and Russians were privileged in the Soviet system. Under the Soviet system, nationalistic aspirations of other groups—Georgians, Ukrainians, and Lithuanians, for example—were tolerated as long as they remained culturally independent, like retention of costume, music, dance, and food, but were crushed when they became political.

The old guard of the Communist Party, hoping to prevent the disintegration of both party control and the Soviet Union, kidnapped Gorbachev and tried to seize control of the government in August 1991. Massive popular resistance and the clever machinations of Yeltsin rescued Gorbachev and restored him to power. The Communist Party was outlawed and its property confiscated, and when Yeltsin declared Russia independent and the other Soviet republics followed suit, the Soviet Union officially died on Christmas Day 1991. Gorbachev no longer had a job and went into temporary exile. A loose and ultimately unimportant confederation of former Soviet republics called the Commonwealth of Independent States provided a structure of unity.

German Reunification and the End of the Cold War

The transformation of East Germany opened up the possibility of German reunification. In October 1989, reform-minded communists in East Germany, supported by dissidents and intellectuals, tried to create a genuinely democratic form of socialism, a third way between capitalism and Soviet-style communism. They feared that reunification with capitalist West Germany would prevent the realization of the third way. But they could not prevent it. Some 9 million East Germans went through the newly opened Wall to West Germany to visit friends and family, and aroused dreams of one Germany. The West German chancellor Helmut Kohl offered a step-by-step plan for unification, promising immediate economic benefits, such as one-for-one exchange of currencies and preserving the value of East German pensions and savings, and financing a conservative-liberal Alliance for Germany, to counter the idea of the third way; it won nearly half the votes in 1990 parliamentary elections. In the summer of 1990, Gorbachev and Kohl negotiated a settlement to allay Russian fears of military threat of a unified and resurgent Germany. Germany was to unify but pledged to abjure biological, chemical, and nuclear weapons and to give the Soviet Union some much-needed loans. Unification was achieved in October 1990.

The difficulties of incorporating former communist states into the capitalist world were easily apparent in the newly unified Germany. Even with huge investments from West Germany, production sagged in the former East Germany and unemployment reached 20 percent in late 1997. Women particularly suffered. They had had jobs and inexpensive child care under communist rule and now had expensive child care and were under pressure to let men take the few jobs there were. They helped defeat Kohl in his bid for reelection.

AP Tip

This third way would have led to the type of mixed economy with substantial cradle-to-grave social welfare programs that were successful in Sweden. It sought to prevent the type of economic and social dislocation that the sudden adoption of capitalism, with its limited protection for those who lose out in free-enterprise competition, did in fact mean for millions of people in former communist states including Russia.

The cold war ended too, when some twenty-two European delegations met with those from the United States and the Soviet Union in November 1990 and agreed to reduce their armed forces and accept existing borders in Europe. In practice, this Paris Accord was the peace treaty that finally ended World War II. The U.S. president George W. H. Bush and Gorbachev ended the twenty-four-hour alert status for their bombing fleets. The Soviet Union had lost its will to be a world power (temporarily, it later proved), and the United States became the world's one and only superpower. It used its new power in the first Gulf War of 1991 to roll back Iraqi annexation of Kuwait, a military effort supported by the United Nations' Security Council as well as Great Britain and France. The quick defeat of the Iraqi forces reinforced the notion of U.S. military superiority and solo superpower status and of the new world order of stability and international cooperation promised by the first President Bush.

AP Tip

Many Europeans were concerned that with the United States as the sole world power, there would be no balance of power to act as counterbalance and restraint. Some Europeans hoped that the European Union, now encompassing most states on the continent, would become a significant power in world politics and the world economy.

BUILDING A NEW EUROPE IN THE 1990S

The fall of the Soviet system and the Soviet Union opened up a new period in European and world history. It is still so recent and so startling a development that historians must be wary of analyzing it so soon. Yet some things seem to be clear. The drive toward European unity intensified as economic unity was accompanied by a growing uniformity of political, economic, and social institutions. There was general acceptance of free-market capitalism, with U.S. prestige high after the end of cold war and its economy strong during the presidency of Bill Clinton. Poland and Hungary adopted market reforms, freeing prices, privatizing state enterprises, strengthening their currencies, and balancing their budgets. Similar programs were adopted in western Europe in the 1980s as states modified their long-standing welfare capitalism toward the model of Great Britain and the United States. The global economy was also turning toward freer movement of goods, services, and capital, as the computer and electronics revolution encouraged new start-up business enterprises around the globe.

Globalization had both positive and negative consequences. Worldwide economic growth sped up, but unemployment in many sectors of the economy increased as corporations downsized or outsourced jobs, labor unions weakened, and many governments reduced social benefits. In places like France and Germany, where socialist parties and labor unions remained strong, there was substantial resistance to such changes. When financial crises in Asia in the 1990s spread around the globe, the dangers of globalization became apparent to many in both poor and wealthy countries, especially as in poor countries, local industries had a hard time competing and wages remained pitifully low at the same time that international financial institutions like the International Monetary Fund (IMF) insisted on austerity budgets and cuts in government social programs as the price of credit. Protests grew more frequent.

Politically, liberal democracy seemed ascendant as civil liberties were guaranteed everywhere in Europe. This encouraged Fukuyama in his 1992 treatise, *The End of History*, to argue that history had ended with the triumph of democracy, although other commentators, such as James Cronin in his *The World the Cold War Made*, 1996, argued that fervid nationalism and ethnic conflict had returned. In fact, Cronin proved correct, as horrific violence in civil wars in Yugoslavia, as well as in Rwanda and other hot spots, revealed lingering hostilities to people who were religiously or ethnically different. Racist violence against immigrants and minorities occurred throughout Europe too but were limited by a concerted effort of the European Union (EU), as the European Community renamed itself in 1993.

RECASTING RUSSIA

Russia, like Poland, adopted shock therapy to quickly establish market capitalism, energize the economy, and bring prosperity. Industry was rapidly privatized, although control tended to remain in the hands of the managers from the Soviet era; prices on most goods were freed from controls; and citizens were encouraged to buy stocks with a voucher program. But many of the results were devastating for the vast majority of Russians. Prices soared and kept soaring, and production, instead of increasing, dropped by 20 percent, so that by 1996, Russia was producing less than one half of what it had produced in 1991. Inflation continued throughout 1995, and general economic decline only ended in the late 1990s. Rapid liberalization in Russia faced many challenges. It was difficult to transition from military to consumer production. Powerful state enterprises became powerful private monopolies given generous subsidies by the government. They raised prices and cut production to increase their profits and allowed criminal elements into the managerial elite, which made it harder for ordinary Russians to enter the economy. Great wealth was generated particularly in the oil and natural resources industries. A powerful capitalist elite emerged in Moscow, while many ordinary Russians became impoverished as their pensions disappeared and inflation ate up their savings and their salaries. Life expectancy declined rapidly from sixty-nine years in 1991 to fifty-eight years in 1996.

The turmoil in Russia also threatened its fledging democracy. Populists, nationalists, and communists opposed Yeltsin, who consolidated his power at the expense of the opposition and of functional representative government. Democracy became tainted with corruption, poverty, and decline. Yeltsin's chosen successor, Vladimir Putin, was reelected by a landslide in 2004, and reestablished authoritarian control, although he retained free markets. Putin also reasserted Russia's presence in world affairs, although he had to contain the bad news from Russia's war with the tiny Muslim republic of Chechnya, which had declared independence in 1991. As oil prices rose and brought greater economic prosperity and an enlarged middle class, many Russians accepted this combination of political authoritarianism, nationalism, and economic freedom.

PROGRESS IN EASTERN EUROPE

Poland, the Czech Republic, and Hungary fared better than other Soviet satellite states because of their earlier experience with market reforms and their energetic and flexible entrepreneurial elites. They also firmly established constitutional governments, with Walesa in Poland and Havel in Czechoslovakia elected president with comfortable majorities. Havel oversaw the Velvet Divorce of the

Czechs and the Slovaks when Slovakia became independent in 1993. The three states joined NATO in 1997 and have joined the EU.

Elsewhere in eastern Europe, the patterns developed in Russia were paralleled. Ordinary people, particularly the elderly, suffered while new elites, mostly young, prospered. The gap between rich and poor grew, and capital cities saw concentrated wealth as never before while provincial cities suffered from economic stagnation and rising crime and gangsterism. At the same time, nationalism surged. Romania and Bulgaria had particularly hard times, as Western influences were less deeply ingrained and they started out poorer than the other states. They made some progress but not nearly as much as the others.

In Yugoslavia, which had brought six ethnicities together as the Kingdom of the South Slavs after World War I, nationalism reared an especially ugly head. When Josip Tito, the hero of the anti-Nazi resistance and longtime ruler of Yugoslavia, died in 1980, the authority of the individual republics grew. The Serbian president Slobodan Milosevic hoped to unite all the Serbs living in the various republics into Greater Serbia. When he abolished self-rule in the mostly Muslim province of Kosovo, separatism grew. Croatia and Slovenia declared their independence in 1991, Bosnia-Herzegovina the next year, only to face Milosevic's armies. Slovenia held the Serbs off, as did Croatia after initial difficulty, but Bosnia was completely vulnerable, partially because its population was 30 percent Serb. The Serbs fought with unexpected fury, rounding up refugees into concentration camps and engaging in mass murder and rape. A particularly nasty incident occurred in the Muslim city of Srebrenica, where Bosnian Serbs killed several thousand civilians.

AP Tip

The ethnic tensions in Yugoslavia were compounded by religion. Most Serbs are Serbian Orthodox, most Bosnians are Muslims, and most Slovenians and Croatians are Catholic. For many decades the various peoples in Yugoslavia had gotten along pretty well, so the vehemence of the violence was surprising and disturbing. A new term for genocide appeared—*ethnic cleansing.*

NATO responded by bombing Bosnian Serb military targets and kept peacekeeping forces there for years. The U.S. president Bill Clinton negotiated a territorial settlement, but this offered little to the people in Kosovo. The Kosovo Liberation Army, formed by militants in 1998 to achieve independence, was heavily attacked by the Serbs, displacing some quarter of a million people. When Milosevic refused to give in to NATO demands to cease his attacks, NATO began bombing, and after a period of increasing violence and civilian casualties, Milosevic was forced to withdraw. Voted out of office, Milosevic was turned over by the new pro-Western Serbian government to the International Court of Justice in the Netherlands for trial for war crimes. He died after five years in custody in The Hague just before the conclusion of the trial.

UNITY AND IDENTITY IN WESTERN EUROPE

In the 1980s, the movement toward European unity generated new energy. In 1986, the Single European Act created a legal framework for a single market adding free movement of labor, capital, and goods to the already existing free trade. In 1991, the members of the European Community signed the Maastricht Treaty, which announced a common currency, the euro, and common fiscal standards and moved toward greater union on defense and foreign policies. Enthusiastically supported by European elites, Maastricht was regarded with widespread popular skepticism, nationalistic resentments, fear over the loss of social welfare benefits, and anger at "Eureaucrats" imposing common standards from the EC headquarters in Brussels. Nevertheless, most of the member states of the European Community (European Union [EU] in 1993) voted, however narrowly, for the common currency, which came into use in 2002. Britain, however, remained committed to the British pound. Maastricht mandated deficit-reducing cuts, and this caused turmoil on the domestic front, creating many doubts about the value of increasing European unification. In France, for example, unions shut down railroad transportation for a month and won much popular support. The socialists, under François Mitterrand, were returned by the electorate to power and reduced the workweek to thirty-five hours to reduce unemployment but avoid budget cuts.

A new European constitution written in 2004 created a centralized federal system with each state retaining veto power on important taxation and social policies. The changes in the EU raised questions on a number of complex issues. How could it remain cohesive in enlarging from twelve to twenty five members? The new members—Sweden, Austria, Finland, Malta, Cyprus, and eight former Soviet republics—made the population of the EU some 455 million. What should it do about the application for admission of Turkey, with its population of nearly 60 million Muslims, or its relations with the United States? These issues clouded the process of ratification of the EU constitution. The parliaments of nine states approved the new constitution; in seven others, ratification was put to popular referenda. The French and Dutch voted against it, stalling further unification. As the EU leadership reconsidered the problem, it worked on fully incorporating the new members.

AP Tip

Because of these changes, citizens of any member EU state have extraordinary opportunities. They can travel to, study in, or live and work in any other member state without needing work permits or visas, and in most cases, they do not even have to change currency. In a sense, a "United States of Europe" is in the process of being created. Europeans are increasingly European in focus; at the same time, most remained attached to their national identities.

New Challenges in the Twenty-first Century

As the new century began, European and most other industrialized nations experienced a baby bust, the opposite of a baby boom, with the dramatic consequence that older people become a larger and larger proportion of the population. Birthrates in Europe dropped to an average of 1.6 children, with Catholic Italy having the lowest birth rate in the world, down to 1.2 babies per woman. Projections for Germany predict that, should these trends continue, its population would decline by 20 million, to 62 million, by 2050. The causes of this Europe-wide population decline include high unemployment and economic uncertainty, and the women's liberation movement allowing women to choose careers over housework and to have just one child or no children at all (some 30 percent of German women were childless in 2000). By 2005, however, it appeared that birthrates had stabilized.

The Growth of Immigration

Western European states suffering from precipitously low birthrates initially encouraged immigration, bringing in guest workers from Turkey and North Africa, but as numerous migrants, fleeing war and economic dislocation in Africa, the Middle East, and eastern Europe came into western Europe, immigration became a hotly contested issue. In the 1990s, illegal immigrants in the EU numbered about a half million, a significant increase from pervious decades. Some applied for political asylum, others were brought in by "people-smuggling" rings for profit, particularly in the coastal areas of Spain and Italy. Since border controls between member states had been abolished in 1998, landing anywhere in the EU would allow the immigrants to get to other places. Many of those smuggled in were young women, from Ukraine and Russia, who quite typically were forced into prostitution.

Politically, immigration became a divisive issue, with the majority of Europeans fearful of the rising numbers of new immigrants, both from an economic point of view, from their taking scarce jobs, and culturally, as many immigrants were Muslim or nonwhite. Nationalist politicians argued that Muslim immigrants would never assimilate into European culture. Others countered that Europe needed legal immigrants, particularly those with technical skills, and urged the EU to tighten border controls to restrict illegal immigration but also guarantee the civil rights of legal immigrants.

Intellectuals began to forge a new mission for Europe—the promotion of human rights as well as domestic peace to be achieved through international agreements, thereby limiting states' rights in favor of human rights. U.S. leaders, particularly George W. Bush, elected president in 2000, disagreed, reserving independent freedom of action for the United States. For the EU, this new mission meant intervention when human rights were threatened, so it joined the United States to stop the fighting in Kosovo and supported international efforts for the elimination of land mines and chemical weapons. EU states abolished the death penalty and criticized those nations, including the United States and China, that still have it. They offered financial aid to combat AIDS in Africa. Socialists took the lead on many of these issues, as they had in the protests against globalization, and in many states, they regained power. Personal liberties also increased; the Netherlands was the path breaker in this regard, legalizing prostitution as early as 1917, and then recreational drugs, gay marriage, and euthanasia.

AP Tip

A highly influential and controversial book by the American Samuel Huntington, *The Clash of Civilizations and the Remaking of World Order,* 1996, argued that the twenty-first century would be dominated by a struggle between the West and Islam, making the nation-state almost irrelevant. It is this sense of a culture clash that lies at the heart of much of the European debate over immigration.

THE AL-QAEDA ATTACK OF SEPTEMBER 11, 2001

Certainly, future historians will depict one of the key issues of the early twenty-first century to have been the deterioration of relations between the West and the Islamic world, highlighted by the 9/11 attacks, U.S.-led wars in Afghanistan and Iraq, and the increasingly tense relations at home between Muslims and Christians. The 9/11 attacks on the World Trade Center in New York, which brought two 110-story skyscrapers down, and on the Pentagon, killed more than 3,000 people. The United States retaliated with attacks on Afghanistan to end the oppressive rule of the Taliban and to ferret out those responsible for 9/11, the al-Qaeda terrorist network organized and led by Saudi millionaire Osama bin Laden (who was not found).

Terrorism—the intentional use of assassination, kidnappings, and bombings—had been since the nineteenth century a tactic of revolutionary and independence movements, and in the 1960s of radicals within Europe and the United States who sharply opposed U.S. involvement in Vietnam, such as the Red Army Faction in Germany and the Red Brigades in Italy. The 1990s and the early twenty-first century witnessed a new wave of terrorism by religious fundamentalists of different faiths. Islamic fundamentalism, also called political Islam, was behind the 9/11 attacks. "Holy warriors" fought not only against the United States, which they saw as the "great Satan," but against what they saw as corrupt and politically oppressive Arab governments, especially the Saudi monarchy, which the United States supported.

AP Tip

Terrorism was developed as an ideology and used, to some success, in nineteenth-century Russia. There too the notion developed that change can only happen if full-time revolutionaries commit themselves completely to the cause. This has been adopted by many movements, particularly when the options for peaceful change via the democratic process are not seen as possible.

The War in Iraq

The United States also responded to 9/11 with a controversial war against Iraq, for which it requested help from its European allies. A long-standing goal of the Bush administration was to topple the regime of Saddam Hussein and replace it with a democratic, pro-U.S. one. Claiming Iraq had weapons of mass destruction (WMDs), the United States prepared for war, although many doubted that Iraq was aggressive or that such a war was legal or wise. France and Germany, as well as China and Russia, argued instead for the continued use of United Nations weapons inspectors to find and control the WMDs, dividing the United Nations Security Council and threatening the stability of the now fifty-year-old alliance between western Europe and the United States. Among the European powers Britain most actively supported the U.S. war in Iraq. With the Security Council deadlocked, U.S. and British troops invaded Iraq in March 2003 on their own and quickly ended Saddam's dictatorship. A tentative constitutional state came into being, but faced ever-increasing sectarian violence and the real threat of disintegration into three states for the main religious or ethnic groups, Kurds, Shi'ite Muslims, and Sunni Muslims, as well as unemployment and economic decline produced by the war and some poor decisions by the U.S. occupiers. The war grew increasingly unpopular both in Europe and the United States, especially as it became clear that the intelligence about Iraq's WMDs had been faulty or even fraudulent.

The West and Its Muslim Citizens

After 9/11, there were no more terrorist attacks in the United States, but there were several in Europe. Some 250 people were killed when extremists planted a bomb on a Spanish commuter train in 2004; a similar although much less deadly attack took place in London a year later. The Dutch filmmaker Theo van Gogh who had made what was seen by some as an anti-Muslim film was brutally murdered on the streets of Amsterdam. In all these cases, the attackers were local Muslims, typically the sons of immigrants, not foreigners. These attacks intensified the debate over immigration, particularly of Muslims, who numbered some 15 million in Europe in 2006, a number predicted to double by 2025. Some argued that the fact that attackers were living in tolerant and liberal Europe showed that Muslim immigrants could and would not be assimilated, and in fact, were in opposition to Enlightenment values of religious toleration and freedom of thought, equal rights, and representative government that are fundamental to European culture. They denounced Muslim clerics preaching from the many mosques that had sprouted up in major cities as promoters of terrorism and the supremacy of Islamic law over that of the state. Others, however, argued that European states must do better to integrate the Muslim minorities and to provide jobs and job training for recent immigrants, who quite typically lived in depressing housing projects on the outskirts of cities without much hope for personal advancement. The debate was crystallized by riots in France in November 2005 in which hundreds of young second- and third-generation immigrants of Arab origin expressed frustration over unemployment and discrimination by burning cars (see Listening to the Past, pp.1054–1055). The situation for Muslim immigrants in Europe, usually from poor peasant backgrounds, was worse than for those in the United States who were typically well educated. This class difference made integration in Europe more complicated. Europeans had also become increasingly nonreligious, with less than 5 percent of the population attending church on Sunday; this made it harder for them to understand the religious fervor of their Muslim neighbors. The French scholar Olivier Roy called on Europeans to recognize that Islam is now a European religion. Tariq Ramadan, a scholar and public lecturer, demonstrates the vitality of that idea (see Individuals in Society, p. 1051). Of Egyptian ancestry, Ramadan was born and educated in Switzerland and married a Swiss woman who converted to Islam. He speaks favorably about the freedom of religion, legal rights, and security, which are offered to Muslims by the West and which they would not have in most Arab states, and urges Muslims to obey Western laws and work with non-Muslims on common concerns. His criticisms of the U.S. war in Iraq, of globalization and Western capitalism, and of Israeli policies, have led his opponents to suggest that he is really anti-Western.

THE FUTURE IN PERSPECTIVE

While the study of history cannot be definitively predictive of the future, it offers an understanding of historical change and a healthy skepticism to help balance the pendulum predictions of doom and gloom or of peace and happiness. Optimism and pessimism about the future form "the great seesaw," each swing reflecting the conditions and issues of the period. Optimistic predictions were common in the 1950s and 1960s, while pessimistic ones dominated in the 1970s and 1980s, underlaid by fear of pollution, the proliferation of nuclear weapons, the weakening of the traditional family structure, looming unemployment or underemployment, and the threat of high energy prices. Since 9/11, fears of terrorism have engendered a still more pessimistic outlook. But there is much to be optimistic about for Europe. Its recovery from the devastation of World War II, the vitality of the EU, the Velvet Revolution in Czechoslovakia, the strong commitment to human rights, and many other positive developments demonstrate the vigor of European civilization.

Multiple-Choice Questions

1. In which eastern Europe state was the challenge to the communist system successful first?
   (A) Romania
   (B) Poland
   (C) Hungary
   (D) Czechoslovakia
   (E) Chechnya

2. In which state was the end of communist rule accompanied by the execution of its former leader?
   (A) Poland
   (B) Hungary
   (C) Yugoslavia
   (D) Romania
   (E) Czechoslovakia

3. Gorbachev's goal in initiating perestroika and glasnost was to
   (A) introduce capitalism but prevent political democracy.
   (B) enforce the Brezhnev Doctrine on the Soviet satellites.
   (C) outmaneuver his rival, Boris Yeltsin.
   (D) reform the Soviet system in order to maintain it.
   (E) respond to criticisms from western European leaders.

4. The disintegration of the Soviet Union began when
   (A) Lithuania declared its independence.
   (B) Yeltsin announced Russian independence.
   (C) East Germany reunified with West Germany.
   (D) Gorbachev became president of the Russian Federation.
   (E) Poland broke free of Soviet control.

5. The success of Gorbachev's reforms can be most accurately summarized as follows:
   (A) neither glasnost nor perestroika were successful.
   (B) both glasnost and perestroika were successful to more or less equal decrees.
   (C) glasnost was more successful than perestroika.
   (D) perestroika was more successful than glasnost.
   (E) it was dependent on help from the West.

6. Hungary's opening of its borders with East Germany
   (A) led to the opening of the Berlin Wall.
   (B) led to the reelection of the reformist communist leadership in Hungary.
   (C) was strongly protested by West Germany.
   (D) led to a mass exodus from Hungary.
   (E) had few consequences beyond the symbolic.

7. Which was *not* a result of the collapse of Soviet communism in Russia?
   (A) A decline in life expectancy
   (B) A growing gap between rich and poor
   (C) Many new businesses, mostly created by many ordinary Russians
   (D) Inflation and the erosion of savings
   (E) A decline in production

8. German reunification was achieved through
   (A) a promise made by the United States to invest in the East German economy.
   (B) the success of the third way in East Germany.
   (C) the careful negotiations of the West German chancellor Helmut Kohl.
   (D) the enthusiastic support of women in the former East Germany.
   (E) resistance to Gorbachev's hostile response to the idea.

9. In the 1990s, most western European countries
   (A) sought the middle way between socialism and capitalism.
   (B) shifted from the welfare state to deregulation and privatization.
   (C) rejected the proposals of the International Monetary Fund.
   (D) drastically cut taxes to stimulate the economy.
   (E) severely restricted immigration.

10. The Maastricht Treaty of 1991
   (A) ended World War II by accepting national borders.
   (B) replaced NATO once the cold war was over.
   (C) promised European intervention to prevent human rights abuses.
   (D) accepted eastern European countries into the European Union.
   (E) established a common currency for most European Union members.

11. The violence accompanying the breakup of Yugoslavia can best be explained by
   (A) the conflicting nationalisms of its former members.
   (B) differing experiences in postcommunist economic life.
   (C) Slav hatred of non-Slavs.
   (D) interference from outside powers.
   (E) conflicts between communists and anticommunists.

12. Post-9/11 terrorist attacks by militant Muslims were particularly disturbing to Europeans because
   (A) they showed that the EU had made it easy for terrorists to live in Europe.
   (B) the terrorists came from Turkey, which was applying for membership in the EU.
   (C) it revealed a fissure in the unity of Europe, as only Great Britain was attacked.
   (D) most of the terrorists were citizens or long-standing residents of the countries they attacked.
   (E) the United States criticized the countries that were attacked for not supporting its war on terror.

13. Illegal immigrants into western and central Europe in the 1990s
   (A) came mostly from Turkey and the Middle East.
   (B) were mostly Muslim.
   (C) tended to come from eastern Europe and Africa.
   (D) got to Europe easily using public means of transportation.
   (E) were generally welcomed.

14. The "baby bust" in Europe in the 1980s and 1990s was a reflection of all of the following *except*
 (A) high unemployment.
 (B) the rejection of motherhood by some women.
 (C) the late age of women at first pregnancies.
 (D) increasing participation of women in the work force.
 (E) similar attitudes of women about family size across class lines.

15. Fukuyama's optimism that liberal capitalism would be permanently triumphant after the fall of communism was contradicted most clearly by
 (A) the EU's indifference to human rights.
 (B) globalization's encouragement of small business enterprises around the globe.
 (C) resurgent nationalism in Europe.
 (D) the entry of Turkey and its 60 million Muslims into the EU.
 (E) a growing trend toward dictatorship in central and eastern Europe.

Free-Response Questions

1. Analyze the factors that led to the disintegration of the Soviet Union and the collapse of the Soviet system in the 1980s and early 1990s.

2. "All politics is local." Analyze the validity of this statement by evaluating to what degree domestic difficulties impeded the further progress of European unity.

Answers

Multiple-Choice Questions

1. (B) It was the Solidarity movement in Poland that led to revolution in eastern Europe. (McKay, *A History of Western Society*, 8th ed., p. 1035/9th ed., p. 1025)

2. (D) Only in Romania was the communist ruler executed. Ceauşescu was executed by military court in 1989. (McKay, *A History of Western Society*, 8th ed., p. 1037/9th ed., p. 1026)

3. (D) Gorbachev sought to reform the Soviet Union in order to save it. Yeltsin came on the scene after the reforms were already in place. Gorbachev renounced the Brezhnev Doctrine. (McKay, *A History of Western Society*, 8th ed., pp. 1032–1033/9th ed., pp. 1022–1024)

4. (A) Lithuania was the first to declare independence. Yeltsin, not Gorbachev, was president of the Russian Federation and announced his intentions to declare Russia independent of the Soviet Union a few months after Lithuania's bold move. (McKay, *A History of Western Society*, 8th ed., pp. 1037–1038/9th ed., pp. 1026–1027)

5. (C) Glasnost, or openness, was highly successful in opening up the floodgates of public discourse. Perestroika, or restructuring, proved to be more complicated and less thoroughgoing. (McKay, *A History of Western Society*, 8th ed., p. 1033/9th ed., p. 1023)

6. (A) When Hungary opened its borders, large numbers of East Germans fled through its gates; this led the East German government to open the Berlin Wall a few months later. (McKay, *A History of Western Society*, 8th ed., p. 1037/9th ed., p. 1025)

7. (C) The transfer of ownership from the Soviet government to its former managers and the intrusion of criminal elements limited opportunities for ordinary citizens to successfully enter the new economy. Privatization resulted in the concentration of wealth and large-scale enterprises which sought to eliminate competition. (McKay, *A History of Western Society*, 8th ed., pp. 1043–1044/9th ed., p. 1033)

8. (C) Kohl negotiated carefully with East Germans, promising them economic bonanzas, and with the international community. Kohl and Gorbachev signed an agreement to allow unification. East German women were generally hostile to the changes Kohl brought. The United States supported unification but did not play an active role. (McKay, *A History of Western Society*, 8th ed., pp. 1039–1040/9th ed., pp. 1029–1030)

9. (B) Western European countries adopted U.S. and British programs reducing the role of the government in the economy and freer movement of goods and capital, adopting the program of the International Monetary Fund. Taxes were sometimes lowered, but not drastically, in order to balance the budget. (McKay, *A History of Western Society*, 8th ed., p. 1041/9th ed., p. 1031)

10. (E) Maastricht established a monetary union. The treaty accepting borders was the Paris Accord. NATO remains in force. (McKay, *A History of Western Society*, 8th ed., pp. 1040, 1049 /9th ed., pp. 1030, 1039)

11. (A) Croatian, Kosovan, and Bosnian nationalist goals of independence conflicted with Serbian nationalist goals for Greater Serbia. All these peoples are Slavs. The violence occurred after the communists lost power and played little further role. (McKay, *A History of Western Society*, 8th ed., pp. 1047–1048/9th ed., pp. 1037–1039)

12. (D) Britain and Spain both suffered lethal terrorist attacks in 2004 and 2005 made by residents or citizens in those counties. Britain was a strong supporter of U.S. foreign policy. (McKay, *A History of Western Society*, not in 8th ed./9th ed., p. 1049)

13. (C) Immigrants from eastern Europe fled poverty and civil war. Illegal immigrants had a hard time getting to western Europe and often were smuggled in, but had an easy time once they landed traveling in Europe because of the EU's open borders. Anti-immigration political movements developed in most European countries in response to the growing immigrant, legal as well as

illegal, population. (McKay, *A History of Western Society*, 8th ed., pp. 1052–1053/9th ed., pp. 1042–1043)

14. (E) The higher the social class of a woman, the more professional and educated, the greater the likelihood of having fewer or no children. (McKay, *A History of Western Society*, 8th ed., pp. 1051–1052/9th ed., pp. 1041–1042)

15. (C) Turkey has not been admitted to the EU, which has committed itself to protecting human rights. Global capitalism's encouragement of small businesses would be applauded by Fukuyama, although not its negative impact on the poor. (McKay, *A History of Western Society*, 8th ed., p. 1042/9th ed., pp. 1032–1033)

FREE-RESPONSE QUESTIONS

1. Separate the factors leading to the end of the Soviet Union and the Soviet system.

Factors leading to the fall of communism in Russia:

- Economic and political stagnation revealed the need for reform. The Solidarity movement in Poland revealed the degree of workers' discontent and offered a model for reform.
- Gorbachev, who became head of the Soviet Union in 1985, initiated a series of reforms called glasnost (openness) and perestroika (restructuring) to allow for freer discourse on the problems facing the Soviet Union and for economic reforms such as the loosening up of price controls and introduction of profit-making cooperatives. Democratization and the end of one-party rule allowed for free elections and the transformation of the Congress of People's Deputies into a bona fide legislature. Glasnost and democratization ultimately went much further than Gorbachev had planned.
- The economic reforms were too little and too meager; inflation, shortages of goods, created hostility to Gorbachev and his reform movement.
- Gorbachev lost further support by not attacking Lithuania when it declared its independence and by not agreeing to election by universal suffrage. Yeltsin, now an advocate of democracy and Russian nationalism, outmaneuvered Gorbachev, although Yeltsin rescued him from kidnapping by the antireformists, and then effectively replaced him when Yeltsin became president of Russia.

Factors leading to the collapse of the Soviet Union:

- Nationalistic urges grew in member states of the Soviet Union.
- Gorbachev renounced the Brezhnev Doctrine and the use of force to impose Soviet will. When Lithuania's newly elected government declared independence, the Soviet Union did not send troops.
- Yeltsin asserted the independence of Russia from the Soviet Union in 1991. All remaining Soviet republics quickly followed suit, and the Soviet Union collapsed.

2. To answer this question properly, first discuss the evidence for a blockage in the continued growth of European unity, and then analyze to what degree domestic concerns explain that blockage.

- Blockages to European unity were revealed by the refusal of Britain to join the common EU currency system and by the rejection by majorities of French and Dutch voters of the new EU constitution proposed in 2004 that would have created a federal form of government for the EU.
- One main reason for the hesitation about the new constitution was nationalistic sentiment and fears over the loss of national sovereignty and about the potential loss of European identity should the EU come to include the distinctly different former Soviet republics of Ukraine and Georgia and the mostly Muslim Turkey. The apportionment of votes in the proposed voting system was based on population; this would limit the influence and power of less populous states.
- Anti-immigration movements arose in response to growing numbers of immigrants, both legal and illegal, in western and central Europe. Cultural and religious differences roused racist elements. The abandonment of border controls within the EU was blamed for the ease of movement of these immigrants within Europe. Militant Muslims, some of whom staged terrorist attacks on Britain and Spain, stirred fears of the undermining of Enlightenment values and the resistance to assimilation on the part of the new immigrants.
- Economic difficulties, particularly unemployment and underemployment, intensified competition for jobs and resentment over the expanding EU, which insisted on certain economic policies from its headquarters in Brussels. The acceptance into the EU of many states still adapting to the end of communist rule meant a wide gap in income and economic development between the original members of the EU and its new ones, and added to the economic burdens of the EU.

Part III

Practice Tests

Practice Test 1

AP EUROPEAN HISTORY EXAMINATION
SECTION I: Multiple-Choice Questions
Time—55 minutes
Number of questions: 80

Directions The questions or incomplete statements below are each followed by five suggested answers. Select the best answer to each question.

MULTIPLE-CHOICE QUESTIONS

1. Compare Map 22.2 with Map 22.3. Which of the following statements is an accurate conclusion based on a comparison of these maps?
   (A) England had more industrialized areas than the continent had emerging industrialized areas.
   (B) England had a greater population than the German Confederation and France combined.
   (C) The continent had more ironworks per capita than England.
   (D) England had 50 percent more coalfields in terms of square miles than the continent did.
   (E) England had a more developed railroad system than the continent did.

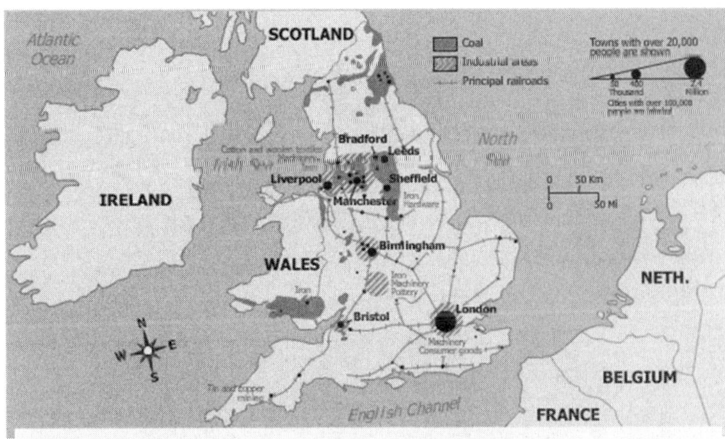

MAP 22.2. THE INDUSTRIALIZED REVOLUTION IN ENGLAND, CA 1850

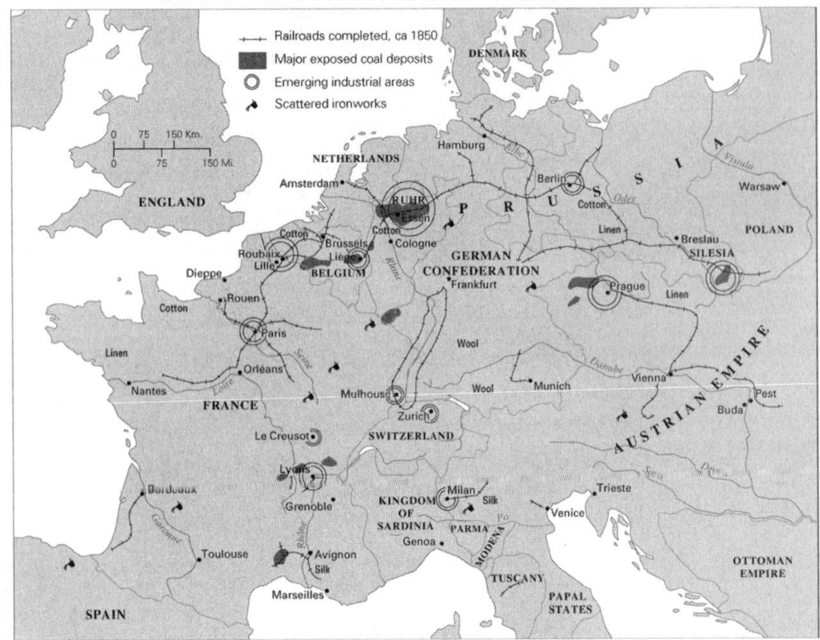

MAP 22.3 CONTINENTAL INDUSTRIALIZATION, CA 1850

GO ON TO NEXT PAGE

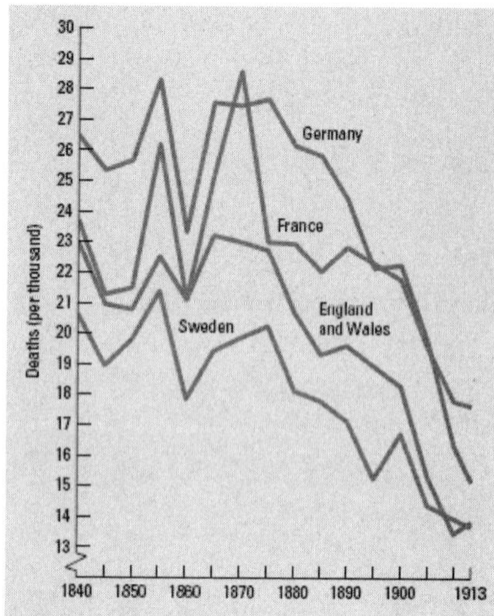

FIGURE 24.1

2. All of the following factors helped contribute to the trend exhibited by the chart above *except*
   (A) a rising standard of living.
   (B) improvements in public health.
   (C) medical advances.
   (D) improved public transportation.
   (E) the development of the germ theory.

3. This painting by Vincent van Gogh, *The Starry Night,* represents the transition between
   (A) impressionism and realism.
   (B) impressionism and expressionism.
   (C) romanticism and impressionism.
   (D) postimpressionism and superrealism.
   (E) postimpressionism and cubism.

4. In Europe, by the mid-sixteenth century, black slaves
   (A) had not begun to arrive.
   (B) were small in number and widely dispersed.
   (C) suffered worse conditions than they did in the colonies.
   (D) typically returned to Africa if they were freed.
   (E) intermarried with serfs and became mulattos.

5. What contributed to Europeans' susceptibility to the Black Death in the fourteenth and fifteenth centuries?
   (A) New farming methods
   (B) Superstition and fear
   (C) Famine and malnutrition
   (D) Dependence on herbal remedies
   (E) Most people living in the countryside

6. The Great Schism refers to
   (A) a split within the Roman Catholic Church around the turn of the fifteenth century.
   (B) the feud between England and France that led to the Hundred Years' War.
   (C) the peasant revolts that arose in Europe during the fourteenth century.
   (D) the devastating effects of the Black Death on Europe.
   (E) the unwillingness of monks from the noble classes to do the work of lay brothers from the peasant classes.

7. The Renaissance was able to begin in Italy because of
   (A) Italy's superior monasteries.
   (B) the dominance of the Catholic Church in Italy.
   (C) strong alliances between Italian city-states.
   (D) wealth created from Italy's extensive trade network.
   (E) Italy's strong sense of nationalism.

8. All of the following are intellectual hallmarks of the Renaissance *except*
   (A) individualism.
   (B) nationalism.
   (C) humanism.
   (D) secularism.
   (E) aestheticism.

9. Italian Renaissance art differed from medieval art in that Renaissance art
   (A) focused more on religious themes and motifs.
   (B) was more impressionistic and less concerned with the realism of the figures that were depicted.
   (C) was funded by the church.
   (D) brought less prestige and acclamation to the artist.
   (E) promoted greater individuality.

10. An educated Renaissance woman
   (A) was expected to bring prestige to her husband and household.
   (B) could teach certain courses at local universities.
   (C) was no better educated than an educated woman from the medieval era.
   (D) had to publish any writings under the name of a man.
   (E) could run for political office.

11. Louis XI, the Spider King, helped curb feudal disorder and expand royal authority in France by
   (A) bringing an end to the Hundred Years' War.
   (B) raising revenues through industry and taxation to improve the army.
   (C) signing treaties with individual feudal lords that declared his supremacy.
   (D) ceding certain territories to Charles the Bold, duke of Burgundy.
   (E) establishing common law.

12. The Inquisition in Spain was spurred by
   (A) rising unrest among the peasants as famine struck the countryside.
   (B) Ferdinand and Isabella's desire to appear tolerant to their subjects.
   (C) mounting anti-Semitism and resentment toward wealthy New Christians.
   (D) Spain's desire for French lands on the continent.
   (E) the intellectual curiosity promoted during the Renaissance.

13. Which of the following statements could be made by a Protestant, rather than a Catholic?
   (A) Salvation comes through faith alone.
   (B) Indulgences demonstrate one's sincerity of repentance.
   (C) Only clergy should interpret scriptures.
   (D) There are seven sacraments.
   (E) In the process of transubstantiation, the bread and wine become the actual body and blood of Christ.

14. Martin Luther wrote the Ninety-five Theses
   (A) hoping to start the Lutheran Church.
   (B) to argue against the practice of selling indulgences.
   (C) on the basis of his belief in predestination.
   (D) to prove his ability to become a priest.
   (E) as a rebuttal to John Calvin's teachings.

15. During the sixteenth century, Geneva became
   (A) a bulwark of Catholic doctrine.
   (B) financially ruined due to the faulty decisions of its leaders.
   (C) religiously neutral to avoid conflict between its citizens.
   (D) a meeting place for the first ecumenical council of the Counter-Reformation.
   (E) a model Christian community established by John Calvin.

GO ON TO NEXT PAGE

16. In terms of her religious preferences, Queen Elizabeth I was best known as a(n)
    (A) staunch Catholic.
    (B) strict Puritan.
    (C) follower of Calvin.
    (D) moderate Protestant.
    (E) Anabaptist.

17. Which of the following was *not* an outcome of the Catholic Reformation?
    (A) The establishment of new religious orders
    (B) A reconciliation with Protestantism
    (C) Greater clerical discipline
    (D) A strong Roman Inquisition to destroy heresy
    (E) Spiritual renewal within the church

18. France experienced riots and civil wars during the sixteenth century because of
    (A) religious conflicts between Catholics and Huguenots.
    (B) religious conflicts between Protestants and Huguenots.
    (C) class conflicts between the aristocracy and the peasants.
    (D) political conflicts between *politiques* and monarchists.
    (E) political conflicts between the republicans and the *politiques*.

19. Philip II
    (A) sailed at the head of the Spanish Armada and invaded England.
    (B) willingly relinquished Spain's hold over the Netherlands.
    (C) supported a plot to assassinate Elizabeth I.
    (D) promoted religious toleration in Spain.
    (E) adopted many of Martin Luther's ideas.

20. The Peace of Westphalia, which marked the end of the Thirty Years' War, was a turning point in Europe because it signified
    (A) an end to the religious wars that began during the Reformation.
    (B) a unified Germany, ruled by the king of Prussia.
    (C) an end to the Holy Roman Empire.
    (D) the dominance of Calvinism throughout Germany.
    (E) a German nation on the rise with a strong economy to support it.

21. The initial leader in Europe's exploration of the world during the fifteenth century was
    (A) France.
    (B) England.
    (C) Spain.
    (D) Portugal.
    (E) Germany.

22. Which of the following was *not* a motive for European exploration during the fifteenth and sixteenth centuries?
    (A) Desire for greater economic opportunities
    (B) Renaissance-inspired curiosity about the physical world and its peoples
    (C) Promoting the Renaissance ideals of education and culture to other peoples
    (D) Increased desire for spices
    (E) Desire to spread Christianity to other lands

23. The exchange of food, animals, plants, and diseases between the Old World and the New World during the sixteenth century is often referred to as
    (A) the Columbian exchange.
    (B) *Mundus Novus.*
    (C) Indian trading.
    (D) the age of discovery.
    (E) the Euro-American trade network.

24. During the sixteenth century, slaves
    (A) were emancipated in Europe.
    (B) were introduced on the European continent as efficient workers.
    (C) converted in large numbers to Christianity, under the influence of European missionaries.
    (D) were used by European explorers to make their fortunes.
    (E) were used as soldiers to supplement dwindling European armies.

25. Which of the following authors, famous for his understanding of human nature, wrote during the Elizabethan and Jacobean eras?
    (A) Geoffrey Chaucer
    (B) William Shakespeare
    (C) William Laud
    (D) John Locke
    (E) Adam Smith

26. Peter Paul Rubens is one of the most famous artists of
    (A) the Baroque era.
    (B) classicism.
    (C) modernism.
    (D) impressionism.
    (E) the Renaissance.

27. Absolutism is similar to totalitarianism in all of the following ways *except* that absolute rulers
    (A) employed fear and intimidation tactics to gain control of the people.
    (B) had better financial resources at their disposal.
    (C) sought to control all aspects of a state's culture.
    (D) sometimes allowed constitutions for the government of their nations.
    (E) lacked the technology and resources to fully control the state.

28. Louis XIV accomplished all of the following *except*
    (A) establishing the palace of Versailles as an artistic wonder.
    (B) appointing Cardinal Richelieu as his chief counselor.
    (C) cooperation with and limited control over the nobility.
    (D) the revocation of the Edict of Nantes.
    (E) appointing Jean-Baptiste Colbert as his chief financial minister.

29. Oliver Cromwell's Protectorate can best be described as a(n)
    (A) Puritan democracy.
    (B) military dictatorship.
    (C) constitutional monarchy.
    (D) absolute monarchy.
    (E) Catholic commonwealth.

30. The Glorious Revolution in England signified an end to
    (A) taxation without representation.
    (B) religious intolerance.
    (C) Queen Elizabeth's reign.
    (D) divine-right monarchy.
    (E) Protestant power.

31. The Dutch Republic in the seventeenth century was best known for
    (A) commercial prosperity.
    (B) peasant unrest and riots.
    (C) being the first country to grant women's suffrage.
    (D) promoting Catholicism over Protestantism.
    (E) dramatic inflation.

32. By the mid-eighteenth century, Frederick William of Prussia had
    (A) expelled all Jews from his land.
    (B) established one of the strongest trade networks in the world.
    (C) colonized parts of Africa.
    (D) established one of the strongest armies in Europe.
    (E) been elected to head a republican government.

33. Peter the Great built St. Petersburg
    (A) because Moscow was too cold in the winter.
    (B) because he wanted a port for trade and military power.
    (C) in order to provide jobs for unemployed Russians.
    (D) because he fell in love with the perfection of the land.
    (E) to show his rejection of all things European and modern.

34. One of the earliest controversial ideas that arose during the scientific revolution was the
(A) geocentric model of the universe.
(B) theory of relativity.
(C) heliocentric model of the universe.
(D) law of universal gravitation.
(E) idea that empiricism was outdated and unscientific.

35. The Enlightenment is associated with all of the following *except*
(A) dependence on reason.
(B) use of the scientific method.
(C) progress of humanity.
(D) existentialism.
(E) secularism.

36. Frederick the Great of Prussia and Catherine the Great of Russia are examples of
(A) enlightened absolutists.
(B) enlightened republicans.
(C) parliamentary leaders.
(D) mercantilists.
(E) imperialists.

37. Europe's surge in population growth in the early eighteenth century was due in part to
(A) Europe's importation of slaves.
(B) more scientific farming methods.
(C) an end to the enclosure movement.
(D) no longer relying on crop rotation.
(E) increased use of chemical fertilizers and pesticides.

38. The putting-out system was a key feature of
(A) the scientific revolution.
(B) the agricultural revolution.
(C) cottage industry.
(D) the Atlantic slave trade.
(E) mercantilism.

39. Which of the following statements regarding foundling hospitals was true in the eighteenth century?
(A) There were long waiting lists to adopt foundlings.
(B) Foundling hospitals were necessary only in the cities.
(C) Foundling hospitals provided care that enabled most foundlings to survive.
(D) Foundling hospitals were labeled legalized infanticide.
(E) Foundling hospitals provided simple education for the older children.

40. All of the following factors played a part in starting the French Revolution *except*
(A) religious struggles between Catholics and Huguenots.
(B) the success of the American Revolution.
(C) rising debts of the French government.
(D) power struggles between the monarchy and the bourgeoisie.
(E) poor harvests and high bread prices.

41. Why did the French so willingly submit themselves to Napoleon Bonaparte's rule?
(A) Napoleon promised the French "peace, bread, and land."
(B) French voters were charmed by his winning personality.
(C) The French were no longer willing to submit themselves to absolute rulers.
(D) Napoleon promised to continue the French Revolution.
(E) The French were looking for stability and authority after years of turmoil.

42. One reason the Industrial Revolution began in Great Britain was
   (A) inadequate farming methods made the British look for other sources of income.
   (B) after years of political turmoil, the British were hoping industry would help them to settle down.
   (C) the British never took part in cottage industry, so the country was waiting for something to fill this void.
   (D) proximity to waterways made shipping raw materials and finished goods relatively easy.
   (E) the high tariffs imposed by the British government encouraged people to create their own manufactured goods.

43. What was one of the more significant impacts of the Industrial Revolution on Europe?
   (A) A dramatic decrease in agricultural output, as farmers abandoned their land to work in factories
   (B) Improved relations between the working class and the middle class
   (C) Significantly better living conditions for city dwellers who worked in factories
   (D) A rise in trade unions
   (E) Greater opportunities and rights for women

44. At the Congress of Vienna, European countries actively sought
   (A) religious reform.
   (B) a balance of power.
   (C) an end to tariffs and other trade restrictions.
   (D) industrial power.
   (E) imperialist policies.

45. All of the following were significant and influential hallmarks of nineteenth-century Europe *except*
   (A) liberalism.
   (B) nationalism.
   (C) socialism.
   (D) communism.
   (E) romanticism.

46. Which of the following suffered the decimation of its population during the mid-nineteenth century?
   (A) England due to enclosures
   (B) Ireland due to famine
   (C) Germany due to war
   (D) Spain's colonies due to rebellion
   (E) Scotland due to invasion

47. All of the following contributed to improvements in public health in the latter half of the nineteenth century *except*
   (A) sewage systems.
   (B) acceptance of the germ theory.
   (C) rejection of the antiseptic principle.
   (D) running water systems in cities.
   (E) vaccinations.

48. As ruler of France, Louis Napoleon's authority in the 1850s and early 1860s most closely resembled that of a(n)
   (A) enlightened despot.
   (B) British prime minister.
   (C) American president.
   (D) British monarch.
   (E) totalitarian dictator.

49. Italy became an officially united nation in 1860 and created a
   (A) socialist government led by Count Camillo di Cavour.
   (B) parliamentary monarchy led by Victor Emmanuel.
   (C) republic led by Giuseppe Garibaldi.
   (D) democracy led by Giuseppe Mazzini.
   (E) dictatorship led by Vincenzo Gioberti.

50. When Russian leaders decided to modernize, one of Russia's first and greatest social reforms of the mid-nineteenth century was the
   (A) emancipation of the serfs.
   (B) formation of the zemstvos.
   (C) abdication of the tsar.
   (D) building of a transcontinental railway.
   (E) the establishment of compulsory education for Russian peasants.

51. Zionism refers to the movement advocating
    (A) suffrage for Jews.
    (B) suffrage for women.
    (C) child labor laws.
    (D) the establishment of a Jewish homeland.
    (E) a balance of power in Europe.

52. The most typical European migrants in the latter half of the nineteenth century were
    (A) desperately impoverished landless peasants.
    (B) small farmers and skilled artisans.
    (C) urban proletarians.
    (D) wealthy aristocrats.
    (E) middle-class merchants and shopkeepers.

53. At the Berlin Conference, the European powers
    (A) agreed on how to divide Africa among themselves.
    (B) brought a halt to imperialism.
    (C) opened the doors to China and Japan.
    (D) barred Asian migrants from entering European countries.
    (E) established a Jewish homeland.

54. Causes of the new imperialism included all of the following *except*
    (A) the desire for international prestige.
    (B) the competition for foreign markets.
    (C) the "white man's burden."
    (D) the lucrative slave trade.
    (E) spreading Christianity.

55. Which country was considered the "jewel of the British Empire" and why?
    (A) Canada for its furs
    (B) India for its spices and tea
    (C) Australia for its land
    (D) New Zealand for its location
    (E) South Africa for its diamonds and gold

56. By 1914, the only two African countries that were independent of European rule were
    (A) Nigeria and the Congo.
    (B) Libya and Egypt.
    (C) Ethiopia and Liberia.
    (D) Sierra Leone and Mozambique.
    (E) Angola and Cameroon.

57. In forming the Triple Alliance, Bismarck was primarily motivated by his desire to
    (A) win favor with the Russians.
    (B) go to war with Great Britain.
    (C) win back Alsace-Lorraine.
    (D) end the Franco-Prussian War.
    (E) isolate France.

58. Though there were many causes for World War I, the spark that ignited the fuse was
    (A) the formation of the Triple Alliance.
    (B) the destruction of the Ottoman Empire.
    (C) the assassination of Archduke Francis Ferdinand.
    (D) Germany's invasion of Poland.
    (E) the Moroccan crisis.

59. The trench warfare of World War I resulted in
    (A) quick victories for the British.
    (B) minuscule gains in territory.
    (C) fewer lives lost than in the Franco-Prussian War.
    (D) protection from gas attacks.
    (E) increased bombing.

60. World War I was considered a total war because
    (A) widespread bombing of civilians became acceptable.
    (B) every country in the world became involved.
    (C) countries were also fighting poverty and illiteracy on the home front.
    (D) newspapers reported all the most gruesome aspects of the war.
    (E) governments controlled social and economic policies on the home front.

61. Russia's involvement in World War I can best be described as
    (A) crucial for turning the tide of the war in favor of the Central Powers.
    (B) insignificant in terms of the outcome of the war.
    (C) the most difficult front for the Germans and Austrians.
    (D) a slaughter of the Russian peasants.
    (E) an exhibition of great military strategy on the part of Russian generals.

62. Lenin came to power in Russia
    (A) with the aid of the Germans.
    (B) after defeating Kerensky in the polls.
    (C) by working closely with the Provisional Government.
    (D) with aid from the United States.
    (E) by working his way up from the bottom of the Moscow government power chain.

63. Which of the following was *not* a reason for Bolshevik success in the Russian Revolution?
    (A) The establishment of war communism
    (B) Intimidation by the Cheka
    (C) Foreign military intervention
    (D) Trotsky forming a disciplined army
    (E) The White Army controlling the center of Russia

64. The Treaty of Versailles resulted in all of the following *except*
    (A) the establishment of the League of Nations.
    (B) an emphasis on national self-determination.
    (C) Alsace-Lorraine remaining part of Germany.
    (D) Germany losing its overseas colonies.
    (E) Germany having to pay war reparations.

65. In the years immediately after World War I, modern philosophers
    (A) expressed optimism in Europe's ability to improve the world.
    (B) turned back to the ancient Greek philosophers for answers to life's questions.
    (C) relied heavily on rational scientific thought.
    (D) challenged the belief in human progress.
    (E) turned to Christianity for help with their struggles.

66. All of the following dominated the art and design world of the twentieth century *except*
    (A) functionalism.
    (B) revisionism.
    (C) postimpressionism.
    (D) cubism.
    (E) Dadaism.

67. In the early 1930s, Europe was marked by
    (A) extreme economic hardship.
    (B) a growing sense of solidarity among the countries.
    (C) outright rejection of the Treaty of Versailles.
    (D) far more opportunities for women to work outside the home.
    (E) a rejection of socialist political practices.

68. Stalin was responsible for all of the following practices or policies in the Soviet Union *except*
    (A) the New Economic Policy (NEP).
    (B) the Five-Year Plans.
    (C) collectivization of the farms.
    (D) rapid industrialization.
    (E) purges.

69. Mussolini's fascists won widespread support from
    (A) socialists.
    (B) communists.
    (C) conservatives.
    (D) parliament.
    (E) Jews.

GO ON TO NEXT PAGE

70. Which of the following was *not* true of Mussolini's Italy and Hitler's Germany?
(A) Both leaders were dictators.
(B) Both leaders made a secret pact with Stalin.
(C) Both governments created fascist youth movements.
(D) Both countries were fiercely nationalistic.
(E) Both societies emphasized the woman's role in the home.

71. Hitler was allowed to reoccupy the Rhineland because of
(A) French retraction of the Treaty of Versailles.
(B) the policy of self-determination.
(C) the German blitzkrieg.
(D) the British policy of appeasement.
(E) the vote cast by the citizens of the Rhineland.

72. All of the following helped the Allies to win World War II in Europe *except*
(A) the United States' policy of Europe first.
(B) the Allies' ability to temporarily overlook political differences.
(C) the atomic bomb attack.
(D) the Allies' principle of unconditional surrender.
(E) the Allies' military resources.

73. All of the following were direct or indirect results of World War II *except* the
(A) cold war.
(B) deaths of more than 6 million Jews.
(C) Great Depression.
(D) dropping of atomic bombs on Hiroshima and Nagasaki.
(E) deaths of more than 50 million soldiers and civilians.

74. After Stalin's death, the Soviet Union
(A) turned in on itself, refusing to become involved with the affairs of other countries.
(B) collapsed.
(C) experienced a dramatic decrease in its standard of living.
(D) went through a process of de-Stalinization.
(E) accepted capitalism as its economic model.

75. The revolutions of 1989
(A) ended in great loss of human lives throughout eastern Europe.
(B) were triggered by the intervention of the United States.
(C) brought Gorbachev to power in the Soviet Union.
(D) brought an end to communism throughout the world.
(E) were largely peaceful in nature.

76. The most compelling cause of European decolonization was that
(A) Asian and African peoples called for national self-determination and equality.
(B) Europeans were losing money from their colonies.
(C) Europeans had already taken all the natural resources from the colonies, so they no longer had use for them.
(D) the Treaty of Versailles called for self-determination.
(E) the colonies had all turned to communism.

77. In the 1990s, western Europe experienced both
(A) a communist resurgence and socialist revolutions.
(B) a baby bust and a surge of illegal immigration.
(C) a genocide and civil war.
(D) decreased employment opportunities for women and increased birthrates.
(E) an educational gap between men and women and a strong economy.

78. The twentieth century differed from the nineteenth century in that
   (A) women were finally allowed to work outside the home in the twentieth century.
   (B) railroads became an indispensable mode of transportation in the twentieth century.
   (C) European birthrates declined in the twentieth century.
   (D) people increasingly looked to science for answers in the twentieth century.
   (E) communism triumphed in parts of Europe and Asia in the twentieth century.

79. Place the following British rulers in the correct chronological order:
   I. James I
   II. Elizabeth I
   III. Charles I
   IV. Oliver Cromwell
   (A) I, II, III, and IV
   (B) II, III, IV, and I
   (C) I, III, II, and IV
   (D) II, I, III, and IV
   (E) III, I, IV, and II

80. Place the following events of the French Revolution in the correct chronological order:
   I. The storming of the Bastille
   II. The Oath of the Tennis Court
   III. The meeting of the Estates General
   IV. The Reign of Terror
   V. Louis XVI executed
   (A) I, II, III, IV, and V
   (B) III, II, I, V, and IV
   (C) II, III, I, IV, and V
   (D) III, I, II, IV, and V
   (E) I, IV, V, II, and III

STOP

END OF SECTION I

IF YOU FINISH BEFORE TIME IS CALLED, YOU MAY CHECK YOUR WORK ON THIS SECTION. DO NOT GO ON TO SECTION II UNTIL YOU ARE TOLD TO DO SO.

AP EUROPEAN HISTORY EXAMINATION
Section II: Free-Response Essays

Section II of the examination has two kinds of questions. Part A is the Document-Based Question, which you must answer. Part B and Part C each have three general free-response essay questions. You are to answer *one* essay question from Part B and *one* essay question from Part C. You will have a total of 130 minutes to complete the document-based essay and two free-response essays.

Part A: Document-Based Question (DBQ)
Suggested reading time—15 minutes
Suggested writing time—45 minutes
Percent of Section II score—45

Directions The following question is based on the accompanying Documents 1–12. The documents have been edited for the purpose of this exercise. Write your answer on the tinted pages of the Section II free-response booklet.

This question is designed to test your ability to work with and understand historical documents.

Write an essay that

- Provides an appropriate, explicitly stated thesis that directly addresses all parts of the question and does *not* simply restate the question
- Discusses a majority of the documents individually and specifically
- Demonstrates understanding of the basic meaning of a majority of the documents
- Supports the thesis with appropriate interpretation of a majority of the documents
- Analyzes the documents by explicitly grouping them in at least three appropriate ways
- Takes into account both the sources of the documents and the authors' point of view

You may refer to relevant historical information not mentioned in the documents.

1. Analyze the changing views held by women about women's nature and their place in society between 1500 and 1900.

   Historical Background: Most European women were granted the right to vote in the early twentieth century, generally after World War I. Before that, women were by and large severely restricted in their rights and opportunities for education or employment, both by law and by custom. While poor women always did productive labor, whether in the fields or in towns, middle- and upper-class women lived more comfortable lives but were barred from the educational, intellectual, and employment opportunities available to men of their station in life. Exceptions were a number of women who played important political roles, such as Queen Elizabeth I of England and Queen Isabella of Spain. Numerous women wrote about women's issues over the centuries.

Document 1

Christine de Pizan, 1364–ca. 1430, French author who supported her family by writing after being widowed. *The Book of the City of Ladies: Advice for a "Wise Princess,"* 1404

The sixth teaching: how the wise princess will keep the women of her court in good order. The women should restrain themselves with seemly conduct among knights and squires and all men. They should speak demurely and sweetly and, whether in dances or other amusements, divert and enjoy themselves decorously and without wantonness. They must not be frolicsome, forward, or boisterous in speech, expression, bearing or laughter. They must not go about with their heads raised like wild deer. This kind of behavior would be very unseemly and greatly derisory in a woman of the court, in whom there should be more modesty, good manners and courteous behavior than in any others, for where there is most honor there ought to be the most perfect manners and behavior.

Document 2

Laura Cereta, 1469–1499, Italian humanist and author, "Letter to Bibulus Sempronius," 13 January 1488, manuscript *Epistolae familiares,* published in 1640

You [Bibulus] brashly and publicly not merely wonder but indeed lament that I am said to possess as fine a mind as nature ever bestowed upon the most learned man. You seem to think so learned a woman has scarcely before been seen in the world. You are wrong. . . . The explanation is clear: women have been able by nature to be exceptional, but have chosen lesser goals. For some women are concerned with parting their hair correctly, adorning themselves with lovely dresses, . . . or standing at mirrors to smear their lovely faces. But those in whom a deeper integrity yearns for virtue, restrain from the start their youthful souls, reflect on higher things, harden the body with sobriety and trials, and curb their tongues, open their ears, compose their thoughts in wakeful hours, their minds in contemplation to letters bonded to righteousness. For knowledge is not given as a gift, but [is gained] with diligence. Nature has generously lavished its gifts upon all people, opening to all the doors of choice through which reason sends envoys to the will. . . . You pretend that I alone am admirable because of the good fortune of my intellect. But I, compared to other women who have won splendid renown, am but a little mousling.

Source: Margaret L. King and Albert Rabil Jr., *Her Immaculate Hand* (SUNY-Binghamton: Medieval and Renaissance Texts and Studies, 1983); Modern History Sourcebook online.

GO ON TO NEXT PAGE

Document 3

St. Teresa of Avila (Teresa de Cepeda y Ahumada), 1515–1582, *Life of St. Teresa of Jesus, of The Order of Our Lady of Carmel* (London: Thomas Baker; New York: Benziger Bros., 1904)

I will relate what I saw, by way of warning to men to be on their guard against women who will do things of this kind. . . . Women—for they are more bound to purity than men—if once they have lost all shame before God, are in nothing whatever to be trusted; and that in exchange for the gratification of their will, and of that affection which the devil suggests, they will hesitate at nothing. . . . All men must have a greater affection for those women whom they see disposed to be good; and even for the attainment of earthly ends, women must have more power over men because they are good. . . . For the rest, it is enough that I am a woman to make my sails droop: how much more, then, when I am a woman, and a wicked one?

Source: Christian Classics Ethereal Library

Document 4

Louise Labé, 1524/1525–1566, French poet, linguist, soldier, trained in Latin. Letter to a friend

Since a time has come, Mademoiselle, when the severe laws of men no longer prevent women from applying themselves to the sciences and other disciplines, it seems to me that those of us who can, should use this long-craved freedom to study and to let men see how greatly they wronged us when depriving us of its honor and advantages. And if any woman becomes so proficient as to be able to write down her thoughts, let her do so and not despise the honor but rather flaunt it instead of fine clothes, necklaces, and rings. For these may be considered ours only by use, whereas the honor of being educated is ours entirely.

Source: Quoted in *Uppity Women of Medieval Times* by Vicki León, 1997
www.feminist.com/resources/quotes/womenshistory.html.

Document 5

Mary Cary, English member of the Fifth Monarchy millenarian sect during the English Revolution, which thought that the end of the world was near and argued that women could be preachers and ministers. *The New Jerusalem's Glory,* 1656

And if there be very few men that are thus furnished with the gift of the Spirit; how few are the women! Not but that there are many godly women, many who have indeed received the Spirit: but in how small a measure is it? how weak are they? and how unable to prophesie? for it is that that I am speaking of, which this text says they shall do; which yet we see not fulfilled. . . . But the time is coming when this promise shall be fulfilled, and the Saints shall be abundantly filled with the spirit; and not only men, but women shall prophesie; not only aged men, but young men; not only superiours, but inferiours; not only those that have University learning, but those that have it not; even servants and handmaids.

Source: Mary Cary, *The New Jerusalem's Glory* (London, 1656), p. 238; Modern History Sourcebook online.

Document 6

Mary Astell, 1668 1731, English writer who never married. *Some Reflections Upon Marriage,* 1700

But how can a Woman scruple entire Subjection, how can she forbear to affirm the Worth and Excellency of the Superior Sex, if she at all considers it! Have not all the great Actions that have been performed in the World been done by Men? Have they not founded Empires and over-turned them? Do they not make Laws and continually repeal and amend them? Their vast Minds lay Kingdoms waste, no Bounds or Measures can be prescribed to their Desires. War and Peace depend on them; they . . . have the Wisdom and Courage to get over all . . . the petty Restraints which Honor and Conscience may lay in the way of their desired Grandeur. What is it they cannot do? They make Worlds and ruin them, form Systems of universal Nature, and dispute eternally about them; their Pen gives Worth to the most trifling Controversy. . . . It is a Woman's Happiness to hear, admire and praise them, especially if a little Ill nature keeps them at any time from bestowing the Applauses to each other! And if she aspires no further, she is thought to be in her proper Sphere of Action, she is as wise and as good as can be expected from her!

Source: http://www.pinn.net/~sunshine/march99/astell4.html.

GO ON TO NEXT PAGE

Document 7

Marianne Loir, 1715–1769, French artist, translator of Newton's Principia Mathematica, and companion of Voltaire. Portrait of Madame du Châtelet.

Document 8

Lady Mary Wortley Montagu, 1689–1762, author, aristocratic wife of a Whig Member of Parliament and ambassador to the Ottoman Empire, credited with bringing Turkish inoculation against smallpox to England, in a paper called *The Nonsense of Common-Sense,* January 24, 1738

Among the most universal errors, I reckon that of treating the weaker sex with a contempt which has a very bad influence on their conduct. How many of them think it excuse enough to say they are women, to indulge any folly that comes into their heads! This renders them useless members of the commonwealth, and only burdensome to their own families . . . what reason nature has given them is thrown away. . .

. . . A woman really virtuous, in the utmost extent of this expression, has virtue of a purer kind than any philosopher has ever shown. . . . I have some thoughts of exhibiting a set of pictures of such meritorious ladies, where I shall say nothing of the fire of their eyes, or the pureness of their complexions, but give them such praises as befit a rational sensible being: virtues of choice, and not beauties of accident. . . . I would not have them place so much value on a quality that can be only useful to one, as to neglect that which may be of benefit to thousands, by precept or by example. There will be no occasion of amusing themselves with trifles, when they consider themselves capable of not only making the most amiable, but the most estimable, figures in life. Begin, then, ladies, by paying those authors with scorn and contempt who, with a sneer of affected admiration, would throw you below the dignity of the human species.

Source: Lady Mary Wortley Montagu, *The Nonsense of Common-Sense, 1727–1738,* ed. Robert Halsband (Evanston, IL: Northwestern University Press, 1947); Modern History Sourcebook online.

GO ON TO NEXT PAGE

Document 9

Mary Wollstonecraft, 1759–1797, English writer, translator, and governess. *A Vindication of the Rights of Women,* 1792

My own sex, I hope, will excuse me, if I treat them like rational creatures, instead of flattering their fascinating graces, and viewing them as if they were in a state of perpetual childhood, unable to stand alone. I earnestly wish to point out in what true dignity and human happiness consists—I wish to persuade women to endeavor to acquire strength, both of mind and body, and to convince them that the soft phrases, susceptibility of heart, delicacy of sentiment, and refinement of taste, are almost synonymous with epithets of weakness, and that those beings who are only the objects of pity will soon become objects of contempt.

Dismissing those soft pretty feminine phrases, which the men condescendingly use to soften our slavish dependence, and despising that weak elegancy of mind, exquisite sensibility, and sweet docility of manners, supposed to be the sexual characteristics of the weaker vessel, I wish to shew that elegance is inferior to virtue, that the first object of laudable ambition is to obtain a character as a human being, regardless of the distinction of sex.

. . . Why must the female mind be tainted by coquettish arts to gratify the sensualist and prevent love from subsiding into friendship, or compassionate tenderness, when there are not qualities on which friendship can be built? Let the honest heart shew itself, and reason teach passion to submit to necessity; or, let the dignified pursuit of virtue and knowledge raise the mind above those emotions.

Document 10

Clara Zetkin, 1857–1933, German socialist, suffragist, later communist, died in exile from Nazi Germany in the Soviet Union. *A Socialist Solution to the Question of Women's Rights,* 1887

Given the fact that many thousands of female workers are active in industry, it is vital for the trade unions to incorporate them into their movement. In individual industries where female labor plays an important role, any movement advocating better wages, shorter working hours, etc., would be doomed from the start because of the attitude of those women workers who are not organized. Battles which begin propitiously enough, ended up in failure because the employers were able to play off non-union female workers against those that are organized in unions. These non-union workers continued to work (or took up work) under any conditions, which transformed them from competitors in dirty work to scabs.

Certainly one of the reasons for these poor wages for women is the circumstances that female workers are practically unorganized. They lack the strength which comes with unity. They lack the courage, the feeling of power, the spirit of resistance, and the ability to resist which is produced by the strength of an organization in which the individual fights for everybody and everybody fights for the individual. Furthermore, they lack the enlightenment and the training which an organization provides.

Document 11

Adelheid Popp, 1869–1939, Viennese socialist, founder of the proletarian women's movement in Austria, and member of Parliament 1919–1934. *The Autobiography of a Working Woman,* 1913

. . . From the women of this factory one can judge how sad and full of deprivation is the lot of a factory worker. In none of the neighboring factories were the wages so high; we were envied everywhere. Parents considered themselves fortunate if they could get their daughters of fourteen in there on leaving school . . . and even, here in this paradise, all were badly nourished. All humbled themselves and suffered the worst injustice from the foreman not to risk losing this good work, not to be without food. . . .

. . . [When I became a Social Democrat], in the factory I became another woman. . . . I told my [female] comrades all that I had read of the workers' movement. Formerly I had often told stories when they had begged me for them. But instead of narrating . . . the fate of some queen, I now held forth on oppression and exploitation. . . . It often happened on that one of the clerks passing by shook his head and said to another clerk "that girl speaks like a man."

Source: Mckay, 9th edition, p. 845.

Document 12

Annie Steel, 1847–1929, bestselling author of books on India, education, and women's issues, as well as novels and stories. *The Complete Indian Housekeeper and Cook,* London, 1902

It is not necessary, or in the least degree desirable, that an educated woman should waste the best years of her life in scolding and petty supervision. Life holds higher duties, and it is indubitable that friction and over-zeal is a sure sign of a bad housekeeper. . . .

The personal attention of the mistress is quite as much needed here as at home. . . . The first duty of a mistress is, of course, to be able to give intelligible orders to her servants, therefore it is necessary she should learn to speak Hindustani. . . . The next duty is obviously to insist on her orders being carried out. . . . The secret lies is making rules and keeping to them. The Indian servant is a child in everything save age, and should be treated as a child, that is to say, kindly but with the greatest firmness. . . . A good mistress in India will try to set a good example to her servants, in routine, method and tidiness. . . . An untidy mistress invariably has untidy, a weak one, idle servants.

<u>*End of Part A*</u>

SECTION II: Free-Response Essay Questions
Parts B and C
Suggested planning and writing time—35 minutes per essay
70 minutes total
Percent of Section II score—27.5 per essay, 55 total

DIRECTIONS You are to answer one question from Part B and one from Part C. *Do not answer two questions from the same group.*

Make your selection carefully, choosing the questions that you are best prepared to answer thoroughly in the time permitted. You should spend 5 minutes organizing or outlining your answer.

Write an essay that

- Has a relevant thesis
- Addresses all parts of the question
- Supports thesis with specific evidence
- Is well organized

[On the actual AP exam, you will read these instructions before Part B and Part C, each of which has three essay questions. You will also be told to write your answer to the question on the lined pages of the Section II free-response booklet, making sure to indicate the question you are answering by writing the appropriate question number at the top of each page. Part A of Section II is the DBQ. In this practice exam, the free-response questions are organized chronologically; Part B is on the early modern period and Part C on the nineteenth and twentieth centuries. Remember to pick only one question from each part; should you pick two from the same part, the second essay will not be read.]

Part B Select *one* question from Part B.

2. In what ways did Britain use war and aggression to achieve great power status by 1763?
3. In what ways did developments during the Renaissance help bring about the age of exploration?
4. Describe the witchcraft craze of the sixteenth and seventeenth centuries and analyze the reasons for both its development and its decline.

Part C Select *one* question from Part C.

5. Compare the processes of industrialization in England and on the European continent.
6. Describe and analyze the challenges to nineteenth-century European artistic values and styles made by twentieth-century artists before World War II.
7. Describe three resistance movements in eastern Europe to Soviet domination from 1946 to 1985 and analyze the reasons for their success or failure.

END OF EXAMINATION

ANSWERS FOR SECTION I

ANSWER KEY FOR MULTIPLE-CHOICE QUESTIONS

1. E	15. E	29. B	43. D	57. E	71. D
2. D	16. D	30. D	44. B	58. C	72. C
3. B	17. B	31. A	45. D	59. B	73. C
4. B	18. A	32. D	46. B	60. E	74. D
5. C	19. C	33. B	47. C	61. D	75. E
6. A	20. A	34. C	48. A	62. A	76. A
7. D	21. D	35. D	49. B	63. E	77. B
8. B	22. C	36. A	50. A	64. C	78. E
9. E	23. A	37. B	51. D	65. D	79. D
10. A	24. D	38. C	52. B	66. B	80. B
11. B	25. B	39. D	53. A	67. A	
12. C	26. A	40. A	54. D	68. A	
13. A	27. E	41. E	55. B	69. C	
14. B	28. B	42. D	56. C	70. B	

SCORING The multiple-choice section counts for 50 percent of your examination grade.

EXPLANATIONS FOR THE MULTIPLE-CHOICE ANSWERS

1. **ANSWER: (E)** According to these maps, England had a more developed railroad system than the continent did. The railroad connected major industrialized areas to key cities and ports; this allowed for the rapid industrialization of Britain before the rest of Europe. (McKay, *A History of Western Society*, 8th ed. pp. 735, 738/9th ed. pp. 725, 729)

2. **ANSWER: (D)** The decline of death rates in many European countries throughout the latter half of the nineteenth century can be attributed to a rising standard of living, public health improvements, better medicine, and an understanding of how diseases are spread (the germ theory). Public transportation did improve during this time, but did not have a direct impact on the decline in the death rate. (McKay, *A History of Western Society*, 8th ed. p. 791/9th ed. p. 783)

3. **ANSWER: (B)** Van Gogh studied impressionism in Paris, but he moved toward expressionism as he established himself as an artist. (McKay, *A History of Western Society*, 8th ed. pp. 930-932/9th ed. pp. 921-926)

4. **ANSWER: (B)** Black slaves constituted as much as 10 percent of the population in Lisbon, Portugal, and typically 3 percent in the country. In general they were a small number, and were dispersed primarily in Portugal and northern Europe. Italy imported white slaves. (McKay, *A History of Western Society*, 8th ed. p. 436/9th ed. p. 429)

5. **ANSWER: (C)** Famine and malnutrition, prevalent during this time, weakened people's immune systems so they were more susceptible to

disease. (McKay, *A History of Western Society*, 8th ed. pp. 381-385/9th ed. pp. 374-378)

6. **ANSWER: (A)** The Great Schism was a split within the Catholic Church that resulted in two men declaring themselves to be the pope. It ended with the Council of Constance in 1414. (McKay, *A History of Western Society*, 8th ed. p. 394/9th ed. pp. 387-388)

7. **ANSWER: (D)** The enormous wealth of the Italian cities, such as Venice and Florence, allowed merchants and others who benefited from trade to patronize artists and intellectuals. This led to a cultural renaissance in Italy, which slowly spread throughout Europe. (McKay, *A History of Western Society*, 8th ed. pp. 413-414/9th ed. pp. 407-408)

8. **ANSWER: (B)** Nationalism was a concept that did not fully develop in Europe until well into the eighteenth century. Though nationalism was present in countries such as England on a limited basis during this time, it was not a significant part of the Renaissance. (McKay, *A History of Western Society*, 8th ed. pp. 419-421/9th ed. pp. 412-414)

9. **ANSWER: (E)** Renaissance art tended to promote individuality by placing greater importance on the merits of individual artists. In addition, Renaissance artists focused on individuals in their work, as seen in the growing popularity of individual portraits. (McKay, *A History of Western Society*, 8th ed. pp. 422-425/9th ed. pp. 421-425)

10. **ANSWER: (A)** Although Renaissance women were better educated than women in the past, they still had limited outlets for their intellect. For the most part, women were expected to grace the home with their learning, but not to reach too far beyond that. (McKay, *A History of Western Society*, 8th ed. pp. 428-429/9th ed. pp. 414-415)

11. **ANSWER: (B)** Louis XI promoted new industries, such as silk weaving, and brought in tradesmen to increase the French revenues. He also increased taxation to help pay for a better army so that he could keep the cities and nobles in check. As a result, the power of the French monarchy grew significantly during his reign. (McKay, *A History of Western Society*, 8th ed. p. 442/9th ed. p. 435)

12. **ANSWER: (C)** Ferdinand responded to the rising anti-Semitic feelings in Spain by asking the pope for permission to launch the Inquisition. In theory, this would punish any new Christians who still clung to their Jewish practices and beliefs. The Inquisition allowed Spaniards to persecute and drive out Jews and Christian converts in the years following the Reconquista. (McKay, *A History of Western Society*, 8th ed. pp. 443-446/9th ed. pp. 436-439)

13. **ANSWER: (A)** Protestants such as Martin Luther disputed the Catholic Church's teaching that salvation comes from both faith and good works. They maintained that faith alone was enough to merit salvation; they also believed that good works would be an inevitable result of gratitude for God's love. (McKay, *A History of Western Society*, 8th ed. pp. 462-463/9th ed. p. 447)

14. **ANSWER: (B)** Martin Luther wrote the "Ninety-five Theses on the Power of Indulgences" to refute the idea that salvation could be achieved through good works, such as indulgences. Though he effectively established a new religious sect, that was not his original intent when he wrote the document. (McKay, *A History of Western Society*, 8th ed. pp. 457-458/9th ed. pp. 448-449)

15. **ANSWER: (E)** John Calvin established a strong Christian community in Geneva, based on his ideas that society should be ruled by God. Geneva was known as a city that was a Church. (McKay, *A History of Western Society*, 8th ed. pp. 470-472/9th ed. pp. 463-465)

16. **ANSWER: (D)** Queen Elizabeth I declared herself the supreme governor of the Church of England. She tried to appease both Catholics and Puritans by maintaining aspects of each group in the Anglican Church in order to unify and strengthen the state. (McKay, *A History of Western Society*, 8th ed. pp. 474-475/9th ed. pp. 461-463)

17. **ANSWER: (B)** The Catholic Reformation came about in response to the Protestant Reformation. In the Council of Trent, Catholic leaders sought to reconcile Catholic and Protestant doctrines, while maintaining the theological backbone of the Catholic Church. While the Catholics did succeed in strengthening and renewing their church, they never achieved reconciliation with Protestants. (McKay, *A History of Western Society*, 8th ed. pp. 479-483/9th ed. pp. 467-469)

18. **ANSWER: (A)** Fighting between Catholics and Huguenots resulted in violent attacks such as the Saint Bartholomew's Day massacre. After years of fighting that weakened France, the *politiques* (moderates) helped to establish a strong monarchy to bring order and stability to France, under the leadership of Henry of Navarre (Henry IV). (McKay, *A History of Western Society*, 8th ed. p. 492/9th ed. pp. 472-473)

19. **ANSWER: (C)** Philip II supported Mary, Queen of Scots, in her attempt to assassinate Elizabeth I because Elizabeth I heavily supported the Netherlands in their revolt against Spain. (McKay, *A History of Western Society*, 8th ed. pp. 496-497/9th ed. pp. 512-513)

20. **ANSWER: (A)** After a century of religious conflicts in Europe, the Peace of Westphalia marked the end to this fighting. While conflicts remained, there were no major wars fought over them after 1648, when the treaty was signed. (McKay, *A History of Western Society*, 8th ed. pp. 498-499/9th ed. pp. 562-563)

21. **ANSWER: (D)** Portugal was not a significant European power, but sought greater prestige through its overseas exploration. Prince Henry the Navigator, Bartholomew Diaz, and Vasco da Gama, all from Portugal, were among the earliest European explorers of this time. (McKay, *A History of Western Society*, 8th ed. pp. 502-503/9th ed. pp. 495-498)

22. **ANSWER: (C)** The European exploration of other lands was primarily fueled by self-serving motives. While some European explorers did express an interest in converting other peoples to Christianity, no one was motivated by a desire to educate other people in the Renaissance

ideals. In fact, many European explorers were only too willing to exploit or enslave other peoples for their own gain. (McKay, *A History of Western Society*, 8th ed. pp. 506-507/9th ed. pp. 492-493)

23. **ANSWER: (A)** The Columbian exchange refers to the introduction and trading of new crops, animals, and diseases between Europe and the Americas that began after Christopher Columbus's exploration of America. (McKay, *A History of Western Society*, 8th ed. p. 511/9th ed. pp. 508-509)

24. **ANSWER: (D)** European explorers captured, bought, and sold many natives of the lands they explored. Europeans used these slaves to work the land for cash crops and to mine for precious gems and minerals, thus increasing their fortunes. (McKay, *A History of Western Society*, 8th ed. pp. 515-519/9th ed. pp. 513-514)

25. **ANSWER: (B)** William Shakespeare (1564-1616) wrote plays during the reigns of Queen Elizabeth I and King James I. (McKay, *A History of Western Society*, 8th ed. p. 520/9th ed. pp. 514-516)

26. **ANSWER: (A)** Peter Paul Rubens's work was highly representative of the Baroque era of art. His paintings were vivid and dramatic, in the Baroque style. (McKay, *A History of Western Society*, 8th ed. p. 523/9th ed. pp. 539-540)

27. **ANSWER: (E)** The totalitarian regimes of the twentieth century had better financial, military, and technological resources with which to control the people of a state. Therefore, totalitarian regimes were more thoroughly centralized than those of absolutists. (McKay, *A History of Western Society*, 8th ed. pp. 532-533/partial information 9th ed. p. 528)

28. **ANSWER: (B)** Cardinal Richelieu was the first minister of the French crown under Louis XIII's reign. Richelieu died in 1642, right before Louis XIV assumed the crown. (McKay, *A History of Western Society*, 8th ed. pp. 534-541/9th ed. pp. 528-533)

29. **ANSWER: (B)** Although the Protectorate was theoretically a commonwealth, with power divided between Parliament and a council of state, the reality was that the army controlled the government. As head of the army, Oliver Cromwell essentially ruled as a military dictator. (McKay, *A History of Western Society*, 8th ed. p. 551/9th ed. pp. 546-547)

30. **ANSWER: (D)** When William and Mary accepted the throne from Parliament in 1688, they essentially established the idea that a monarch's power came from the Parliament and not from divine authority. From this point forward, monarchs and Parliament had to work together to govern the people of England. (McKay, *A History of Western Society*, 8th ed. pp. 553-554/9th ed. pp. 548-549)

31. **ANSWER: (A)** The Dutch had the largest merchant marine in Europe in the seventeenth century. They used these ships to establish an extensive trade network around the world. The Dutch East India Company and other merchants brought in phenomenal wealth to the

small country. (McKay, *A History of Western Society*, 8th ed., pp. 555-559/9th ed. pp. 549-553)

32. **ANSWER: (D)** The Prussians were known for their military prowess because of Frederick William's influence as an absolute ruler. He was particularly interested in armies, so he made it his lifelong ambition to establish a strong Prussian army. (McKay, *A History of Western Society*, 8th ed. pp. 575-576/9th ed. pp. 571-572)

33. **ANSWER: (B)** Peter the Great had fought Sweden for years over access to a warm-water port for Russia. When he had the opportunity to build a city at the mouth of the Neva River, he seized it, even though the land was far from ideal. (McKay, *A History of Western Society*, 8th ed. p. 587/9th ed. pp. 578-580)

34. **ANSWER: (C)** Copernicus and Galileo helped to advance the concept of a heliocentric universe, but as this detracted from the importance of Earth and seemingly contradicted literal interpretations of the Bible, it was a highly controversial idea. (McKay, *A History of Western Society*, 8th ed. pp. 596-600/9th ed. pp. 590-594)

35. **ANSWER: (D)** Although some Enlightenment thinkers criticized the church, most were deists. Existentialism was a twentieth-century movement. (McKay, *A History of Western Society*, 8th ed. pp. 605-607/9th ed. pp. 598-600)

36. **ANSWER: (A)** Frederick the Great and Catherine the Great embraced many of the Enlightenment ideals during their reigns, while maintaining their roles as absolute monarchs. (McKay, *A History of Western Society*, 8th ed. pp. 615-619/9th ed. pp. 609-613)

37. **ANSWER: (B)** The scientific revolution helped inspire people to reexamine farming methods in the light of their scientific discoveries. This contributed to improved farming methods, which led to the agricultural revolution. (McKay, *A History of Western Society*, 8th ed. pp. 631-633/9th ed. pp. 622-623)

38. **ANSWER: (C)** In the putting-out system, a merchant gave basic materials to cottage workers who processed the materials in their own homes and returned finished goods to the merchant. It was all part of the cottage industry. (McKay, *A History of Western Society*, 8th ed. p. 639/9th ed. pp. 629-630)

39. **ANSWER: (D)** Survival rates for infants and children were low during the eighteenth century. Many infants were abandoned and other infants and children died due to malnutrition and disease. The foundling hospitals did not provide an answer, since 50 percent of the foundlings died within the first year, and often 90 percent did not survive. (McKay, *A History of Western Society*, 8th ed. pp. 666-671/9th ed. pp. 658-663)

40. **ANSWER: (A)** The French Revolution was fueled by desires for liberty and equality within society. The extreme poverty of the lowest classes made these people all the more willing to revolt against the monarchy. The bourgeoisie also clashed with the monarchy, when the monarchy

tried to find ways to pay the government's debts. Religious differences in France were not an important factor in starting the French Revolution. (McKay, *A History of Western Society*, 8th ed. pp. 697-699/9th ed. pp. 688-689)

41. **ANSWER: (E)** The French were willing to give up some of their liberty in exchange for stability within their country, so they willingly allowed Napoleon Bonaparte to lead them as an absolute ruler. Napoleon came after the years of turmoil due to the French Revolution and the ensuing Directory. (McKay, *A History of Western Society*, 8th ed. pp. 712-714/9th ed. pp. 703-705)

42. **ANSWER: (D)** Surrounded by water, with many rivers and canals inland, Great Britain was able to ship goods quickly and efficiently. This fact, along with their stable government and bountiful harvests, was one of the main reasons that Britain was ready for the Industrial Revolution before other European nations. (McKay, *A History of Western Society*, 8th ed. p. 726/9th ed. p. 718)

43. **ANSWER: (D)** Working-class solidarity gave rise to trade unions. Though these were outlawed in many countries, the labor movement could not be so easily suppressed, and it continued to grow from the time of the Industrial Revolution. (McKay, *A History of Western Society*, 8th ed. pp. 740-749/9th ed. pp. 732-741)

44. **ANSWER: (B)** In 1814, European powers met at the Congress of Vienna to establish a balance of power following the defeat of Napoleon. They were eager to ensure that no one could ever come so close to taking over Europe as Napoleon had. (McKay, *A History of Western Society*, 8th ed. pp. 757-758/9th ed. pp. 749-751)

45. **ANSWER: (D)** Though Karl Marx and Friedrich Engels wrote *The Communist Manifesto* in 1848, communism was not particularly influential in the nineteenth century. It was not until the twentieth century that communism became so widespread. (McKay, *A History of Western Society*, 8th ed. pp. 761-767/9th ed. pp. 753-758)

46. **ANSWER: (B)** The potato blight wiped out nearly all the potatoes in Ireland in the mid-nineteenth century. Without this staple crop, the Irish experienced a famine that devastated the country. (McKay, *A History of Western Society*, 8th ed. p. 775/9th ed. pp. 766-767)

47. **ANSWER: (C)** Joseph Lister's antiseptic principle held that a chemical disinfectant could be used to kill harmful bacteria around a wound. When doctors applied this principle to all equipment in an operating room, the mortality rate from surgery declined. (McKay, *A History of Western Society*, 8th ed. pp. 791-792/9th ed. p. 783)

48. **ANSWER: (A)** Louis Napoleon declared himself emperor of France in 1852. He had nearly absolute control over the government, though he did maintain the elected Assembly. He was like an enlightened despot in that he had full power, yet exhibited some progressive principles. (McKay, *A History of Western Society*, 8th ed. pp. 824-826/9th ed. pp. 816-818)

49. **ANSWER: (B)** All of these men played a role in uniting Italy, but it was Victor Emmanuel who became the first king of the parliamentary monarchy. Mazzini inspired nationalism, Garibaldi's Red Shirts conquered southern Italy, and Cavour brokered *realpolitik* diplomacy. (McKay, *A History of Western Society*, 8th ed. pp. 826-829/9th ed. pp. 818-821)

50. **ANSWER: (A)** Russian leaders realized that they could not hope to modernize their country with the institution of serfdom holding them back. In 1861, Tsar Alexander II freed the serfs in the first of many great reforms in Russia. (McKay, *A History of Western Society*, 8th ed. p. 835/9th ed. p. 826)

51. **ANSWER: (D)** Theodor Herzl led the Zionist movement, which called for a Jewish homeland, at the turn of the twentieth century. (McKay, *A History of Western Society*, 8th ed. pp. 846-847/9th ed. pp. 837-838)

52. **ANSWER: (B)** There was too little land in Europe to accommodate all the small farmers, so many of them moved to countries where land was bountiful and cheap. Also, skilled artisans were competing against the cheap manufactured goods of the Industrial Revolution, so they were also seeking a new way to make a living. (McKay, *A History of Western Society*, 8th ed. p. 865/9th ed. p. 856)

53. **ANSWER: (A)** In 1884 and 1885, European powers met at the Berlin Conference to discuss their claims on African territories. They established the principle that in order to claim a colony as their own, they had to have effective occupation of that land. (McKay, *A History of Western Society*, 8th ed. p. 870/9th ed. pp. 861-862)

54. **ANSWER: (D)** The new imperialism took place around the turn of the twentieth century, when slavery had been outlawed in nearly all European countries and America. Many missionaries and abolitionists used imperialism to help stop the slave trade at this time. (McKay, *A History of Western Society*, 8th ed. pp. 873-876/9th ed. pp. 865-867)

55. **ANSWER: (B)** India was the jewel of the British Empire because of the wealth it brought to the British. India had many natural resources and cash crops for the British to trade. In addition, the Indian people provided a market for British goods. (McKay, *A History of Western Society*, 8th ed. pp. 877-879/9th ed. pp. 868-870)

56. **ANSWER: (C)** Ethiopia drove out Italian invaders to remain independent. Liberia was established as an independent nation for former slaves from the Americas to settle in. (McKay, *A History of Western Society*, 8th ed. pp. 869-870/9th ed. pp. 859-860)

57. **ANSWER: (E)** After defeating France in the Franco-Prussian War, Bismarck wanted to ensure that France remained politically isolated. With this in mind, he formed the Triple Alliance with Austria and Italy. (McKay, *A History of Western Society*, 8th ed. p. 889/9th ed. pp. 880-881)

58. **ANSWER: (C)** After the assassination of the Archduke Francis Ferdinand by Serbian terrorists, Austria-Hungary issued an ultimatum

to Serbia. When the Serbians did not accept the ultimatum, Austria declared war on Serbia. Germany gave Austria support, which mobilized other European countries to get involved and soon a world war had begun. (McKay, *A History of Western Society*, 8th ed. pp. 892-893/9th ed. pp. 883-884)

59. **ANSWER: (B)** Trench warfare led to stalemate as each side tried to outlast the other. The cost in lives was enormous, yet the gain in territory was almost nonexistent. Battles would go on for weeks, with the only result being a gain of a few yards of territory for one side. (McKay, *A History of Western Society*, 8th ed. p. 895/9th ed. pp. 887-888)

60. **ANSWER: (E)** World War I was a total war in that every aspect of life was affected in some way. Governments had control over all the resources of a country to use for the good of their military. Governments could ration food, draft soldiers, force people to work in factories, or do anything else that might further their cause in the war. (McKay, *A History of Western Society*, 8th ed. pp. 900-901/9th ed. pp. 892-894)

61. **ANSWER: (D)** There were 2 million Russian casualties in 1915 alone. By the time Russia withdrew from the war in 1917, they had lost millions of their people, almost all of them from the peasant class. (McKay, *A History of Western Society*, 8th ed. pp. 904-905/9th ed. p. 895)

62. **ANSWER: (A)** Lenin had been exiled in Switzerland during the war. When the Germans saw that the Russian government was in turmoil in 1917, they helped Lenin and some of his Bolshevik followers get back to Russia so that they could undermine the Russian government and force them to withdraw from the war. (McKay, *A History of Western Society*, 8th ed. p. 908/9th ed. p. 898)

63. **ANSWER: (E)** The White Army, which fought the Bolshevik Red Army, was on the fringes of Russia and was very disunited. This made it easier for the Bolsheviks to defeat them. (McKay, *A History of Western Society*, 8th ed. pp. 909-910/9th ed. pp. 899-901)

64. **ANSWER: (C)** Alsace-Lorraine, desirable for its resources, was returned to France at the end of World War I as part of the Treaty of Versailles, but was seized by Hitler in World War II. (McKay, *A History of Western Society*, 8th ed. pp. 914-915/9th ed. pp. 902-903)

65. **ANSWER: (D)** World War I was so devastating that it left people emotionally and psychologically scarred. Modern philosophers responded by attacking the idea that humanity was progressing and that rational thought could be relied on. (McKay, *A History of Western Society*, 8th ed. pp. 923-925/9th ed. pp. 915-917)

66. **ANSWER: (B)** Revisionism refers to a socialist movement to update Marxist doctrines to reflect the changing lifestyles at the turn of the twentieth century. This did not influence the art or design world. (McKay, *A History of Western Society*, 8th ed. pp. 849-850, 930-933/9th ed. pp. 840-842, 921-926)

67. **ANSWER: (A)** The Great Depression of 1929 triggered a downward financial spiral that devastated the European economy. (McKay, *A History of Western Society*, 8th ed. pp. 942-944/9th ed. pp. 933-936)

68. **ANSWER: (A)** The NEP was Lenin's policy, which Stalin brought to an end with his Five-Year Plans. (McKay, *A History of Western Society*, 8th ed. pp. 957-959/9th ed. pp. 949-950)

69. **ANSWER: (C)** Mussolini did start out as a socialist, but when he broke from their party to form the fascists and started to attack the Socialist Party, his words appealed to conservatives and others who were afraid of the socialist agitation in Italy. (McKay, *A History of Western Society*, 8th ed. p. 964/9th ed. p. 955)

70. **ANSWER: (B)** Though Germany and Italy shared many characteristics under the rules of Hitler and Mussolini, respectively, Italy was not part of Germany's secret pact with Stalin. (McKay, *A History of Western Society*, 8th ed. p. 966/9th ed. p. 957)

71. **ANSWER: (D)** The British were following a policy of appeasement, allowing Hitler to do what he wanted as long as they could avoid another war. The French were unwilling to fight the Germans without British support, so Hitler was able to take over the Rhineland with no opposition. (McKay, *A History of Western Society*, 8th ed. p. 972/9th ed. p. 962)

72. **ANSWER: (C)** The United States dropped atomic bombs on Hiroshima and Nagasaki in Japan, but no one ever dropped one on Germany. By the time the United States bombed Japan, Germany had already lost to the Allies. (McKay, *A History of Western Society*, 8th ed. pp. 980-983/9th ed. pp. 972-975)

73. **ANSWER: (C)** The Great Depression struck in 1929, ten years before the start of World War II. (McKay, *A History of Western Society*, 8th ed. pp. 942, 983-984, 990/9th ed. pp. 933, 974-975, 981-982)

74. **ANSWER: (D)** When Stalin died in 1953, the Soviet Union went through a decade of de-Stalinization that brought a better standard of living and somewhat greater freedom to the Soviet people. (McKay, *A History of Western Society*, 8th ed., pp. 1003-1006/9th ed. pp. 995-997)

75. **ANSWER: (E)** With the exception of Romania's revolution, the collapse of communism in eastern Europe was peaceful. (McKay, *A History of Western Society*, 8th ed. pp.1034-1037/9th ed. pp. 1024-1028)

76. **ANSWER: (A)** With the African and Asian peoples calling for freedom from European rule and in some places, starting to revolt, the Europeans began to think more seriously about relinquishing them. After World War II, the clamor for independence increased, and the European countries eventually gave in (or lost) to these demands. (McKay, *A History of Western Society*, 8th ed. pp. 999-1000/9th ed. pp. 989-992)

77. **ANSWER: (B)** Birthrates declined dramatically in Europe as more women were educated and working outside the home. At the same

time, there was a surge of illegal immigrants into western Europe, many of whom were refugees from war-torn countries. (McKay, *A History of Western Society*, 8th ed. pp. 1051-1052/9th ed. pp. 1041-1042)

78. **ANSWER: (E)** Answers A-D were all similarities between the two centuries. The only difference listed here is that communism became an important political practice in the twentieth century, beginning with the Russian Revolution. (McKay, *A History of Western Society*, 8th ed. pp. 732, 811, 904/9th ed. pp. 723-724, 802, 895)

79. **ANSWER: (D)** Elizabeth I was succeeded by her cousin James I, in 1603. His son, Charles I, succeeded him in 1625. Charles I was defeated by Oliver Cromwell's Puritan army and beheaded in 1649. (McKay, *A History of Western Society*, 8th ed. pp. 548-551/9th ed. pp. 542-546)

80. **ANSWER: (B)** The Estates General convened on May 5, 1789. On June 20, the Oath of the Tennis Court was sworn. On July 14, French citizens stormed the Bastille. Later in the revolution, Louis XVI was executed (January 1793), and the Reign of Terror began shortly thereafter. (McKay, *A History of Western Society*, 8th ed. p. 709/9th ed. p. 699)

ANSWER FOR SECTION II, PART A: DOCUMENT-BASED QUESTION (DBQ)

Below are short analyses of the documents.

Document 1 Christine de Pizan exhorts women at court to be demure, modest, and well-behaved and emphasizes the role of the princess in maintaining such behavior.

POV: Although seeking to enhance the prestige of women, the author is careful not to do so at the expense of their modesty. She may be seeking the patronage of a princess and therefore wants to emphasize the importance of the leadership of the princess at court. As a widow, she had to take care to preserve her own reputation and therefore stressed the importance of modest behavior

Document 2 Laura Cereta criticizes a male correspondent for praising her intellect, saying that all women are born with such possibilities but only some choose to pursue them. She connects intellectual pursuit with virtue and implicitly criticizes women who spend their energies adorning themselves.

POV: As a woman humanist, Cereta sought acceptance from male humanists, which was not easy. Her sense of the capabilities of humans that she expresses reflects Renaissance Neoplatonism; it is an insult to that sense if she is seen as unique among women. She also wants to show that she has worked as hard as any male humanist to acquire classical skills and knowledge; this is why she emphasizes the importance of diligence. Renaissance women adorned themselves with beautiful fabrics and jewels to express the wealth of their families, but Cereta is rejecting this as the most useful activity for women.

Document 3 Teresa of Avila complains about the looseness and immorality of women and the dangers these pose to men and argues that women who act in such ways have turned away from God. Women, she says, are naturally pure and inclined to the good and deserve respect from men for that.

POV: As a religious figure, Teresa of Avila is little concerned with women's scholarship or prestige; she is concerned about morality and goodness. She also is very modest and sees that being a woman is itself enough to lower her self-esteem; this reflects a Christian sense of the moral weakness of women beginning with Eve. As an author, she is also trying to avoid the sin of pride. She argues that good women must be given respect and power; religious women, nuns like herself, belong in this category.

Document 4 Louise Labé criticizes women for superficial preoccupations when it was possible at the time for women to become educated in science and the humanities. She applauds those women who take advantage of these new freedoms and comments that education and culture truly belong to the women who acquire them unlike jewels and the like which they can but use.

POV: Labé is writing during the French Renaissance in the sixteenth century and reflects the increasing possibilities for women of that period. Because she is a well-known poet, she wants to be respected for that rather than typical womanly traits. As this is a private letter to a woman, her intent is to encourage her friend to engage in literary pursuits and so it probably reflects her true feelings.

Document 5 Mary Cary laments how few men and even fewer women are ready for the highest spiritual level and are ready to act like prophets. She expects that soon not only men will be able to prophesize but women will too–a time in which there will be greater equality all around.

POV: Cary reflects the egalitarian spirit of the radical millenarian group to which she belonged during the English Revolution. Radicals could imagine not only social equality but also gender equality, which for her, a religious person, meant the equal ability and opportunity to prophesize. Her writing a book about the New Jerusalem indicates her belief that she was already able to do so.

Document 6 Mary Astell condemns marriage in a passage that is highly ironical in tone. She lambastes men for depriving women of their equality but doing harm to people and spinning their wheels in their search for power. She defines marriage as subjugation, as little more than slavery, and laments that women with few aspirations are the ones who are considered praiseworthy.

POV: As Astell never married, her views on marriage are theoretical and not based on personal experience.

Document 7 Marianne Loir portrays Madame du Châtelet in a beguilingly feminine way.

POV: Although a woman artist, Loir focuses on Madame du Châtelet's feminine attractions rather than her scholarship. There are no notebooks or any symbols of scholarship in the portrait, even though Madame du Châtelet was widely admired for her intellectual gifts.

Document 8 Lady Montagu condemns women for being frivolous and rejecting the use of reason, which she says makes them useless in society and even in their own families. She calls on women to reject those authors who disparage women and to give up being amiable in order to become estimable.

POV: Lady Montagu actively promoted her knowledge of inoculation against smallpox, which she had observed in the Ottoman Empire, so she defined her social role as much greater than aristocratic elegance. Although she herself was an aristocrat, she condemned the typical virtues associated with women of her class.

Document 9 Mary Wollstonecraft condemns the frivolities of women and exhorts them to live up to their rational potential. Such frivolities make women weak and are encouraged by men.

POV: Written during the French Revolution, *A Vindication of the Rights of Women* was a crucial feminist tract that sought to extend the rights won by French men in 1789 to women. Recognizing that these rights were unlikely to be given to women by men, she focuses on getting women to change themselves, as she herself has done by becoming educated and a serious writer.

Document 10 Clara Zetkin condemns women for being easily swayed into becoming scabs and weakening the labor movement. Women need the strength and training that will come with being members of a labor union.

POV: As a socialist, Zetkin is concerned about proletarian women specifically and believes that only membership in labor unions can save them. For her, enlightenment for women comes from participation in the socialist movement, not by study and use of reason on their own. That she is German reflects the great importance of the socialist movement there.

Document 11 Adelheid Popp describes the sorry conditions for working women in Vienna, even in a good factory, and reveals how empowering it was for her to become a socialist and tell her fellow workers what she had read about the workers' movement rather than inconsequential stories.

POV: Popp's statement seems to verify Zetkin's exhortation that participation in the socialist movement is empowering. As a woman who took on roles that typically were men's, she makes the point that speaking as a socialist made her sound like a man, that is, someone with authority. As a socialist, she also shows that even improvements in the factory system will not change things enough, as workers will still be beholden to the foremen.

Document 12 Annie Steel reflects two aspects of English attitudes in India. On the one hand, she exhorts women to learn Hindustani and not to waste their time on overzealousness in housework. On the other hand, she articulates that the main role of educated women is to run an efficient and orderly household by being efficient and orderly themselves. She describes the Indians as childlike.

POV: Steel's portrayal of the Indians as inferior and childlike is similar to Kipling's in "The White Man's Burden" and reflects the typical attitude of the British colonialists. Her definition of women's role is limited to the household, so although she calls for education and learning the native language, it is not so that women can make contributions to society but so that they can better manage their households. Her book is clearly written for the housekeeping market, so perhaps she tailored her views to homemakers, contradicting her own activities as a writer in the public sphere.

GROUPS: Numbers in brackets refers to the document number.

French: Christine de Pizan [1], Louise Labé [4], Marianne Loir [7]

English: Mary Cary [5], Mary Astell [6], Lady Montagu [8], Mary Wollstonecraft [9], Annie Steel [12]

Fifteenth century: Christine de Pizan [1], Laura Cereta [2]

Sixteenth century: Teresa of Avila [3], Laura Labé [4]

Eighteenth century: Mary Astell [6], Marianne Loir [7], Lady Montagu [8], Lady Wollstonecraft [9]

Nineteenth and twentieth centuries: Clara Zetkin [10], Adelheid Popp [11], Annie Steel [12]

Condemns women for being frivolous: Labé [4], Lady Montagu [8], Mary Wollstonecraft [9]

Exhorts women to provide good examples: Christine de Pizan [1], Annie Steel [12]

Is concerned about virtue: Laura Cereta [2], Teresa de Avila [3], Lady Montagu [8], Mary Wollstonecraft [9]

Calls on women to make contributions to society: Lady Montagu [8], Clara Zetkin [10], Adelheid Popp [11]

Claims women are rational beings: Laura Cereta [2], Louise Labé [4], Lady Montagu [8], Mary Wollstonecraft [9]

Religious orientation: Teresa de Avila [3], Mary Cary [5]

Humanistic training: Laura Cereta [2], Louise Labé [5]

Socialists: Clara Zetkin [10], Adelheid Popp [11]

SCORING

Remember that the two parts of the exam—Section I, multiple choice, and Section II, three essays—are equally weighted at 50 percent each in determining the final score. Of the three essays, the DBQ counts for 45 percent of the Section II score, and each FRQ essay counts for 27.5 percent, together counting for 55 percent of the Section II score.

SCORING THE DATA-BASED ESSAY: THE CORE SCORING STANDARDS

1. Do you have a thesis that derives from the documents and does more than restate the question?

Example of a thesis that would not be accepted:

Women had many views about their roles over the centuries.
Or
Women have always been opposed to and unhappy about their role.

Example of an acceptable thesis:

Women had many views about their roles in society. Some argued that women had to serve as examples to others, while others argued that women were rational beings who should devote themselves to their intellect.

Example of a strong thesis:

Women writers reflected their historical times by asserting the roles women should play. During the Renaissance, women sought education and a role in literary and intellectual circles. In the seventeenth and eighteenth centuries, writers focused on the importance of education for women and their rejection of superficial roles. In the nineteenth and twentieth centuries, women socialists saw the solution to women's rights in the labor movement.

2. Have you used more than half the documents [in this case, 7]?
3. Have you made no more than one major error in your analysis of the documents?
4. Have you supported your thesis with evidence from the documents?
5. Have you grouped the documents in at least three ways?
6. Have you analyzed POV in at least three documents?

Give yourself one point for each affirmative answer. If you have earned the 6 core points, evaluate how much better than the minimum you have done and give yourself an additional 1, 2, or 3 points. If you missed a core point, go back over the DBQ to see what you could have done differently.

ANSWERS FOR SECTION II, PART B AND PART C: FREE-RESPONSE QUESTIONS (FRQS)

QUESTION 2

This question requires a knowledge of British political and military history. Make sure you can discuss at least three wars. You will need to explain why Britain was able to win these wars (its commercial strength, its well-developed sense of nationalism, its competent leadership) and what its motivations were (commercial, maintaining the balance of power, religious).

- Thesis: Britain aimed its military might against its chief rivals over the course of three centuries, defeating one enemy and moving on the next one. It forged alliances with other states that also sought to attack its enemies. By the end of the Seven Years' War, Britain was the dominant power in the New World and a great power on the continent, rivaled only by France.
- Britain's first competitor was Spain. The tensions between the two states were partially religious, as Spain was the great defender of Catholicism and England had broken away from the Catholic Church. Spain tried to invade England in 1588 with the Armada, only to meet with disastrous defeat. Queen Elizabeth encouraged Sir Francis Drake and others to engage in acts of piracy to steal or sink Spanish ships carrying gold and silver back to Spain from the New World. While it was only one reason for the decline of Spain in the seventeenth century, England's hostility to Spain was certainly an important factor.
- Britain then turned its attention to the Netherlands, which by the seventeenth century was the dominant force in international trade. Britain went to war with the Dutch three times in the seventeenth century, twice in alliance with France. In 1664, the Dutch ceded their colony of New Amsterdam to the British; it became New York. Dutch trade and finances were seriously affected by these wars; so many Dutch ships were damaged and the wars were so costly that the Dutch ceased to be the dominant economic power in Europe.
- Britain's chief rival then became France. During the War of the Spanish Succession, Britain, along with Austria, fought against France and prevented the union of the crowns of Spain and France. Britain acquired Gibraltar, Minorca, and the lucrative control of the slave trade. Some thirty years later, Britain aided Maria Theresa during the War of the Austrian Succession, to prevent a power vacuum from developing in the Austrian Empire and tilting the effective balance of power to France. Britain and France fought each other in the Seven Years' War. In the New World, Britain won hands down, and France was forced to cede its Quebec colony in Canada to Britain. On the continent, the settlement ended with modest but crucial gains for Britain. The French ceded their trading colony along the Indian coast to Britain; this laid the basis for British domination of India in the next century.
- Thus, by the end of the Seven Years' War, Britain had eliminated Spain and Holland as economic and imperial competitors and had prevented French expansion. When Napoleon took France into an expansionist course again in the early nineteenth century, it was Britain that stood firm against him and ultimately played a crucial role in his defeat.

QUESTION 3

In this question, you are asked to discuss not the Italian Renaissance per se but what aspects of it promoted the age of exploration. You do not need to spend time explaining what the Renaissance was, unless it is relevant to your thesis, or, for example, the role the Medici played as patrons of the arts.

- Thesis: The Renaissance provided crucial foundations for the age of exploration but was not itself its direct cause.
- The Renaissance passion for antiquity brought into the public eye ancient geographic texts, the most important of which was Ptolemy's *Geography*. This confirmed notions of the roundness of the Earth and implied a relatively short distance from Asia if one went west from Europe.
- Renaissance cities thrived on international trade with the East. They encouraged the importation of products, technologies, and ideas from what remained of the Byzantine Empire, as well as Asia and the Middle East, and stimulated the market for such goods.
- Italians, particularly Florentines, played a crucial role in the exploration of the New World. Many of the earliest explorers were Italians, for example, Christopher Columbus, John Cabot, and Amerigo Vespucci, who gave his name to the New World when he wrote about his adventures.
- The lack of a unified Italian state meant that the Italians were explorers not conquerors. They worked on behalf of or for nation-states like England and Spain.
- Renaissance Neoplatonism stressed mathematical thinking, which allowed explorers to believe that they could rely on their computations, even if these were often wrong, and encouraged notions of the enormous potential of human achievement.
- The printing press made possible the dissemination of relatively inexpensive books, which spread new ideas and encouraged new ways of thinking. Such popular works as the stories of the mythical king Prester John or the legendary traveler John Mandeville did a great deal to spark curiosity and a thirst for travel. The publication of maps of the seas also smoothed the way for exploration.
- Northern Renaissance cities, such as Amsterdam and Rotterdam, had a thriving trade with the East, which brought a wide variety of peoples into contact with each other and created a relatively tolerant international culture. Dutch innovations encouraged exploration.
- The Renaissance was marked by intense curiosity about not only the world of the past but the physical universe.
- On the other hand, there were many motivations for the explorations that contradicted the Renaissance spirit, particularly the religious, missionary fervor. On balance, the Renaissance may have been a precondition of the explorations rather than their cause.

QUESTION 4

In this question you are asked to both describe the witchcraft persecution craze and analyze the reasons for its development and its decline. You need therefore to write about three aspects of witchcraft; this makes it easy to organize the essay into three paragraphs. Remember you need a thesis; one possible example is given here.

- Thesis: The intense persecution of witches during the sixteenth and seventeenth centuries was a part of great struggles over religious issues in that period and abated when those struggles were resolved.
- Description of the witchcraft craze: Persecution of witches began in the 1480s but intensified after 1560, following the Protestant Reformation. Between 100,000 and 200,000 people were tried for witchcraft and about half of them were executed. Approximately three-quarters of the victims of persecution were women, often older women. Witches were persecuted by both Catholics and Protestants. The most intense witchcraft persecutions occurred in the Holy Roman Empire and parts of France. Witchcraft persecution abated at the end of the seventeenth century and was outlawed in the next.
- Reasons for its development: Ideas of the power of God and of Satan encouraged the development of demonology and the increased fear of these powers. The high proportion of women reflected various ideas about women: their inferiority, their associations with nature and its disorder, their lack of power, and their roles in preparing food, acting as midwives in childbirth, and taking care of children and animals. Accusations of witchcraft were also a way of enforcing conformist behavior. The use of inquisitional procedures, which often involved torture, rather than accusatorial procedures, ironically did not necessarily lead to higher death rates: The places where the Inquisition was long active—Spain, Portugal, and Rome—executed few people.
- Reasons for its decline: Skepticism grew, particularly when witch panics seem to create obviously exaggerated persecutions and torture often produced questionable results. The scientific revolution over time reduced or eliminated the belief in demonology. The general reduction in religious violence after the end of the Thirty Years' War also was a factor.

QUESTION 5

This is a comparison question, so it is important to show similarities and differences. Your thesis can focus on one or more of these, such as the role of governments.

- Thesis: Continental countries had advantages and disadvantages over Britain. Advantages included well-established artisanal and commercial communities, which could build on already developed technologies. Continental countries also had strong governments that played a greater role than the British government in promoting industry, issuing bonds or guaranteeing investments, and establishing corporate banks. Disadvantages included the difficulties of competing with British manufactured goods and of mastering the complicated British machines. Britain had decades of economic superiority over the continental industrial states so it continued to produce its goods so cheaply that other countries could not easily compete.

- Similarities: Industrialization was accompanied by urbanization, deplorable working and housing conditions, which slowly ameliorated, and labor unions and political parties representing the interests of workers, which became important. Labor legislation was initiated by conservative political leaders. Mercantilism was adopted to protect local industries. Per capita productivity and income increased within a half century.
- Differences: British industrialization began in the eighteenth century, while on the continent it began first in Belgium in the 1830s and later elsewhere. British industrialization was almost completely a result of private initiative, with little government involvement; but on the continent governments played a greater role, particularly in Prussia and later in Russia. British industrialization began in the textile industry, but as it was hard for other nations to compete with British goods, other industries became dominant on the continent, especially steel and iron. In Britain there were transformative inventions like the steam engine; continental technological advancements increased productivity but were less revolutionary. Britain abandoned protectionism and adopted free trade with the repeal of the Corn Laws in 1846, while most states on the continent retained protectionist tariffs. In Britain, industrialization was thorough and deep, and maintained its momentum over time; it was much more gradual and more inconsistent, often accompanied by economic dislocation and inflation, on the continent and less widespread in France and Russia.

QUESTION 6

This question asks you to evaluate how twentieth-century artists broke away from nineteenth-century artistic styles and values. You will need to know about the arts in both centuries and to develop a thesis that connects the changes in art to changes in social and political conditions.

- Thesis: Nineteenth-century art reflected the optimism and confidence of a Europe that had become the dominant force in the world, with a thriving economy and political progress toward greater democracy. The new values and styles of the twentieth century reflected the social, political, and psychological dislocations caused by the World Wars, which undermined Europe's sense of security, superiority, and identity.
- Nineteenth-century art was dominated by three movements: romanticism, realism, and impressionism. While each had different values and styles, they all involved a portrayal of real people and real landscapes. They all used three-dimensional perspective.
- Twentieth-century art was marked by cubism, abstractionism, expressionism, surrealism, and Dadaism. The artists broke away from the notion that the function of art was to depict reality, whether the power of individuals or nature (romanticism), the lives of ordinary people (realism), or the

immediate impression made by a scene or the way light breaks up landscape (impressionism). Twentieth-century artists were fascinated by form rather than content or light. Two-dimensionality replaced three-dimensionality. Cubists broke images into geometric shapes (Picasso); expressionists (Matisse) and abstractionists (Kandinsky) sought to express the inner world of the artist and used bright colors and rapidly moving lines. Surrealists (Dali, Ernst) went even further away from reality by painting the odd images and symbols of dreams. Dadaists challenged the very basic notions of Western art by using outrageous images; *dada* itself is a nonsensical word.

QUESTION 7

This essay asks you to address several decades of eastern European history focusing on attempts to overthrow or resist Soviet rule or Soviet-dominated regimes and evaluating the reasons for their success and failure. You can easily break the resistance into three decades. Your thesis can be general or specific, as the two examples below.

- Thesis 1: Resistance movements in the Soviet Bloc had no chance of achieving the reforms they demanded if Soviet troops were present or easily available. Thesis 2: Poland, more than any other eastern European state other than Yugoslavia, successfully resisted Soviet domination by cautiously avoiding direct challenges to the Soviet Union.
- 1948: Tito broke away from Soviet control and established an independent communist state in Yugoslavia. He succeeded because there were no Soviet troops there. Yugoslavia, a multiethnic state, became more prosperous and modernized than the states under Soviet domination and pursued an independent foreign policy while remaining communist.
- 1950s: Poles and Hungarians both revolted in 1956 for nationalistic reasons and for greater political and economic democracy. Widespread rioting in Poland brought about a change of government with a greater degree of autonomy. But when a liberal communist regime that promised free elections and other reforms took power in Hungary in October 1956, the Soviet troops, which had been forced to leave, returned with Warsaw Pact troops and tanks. The Hungarians, hoping in vain for help from the United States, fought back against the tanks but were crushed. The disappointment of the Hungarian reform movement led most eastern Europeans to believe that they had to accommodate Soviet demands.
- 1968: A liberal reform movement successfully took the reins of power in Czechoslovakia. Alexander Dubçek, the leader of the reformers in the Czech Communist Party, was elected in January and initiated a series of reforms known as the Prague Spring. These included a reduction of censorship and bureaucratic planning, greater political and artistic freedom, and substantial democracy within the party as well as in industry. In August 1968, Warsaw Pact troops invaded and occupied Czechoslovakia ending the reform program and replacing the leadership. The Soviet Union announced the

Brezhnev Doctrine which claimed the right to intervene in the internal affairs of members of the Warsaw Pact.

- 1980: A strike of thousands of workers in the Gdansk shipyards in Poland developed into a movement called Solidarity, which demanded not only redress of economic grievances but also free trade unions, civil liberties, and economic reforms. The members of the movement occupied the shipyards to stay until the government gave in to Solidarity's demands. The support of a new pope of Polish origin helped fuel the resistance. Led by Lech Walesa, Solidarity drew millions of members, but did not try to take power directly, settling for some concessions. Nevertheless, the Communist leader of Poland crushed the movement, arresting its leaders and outlawing it in December 1981. But as the government was unwilling to impose full-scale repression, Solidarity continued to be an important voice for reform. There was greater political and artistic freedom in Poland in the 1980s than elsewhere in the Soviet bloc. Solidarity emerged later in the decade as the fulcrum around which the end of Communist rule in Poland was achieved.

SCORING THE FREE-RESPONSE ESSAYS

The essays are scored on a scale of 0 to 9, with 0 being a real score. A response that is completely off task does not even earn a zero. Here are scoring guidelines for the essays.

9–8 Has a clear, well-developed thesis
Is well organized
Addresses the terms of the question
Supports the thesis with substantial specific evidence
Has sophisticated analysis
May contain minor errors; even a 9 need not be flawless

7–6 Has a clear thesis
Addresses all parts of the question but discussion is uneven
Has competent analysis, but it may be superficial
Supports the thesis with some specific evidence

5–4 Contains a thesis, perhaps superficial or simplistic
Has uneven responses to the question's terms
May contain errors, factual or interpretative
Addresses the question with generally accurate discussion but without specific evidence; analysis is implicit or superficial
May contain major errors within a generally accurate and appropriate discussion
Is descriptive rather than analytical

3–2 Has weak or muddled thesis, perhaps suggesting false or inappropriate dichotomies or connections
Contains significant errors of chronology or fact
Has minimal discussion
Offers limited evidence

1–0 Has confused or absent thesis or merely restates the question
Misconstrues the question or omits major tasks
May contain major errors or irrelevant historical information
Addresses only one part of the question
Offers minimal or no evidence

Reread your essay or, if you can work with a fellow student in APEH, read each other's essays and ask the following questions:

1. How well organized is the essay? Is it clearly divided into distinct paragraphs? Is there an introduction and a conclusion?
2. How clear is the thesis? Is the thesis statement at the beginning of the essay or in the conclusion?
3. How many arguments support the thesis?
4. How much evidence is used to support the thesis? How specific was it?
5. Were all parts of the question addressed? Was the discussion of the different parts more or less balanced?
6. How many of the points noted in the explanations of the answer were made in the essay?
7. Were there major factual, chronological, or interpretative errors? Or minor errors?
8. Was the analysis explicit or implicit? Was it sophisticated or minimal?

Now reread the scoring guidelines and give yourself a score.

In general, the scores on the DBQ average higher than those of the FRQs, because the DBQ is a skill-based question while the FRQs are content based. The median score on the DBQ is 5 usually because of lack of POV analysis, while the median scores on the FRQs are typically 4 to 5 in Part B and often 3 to 4 on the Part C, frequently because students run out of time.

CALCULATING YOUR SCORE ON THE AP EXAM

SECTION 1: MULTIPLE-CHOICE QUESTIONS

__________ – (1/4 × __________) × 1.1250 = __________

number correct out of 80 — number wrong — Weighted Section I score (if less than zero, enter zero; do not round)

SECTION II: FREE-RESPONSE QUESTIONS

Question 1 (Part A)	________ Out of 9	× 4.5000 =	________ (do not round)
Question 2 (Part B)	________ Out of 9	× 2.7500 =	________ (do not round)
Question 3 (Part C)	________ Out of 9	× 2.7500 =	________ (do not round)
		Sum =	________ Weighted Section II score (do not round)

COMPOSITE SCORE:

________ + ________ = ________

Weighted Section I   Weighted Section II   Composite Score (round to the nearest whole number)

COMPOSITE SCORE RANGE	AP GRADE
121–180	5
99–120	4
67–98	3
49–66	2
0-48	1

HOW TO INTERPRET YOUR PRACTICE TEST RESULTS

1. First, look at the multiple-choice score. It is a fair indicator of what your overall score will be. How many out of 80 did you get right? How many points off did you lose for incorrect answers?

   According to College Board statistics on the 2004 Released Exam, most students who got a score of 4 or 5 on the examination earned a weighted score of 61 or over on the multiple-choice section. A weighted score of 31 to 45 on the multiple-choice section was typical of the vast majority of students earning a 3 on the exam; the rest of the students, about a third, earning a 3 received a weighted score of 16 to 30. More than 60% of students with a weighted score of 16 to 30 earned an exam score of 1 or 2. Students with a weighted score below 15 were mostly likely to get a 1 on the exam.

2. Check to see if you lost too many points for wrong answers. Look back at the ones you got wrong to see if you got them wrong because you did not know the answer or because you guessed. If you discover that you guessed a lot and guessed wrong, then on the AP exam, don't guess!

3. Examine your essay scores. What strengths and weaknesses do you find? If you did not do as well as you would have liked, try to focus on what problems you had in writing the essays. Was it your thesis statement, use of evidence, errors, or lack of organization? Once you identify your difficulties, you can focus your attention on addressing them.

4. Set a realistic goal for yourself. If you want a score of 4, for example, then your goal should be 55 out of 80 multiple-choice answers correct, a 6 or 7 on the data-based question, and a 5 or 6 on each free-response question. For an exam score of 5, raise the ante to 60 multiple-choice answers correct and essay scores of 8, 7, and 7. If you have used this book and prepared well for the examination, you have every right to expect a score of 4 or 5. Make it happen!

Practice Test 2

AP EUROPEAN HISTORY EXAMINATION
SECTION I: Multiple-Choice Questions
Time—55 minutes
Number of questions: 80

Directions The questions or incomplete statements below are each followed by five suggested answers. Select the best answer.

MULTIPLE-CHOICE QUESTIONS

1. The results of the Hundred Years' War included all of the following *except*
   (A) losses in the number of knights led to a decline in the number of local magistrates and an increase in disorder.
   (B) English wool exports declined significantly.
   (C) representative assemblies developed in Britain, Germany, and Spain.
   (D) France established a single national assembly from its many provincial assemblies.
   (E) nationalism rose in Britain and France.

2. Before the Renaissance,
   (A) literature, literacy, and the use of the vernacular increased.
   (B) only the clergy were allowed to read.
   (C) all works of literature were published in Latin.
   (D) major works of literature were written but banned by the Catholic Church.
   (E) the number of schools increased dramatically in the urban areas.

3. Slavery of Africans in Europe during the Renaissance involved
   (A) numerous slave revolts.
   (B) escaped slaves returning to Africa.
   (C) plantation life similar to that of North America.
   (D) slaves used as entertainment as well as labor.
   (E) a decline in the slave trade after the Black Plague.

4. The paintings in the Sistine Chapel demonstrate all of the following characteristics of Renaissance art *except*
   (A) classical influence.
   (B) individualism.
   (C) religious themes.
   (D) iconography.
   (E) patronage by the Catholic Church.

5. In spite of Machiavelli's advice and due to a number of problems, Italy experienced all of the following *except*
   (A) invasion by Charles V.
   (B) division until the late nineteenth century.
   (C) continual warfare.
   (D) creation of a common foreign policy by the states.
   (E) subjection to outside invaders for many years.

6. Erasmus of Rotterdam emphasized
   (A) a utopian society.
   (B) the importance of civic virtue.
   (C) the importance of simplicity and education in religion.
   (D) sensual tales.
   (E) the discovery that the Donation of Constantine was a forgery.

7. Henry VII of England instituted the Court of Star Chamber as a method of
   (A) implementing the beginning stages of democracy.
   (B) intimidating aristocrats who might compete for his power.
   (C) punishing rebellious peasants.
   (D) support for the Inquisition.
   (E) the initial foundation of a judicial system.

8. "I cannot and will not recant anything for it is neither safe nor right to go against conscience. God help me." The statement was made by the critic of the Catholic Church
   (A) Jan Hus.
   (B) John Wycliffe.
   (C) Erasmus.
   (D) Martin Luther.
   (E) John Calvin.

9. Elizabeth I resolved the religious issue in England by
   (A) eliminating all Catholic elements in the Church of England.
   (B) requiring all subjects to attend church but not caring what they believed.
   (C) returning England to its Catholic roots.
   (D) being willing to convert to Catholicism for the sake of peace in her country.
   (E) remaining Protestant but marrying a Catholic.

10. Calvin's followers
(A) were held to a high standard of morality.
(B) believed that baptism should be granted only to adults.
(C) objected to the English Puritans.
(D) were granted freedom of religion with the Peace of Augsburg.
(E) were most known for their missionary work.

11. The Council of Trent resulted in all of the following *except*
(A) increased missionary work.
(B) improved education for priests.
(C) influence of Ignatius of Loyola.
(D) affirmation of all Catholic doctrines.
(E) reduction of sacraments.

12. Which of the following resisted Spanish invasion during the sixteenth century?
(A) The Netherlands
(B) France
(C) Portugal
(D) Scotland
(E) The Holy Roman Empire

13. Calvinists attracted large numbers of converts in all of the following countries *except*
(A) Scotland.
(B) the Netherlands.
(C) Switzerland.
(D) Ireland.
(E) France.

14. Which of the following was *not* involved in transcontinental trade in the fifteenth century?
(A) Africa
(B) China
(C) India
(D) Ottoman Empire
(E) Mesoamerica

15. The Spanish conquered the Incas by use of
(A) force.
(B) disease and force.
(C) bribery and deception.
(D) diplomacy and ransom money.
(E) trade and religion.

16. The most profitable crop in the New World during the sixteenth century was
(A) tobacco.
(B) rice.
(C) cotton.
(D) sugar.
(E) corn.

17. Seventeenth-century European absolutism was *not* associated with
(A) *"L'etat, c'est moi."*
(B) Divine right rule
(C) Limited bureaucracies
(D) Standing armies
(E) Reduction of noble power

18. Both absolute and constitutional monarchs were concerned with
(A) responding to the needs of the people.
(B) developing relationships with representative bodies.
(C) attending to provincial concerns.
(D) protection, taxation, and state control.
(E) the development of a single language.

19. Which of the following was the greatest threat to the sixteenth century French monarchy's goal of centralizing the government?
(A) Nobility
(B) Peasantry
(C) Clergy
(D) Basque minorities
(E) Bourbon siblings

20. Mercantilism included all of the following strategies *except*
(A) colonies.
(B) tariffs.
(C) subsidies.
(D) infrastructure.
(E) free-market trade.

21. The Pragmatic Sanction
(A) was ignored by Prussia.
(B) protected Austria from Prussia.
(C) created an alliance system against England.
(D) sent an intimidating message to Peter the Great.
(E) protected central Europe from the Turks.

GO ON TO NEXT PAGE

22. Suleiman the Magnificent encouraged all of the following *except*
    (A) religious toleration.
    (B) trade.
    (C) cultural autonomy for minority groups.
    (D) a slave corps in the bureaucracy.
    (E) private property.

23. Peter the Great used all of the following means to strengthen his state *except*
    (A) bureaucracy.
    (B) war.
    (C) freedom for the serfs.
    (D) power over the nobles.
    (E) the military.

24. After the Thirty Years' War, the strongest province in the northern part of the Holy Roman Empire was
    (A) Brandenburg-Prussia.
    (B) Silesia.
    (C) Bohemia.
    (D) Austria.
    (E) Transylvania.

25. Among the results of the scientific revolution was
    (A) a competitive scientific community.
    (B) immediate practical applications of its ideas.
    (C) a significant impact on European economies.
    (D) the rejection of all science by the church.
    (E) a theoretical approach to science.

26. Voltaire did *not*
    (A) consider Newton history's greatest man.
    (B) criticize the Catholic Church for its intolerance.
    (C) satirize war.
    (D) admire England.
    (E) hope for a democracy.

27. Madame du Châtelet
    (A) was an aristocrat who had a passion for science.
    (B) hosted many salons for the philosophes.
    (C) opposed expansion of education for women other than scientists.
    (D) predicted the rebellion of the peasants in the French Revolution.
    (E) funded the *Encyclopedia*.

28. The most common element of the Enlightenment accepted by Frederick the Great, Catherine the Great, and Joseph II was the
    (A) rejection of war.
    (B) acceptance of the idea of a constitution.
    (C) abolishment of serfdom.
    (D) acceptance of the cultural values of the Enlightenment.
    (E) consideration of compulsory education.

29. Moses Mendelssohn
    (A) fostered the Jewish Enlightenment.
    (B) led the Polish uprising against partitioning of the country.
    (C) joined the Royal Academy of Sciences.
    (D) persuaded Frederick the Great to become more tolerant.
    (E) corresponded with Catherine the Great.

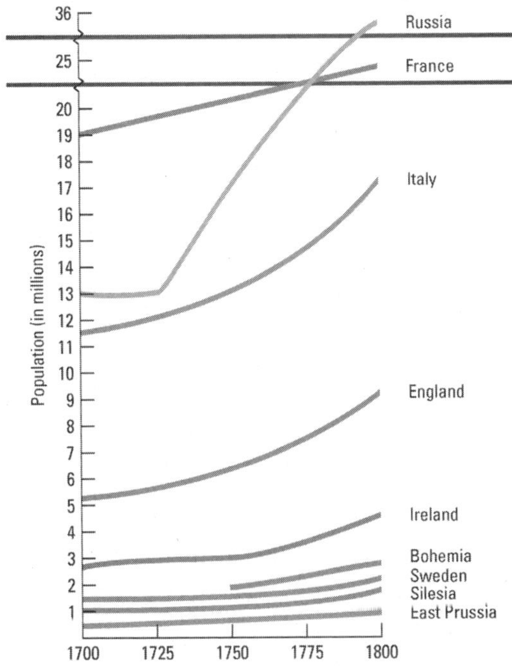

30. Using the chart, which of the following did *not* contribute to the rise in population in Europe during the eighteenth century?
    (A) Decline in mortality rates
    (B) Agricultural improvements
    (C) Improvements in transportation
    (D) Less destructive wars
    (E) Industrial Revolution

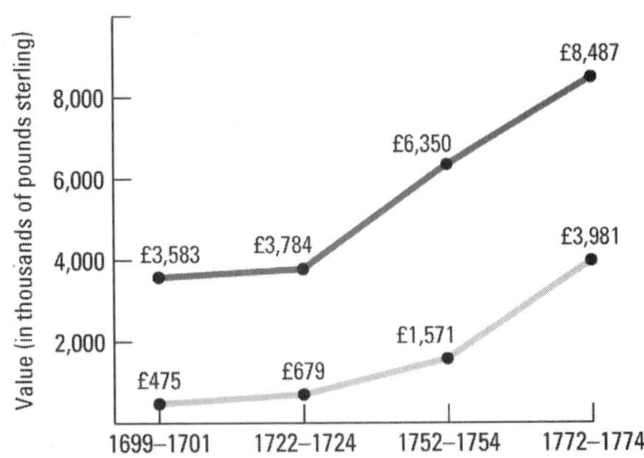

31. According to the chart,
    (A) exports to the transatlantic area paralleled the total growth of exports.
    (B) exports from England to Europe expanded dramatically after 1700.
    (C) slaves were the predominant trading item after 1722.
    (D) imports to England outgrew exports.
    (E) exports from the Atlantic economy included sugar, tobacco, and cotton.

32. Slave labor created what percentage of the products traded by North America from 1761–1800?
    (A) none
    (B) 25 percent
    (C) 50 percent
    (D) 80 percent
    (E) all

33. Adam Smith
    (A) was critical of mercantilism.
    (B) wrote a rationale for having a command economy.
    (C) opposed Marxism.
    (D) hoped to combine government and business.
    (E) attempted to implement social welfare practices.

34. During the eighteenth century, attitudes toward children softened as a result of
    (A) government policies.
    (B) child-rearing manuals.
    (C) the evolution of psychology.
    (D) the Enlightenment.
    (E) medical improvements.

35. The most remarkable dietary change in the eighteenth century was the dramatic increase in consumption of
    (A) meat.
    (B) dairy products.
    (C) tea and sugar.
    (D) beer.
    (E) semitropical fruits.

36. All of the following was true about eighteenth-century medical practice *except*
    (A) physicians used blood letting and purging to cure illness.
    (B) scientists discovered that germs cause disease.
    (C) surgeons did not have anesthesia for their patients.
    (D) surgeons learned to cauterize wounds.
    (E) smallpox inoculations eradicated much of the disease.

37. Eighteenth-century religious trends of significant interest included all of the following *except*
    (A) Pietism.
    (B) Methodism.
    (C) deism.
    (D) Jansenism.
    (E) existentialism.

38. Eighteenth-century leisure included
    (A) blood sports.
    (B) popular magazines.
    (C) proliferation of novels.
    (D) organized teams.
    (E) regional competitions for youth.

39. The ancien régime in eighteenth-century France included all of the following *except*
    (A) peasants could attain noble status.
    (B) some nobles were aggressive capitalists.
    (C) some merchants wanted to be landowners.
    (D) legally, society was no longer based on rigid social orders.
    (E) the clergy owned approximately 10 percent of the land.

40. Which of the following was the most radical element in the Terror?
    (A) Jacobins
    (B) Girondists
    (C) Mountain
    (D) Third Estate
    (E) Robespierre and the Committee of Public Safety

41. Women were involved in the French Revolution in all of the following ways *except*
    (A) the march on Versailles to accost the king and queen.
    (B) support of Mary Wollstonecraft's vision for women.
    (C) part of the *sans culottes* radicals.
    (D) sewing tents and clothes for the war.
    (E) serving on the Committee of Public Safety.

42. Napoleon met France's desire for "confidence from below, authority from above" because he
    (A) sought to create a republic where people would vote for him among other candidates.
    (B) provided dictatorial rule.
    (C) offered military leadership and gained the support of powerful groups.
    (D) took the initiative in strengthening the National Assembly.
    (E) sought the support of the Catholic Church.

43. Ultimately, the Napoleonic empire, including dependent states and allies, included all of the following *except*
    (A) the Grand Duchy of Warsaw.
    (B) Russia.
    (C) Great Britain and Russia.
    (D) Spain.
    (E) Italy.

44. During the first Industrial Revolution, the steam engine was a critical improvement in technology in all of the following areas *except*
    (A) draining mines.
    (B) replacing water power in mills.
    (C) replacing charcoal with coke.
    (D) improving the iron industry.
    (E) expanding the steel industry.

Per Capita Levels of Industrialization, 1750–1913

	1750	1800	1830	1860	1880	1900	1913
Great Britain	10	16	25	64	87	100	115
Belgium	9	10	14	28	43	56	88
United States	4	9	14	21	38	69	126
France	9	9	12	20	28	39	59
Germany	8	8	9	15	25	52	85
Austria-Hungary	7	7	8	11	15	23	32
Italy	8	8	8	10	12	17	26
Russia	6	6	7	8	10	15	20
China	8	6	6	4	4	3	3
India	7	6	6	3	2	1	2

Note: All entries are based on an index value of 100, equal to the per capita level of industrialization in Great Britain in 1900. Data for Great Britain are actually for the United Kingdom, thereby including Ireland with England, Wales, and Scotland.

45. The table above illustrates
    (A) the gap between Great Britain's textile production and other countries between 1860 and 1880.
    (B) that Great Britain's per capita income increased four times that of France during 1860.
    (C) that all of the European states increased their per capita industrial levels between 1750 and 1913.
    (D) that Germany was an industrial competitive force during the early nineteenth century.
    (E) that East Asia was exhibiting its industrial potential in the nineteenth century.

46. Which of the following did *not* criticize the Industrial Revolution?
    (A) Luddites
    (B) Romantics
    (C) Marxists
    (D) Malthus
    (E) Owen

47. Which of the following is true of the Congress of Vienna?
    (A) It fomented a spirit of bitterness in defeated France.
    (B) It contributed to a century without generalized war.
    (C) It disrupted the European balance of power.
    (D) Metternich refused to relinquish any conquered territory.
    (E) France was not represented in the negotiations.

48. Most nineteenth-century liberals favored all of the following *except*
    (A) laissez-faire economics.
    (B) universal voting rights.
    (C) representative government.
    (D) equality before the law.
    (E) freedom of press and speech.

49. Marxism differed from Utopian socialism in that Marx
    (A) appealed to the middle class to help the poor.
    (B) appealed to the government to help the poor.
    (C) favored a strong leader, temporarily, to implement change.
    (D) predicted violent revolution.
    (E) sought to avoid class struggle.

50. Early nineteenth-century romantic artists and literary figures would applaud all of the following *except*
    (A) the repeal of the Corn Laws.
    (B) the defeat of the Turks in Greece.
    (C) the revolutions of 1848.
    (D) expanded urbanization.
    (E) Jean Jacques Rousseau.

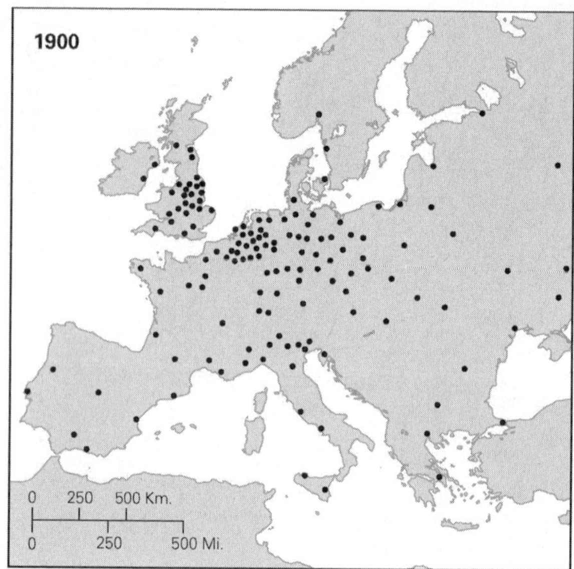

51. According to the map provided, which shows the number of European cities of 100,000 or more in 1800 and 1900,
    (A) there were more large cities in Great Britain in 1900 than in all of Europe in 1800.
    (B) cities demonstrated slower growth at the end of the nineteenth century.
    (C) many cities grew due to migration among European countries.
    (D) most populous areas grew due to immigration from the state's colonies.
    (E) the largest cities emerged along sixteenth-century trade routes.

52. One important solution to overcrowding in the nineteenth century was
    (A) government housing to supply decent homes.
    (B) public transportation to allow people to move out of the city's center.
    (C) welfare to increase income for the poor.
    (D) compulsory education to improve social mobility.
    (E) new leadership so that centralized action could occur.

53. Which of the following was *not* a common disease in nineteenth-century Europe?
    (A) Diphtheria
    (B) Typhoid
    (C) Typhus
    (D) Cholera
    (E) Polio

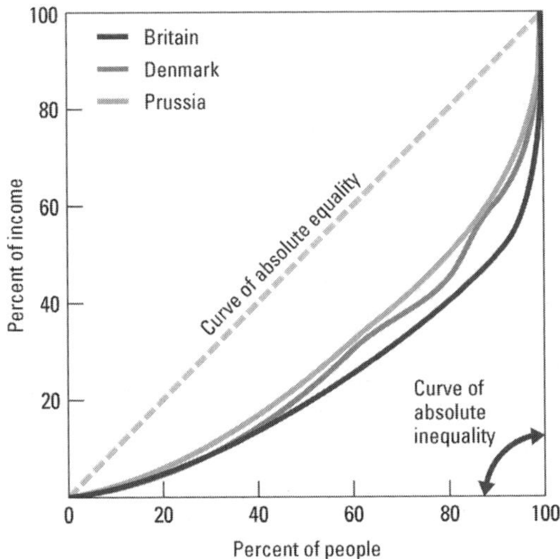

Distribution of Income

	Richest 5%	Richest 10%	Richest 20%	Poorest 60%
Britain	43%		59%	
Denmark	30%	39%	55%	31%
Prussia	30%		50%	33%

54. The chart and table above demonstrate
    (A) the gap between rich and poor grew smaller as a result of the Industrial Revolution.
    (B) England had the largest gap between rich and poor.
    (C) the incomes in Prussia were less equal than those in Britain.
    (D) Prussia had the largest number of poor.
    (E) Britain, Denmark, and Prussia had the best economies in Europe.

55. Late-nineteenth-century responses to crisis in urban families typically led to support from
    (A) extended families and the government.
    (B) only the nuclear family.
    (C) only the government.
    (D) only private charities.
    (E) none of the above.

56. Which of the following was *not* a common strategy of both Germany and Italy in their unification efforts?
    (A) Defeat the key enemies, Austria and France
    (B) Utilize inspiration from nationalist movements
    (C) Aggressive armies, which proved their military might
    (D) Machiavellian tactics that enabled progress toward the goal
    (E) Strong leadership that effected change

57. Which of the following was *not* true of Alexander II's rule in nineteenth-century Russia?
    (A) He freed the serfs.
    (B) Industrialization increased.
    (C) He was assassinated.
    (D) Local zemstvos were established.
    (E) Marxist thought almost disappeared.

58. Which of the following countries was most industrialized, socialized, and unionized by 1914?
    (A) Great Britain
    (B) France
    (C) Germany
    (D) Italy
    (E) Russia

4. The paintings in the Sistine Chapel demonstrate all of the following characteristics of Renaissance art *except*
   (A) classical influence.
   (B) individualism.
   (C) religious themes.
   (D) iconography.
   (E) patronage by the Catholic Church.

5. In spite of Machiavelli's advice and due to a number of problems, Italy experienced all of the following *except*
   (A) invasion by Charles V.
   (B) division until the late nineteenth century.
   (C) continual warfare.
   (D) creation of a common foreign policy by the states.
   (E) subjection to outside invaders for many years.

6. Erasmus of Rotterdam emphasized
   (A) a utopian society.
   (B) the importance of civic virtue.
   (C) the importance of simplicity and education in religion.
   (D) sensual tales.
   (E) the discovery that the Donation of Constantine was a forgery.

7. Henry VII of England instituted the Court of Star Chamber as a method of
   (A) implementing the beginning stages of democracy.
   (B) intimidating aristocrats who might compete for his power.
   (C) punishing rebellious peasants.
   (D) support for the Inquisition.
   (E) the initial foundation of a judicial system.

8. "I cannot and will not recant anything for it is neither safe nor right to go against conscience. God help me." The statement was made by the critic of the Catholic Church
   (A) Jan Hus.
   (B) John Wycliffe.
   (C) Erasmus.
   (D) Martin Luther.
   (E) John Calvin.

9. Elizabeth I resolved the religious issue in England by
   (A) eliminating all Catholic elements in the Church of England.
   (B) requiring all subjects to attend church but not caring what they believed.
   (C) returning England to its Catholic roots.
   (D) being willing to convert to Catholicism for the sake of peace in her country.
   (E) remaining Protestant but marrying a Catholic.

62. The Treaty of Brest-Litovsk involved the
   (A) Armenian atrocities.
   (B) German defeat due to severe winter conditions.
   (C) Russian heroism during the siege of Leningrad.
   (D) occupation of the Balkans by the Allies.
   (E) Russian surrender to the Germans.

63. The causes of World War I included all of the following *except*
   (A) worldwide economic downturn from over speculation.
   (B) military stockpiling.
   (C) aggressive motives on the part of most western European countries.
   (D) shifting alliances.
   (E) public support as a result of propaganda.

64. The Treaty of Versailles
   (A) urged the reduction of nationalism in smaller nations.
   (B) created a League of Nations.
   (C) included Germany in the negotiations.
   (D) stated that Germany was not the only country responsible for the war.
   (E) was ratified by the U.S. Senate with little disagreement.

65. The map below illustrates
   (A) the expansion of the Ottoman Empire during the seventeenth century.
   (B) Muslim versus Christian areas during the late nineteenth century.
   (C) the partition of the Ottoman Empire after World War I.
   (D) the independence of former colonies in the Middle East.
   (E) the spread of terrorism during the late twentieth century.

66. Postwar disillusionment contributed to increased interest in all of the following *except*
   (A) Nietzsche.
   (B) Christianity.
   (C) existentialism.
   (D) the Newtonian worldview.
   (E) Freudian psychology.

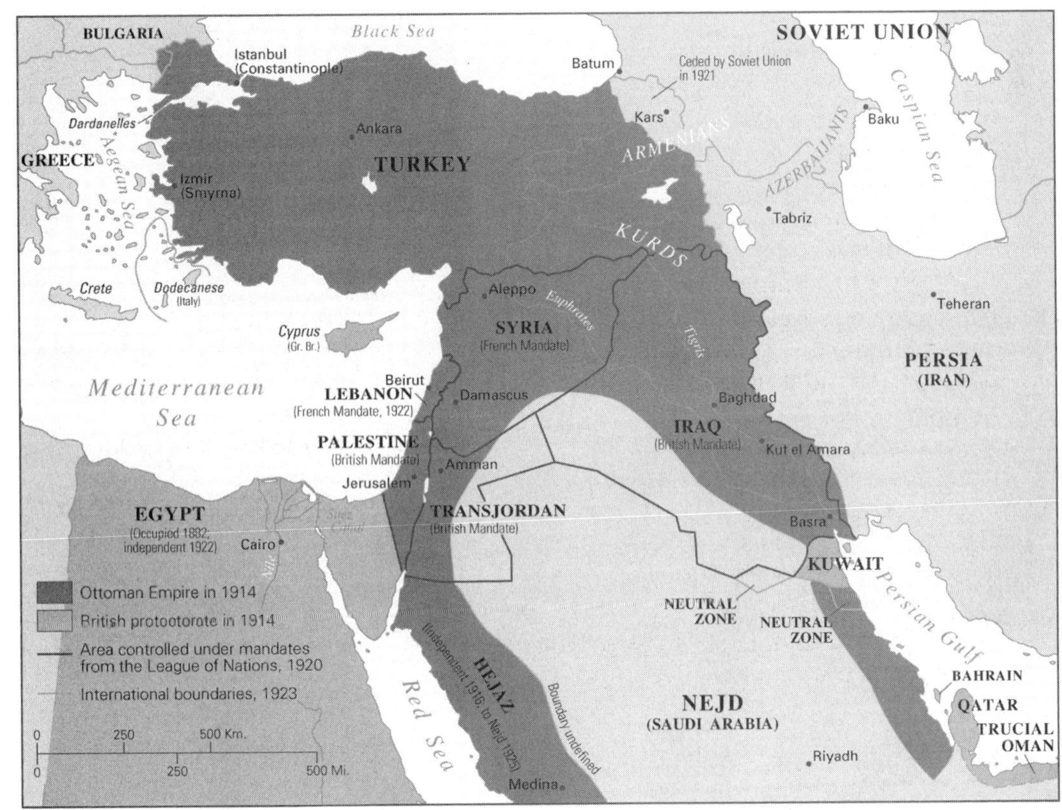

GO ON TO NEXT PAGE

67. The poster above represents horror at
    (A) the German invasion of Belgium.
    (B) the Russian Revolution.
    (C) the French occupation of the Ruhr.
    (D) the German arms race.
    (E) British industrialization.

68. Which of the following was *not* a response to the Great Depression?
    (A) The output of goods fell significantly throughout the world.
    (B) Britain devalued its currency.
    (C) Most countries became isolationist.
    (D) Germany, northern Britain, and the American Midwest were hit hardest.
    (E) France established a stable government.

69. Collectivization in Stalin's Soviet Union resulted in
    (A) rapid industrialization.
    (B) success of the Five Year Plan.
    (C) the New Economic Policy.
    (D) the deaths of millions of people.
    (E) diversity of production.

70. The poster illustrates the artistic style of
    (A) expressionism.
    (B) surrealism.
    (C) socialist realism.
    (D) romanticism.
    (E) cubism.

71. Mussolini was supported by all of the following *except*
    (A) the Catholic Church.
    (B) conservatives.
    (C) socialists.
    (D) property owners.
    (E) revolutionary socialists.

72. Hitler gained power in Germany because
    (A) he pitched his speeches to the upper class.
    (B) he created a powerful coalition with the Communists.
    (C) he appealed to the youth, military, and businessmen.
    (D) he appealed to the youth and working class.
    (E) even working together, the Communists and Social Democrats could not overcome the Nazis.

73. The cartoon illustrates the idea that Hitler
   (A) overcame the resistance of the peasants.
   (B) gained power over the silent majority.
   (C) succeeded due to weak leadership by the European powers.
   (D) used various organizations as the foundation of his rise to success.
   (E) created an image that prompted the public to bow before him.

74. The map below illustrates
   (A) movements of post–World War II refugees.
   (B) the Axis strategy during World War II.
   (C) troops gathered to defeat Napoleon.
   (D) the spread of Protestant denominations.
   (E) the Soviet strategy to defeat Germany in World War II.

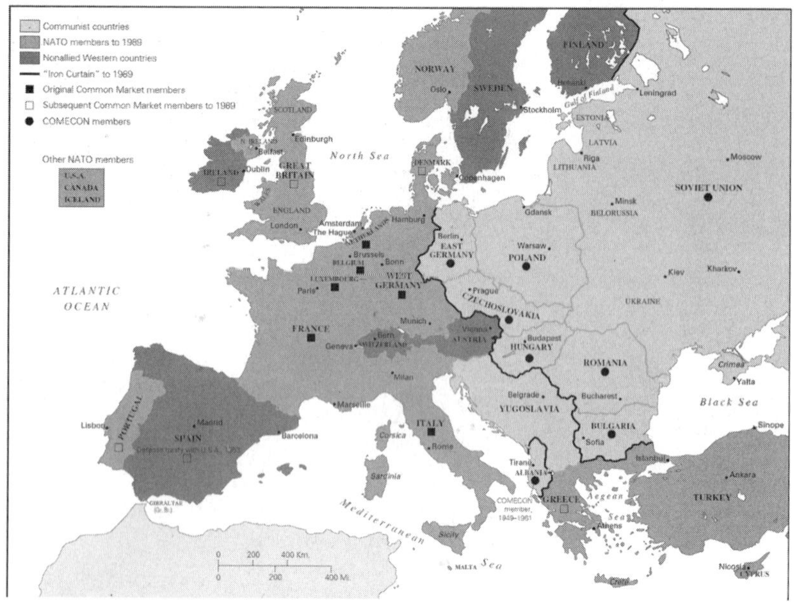

75. The map above represents
   (A) the Thirty Years; War.
   (B) NATO and communist countries after World War II.
   (C) Catholic versus Eastern Orthodox countries.
   (D) the spread of the Reformation.
   (E) the Napoleonic empire before his invasion of Russia.

76. Which of the following is *not* associated with attempts to establish a European Union?
   (A) Treaty of Rome
   (B) Common Market
   (C) Maastricht Treaty
   (D) Gaullist policies
   (E) Coal and Steel Community

77. Which of the following was *not* evidence of the Soviet Union's harsh communism?
   (A) Brezhnev Doctrine
   (B) Prague Spring
   (C) Response to Hungary 1956
   (D) Khrushchev's "secret speech"
   (E) Berlin Wall

78. The best title for the map would be
   (A) Most Devastated Cities During the Plague.
   (B) Early Nineteenth-Century Revolutions
   (C) World War I Battles.
   (D) Sites of Nazi Concentration Camps During World War II.
   (E) Democratic Movements in 1989.

79. German reunification in 1989 was swift due to all of the following *except*
   (A) Chancellor Kohl promised the East Germans an even exchange for their weak currency.
   (B) the Soviet Union allowed reunification if Germany agreed to prohibit the development of nuclear weapons.
   (C) West Germany committed government funds to build housing for the former East Germans.
   (D) half of the East German population poured into West Germany when it occurred.
   (E) the Paris Accord affirmed the new borders, solidifying reunification.

80. Which of the following twentieth-century Soviet rulers would be considered most appreciated by the West?
   (A) Lenin
   (B) Stalin
   (C) Gorbachev
   (D) Yeltsin
   (E) Putin

STOP

END OF SECTION I

IF YOU FINISH BEFORE TIME IS CALLED, YOU MAY CHECK YOUR WORK ON THIS SECTION. DO NOT GO ON TO SECTION II UNTIL YOU ARE TOLD TO DO SO.

AP EUROPEAN HISTORY EXAMINATION
Section II: Free-Response Essays

Section II of the examination has two kinds of questions. Part A is the Document-Based Question, which you must answer. Part B and Part C each have three general free-response essay questions. You are to answer *one* essay question from Part B and *one* essay question from Part C. You will have a total of 130 minutes to complete the document-based essay and two free-response essays.

Part A: Document-Based Question (DBQ)
Suggested reading time—15 minutes
Suggested writing time—45 minutes
Percent of Section II score—45

Directions The following question is based on the accompanying Documents 1–14. The documents have been edited for the purpose of this exercise. Write your answer on the tinted pages of the Section II free-response booklet.

This question is designed to test your ability to work with and understand historical documents.

Write an essay that

- Provides an appropriate, explicitly stated thesis that directly addresses all parts of the question and does *not* simply restate the question
- Discusses a majority of the documents individually and specifically
- Demonstrates understanding of the basic meaning of a majority of the documents
- Supports the thesis with appropriate interpretation of a majority of the documents
- Analyzes the documents by explicitly grouping them in at least three appropriate ways
- Takes into account both the sources of the documents and the authors' point of view

You may refer to relevant historical information not mentioned in the documents.

1. Analyze the various views of British leaders about the Eastern Question and the Russo-Turkish War of 1877–1878.

   Historical Background: Britain, then under the leadership of Prime Minister Benjamin Disraeli, was divided over how best to respond to growing tensions in the Balkans in the 1870s. British concerns about the Middle East intensified after the purchase of the Suez Canal in 1875. In 1875 a revolt against their Ottoman rulers by Christians in Bosnia was militarily supported by Serbia and Montenegro; the next year, Serbia and Turkey negotiated a settlement. There was also unrest in Bulgaria, still under Ottoman rule. In 1877, the Russians invaded the Ottoman Empire and nearly reached Constantinople to defend their fellow Orthodox Slavs and fulfill a long-standing Russian territorial ambition to obtain access to the Mediterranean. The Russian advance was temporarily stopped by the Turks at Plevna in September 1877, but when it continued, Turkey asked Britain to mediate. In 1878, Britain sent its fleet to Constantinople. In March 1878, the Russo-Turkish War ended with the signing by Turkey and Russia of the Treaty of San Stefano, in which the Ottoman Empire granted independence to Serbia, Montenegro, and Rumania, and parts of Bulgaria were put under Russian protection. This settlement was unsatisfactory to the other great powers of Europe, who met at the Congress of Berlin and arrived at a new settlement putting Bosnia and Herzegovina under Austrian occupation and checking Russian expansion.

Document 1

Sir Edwin Pears, 1835–1919, British lawyer, president of European Bar Association, resident of Constantinople after 1873, correspondent for the *Daily News. Forty Years in Constantinople, 1873–1915,* 1916

Mr. Disraeli was then Prime Minister, and treated the matter very lightly. He declared, in reply to a statement that persons had been tortured as well as killed, that he doubted whether torture was practiced among a people "who generally terminated their connection with culprits in a more expeditious manner." . . . His light manner of speaking on the subject irritated Members on both sides of the House, who recognized that if my statements were true they constituted a damning charge against Turkish methods of government in Bulgaria, and demanded at least serious examination. . . .

It should be understood that at this time there was no revolt in Bulgaria, though there had been considerable expression of discontent. The idea of the Turks was to crush out the spirit of the Bulgarian people, and thus prevent revolt. . . . The London Daily News sent Mr. MacGahan, an Irish-American of great experience and fine character, to Bulgaria to report more fully than I had been able to do. . . . [He] had been in Central Asia and knew something of Russia, and could not be charged with having any prejudice against the Turks.

One of the first places they visited was Batak, . . . a thriving town, rich and prosperous in comparison with neighboring Moslem villages. . . . Its prosperity had excited the envy and jealousy of its Moslem neighbors. . . . In all the Moslem atrocities, Chiot, Bulgarian, and Armenian, the principal incentive has been the larger prosperity of the Christian population; for, in spite of centuries of oppression and plunder, Christian industry and Christian morality everywhere make for national wealth and intelligence. . . .

Source: Sir Edwin Pears, *Forty Years in Constantinople, 1873–1915* (New York: D. Appleton and Co., 1916), pp. 16-19; reprinted in Alfred J. Bannan and Achilles Edelenyi, eds., *Documentary History of Eastern Europe,* (New York: Twayne Publishers, 1970), pp. 191–194; Modern History Sourcebook online.

Document 2

W. T. Stead, 1849–1912, British educator, social reformer, and journalist, editor of the *Pall Mall Gazette,* 1880–1890. Articles in the *Northern Echo,* June 24, 1876, and July 5, 1876

A War of extermination is being carried on against the Christians in Bulgaria. . . . England is Turkey's friend. The Mussulmans [sic] are going about saying that England will not see the Empire broken up—that, if necessary, it will help to put down insurrections. . . . Serbia and Montenegro are at war with Turkey. . . . Much as war is to be detested, in cases like the present, war is the only solution which has yet been devised. . . . It is a war of Liberation. . . . The Premier [Prime Minister] . . . is quite capable of plunging the country into a disastrous war in order to perpetuate the dying agonies of the Turkish Empire by opposing the liberators of Bosnia. Our duty is to stand aloof, extending merely as moral support to the insurgents. . . . Woe be unto that man, be he Premier or be he Earl, who in the name of England . . . [or] from jealousy of Russia . . . dares to oppose the brave men who are struggling for liberty among the Bosnian hills.

Source: W. T. Stead Resource Site, www.attackingthedevil.co.uk.

Document 3

J. A. MacGahan, 1844–1878, American journalist, war correspondent. Dispatch to the *London Daily News,* August 22, 1876

Since . . . yesterday, I have supped full of horrors. Nothing has as yet been said of the Turks that I do not now believe; nothing could be said of them that I should not think probable and likely. . . . Let me tell you what we saw at Batak. . . . As we ascended, bones, skulls, and skeletons became more frequent . . . fragments of half dry, half putrid flesh attached to them. . . . We drew rein with an exclamation of horror, for right before us, almost beneath our horse's feet, was a sight that made us shudder. It was a heap of skulls . . . it emitted a sickening odor, and it was here that the dogs had been seeking a hasty repast. . . . We looked again at the heap of skulls and skeletons before us, and we observed that they were all small and that the articles of clothing intermingled with them and laying about were all women's apparel. These then, were all women and girls. . . . These women had all been beheaded. . . . The Turkish authorities did not even pretend that there was any Turk killed here or that the inhabitants offered any resistance. . . . Of the 8,000 to 9,000 people who made up the population of the place only 1200 to 1500 are left, and they have neither tools to dig graves with, nor strength to use spades if they had them.

Document 4

Benjamin Disraeli, Conservative Party leader and prime minister of Great Britain, 1868, 1874–1878. Letter to Lady Bradford, September 2, 1876

All the papers are arguing whether the great victory of the Serbians may not retard peace. Fortunately, we now have a military attaché, a General officer of our own, at Turkish Headquarters, and he informs up that there has been no victory, no battle, scarcely any fighting; things remain the same.

Document 5

William Gladstone, 1809–1898, Liberal Party statesman and four-time prime minister of England. *Bulgarian Horrors and The Question of the East,* pamphlet, September 6, 1876

The Turkish race. . . were, upon the whole, from the black day when they first entered Europe, the one great anti-human specimen of humanity. Wherever they went a broad line of blood marked the track behind them, and as far as their dominion reached, civilization disappeared from view. They represented everywhere government by force as opposed to government by law. . . . That which has been done, which has too late been examined but which remains unavenged, which has left behind all the foul and all the fierce passion which produced it and which may again spring up in another murderous harvest from the soil soaked and reeking with blood and in the air tainted with every imaginable deed of crime and shame. That such things should be done once is a damning disgrace to the portion of our race which did them; that the door should be left open to their ever so barely possibly repetition would spread that shame over the world.

Source: Quoted in George Horton, *The Blight of Asia* (Indianapolis, IND: 1926); Hellenic Resources Network online, www.hri.org/docs/Horton/HortonBook.htm#_CHAPTER _II.

Document 6

Lord Salisbury, 1830–1903, foreign minister 1878, Conservative Party leader and three-time prime minister. Letter to Benjamin Disraeli, September 23, 1876

We have not the power, even if we have the wish, to give back any of the protected districts to the . . . government of the Porte.* . . . We must have something more than promises. . . . Let there be an Officer of state established at Constantinople who shall be in fact if not in name Protector of Christians . . . nominated in concert with the Powers and for a term of year. He should always have access to the Sultan, and it should be his duty to call the attention of the Turkish Government to any breach of the decrees which have been issued in protection of the Christians. . . . It should further be his duty to submit to the Turkish government a list of persons fit to hold office as Governors of Bosnia, Herzegovina, and Bulgaria, and the Porte should be forced to choose the governors from that list. . . . The problem is solved, if you can get good governors for these oppressed provinces, men who will be just for the Christians but not disloyal to the Porte and who cannot be driven or dismissed by the corrupted intrigues of the seraglio.†

* The Turkish government.

† The harem at the sultan's palace.

Source: www.bodley.ox.ac.uk/dept/scwmss/projects/disraeli/modpol001-aes.html.

Document 7

Pall Mall Gazette, Conservative newspaper until 1880, Liberal and social reformist from 1880 to 1890. Reported in Latest News by Cable, *New York Times,* London, March 22, 1877

That Lord Derby was thoroughly justified—more than justified—in his determination that a clear undertaking on Russia's part to recall her armies from the frontier is an indispensable condition of accepting any such engagement as the protocol implies, will be the universal opinion in England, and it may be taken for certain by all whom it concerns that the Government will abide by its decision.

A special dispatch from Paris to the *Times* says: "when Russian demobilization is once ordered, Europe will be surprised with the speed with which it will be effected. Numerous regiments are already encamped away from the frontier, and the protocol once signed the Czar will address a proclamation ordering demobilization to an almost empty camp.

Document 8

"An Ugly outlook for the Czar," special dispatch by cable to the *New York Times,* September 15, 1877

London: September 15. A week of bloodier work than even that terrible one when Suleiman Pasha encountered such heavy losses in the Schipka Pass, closes with 10,000 dead and wounded Russian and Rumanian soldiers lying around Plevna. The sacrifice of life has been immense in the efforts made to dislodge the troops of Osman Pasha, but the Turkish flag still floats victorious and defiant over as brave an Army as ever defended an entrenched position. American rifles, Krupp guns, and the stubborn resistance and endurance so characteristic of the Ottoman soldiers has completely frustrated the supreme effort of the Muscovites. . . . Only another month of weather fit for fighting remains, and the army of invasion is further off than ever from their attempted conquest of Turkey. . . . Serbia now appears upon the scene as an armed ally of the Defender so called of the Christian faith. She makes most arrogant demands in return for proffered aid and meanwhile poses as the champion of the Slavonic race.

Source: New York Times, September 16, 1877.

Document 9

Lord Derby (Edward Henry Stanley), 1826–1893, foreign secretary in Disraeli's cabinet 1874–1878, became a member of the Liberal Party in 1880, member of Gladstone's cabinet, and in 1882 secretary of state for the colonies. Letter to Benjamin Disraeli, January 23, 1878

After our . . . discussions in Cabinet on the question of sending up the fleet to Constantinople and the decision which was come to this afternoon, you will feel as I do that only one result is possible as far as I am concerned.

The question which we were unable to agree is obviously one of grave importance; it is certain to be eagerly and frequently discussed both in and out of Parliament. The Foreign Secretary more than any other minister would in the ordinary course of things be charged with the duty of defending the decision taken. And as I cannot think it, or say that I think it, a safe or wise one, it is clear that no alterative is left me except to ask you to allow me to retire from the post I hold.

Source: www.bodley.ox.ac.uk/dept/scwmss/projects/disraeli/modpol001-aeu-2.html.

Document 10

Queen Victoria, 1819–1901, r. 1837–1901, empress of India 1877. Letter to Benjamin Disraeli, January/February 1878

The Queen is feeling terribly anxious lest delay should cause us to be too late and lose our prestige for ever! It worries her night and day. . . . And the language, the insulting language—used by the Russians against us! It makes the Queen's blood boil. . . . Oh, if the Queen were a man, she would like to go and give those Russians, whose word one cannot believe, such a beating! We shall never be friends again till we have it out This the Queen feels sure of. This delay, this uncertainty by which abroad, we are losing our prestige and our position while Russia is advancing and will be before Constantinople in no time! Then the Government will be fearfully blamed and the Queen so humiliated that she thinks she would abdicate at once. Be Bold! . . . She feels, she cannot remain the sovereign of a country that is letting itself down to kiss the feet of the great barbarians, the retarders of all liberty and civilization that exists.

Source: Quoted in Lytton Strachey, *Queen Victoria,* 1921 biography, Chap. 8; http//womenshistory.about.com/libraty/etext/ls/bl_lsqv.08.htm online.

Document 11

Popular song sung in streets of London early in 1878

We don't want to fight,

But, by Jingo! if we do,

We've got the ships,

We've got the men,

We've got the money too!

We've fought the Bear before

And while we're Britons true,

The Russians shall not have Constantinople.

Source: Turkish Odyssey: Russo---turkish-war.html.

Document 12

A "HAPPY FAMILY" AT BERLIN.

SHOWMAN. "*The British Lion and the Rooshian Bear will now embrace!* (Aside.) *It's all right, ladies and gentlemen, this effect has been* WELL REHEARSED!"

Showman: "The British Lion and the Russian Bear will now embrace. [Aside: It's all right, Ladies and Gentlemen, this effect will be explained.]

Document 13

Cyprus Convention, Convention of Defensive Alliance between Great Britain and Turkey, with respect to the Asiatic Provinces of Turkey. Signed at Constantinople 4th June 1878

Article 1: . . . If any attempt shall be made at any future time by Russia to take possession of any further territories of His Imperial Majesty the Sultan in Asia . . . England engages to join His Imperial Majesty the Sultan in defending them by force of arms.

In return, His Imperial Majesty the Sultan promises to England to introduce necessary Reforms . . . for the protection of Christen and other subjects of the Porte in these territories. . . .

And in order to enable England to make necessary provision for executing her engagement, His Imperial Majesty the Sultan further consents to assign the Island of Cyprus to be occupied and administrated by England.

Source: Wikipedia.org/wiki/Cyprus_Convention online.

Document 14

Disraeli, quoted in the *Times of London,* on return from the Berlin Conference, July 17, 1878

Lord Salisbury and myself have brought you back peace but a peace I hope with honour.

Source: Quotations from Benjamin Disraeli, PoetHßßunter.com online.

End of Part A

SECTION II: Free-Response Essay Questions
Parts B and C:
Suggested planning and writing time—35 minutes per essay; 70 minutes
Percent of Section II score—27.5 per essay, 55 in total

DIRECTIONS You are to answer one question from Part B and one from Part C. *Do not answer two questions from the same group.*

Make your selection carefully, choosing the questions that you are best prepared to answer thoroughly in the time permitted. You should spend 5 minutes organizing or outlining your answer.

Write an essay that

- Has a relevant thesis
- Addresses all parts of the question
- Supports the thesis with specific evidence
- Is well organized

[On the actual AP exam, you will read these instructions before Part B and Part C, each of which has three essay questions. You will also be told to write your answer to the question on the lined pages of the Section II free-response booklet, making sure to indicate the question you are answering by writing the appropriate question number at the top of each page. Part A of Section II is the DBQ. In this practice exam, the free-response questions are organized chronologically; Part B is on the early modern period and Part C on the nineteenth and twentieth centuries. Remember to pick only one question from each part; should you pick two from the same part, the second essay will not be read.]

Part B Select *one* question from Part B.

2. Describe the roles in intellectual life played by women from the Renaissance through the eighteenth century, and analyze the views of male intellectuals about women's intellect and scholarship.
3. Discuss the differences between the empirical and the mathematical approaches to science during the seventeenth century, and analyze the approach taken by each of Copernicus, Galileo, Kepler, and Newton.
4. Compare the societies that produced Renaissance art in Italy in the fifteenth century and the impressionist movement in France in the nineteenth century, and discuss the relationship of the artist to society in each case.

Part C Select *one* question from Part C.

5. Evaluate the importance of the alliance system in causing World War I.
6. Analyze the reasons for the rise of a successful fascist movement in Italy and describe how it implemented its ideology from when it took power in 1922 to when Italy signed the Axis Pact in 1936.
7. In what ways were the goals of European colonizers in the late nineteenth century different from those of European colonizers in the fifteenth and sixteenth centuries?

END OF EXAMINATION

ANSWERS FOR SECTION I

ANSWER KEY FOR MULTIPLE-CHOICE QUESTIONS

1. D	15. A	29. A	43. C	57. E	71. C
2. A	16. D	30. E	44. E	58. C	72. C
3. D	17. C	31. A	45. C	59. B	73. C
4. D	18. D	32. D	46. D	60. A	74. A
5. D	19. A	33. A	47. D	61. D	75. B
6. C	20. E	34. D	48. B	62. E	76. D
7. B	21. A	35. C	49. D	63. A	77. D
8. D	22. E	36. B	50. D	64. B	78. E
9. B	23. C	37. E	51. A	65. C	79. C
10. A	24. A	38. A	52. B	66. D	80. C
11. E	25. A	39. D	53. E	67. C	
12. A	26. E	40. E	54. B	68. E	
13. D	27. A	41. E	55. A	69. D	
14. E	28. D	42. C	56. C	70. C	

SCORING The multiple-choice section counts for 50 percent of your examination grade.

EXPLANATIONS FOR THE MULTIPLE-CHOICE ANSWERS

1. **ANSWER: (D)** France was not able to create a central representative body. (McKay, *A History of Western Society*, 8th ed. pp. 392-393/9th ed. pp. 385-387)

2. **ANSWER: (A)** Although they grew slowly, all did increase. (McKay, *A History of Western Society*, 8th ed. pp. 405-407/9th ed. pp. 399-401)

3. **ANSWER: (D)** Slaves were sometimes expected to be the court buffoon, others actresses, musicians, or dancers. (McKay, *A History of Western Society*, 8th ed. pp. 436-438/9th ed. pp. 429-431)

4. **ANSWER: (D)** Iconography, painting symbolizing religious figures rather than reproducing them realistically, was characteristic of the medieval period. (McKay, *A History of Western Society*, 8th ed. pp. 419-426/9th ed. pp. 412-416, 421-428)

5. **ANSWER: (D)** The lack of a central government caused Italy to be vulnerable to outside invasion. (McKay, *A History of Western Society*, 8th ed. pp. 418-419/9th ed. pp. 410-411)

6. **ANSWER: (C)** In *Praise of Folly* was a critique of the Catholic Church in favor of simplicity of faith. (McKay, *A History of Western Society*, 8th ed. pp. 438-441/9th ed. pp. 417-418)

7. **ANSWER: (B)** Henry VII used the court to punish any nobles who seemed to threaten his power. (McKay, *A History of Western Society*, 8th ed. p. 442/9th ed. p. 435)

8. **ANSWER: (D)** Luther was the only critic who was brought before a Diet and expected to recant, which he refused to do. (McKay, *A History of Western Society,* 8th ed. p. 458/9th ed. p. 449)

9. **ANSWER: (B)** Those who did not attend church were subject to a fine. In general Elizabeth chose a middle ground between Protestants and Catholics, while glorifying England and her own position. (McKay, *A History of Western Society,* 8th ed. p. 474/9th ed. p. 463)

10. **ANSWER: (A)** Calvin believed that the purity of Christians would draw others to become believers and even promoted theocracy based on the idea of a city on a hill. (McKay, *A History of Western Society,* 8th ed. p. 471/9th ed. p. 463-464)

11. **ANSWER: (E)** The Catholic Church affirmed its belief in seven sacraments. (McKay, *A History of Western Society,* 8th ed. pp. 481-482/9th ed. p. 467)

12. **ANSWER: (A)** The Netherlands resisted the Spanish invasion and became the most tolerant of the European countries. (McKay, *A History of Western Society,* 8th ed. p. 471/9th ed. p. 474)

13. **ANSWER: (D)** Ireland remained staunchly Catholic even though Scotland became Calvinist. (McKay, *A History of Western Society,* 8th ed. p. 478/9th ed. p. 462)

14. **ANSWER: (E)** Although various tribes warred, they did not establish transcontinental trade. (McKay, *A History of Western Society,* 8th ed. pp. 502-507/9th ed. pp. 492-498)

15. **ANSWER: (A)** Pizarro crushed the Inca Empire and established a Spanish viceroyalty in Peru. Also, Cortés used disease as a tool of war during his defeat of the Aztecs. (McKay, *A History of Western Society,* 8th ed. p. 510-512/9th ed. pp. 502-504, 509)

16. **ANSWER: (D)** Sugar was the most important crop but required intensive labor and therefore increased the use of slavery. (McKay, *A History of Western Society,* 8th ed. p. 516/9th ed. pp. 505-508)

17. **ANSWER: (C)** Expanded bureaucracies contributed to loyalty to the monarchs who hired the bureaucrats, and the new civil servants could collect ever increasing taxes. (McKay, *A History of Western Society,* 8th ed. pp. 532-535/9th ed. pp. 528-530)

18. **ANSWER: (D)** Even developing democracies, such as England and the Netherlands, were primarily concerned with establishing a strong central government. (McKay, *A History of Western Society,* 8th ed. pp. 531-532/9th ed. pp. 523-526)

19. **ANSWER: (A)** Various nobles competed for power. (McKay, *A History of Western Society,* 8th ed. p. 534/9th ed. pp. 528-529)

20. **ANSWER: (E)** Laissez-faire capitalism rejected the government involvement of mercantilism. (McKay, *A History of Western Society,* 8th ed. pp. 539-541/9th ed. pp. 532-533)

21. ANSWER: (A) Frederick the Great invaded Austria even though Charles VI had attempted to prevent European nations from invading when his daughter took the throne at his death. (McKay, *A History of Western Society*, 8th ed. p. 573/9th ed. pp. 567-571)

22. ANSWER: (E) All agricultural property officially belonged to the sultan. (McKay, *A History of Western Society*, 8th ed. p. 573/9th ed. p. 567)

23. ANSWER: (C) Peter actually forced thousands of peasants to work to build St. Petersburg, and many peasants were assigned to work in mines and factories. The serfs were not freed until 1866. (McKay, *A History of Western Society*, 8th ed. pp. 581-585/9th ed. pp. 576-580)

24. ANSWER: (A) Brandenburg-Prussia became the foundation of what would become Germany in the nineteenth century. (McKay, *A History of Western Society*, 8th ed. pp. 573-576/9th ed. pp. 567-571)

25. ANSWER: (A) Members of the scientific community had similar goals and worked together, but became increasingly competitive. (McKay, *A History of Western Society*, 8th ed. pp. 604-605/9th ed. pp. 597-598)

26. ANSWER: (E) Voltaire, a member of the aristocracy, was a reformer not a revolutionary. (McKay, *A History of Western Society*, 8th ed. p. 609/9th ed. pp. 601-602)

27. ANSWER: (A) An extraordinary intellect, Madame du Châtelet was excluded from the Academy of Sciences because of her gender. (McKay, *A History of Western Society*, 8th ed. p. 609/9th ed. p. 601)

28. ANSWER: (D) Although the enlightened despots did not implement radical change, they could appreciate the value of education and that knowledge was power while maintaining their role as absolutists. (McKay, *A History of Western Society*, 8th ed. p. 623/9th ed. pp. 615-616)

29. ANSWER: (A) Mendelssohn, well read and a bold thinker, was convinced that Enlightenment ideas could complement religion. (McKay, *A History of Western Society*, 8th ed. p. 617/9th ed. p. 611)

30. ANSWER: (E) The Industrial Revolution occurred after the agricultural revolution. (McKay, *A History of Western Society*, 8th ed. pp. 637-638/9th ed. pp. 627-628)

31. ANSWER: (A) The exports to the Atlantic economy helped to improve the economy of England. (McKay, *A History of Western Society*, 8th ed. p. 647/9th ed. pp. 637-640)

32. ANSWER: (D) Slave labor created a flood of trade in labor intensive products and made them accessible to more people. (McKay, *A History of Western Society*, 8th ed. p. 651/9th ed. p. 642)

33. ANSWER: (A) Smith recognized the restrictions of government involvement in the economy as practiced under mercantilism. Although Smith's views are often considered as the antithesis to

Marxist theory, Smith's *Wealth of Nations* (1776) predates the *Communist Manifesto* (1848). (McKay, *A History of Western Society*, 8th ed. pp. 654-656/9th ed. pp. 647-648)

34. **ANSWER: (D)** The Enlightenment emphasized the innate goodness of man and encouraged parents to follow the laws of nature in rearing children. (McKay, *A History of Western Society*, 8th ed. pp. 668-669/9th ed. pp. 660-661)

35. **ANSWER: (C)** Slave labor in the colonies, which grew sugar cane and tea, enabled the prices to drop, and they became dietary staples. (McKay, *A History of Western Society*, 8th ed. p. 675/9th ed. pp. 664-665)

36. **ANSWER: (B)** The germ theory was not discovered until the mid-nineteenth century. (McKay, *A History of Western Society*, 8th ed. pp. 675-679/9th ed. pp. 667-671)

37. **ANSWER: (E)** Existentialism, which did not attract significant interest until the twentieth century, was an intellectual movement that rejected belief in God. (McKay, *A History of Western Society*, 8th ed. pp. 681-682/9th ed. pp. 672-673)

38. **ANSWER: (A)** Blood sports, such as bull baiting and cockfighting, were popular with the masses. (McKay, *A History of Western Society*, 8th ed. p. 684/9th ed. pp. 675-676)

39. **ANSWER: (D)** In spite of some fluidity within classes, the social orders remained rigid legally; this contributed to significant discontent. (McKay, *A History of Western Society*, 8th ed. pp. 698-699/9th ed. pp. 684-685)

40. **ANSWER: (E)** Robespierre drew from the most radical of the Jacobins and Mountain to create his Committee of Public Safety. (McKay, *A History of Western Society*, 8th ed. pp. 706-707/9th ed. pp. 696-697)

41. **ANSWER: (E)** Robespierre did not invite any women to serve as leaders of the radicals during the Terror. (McKay, *A History of Western Society*, 8th ed. pp. 703-711/9th ed. pp. 691-702)

42. **ANSWER: (C)** Abbé Sieyes originated the quotation, which described the desire of the French for a strong leader to bring stability to the chaotic situation in their country, and yet consider the needs of the people. (McKay, *A History of Western Society*, 8th ed. p. 713/9th ed. pp. 703-704)

43. **ANSWER: (C)** Only Great Britain and Russia were able to prevent Napoleon from having a powerful presence in their countries. Napoleon was actually defeated in Russia and retreated in brutal winter conditions. Napoleon's Continental System, designed to strangle Britain's economy, failed. (McKay, *A History of Western Society*, 8th ed. p. 716/9th ed. pp. 708-711)

44. **ANSWER: (E)** The steel industry expanded during the second industrial revolution, which occurred in the late nineteenth century.

(McKay, *A History of Western Society,* 8th ed. pp. 731-732/9th ed. pp. 721-723)

45. **ANSWER: (C)** Although Great Britain was in the forefront, all countries profited from the Industrial Revolution. (McKay, *A History of Western Society,* 8th ed. p. 736, Table 22/9th ed. p. 728, Table 22.1)

46. **ANSWER: (D)** Malthus did not criticize the Industrial Revolution, but showed concern that the population would grow faster than the food supply and therefore hoped that working class people would marry late and have fewer children. (McKay, *A History of Western Society,* 8th ed. pp. 742-744/9th ed. pp. 734-736)

47. **ANSWER: (D)** Metternich, leader of the congress, agreed to return Belgium and southern Germany, but expanded elsewhere. (McKay, *A History of Western Society,* 8th ed. pp. 757-759/9th ed. pp. 749-751)

48. **ANSWER: (B)** Some intellectuals criticized the liberals because they did not favor full democracy. (McKay, *A History of Western Society,* 8th ed. pp. 761-762/9th ed. pp. 753-754)

49. **ANSWER: (D)** Marx assumed that the proletariat would become sufficiently frustrated to overthrow capitalism. (McKay, *A History of Western Society,* 8th ed. pp. 764-765/9th ed. pp. 756-758)

50. **ANSWER: (D)** The romantics glorified nature and decried the polluted cities. (McKay, *A History of Western Society,* 8th ed. pp. 767-771/9th ed. p. 758)

51. **ANSWER: (A)** Great Britain was in the forefront of industrialization during the early nineteenth century; this resulted in rapid urbanization. (McKay, *A History of Western Society,* 8th ed. p. 788/9th ed. p. 780)

52. **ANSWER: (B)** Overcrowding occurred in part because people needed to walk to work and shops. (McKay, *A History of Western Society,* 8th ed. p. 789/9th ed. pp. 780-781)

53. **ANSWER: (E)** Polio was a twentieth-century phenomenon. (McKay, *A History of Western Society,* 8th ed. p. 789/9th ed. p. 781)

54. **ANSWER: (B)** Although the Industrial Revolution raised the overall standard of living and Britain was in the forefront, Britain continued to have the largest gap between rich and poor. (McKay, *A History of Western Society,* 8th ed. p. 796/9th ed. p. 788)

55. **ANSWER: (A)** Extended families supported their relatives in crises, such as a death and need for a funeral, which could be stressful and expensive. (McKay, *A History of Western Society,* 8th ed. p. 807/9th ed. p. 799)

56. **ANSWER: (C)** Italy did not have a strong military, but Cavour's diplomatic skills, Napoleon's temporary support, and the distraction provided by the unification war in Germany contributed significantly

to success. (McKay, *A History of Western Society,* 8th ed. pp. 826-832/9th ed. pp. 818-824)

57. **ANSWER: (E)** Marxist thought spread in response to industrialization. (McKay, *A History of Western Society,* 8th ed. pp. 835-836/9th ed. pp. 826-827)

58. **ANSWER: (C)** German union membership skyrocketed after legal harassments were eliminated. (McKay, *A History of Western Society,* 8th ed. p. 849/9th ed. p. 840-841)

59. **ANSWER: (B)** In 1908 an international human rights campaign forced the Belgian king Leopold to cede his personal right to the Congo due to the brutal practices he had enforced there, including cutting off hands of Africans who did not gather enough rubber. (McKay, *A History of Western Society,* 8th ed. p. 872/9th ed. p. 862)

60. **ANSWER: (A)** China responded with the Taiping rebellions and the Boxer Rebellion, hoping to stave off Western imperialism. (McKay, *A History of Western Society,* 8th ed. pp. 877-882/9th ed. pp. 868-873)

61. **ANSWER: (D)** Three-fourths of the trade in the late nineteenth century went to other European countries. (McKay, *A History of Western Society,* 8th ed. p. 859/9th ed. p. 851)

62. **ANSWER: (E)** During the first year of the war, 2.5 million Russians were killed, wounded, or taken prisoner. After the Russian Revolution, the Soviet Union ceded territory to Germany in the Treaty of Brest-Litovsk. (McKay, *A History of Western Society,* 8th ed. pp. 907-909/9th ed. pp. 897-899)

63. **ANSWER: (A)** The Great Depression, which resulted in a worldwide downturn in the economy, was caused in part by over speculation, but it occurred during the 1930s, not as a cause of World War I. (McKay, *A History of Western Society,* 8th ed. pp. 887-891, 942/9th ed. pp. 879-883, 933)

64. **ANSWER: (B)** Even though the United States did not join the League of Nations, the League existed until World War II. (McKay, *A History of Western Society,* 8th ed. pp. 912-916/9th ed. pp. 902-908)

65. **ANSWER: (C)** World War I marked the end of the Ottoman Empire, and the divided area was ceded as protectorates to Great Britain and France. (McKay, *A History of Western Society,* 8th ed. pp. 913, 915/9th ed. pp. 904, 906)

66. **ANSWER: (D)** The Newtonian worldview, which began with physical laws of nature, contributed to a sense of certainty and to the Enlightenment philosophy of progress and optimism. The horrors of World War I dispelled some of the optimism. (McKay, *A History of Western Society,* 8th ed. pp. 921-928/9th ed. pp. 913-920)

67. **ANSWER: (C)** The French hoped to collect reparations by occupying the Ruhr valley in Germany, which prompted indignation from the

Germans. (McKay, *A History of Western Society*, 8th ed. p. 938/9th ed. p. 929)

68. **ANSWER: (E)** Although France experienced the effects of the Great Depression later than other countries, it struggled with instability and a variety of governments. (McKay, *A History of Western Society*, 8th ed. pp. 942-947/9th ed. pp. 933-939)

69. **ANSWER: (D)** One historian wrote that "The number dying in Stalin's war against the peasants was higher than the total deaths of all the countries in World War I." (McKay, *A History of Western Society*, 8th ed. pp. 959-961/9th ed. pp. 951-952)

70. **ANSWER: (C)** Soviet social realism depicted objects in a literal style and promoted pride and patriotism. (McKay, *A History of Western Society*, 8th ed. p. 962/9th ed. p. 953)

71. **ANSWER: (C)** Although originally Mussolini's platform included socialist reforms, he attacked the socialists as his enemies. (McKay, *A History of Western Society*, 8th ed. pp. 964-966/9th ed. pp. 955-957)

72. **ANSWER: (C)** In 1931 almost 40 percent of the population was under the age of thirty, and the exciting change promoted by the Nazis appealed to them. Hitler gained further support from key people in the army and business. (McKay, *A History of Western Society*, 8th ed. pp. 967-968/9th ed. p. 958-960)

73. **ANSWER: (C)** The European powers adopted a policy of appeasement in the wake of economic woes and then regretted that they had allowed Hitler to expand as he did. (McKay, *A History of Western Society*, 8th ed. p. 974/9th ed. p. 965)

74. **ANSWER: (A)** Millions of refugees from World War II migrated westward. (McKay, *A History of Western Society*, 8th ed. p. 994/9th ed. p. 986)

75. **ANSWER: (B)** The Iron Curtain separated communist countries from the NATO countries; there were only a few nonaligned countries. (McKay, *A History of Western Society*, 8th ed. pp. 992, 996/9th ed. 983-984, 988)

76. **ANSWER: (D)** Charles de Gaulle, president of France, was such a nationalist that he thwarted efforts at European unity. (McKay, *A History of Western Society*, 8th ed. p. 997/9th ed. p. 989)

77. **ANSWER: (D)** Khrushchev shocked the world when he criticized Stalin after Stalin's death. The West hoped that the speech was a signal of liberal policies to follow, but Khrushchev disappointed them. (McKay, *A History of Western Society*, 8th ed. pp. 1006-1007, 872/9th ed. pp. 997-998)

78. **ANSWER: (E)** When Gorbachev relaxed policies in the Soviet Union, many satellite nations pushed for freedom. (McKay, *A History of Western Society*, 8th ed. p. 1034/9th ed. p. 1024)

79. **ANSWER: (C)** The even exchange of currency was a generous gesture, but the government did not promise new housing. (McKay, *A History of Western Society*, 8th ed. pp. 1038-1040/9th ed. pp. 1028-1030)

80. **ANSWER: (C)** Although Gorbachev lost popularity due to economic problems, he was appreciated by the West for his efforts to change communism. (McKay, *A History of Western Society*, 8th ed. pp. 1043-1044/9th ed. pp. 1033)

ANSWER FOR SECTION II, PART A: DOCUMENT-BASED QUESTION (DBQ)

Below are short analyses of the documents.

Document 1 Sir Edwin Pears condemned Disraeli for his casual response to reports of atrocities in Bulgaria against Christians, which he said, was part of intentional plans. He noted that a knowledgeable and objective reporter, the Irish-American MacGahan, was sent to the area to investigate. He also gave a reason for Turkish hostility to the Christians in Bulgaria, namely economic competition.

POV: Having lived in Constantinople for forty years, Pears could be judged to be a reliable witness. He had a clear bias toward Christians, seeing them as more industrious, moral, and intelligent than the Turks or Muslims in the Balkans; this may be because he, most likely, was a Christian himself. He said that economic competition was at the heart of Christian-Muslim tensions; this may have been because he lived in Constantinople for forty years presumably safely as a Christian and therefore did not see religion as the key factor in and of itself.

Document 2 W. T. Stead argued forcefully against British intervention on behalf of the Turks, whom he vilified for what he described as a campaign against the Christians, whom he labeled freedom fighters.

POV: Stead was a social reformer who saw the Ottoman Empire as oppressive as well as decaying and was opposed to Conservatives like Disraeli. As someone who saw war as terrible, he was opposed to what he saw as an unnecessary war to prop up an oppressive regime. Stead later became editor of the *Pall Mall Gazette* (see Document 2).

Document 3 MacGahan describes Turkish atrocities he witnessed in Batak, including the murder of children and the beheading of women. Batak's population was mostly gone. He said that he now could believe any accusation against the Turks.

POV: MacGahan was the reporter described by Pears in Document 1 as not prejudiced against the Turks, but in this document he certainly vilified them. His views may have been changed as a result of what he witnessed.

Document 4 Disraeli said in a private letter that Britain now had a general in Turkish headquarters; this challenged the view that the Serbs had won an important victory.

POV: Disraeli was probably expressing his true views because they were in a private letter. He was writing to an aristocrat who may have been a Conservative like himself. As prime minister he may have sent the general to Turkish headquarters. Since he had been instrumental in the acquisition of the Suez Canal, he was concerned that the Middle East remain stable. A Serbian victory would have destabilized the region. Disraeli might have underestimated the strength of the Serbs for this reason.

Document 5 William Gladstone described the Turks as brutal, uncivilized, and inherently opposed to European values. The title of his pamphlet refers to the horrors in Bulgaria. He warned that atrocities might be committed again.

POV: Gladstone and Disraeli were perpetual rivals, and when Gladstone wrote this pamphlet about Bulgaria, it may have been an attempt to win popular support for the next election. Gladstone was the leader of the Liberal Party and would oppose the Ottoman regime because it lacked democracy and social reforms.

Document 6 Lord Salisbury suggested in this letter to Disraeli a solution to the problem of Christians within the Ottoman Empire that would avoid direct British involvement by creating a new position to protect the Christians. He warned against the idea that any liberated territories could be returned to the Turkish government.

POV: Lord Salisbury was a member of Disraeli's cabinet after Lord Derby resigned (see Document 9) and played an important role in the Congress of Berlin (see Document 14). He was trying to find a solution to the problem that would appease those like Gladstone anxious to protect Christians in the Ottoman Empire. As Lord Salisbury wrote this in a letter, it may have been only for Disraeli's private consideration and may therefore have expressed his true views.

Document 7 The newspaper praised Lord Derby for this support of the protocol that was signed by Russia and Serbia. Russian demobilization was praised.

POV: The *Pall Mall Gazette* was a Conservative newspaper when this article was published, so it spoke in praise of the Conservative foreign secretary Lord Derby. It later became a Liberal Party newspaper, and W. T. Stead (author of Document 2) became its editor. Russian withdrawal was promised. The Russians invaded a few months after this article appeared.

Document 8

The *New York Times* reported from London that the Russian advance was stopped by the brave and heroic Turks. The Serbs were described as arrogant aggressors claiming to defend Christians.

POV: Although the source of the news from London was not identified, the views represent those of the Conservatives, which doubted the claims of the Serbs to be protectors of Christians.

Document 9 Lord Derby resigned from the cabinet in 1878 because he disagreed with Disraeli's decision to send the fleet to protect Constantinople.

POV: Lord Derby's disillusionment with Conservative policies in the Balkans is reflected by the fact that he switched parties and served under Prime Minister Gladstone. He may have been influenced by Gladstone's pamphlet (Document 5) in his views on the matter.

Document 10 Queen Victoria expressed her rage at the Russians and her concern for Britain's reputation. She urged in a letter to Disraeli that he take military action to prevent the Russian conquest of Constantinople. She threatened to abdicate if no action was taken.

POV: The queen expressed herself emotionally because she was writing a letter to Disraeli. As she had just become empress of India, she was all the more anxious to defend the British Empire.

Document 11 This song represented jingoism or the willingness to fight for nationalistic reasons. It was popular on the streets of London in early 1878.

POV: The popularity of the song indicates that there may have been support by the people, perhaps stirred by Gladstone's pamphlet two years earlier, for British intervention against the Ottoman Empire. Liberals in favor of aiding the rebels against the Turks had the support of the working classes; the Conservative Party's support of the Turks was seen favorably by the aristocrats.

Document 12 This cartoon shows Disraeli at the Berlin Conference with the British Lion and the Russian Bear about to embrace. Disraeli gives an aside that says that this will be explained and the crowd need not worry.

POV: This is clearly a nationalistic cartoon, which can be seen as satirical and opposing Disraeli's compromise with Russia at the Conference of Berlin. Disraeli is depicted in Roman military dress and as the ringmaster of a circus; his Jewish ancestry is also indicated, rather negatively, in the cartoon.

Document 13 The treaty convention showed that Britain gained a strategic territory from the Ottoman Empire, Cyprus, before the Berlin Conference, in exchange for promises of military support to preserve the empire's territorial integrity. At the same time, the Ottoman Empire promised reforms and protection of Christians.

POV: Cyprus strengthened Britain's military presence in the eastern Mediterranean and allowed it to check further Russian advances; this is clearly a victory for the Conservative position as well as the Turks. This convention was a way to show the British people that Conservative policies would benefit them.

Document 14 Disraeli says that he and Lord Salisbury had brought back a peace treaty with honor from the Berlin Conference.

GROUPS:

Social reformers/Liberals: 2, 5

Describing Turks as oppressors of Christians: 2, 5, 6,

Outraged by atrocities: 1, 3

Conservatives: 4, 6, 7, 9

Opposing war: 2, 6, 7, 9

Opposing Russian expansion: 8, 10, 11, 12, 13

SCORING

Remember that the two parts of the exam—Section I, multiple choice, and Section II, three essays—are equally weighted at 50 percent each in determining the final score. Of the three essays, the DBQ counts for 45 percent of the Section II score, and each FRQ essay counts for 27.5 percent, together counting for 55 percent of the Section II score.

SCORING THE DATA-BASED ESSAY: THE CORE SCORING STANDARDS

1. Do you have a thesis that derives from the documents and does more than restate the question?

Example of a thesis that would not be accepted:

There were many views on the issue of what to do about unrest in the Balkans, and people were very emotional about it.

Example of an acceptable thesis:

Conservatives [Tories] and Liberals were divided on how to deal with the trouble in the Balkans that broke out among the Christian subjects of the Ottoman Empire. Tories in general supported the Ottoman Empire and the Liberals supported the rebels.

Example of a strong thesis:

British leaders were sharply divided in their attitudes toward the Ottoman Empire and how to protect the Christian subjects under Turkish rule. While many were appalled by atrocities reported in 1876 against the Bulgarians and called for British military intervention on behalf of the Christians, more called for a hands-off policy to allow those fighting the Turks to win. Others were afraid that military intervention would bring disastrous war and undermine the security of the Ottoman Empire and the stability of the region in which Britain had many important investments, including the Suez Canal. Still others were more concerned about the danger of Russian expansion there should the Turks prove vulnerable. This issue was so divisive that at least one cabinet member, Lord Derby, resigned over the issue and even changed his political party.

2. Have you used more than half the documents (in this case, 8)?
3. Have you made no more than one major error in your analysis of the documents?
4. Have you supported your thesis with evidence from the documents?
5. Have you grouped the documents in at least three ways?
6. Have you analyzed POV in at least three documents?

Give yourself one point for each affirmative answer. If you have earned the 6 core points, evaluate how much better than the minimum you have done and give yourself an additional 1, 2, or 3 points. If you missed a core point, go back over the DBQ to see what you could have done differently.

ANSWERS FOR SECTION II, PART B AND PART C: FREE-RESPONSE QUESTIONS (FRQS)

QUESTION 2

This question asks about women's roles in intellectual life and education from the fifteenth through the eighteenth century.

- Thesis: Although women were generally excluded from primary and secondary educational institutions until the nineteenth century and most Europeans believed that women were inferior in intellect and that formal education would be wasted on them, women were in fact active in intellectual life throughout the period, albeit on the margins.
- In the late medieval period, schools were established for boys in some city-states, and a few admitted girls. But although no humanist schools were established for girls during the Renaissance and most male humanists thought that humanist studies were not suitable for women, a few women were tutored in humanist studies at home and wrote Latin treatises. They challenged the views of humanists like Alberti who asserted in his treatise *On the Family* that the home was the proper sphere for women. Christine de Pizan was a successful fifteenth-century woman writer who advocated on behalf of women by listing many notable women and exploring the reasons for the inferior position of women.
- During the Reformation, women were encouraged to become literate in order to read the Bible. Protestants argued that women were spiritually equal before God and, by allowing divorce, stressed the importance of compatibility in marriage, although women were expected to be obedient wives. However, as monasteries and convents were closed in most Protestant states, women only had one option open to them: marriage. During the Counter-Reformation, the Ursuline Order was established to educate Catholic girls. Within the convent world, there remained substantial roles for unmarried women to play in scholarship and education.

- In the seventeenth century the debate over women intensified, with some schools established for aristocratic women but with a limited curriculum. Women themselves debated the issue: Some thought that women needed education only to manage their households and raise their children, while others advocated for full participation of women in society. During the scientific revolution, a few women played a notable role in scientific work, such as Maria Sibylla Merian who went off to Surinam with her daughter for two years to do botanical research. While the newly established scientific societies or academies were closed to women, women were illustrators and makers of anatomical models and attended informal salons. Some women such as Margaret Cavendish and Mary Astrell wrote philosophical works on Cartesian dualism. Madame du Châtelet brought Newton's work to France by translating his *Principia Mathematica*.
- During the Enlightenment, women played a pivotal role as organizers of salons and patrons of philosophes. They brought aristocrats and well-educated middle-class intellectuals together for free-ranging discussions. One of these, Madame Geoffrin, also gave crucial financial support for the publication of the *Encyclopedia*. Nevertheless, most philosophes did not advocate equality for women. Rousseau declared that men and women had fundamentally different natures and that women should play a passive role at home nurturing their children and breastfeeding them, in order to return to natural ways; women acting within the public sphere would be a corrupting influence. Montesquieu criticized the influence of women at the courts of the absolute monarchs.
- Toward the end of the Enlightenment, in 1792, Mary Wollstonecraft wrote a definitive feminist work, *A Vindication of the Rights of Women*, in which she argued that to limit women to the household deprived humanity of their enormous talents and that women needed to be educated to be proper companions to their husbands and provide solid training for their children. It was a matter of justice for women, who would, if they were given a rigorous education, be able to participate fully in public life and help reform the world.

QUESTION 3

This question asks you to specifically discuss two approaches to science developed in the seventeenth century. You need to articulate both and develop a thesis that either emphasizes the importance of one over the other or shows the limitations of each approach and how they combine in the modern scientific method.

- Thesis: Both the empirical and mathematical approaches to science were crucial to the success of the Scientific Revolution and the establishment of the modern scientific method.
- Empiricism was developed and defended by Francis Bacon, who argued that only experiments and scientific observations could serve as the basis for scientific truth. He supported the inductive method of reasoning, that is, going from the specific to the general. Galileo was an empiricist who performed many

experiments to test Aristotelian physics, which ultimately he disproved. He derived the law of inertia from his experiments, which overturned Aristotle's conclusions. Similarly, with the telescope, he saw sunspots, the craters on the moon, and moons around Jupiter, which provided the observations necessary to prove the Copernican hypothesis. There were many other experimenters during the scientific revolution, such as Pascal.

- On the other hand, many important figures in the scientific revolution were mathematicians who relied on logic and mathematics rather than empirical data to derive their theories or their laws. Copernicus rejected the Ptolemaic system not because of observations that contradicted it but because it did not make sense mathematically. Descartes rejected empiricism entirely, which he said could provide faulty data, and argued instead for logical and mathematic analysis in the mind. He created analytic geometry when he saw the connections between geometry and algebra. Cartesian dualism separated mind from matter. Kepler used mathematic analysis of data observed by Tycho Brahe, who had rejected Copernicanism, to derive his three laws of planetary motion. Newton used mathematics and logic to derive the theory of universal gravitation, which explained both the mathematic work of Kepler and the observations of Galileo. Copernicus, Kepler, and Newton proved the value of mathematic proof in science, while Galileo demonstrated the value of experiments and observations.

QUESTION 4

This is a comparative question so you need to discuss both societies in some depth. You also need to evaluate the relationship of artists to their society. This includes the prestige of the artist and patronage.

- Thesis: New artistic movements respond to changes in economic and social life, particularly where democracy and economic opportunity are expanding. Italian Renaissance artists were intimately connected to their society, while Impressionists tended more to be outsiders.
- Renaissance art was born in the city-states of Italy, not in a unified state. Florence was a guild republic, in which aristocrats had no role per se and political rights were dependent on membership in one of twenty-one guilds. Although later it would come under the domination of the Medicis, during the crucial decades in which artistic innovations occurred, the Republic of Florence was strong, triumphant militarily, and economically prosperous. The 1420s, a decade before the Medici became dominant, was when Donatello sculpted the first nude since antiquity; Brunelleschi designed the first true Renaissance building, the Foundling Hospital; and Masaccio painted the frescos in the Carmine Chapel and the first nudes–Adam and Eve–since antiquity. They revived the principles of classical art—proportion, balance, and self-awareness—and used the newly developed techniques of vanishing-point perspective.

- Patrons during the Renaissance were various churches, guilds, city-state governments, and wealthy merchants like the Medici. Most Renaissance artists worked on commission and reflected the values of their patrons: humanism, individualism, and patriotism. While early Renaissance artists included landscapes in their portraits and paintings, they were profoundly urban, based in Florence and later in Rome. They had great prestige and fame, and many were quite wealthy.
- Impressionism was born in late-nineteenth-century France, which was very different from Renaissance Italy. It was a long-standing, powerful, and influential unified state, recently restored to republicanism after twenty years of the Third Empire under Napoleon III and expanding economically through industrialization and internationally through imperialism.
- Impressionists sought to find a new value for art beyond realistic portrayals of people and landscapes that could be easily made through the brand-new technology of photography. Renoir, Monet, Pissarro, and other impressionists were interested particularly in conveying the varieties of light and in capturing impressions of particular scenes, especially rural ones. Many abandoned Paris and moved to the countryside, resisting the rapid urbanization that was under way, though some painted scenes of Parisian life and some were fascinated by the industrial cities. Monet for example painted train stations; Toulouse-Lautrec painted dance halls and other scenes of night life. But the most famous impressionist paintings were landscapes.
- While in the Renaissance artists worked generally on commission, impressionists generally painted works to fulfill their inner visions, and then showed them in salons or in galleries. Some wealthy middle-class individuals supported the artists or bought their works, but some artists, such as the postimpressionist van Gogh, were quite poor.
- Thus Renaissance artists were intimately connected to their society, while impressionists saw themselves more as outsiders.

QUESTION 5

This is a mainstream question for which there are a number of acceptable theses: you could argue, for example, that the alliance system was the main reason for the war or that it was a factor but not the most important cause, which is the thesis given here as an example.

- Thesis: The division of the great powers into two allied camps increased tensions in the decade before the war, but the actual outbreak of the war had less to do with alliances than with long-standing national interests and short-term military needs.
- When the Archduke Francis Ferdinand was assassinated in June 1914, war did not begin for six weeks. When Austria challenged and then declared war on Serbia, Russia mobilized on her behalf. But Serbia was not part of the Triple Alliance, so

it was the historic, ethnic, and religious ties between them and not the alliance system that led Russia to act.

- Germany gave Austria the so-called blank check of unconditional support in the month after the assassination, but it did so not primarily because of the terms of the Alliance but because of its own nationalistic goals. Italy, the third member of the Triple Alliance, acted completely differently. It did not judge Austria to be the victim of aggression, and therefore did not believe itself obligated by the terms of the treaty to defend Austria.
- The Triple Entente was not a military alliance, and it was unclear until a few days just before the actual outbreak of war whether England would fight. Germany hoped that England would stay out, believing the Britain would not go to war in defense of Russia, but its aggressive invasion of Belgium led England to join the war. This invasion was prompted by the Schlieffen war plan, which called for a quick defeat of France, a gamble that fizzled miserably.
- What caused the war was not the alliance system but nationalism: Serbian nationalistic dreams of a unified and enlarged Slavic state, Austrian nationalistic desires to hold its empire together, German nationalistic desires to remain the dominant power on the continent, Russian nationalistic desires to expand its influence in the Balkans, and French nationalistic desires to win back Alsace-Lorraine. Nationalism sparked an arms race among all the great powers and tensions over imperialistic competition.

QUESTION 6

This is another mainstream question; the key element is your ability to analyze fascist ideology in comparison with fascist practice.

- Thesis: In spite of their ideology, Italian fascists took power legally and were cautious and limited in their implementation of fascism.
- The ideology of Italian fascism, as articulated by its leader Benito Mussolini, was a fundamental rejection of constitutionalism, liberalism, democracy, and pacifism. Instead, fascists promoted action and the use of violence as legitimate political tools, and they demanded a state that would end the class rivalries that were impeding Italian unity. They wanted a state led by a single leader who would represent the soul of Italy and return it to greatness. Political parties, labor unions, representative government, all would be abolished. Fascist bands attacked socialists and destroyed their newspaper, offices, and union halls.
- Nevertheless, the fascists took power legally, after the March on Rome when the king asked Mussolini to become prime minister. Although it considered itself revolutionary, the Fascist Party never abolished the monarchy. Nor did the fascists challenge the church, a major political power in Italy. Instead, they negotiated a settlement with the papacy, which had rejected the new Italian state since its formation in 1870. The Lateran Agreement returned to the church important

rights, such as a role in the education of children. Thus, the Italian Fascists left in place two important traditional authorities, the monarchy and the church.

- Because they were a minority party in the Chamber of Deputies, it was several years before the Fascists could eliminate the other parties and restrict civil liberties. The first cabinet under Mussolini included ministers from other parties. The electoral law reform, the Acerbo Law of 1923, ended up giving the Fascists an absolute majority after the election that year. The leader of the Socialist Party in the Chamber of Deputies, Matteotti, was assassinated by the Fascists. The Fascists soon thereafter arrested political opponents, abolished civil liberties, and ended freedom of the press; by 1926 Italy became a one-party state. But elections were held, even if they were fixed, and the Fascists collaborated with the old conservative classes, taking little radical action on social and economic issues. Relatively few people were executed for political reasons under Mussolini.
- But parts of fascist ideology were enacted. Fascists created a youth movement to indoctrinate the young, and restricted the rights of women in the workforce and at home, especially when they abolished divorce. The Fascist regime abolished labor unions, and big business was free to regulate itself. The end result was that workers lost benefits and political power.
- Thus, Italian fascism was more authoritarian and conservative than radical in practice and in its ideology where rhetoric remained revolutionary.

QUESTION 7

This is another mainstream question. Be sure you know both time periods of European colonization before you select this answer.

- Thesis: While the phrase "God, Gold, and Glory" would apply in both periods, Europeans had different ways to achieve those aims in each period. The goals of Europeans in the fifteenth and sixteenth centuries were largely religious and commercial, while the goals of the European colonizers in the nineteenth century were to meet industrial needs and to establish strategic colonies to ensure their status as naval powers.
- In the fifteenth and sixteenth centuries, "God, Gold, and Glory" were the goals of European colonizers of Asia, Africa, and the New World. Glory was as much about the individual pride of the conquerors and explorers as about national pride. Religious zeal to convert the heathen motivated many to travel to distant lands, where missions were set up, although many of the conversions, particularly in the Americas, were forced. Gold was a literal motive in this period, as the gold of the Americas was a major impetus to colonization there. Silver became even more important when it was discovered in Peru in the early sixteenth century; it was what the Chinese wanted in exchange for their desirable goods. By the end of that century, Europeans were also making money from agricultural plantations in Asia and the New World, especially those producing sugar cane, and from the lucrative trade in slaves

who were the main labor force on such plantations. Another source of great wealth was the trade in spices, particularly for the Dutch, in their valuable colony of the Dutch East Indies. By and large, European colonies were limited to coastal regions. Europeans acquired political control of their colonies in the New World and in parts of Asia either from concession or conquest. But China and Japan retained their political independence. The Japanese shogunate severely restricted the presence of foreigners in Japan. China was little interested in the goods Europeans had to offer and was willing to sell silk to them only in exchange for silver. Various forms of triangle trade took place: Goods, such as Chinese silks, imported from one part of Asia, were paid for with goods from another part of Asia, such as Indian textiles, or goods from the New World, such as sugar. European goods, such as guns, were sold in Africa, and slaves were bought with the profits and brought to the New World. The dominant seafaring powers in the fifteenth and sixteenth centuries were the Spanish, Portuguese, and Dutch.

- In the nineteenth century, "God, Gold, and Glory" still applied but with new meanings. European colonization focused on Asia, Africa, and the Middle East as the American colonies became independent. Missionaries from Europe set up missions, particularly in Africa, but often soon asked for protection from the home country. Much of Africa was converted to Christianity in this way, but missionaries had less success in Asia and the Middle East. National glory was now defined as being a great naval power and possessing a colonial empire. British control over the Suez Canal and later Egypt was a crucial step in establishing British naval supremacy. Colonies were no longer just strategically located ports but entire states. With quinine and the machine gun, Europeans were able to go into and then take over tropical and inland areas of Africa and Asia. Europeans acquired political control over those colonies, ruling either directly or indirectly. Racism and notions of the white man's burden justified European control of the internal affairs of its colonies. Britain had over fifty colonies, France had several dozen, and a newcomer to the imperial game, Germany, took important regions on both sides of Africa and a sphere of influence in China.
- China and Japan were forced to trade with the West by war or threat of war. China was forced to give westerners significant concessions after its defeat in the Opium Wars with Britain in the 1840s. It was even required to grant extraterritoriality, which meant that it had little legal control over the foreigners in its midst. Japan was threatened with bombardment by the American commodore Perry in the 1850s and, under this threat, ended its long centuries of isolation.
- Gold too had a different meaning. Europeans were still interested in agricultural crops like sugar, but new crops—tobacco, tea, and coffee—became even more important. Moreover Europeans were now seeking new agricultural or natural products that could fuel their industrial economies at home, for example, Indian and Egyptian raw cotton, to be

shipped to factories in Britain to be made into cloth, or rubber from the Belgian Congo, for a variety of industrial uses. As industrial competition among the European states intensified, the importance of colonies as markets for manufactured goods became increasingly important. Colonies were also seen as valuable places for the investment of European surplus capital.

- Thus, economic and political motives had different sources in nineteenth-century Europe from what they had had in the fifteenth and sixteenth centuries, mostly because of industrialization.

SCORING THE FREE-RESPONSE ESSAYS

The essays are scored on a scale of 0 to 9, with 0 being a real score. A response that is completely off task does not even earn a zero. Here are scoring guidelines for the essays.

9–8 Has a clear, well-developed thesis
Is well organized
Addresses the terms of the question
Supports the thesis with substantial specific evidence
Has sophisticated analysis
May contain minor errors; even a 9 need not be flawless

7–6 Has a clear thesis
Addresses all parts of the question but discussion is uneven
Has competent analysis, but it may be superficial
Supports the thesis with some specific evidence

5–4 Contains a thesis, perhaps superficial or simplistic
Has uneven responses to the question's terms
May contain errors, factual or interpretative
Addresses the question with generally accurate discussion but without specific evidence; analysis is implicit or superficial
May contain major errors within a generally accurate and appropriate discussion
Is descriptive rather than analytical

3–2 Has weak or muddled thesis, perhaps suggesting false or inappropriate dichotomies or connections
Contains significant errors of chronology or fact
Has minimal discussion
Offers limited evidence

1–0 Has confused or absent thesis or merely restates the question
Misconstrues the question or omits major tasks
May contain major errors or irrelevant historical information
Addresses only one part of the question
Offers minimal or no evidence

Reread your essay or, if you can work with a fellow student in APEH, read each other's essays and ask the following questions:

1. How well organized is the essay? Is it clearly divided into distinct paragraphs? Is there an introduction and a conclusion?

2. How clear is the thesis? Is the thesis statement at the beginning of the essay or in the conclusion?
3. How many arguments support the thesis?
4. How much evidence is used to support the thesis? How specific was it?
5. Were all parts of the question addressed? Was the discussion of the different parts more or less balanced?
6. How many of the points noted in the explanations of the answer were made in the essay?
7. Were there major factual, chronological, or interpretative errors? Or minor errors?
8. Was the analysis explicit or implicit? Was it sophisticated or minimal?

Now reread the scoring guidelines and give yourself a score.

In general, the scores on the DBQ average higher than those of the FRQs, because the DBQ is a skill-based question while the FRQs are content based. The median score on the DBQ is 5 usually because of lack of POV analysis, while the median scores on the FRQs are typically 4 to 5 in Part B and often 3 to 4 on the Part C, frequently because students run out of time.

CALCULATING YOUR SCORE ON THE AP EXAM

SECTION 1: MULTIPLE-CHOICE QUESTIONS

__________ —(1/4 × __________) × 1.1250 = __________

number correct out of 80 — number wrong — Weighted Section I score (if less than zero, enter zero; do not round)

SECTION II: FREE-RESPONSE QUESTIONS

Question 1 (Part A) __________ Out of 9 × 4.5000 = __________ (do not round)

Question 2 (Part B) __________ Out of 9 × 2.7500 = __________ (do not round)

Question 3 (Part C) __________ Out of 9 × 2.7500 = __________ (do not round)

Sum = __________ Weighted Section II score (do not round)

COMPOSITE SCORE:

__________ + __________ = __________

Weighted Section I — Weighted Section II — Composite Score (round to the nearest whole number)

COMPOSITE SCORE RANGE	AP GRADE
121–180	5
99–120	4
67–98	3
49–66	2
0-48	1

HOW TO INTERPRET YOUR PRACTICE TEST RESULTS

1. First, look at the multiple-choice score. It is a fair indicator of what your overall score will be. How many out of 80 did you get right? How many points off did you lose for incorrect answers?

   According to College Board statistics on the 2004 Released Exam, most students who got a score of 4 or 5 on the examination earned a weighted score of 61 or over on the multiple-choice section. A weighted score of 31 to 45 on the multiple-choice section was typical of the vast majority of students earning a 3 on the exam; the rest of the students, about a third, earning a 3 received a weighted score of 16 to 30. More than 60% of students with a weighted score of 16 to 30 earned an exam score of 1 or 2. Students with a weighted score below 15 were mostly likely to get a 1 on the exam.

2. Check to see if you lost too many points for wrong answers. Look back at the ones you got wrong to see if you got them wrong because you did not know the answer or because you guessed. If you discover that you guessed a lot and guessed wrong, then on the AP exam, don't guess!

3. Examine your essay scores. What strengths and weaknesses do you find? If you did not do as well as you would have liked, try to focus on what problems you had in writing the essays. Was it your thesis statement, use of evidence, errors, or lack of organization? Once you identify your difficulties, you can focus your attention on addressing them.

4. Set a realistic goal for yourself. If you want a score of 4, for example, then your goal should be 55 out of 80 multiple-choice answers correct, a 6 or 7 on the data-based question, and a 5 or 6 on each free-response question. For an exam score of 5, raise the ante to 60 multiple-choice answers correct and essay scores of 8, 7, and 7. If you have used this book and prepared well for the examination, you have every right to expect a score of 4 or 5. Make it happen!